FOUNDATIONS OF PROBABILISTIC PROGRAMMING

What does a probabilistic program actually compute? How can one formally reason about such probabilistic programs? This valuable guide covers such elementary questions and more. It provides a state-of-the-art overview of the theoretical underpinnings of modern probabilistic programming and their applications in machine learning, security, and other domains, at a level suitable for graduate students and non-experts in the field. In addition, the book treats the connection between probabilistic programs and mathematical logic, security (what is the probability that software leaks confidential information?), and presents three programming languages for different applications: Excel tables, program testing, and approximate computing. This title is also available as Open Access on Cambridge Core.

GILLES BARTHE is Scientific Director at the Max Planck Institute for Security and Privacy and Research Professor at the IMDEA Software Institute, Madrid. His recent research develops programming language techniques and verification methods for probabilistic languages, with a focus on cryptographic and differentially private computations.

JOOST-PIETER KATOEN is Professor at RWTH Aachen University and University of Twente. His research interests include formal verification, formal semantics, concurrency theory, and probabilistic computation. He co-authored the book *Principles of Model Checking* (2008). He received an honorary doctorate from Aalborg University, is member of the Academia Europaea, and is an ERC Advanced Grant holder.

ALEXANDRA SILVA is Professor of Algebra, Semantics, and Computation at University College London. A theoretical computer scientist with contributions in the areas of semantics of programming languages, concurrency theory, and probabilistic network verification, her work has been recognized by multiple awards, including the Needham Award 2018, the Presburger Award 2017, the Leverhulme Prize 2016, and an ERC Starting Grant in 2015.

FOUNDATIONS OF PROBABILISTIC PROGRAMMING

Edited by

GILLES BARTHE

Max-Planck-Institut für Cybersicherheit und Schutz der Privatsphäre, Bochum, Germany

JOOST–PIETER KATOEN

Rheinisch–Westfälische Technische Hochschule, Aachen, Germany

ALEXANDRA SILVA

University College London

CAMBRIDGE
UNIVERSITY PRESS

CAMBRIDGE
UNIVERSITY PRESS

University Printing House, Cambridge CB2 8BS, United Kingdom

One Liberty Plaza, 20th Floor, New York, NY 10006, USA

477 Williamstown Road, Port Melbourne, VIC 3207, Australia

314–321, 3rd Floor, Plot 3, Splendor Forum, Jasola District Centre, New Delhi – 110025, India

79 Anson Road, #06–04/06, Singapore 079906

Cambridge University Press is part of the University of Cambridge.

It furthers the University's mission by disseminating knowledge in the pursuit of education, learning, and research at the highest international levels of excellence.

www.cambridge.org
Information on this title: www.cambridge.org/9781108488518
DOI: 10.1017/9781108770750   .

First published 2021

Printed in the United Kingdom by TJ Books Limited, Padstow Cornwall

A catalogue record for this publication is available from the British Library.

ISBN 978-1-108-48851-8 Hardback

Contents

Contributors   *page* vii

Preface   xi

1   **Semantics of Probabilistic Programming: A Gentle Introduction**
    Fredrik Dahlqvist, Alexandra Silva and Dexter Kozen   1

2   **Probabilistic Programs as Measures**
    Sam Staton   43

3   **Application of Computable Distributions to the Semantics of Probabilistic Programs**
    Daniel Huang, Greg Morrisett and Bas Spitters   75

4   **On Probabilistic λ-Calculi**
    Ugo Dal Lago   121

5   **Probabilistic Couplings from Program Logics**
    Gilles Barthe and Justin Hsu   145

6   **Expected Runtime Analyis by Program Verification**
    Benjamin Lucien Kaminski, Joost-Pieter Katoen and Christoph Matheja   185

7   **Termination Analysis of Probabilistic Programs with Martingales**
    Krishnendu Chatterjee, Hongfei Fu and Petr Novotný   221

8   **Quantitative Analysis of Programs with Probabilities and Concentration of Measure Inequalities**
    Sriram Sankaranarayanan   259

9   **The Logical Essentials of Bayesian Reasoning**
    Bart Jacobs and Fabio Zanasi   295

10 **Quantitative Equational Reasoning**
Giorgio Bacci, Radu Mardare, Prakash Panangaden and Gordon Plotkin   333

11 **Probabilistic Abstract Interpretation: Sound Inference and Application to Privacy**
José Manuel Calderón Trilla, Michael Hicks, Stephen Magill, Piotr Mardziel and Ian Sweet   361

12 **Quantitative Information Flow with Monads in Haskell**
Jeremy Gibbons, Annabelle McIver, Carroll Morgan and Tom Schrijvers   391

13 **Luck: A Probabilistic Language for Testing**
Lampropoulos Leonidas, Benjamin C. Pierce, Li-yao Xia, Diane Gallois-Wong, Cătălin Hrițcu, John Hughes   449

14 **Tabular: Probabilistic Inference from the Spreadsheet**
Andrew D. Gordon, Claudio Russo, Marcin Szymczak, Johannes Borgström, Nicolas Rolland, Thore Graepel and Daniel Tarlow   489

15 **Programming Unreliable Hardware**
Michael Carbin and Sasa Misailovic   533

Contributors

Giorgio Bacci   *Department of Computer Science, Aalborg University, Selma Lagerlöfs Vej 300, DK-9220 Aalborg, Denmark*

Gilles Barthe   *Max Planck Institute for Cybersecurity and Privacy, Exzenterhaus, Universitätsstr. 60, 44789 Bochum, Germany*

Johannes Borgström   *Department of Information Technology, Uppsala University, 752 37 Uppsala, Sweden*

Jose Manuel Calderón Trilla   *Galois, Inc., Arlington, VA 22203, USA*

Michael Carbin   *MIT CSAIL, 77 Massachusetts Ave, 32-G782 Cambridge, MA 02139, USA*

Krishnendu Chatterjee   *Am Campus 1, IST Austria, A-3400 Klosterneuburg, Austria*

Fredrik Dahlqvist   *University College London, Department of Computer Science, Gower Street, London WC1E 6BT, UK*

Ugo Dal Lago   *Dipartimento di Informatica – Scienza e Ingegneria Università degli Studi di Bologna, Mura Anteo Zamboni, 7, 40127 Bologna, Italy*

Hongfei Fu   *John Hopcroft Center for Computer Science, Shanghai Jiao Tong University, 800 Dongchuan Road, Minhang District, Shanghai 200240, China*

Diane Gallois-Wong   *Inria de Paris 2, rue Simone Iff, CS 42112, 75589 Paris CEDEX 12, France*

Jeremy Gibbons   *University of Oxford, Department of Computer Science, Parks Road, Oxford OX1 3QD, UK*

Andrew D. Gordon   *Microsoft Research Ltd, 21 Station Road, Cambridge CB1 2FB, UK*

Thore Graepel   *University College London, Department of Computer Science, Gower Street, London WC1E 6BT, UK*

Michael Hicks   *Department of Computer Science, University of Maryland, College Park, MD 20742, USA*

Cătălin Hrițcu   *Inria de Paris 2, rue Simone Iff, CS 42112, 75589 Paris CEDEX 12, France*

John Hughes   *Department of Computer Science and Engineering, SE-412 96, Gothenburg, Sweden*

Justin Hsu   *School of Computer, Data and Information Sciences, 1210 W. Dayton Street Madison, WI 53706-1613, USA*

Daniel Huang   *EECS, University of California, Berkeley, CA 94720-1770, USA*

Benjamin Lucien Kaminski   *Software Modeling and Verification Group, RWTH Aachen University D-52056 Aachen, Germany*

Joost-Pieter Katoen   *Software Modeling and Verification Group, RWTH Aachen University D-52056 Aachen, Germany*

Dexter Kozen   *Computer Science Department, 436 Gates Hall, Cornell University, Ithaca, New York 14853–7501, USA*

Bart Jacobs   *Interdisciplinary Hub for Security, Privacy, and Data Governance, Radboud University Nijmegen, Erasmusplein 1, 6525 HT Nijmegen, The Netherlands*

Lampropoulos Leonidas   *University of Pennsylvania, Department of Computer and Information Science, 3330 Walnut Street, Philadelphia, PA 19104-6389, USA*

Stephen Magill   *Galois, Inc., Arlington, VA 22203, USA*

Radu Mardare   *Computer and Information Sciences University of Strathclyde, 26 Richmond Street, Glasgow G1 1XH, UK*

Piotr Mardziel   *Electrical and Computer Engineering Department, Carnegie Mellon University, 5000 Forbes Avenue, Pittsburgh, PA 15213, USA*

Christoph Matheja   *Software Modeling and Verification Group, RWTH Aachen University D-52056 Aachen, Germany*

Annabelle McIver   *Department of Computing, Macquarie University, Sydney, NSW 2109, Australia*

Sasa Misailovic   *Department of Computer Science, University of Illinois, 4110 Siebel Center, Urbana, IL 61801, USA*

Carroll Morgan   *Faculty of Engineering, UNSW, Sydney, NSW 2052, Australia*

Greg Morrisett   *Cornell Tech, Cornell University, 2 West Loop Road, New York, New York 10044, USA*

Petr Novotný   *Faculty of Informatics, Masaryk University, Botanickà 68a, 60200 Brno, Czech Republic*

Prakash Panangaden   *School of Computer Science, McGill University, 3480 rue University, Montreal, Quebec H3A 0E9, Canada*

Benjamin C. Pierce   *University of Pennsylvania, Department of Computer and Information Science, 3330 Walnut Street, Philadelphia, PA 19104-6389, USA*

Gordon Plotkin   *Laboratory for Foundations of Computer Science, School of Informatics, Informatics Forum, 10 Crichton Street, Edinburgh EH8 9AB, UK*

Nicolas Rolland   *University College London, Department of Computer Science, Gower Street, London WC1E 6BT, UK*

Claudio Russo   *DFINITY, Stockerstrasse 47, 8002 Zürich, Switzerland*

Sriram Sankaranarayanan   *Department of Computer Science, University of Colorado, Boulder CO 80309–0430, USA*

Tom Schrijvers   *Department of Computer Science. KU Leuven. Celestijnenlaan 200A. 3001 Leuven. Belgium*

Alexandra Silva   *University College London, Department of Computer Science, Gower Street, London WC1E 6BT, UK*

Bas Spitters   *Department of Computer Science, Aarhus University, Nygaard-268 Aabogade 34, DK-8200 Aarhus N, Denmark*

Sam Staton   *Department of Computer Science, University of Oxford Wolfson Building, Parks Road, Oxford OX1 3QD, UK*

Ian Swect   *Department of Computer Science, University of Maryland, College Park, MD 20742, USA*

Marcin Szymczak   *Lehrstuhl für Informatik 2, RWTH Aachen University, 52056 Aachen, Germany*

Daniel Tarlow   *Google Research, Brain Team, Montreal, Quebec H3B 2Y5, Canada*

Li-yao Xia   *University of Pennsylvania, Department of Computer and Information Science, 3330 Walnut Street, Philadelphia, PA 19104-6389, USA*

Fabio Zanasi   *University College London, Department of Computer Science, Gower Street, London WC1E 6BT, UK*

Preface

Probabilistic programs

Probabilistic programs describe recipes for inferring statistical conclusions from a complex mixture of uncertain data and real-world observations. They can represent probabilistic graphical models far beyond the capabilities of Bayesian networks and are expected to have a major impact on machine intelligence. Probabilistic programs are ubiquitous. They steer autonomous robots and self-driving cars, are key to describe security mechanisms, naturally code up randomised algorithms for solving NP-hard or even unsolvable problems, and are rapidly encroaching on AI. Probabilistic programming aims to make probabilistic modelling and machine learning accessible to the programmer.

What is this book all about?

Probabilistic programs, though typically relatively small in size, are hard to grasp, let alone check automatically. Elementary questions are notoriously hard – even the most elementary question "does a program halt with probability one? – is "more un-decidable" than the halting problem. This book is about the theoretical foundations of probabilistic programming. It is primarily concerned with fundamental questions such as the following: What is Bayesian probability theory? What is the precise mathematical meaning of probabilistic programs? How show almost-sure termination? How determine the (possibly infinite) expected runtime of probabilistic programs? How can two similar programs be compared? It covers several analysis techniques on probabilistic programs such as abstract interpretation, algebraic reasoning and determining concentration measures.

These chapters are complemented with chapters on the formal definition of concrete probabilistic programming languages and some possible applications of the use of probabilistic programs.

How to read this volume?

The volume consists of five parts: semantics, verification, logic, security, and programming languages.

Semantics.

The first part on semantics consists of four chapters on different aspects of the formal semantics of probabilistic programming languages. Dahlqvist *et al.* start off in Chapter 1 by presenting an operational and denotational semantics of an imperative language with discrete and continuous distributions. The chapter by Staton presents a compositional measure-theoretic semantics for a first-order probabilistic language with arbitrary soft conditioning. Chapter 3 by Huang *et al.* studies semantics with a focus on computability. Motivated by the tension between the discrete and the continuous in probabilistic modelling, type-2 computable distributions are introduced as the elementary mathematical objects to give semantics to probabilistic languages. Dal Lago's Chapter 4 completes the semantics part by treating a probabilistic version of the λ-calculus, the backbone language for functional programming languages.

Verification.

The second part on formal verification starts with a chapter by Barthe and Hsu on the use of couplings, a well-known concept in probability theory for verifying probabilistic programs. Kaminski *et al.* present a weakest pre-condition calculus in the style of Dijkstra for determining the expected run-time of a probabilistic program. This can be used to determine whether a program needs infinitely many steps to terminate with probability one. Chapter 7 by Chatterjee *et al.* presents various techniques based on supermartingales to decide the almost-sure termination of a probabilistic program, i.e., does a program terminate with probability one on all possible inputs? The verification part ends with a chapter by Sankaranarayanan about the quantitative analysis of probabilistic programs by means of concentration of measure inequalities. This includes Chernoff–Hoeffding and Bernstein inequalities.

Logic.

The third part focuses on logic and consists of two chapters. In Chapter 9, Jacobs and Zanasi present an insightful new perspective on fundamental aspects of probability theory which are relevant for probabilistic programming. Their chapter introduces a category-theoretic formalization of Bayesian reasoning, and in particular a string-diagram-friendly one. This contribution is complemented by the chapter by Bacci *et al.* which surveys some recent contributions on extending the classical

Birkhoff/Lawvere theory of equational reasoning to the quantitative setting. In that setting, compared entities are not necessarily equal but rather treated by a notion of distance.

Security.

Part four is concerned with security, an important application field in which probabilities are pivotal. Chapter 11 by Calderon *et al.* collects together results on probabilistic abstract interpretation and applies them to probabilistic programming in the context of security. Chapter 12 by Gibbons *et al.* presents an embedded domain-specific language in Haskell to compute hyper-distributions induced by programs. This is used to compute the amount of leakage of a program by measuring variations on post-distributions that include Shannon entropy and Bayes' risk (that is, the maximum information an attacker can learn in a single run).

Programming languages.

The final part of this volume is concerned with three concrete probabilistic programming languages: Luck, Tabular, and Rely. Chapter 13 describes Luck, proposed by Lampropoulos *et al.*, a language for test generation and a framework for property-based testing of functional programs. Luck combines local instantiation of unknown variables and global constraint solving to make test generation more efficient than existing approaches. Gordon *et al.* introduce Tabular, a domain-specific programming language designed to express probabilistic models and to perform probabilistic inference over relational data. Tabular can be used from Microsoft Excel or as stand-alone software. Chapter 14 presents the syntax, semantics and type system of Tabular and shows how it can be used to design probabilistic models and to perform probabilistic inference. Chapter 15, the last chapter of this volume, by Carbin and Misailovic, presents Rely, a programming language that enables reasoning about the probability that a program produces the correct result when executed on unreliable hardware.

How this volume emerged

This book consists of 15 contributed chapters and a preface. The idea for this volume emerged at the first summer school on Foundations of Programming and Software Systems held in Braga, Portugal, May–June 2017. This biennial school series is supported by EATCS (European Association for Theoretical Computer Science), ETAPS (European Conference on Theory and Practice of Software), ACM SIGPLAN (Special Interest Group on Programming Languages) and ACM SIGLOG (Special Interest Group on Logic and Computation). It was felt that there is no comprehensive book on the theoretical foundations of probabilistic programming languages. We sincerely hope that this volume contributes to filling this gap. Enjoy reading!

Acknowledgements

Many people have helped us to make this volume possible. First and foremost, we like to thank all authors for their fine contributions and for their patience in this book process. All chapters have been subject to peer reviews. We thank the reviewers Alejandro Aguirre, Krishnendu Chatterjee, Ugo Dal Lago, Thomas Ehrhard, Claudia Faggian, Marco Gaboardi, Francesco Gavazzo, Jeremy Gibbons, Andrew D. Gordon, Ichiro Hasuo, Jan Hoffmann, Justin Hsu, Bart Jacobs, Benjamin Lucien Kaminski, Pasquale Malacaria, Radu Mardare, Christoph Matheja, Annabelle McIver, Sasa Misailovic, Petr Novotný, Prakash Panangaden, Corina Pasareanu, Alejandro Russo, Sriram Sankaranarayanan, Steffen Smolka, and Marcin Szymczak for their thorough reviewing work.

We thank Luis Barbosa, Catarina Fernandes and Renato Neves for their invaluable efforts in the local organisation of the FoPPS 2017 summer school. We thank Joshua Moerman for his efforts in the editing process. David Tranah and Anna Scriven from Cambridge University Press are thanked for their support during this process. We thank Hanna Schraffenberger for designing the cover of the book. Finally, we are grateful for the financial support from the ERC (AdG FRAPPANT and StG ProFoundNet) and the MPI on Security and Privacy which enabled to publish this volume under gold open access.

1

Semantics of Probabilistic Programming:
A Gentle Introduction

Fredrik Dahlqvist and Alexandra Silva
University College London
Dexter Kozen
Cornell University

Abstract: Reasoning about probabilistic programs is hard because it compounds the difficulty of classic program analysis with sometimes subtle questions of probability theory. Having precise mathematical models, or *semantics*, describing their behaviour is therefore particularly important. In this chapter, we review two probabilistic semantics. First an operational semantics which models the local, step-by-step, behaviour of programs, then a denotational semantics describing global behaviour as an operator transforming probability distributions over memory states.

1.1 Introduction

A *probabilistic program* is any program whose execution is probabilistic. This usually means that there is a source of randomness that allows weighted choices to be made during execution. Given an initial machine-state, in the event that the program halts, there will be a distribution describing the probability of output events. Any deterministic program is trivially a probabilistic program that does not make any random choices. The source of randomness is typically a *random number generator*, which is assumed to provide independent samples from a known distribution. In practice, these are often *pseudo-random number generators*, which do not provide true randomness, but only an approximation; however, it is possible to construct hardware random number generators that provide true randomness, for example by measuring a noisy electromagnetic process.

Reasoning about deterministic programs usually involves answering binary yes/no questions: *Is the postcondition always satisfied? Does this program halt on all inputs? Does it always halt in polynomial time?* On the other hand, reasoning about probabilistic programming usually involves more *quantitative* questions: *What is the probability that the postcondition is satisfied? What is the probability that this*

[a] From *Foundations of Probabilistic Programming*, edited by Gilles Barthe, Joost-Pieter Katoen and Alexandra Silva published 2020 by Cambridge University Press.

program halts? Is its expected halting time polynomial? In order to answer questions like these, the first step should be to develop a formal mathematical semantics for probabilistic programs, which will allow us to formalise such questions precisely. This is the main purpose of this chapter.

Reasoning about probabilistic programs is in general difficult because it compounds the difficulty of deterministic program analysis with questions of probability theory, which can sometimes be counterintuitive. We will use examples to illustrate all the main ideas presented in this chapter. We introduce these examples here and will return to them as we develop the semantics of probabilistic programs. We start with two examples involving *discrete probabilities* for which naive probability theory provides a sufficient framework for reasoning. We will then present two programs that involve *continuous* distributions for which a more general theory known as *measure theory* is needed. The requisite background for understanding these concepts is presented in Section 1.2.

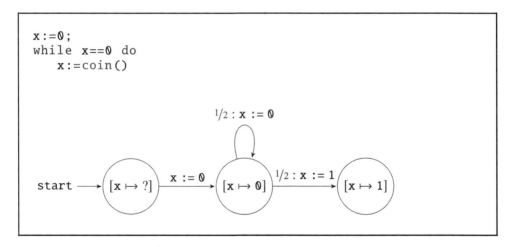

Figure 1.1 A simple coin-toss program

We start with the simple program of Fig. 1.1 displayed next to the small probabilistic automaton it implements. Here the construct coin() is our random number generator; each successive call returns 0 or 1, each with probability $1/2$, and successive calls are *independent*, which means that n successive calls will yield one of the 2^n possible sequences of n binary digits, each with probability 2^{-n}. A distribution on $\{0, 1\}$ that takes value 1 with probability p and 0 with probability $1 - p$ is called a *Bernoulli distribution with (success) parameter p*. Thus coin() is a Bernoulli distribution with success parameter $1/2$.

It is intuitively clear that this program eventually halts with probability 1. Looking at the automaton of Fig. 1.1, one can see that the probability of the program going through n iterations of the body of the loop is 2^{-n}. Moreover, the expected number of iterations of the body of the loop is given by

$$\sum_{n=1}^{\infty} n2^{-n} = 2.$$

This type of simple probabilistic process involving repeated independent trials until some fixed "success" event occurs is called a *Bernoulli process*. If the probability of success in each trial is p, then the expected time until success is $1/p$. In this example, $p = 1/2$. We will show in Section 1.3 how the mathematical interpretation of this program (its *semantics*) can be constructed *compositionally*, that is to say line-by-line, and how it agrees with these simple observations.

Our second example is also discrete, but intuitively less obvious. The program of Fig. 1.2 implements a random walk on the two-dimensional grid $\mathbb{Z} \times \mathbb{Z}$. In each iteration of the body of the loop, the function `step` updates the current coordinates by moving left, right, down, or up, each with equal probability $1/4$.

```
main{
    u:=0;
    v:=0;
    step(u,v);
    while u!=0 || v!=0 do
        step(u,v)
}

step(u,v){
    x:=coin();
    y:=coin();
    u:=u+(x-y);
    v:=v+(x+y-1)
}
```

Figure 1.2 A random walk on a two-dimensional grid

The loop continues until the random walk returns to the origin. The first call to `step` outside the loop ensures that the program takes at least one step, so it does not halt immediately. The question of the halting probability is now much less obvious. The state space is infinite, and there is no constraint on how far the random walk can travel from the origin. Indeed, for any distance, there is a nonzero probability that it goes at least that far. However, it turns out that the probability that the program halts is 1. In the terminology of probability theory, we would say that the two-dimensional random walk is *recurrent* at every point. This example illustrates how the analysis of probabilistic programs can rely on results from probability theory that are far from obvious. Indeed, the three-dimensional version is not recurrent; the probability that a random walk on $\mathbb{Z}^3$ eventually returns to the origin is strictly less than 1.

We now consider two programs that require *continuous* distributions. The semantics of such programs cannot be defined without the full power of *measure theory*, the mathematical foundation of probabilities and integration. The program of Fig. 1.3 approximates the constant π using *Monte Carlo integration*, a probabilistic integration method. The program works by taking a large number of independent, uniformly distributed random samples from the square $[0, 1] \times [0, 1]$ and counting the number that fall inside the unit circle. As the area of the square is 1 and the area of the part of the unit circle inside that square is $\pi/4$, by the law of large numbers we expect to see a $\pi/4$ fraction of sample points lying inside the circle.

```
i:=0;
n:=0;
while i<1e9 do
    x:=rand();
    y:=rand();
    if (x*x+y*y) < 1 then n:=n+1;
    i:=i+1
i:=4*n/1e9;
```

Figure 1.3 Probabilistic computation of π.

In this example, the random number generator `rand()` samples from the uniform distribution on the interval $[0, 1]$. This distribution is often called *Lebesgue measure*. Here the state space $[0, 1]$ is uncountable and the probability of drawing any particular $x \in [0, 1]$ is zero. Such probability distributions are called *continuous*. The natural question to ask about this program is not whether it terminates (it clearly does) but whether it returns a good approximation of π with high probability. We will answer this question in Section 1.3.

Finally, the program in Fig. 1.4 generates a real number between $[0, 1]$ whose expansion in base 3 does not contain any 1's. This program is not like the others in that it does not halt (nor is it meant to). The program generates a sample from a curious and in many respects counterintuitive distribution called the *Cantor distribution*. It cannot be described using discrete probability distributions (i.e. finite or countable weighted sums of point masses), although the program only uses a discrete fair coin as a source. The Cantor distribution is also an example of *continuous* probability distribution, which assigns probability zero to every element of the state space. It is also an example of a so-called *singular* distribution, since it can be shown that the set of all its possible outcomes—that is to say the set of all real numbers whose base-3 expansion contains no 1's—has measure 0 in the Lebesgue measure on $[0, 1]$.

```
x:=0;
d:=1;
while true do
    d:=d/3;
    x:=x+2*coin()*d
```

Figure 1.4 Cantor distribution program.

1.2 Measure theory: What you need to know

Measures are a generalization of the concepts of length, area, or volume of Euclidean geometry to other spaces. They form the basis of probability and integration theory. In this section, we explain what it means for a space to be a *measurable space*, we define *measures* on these spaces, and we examine the rich structure of *spaces of measures*, which will be essential to the semantics of probabilistic programs defined in Section 1.3.5. When not specified otherwise we use the word measure to refer to finite measures.

1.2.1 Some intuition

The concepts of length, area, and volume on Euclidean spaces are examples of *(positive) measures*. These are sufficient to illustrate most of the desired properties of measures and some pitfalls to avoid. For the sake of simplicity, let us examine the concept of *length*. Given an interval $[a, b] \subseteq \mathbb{R}$, its length is of course $\ell([a, b]) = b - a$. But the length function ℓ makes sense for other subsets of $\mathbb{R}$ besides intervals. So we will begin with two related questions:

(a) Which subsets of $\mathbb{R}$ can meaningfully be assigned a "length" consistent with the length of intervals? I.e., what should the domain of ℓ be?
(b) Which properties should the length function ℓ satisfy?

The answer to question (a) will give rise to the notion of *measurable space*, and the answer to question (b) will give rise to the notion of *measure*, both defined formally in Section 1.2.2.

Note that larger intervals have larger lengths: if $[a, b] \subseteq [c, d]$, then we have that $\ell([a, b]) = b - a \le d - c = \ell([c, d])$. This intuitively obvious property is a general feature of all positive measures: they associate nonnegative real numbers to subsets monotonically with respect to set inclusion. Let us now take two disjoint intervals

$[a_1, b_1]$ and $[a_2, b_2]$ with $b_1 < a_2$. It is natural to define the length of $[a_1, b_1] \cup [a_2, b_2]$ as the sum of the length of the respective intervals, i.e.

$$\ell([a_1, b_1] \cup [a_2, b_2]) = \ell([a_1, b_1]) + \ell([a_2, b_2]) = (b_1 - a_1) + (b_2 - a_2).$$

We can draw two conclusions from this natural definition. First, if A, B are two disjoint subsets of $\mathbb{R}$ in the domain of ℓ, then their union should also belong to the domain of ℓ, and the measure of the union should be the sum of the measures. More generally, if A_i, $1 \leq i \leq n$, is any finite collection of pairwise disjoint sets in the domain of ℓ, then $\bigcup_{i=1}^{n} A_i$ should also be in the domain of ℓ, and the measure of the union should be the sum of the measures of the A_i; that is,

$$\ell \left(\bigcup_{i=1}^{n} A_i \right) = \sum_{i=1}^{n} \ell(A_i). \tag{1.1}$$

A real-valued function on subsets satisfying (1.1) is called (finitely) *additive*. All measures will be finitely additive, and in fact more. Consider the countable collection of pairwise disjoint intervals $[n, n + 2^{-n})$, $n \in \mathbb{N}$. Generalising (1.1), it is natural to define ℓ on the union of these intervals as

$$\ell \left(\bigcup_{n=0}^{\infty} [n, n + 2^{-n}) \right) = \sum_{n=0}^{\infty} 2^{-n} = 2.$$

Again, we can draw two conclusions from this natural definition. First, if A_i for $i \in \mathbb{N}$ is a *countable* collection of pairwise disjoint sets in the domain of ℓ, then $\bigcup_{i \in \mathbb{N}} A_i$ should be in the domain of ℓ; second, that (1.1) should be extended to such countable collections, so that

$$\ell \left(\bigcup_{i=0}^{\infty} A_i \right) = \sum_{i=0}^{\infty} \ell(A_i). \tag{1.2}$$

A function ℓ satisfying (1.2) is called *countably additive* or *σ-additive*. Every measure will be countably additive. The reader will now legitimately ask: what happens if the sum in (1.2) diverges? To deal with this behaviour, one simply allows ∞ as a possible length, that is to say the codomain of ℓ can be the extended real line $\mathbb{R}^+ \cup \{\infty\}$. In particular, this allows us to define the length of $\mathbb{R}$ via (1.2) as:

$$\ell(\mathbb{R}) = \ell \left(\bigcup_{n \in \mathbb{Z}} [n, n + 1) \right) = \infty.$$

However, for the purpose of semantics of probabilistic programs, we will not need measures taking the value ∞. A measure is called *finite* if it only assigns finite values in $\mathbb{R}$ to any set in its domain. *For the remainder of this chapter, the term "measure", otherwise unqualified, will refer to finite measures.*

Consider now subsets $A \subseteq B$ of $\mathbb{R}$ in the domain of ℓ such that $\ell(A) \le \ell(B) < \infty$. From finite additivity, it would make sense to define $\ell(B \setminus A) = \ell(B) - \ell(A)$, since $B = A \cup (B \setminus A)$ is a partition of B. In other words, it would also be natural to require that if $A \subseteq B$ and A and B are in the domain of ℓ, then so should be $B \setminus A$, and $\ell(B \setminus A) = \ell(B) - \ell(A)$. Thus the domain of ℓ should be closed under complementation.

The reader may now be wondering: If the domain of ℓ contains all intervals and is closed under countable pairwise disjoint unions and complementation, that is already a very large set of subsets of $\mathbb{R}$. Is it possible that a length can be sensibly assigned to *all* subsets of $\mathbb{R}$? In other words, can we extend ℓ to domain $\mathcal{P}(\mathbb{R})$? Alas, it turns out that this is not possible. An important and desirable property of the length function ℓ is that it is *translation invariant*: given a set A with length $\ell(A)$ (for example an interval), if the entire set A is translated a fixed distance, say d, then its length should be unchanged; that is, $\ell(A) = \ell(\{x + d \mid x \in A\})$. Vitali (1905) constructed a countable set of subsets of the interval $[0, 1)$, called *Vitali sets*, which are pairwise disjoint, translates of each other (modulo 1), and whose union is $[0, 1)$. They would all have to have the same measure, which would break the countable additivity axiom (1.2). Vitali sets are examples of *non-measurable sets*. They provide an example of subsets of $\mathbb{R}$ which are incompatible with the basic assumptions of how the length function should behave. Thus the domain of the length function cannot be $\mathcal{P}(\mathbb{R})$, because it cannot contain the Vitali sets.

The length function ℓ described in the preceding paragraphs is called the *Lebesgue measure* on $\mathbb{R}$. We now turn our attention to axiomatizing the intuitive ideas presented thus far.

1.2.2 Measurable spaces and measures

We start by axiomatizing the closure properties of the domain of a measure (such as the length function) which we have described informally in the previous section.

A σ-*algebra* $\mathcal{B}$ on a set S is a collection of subsets of S containing the empty set $\varnothing$ and closed under complementation in S and countable union (hence also under countable intersection). A pair $(S, \mathcal{B})$, where S is a set and $\mathcal{B}$ is a σ-algebra on S, is called a *measurable space*. The elements of $\mathcal{B}$ are called the *measurable sets* of the space. In a probabilistic setting, elements of S and $\mathcal{B}$ are often called *outcomes* and *events*, respectively. The domain of a measure, for example the length function, will always be a σ-algebra. If the σ-algebra is obvious from the context, we simply say that S is a measurable space. The set of all subsets $\mathcal{P}(S)$ is a σ-algebra called the *discrete σ-algebra*, but as noted above, it may not be an appropriate choice since it may not allow the definition of certain measures. However, it is always an acceptable choice for finite or countable sets, and we will always assume that finite and countable sets are equipped with the discrete σ-algebra.

If $\mathcal{F}$ is a collection of subsets of a set S, we define $\sigma(\mathcal{F})$, the σ-algebra *generated* by $\mathcal{F}$, to be the smallest σ-algebra containing $\mathcal{F}$. That is, $\sigma(\mathcal{F})$ is the smallest collection of subsets of S containing $\mathcal{F}$ and $\varnothing$ and closed under countable union and complement. Equivalently,

$$\sigma(\mathcal{F}) \triangleq \bigcap \{\mathcal{A} \mid \mathcal{F} \subseteq \mathcal{A} \text{ and } \mathcal{A} \text{ is a } \sigma\text{-algebra}\}.$$

Note that $\sigma(\mathcal{F})$ is well-defined, since the intersection is nonempty, as $\mathcal{F} \subseteq \mathcal{P}(S)$ and $\mathcal{P}(S)$ is a σ-algebra. If $(S, \mathcal{B})$ is a measurable space and $\mathcal{B} = \sigma(\mathcal{F})$, we say that the space is *generated* by $\mathcal{F}$.

Measurable functions. Let $(S, \mathcal{B}_S)$ and $(T, \mathcal{B}_T)$ be measurable spaces. A function $f: S \rightarrow T$ is *measurable* if the inverse image $f^{-1}(B) = \{x \in S \mid f(x) \in B\}$ of every measurable subset $B \in \mathcal{B}_T$ is a measurable subset of S. When $\mathcal{B}_T$ is generated by $\mathcal{F}$, then f is measurable if and only if $f^{-1}(B)$ is measurable for every $B \in \mathcal{F}$.

An example of a measurable function is $\chi_B: S \rightarrow \{0, 1\}$, the *characteristic function* of a measurable set B:

$$\chi_B(s) = \begin{cases} 1, & s \in B, \\ 0, & s \notin B. \end{cases}$$

Here, $(S, \mathcal{B})$ is a measurable space, $B \in \mathcal{B}$, and $\{0, 1\}$ is the discrete space.

Measures. A *signed (finite) measure* on $(S, \mathcal{B})$ is a countably additive map $\mu: \mathcal{B} \rightarrow \mathbb{R}$ such that $\mu(\varnothing) = 0$. Recall that *countably additive* means that if $\mathcal{A}$ is a countable set of pairwise disjoint events, then $\mu(\bigcup \mathcal{A}) = \sum_{A \in \mathcal{A}} \mu(A)$. Equivalently, if $A_0, A_1, A_2, \ldots$ is a countable chain of events (a countable collection of measurable sets such that $A_n \subseteq A_{n+1}$ for all $n \geq 0$), then $\lim_n \mu(A_n)$ exists and is equal to $\mu(\bigcup_n A_n)$.

A signed measure on $(S, \mathcal{B})$ is called *positive* if $\mu(A) \geq 0$ for all $A \in \mathcal{B}$. A positive measure on $(S, \mathcal{B})$ is called a *probability measure* if $\mu(S) = 1$ and a *subprobability measure* if $\mu(S) \leq 1$. A measurable set B such that $\mu(B) = 0$ is called a *μ-nullset*, or simply a *nullset* if there is no ambiguity. A property is said to hold *μ-almost surely* (μ-a.s.) or *μ-almost everywhere* (μ-a.e.) if the set of points on which it does *not* hold is contained in a nullset.

In probability theory, measures are sometimes called *distributions*. We will use the terms *measure* and *distribution* synonymously.

For $s \in S$, the *Dirac measure*, or *Dirac delta*, or *point mass* on s is the probability measure

$$\delta_s(B) = \begin{cases} 1, & s \in B, \\ 0, & s \notin B. \end{cases}$$

A measure is *discrete* if it is a countable weighted sum of Dirac measures. In particular a convex sum of Dirac measures is a discrete probability measure. These are finite or countable sums of the form $\sum_{s \in C} a_s \delta_s$, where all $a_s \geq 0$ and $\sum_{s \in C} a_s = 1$.

A measure μ on a measurable set $(S, \mathcal{B})$ is called *continuous* if $\mu(\{s\}) = 0$ for all singleton sets $\{s\}$ in $\mathcal{B}$. The Lebesgue measures on $\mathbb{R}^n$ for $n \in \mathbb{N}$, that is, the lengths, areas, volumes, etc., are the best known examples of continuous measures.

Pushforward measure. Given $f : (S, \mathcal{B}_S) \to (T, \mathcal{B}_T)$ measurable and a measure μ on $\mathcal{B}_S$, one defines the *pushforward measure* $f_*(\mu)$ on $\mathcal{B}_T$ by

$$f_*(\mu)(B) = \mu(f^{-1}(B)), \quad B \in \mathcal{B}_T. \tag{1.3}$$

This measure is well defined; since f is measurable, f^{-1} maps measurable sets of $\mathcal{B}_T$ to measurable sets of $\mathcal{B}_S$.

Lebesgue integration. An important operation on measures and measurable functions is *Lebesgue integration*. Let $(S, \mathcal{B})$ be a measurable space. Given a measure $\mu : \mathcal{B} \to \mathbb{R}$ and bounded measurable function $f : S \to \mathbb{R}$, say bounded above by M and below by m, the *Lebesgue integral* of f with respect to μ, denoted $\int f \, d\mu$, is a real number obtained as the limit of finite weighted sums of the form

$$\sum_{i=0}^{n} f(s_i)\mu(B_i), \tag{1.4}$$

where $B_0, \ldots, B_n$ is a measurable partition of S, the value of f does not vary more than $(M - m)/n$ in any B_i, and $s_i \in B_i$, $1 \leq i \leq n$. The limit is taken over increasingly finer measurable partitions of the space. For the details of this construction, see for example (Dudley, 2002, Ch. 4) or (Aliprantis and Border, 1999, Ch. 11).

For a finite discrete space $n = \{1, 2, \ldots, n\}$, the integral reduces simply to a weighted sum: $\int f \, d\mu = \sum_{i=1}^{n} f(i)\mu(i)$.

The *bounded integral* $\int_B f \, d\mu$, where $B \in \mathcal{B}$, is obtained by integrating over the set B instead of all of S; equivalently,

$$\int_B f \, d\mu \triangleq \int \chi_B \cdot f \, d\mu, \tag{1.5}$$

where χ_B is the characteristic function of B and $\chi_B \cdot f$ is the pointwise product of real-valued functions.

Absolute continuity. Given two measures μ, ν, we say that μ is *absolutely continuous* with respect to ν and write $\mu \ll \nu$ if for all measurable sets B, if $\nu(B) = 0$, then $\mu(B) = 0$. Informally, if ν assigns no mass to B, then neither does μ. Although we will not need it, we cannot fail to mention the following theorem, which is one the pillars of probability theory.

Theorem 1.1 (Radon–Nikodym)   *Let μ, ν be two finite measures on a measurable space $(S, \mathcal{B})$ and assume that μ is absolutely continuous with respect to ν. Then there exists a measurable function $f \colon S \to \mathbb{R}$ defined uniquely up to a μ-nullset such that*

$$\mu(B) = \int_B f \, d\nu.$$

The function f is called the Radon–Nikodym derivative *of μ with respect to ν.*

Radon–Nikodym derivatives are known in probability theory as *probability density functions*. For example, the standard Gaussian probability measure is absolutely continuous with respect to Lebesgue measure (the length function) on $\mathbb{R}$. Its Radon–Nikodym derivative with respect to Lebesgue measure is the Gaussian density function $f(t) = \frac{1}{\sqrt{2\pi}} e^{-t^2/2}$.

Products. Given two measurable spaces $(S_1, \mathcal{B}_1)$ and $(S_2, \mathcal{B}_2)$, one can construct the *product space* $(S_1 \times S_2, \mathcal{B}_1 \otimes \mathcal{B}_2)$, where $S_1 \times S_2$ is the cartesian product and $\mathcal{B}_1 \otimes \mathcal{B}_2$ is the σ-algebra on $S_1 \times S_2$ generated by all *measurable rectangles* $B_1 \times B_2$ for $B_1 \in \mathcal{B}_1$ and $B_2 \in \mathcal{B}_2$. In other words,

$$\mathcal{B}_1 \otimes \mathcal{B}_2 \triangleq \sigma\left(\{B_1 \times B_2 \mid B_1 \in \mathcal{B}_1, B_2 \in \mathcal{B}_2\}\right). \tag{1.6}$$

The measurable rectangles $B_1 \times B_2$ are a generalisation of the case where $S_1 = S_2 = \mathbb{R}$ and B_1, B_2 are intervals. The product of two measurable spaces is thus the measurable space generated by the corresponding measurable rectangles.

A measure on the product space $(S_1 \times S_2, \mathcal{B}_1 \otimes \mathcal{B}_2)$ is sometimes called a *joint distribution*. Due to the inductive construction (1.6) of $\mathcal{B}_1 \otimes \mathcal{B}_2$ from measurable rectangles $B_1 \times B_2$, joint distributions are uniquely determined by their values on measurable rectangles. For details of this extension, see (Dudley, 2002, §4.4).

A special class of joint distributions are the *product measures* $\mu_1 \otimes \mu_2$ formed from a measure μ_1 on $(S_1, \mathcal{B}_1)$ and a measure μ_2 on $(S_2, \mathcal{B}_2)$, defined on measurable rectangles by

$$(\mu_1 \otimes \mu_2)(B_1 \times B_2) \triangleq \mu_1(B_1)\mu_2(B_2).$$

As mentioned, this extends uniquely to a joint distribution $\mu_1 \otimes \mu_2 \colon \mathcal{B}_1 \otimes \mathcal{B}_2 \to \mathbb{R}$. Product measures capture the idea of *independence*: sampling $\mu_1 \otimes \mu_2$ to obtain an element of $S_1 \times S_2$ is equivalent to independently sampling μ_1 on S_1 and μ_2 on S_2.

Markov Kernels. Let $(S, \mathcal{B}_S)$ and $(T, \mathcal{B}_T)$ be measurable spaces. A function $P\colon S \times \mathcal{B}_T \to \mathbb{R}$ is called a *Markov kernel* (also called a Markov transition, measurable kernel, stochastic kernel, or stochastic relation) if

- for fixed $A \in \mathcal{B}_T$, the map $\lambda s.P(s, A)\colon S \to \mathbb{R}$ is a measurable function on $(S, \mathcal{B}_S)$; and
- for fixed $s \in S$, the map $\lambda A.P(s, A)\colon \mathcal{B}_T \to \mathbb{R}$ is a probability measure on $(T, \mathcal{B}_T)$.

These properties allow integration on the left and right, respectively.

The measurable spaces and Markov kernels form a category, the *Kleisli category of the Giry monad*; see Panangaden (1998, 2009); Doberkat (2007); Giry (1982). In this context, we occasionally write $P\colon (S, \mathcal{B}_S) \to (T, \mathcal{B}_T)$ or just $P\colon S \to T$. Composition is given by integration: for $P\colon S \to T$ and $Q\colon T \to U$,

$$(P \; ; \; Q)(s, A) = \int_{t \in T} P(s, dt) \cdot Q(t, A). \tag{1.7}$$

Associativity of composition follows essentially from Fubini's theorem (see Chung, 1974, or Halmos, 1950). Markov kernels were introduced in Lawvere (1962) and were proposed as a model of probabilistic while programs in Kozen (1985).

The definition of the pushforward of a measure can be extended to Markov kernels as follows. Given a measure μ on $\mathcal{B}_S$, its *pushforward* under the Markov kernel $P\colon (S, \mathcal{B}_S) \to (T, \mathcal{B}_T)$ is the measure $P_*(\mu)$ on $\mathcal{B}_T$ defined by

$$P_*(\mu)(B) = \int_{s \in S} P(s, B) \, \mu(ds). \tag{1.8}$$

Any measurable map $f\colon (S, \mathcal{B}_S) \to (T, \mathcal{B}_T)$ determines a trivial Markov kernel $s \mapsto \delta_{f(s)}$, and under this definition the pushforward operation defined in Eq. (1.3) is just a special case of Eq. (1.8).

The reader will note that we changed notation in displaying the Lesbegue integrals in Equations (1.7) and (1.8) when compared to Eq. (1.5). This is standard notation in measure theory, in particular in the presence of Markov kernels, but for clarity we note that these could have been written as:

$$(P \; ; \; Q)(s, A) = \int_T Q(-, A) \, dP(s, -)$$

$$P_*(\mu)(B) = \int_S P(-, B) \, d\mu.$$

Recall that because P and Q are Markov kernels the functions $Q(-, A)$ and $P(-, B)$ are measurable and $P(s, -)$ is a probability measure.

1.2.3 Spaces of measures

The set of all (finite, signed) measures on a measurable set $(S, \mathcal{B})$ will be denoted $\mathcal{M}(S, \mathcal{B})$, or simply $\mathcal{M}S$ if $\mathcal{B}$ is understood. The spaces $\mathcal{M}S$ carry a very rich structure which lies at the heart of the denotational semantics described in Section 1.3.5. We now describe this structure.

Vector space structure. First, $\mathcal{M}S$ is always a *real vector space* whose addition operation and scalar multiplication are defined pointwise:

$$(\mu + \nu)(B) \triangleq \mu(B) + \nu(B) \qquad\qquad (a\mu)(B) \triangleq a\mu(B)$$

for $B \in \mathcal{B}$, $\mu, \nu \in \mathcal{M}S$, and $a \in \mathbb{R}$. It is easily argued that $\mu + \nu$ and $a\mu$ defined in this way are measures whenever μ, ν are.

The set of measures on a finite set $n = \{0, 1, \ldots, n - 1\}$ is isomorphic as a real vector space to $\mathbb{R}^n$: the mass $\mu(i)$ of the element i corresponds to the ith coordinate of a vector in $\mathbb{R}^n$ in the standard basis. This perspective is well established in the theory of Markov chains, where initial or stationary distributions are represented as row or column vectors depending on the convention (see e.g. Norris (1997)).

Normed space structure. The second important structure carried by $\mathcal{M}S$ is its *norm*. Combined with the vector space structure, this makes $\mathcal{M}S$ a *Banach space*. The norm $\|\mu\|$ of a measure μ is called the *total variation norm* and defined by

$$\|\mu\| \triangleq \sup \left\{ \sum_{i=1}^{n} |\mu(B_i)| : \{B_1, \ldots, B_n\} \text{ is a finite measurable partition of } S \right\}. \quad (1.9)$$

For a positive measure μ, the norm is always $\|\mu\| = \mu(S)$, and for a probability measure, $\|\mu\| = 1$. In other words, probability measures lie on the boundary of the unit ball of the space of measures. However, a general (signed) measure can assign positive mass to some regions of S and negative mass to others, hence the idea of partitioning the space and the presence of the absolute value in (1.9).

The total variation norm interacts with the vector space structure to make $\mathcal{M}S$ a normed vector space: $\|x\| \geq 0$, $\|x\| = 0$ iff $x = 0$, $\|a\mu\| = |a| \|\mu\|$, and $\|\mu + \nu\| \leq \|\mu\| + \|\nu\|$. Moreover, the normed vector space $\mathcal{M}S$ is *complete*, which means that all Cauchy sequences of measures converge to a limit in $\mathcal{M}S$. A complete normed vector space is called a *Banach space*.

In the case of a finite set n, using the vector space representation of $\mathcal{M}n$ described above, the norm of a finite measure $\mu \in \mathcal{M}n$ is simply the usual ℓ_1-norm, sometimes also called *Manhattan* or *taxicab norm* $\|\mu\| = \sum_{i=1}^{n} |\mu(i)|$. A probability measure on n is thus always a vector in $\mathbb{R}^n$ of ℓ_1-norm 1.

Order structure. The final piece of structure is a *partial order*. Measures have a natural pointwise order: $\mu \leq \nu$ if $\mu(B) \leq \nu(B)$ for every $B \in \mathcal{B}$.

Any pair of distinct probability measures are incomparable in this order, as $\mu(B) < \nu(B)$ for a some $B \in \mathcal{B}$ implies $\nu(B^c) < \mu(B^c)$, where B^c is the complement of B, since $\mu(B) + \mu(B^c) = 1 = \nu(B) + \nu(B^c)$. A measure μ is positive if $0 \leq \mu$. The set of all positive measures is called the *positive cone* of $\mathcal{MS}$ and denoted $(\mathcal{MS})^+$. Probability measures are of course positive measures, so the probability measures in $\mathcal{MS}$ are precisely the positive measures of norm 1, and the subprobability measures are the positive measures of norm at most 1. In other words, the subprobability measures comprise the positive orthant of the unit ball of $\mathcal{MS}$.

The partial order is compatible with the vector space structure in the sense that

- if $\mu \leq \nu$, then $\mu + \rho \leq \nu + \rho$; and
- if $0 \leq a \in \mathbb{R}$ and $\mu \leq \nu$, then $a\mu \leq a\nu$.

We say that the operations of addition and multiplication by a positive scalar are *monotone*. Moreover, the partial order in fact defines a *lattice structure*, that is to say every pair of measures μ, ν have a least upper bound and a greatest lower bound with respect to the partial order, defined explicitly by

$$(\mu \vee \nu)(B) \triangleq \sup \{\mu(A \cap B) + \nu(A^c \cap B) \mid A \in \mathcal{B}\}$$
$$(\mu \wedge \nu)(B) \triangleq \inf \{\mu(A \cap B) + \nu(A^c \cap B) \mid A \in \mathcal{B}\}.$$

In particular, the *positive part* of a measure μ can be defined as $\mu^+ = \mu \vee 0$, and its negative part as $\mu^- = (-\mu) \vee 0$. Note that both μ^+ and μ^- are positive measures, and in fact every measure can be decomposed as the difference of two positive measures, since $\mu = \mu^+ - \mu^-$. Moreover, there is a measurable set C such that $\mu^+ = \mu_C$ and $\mu^- = -\mu_{C^c}$, where μ_C is the measure $\mu_C(A) = \mu(A \cap C)$; equivalently, $\mu(B) \geq 0$ for all measurable sets $B \subseteq C$ and $\mu(B) \leq 0$ for all measurable sets $B \subseteq C^c$. The set C is *essentially unique* in the sense that if C' is any other measurable set satisfying these properties, then all measurable subsets of the symmetric difference $C \triangle C'$ are μ-nullsets. This is known as the *Hahn–Jordan decomposition theorem*; see e.g. (Dudley, 2002, Th. 5.6.1). The sum of the positive and negative part is called the *modulus* of μ and is denoted $|\mu| = \mu^+ + \mu^-$.

The order is compatible with the norm in the sense that $|\mu| \leq |\nu|$ implies $\|\mu\| \leq \|\nu\|$. A Banach space with a lattice structure that is compatible with both the linear and normed structures in the sense detailed above is called a *Banach lattice*. Thus $\mathcal{MS}$ is always a Banach lattice.

In order to interpret `while` loops in Section 1.3.5, we will need one last order-theoretic concept. A Banach lattice is said to be *σ-order-complete* or *σ-Dedekind-complete* if every countable order-bounded set of measures in $\mathcal{MS}$ has a supremum in $\mathcal{MS}$. From the perspective of theoretical computer science, this notion is similar to the completeness property for ω-complete partial orders (ω-CPOs) in domain theory, the key difference being that only sets of elements with a common upper bound are considered. In particular, the set $\mathcal{M}1 \cong \mathbb{R}$ is σ-order complete but is not an ω-CPO, because this would require adding a point at infinity, thereby losing the vector space structure. In fact, every space of measures $\mathcal{MS}$ is σ-order complete.

In the case of a finite set $\{1, \ldots, n\}$, the order is just the usual pointwise order on $\mathbb{R}^n$: $(x_1, \ldots, x_n) \leq (y_1, \ldots, y_n)$ if $x_i \leq y_i$, $1 \leq i \leq n$, and the lattice structure on $\mathcal{M}n \cong \mathbb{R}^n$ simplifies to $(\mu \vee \nu)(\{i\}) = \max\{\mu(\{i\}), \nu(\{i\})\}$ and $(\mu \wedge \nu)(\{i\}) = \min\{\mu(\{i\}), \nu(\{i\})\}$.

Operators. One of the advantages of working with spaces of measures is that, since they are vector spaces, we can do linear algebra on them. In the case of measure spaces over finite sets, i.e. spaces of the form $\mathbb{R}^n$, this means the usual matrix-based linear algebra. In the general case, we have the infinite-dimensional generalisation in terms of *linear operators*.

A *linear operator* (or simply an *operator*) $T \colon V \to W$ between two vector spaces over the reals is a map satisfying $T(x + y) = T(x) + T(y)$ and $T(ax) = aT(x)$ for $x, y \in V$ and $a \in \mathbb{R}$. In the finite-dimensional case, if we choose bases $(v_1, \ldots, v_m)$ and $(w_1, \ldots, w_n)$ for V and W respectively, T can be represented as an $n \times m$ matrix $\mathbf{T}$ whose ij^{th} component $\mathbf{T}_{ij}$ is the jth coordinate of $T(v_i)$ in the basis of W.

We will be mostly interested in operators that send probability measures to subprobability measures. Recall that probability measures are precisely the positive measures of norm 1. A *positive operator* between Banach lattices is an operator that sends positive vectors to positive vectors, i.e. $Tv \geq 0$ whenever $v \geq 0$. A *stochastic operator* is a positive operator preserving the norm of positive vectors, i.e. such that $\|Tv\| = \|v\|$ whenever $v \geq 0$. Similarly, an operator sending probabilities to subprobabilities is characterised as a positive operator contracting the norm of positive vectors, i.e. such that $\|Tv\| \leq \|v\|$ whenever $v \geq 0$.

In the case of measures over finite spaces $\mathcal{M}n \cong \mathbb{R}^n$, we can represent stochastic operators as *(right) stochastic matrices*, matrices with nonnegative entries whose rows each sum to 1.[1] Indeed, any operator A sending probability measures $p = (p_1, \ldots, p_n)$ to probability measures must be stochastic, as the kth row of A is the result of applying A to the Dirac delta δ_k:

$$(\delta_k A)_j = \sum_{i=1}^{n} \delta_k(i) A_{ij} = A_{kj}.$$

---

[1] We follow the convention adopted in the literature on Markov chains, where measures are represented as row vectors and operators are applied from the right (hence "right stochastic").

1.3 Semantics of a simple imperative probabilistic language

Now we are ready to give the formal semantics of a simple imperative programming language with two types of probabilistic operations: a function sampling from a Bernoulli distribution with parameter $p = 1/2$, and a function sampling from the uniform distribution on the interval $[0, 1]$. This simple language will cover the examples in Figs. 1.1, 1.2, 1.3, and 1.4.

1.3.1 Syntax

We start by defining the syntax of the language.

(i) Deterministic terms:

$$
\begin{aligned}
d ::=\ & a & a \in \mathbb{R}, \text{ constants} \\
 | \ & x & x \in \text{Var, a countable set of variables} \\
 | \ & d \text{ op } d & \text{op} \in \{+, -, *, \div\}
\end{aligned}
$$

(ii) Terms:

$$
\begin{aligned}
t ::=\ & d & d \text{ a deterministic term} \\
 | \ & \texttt{coin()} \ | \ \texttt{rand()} & \text{sample in } \{0, 1\} \text{ and } [0, 1], \text{ respectively} \\
 | \ & t \text{ op } t & \text{op} \in \{+, -, *, \div\}
\end{aligned}
$$

(iii) Tests:

$$
\begin{aligned}
b ::=\ & \texttt{true} \ | \ \texttt{false} \\
 | \ & d == d \ | \ d < d \ | \ d > d & \text{comparison of deterministic terms} \\
 | \ & b \text{ \&\& } b \ | \ b \text{ || } b \ | \ !b & \text{Boolean combinations of tests}
\end{aligned}
$$

(iv) Programs:

$$
\begin{aligned}
e ::=\ & \texttt{skip} \\
 | \ & x := t & \text{assignment} \\
 | \ & e \ ; \ e & \text{sequential composition} \\
 | \ & \texttt{if } b \texttt{ then } e \texttt{ else } e & \text{conditional} \\
 | \ & \texttt{while } b \texttt{ do } e & \texttt{while} \text{ loop}
\end{aligned}
$$

Remark 1.2 We disallow probabilistic terms in tests for simplicity in the presentation. This restriction is without loss of generality, as one could consider such expressions as syntactic sugar; the probabilistic term can always be removed using auxiliary variables. For example, the right-hand program below is the de-sugared version of the left-hand program using a fresh auxiliary variable x:

$$\texttt{if coin()} == 1 \texttt{ then } e_1 \texttt{ else } e_2 \qquad x := \texttt{coin() ; if } x == 1 \texttt{ then } e_1 \texttt{ else } e_2$$

1.3.2 Operational versus denotational semantics

As we outlined in the introduction, the main purpose of this chapter is to define a formal mathematical interpretation—a *semantics*—for probabilistic programs. Having a semantics provides the tools necessary to reason about the properties of programs, as we will show with a few concrete examples. However, the focus of this chapter will primarily be on defining the semantics itself.

We will present two classical types of semantics: *operational* and *denotational*. The purpose of operational semantics is to model the step-by-step executions of the program on a machine. It will model the evolution of the state of the machine described by its *memory-state*, the values assigned to each variable and to each random number generator in a program, together with a stack of instructions. On the other hand, the purpose of denotational semantics is to model the intended mathematical meaning of a probabilistic program in terms of probability distributions.

1.3.3 Operational semantics of probabilistic programs

The random number generator $\texttt{coin()}$ is represented by an independent and identically distributed (i.i.d.) sequence of random variables distributed according to the Bernoulli distribution on $\{0, 1\}$ with parameter $p = 1/2$. Similarly, $\texttt{rand()}$ is represented by an i.i.d. sequence distributed according to the uniform distribution on $[0, 1]$. When a program runs, we fix at the beginning two infinite streams $m_0 m_1 m_2 \cdots$ and $p_0 p_1 p_2 \cdots$, where each $m_i \in \{0, 1\}$ is an independent sample from the Bernoulli distribution with $p = 1/2$ and each $p_i \in [0, 1]$ is an independent sample from the uniform distribution on $[0, 1]$. Intuitively, these sequences represent infinite stacks of random numbers that are available to the program. Each time the function $\texttt{coin()}$ or $\texttt{rand()}$ is called, the next random number is popped from the stack. We use the auxiliary head and tail functions $\mathsf{hd}(m_0 m_1 m_2 \cdots) = m_0$ and $\mathsf{tl}(m_0 m_1 m_2 \cdots) = m_1 m_2 m_3 \cdots$ to implement this. This deterministic behaviour reflects the behaviour of pseudo-random number generators which, given a seed, deterministically generate such sequences (or to be precise, seemingly random cyclical sequences with very long periods).

Given a program containing n variables $\{x_1, \ldots, x_n\}$, as described in Section 1.3.1, a *memory-state* is modelled as a triple (s, m, p) consisting of a store $s \colon n \to \mathbb{R}$ and a pair of infinite streams $m \in \{0, 1\}^\omega$ and $p \in [0, 1]^\omega$ representing the current streams of available random digits. A machine-state is a 4-tuple (e, s, m, p), where e corresponds to a stack of instructions and (s, m, p) is a memory-state.

We can now define the operational semantics of our language. The operational semantics is defined in terms of a single-step *reduction relation* $(e, s, m, p) \longrightarrow (e', s', m', p')$ between machine-states. The reduction relation describes the step-by-step evaluation of a program and its corresponding effect on the state of the machine. The reflexive transitive closure of this relation will be denoted $\overset{*}{\longrightarrow}$ and will be used to talk about multi-step transitions.

In order to define the reduction relation, we first define the semantics of terms. Each term t will be interpreted as a function

$$[\![t]\!] : \mathbb{R}^n \times \mathbb{N}^\omega \times \mathbb{N}^\omega \to \mathbb{R} \times \mathbb{N}^\omega \times \mathbb{N}^\omega.$$

Intuitively, the value of $[\![t]\!]$ on (s, m, p) is a triple (a, m', p'), where a is the real value of the term and m' and p' are the new stacks of random numbers. Formally, $[\![t]\!]$ is defined inductively:

$$[\![r]\!] : (s, m, p) \mapsto (r, m, p)$$
$$[\![x_i]\!] : (s, m, p) \mapsto (s(i), m, p)$$
$$[\![\mathtt{coin}()]\!] : (s, m, p) \mapsto (\mathsf{hd}\, m, \mathsf{tl}\, m, p)$$
$$[\![\mathtt{rand}()]\!] : (s, m, p) \mapsto (\mathsf{hd}\, p, m, \mathsf{tl}\, p)$$
$$
\begin{aligned}
[\![t_1 \ \mathtt{op}\ t_2]\!] : (s, m, p) \mapsto \ & \mathtt{let}\ (a_1, m', p') = [\![t_1]\!](s, m, p)\ \mathtt{in} \\
& \mathtt{let}\ (a_2, m'', p'') = [\![t_2]\!](s, m', p')\ \mathtt{in} \\
& (a_1\ \mathtt{op}\ a_2, m'', p'')
\end{aligned}
$$

where $\mathtt{op} \in \{+, -, *, \div\}$. In other words, we evaluate t_1 first, which produces a value a_1 but might consume some values from m and p, popping those stacks to leave m' and p'; these new stacks are then used in the evaluation of t_2, which in turn changes them to m'' and p'' and yields a value a_2. The values a_1 and a_2 are combined with the appropriate arithmetic operation, and that is returned with the stacks m'' and p''.

There is already an interesting question to consider. Note that we are evaluating $t_1 \ \mathtt{op}\ t_2$ from left to right, i.e. starting with t_1. This is an arbitrary decision. Would evaluation from right to left be equally valid? It clearly would not always give the same value; e.g., the program $\mathtt{rand}() \div \mathtt{rand}()$ evaluated on $(s, m, (.2, .5, p))$ from left to right would give $(.4, m, p)$, but evaluated from right to left would give $(2.5, m, p)$. However, perhaps surprisingly, the two methods of evaluation are *probabilistically* equivalent, which means they give the same values with equal probability. The denotational semantics to be given below will allow us to reason more easily about such facts.

We now define the semantics of tests. Each test b will be interpreted as a function

$$[\![b]\!] : \mathbb{R}^n \times \mathbb{N}^\omega \times \mathbb{N}^\omega \to \{\mathtt{true}, \mathtt{false}\}$$

defined inductively by

$$[\![t_1 == t_2]\!] : (s,m,p) \mapsto \begin{cases} \texttt{true} & \text{if } [\![t_1]\!](s,m,p) = [\![t_2]\!](s,m,p) \\ \texttt{false} & \text{otherwise} \end{cases}$$

$$[\![t_1 < t_2]\!] : (s,m,p) \mapsto \begin{cases} \texttt{true} & \text{if } [\![t_1]\!](s,m,p) < [\![t_2]\!](s,m,p) \\ \texttt{false} & \text{otherwise} \end{cases}$$

$$[\![t_1 > t_2]\!] : (s,m,p) \mapsto \begin{cases} \texttt{true} & \text{if } [\![t_1]\!](s,m,p) > [\![t_2]\!](s,m,p) \\ \texttt{false} & \text{otherwise} \end{cases}$$

$$[\![b_1 \ \&\& \ b_2]\!] : (s,m,p) \mapsto [\![b_1]\!](s,m,p) \wedge [\![b_2]\!](s,m,p)$$

$$[\![b_1 \ || \ b_2]\!] : (s,m,p) \mapsto [\![b_1]\!](s,m,p) \vee [\![b_2]\!](s,m,p)$$

$$[\![!b]\!] : (s,m,p) \mapsto \neg [\![b]\!](s,m,p)$$

where $\wedge, \vee$ and $\neg$ are the usual Boolean operations on $\{\texttt{true}, \texttt{false}\}$. Note that in the definition of the three base cases above, m,p are arguments of both $[\![t_1]\!]$ *and* $[\![t_2]\!]$, unlike in the semantics of terms. This is because we only allow deterministic terms in tests, thus $[\![t_1]\!]$ does not consume any random numbers, leaving the stacks m,p unchanged for the evaluation of $[\![t_2]\!]$. For the same reason, it is unnecessary to include m,p in the output of $[\![b]\!]$.

We can now define the reduction relation $\longrightarrow$. The relation is given by the rules gathered in Table 1.1. We use the traditional notation $s[i \mapsto l]$ to denote the n-tuple defined exactly as s apart from at position i where value l is used instead. We will say that the execution of a program e *terminates* from the memory-state (s,m,p) if there exists a memory-state (s',m',p') such that

$$(e,s,m,p) \xrightarrow{*} (\texttt{skip}, s', m', p').$$

We will say that a program e *diverges* from a state (s,m,p) if it does not terminate.

1.3.4 Operational semantics through examples

To illustrate how the system described above works concretely, let us examine the operational semantics of the programs described in Section 1.1.

Example 1: A simple Markov chain

We start with the very simple program displayed in Fig. 1.1. Using the rule for assignments, the rule for sequential composition and the definition of the reflexive transitive closure $\xrightarrow{*}$ we get the following derivation, where for notational convenience we write e for while $x == 0$ do $x := $ coin():

Assignment:

$$\frac{[\![t]\!](s,m,p) = (a,m',p')}{(x_i := t,s,m,p) \longrightarrow (\texttt{skip}, s[i \mapsto a], m',p')}$$

Sequential composition:

$$\frac{(e_1,s,m,p) \longrightarrow (e_1',s',m',p')}{(e_1 \text{ ; } e_2,s,m,p) \longrightarrow (e_1' \text{ ; } e_2,s',m',p')} \qquad \frac{}{(\texttt{skip} \text{ ; } e,s,m,p) \longrightarrow (e,s,m,p)}$$

Conditional:

$$\frac{[\![b]\!](s,m,p) = \texttt{true}}{(\texttt{if } b \texttt{ then } e_1 \texttt{ else } e_2, s,m,p) \longrightarrow (e_1,s,m,p)}$$

$$\frac{[\![b]\!](s,m,p) = \texttt{false}}{(\texttt{if } b \texttt{ then } e_1 \texttt{ else } e_2, s,m,p) \longrightarrow (e_2,s,m,p)}$$

whi*le loops:*

$$\frac{}{(\texttt{while } b \texttt{ do } e, s,m,p) \longrightarrow (\texttt{if } b \texttt{ then } (e \text{ ; } \texttt{while } b \texttt{ do } e) \texttt{ else } \texttt{skip}, s,m,p)}$$

Reflexive-transitive closure:

$$\frac{}{(e,s,m,p) \overset{*}{\longrightarrow} (e,s,m,p)} \qquad \frac{(e_1,s_1,m_1,p_1) \longrightarrow (e_2,s_2,m_2,p_2)}{(e_1,s_1,m_1,p_1) \overset{*}{\longrightarrow} (e_2,s_2,m_2,p_2)}$$

$$\frac{(e_1,s_1,m_1,p_1) \overset{*}{\longrightarrow} (e_2,s_2,m_2,p_2) \qquad (e_2,s_2,m_2,p_2) \overset{*}{\longrightarrow} (e_3,s_3,m_3,p_3)}{(e_1,s_1,m_1,p_1) \overset{*}{\longrightarrow} (e_3,s_3,m_3,p_3)}$$

Table 1.1 *Rules of the operational semantics*

$$\frac{\dfrac{\dfrac{(x := 0, s,m,p) \longrightarrow (\texttt{skip}, s[x \mapsto 0], m, p)}{(x := 0 \text{ ; } e, s,m,p) \longrightarrow (\texttt{skip} \text{ ; } e, s[x \mapsto 0], m, p)} \quad (\texttt{skip} \text{ ; } e, s[x \mapsto 0], m, p) \longrightarrow (e, s[x \mapsto 0], m, p)}{(x := 0 \text{ ; } e, s,m,p) \overset{*}{\longrightarrow} (\texttt{skip} \text{ ; } e, s[x \mapsto 0], m, p) \quad (\texttt{skip} \text{ ; } e, s[x \mapsto 0], m, p) \overset{*}{\longrightarrow} (e, s[x \mapsto 0], m, p)}}{(x := 0 \text{ ; } e, s,m,p) \overset{*}{\longrightarrow} (e, s[x \mapsto 0], m, p)}$$

We now turn our attention to $(e, s[x \mapsto 0], m, p)$. Using the rule for while loops and conditionals we get (using the same definition of e as above)

$$(e, s[x \mapsto 0], m, p) \overset{*}{\longrightarrow} (x := \texttt{coin}() \text{ ; } e, s[x \mapsto 0], m, p) \qquad (1.10)$$

since $[\![x == 0]\!](s[x \mapsto 0], m, p) = \texttt{true}$. We now encounter our first probabilistic behaviour:

$$(x := \texttt{coin}() \text{ ; } e, s[x \mapsto 0], m, p) \overset{*}{\longrightarrow} (e, [s \mapsto \texttt{hd } m], \texttt{tl } m, p).$$

If hd m = 0, then s does not change, and we are back at the left-hand state of (1.10), but with tl m instead of m. This same sequence of steps continues until encountering a suffix of m of the form $1m'$, at which time, combining the rule for while loops and conditionals, we get

$$(e, s[x \mapsto 1], m', p) \xrightarrow{*} (\text{skip}, s[x \mapsto 1], m', p)$$

since $[\![x == 0]\!](s[x \mapsto 1], m', p) = \text{false}$. If no such suffix $1m'$ exists, then (1.10) continues forever. We can conclude that

$$(x := 0 \; ; \; e, s, m, p) \xrightarrow{*} (\text{skip}, s[x \mapsto 1], m', p)$$

for some m', that is, the program terminates in some state $(s[x \mapsto 1], m', p)$ when started in state (s, m, p), if and only if there exists a suffix of m of the form $1m'$, that is, there exist $k \geq 0$ and $m' \in \{0, 1\}^\omega$ such that $m = 0^k 1m'$. We can compute the probability of termination with a simple calculation:

$$\mathbb{P}\left[\exists m' \; (x := 0 \; ; \; e, s, m, p) \xrightarrow{*} (\text{skip}, s[x \mapsto 1], m', p)\right]$$

$$= \mathbb{P}\left[\exists k \geq 0 \; \exists m' \; m = 0^k 1m'\right]$$

$$= \sum_{k=1}^{\infty} 2^{-k} = 1$$

as claimed in the introduction.

Example 2: A random walk on $\mathbb{Z}^2$

We now turn our attention to the program of Fig. 1.2, which implements a random walk on the set $\mathbb{Z}^2$. We show fewer details, since the previous example already described some of the simplest derivations. The program is written with the function step for readability and notational convenience, but it is of course equivalent to the inline program where each instance of step in main is substituted by its definition. For any $s \in \mathbb{R}^4$ and $m, p \in \mathbb{N}$, there can be one of four actions:

$$(\text{step}, s, 00m, p) \xrightarrow{*} (\text{skip}, s[(\mathsf{u}, \mathsf{v}) \mapsto (0, -1), (\mathsf{x}, \mathsf{y}) \mapsto (0, 0)], m, p)$$

$$(\text{step}, s, 01m, p) \xrightarrow{*} (\text{skip}, s[(\mathsf{u}, \mathsf{v}) \mapsto (-1, 0), (\mathsf{x}, \mathsf{y}) \mapsto (0, 1)], m, p)$$

$$(\text{step}, s, 10m, p) \xrightarrow{*} (\text{skip}, s[(\mathsf{u}, \mathsf{v}) \mapsto (1, 0), (\mathsf{x}, \mathsf{y}) \mapsto (1, 0)], m, p)$$

$$(\text{step}, s, 11m, p) \xrightarrow{*} (\text{skip}, s[(\mathsf{u}, \mathsf{v}) \mapsto (0, 1), (\mathsf{x}, \mathsf{y}) \mapsto (1, 1)], m, p)$$

The probability of each of these outcomes is $1/4$, and in all cases the program enters the loop, since $[\![\,!(\mathsf{u} == \mathbb{0}) \; || \; !(\mathsf{v} == \mathbb{0})]\!] = \text{true}$.

Now define the i.i.d. random variables $X_1, X_2, \ldots$ on $\mathbb{Z}^2$ such that each X_i takes one of the values $(0,1),(0,-1),(1,0),(-1,0)$, each with probability $1/4$, as well as the random variables

$$S_n = \sum_{i=1}^{n} X_i$$

where the sum is the usual componentwise sum on $\mathbb{Z}^2$. With these definitions in place, and since the loop is entered at least once, the first few steps of the reduction relation give

$$(\texttt{main}, s, m, p) \xrightarrow{*}$$

$$(\texttt{while !(u == 0) || !(v == 0) do step(u,v)}, s[(\texttt{u},\texttt{v}) \mapsto (i,j)], \texttt{tl}^4(m), p)$$

where (i,j) is distributed according to S_2 and the $\texttt{tl}^4(m)$ indicates that four random bits were consumed. The program will exit the loop if there exists n such that $S_{2n} = (0,0)$; the factor 2 is because a return to 0 is only possible after an even number of calls to the function $\texttt{step}$. If such an n exists, then the rule for $\texttt{while}$ loops gives

$$(\texttt{main}, s, m, p) \xrightarrow{*} (\texttt{skip}, s[(\texttt{u},\texttt{v}) \mapsto (0,0)], \texttt{tl}^{4n}(m), p).$$

It follows that to compute the probability that the program terminates amounts to computing

$$\mathbb{P}\left[\exists n \; (\texttt{main}, s, m, p) \xrightarrow{*} (\texttt{skip}, s[(\texttt{u},\texttt{v}) \mapsto (0,0)], \texttt{tl}^{4n}(m), p)\right]$$

$$= \mathbb{P}\left[\bigvee_{n=0}^{\infty} S_{2n} = (0,0)\right] \tag{1.11}$$

In order for $S_{2n} = (0,0)$, there must exist m such that the walk performed m steps up, m steps down, $n - m$ steps left and $n - m$ steps right. Following Durrett (1996),

$$\mathbb{P}\left[S_{2n} = (0,0)\right] = 4^{-2n} \sum_{m=0}^{n} \frac{(2n)!}{m!m!(n-m)!(n-m)!}$$

$$= 4^{-2n} \binom{2n}{n} \sum_{m=0}^{n} \binom{n}{m}^2$$

$$= 4^{-2n} \binom{2n}{n}^2. \tag{1.12}$$

Since the events $S_{2n} = (0,0)$ for $n \in \mathbb{N}$ are not disjoint—one can return to $(0,0)$ twice in $2n$ steps if $n > 1$—one cannot simply sum these contributions to get the probability of termination as we did in the previous example. However, it can be shown that

$$\sum_{n=0}^{\infty} \mathbb{P}\left[S_{2n} = (0,0)\right] = \sum_{m=0}^{\infty} \mathbb{P}\left[\bigvee_{n=0}^{\infty} S_{2n} = (0,0)\right]^{m}, \tag{1.13}$$

as both expressions describe the expected number of visits to the origin in an infinite random walk (Durrett, 1996, Ch. 3, Thm. 2.2). Moreover, using Stirling's approximation with (1.12), it can be shown that the sums in (1.13) diverge (Durrett, 1996, Ch. 2, Thm. 1.4), which occurs iff the probability (1.11) is 1; that is, the program of Fig. 1.2 terminates with probability one. However, the *expected time to termination* is infinite: in probabilistic terms, the random walk on $\mathbb{Z}^2$ is recurrent but not positively recurrent.

Example 3: Probabilistic computation of π

The program given in Fig. 1.3 is different from the previous two examples in several ways. First of all, it samples from a *continuous* distribution, therefore relies on the full power of measure theory. Secondly, it clearly terminates, so the question this time is not to determine the probability of termination, but rather to evaluate the correctness of the program. Considering the intended purpose of the program, which is to compute an approximation of π, the question we will answer is the following: Given an error tolerance $\varepsilon > 0$, what is the probability that the final numerical value of `pi` is within ε of π?

Let $N = 1e9$ (one billion), the number of iterations of the loop. It is not difficult to see that, starting from a state (s, m, p), the program halts in a state

$$(\texttt{prog}, s, m, p) \xrightarrow{*} (\texttt{skip}, s[\texttt{i} \mapsto 4n/N, \texttt{n} \mapsto n, \ldots], m, \texttt{tl}^{2N}(p))$$

for some integer $0 \le n \le N$. The value n/N is the average of N samples of the random variable

$$Z = \begin{cases} 1 & \text{if } X^2 + Y^2 < 1 \\ 0 & \text{else} \end{cases}$$

where X and Y are independent random variables distributed uniformly on $[0, 1]$.

Let us compute the expected value of Z. First, it is easy to compute the density function for X^2 (and thus Y^2):

$$\mathbb{P}\left[X^2 \le t\right] = \mathbb{P}\left[X \le \sqrt{t}\right] = \int_0^{\sqrt{t}} \mathbb{1}_{[0,1]}(x)\, dx = \sqrt{t}$$

for $0 \le t \le 1$. The density of X^2 is thus given by

$$f(t) = \frac{\partial \mathbb{P}\left[X^2 \le t\right]}{\partial t} = \frac{1}{2\sqrt{t}}\mathbb{1}_{[0,1]}(t)$$

It is well known that the density of the sum of two independent distributions is given by the convolution of their densities, i.e.

$$(f * f)(t) = \int_{-\infty}^{\infty} \frac{1}{2\sqrt{x}} \mathbb{1}_{[0,1]}(x) \frac{1}{2\sqrt{t-x}} \mathbb{1}_{[0,1]}(t-x) \, dx$$

$$= \begin{cases} \int_0^t \frac{1}{4\sqrt{x}\sqrt{t-x}} \, dx & \text{if } 0 \le t \le 1 \\ \int_{t-1}^1 \frac{1}{4\sqrt{x}\sqrt{t-x}} \, dx & \text{if } 1 < t \le 2 \end{cases}$$

Since we are only interested in computing $\mathbb{P}\left[X^2 + Y^2 \le 1\right]$, we need only compute the first expression above, which under the substitution $u = \sqrt{x/t}$ yields:

$$\int_0^t \frac{1}{4\sqrt{x}\sqrt{t-x}} \, dx = \int_0^1 \frac{1}{2\sqrt{1-u^2}} \, du = \frac{1}{2}(\sin^{-1}(1) - \sin^{-1}(0)) = \frac{\pi}{4}.$$

Thus

$$\mathbb{P}\left[X^2 + Y^2 \le 1\right] = \int_0^1 (f * f)(t) \, dt - \int_0^1 \frac{\pi}{4} \, dt = \frac{\pi}{4}$$

We have therefore computed that Z is a Bernoulli variable with probability of success $\pi/4$. In particular, its variance is $\sigma^2 = \pi/4 - (\pi/4)^2$. We can now use Chebyshev's inequality to get:

$$\mathbb{P}\left[\left|\frac{n}{N} - \frac{\pi}{4}\right| > \varepsilon\right] \le \frac{\sigma^2}{N\varepsilon^2}.$$

For example, for $\varepsilon = 0.0005$ and $N = 1e9$, the program outputs an approximation of π which is correct up to 2 significant digits with probability greater than 99.9%. In terms of the operational semantics, we can write the probability of the informal Hoare triple

$$\mathbb{P}\left[\{\} \, (\texttt{prog}, s, m, p) \xrightarrow{*} (\texttt{skip}, s', m', p') \, \{s'(\texttt{i}) \in [3.139, 3.144]\}\right] \ge 0.999.$$

We will show in Section 1.3.6 that much tighter bounds can be obtained using a more sophisticated inequality than Chebyshev's inequality.

Example 4: The Cantor distribution

The final example given in Fig. 1.4 constructs a curious object know as the Cantor distribution. This is a distribution on $[0,1]$ that has uncountable support (it is therefore continuous), yet this support has Lebesgue measure (that is to say length) zero. It is an example of a so-called *singular distribution*.

A simple look at the program given by Fig. 1.4 shows that it does not terminate. However, it is possible to give it an operational (and denotational) semantics.

Starting from an initial configuration (s, m, p) where $m = m_0 m_1 m_2 \cdots$, it is not difficult to see from the rules of the operational semantics that the program generates an the infinite sequence

$$(\mathsf{x} := \mathbf{0}; \mathsf{d} := 1; \mathsf{w}, s, m, p) \xrightarrow{*}$$

$$(\mathsf{w}, s\, [\mathsf{x} \mapsto 0, \mathsf{d} \mapsto 1], m, p) \xrightarrow{*}$$

$$\left(\mathsf{w}, s\, \left[\mathsf{x} \mapsto \frac{2m_0}{3}, \mathsf{d} \mapsto \frac{1}{3}\right], \mathsf{tl}(m), p\right) \xrightarrow{*}$$

$$\left(\mathsf{w}, s\, \left[\mathsf{x} \mapsto \sum_{i=1}^{k} \frac{2m_{i-1}}{3^i}, \mathsf{d} \mapsto \frac{1}{3^k}\right], \mathsf{tl}^k(m), p\right) \xrightarrow{*} \cdots \qquad (1.14)$$

The program can thus be understood as generating a random real number between 0 and 1 whose base-3 expansion does not contain any ones. After k iterations of the loop, the probability that the base-3 expansion of the number is given by a particular sequence $a_1 \cdots a_k$, where $a_i \in \{0, 2\}$, is 2^{-k}. We now show how this interpretation of the program relates to the Cantor measure.

We first look at a σ-algebra. For $a_1 \cdots a_k \in \{0, 1, 2\}^k$, each set

$$C_{a_1 \cdots a_k} := \{x \in [0, 1] \mid \text{the base-3 expansion of } x \text{ starts with } a_1 \cdots a_k\}$$

is a measurable set for the usual σ-algebra on $[0, 1]$. Moreover, it can be shown that the σ-algebra generated by all these sets is in fact the usual σ-algebra on $[0, 1]$.

With the σ-algebra in place, we can define a measure. Following the behaviour of the program above, it makes sense to define

$$\mu(C_{a_1 \cdots a_k}) = \begin{cases} 2^{-k} & \text{if } a_1 \cdots a_k \in \{0, 2\}^k \\ 0 & \text{otherwise.} \end{cases} \qquad (1.15)$$

It can be shown that this definition extends to the entire σ-algebra on $[0, 1]$, thereby defining a *bona fide* measure (in the same way that the definition of the product measure on rectangles extends to the entire product σ-algebra, see Section 1.2.2). This measure is the *Cantor measure*, which we shall denote by κ. Note that for any $x \in [0, 1]$, the probability of any singleton must satisfy $\kappa(\{x\}) \leq 2^{-k}$ for all k, thus $\kappa(\{x\}) = 0$ and the Cantor measure is therefore continuous. If the base-3 expansion of x contains a 1, the inequality above is trivially satisfied. If it does not, it follows from the fact that $\{x\} \subseteq C_{a_1 \cdots a_k}$, where $a_1 \cdots a_k$ consists of the first k digits in the base-3 expansion of x. It can also be shown that the set

$$C = \{x \in [0, 1] \mid \text{the base-3 expansion of } x \text{ has no ones}\}$$

has Lebesgue measure 0, but Cantor measure 1. This set, called the *Cantor set*, is clearly in one-to-one correspondence with the set of possible traces described by the operational semantics described by (1.14).

1.3.5 Denotational semantics of probabilistic programs

Consider the simple program $\mathtt{x} := \mathtt{coin()}$. As we have just seen, the operational semantics models the two possible machine-state transitions defined by this program, viz.

$$(\mathtt{x} := \mathtt{coin()}, s, m, p) \longrightarrow (\mathtt{skip}, s[\mathtt{x} \mapsto 0], \mathtt{tl}\, m, p)$$
$$(\mathtt{x} := \mathtt{coin()}, s, m, p) \longrightarrow (\mathtt{skip}, s[\mathtt{x} \mapsto 1], \mathtt{tl}\, m, p)$$

depending on the value of hd m, each associated with the probability $1/2$. Thus two possible executions are explored *separately*. The denotational approach explores both possibilities *simultaneously*. It does so by changing the notion of state. Operationally, a state is a machine state, i.e. a mathematical representation of the memory state and of the stack of instructions. Denotationally, a state is a *probability distribution over memory states*. The two possible memory states $s[\mathtt{x} \mapsto 0]$ and $s[\mathtt{x} \mapsto 1]$, which correspond operationally to two distinct executions, are combined into a single state $\frac{1}{2}s[\mathtt{x} \mapsto 0] + \frac{1}{2}s[\mathtt{x} \mapsto 1]$. As a consequence, the program $\mathtt{x} := \mathtt{coin()}$ can be interpreted as the operation which associates to a state s the *distribution over states* $\frac{1}{2}s[\mathtt{x} \mapsto 0] + \frac{1}{2}s[\mathtt{x} \mapsto 1]$.

More generally, since a state s can be identified with the Dirac measure δ_s (see Section 1.2.2), the denotational semantics will view the program $\mathtt{x} := \mathtt{coin()}$ as an *operator* (we will justify this term in a moment) which maps the probability distribution δ_s to the probability distribution $\frac{1}{2}s[\mathtt{x} \mapsto 0] + \frac{1}{2}s[\mathtt{x} \mapsto 1]$. This is the essence of the denotational perspective: a program is interpreted as an operator mapping probability distributions to (sub)probability distributions. It follows that denotationally, a program has a single trace (or execution) for a given input, but this trace keeps track of all possible memory state transitions and their probabilities simultaneously. It also follows that an input state could be a nontrivial distribution, for example $\frac{1}{2}s[\mathtt{x} \mapsto 0] + \frac{1}{2}s[\mathtt{x} \mapsto 1]$ could be an *input* for the program $\mathtt{x} := \mathtt{coin()}$.

We now formalize the intuition given above following Kozen (1981). Given a program obeying the syntax of Section 1.3.1 and containing n variables $\{x_1, \ldots, x_n\}$ ranging over $\mathbb{R}$, a *state* will be modelled as a probability distribution μ on $\mathbb{R}^n$ and a program e will be interpreted as an operator $[\![e]\!]: \mathcal{M}\mathbb{R}^n \to \mathcal{M}\mathbb{R}^n$ called a *state transformer*. To define this interpretation formally, we start with the semantics of terms. Each term t denotes a map $[\![t]\!]: \mathbb{R}^n \to \mathcal{M}\mathbb{R}$ defined inductively as follows.

Here a_i represents the value of the variable x_i, $1 \le i \le n$.

$$[\![r]\!](a_1, \ldots, a_n) = \delta_r, \ r \in \mathbb{R}$$

$$[\![x_i]\!](a_1, \ldots, a_n) = \delta_{a_i}$$

$$[\![\mathtt{coin}()]\!](a_1, \ldots, a_n) = \frac{1}{2}\delta_0 + \frac{1}{2}\delta_1$$

$$[\![\mathtt{rand}()]\!](a_1, \ldots, a_n) = \lambda$$

$$[\![t_1 \ \mathtt{op} \ t_2]\!](a_1, \ldots, a_n) = \mathtt{op}_*([\![t_1]\!](a_1, \ldots, a_n) \otimes [\![t_2]\!](a_1, \ldots, a_n))$$

where $\mathtt{op} \in \{+, -, \times, \div\}$ and λ is the Lebesgue (uniform) measure on $[0, 1]$. Recall that $\mu \otimes \nu$ is the product of the measures μ and ν and that $\mathtt{op}_*$ denotes the pushforward operation (see Section 1.2.2). In this case, $[\![t_1]\!](a_1, \ldots, a_n) \in \mathcal{M}\mathbb{R}$ and $[\![t_2]\!](a_1, \ldots, a_n) \in \mathcal{M}\mathbb{R}$, $[\![t_1]\!](a_1, \ldots, a_n) \otimes [\![t_2]\!](a_1, \ldots, a_n) \in \mathcal{M}(\mathbb{R}^2)$, $\mathtt{op} \colon \mathbb{R}^2 \to \mathbb{R}$, and $\mathtt{op}_* \colon \mathcal{M}(\mathbb{R}^2) \to \mathcal{M}\mathbb{R}$. By definition, for B a measurable subset of $\mathbb{R}$,

$$\mathtt{op}_*([\![t_1]\!](a_1, \ldots, a_n) \otimes [\![t_2]\!](a_1, \ldots, a_n))(B)$$

$$= [\![t_1]\!](a_1, \ldots, a_n) \otimes [\![t_2]\!](a_1, \ldots, a_n) \left\{ (u, v) \in \mathbb{R}^2 \mid u \ \mathtt{op} \ v \in B \right\}.$$

It follows almost immediately from this definition that:

Proposition 1.3   *The denotational semantics of any term is a Markov kernel* $\mathbb{R}^n \to \mathcal{M}\mathbb{R}$.

The denotational semantics of tests is given by *subsets of* $\mathbb{R}^n$ defined inductively as follows:

$$[\![t_1 \ \mathtt{==} \ t_2]\!] = \{(a_1, \ldots, a_n) \in \mathbb{R}^n \mid [\![t_1]\!](a_1, \ldots, a_n) = [\![t_2]\!](a_1, \ldots, a_n)\}$$

$$[\![t_1 \ \mathtt{<} \ t_2]\!] = \{(a_1, \ldots, a_n) \in \mathbb{R}^n \mid [\![t_1]\!](a_1, \ldots, a_n) < [\![t_2]\!](a_1, \ldots, a_n)\}$$

$$[\![t_1 \ \mathtt{>} \ t_2]\!] = \{(a_1, \ldots, a_n) \in \mathbb{R}^n \mid [\![t_1]\!](a_1, \ldots, a_n) > [\![t_2]\!](a_1, \ldots, a_n)\}$$

$$[\![b_1 \ \mathtt{\&\&} \ b_2]\!] = [\![b_1]\!] \cap [\![b_2]\!]$$

$$[\![b_1 \ \mathtt{||} \ b_2]\!] = [\![b_1]\!] \cup [\![b_2]\!]$$

$$[\![!b]\!] = [\![b]\!]^c.$$

Note that since we limit ourselves to deterministic guards, the comparisons in the right-hand side of the first three cases above are between Dirac deltas, thus between elements of $\mathbb{R}^n$, as one would expect. It is not hard to show the following result:

Proposition 1.4   *The denotational semantics of any test is a measurable subset of* $\mathbb{R}^n$.

Each measurable subset $B \subseteq \mathbb{R}^n$ defines a linear operator $T_B \colon \mathcal{M}\mathbb{R}^n \to \mathcal{M}\mathbb{R}^n$ defined as

$$T_B(\mu)(C) = \mu(B \cap C). \tag{1.16}$$

In particular, every test defines such an operator. Note that the operator T_B does not in general send probability distributions to probability distributions, since the mass outside of B is lost. Thus T_B sends probability distributions to *sub-probability distributions*, that is to say measures whose total mass is *at most* 1.

We can now define the denotational semantics of programs. Programs will be interpreted as (linear) *operators* $\mathcal{M}\mathbb{R}^n \rightarrow \mathcal{M}\mathbb{R}^n$. The inductive definition is as follows:

(i) $[\![\texttt{skip}]\!] = \mathrm{Id}_{\mathcal{M}\mathbb{R}^n} : \mathcal{M}\mathbb{R}^n \rightarrow \mathcal{M}\mathbb{R}^n$, the identity operator $\mu \mapsto \mu$.

(ii) Assignments: Prop. 1.3 interprets terms t as Markov kernels $[\![t]\!] : \mathbb{R}^n \rightarrow \mathcal{M}\mathbb{R}$. Given such a term t and an index $1 \leq i \leq n$, we define the Markov kernel $F_t^i : \mathbb{R}^n \rightarrow \mathcal{M}\mathbb{R}^n$ as

$$F_t^i(x_1, \ldots, x_n) = \delta_{x_1} \otimes \ldots \otimes \delta_{i-1} \otimes [\![t]\!](x_1, \ldots, x_n) \otimes \delta_{x_{i+1}} \otimes \ldots \otimes \delta_{x_n}$$

Using this definition, we define $[\![x_i := t]\!]$ as the operator

$$[\![x_i := t]\!](\mu) = (F_t^i)_*(\mu) \tag{1.17}$$

where $(F_t^i)_*$ is the pushforward of Markov kernels defined in (1.8). It is useful to consider special cases of this formula. Consider first the expression $x_i := r$ for some constant $r \in \mathbb{R}$. The definition above becomes

$$[\![x_i := r]\!](\mu)(B_1 \times \cdots \times B_n)$$
$$= \int_{\mathbb{R}^n} \delta_{x_1} \otimes \cdots \otimes \delta_{x_{i-1}} \otimes \delta_r \otimes \delta_{x_{i+1}} \otimes \cdots \otimes \delta_{x_n} (B_1 \otimes \cdots \otimes B_n)\, d\mu$$
$$= \int_{\mathbb{R}^n} \delta_{x_1}(B_1) \cdots \delta_{x_{i-1}}(B_{i-1})\delta_r(B_i)\delta_{x_{i+1}}(B_{i+1}) \cdots \delta_{x_n}(B_n)\, d\mu$$
$$= \mu(B_1 \times \cdots \times B_{i-1} \times \mathbb{R} \times B_{i+1} \times \cdots \times B_n)\delta_r(B_i).$$

Similarly, for $x_i := \texttt{coin}()$ we get

$$[\![x_i := \texttt{coin}()]\!](\mu)(B_1 \times \cdots \times B_n)$$
$$= \mu(B_1 \times \cdots \times B_{i-1} \times \mathbb{R} \times B_{i+1} \times \cdots \times B_n)\left(\frac{1}{2}\delta_0 + \frac{1}{2}\delta_1\right)(B_i).$$

(iii) $[\![e_1 ; e_2]\!] = [\![e_2]\!] \circ [\![e_1]\!]$, the usual composition of operators.

(iv) $\texttt{if } b \texttt{ then } e_1 \texttt{ else } e_2$ is the operator defined by

$$[\![\texttt{if } b \texttt{ then } e_1 \texttt{ else } e_2]\!] = [\![e_1]\!] \circ T_{[\![b]\!]} + [\![e_2]\!] \circ T_{[\![b]\!]^c} \tag{1.18}$$

where $T_{[\![b]\!]}$ and $T_{[\![b]\!]^c}$ are defined as in (1.16).

(v) To define the semantics of $\texttt{while}$ loops, we use the equivalence of the following two programs,

$$\texttt{while } b \texttt{ do } e \qquad \texttt{if } b \texttt{ then } (e ; \texttt{while } b \texttt{ do } e) \texttt{ else skip},$$

to write a fixpoint equation which will define the semantics of $[\![\texttt{while } b \texttt{ do } e]\!]$. Formally, and following (1.18), the equivalence of programs above implies that

$$[\![\texttt{while } b \texttt{ do } e]\!] = [\![\texttt{while } b \texttt{ do } e]\!] \circ [\![e]\!] \circ T_{[\![b]\!]} + T_{[\![b]\!]^c}$$

We therefore *define* $[\![\texttt{while } b \texttt{ do } e]\!]$ to be the least fixpoint of the transformation on operators defined by

$$\tau(S) = S \circ [\![e]\!] \circ T_{[\![b]\!]} + T_{[\![b]\!]^c} \tag{1.19}$$

This least fixpoint can be constructed explicitly by the familiar construction

$$[\![\texttt{while } b \texttt{ do } e]\!] = \bigvee_{n \geq 0} \tau^n(0) = \sum_{k=0}^{\infty} T_{[\![b]\!]^c} \circ \left([\![e]\!] \circ T_{[\![b]\!]} \right)^k , \tag{1.20}$$

invoking the fact that countable norm-bounded directed sets have suprema and that τ preserves such suprema.

Theorem 1.5   *The denotational semantics of any program given by the syntax of Section 1.3.1 is a positive operator of norm at most one.*

A comment on non-terminating programs

As we will see when examining the Cantor program (see Fig. 1.4) in Section 1.3.6, the construction of the least fixpoint via Eq. (1.20) returns the constant linear operator 0 for non-terminating programs of the form

$$\texttt{while true do } e.$$

This is in complete agreement with what happens in the formalism of Kleene Algebras with Tests (Kozen, 1997) where the following equivalence holds:

$$\texttt{while true do } e \triangleq (\texttt{true}; e)^*; \texttt{false} = \texttt{false}.$$

Here, $\texttt{false}$ is the program that always aborts corresponding to the constant linear operator 0.

Recall that we also saw in Section 1.3.4 that the Cantor program can be given a non-trivial operational semantics in terms of infinite traces. How can we reconcile these two seemingly conflicting semantics?

There are (at least) two ways. The first is to declare that infinite traces are not valid, and identify diverging executions with a crash behaviour. The second, mathematically much more interesting solution, is not to consider the *least* fixpoint solution to the equation $\tau(S) = S$ (where τ is defined in Eq. (1.19)), but another fixpoint given by the *mean ergodic theorem*. When the guard of the $\texttt{while}$ loop is $\texttt{true}$, Eq. (1.19) simplifies to $\tau(S) = S \circ [\![e]\!]$. Now suppose for simplicity's sake that e does not contain any $\texttt{while}$ loop, and note that by Theorem 1.5 $[\![e]\!]$:

$\mathcal{M}\mathbb{R}^n \to \mathcal{M}\mathbb{R}^n$ is a is a positive operator of norm at most one. It can be shown (see e.g. Dunford et al., 1971; Eisner et al., 2015) that $[\![e]\!]$ is *mean ergodic*, that is to say that for any measure $\mu \in \mathbb{R}^n$ the limit

$$P_{[\![e]\!]}(\mu) \triangleq \lim_{n\to\infty} \frac{1}{n} \sum_{j=0}^{n-1} [\![e]\!]^j(\mu) \tag{1.21}$$

exists. Moreover, $P_{[\![e]\!]}$ is a projection $\mathcal{M}\mathbb{R}^n \to \text{fix}([\![e]\!])$, the subspace of $[\![e]\!]$-invariant measures, and satisfies the fixpoint equation defining the `while` loop:

$$\tau\left(P_{[\![e]\!]}\right) = P_{[\![e]\!]} \circ [\![e]\!] = P_{[\![e]\!]}.$$

This provides an alternative fixpoint semantics in the case of the non-terminating `while` true program, which is the denotational counterpart to the operational semantics in terms of infinite traces. In fact, it would be tempting to decompose the semantics of *any* `while` loop into its terminating component, defined via the least fixpoint construction of Eq. (1.20), and its non-terminating component, defined via the mean ergodic theorem as we have just described. We leave this possibility to be explored in future work.

1.3.6 Denotational semantics through examples

Example 1: Simple Markov chain
We start by looking at the very simple program of Fig. 1.1. Since it contains a single variable, its denotational semantics is given by an operator

$$[\![\texttt{x := 0 ; while x == 0 do x := coin()}]\!] : \mathcal{M}\mathbb{R} \to \mathcal{M}\mathbb{R}$$

which we compute *compositionally*, that is to say line-by-line. Following the definition of the denotational semantics of assignments given in the previous section, the first line of the program is interpreted as:

$$[\![\texttt{x := 0}]\!] : \mathcal{M}\mathbb{R} \to \mathcal{M}\mathbb{R} \qquad\qquad \mu \mapsto \mu(\mathbb{R})\delta_0,$$

since $[\![\texttt{0}]\!] = \delta_0$. Note how the presence of the term $\mu(\mathbb{R})$ is what makes this operator linear: the constant function $\mu \mapsto \delta_0$—which might be a tempting semantics for assignments—would not be linear; assignments must be weighted by the total mass of the input measure. Analogously, we have

$$[\![\texttt{x := coin()}]\!] : \mathcal{M}\mathbb{R} \to \mathcal{M}\mathbb{R} \qquad\qquad \mu \mapsto \mu(\mathbb{R})(\tfrac{1}{2}\delta_0 + \tfrac{1}{2}\delta_1).$$

Next, we evaluate the interpretation of the `while` loop using (1.20). It is easy to see from the definition that the denotation of the test $[\![\texttt{x == 0}]\!]$ is simply the measurable singleton $\{0\}$. Now consider the first two nonzero terms in the join of (1.20):

$$\tau^0(0)(\mu) = 0$$

$$\tau^1(0)(\mu) = T_{\{0\}^c}(\mu) = \mu(-\cap \{0\}^c)$$

$$\tau^2(0)(\mu) = \left(T_{\{0\}^c} + T_{\{0\}^c} \circ [\![x := \text{coin}()]\!] \circ T_{\{0\}}\right)(\mu)$$

$$= \mu(-\cap \{0\}^c) + \frac{\mu(\{0\})}{2}\delta_1.$$

One can show by induction that

$$\tau^k(0)(\mu) = \mu(-\cap \{0\}^c) + \sum_{i=1}^{k-1} \frac{\mu(0)}{2^i}\delta_1$$

$$= \mu(-\cap \{0\}^c) + (1 - 2^{-(k-1)})\mu(\{0\})\delta_1,$$

which for positive μ is an increasing sequence with limit $\mu(-\cap \{0\}^c) + \mu(\{0\})\delta_1$. It follows that $[\![\text{while } x == 0 \text{ do } x := \text{coin}()]\!] : \mathcal{M}\mathbb{R} \to \mathcal{M}\mathbb{R}$ is the operator defined by

$$\mu \mapsto \mu(-\cap \{0\}^c) \cap \mu(\{0\})\delta_1 = \mu(\{0,1\})\delta_1 + \mu(-\cap \{0,1\}^c).$$

The interpretation of the entire program is now obtained by operator composition:

$$[\![x := 0 \text{ ; while } x == 0 \text{ do } x := \text{coin}()]\!] : \mathcal{M}\mathbb{R} \to \mathcal{M}\mathbb{R} \qquad \mu \mapsto \mu(\mathbb{R})\delta_1.$$

In other words, given any input measure, the program outputs the Dirac delta over 1 up to the scalar factor required to make the operator linear. In particular, if the input is a probability distribution, then the output is simply δ_1, which is clearly consistent with the behaviour of the Markov chain of Fig. 1.1.

Example 2: Random walk on $\mathbb{Z}^2$

We start by computing the semantics of step. Since there are four variables u, v, x, y, we will get an operator $\mathcal{M}\mathbb{R}^4 \to \mathcal{M}\mathbb{R}^4$ (assume that the variables are ordered alphabetically; i.e., u corresponds to the first component of $\mathbb{R}^4$, etc.) Working line-by-line, we get

(1) $[\![x := \text{coin}()]\!] : \mathcal{M}\mathbb{R}^4 \to \mathcal{M}\mathbb{R}^4$

$$\mu \mapsto \lambda(B_1 \times B_2 \times B_3 \times B_4).\mu(B_1 \times B_2 \times \mathbb{R} \times B_4)\left(\frac{1}{2}\delta_0 + \frac{1}{2}\delta_1\right)(B_3)$$

(2) $[\![x := \text{coin}() \text{ ; } y := \text{coin}()]\!] : \mathcal{M}\mathbb{R}^4 \to \mathcal{M}\mathbb{R}^4$

$$\mu \mapsto \lambda(B_1 \times B_2 \times B_3 \times B_4).$$

$$\mu(B_1 \times B_2 \times \mathbb{R} \times \mathbb{R})\left(\frac{1}{2}\delta_0 + \frac{1}{2}\delta_1\right)(B_3)\left(\frac{1}{2}\delta_0 + \frac{1}{2}\delta_1\right)(B_4)$$

(3) $[\![\mathtt{x} := \mathtt{coin}() \; ; \; \mathtt{y} := \mathtt{coin}() \; ; \; \mathtt{u} := \mathtt{u} + (\mathtt{x} - \mathtt{y})]\!] \colon \mathcal{M}\mathbb{R}^4 \to \mathcal{M}\mathbb{R}^4$

$\mu \mapsto \lambda(B_1 \times B_2 \times B_3 \times B_4).$

$$\int_{\mathbb{R}^4} \delta_{u+(x-y)}(B_1)\delta_v(B_2)\delta_x(B_3)\delta_y(B_4) \, d[\![\mathtt{x} := \mathtt{coin}() \; ; \; \mathtt{y} := \mathtt{coin}()]\!](\mu)$$

$$= \mu(\mathbb{R}^4)\left(\frac{1}{4}\mu(B_1 \times B_2 \times \mathbb{R}^2)\delta_0(B_3)\delta_0(B_4)\right.$$

$$+ \frac{1}{4}\mu(B_1 - 1 \times B_2 \times \mathbb{R}^2)\delta_0(B_3)\delta_1(B_4)$$

$$+ \frac{1}{4}\mu(B_1 + 1 \times B_2 \times \mathbb{R}^2)\delta_1(B_3)\delta_0(B_4)$$

$$\left.+ \frac{1}{4}\mu(B_1 \times B_2 \times \mathbb{R}^2)\delta_1(B_3)\delta_1(B_4)\right)$$

(4) $[\![\mathtt{x} := \mathtt{coin}() \; ; \; \mathtt{y} := \mathtt{coin}() \; ; \; \mathtt{u} := \mathtt{u} + (\mathtt{x} - \mathtt{y}) \; ; \; \mathtt{v} := \mathtt{v} + (\mathtt{x} + \mathtt{y} - 1)]\!] \colon$
$\mathcal{M}\mathbb{R}^4 \to \mathcal{M}\mathbb{R}^4$

$$\mu \mapsto \lambda(B_1 \times B_2 \times B_3 \times B_4).\mu(\mathbb{R}^4)\left(\frac{1}{4}\mu(B_1 \times B_2 - 1 \times \mathbb{R}^2)\delta_0(B_3)\delta_0(B_4)\right.$$

$$+ \frac{1}{4}\mu(B_1 - 1 \times B_2 \times \mathbb{R}^2)\delta_0(B_3)\delta_1(B_4)$$

$$+ \frac{1}{4}\mu(B_1 + 1 \times B_2 \times \mathbb{R}^2)\delta_1(B_3)\delta_0(B_4)$$

$$\left.+ \frac{1}{4}\mu(B_1 \times B_2 + 1 \times \mathbb{R}^2)\delta_1(B_3)\delta_1(B_4)\right)$$

where $B_1 + 1 = \{x + 1 \mid x \in B_1\}$ and similarly for the other combinations. It now follows that

$$[\![\mathtt{u} := \mathtt{0} \; ; \; \mathtt{v} := \mathtt{0} \; ; \; \mathtt{step}(\mathtt{u},\mathtt{v})]\!](\mu)(B_1 \times B_2 \times B_3 \times B_4)$$

$$= \frac{\mu(\mathbb{R}^4)}{4}\left(\delta_0(B_1)\delta_{-1}(B_2)\delta_0(B_3)\delta_0(B_4) + \delta_{-1}(B_1)\delta_0(B_2)\delta_0(B_3)\delta_1(B_4)\right.$$

$$\left.+ \; \delta_1(B_1)\delta_0(B_2)\delta_1(B_3)\delta_0(B_4) + \delta_0(B_1)\delta_1(B_2)\delta_1(B_3)\delta_1(B_4)\right), \qquad (1.22)$$

where each summand corresponds to one of the four possible execution paths. This will be the input distribution to the operator denoted by the **while** loop. Let us now compute this operator. For notational clarity, we write

$$E \triangleq [\![\mathtt{!(u == 0)} \; || \; \mathtt{!(v == 0)}]\!]^c = \{0\} \times \{0\} \times \mathbb{R} \times \mathbb{R}$$

As in the previous example, we look at the first terms of the formula (1.20).

$$T_E \qquad T_E + T_E \circ [\![\mathtt{step}]\!] \circ T_{E^c}$$

$$T_E + T_E \circ [\![\mathtt{step}]\!] \circ T_{E^c} + T_E \circ ([\![\mathtt{step}]\!] \circ T_{E^c})^2$$

For notational clarity, we consider measurable rectangles of the form $A \times B$, where A, B are measurable subsets of $\mathbb{R}^2$ corresponding to events involving the variables u, v and x, y, respectively. For such an $A \times B \subseteq \mathbb{R}^4$, we have

$$T_E(\mu)(A \times B) = \mu((A \times B) \cap E) = \delta_{(0,0)}(A)\mu(\{(0,0)\} \times B).$$

This is the probability that the while loop exits immediately. Similarly,

$$
\begin{aligned}
&T_E \circ [\![\text{step}]\!] \circ T_{E^c}(\mu)(A \times B) \\
&= \delta_{(0,0)}(A)[\![\text{step}]\!] \circ T_{E^c}(\mu)((0,0) \times B) \\
&= \frac{\delta_{(0,0)}(A)}{4}(\mu((0,-1) \times \mathbb{R}^2)\delta_{(0,0)}(B) + \mu((-1,0) \times \mathbb{R}^2)\delta_{(0,1)}(B) \\
&\qquad + \mu((1,0) \times \mathbb{R}^2)\delta_{(1,0)}(B) + \mu((0,1) \times \mathbb{R}^2))\delta_{(1,1)}(B)
\end{aligned}
$$

where we have omitted curly brackets around singletons for readability's sake, i.e. $(1,0)$ stands for $\{(1,0)\}$, etc. We can already see that μ is evaluated at the points of $\mathbb{Z}^2$ which can reach $(0,0)$ in exactly one step. Similarly, we have

$$
\begin{aligned}
&T_E \circ [\![\text{step}]\!] \circ T_{E^c} \circ [\![\text{step}]\!] \circ T_{E^c}(\mu)(A \times B) \\
&= \delta_{(0,0)}(A)[\![\text{step}]\!] \circ T_{E^c} \circ [\![\text{step}]\!] \circ T_{E^c}(\mu)((0,0) \times B) \\
&= \frac{\delta_{(0,0)}(A)}{4}([\![\text{step}]\!] \circ T_{E^c}(\mu)((0,-1) \times \mathbb{R}^2)\delta_{(0,0)}(B) \\
&\qquad + [\![\text{step}]\!] \circ T_{E^c}(\mu)((-1,0) \times \mathbb{R}^2)\delta_{(0,1)}(B) \\
&\qquad + [\![\text{step}]\!] \circ T_{E^c}(\mu)((1,0) \times \mathbb{R}^2)\delta_{(1,0)}(B) \\
&\qquad + [\![\text{step}]\!] \circ T_{E^c}(\mu)((0,1) \times \mathbb{R}^2)\delta_{(1,1)}(B)) \\
&= \frac{\delta_{(0,0)}(A)}{4}\left(\frac{\delta_{(0,0)}(B)}{4}\mu((0,-2) \cup (-1,-1) \cup (1,-1) \times \mathbb{R}^2)\right. \\
&\qquad + \frac{\delta_{(0,1)}(B)}{4}\mu((-1,-1) \cup (-2,0) \cup (-1,1) \times \mathbb{R}^2) \\
&\qquad + \frac{\delta_{(1,0)}(B)}{4}\mu((1,-1) \cup (2,0) \cup (1,1) \times \mathbb{R}^2) \\
&\qquad + \left.\frac{\delta_{(1,1)}(B)}{4}\mu((-1,1) \cup (1,1) \cup (0,2) \times \mathbb{R}^2)\right).
\end{aligned}
$$

The expression above enumerates all the points that can reach $(0,0)$ in exactly two steps and keeps track of the last move via the terms $\delta_{(i,j)}(B)$. The operators T_{E^c} annihilate any combination of two steps corresponding to a path visiting $(0,0)$ in two or fewer steps. For example, the path "down followed by up" from $(0,0)$ also reaches $(0,0)$ in zero steps, so is excluded. Note also that there is some double counting, as some paths are more likely than others.

To describe the operator corresponding to the kth iteration of the loop, we define $P(x, y, k, l)$ as the set of paths of length $k - 1$ from (x, y) to $(1, 0)$ that do not visit $(0, 0)$. A single additional "left" (l) step thus defines a path of length k to $(0, 0)$ which only visits $(0, 0)$ at the last step, hence the notation. We similarly define the obvious corresponding sets where l is replaced by d for "down", u for "up" and r for "right". With this notation, we get for $k \geq 1$

$$T_E \circ (\llbracket \text{step} \rrbracket \circ T_{E^c})^k (\mu)(A \times B)$$

$$= \frac{\delta_{(0,0)}(A)}{4^k} \left(\delta_{(0,0)}(B) \sum_{(x,y) \in \mathbb{Z}^2} \#P(x, y, k, l) \mu((x, y) \times \mathbb{R}^2) \right.$$

$$+ \delta_{(0,1)}(B) \sum_{(x,y) \in \mathbb{Z}^2} \#P(x, y, k, d) \mu((x, y) \times \mathbb{R}^2)$$

$$+ \delta_{(1,0)}(B) \sum_{(x,y) \in \mathbb{Z}^2} \#P(x, y, k, u) \mu((x, y) \times \mathbb{R}^2)$$

$$\left. + \delta_{(1,1)}(B) \sum_{(x,y) \in \mathbb{Z}^2} \#P(x, y, k, r) \mu((x, y) \times \mathbb{R}^2) \right). \tag{1.23}$$

Of course, $P(x, y, k, l)$ is nonempty for only finitely many (x, y). The expression (1.23) is uniquely determined by its values on B replaced by one of:

$$\{(0, 0)\}, \{(0, 1)\}, \{(1, 0)\}, \text{ and } \{(1, 1)\}.$$

Since this holds for any k, it also holds for the full expansion

$$\sum_{k=0}^{\infty} T_E \circ (\llbracket \text{step} \rrbracket \circ T_{E^c})^k (\mu)(A \times B).$$

By plugging (1.23) into the above expression and regrouping the coefficients of each term $\mu((x, y) \times \mathbb{R}^2)$, we get for $B = \{(0, 0)\}$

$$\delta_{(0,0)}(A) \left(\mu((0, 0) \times \mathbb{R}^2) + \sum_{(x,y) \in \mathbb{Z}^2 \setminus (0,0)} \mu((x, y) \times \mathbb{R}^2) \left(\sum_{k=1}^{\infty} \frac{\#P(x, y, k, l)}{4^k} \right) \right), \tag{1.24}$$

and similarly for $B = \{(0, 1)\}, \{(1, 0)\}, \{(1, 1)\}$. Since $\frac{\#P(x,y,k,l)}{4^k}$ is precisely the probability that the random walk reaches $(0, 0)$ from (x, y) in exactly k steps by avoiding $(0, 0)$ until the last step, it follows that (1.24) simplifies to

$$\sum_{(x,y) \in \mathbb{Z}^2} \mu((x, y) \times \mathbb{R}^2) = \mu(\mathbb{Z}^2 \times \mathbb{R}^2),$$

since the probability of reaching $(0, 0)$ from (x, y) in some number of steps is 1. We conclude that the semantics of the entire loop is the operator which sends μ to

$$\mu(\mathbb{Z}^2 \times \mathbb{R}^2)\delta_{(0,0)} \otimes \frac{1}{4} \left(\delta_{(0,0)} + \delta_{(0,1)} + \delta_{(1,0)} + \delta_{(1,1)} \right).$$

Intuitively, if the starting point is in $\mathbb{Z}^2$, then $(0,0)$ is reached with probability one.

By applying the loop operator to the initialized measure described in (1.22), it now follows that the denotation of the entire program is simply the operator mapping a measure μ to the measure

$$\mu(\mathbb{R}^4)\delta_{(0,0)},$$

as expected from the operational semantics.

Example 3: Probabilistic computation of π

Before computing the denotational semantics of the program in Fig. 1.3, it is instructive as a warm-up exercise to compute the denotational semantics of the frequent loop-iterator pattern

$$[\![\texttt{while i} < N \texttt{ do i} := \texttt{i} + 1]\!],$$

where N is some arbitrary constant. There is a single variable, so the semantics will be given by a linear operator $\mathcal{M}\mathbb{R} \to \mathcal{M}\mathbb{R}$. It is not hard to see from the definitions that

$$[\![\texttt{i} := \texttt{i} + 1]\!](\mu)(B) = \mu(\{x \mid x + 1 \in B\}) = \mu(B - 1).$$

Let us compute the first few terms of (1.20) applied to $[\![\texttt{i} := \texttt{i} + 1]\!]$. For $n = 1$ we get

$$\tau^1(0)(\mu)(B) = \mu(B^{\geq N}) + \mu((B^{\geq N} - 1)^{<N})$$

where $X^{\geq N} \triangleq \{x \in X \mid x \geq N\}$, $X^{<N} \triangleq \{x \in X \mid x < N\}$, and

$$(B^{\geq N} - 1)^{<N} = \{x \in \mathbb{R} \mid N \leq x + 1 \in B\}^{<N} = \{x \mid x < N \leq x + 1 \in B\},$$

where $x < N \leq x + 1 \in B$ is shorthand for $x < N \leq x + 1$ and $x + 1 \in B$. Similarly,

$$\begin{aligned}
\tau^2(0)(\mu)(B) &= \mu(B^{\geq N}) + \mu((B^{\geq N} - 1)^{<N}) + \mu(((B^{\geq N} - 1)^{<N}) - 1)^{<N}) \\
&= \mu(B^{\geq N}) + \mu(\{x \mid x < N \leq x + 1 \in B\}) \\
&\quad + \mu(\{x \mid x + 1 < N \leq x + 2 \in B\}).
\end{aligned}$$

More generally, for $n \geq 1$:

$$\tau^n(0)(\mu)(B) = \mu(B^{\geq N}) + \sum_{k=0}^{n} \mu(\{x \mid x + k < N \leq x + (k+1) \in B\}).$$

It follows that the operator $[\![\text{while } i < N \text{ do } i := i + 1]\!]$ maps a measure μ to the measure

$$[\![\text{while } i < N \text{ do } i := i + 1]\!](\mu)(B)$$

$$= \mu(B^{\geq N}) + \sum_{k=0}^{\infty} \mu(\{x \mid x + k < N \leq x + (k + 1) \in B\}).$$

The intuition behind this operator is as follows. Considering the interval $B = [N, N + 1]$, it is clear that if $x + k \leq N < x + k + 1$, then it will hold that $x + k + 1 \in [N, N + 1]$, and thus

$$[\![\text{while } i < N \text{ do } i := i + 1]\!](\mu)([N, N + 1])$$

$$= \mu([N, N + 1]) + \sum_{k=0}^{\infty} \mu((N - k - 1, N - k])$$

$$= \mu((-\infty, N + 1]).$$

In other words, all the μ-mass below N accumulates in $[N, N + 1]$ because it corresponds to the program exiting the loop from an initial state not satisfying its guard. Conversely,

$$[\![\text{while } i < N \text{ do } i := i + 1]\!](\mu)((N + 1, \infty)) = \mu((N + 1, \infty)),$$

since this is the μ-mass of states that never enter the loop. It follows that $[\![\text{while } i < N \text{ do } i := i + 1]\!](\mu)([N, \infty)) = \mu(\mathbb{R})$, i.e. any measure gets mapped to a measure whose support is $[N, \infty)$, which makes good semantic sense. Note also that if the input distribution is a Dirac delta δ_x with $x < N$, then as expected, the definition above gives

$$[\![\text{while } i < N \text{ do } i := i + 1]\!](\delta_x) = \delta_{x + \lceil N - x \rceil},$$

where $\lceil N - x \rceil$ is the ceiling function applied to $N - x$, i.e. the smallest integer above $N - x$.

With this understanding of the interpretation of the common loop-iterator pattern, let us turn to the program in Fig. 1.3. We start by examining the body of the loop, namely:

```
x:=rand();
y:=rand();
if (x*x+y*y) < 1 then n:=n+1;
i:=i+1
```

which we will denote by **body**. By applying the rules defining the denotational semantics, we see that the operator $[\![\text{body}]\!]: \mathcal{M}\mathbb{R}^4 \to \mathcal{M}\mathbb{R}^4$ is

$$
\begin{aligned}
&[\![\text{body}]\!](\mu)(B_i \times B_n \times B_x \times B_y) \\
&\quad = \lambda(B_x \times B_y \cap D)\mu(B_i - 1 \times B_n - 1 \times \mathbb{R} \times \mathbb{R}) \\
&\quad + \lambda(B_x \times B_y \cap D^c)\mu(B_i - 1 \times B_n \times \mathbb{R} \times \mathbb{R}),
\end{aligned}
$$

where $D = \{(x,y) \mid x^2 + y^2 \leq 1\}$ is the unit disk and λ is the two-dimensional Lebesgue measure (area) restricted to $[0,1]^2$, which is equivalently given by the product of two copies of the uniform distribution on $[0,1]$ corresponding to the two occurrences of $\texttt{rand()}$.

We iteratively compute $[\![\texttt{while i} < N \texttt{ do body}]\!]$ by evaluating the terms in the monotone sequence (1.20). The computation is similar to the simple warmup loop-iterator pattern above, with the operator $[\![\text{body}]\!]$ replacing $[\![\texttt{i := i + 1}]\!]$ as body of the loop.

$$
\begin{aligned}
&\tau^1(0)(\mu)(B_i \times B_n \times B_x \times B_y) \\
&\quad = \mu(B_i^{\geq N} \times B_n \times B_x \times B_y) \\
&\quad + \lambda(B_x \times B_y \cap D)\mu((B_i^{\geq N} - 1)^{<N} \times B_n - 1 \times \mathbb{R} \times \mathbb{R}) \\
&\quad + \lambda(B_x \times B_y \cap D^c)\mu((B_i^{\geq N} - 1)^{<N} \times B_n \times \mathbb{R} \times \mathbb{R}).
\end{aligned}
$$

Iterating once more, we get

$$
\begin{aligned}
&\tau^2(0)(\mu)(B_i \times B_n \times B_x \times B_y) \\
&\quad = \tau^1(0)(\nu)(B_i \times B_n \times B_x \times B_y) \\
&\quad + \lambda(B_x \times B_y \cap D)\left[\frac{\pi}{4}\mu(((B_i^{\geq N} - 2)^{<N} - 1)^{<N} \times B_n - 2 \times \mathbb{R} \times \mathbb{R})\right. \\
&\qquad\qquad \left. + \left(1 - \frac{\pi}{4}\right)\mu(((B_i^{\geq N} - 1)^{<N} - 1)^{<N} \times B_n - 1 \times \mathbb{R} \times \mathbb{R})\right] \\
&\quad + \lambda(B_x \times B_y \cap D^c)\left[\frac{\pi}{4}\mu(((B_i^{\geq N} - 1)^{<N} - 1)^{<N} \times B_n - 1 \times \mathbb{R} \times \mathbb{R})\right. \\
&\qquad\qquad \left. + \left(1 - \frac{\pi}{4}\right)\mu(((B_i^{\geq N} - 1)^{<N} - 1)^{<N} \times B_n \times \mathbb{R} \times \mathbb{R})\right]
\end{aligned}
$$

since $\lambda(D) = \pi/4$ and $\lambda(D^c) = 1 - \pi/4$. Generally,

$$\tau^{n+1}(0)(\mu)(B_{\mathtt{i}} \times B_{\mathtt{n}} \times B_{\mathtt{x}} \times B_{\mathtt{y}})$$

$$= \tau^n(0)(\nu)(B_{\mathtt{i}} \times B_{\mathtt{n}} \times B_{\mathtt{x}} \times B_{\mathtt{y}})$$

$$+ \lambda(B_{\mathtt{x}} \times B_{\mathtt{y}} \cap D) \left[\sum_{k=0}^{n} \binom{n}{k} \left(\frac{\pi}{4}\right)^k \left(1 - \frac{\pi}{4}\right)^{n-k} \right.$$

$$\left. \mu(B_{\mathtt{i}}(n+1, N) \times B_{\mathtt{n}} - k - 1 \times \mathbb{R}^2) \right]$$

$$+ \lambda(B_{\mathtt{x}} \times B_{\mathtt{y}} \cap D^c) \left[\sum_{k=0}^{n} \binom{n}{k} \left(\frac{\pi}{4}\right)^k \left(1 - \frac{\pi}{4}\right)^{n-k} \right.$$

$$\left. \mu(B_{\mathtt{i}}(n+1, N) \times B_{\mathtt{n}} - k \times \mathbb{R}^2) \right]$$

where we have defined $B_{\mathtt{i}}(n, N) \triangleq \{x \mid x + n - 1 < N \le x + n \in B_{\mathtt{i}}\}$. The limit distribution can be seen as an infinite sum of disjoint cases indexed by n, the number of iterations of the loop. To each n corresponds a binomial distribution with parameters $(\frac{\pi}{4}, n)$ counting the number of times $(\mathtt{x} * \mathtt{x} + \mathtt{y} * \mathtt{y} < 1)$—and thus the increment $\mathtt{n} := \mathtt{n} + 1$—was realized.

The denotation simplifies considerably when we pre-compose with the two initialisation steps of the program, namely $\mathtt{i} := 0$; $\mathtt{n} := 0$. Assuming a probability distribution $\mu \in \mathcal{M}\mathbb{R}^4$ as input, the denotational semantics is then given by

$$[\![\mathtt{i} := 0 ; \mathtt{n} := 0 ; \mathtt{while}\ \mathtt{i} < \mathtt{1e9}\ \mathtt{do}\ \mathtt{body}]\!](\mu)(B_{\mathtt{i}} \times B_{\mathtt{n}} \times B_{\mathtt{x}} \times B_{\mathtt{y}})$$

$$= [\![\mathtt{while}\ \mathtt{i} < \mathtt{1e9}\ \mathtt{do}\ \mathtt{body}]\!]\mu(\mathbb{R} \times \mathbb{R} \times B_{\mathtt{x}} \times B_{\mathtt{y}})\delta_0(B_{\mathtt{i}})\delta_0(B_{\mathtt{n}})$$

$$= \lambda(B_{\mathtt{x}} \times B_{\mathtt{y}} \cap D) \left[\sum_{k=0}^{\mathtt{1e9}} \binom{\mathtt{1e9}}{k} \left(\frac{\pi}{4}\right)^k \left(1 - \frac{\pi}{4}\right)^{n-k} \delta_{\mathtt{1e9}}(B_{\mathtt{i}})\delta_{k+1}(B_{\mathtt{n}}) \right]$$

$$+ \lambda(B_{\mathtt{x}} \times B_{\mathtt{y}} \cap D^c) \left[\sum_{k=0}^{\mathtt{1e9}} \binom{\mathtt{1e9}}{k} \left(\frac{\pi}{4}\right)^k \left(1 - \frac{\pi}{4}\right)^{n-k} \delta_{\mathtt{1e9}}(B_{\mathtt{i}})\delta_k(B_{\mathtt{n}}) \right].$$

Finally, we compose with $[\![\mathtt{i} := 4 * \mathtt{n}/\mathtt{1e9}]\!]$. Since we are only interested in the register $\mathtt{i}$ containing the approximation of π, we compute the $\mathtt{i}$-marginal given by

$$(\pi_i)_* \left(\llbracket \text{i} := 0 \text{ ; } \text{n} := 0 \text{ ; while i} < 1e9 \text{ do body ; i} := 4 * \text{n}/1e9 \rrbracket\right)(\mu)(B_i)$$

$$= \llbracket \text{i} := 0 \text{ ; } \text{n} := 0 \text{ ; while i} < 1e9 \text{ do body ; i} := 4 * \text{n}/1e9 \rrbracket(\mu)(B_i \times \mathbb{R}^3)$$

$$= \lambda(D) \left[\sum_{k=0}^{1e9} \binom{1e9}{k} \left(\frac{\pi}{4}\right)^k \left(1 - \frac{\pi}{4}\right)^{n-k} \delta_{k+1}(\{x \mid 4x/1e9 \in B_i\}) \right]$$

$$+ \lambda(D^c) \left[\sum_{k=0}^{1e9} \binom{1e9}{k} \left(\frac{\pi}{4}\right)^k \left(1 - \frac{\pi}{4}\right)^{n-k} \delta_k(\{x \mid 4x/1e9 \in B_i\}) \right]$$

$$= \sum_{k=0}^{1e9+1} \binom{1e9+1}{k} \left(\frac{\pi}{4}\right)^k \left(1 - \frac{\pi}{4}\right)^{n-k} \delta_k(\{x \mid 4x/1e9 \in B_i\})$$

$$= \text{Binomial}\left(\frac{\pi}{4}, 1e9+1\right)(\{x \mid 4x/1e9 \in B_i\}).$$

In other words, from a denotational standpoint, our program returns a distribution whose i-marginal is the pushforward under the rescaling map $x \mapsto 4x/1e9$ of the binomial distribution Binomial $(\pi/4, 1e9+1)$. Since the binomial distribution is just a sum of Bernoulli distributions with parameter $\pi/4$, the connection with the operational semantics of Section 1.3.4 is evident. However, note that the final output of the denotational semantics captures all possible branches of the operational semantics in one single object, namely the distribution Binomial $(\pi/4, 1e9+1)$.

As promised in Section 1.3.4, we will provide a tighter bound on the probability of getting a good approximation of π via the program of Fig. 1.3. Hoeffding's inequality (Hoeffding (1994)) with X a random variable distributed as Binomial (p, n) says that

$$\mathbb{P}\left[|X - pn| \leq \varepsilon n\right] \geq 1 - 2\exp(-2\varepsilon^2 n).$$

For example, with error tolerance $\varepsilon = 0.00007$, we get that

$$\text{Binomial}\left(\frac{\pi}{4}, 1e9+1\right)(\{x \mid 4x/1e9 \in [\pi - \varepsilon, \pi + \varepsilon]\}) \geq 0.999,$$

which is a much tighter bound than the one provided by the Chebyshev inequality in Section 1.3.4. This shows that proving probabilistic guarantees about a program such as

$$(\pi_i)_* \llbracket \text{prog} \rrbracket([\pi - \varepsilon, \pi + \varepsilon]) \geq 0.999$$

can depend on the difficult and purely mathematical problem of finding sufficiently tight bounds to concentration of measure inequalities.

Example 4: The Cantor distribution

We finish by computing the denotational semantics of the program of Fig. 1.4. As mentioned at the end of Section 1.3.5, the least fixpoint denotational semantics of *any* program containing a while true loop is simply the constant operator to 0 since the program never halts. Formally, if we denote by `cantor` the program of Fig. 1.4, then for every $\mu \in \mathcal{M}\mathbb{R}^2$ (since the program contains two variables)

$$[\![\text{cantor}]\!](\mu) = 0.$$

However, as we also discussed above, the mean ergodic theorem provides an alternative semantics to non-terminating `while true` programs. We compute this semantics explicitly for the `cantor` program and, as expected, recover the Cantor measure which we encountered when we computing the operational semantics of `cantor` in Section 1.3.4.

Once again we start by examining the body of the loop. By unravelling the definition of the denotational semantics of terms, it is not hard to compute the semantics of the body of the loop which is given by the operator sending μ to the measure

$$[\![\text{body}]\!](\mu)(B_x \times B_d) = \frac{1}{2}\mu\left(\left\{(x,d) \mid x \in B_x, \frac{d}{3} \in B_d\right\}\right)$$
$$+ \frac{1}{2}\mu\left(\left\{(x,d) \mid x + \frac{2d}{3} \in B_x, \frac{d}{3} \in B_d\right\}\right).$$

It is much easier to reason about the semantics of `cantor` in terms of Markov kernels. The body of the loop in particular is the pushforward (defined in Eq. (1.8)) of the kernel $[\![\text{body}]\!]^{\text{ker}} : \mathbb{R}^2 \to \mathcal{M}\mathbb{R}^2$ defined by

$$[\![\text{body}]\!]^{\text{ker}}(x,d) \triangleq \frac{1}{2}\delta_{(x,\frac{d}{3})} + \frac{1}{2}\delta_{(x+\frac{2d}{3},\frac{d}{3})}$$

It is easy to check that $[\![\text{body}]\!]^{\text{ker}}_* = [\![\text{body}]\!]$, and since the pushforward operation $(-)_*$ is functorial we can compose these kernels to get a kernel representation $\left([\![\text{body}]\!]^j\right)^{\text{ker}}$ of the operator $[\![\text{body}]\!]^j$ for each $j \geq 1$:

$$\left([\![\text{body}]\!]^j\right)^{\text{ker}}(x,d) = \frac{1}{2^j}\sum_{w \in \{0,2\}^j} \delta_{(x+\sum_{i=1}^{j}\frac{w_i d}{3^i}, \frac{d}{3^j})}$$

Using this kernel representation of $[\![\text{body}]\!]^j$ it becomes relatively straightforward to compute the mean ergodic limit given by Eq. (1.21), viz.

$$\lim_{n\to\infty} \frac{1}{n}\sum_{j=0}^{n-1}[\![\text{body}]\!]^j \tag{1.25}$$

In order to compute this limit we start by defining the σ-algebra $\mathcal{B}_{x,d}$ generated by the sets

$$C_w^{x,d} = \left\{y \mid x + \sum_{i=1}^{|w|}\frac{w_i d}{3^i} \leq y < x + \sum_{i=1}^{|w|}\frac{w_i d}{3^i} + \frac{d}{3^{|w|}}\right\},$$

where w is a word of $\{0, 1, 2\}^*$, $|w|$ is the length of this word, and w_i is the ith letter in w. The sets $C_w^{x,d}$ are variants of the sets $C_{a_1 \cdots a_k}$ which we defined when discussing the operational semantics of the cantor program in Section 1.3.4, stretched and shifted to fit the intervals $[x, x + d]$. In particular, $C_{w_1 \cdots w_k} = C_{w_1 \cdots w_k}^{0,1}$. In exactly the same way, these sets generate the usual (Borel) σ-algebra on each interval $[x, x + d]$.

Consider now the Markov kernel on $\mathbb{R}^2$ defined at each (x, d) by the measure $\gamma(x, d)$ on $[x, x + d]$ specified uniquely by its values on the generators $C_w^{x,d}$ via

$$\gamma(x, d)(C_w^{x,d} \times B_{\mathrm{d}}) = \begin{cases} 2^{-|w|}\delta_{(0)}(B_{\mathrm{d}}) & \text{if } w \in \{0, 2\}^*, \\ 0 & \text{otherwise} \end{cases}$$

where $\delta_{(0)}$ is a curious measure defined as follows:

$$\delta_{(0)}(B) = \begin{cases} 1 & \text{if } B \text{ contains an interval } (0, \epsilon) \\ 0 & \text{otherwise} \end{cases}$$

We will see in an instant how $\delta_{(0)}$ arises, but note first that, modulo the $\delta_{(0)}$ term, the measure $\gamma(x, d)$ is simply a stretched and shifted version of the Cantor measure defined in Eq. (1.15), Section 1.3.4. In particular, $\gamma(0, 1)$ is simply the product $\kappa \otimes \delta_{(0)}$ of the Cantor measure κ with $\delta_{(0)}$. We claim that γ is the Markov kernel corresponding to the mean ergodic limit Eq. (1.25). To see this we simply compute that

$$\frac{1}{n}\sum_{j=0}^{n-1}\left(\llbracket \mathtt{body} \rrbracket^j\right)^{\mathrm{ker}}(x, d)(C_w^{x,d} \times B_{\mathrm{d}}) = \begin{cases} 0 & n < |w| \\ \frac{1}{2^{|w|}}\frac{1}{n}\sum_{i=|w|}^{-1n}\delta\frac{d}{3^i} & \text{otherwise.} \end{cases}$$

It follows that for any rectangle $C_w^{x,d} \times B_{\mathrm{d}}$

$$\lim_{n \to \infty} \frac{1}{n}\sum_{j=0}^{n-1}\left(\llbracket \mathtt{body} \rrbracket^j\right)^{\mathrm{ker}}(x, d)(C_w^{x,d} \times B_{\mathrm{d}}) = \gamma(x, d)(C_w^{x,d} \times B_{\mathrm{d}}) \qquad (1.26)$$

Indeed, the $C_w^{x,d}$ contribution to the product is the constant $\frac{1}{2^{|w|}}$ as soon as $n \geq |w|$, and it is not hard to convince oneself that $\lim_{n \to \infty} \frac{1}{n}\sum_{i=|w|}^{n}\delta\frac{d}{3^i}(B_{\mathrm{d}})$, the B_{d} contribution, is precisely given by $\delta_{(0)}(B_{\mathrm{d}})$: if B_{d} contains an interval $(0, \epsilon)$ then there will exist an N such that $\frac{d}{3^n} \in (0, \epsilon) \subseteq B_{\mathrm{d}}$ for all $n \geq N$ and the limit $\frac{1}{n}\sum_{i=|w|}^{n-1}\delta\frac{d}{3^i}(B_{\mathrm{d}})$ will thus converge to 1. In all other cases the limit converges to 0. We can then conclude that the measures on the LHS and RHS of Eq. (1.26) agree on the usual (Borel) product σ-algebra on $[x, x + d] \times \mathbb{R}$ (this follows from Dynkin's π-λ lemma (Aliprantis and Border, 1999, 4.11) because the collection of sets $C_w^{x,d}$ are closed under intersection, i.e. form a π-system).

We can now conclude that the mean ergodic denotational semantics of the program $[\![\texttt{while true do body}]\!]$ is the operator given by the pushforward of the kernel γ. In particular, the semantics of the entire $\texttt{cantor}$ program is given by

$$
\begin{aligned}
[\![\texttt{cantor}]\!](\mu) &= [\![\texttt{x} := \texttt{0}; \texttt{d} := 1; \texttt{while true do body}]\!](\mu) \\
&= \gamma_*([\![\texttt{x} := \texttt{0}; \texttt{d} := 1]\!])(\mu) \\
&= \mu(\mathbb{R}^2)\gamma_*(\delta_{(0,1)}) \\
&= \mu(\mathbb{R}^2)\gamma(0,1) \\
&= \mu(\mathbb{R}^2)(\kappa \otimes \delta_{(0)})
\end{aligned}
$$

and we recover the Cantor measure which we obtained from the operational semantics in Section 1.3.4, as expected.

References

Aliprantis, C., and Border, K. 1999. *Infinite Dimensional Analysis*. Springer.

Chung, K. L. 1974. *A Course in Probability Theory*. 2nd edn. Academic Press.

Doberkat, Ernst-Erich. 2007. *Stochastic Relations: Foundations for Markov Transition Systems*. Studies in Informatics. Chapman Hall.

Dudley, R.M. 2002. *Real Analysis and Probability*. Cambridge Studies in Advanced Mathematics. Cambridge University Press.

Dunford, N., Schwartz, J. T., Bade, W. G, and Bartle, R. G. 1971. *Linear Operators I*. Wiley-interscience New York.

Durrett, R. 1996. *Probability: Theory and Examples*. The Wadsworth & Brooks/-Cole Statistics/Probability Series. Duxbury Press.

Eisner, T., Farkas, B., Haase, M., and Nagel, R. 2015. *Operator Theoretic Aspects of Ergodic Theory*. Vol. 272. Springer.

Giry, Michele. 1982. A categorical approach to probability theory. Pages 68–85 of: *Categorical Aspects of Topology and Analysis*. Springer.

Halmos, P. R. 1950. *Measure Theory*. Van Nostrand.

Hoeffding, Wassily. 1994. Probability inequalities for sums of bounded random variables. Pages 409–426 of: *The Collected Works of Wassily Hoeffding*. Springer.

Kozen, Dexter. 1981. Semantics of probabilistic programs. *J. Comput. Syst. Sci.*, **22**(3), 328–350.

Kozen, Dexter. 1985. A probabilistic *PDL*. *J. Comput. Syst. Sci.*, **30**(2), 162–178.

Kozen, Dexter. 1997. Kleene algebra with tests. *ACM Trans. Programming Languages and Systems (TOPLAS)*, **19**(3), 427–443.

Lawvere, W. 1962. *The category of probabilistic mappings*. Manuscript, 12 pages.

Norris, J. R. 1997. *Markov Chains*. Cambridge Series in Statistical and Probabilistic Mathematics. Cambridge University Press.

Panangaden, Prakash. 1998. Probabilistic relations. Pages 59–74 of: *Proceedings of PROBMIV*.

Panangaden, Prakash. 2009. *Labelled Markov Processes*. Imperial College Press.

Vitali, Giuseppe. 1905. *Sul problema della misura dei Gruppi di punti di una retta: Nota*. Tip. Gamberini e Parmeggiani.

2

Probabilistic Programs as Measures

Sam Staton
University of Oxford

Abstract: This chapter is a tutorial about some of the key issues in semantics of the first-order aspects of probabilistic programming languages for statistical modelling – languages such as Church, Anglican, Venture and WebPPL. We argue that s-finite measures and s-finite kernels provide a good semantic basis.

2.1 Introduction

This Chapter is about a style of probabilistic programming for building statistical models, the basis of languages such as Church (Goodman et al., 2008), WebPPL (Goodman and Stuhlmüller, 2014), Venture (Mansinghka et al., 2014), Anglican (Wood et al., 2014) and Hakaru (Narayanan et al., 2016).

The key idea of these languages is that the model is a combination of three things:

Sample: A generative model is described by a program involving not only binary random choices but also by sampling from continuous real-valued distributions. In Bayesian terms, we think of this as describing the prior probabilities.

Observe: Observations about data can be incorporated into the model, and these are typically used as weights in a Monte Carlo simulation. In Bayesian terms, we think of this as describing the likelihood of the data.

Normalize: Given a model, we run an inference algorithm over it to calculate the posterior probabilities.

Probabilistic programming languages bring many of the abstract ideas of high-level programming to bear on statistical modelling. Perhaps the most compelling aspect is the idea of rapid development, first of quickly creating models, and second quickly combining them with inference algorithms.

[a] From *Foundations of Probabilistic Programming*, edited by Gilles Barthe, Joost-Pieter Katoen and Alexandra Silva published 2020 by Cambridge University Press.

There remain many practical and theoretical challenges with probabilistic languages of these kinds. The purpose of this chapter is to explain, for simple first order programs, how we can understand them as measures in a compositional way.

We begin in Section 2.2 by introducing the general approach to probabilistic programming and giving informal consideration to various aspects of the semantics of probabilistic programs. We are led to the issue of unnormalizable posteriors (§2.2.4). In Section 2.3 we develop the informal semantics from a measure-theoretic perspective, demonstrating through examples why a naive semantics is not so straightforward (§2.3.3).

In Section 2.4 we give a formal semantics for first order probabilistic programs as measures. We do this by understanding expressions with free variables as *s-finite kernels* (Def. 2.6). An s-finite kernel is, roughly, a parameterized measure that is uniformly built from finite measures. Once this semantics is given, one can easily reason about probabilistic programs in a compositional way by using measure theory, the standard basis of probability. We give some simple examples in Section 2.5.

2.2 Informal semantics for probabilistic programming

2.2.1 A first example: discrete samples, discrete observation

To illustrate the key ideas of probabilistic programming, consider the following simple problem, which we explain in English, then in statistical notation, and then as a probabilistic program.

(i) I have forgotten what day it is.
(ii) There are ten buses per hour in the week and three buses per hour at the weekend.
(iii) I observe four buses in a given hour.
(iv) What is the probability that it is the weekend?

This is a very simple scenario, to illustrate the key points, but in practice, probabilistic programming is used for scenarios with dozens of interconnected random parameters and thousands of observations.

We assume that buses arrive as a Poisson process, meaning that their rate is given but they come independently. So the number of buses forms a Poisson distribution (Figure 2.1). We model the idea that the day is unknown by putting a prior belief that all the days are equiprobable. The problem would be written in statistical notation as follows:

(i) Prior: $x \sim \text{Bernoulli}(\frac{2}{7})$
(ii) Observation: $d \sim \text{Poisson}(r)$ where $r = 3$ if x and $r = 10$ otherwise;
(iii) $d = 4$;
(iv) What is the posterior distribution on x?

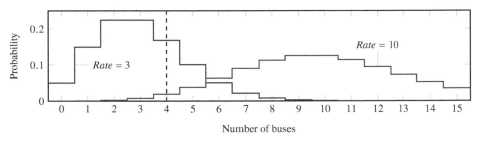

Figure 2.1 The Poisson distributions with rates 3 and 10.

We describe this as a probabilistic program as follows:

```
1.  normalize(
2.      let x = sample(bernoulli(2/7)) in
3.      let r = if x then 3 else 10 in
4.      observe 4 from poisson(r);
5.      return(x))
```

Lines 2–5 describe the combination of the likelihood and the prior. First, on line 2, we sample from the prior: the chance that it is the weekend is $\frac{2}{7}$; this matches line (i) above. On line 3, we set the rate r of buses, depending on whether it is a week day. On line 4 we record the observation that four buses passed when the rate was r, using the Poisson distribution. So lines 3 and 4 match lines (ii) and (iii) above (but not individually). The normalize command on line 1 is wrapped around the whole program up to the return value on line 5, and corresponds to line (iv) above.

There are three naive ways to calculate the answer:

Posterior calculation 1: direct calculation using Bayes' law. The first approach is to calculate the posterior probability using Bayes' law directly

$$\text{Posterior} \propto \text{Likelihood} \times \text{Prior}. \tag{2.1}$$

For a discrete distribution, the likelihood is the probability of the observation point d, which for the Poisson distribution with rate r is $\frac{1}{d!}r^d e^{-r}$.

- The prior probability that it is the weekend is $\frac{2}{7}$, and then the likelihood of the observation is $\frac{1}{4!}3^4 e^{-3} \approx 0.168$; so the posterior probability that it is the weekend is proportional to $0.168 \times \frac{2}{7} \approx 0.048$ (likelihood×prior).
- The prior probability that it is a week day is $\frac{5}{7}$, and then the rate is 10 and the likelihood of the observation is $\frac{1}{4!}10^4 e^{-10} \approx 0.019$. So the posterior probability that it is a week day is proportional to $0.019 \times \frac{5}{7} \approx 0.014$.

- The measure (true $\mapsto 0.048$, false $\mapsto 0.014$) is not a probability measure because it doesn't sum to 1. To build a probability measure we divide by $0.048 + 0.014 = 0.062$, to get a posterior probability measure (true $\mapsto 0.22$, false $\mapsto 0.78$). The normalizing constant, 0.062, is sometimes called model evidence; it is an indication of how well the data fits the model.

Posterior Calculation 2: Monte Carlo simulation with rejection. In more complicated scenarios, it is often impractical to manage a direct numerical calculation like the above, and so people often turn to approximate simulation methods. A simulation with rejection works as follows:

- We run through the inner program (lines 2–5) a large number of times (say N).
- At a sample statement, we randomly sample from the given distribution. In Line 2, there is a Bernoulli trial that produces true with probability $\frac{2}{7}$ and false with probability $\frac{5}{7}$. We might perform this by uniformly generating a random number between 1 and 7 (the day of the week) and then returning true if the number is 6 or 7.
- At an observe statement, we also randomly sample from the given distribution, but we reject the run if the sample does not match the observation. In Line 4, we would sample a number k from the Poisson distribution with rate either 3 or 10, depending on the outcome of Line 2 (according to Line 3) and then reject the run if $k \neq 4$. This amounts to running a simulation of the bus network, but then rejecting the run if the outcome of the simulation did not match our observation. That is to say, we disregard or ignore the runs where the prior sample is inconsistent with the observation.
- Line 5 says that the result of the run is $x =$ true if it is the weekend on that run.
- Line 1, wrapped around the whole program, says that of the non-rejected runs, we see what proportion of runs returns $x =$ true. As $N \to \infty$, the ratio will tend towards $(0.22 : 0.78)$, the true posterior distribution. Thus the normalize command converts the sampler described by Lines 2–5 into a proper probability distribution.

Posterior Calculation 3: Monte Carlo simulation with weights. The rejection method is rather wasteful, and doesn't scale clearly to the continuous situations that we turn to later. An alternative is a simulation with likelihood weights, which works as follows:

- We run through the inner program (Lines 2–5) a large number N of times.
- As before, at a sample statement, we randomly sample from the given distribution.
- At an observe statement, we do not sample. Rather, we use the density function of the given distribution to weight the run. In Line 4, the density function of the

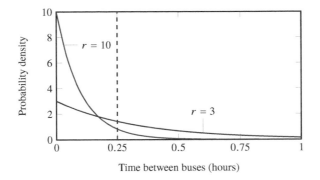

Figure 2.2 The exponential distributions with rates $r = 3$ and $r = 10$.

Poisson distribution is $\frac{1}{d!}r^d e^{-r}$, so we weight the run by either 0.168 or 0.019, depending on the outcome of Line 2. In a program with multiple observations, we accumulate the weights multiplicatively. (In practice it is numerically prudent to use log-weights and add them.)

- Looking at all the runs, we see what weighted proportion of runs returns x − true. As $N \to \infty$, the ratio will tend towards $(0.22 : 0.78)$.

In this discrete setting we can encode rejection sampling using a Monte Carlo simulation with weights, by replacing Line 4 with

4′.   let $d =$ sample($poisson(r)$) in observe 4 from $dirac(d)$

so that the weight will be either 1 (if $d = 4$) or 0 (if $d \neq 4$). When the weight is zero the run is as good as rejected.

2.2.2 A second example: discrete samples, continuous observation

Now consider the following situation, which is almost the same but the observation is different: we observe a 15 minute gap rather than four buses.

(i) I have forgotten what day it is.
(ii) There are ten buses per hour in the week and three buses per hour at the weekend.
(iii) I observe a 15 minute gap between two buses.
(iv) What is the probability that it is a week day?

In this example, since the buses are run as a Poisson process, the gap between them is exponentially distributed (Figure 2.2). The exponential distribution is a continuous probability measure on the positive reals; when the rate is r it has density function $t \mapsto re^{-rt}$. which means that the probability that the gap between events will lie in a given interval U is given by $\int_U re^{-rt}\,dt$.

In statistical notation, this example would be described as follows:

(i) Prior: $x \sim \text{Bernoulli}(\frac{2}{7})$

(ii) Observation: $d \sim \text{Exponential}(r)$ where $r = 3$ if x and $r = 10$ otherwise;

(iii) $d = \frac{15}{60} = 0.25$;

(iv) What is the posterior distribution on x?

The program for this example differs from the previous one only on Line 4:

$4''$.   observe 0.25 from *exponential*(r);

Posterior calculation 1 (direct mathematical calculation) is easily adapted to this situation. Here the likelihood of the observation (15 mins) is again the value of the density function, which is $3 \times e^{-3 \times 0.25} \approx 1.42$ when it is the weekend and $10 \times e^{-10 \times 0.25} \approx 0.82$ when it is a week day. So the unnormalized posterior has (true $\mapsto \frac{2}{7} \times 1.42 \approx 0.405$, false $\mapsto \frac{5}{7} \times 0.82 \approx 0.586$). In this example the normalizing constant is 0.991, and the normalized posterior is $(0.408 : 0.592)$. Notice that likelihood is not the same as probability — it is not even less than 1.

Posterior calculation 2 (rejection sampling) cannot easily be adapted to this situation. The problem is that although sampling from an exponential distribution will often produce numbers that are close to 0.25, it will almost never produce exactly 0.25, so almost all the runs will be rejected.

Posterior calculation 3 (weighted sampling) is easily adapted to this situation. The weight on Line $4''$ will either be 1.42 or 0.82.

Calculation Method 2 (Rejection) is perhaps the most intuitive, so it is unfortunate that it does not apply to this situation – not even theoretically. One way to resolve this is to say that our observation is not *precisely* 15 minutes, but $15 \pm \epsilon$ minutes. For all $\epsilon > 0$ we can make a rejection sampling algorithm which rejects all runs where the gap is not within $15 \pm \epsilon$. In an analogous way to line $4'$, we can encode rejection sampling in an interval with weighted sampling, by replacing line $4''$ by

$4'''$a.   let $d = $ sample$(exponential(r))$ in

$4'''$b.   observe d from *uniform*$(0.25 - \epsilon, 0.25 + \epsilon)$

As $\epsilon \to 0$, in this example, the posterior probability from rejection sampling tends to the posterior probability from weighted sampling.

  (This is not a practical approach at all because, for small ϵ, the vast majority of runs will be rejected. One practical solution to soften the hard rejection constraint using noise from a normal distribution, e.g.

$4'''$b$'$.   observe d from *normal*$(0.25, \frac{\epsilon}{2})$

Here we use $\frac{\epsilon}{2}$ as a small standard deviation.)

  The correctness of this argument depends on some continuity issues, which have been investigated in the setting of conditional probability by Tjur (1980, §9.12) and

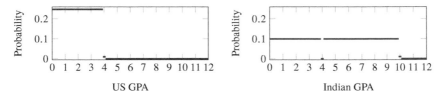

Figure 2.3 Discontinuous density functions for the GPA problem. See also Wu et al. (2018) and Section 2.3.2. The idea is this: suppose that grades are distributed uniformly, except the top 1% are given the maximum grade, which is 4 in the US and 10 in India. The problem is: given that I observe a GPA of 4, what is probable nationality of the student? The answer: certainly US.

Ackerman et al. (2015). On the other hand, densities that arise in practice are not always continuous: the GPA problem is an example of this that has been studied in the probabilistic programming context (see e.g. Figure 2.3, and §2.3.2, and Nitti et al., 2016; Wu et al., 2018).

In order to describe a situation as a program in this way, especially in a way that is amenable to Calculation Method 3 (Weighted sampling), the likelihood function of the observation distribution must be known. Research on automatic density calculation is ongoing (Bhat et al., 2017; Gehr et al., 2016; Ismail and chieh Shan, 2016).

2.2.3 A third example: continuous samples, continuous observations

For a third example, we use a similar story but now with bikes rather than buses, and rather than guess the day of the week we guess the time of day.

(i) I have forgotten what time it is.
(ii) The rate of bikes per hour is determined by a function of the time of day.
(iii) I observe a 1 minute gap between two bikes.
(iv) What time is it?

We model the idea that the time is unknown by picking the uniform distribution on the continuous interval $(0, 24)$. Suppose that we have some idea of the number of bikes per hour; the rate $f(t)$ will vary according to the time t. A possible f is given in Figure 2.4. In statistics notation, we would write:

(i) Prior: $t \sim \text{Uniform}(0, 24)$;
(ii) Observation: $d \sim \text{Exponential}(f(t))$;
(iii) $d = 0.0167$;
(iv) What is t?

The program for this example has the same outline as the previous one:

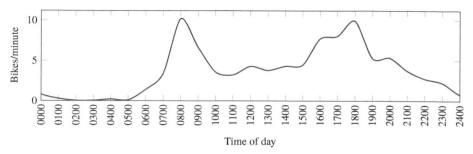

Figure 2.4 The rate of bikes as a function of the current time. The function is fictitious but based on real observations by "Bells on Bloor" in Toronto (Koehl et al., 2017).

```
1.  normalize(
2.      let t = sample(uniform(0, 24)) in
3.      let r = f(t) in
4.      observe 0.0167 from exponential(r);
5.      return(x))
```

Now to make Calculation Method 3 (weighted sampling) work, we need to accept that the prior and posterior distributions are on an uncountable space. On a discrete computer it is not really possible to sample from an uncountable continuous distribution. One way to deal with this is to approximate the prior (and hence the posterior) by discrete distributions; the finer the granularity the closer the approximation is to the continuous distribution.

A secondary problem is that even a discretized sample space is too large to explore naively; many runs will have low weights (i.e. improbable) which is a waste of resources. There are Monte Carlo algorithms that perform this more efficiently, and can be applied to probabilistic programs, for example:

- Markov Chain Monte Carlo / Metropolis Hastings: with each run, we do not resample all the random choices, but only some, and we randomly reject or accept the resample depending on the change in weight. In other words, we build a Markov chain from the program and perform a random walk over it.
- Sequential Monte Carlo: we can run N times up to a checkpoint (typically an observation), pause, and redistribute the effort so that not too many of the running threads have low weight.

There are elaborations and combinations of these methods, together with other methods (such as variational ones). The introduction by van de Meent et al. (2018) covers many of these different methods.

For Posterior Calculation 1 (direct mathematical calculation), in this instance, we

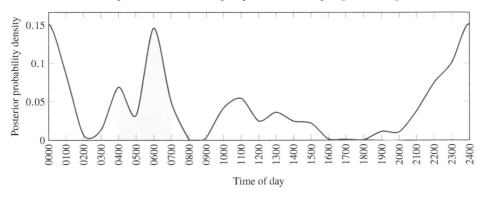

Figure 2.5 Posterior density for the current time given that I noticed a one minute gap between bikes when the rate is as shown in Figure 2.4. The probability that the time is between 4am and 7am is the purple area.

can give a posterior probability in terms of a probability density function. Recall that the meaning of density functions applied to probabilities (as opposed to likelihoods) is as follows: although the probability that the time is exactly 05:30 is zero, we can give a probability that the time is in some interval (more generally, a measurable set), as the integral of the density function. For instance, the posterior probability that the time is between 4am and 7am is shaded in Figure 2.5. The density function in this case is given by multiplying the likelihood function by the density of the prior distribution, which is uniform:

$$\text{Posterior} \quad \propto \quad \text{Likelihood} \quad \times \quad \text{Prior}$$
$$\text{posterior pdf}(t) \quad \propto \quad f(t)e^{-0.016 \times f(t)} \quad \times \quad \tfrac{1}{24}$$

The density function $t \mapsto f(t)e^{-0.016 \times f(t)} \times \tfrac{1}{24}$ is not normalized, but we can divide by the normalizing constant to get a true posterior density function:

$$t \mapsto \frac{f(t)e^{-0.016 \times f(t)} \times \tfrac{1}{24}}{\int_0^{24} f(t)e^{-0.016 \times f(t)} \times \tfrac{1}{24}\, dt} = \frac{f(t)e^{-0.016 \times f(t)}}{\int_0^{24} f(t)e^{-0.016 \times f(t)}\, dt} \tag{2.2}$$

In general, we cannot naively use density functions for a full compositional semantics because some basic programs do not have density functions. We return to this point in Section 2.3.

Aside on probabilistic programming for rapid prototyping

To briefly demonstrate the power of probabilistic programming for rapid prototyping, we consider a few elaborations on the last example. Supposing that the frequency $f(t)$ is uncertain, say we only know the frequency ±1, then we can quickly introduce an extra random variable by changing line 3 to

3'.   let r = sample($normal(f(t), 1)$) in ...

If the error in the frequency $f(t)$ is itself unknown, we can introduce yet another random variable σ for the error, for example,

3"a.   let σ = sample($inv\text{-}gamma(2, 1)$) in
3"b.   let r = sample($normal(f(t), \sigma)$) in ...

2.2.4 Unnormalizable posteriors

This chapter is about semantics of probabilistic programs and so it is informative to consider some corner cases. Recall that when we calculate a posterior we must divide by a normalizing constant. If this constant is 0 or ∞, we cannot find a posterior. In practice, if the constant is very low or very high, it suggests the model is bad, and it is numerically inconvenient to find the posterior, but if it is 0 or ∞ it is impossible even in theory.

Zero normalizing constant

A normalizing constant of 0 occurs when an observation is not only improbable, but impossible. For example, in the first example, suppose that we say that we claim to observe (-42) buses – a negative number of buses. This is impossible, nonsense, and the likelihood is not just very small but 0. In the rejection sampling semantics, all runs will be rejected.

Whether a normalizing constant is 0 is undecidable in general. For example, consider a Turing machine M with initial tape, and the following scenario.

(i) We toss a coin repeatedly until the outcome is heads. Call the number of tosses k.

(ii) We observe that Turing machine M terminates after exactly k steps.

(iii) What is k?

The prior distribution on k is a geometric distribution. The normalizing constant is non-0 if and only if the machine M terminates, in which case the posterior probability is the Dirac distribution on the number of steps required. For this reason, finding the normalizing constant is undecidable in general.

This manifests in practice as follows. For many Monte Carlo methods, it is guaranteed that sampling will converge eventually. However, it is difficult in practice to know when a Monte Carlo process has converged, and as this example shows, it may be impossible to know.

Infinite normalizing constant

Very high normalizing constants can occur when the observations are considerably more likely for improbable prior parameters. To demonstrate this we consider a scenario of a similar shape to the previous stories. An astronomer has invented a telescopic device which she is using to measure the distance between two stars, which are in fact precisely 1 light-year apart.

(i) The device is unreliable and breaks down every hour on average.
(ii) Every 2.89 hours that she uses the device, she is able to double the precision (inverse variance) of her measurement; the initial precision is $6.3 \, \text{ly}^{-2}$. At the point that the machine breaks down, she estimates that the distance is 1 light-year – coinciding with the true distance.
(iii) How long was the scientist using the machine for?

The story is set up so that the likelihood is inverse to the prior. The numbers have been chosen so that the initial precision (6.3) is approximately 2π, and the precision doubles every $\frac{2}{\ln 2}$ hours (≈ 2.9), so that the precision τ_t at time t is approximately $\tau_t = 2\pi e^{2t}$. If we model the measurement inaccuracy by a normal distribution, the likelihood function of data d is $\sqrt{\frac{\tau_t}{2\pi}} e^{-\frac{1}{2}(d-1)^2 \tau_t}$. When $d = 1$, the likelihood is e^t. So the prior density is e^{-t}, but the likelihood is e^t.

In statistical notation:

(i) Prior: $t \sim \text{Exponential}(1)$;
(ii) Likelihood: $d \sim \text{Normal}(1, (2\pi e^{2t})^{-\frac{1}{2}})$, with $d = 1$;
(iii) What is the posterior probability on t?

As a probabilistic program:

```
1. normalize(
2.     let x = sample(exponential(1)) in
3.     observe 1 from normal(1, (2πe²ᵗ)⁻¹/²);
4.     return(x))
```

In the Posterior Calculation Method 3, the problem is that we are very unlikely to pick long times, but when we do they receive very high weights.

In the Calculation Method 1, the unnormalized posterior density is

$$\text{Posterior} \quad \propto \quad \text{Likelihood} \quad \times \quad \text{Prior}$$
$$\text{posterior-pdf}(t) \quad \propto \quad e^t \quad \times \quad e^{-t}$$

and so the probability that the time lies in a set U is

$$\int_U e^t e^{-t} \, dt \; = \; \int_U 1 \, dt \qquad (2.3)$$

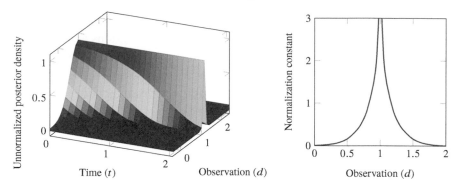

Figure 2.6 The posterior distribution on time spent using the device t given the observation d, in the context of the story about the scientist measuring the distance between stars. Notice that when $d = 1$ the unnormalized posterior density is constant, and the normalization constant is infinite.

which is the Lebesgue measure. For instance, on an interval (a, b), the unnormalized posterior is $b - a$. Across the entire positive reals $(0, \infty)$, the normalizing constant is infinite. So the question does not have an answer. We cannot form a posterior probability on the time that the scientist used the device: every time is equiprobable.

There are several contrivances in the story, the most ridiculous of which is that the observed distance happens to perfectly match the true distance. If the observed distance had been even slightly different from the true distance, the infinite normalization constant would not occur. Indeed, if the observed distance was very different from the true distance, we could easily conclude that the device broke quickly (see Fig. 2.6). This means that in practice we do not need to worry about the story, because a problem-causing observation almost never occurs. In principle, however, we do need to consider infinite measures like this, in part because they can legitimately arise as fragments of reasonable programs, as we now discuss. (For further examples of improper posteriors such as this, see e.g. Robert, 2007, Ex. 1.49–1.52.)

Improper priors and posteriors

When a normalizing constant is infinite, this is sometimes called an 'improper' distribution. Although an improper distribution is problematic as the end result of an inference problem, the distributions are incredibly useful when used as part of a model. To analyze this we consider a construction score(r) which weights the current run by r. This is equivalent to observe 0 from *exponential*(r).

Suppose for a moment that we have a program *Lebesgue*, such as Lines 2-4 of our astronomy example, that behaves as the Lebesgue measure. Suppose too that we have a probability distribution on $[0, \infty)$ that has a probability density function

$f : [0, \infty) \to [0, \infty)$, and we want to sample from it. We can do this by:

$$\text{let } x = Lebesgue \text{ in score}(f(x)); \text{return}(x)$$

since this is the definition of density functions. This composite program has normalizing constant 1. In fact, when we expand the definition of *Lebesgue* as above, this becomes the "importance sampling algorithm":

$$\text{let } x = \text{sample}(exponential(1)) \text{ in score}(e^x); \text{score}(f(x)); \text{return}(x)$$

In words: to build a sampler for one distribution from a sampler for another distribution, sample from the first distribution and then weight each run by the ratio of the density functions.

So although infinite normalizing constants are problematic at the top level, it is often useful to reason about programs where subexpressions do have infinite normalizing constants.

2.2.5 Summary of informal semantics

We have discussed three approaches to semantics for probabilistic programs:

- mathematical semantics defined using densities and measures;
- Monte Carlo semantics with rejection;
- Monte Carlo semantics with weighting.

In Section 2.2.4, we have seen that, no matter what approach is taken, some care is needed because the normalizing constant may be infinite or zero.

2.3 Introduction to measurability issues

In Section 2.4 we will give a formal semantics for probabilistic programs in terms of measures. In this section, we introduce the basics of a measure-theoretic approach to probability (see also Pollard, 2002) and use it to illustrate why such a formal semantics is not entirely trivial.

The idea of weighted simulation already gives us an interpretation of a probabilistic program. We define an underlying probability space $\Omega = [0, 1]^d$ where d is the number of sample statements in the program. If the program includes recursion, d may be countably infinite, but that is not a problem. We can think of each element of Ω as a list of random seeds. Given such a list, we can execute a program deterministically, leading to a weight (the product of all the observes) and a deterministic result, because the results of the sample statements are fixed.

(Here we are using the fact that uniform random numbers in $[0, 1]$ are a sufficient seed for sampling from any probability distribution with parameters. For example,

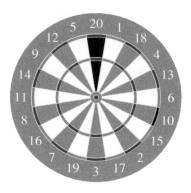

Figure 2.7 A dartboard with the areas scoring 20 highlighted in black. Reproduced under a
Creative Commons Licence from Robert Bonvallet.

sampling from a Bernoulli distribution can be simulated by testing the position of a
uniform random number,

$$\text{sample}(bernoulli(r)) \;=\; \text{let } x = \text{sample}(uniform) \text{ in return}(x < r)$$

and more generally, sampling from a general distribution can be simulated using the
inverse-cdf method, e.g.:

$$\text{sample}(normal(m, s)) \;=$$

$$\text{let } x = \text{sample}(uniform) \text{ in return(norm-invcdf}(m, s, x)).)$$

Thus a probabilistic program of type X determines two functions:

$$result : \Omega \rightarrow X \qquad weight : \Omega \rightarrow [0, \infty) \tag{2.4}$$

and each run of the weighted simulation corresponds to randomly picking seeds
$\omega \in \Omega$ and returning the pair $(weight(\omega), result(\omega))$.

In general this (2.4) is a very intensional representation of a probabilistic program:
programs that describe the same probabilistic scenarios have different different
representations, because the functions *result* and *weight* will differ. For example, the
following two programs implementing sample($bernoulli2/7$):

$$\text{let } x = \text{sample}(uniform) \text{ in return}(x < \tfrac{2}{7})$$

$$\text{let } x = \text{sample}(uniform) \text{ in return}(x > \tfrac{5}{7})$$

will have different representations; introducing redundant sample statements will
give different representations; and so on. What we ultimately care about is the
posterior probability on the results. In general, this will be a measure.

Measure theory generalizes the ideas of size and probability distribution from
countable discrete sets to uncountable sets. To motivate, think of the game of darts.

No matter how good a player I am, the chance of hitting the point at the centre of the dartboard is zero. The chance of hitting any given point is zero. Nonetheless I will hit a point when I throw. We resolve this apparent paradox by giving a probability of hitting each region. The probability of scoring 20 points is the sum of the probabilities of hitting one of the three regions that score 20 points (Figure 2.7). And so on. We can think of these regions of the dartboard as measurable sets with positive probability.

With this in mind, we are interested in the posterior probability that the result of a probabilistic program is within a certain set; for example, that the day is a weekend day, or that the time is between 4am and 7am, or that I scored 20 on the dartboard. If we run a weighted simulation k times, picking seeds $\omega_1 \ldots \omega_k \in \Omega$, we obtain an empirical posterior probability that the result is in the set U:

$$\frac{\sum_{i=1}^{k} [result(\omega_i) \in U] \cdot weight(\omega_i)}{\sum_{i=1}^{k} weight(\omega_i)} \tag{2.5}$$

(Here and elsewhere we regard a property, e.g. $[x \in U]$, as its characteristic function $X \to \{0, 1\}$.) Although this empirical probability is itself random, in that it depends on the choices ω_i, we would like to use the law of large numbers to understand that as $k \to \infty$ the empirical posterior (2.5) converges to a true posterior

$$\frac{\int_{\Omega} [result(\omega) \in U] \cdot weight(\omega) \, d\omega}{\int_{\Omega} weight(\omega) \, d\omega}. \tag{2.6}$$

Then two programs should be regarded as the same if they give the same posterior probability measure. There are two issues:

- We need to understand why the integrals in (2.6) exist;
- We need to also understand program fragments in this way, so that we can reason about program equality bit by bit, compositionally.

To address these, we interpret probabilistic programs as unnormalized measures and kernels.

2.3.1 Rudiments of measure-theoretic probability

We recall some basic definitions of measure theory. These are well-motivated by the illustration in Figure 2.7: the probability of scoring 20 is the sum of the probabilities of hitting the three regions shown. Thus countable disjoint unions are crucial for formulating measures.

Definition 2.1 A σ-*algebra* on a set X is a collection of subsets of X that contains $\emptyset$ and is closed under complements and countable unions. A *measurable space* is a pair (X, Σ_X) of a set X and a σ-algebra Σ_X on it. The sets in Σ_X are called *measurable sets*.

For example, we equip the set $\mathbb{R}$ of reals with the Borel sets. The Borel sets are the smallest σ-algebra on $\mathbb{R}$ that contains the intervals. The plane $\mathbb{R}^2$ is equipped with the least σ-algebra containing the rectangles $(U \times V)$ with U and V Borel. For example, the dartboard (Fig 2.7) is a subset of $\mathbb{R}^2$, and the set of points that would score 20 points is measurable.

Definition 2.2   A *measure* on a measurable space (X, Σ_X) is a function $\mu : \Sigma_X \to [0, \infty]$ into the set $[0, \infty]$ of extended non-negative reals that is σ-additive, i.e. $\mu(\emptyset) = 0$ and $\mu(\biguplus_{n \in \mathbb{N}} U_n) = \sum_{n \in \mathbb{N}} \mu(U_n)$ for any $\mathbb{N}$-indexed sequence of disjoint measurable sets U. A *probability measure* is a measure μ such that $\mu(X) = 1$.

For example, the Lebesgue measure λ on $\mathbb{R}$ is determined by saying that the measure of a line segment is its length ($\lambda(a, b) = b - a$), and the Lebesgue measure on $\mathbb{R}^2$ is determined by saying that the measure of a rectangle is its area. For any $x \in X$, the Dirac measure δ_x has $\delta_x(U) = [x \in U]$. To give a measure on a countable discrete measurable space X it is sufficient to assign an element of $[0, \infty]$ to each element of X. For example, the counting measure γ is determined by $\gamma(\{x\}) = 1$ for all $x \in X$.

Measures can be equivalently understood as integration operators. A function between measurable spaces, $f : X \to Y$, is said to be measurable if $f^{-1}(U) \in \Sigma_X$ when $U \in \Sigma_Y$. If $f : X \to [0, \infty]$ is measurable and μ is a measure on X then we can integrate f with respect to μ, written $\int_\mu f(x) \, dx$, giving a number in $[0, \infty]$.

2.3.2 Relationship to Bayesian statistics

The measure-theoretic semantics that we discuss in this chapter is inspired by Bayes' law, but it is not tied to it. Indeed, sometimes a language for weighted Monte Carlo simulation is useful without a formal Bayesian intuition; for example, one might use weights coming from image similarity without making a formal connection to likelihood. Nonetheless in this section we make a connection with the measure-theoretic treatment of Bayes' law.

Measures are closely related to density functions.

Definition 2.3   If $f : X \to [0, \infty]$ is measurable, and μ is a measure on X, then

$$\nu(U) = \int_\mu [x \in U] f(x) \, dx$$

is also a measure. We say that ν has *density* f with respect to μ. A density is sometimes called a *Radon-Nikodym derivative*. If $\nu(X) = 1$, it is a *probability density*. If a measurable function $f : X \times Y \to [0, \infty]$ has the property that $\int_\mu f(x, y)\, \mathrm{d}x = 1$ for all y then it is a *conditional probability density* with respect to μ.

For example, the density function of the exponential distribution $(r, x) \mapsto re^{-x}$ is a conditional density with respect to the Lebesgue measure, and this induces the exponential probability measures on $\mathbb{R}$. The Dirac measure has no density with respect to the Lebesgue measure, but it does have a density with respect to itself, as does every measure.

Throughout the above analysis, we have used densities as weights. The observed data has been fixed in our examples, for example, 4 buses or 15 minutes, but it would be reasonable to make the function *weight*: $\Omega \to [0, \infty)$ parametrized in the data. Thus, supposing our data lies in a space D, the data-parameterized weight function is a measurable function *likelihood*: $D \times \Omega \to [0, \infty)$, such that *weight*$(\omega) = $ *likelihood*(d, ω) where d is the specific data that is hard-coded into the program. The Bayesian approach is that *likelihood* should be a conditional probability density with respect to some measure λ on D.

The posterior (2.6) can then be made a measurable function of $y \in D$, i.e. a regular conditional probability:

$$q_y(U) = \frac{\int_\Omega [result(\omega) \in U] \cdot likelihood(y, \omega)\, \mathrm{d}\omega}{\int_\Omega likelihood(y, \omega)\, \mathrm{d}\omega}.$$

This can also now be connected formally to Bayes' theorem of conditional probability, see e.g. Schervish (1995, Thm. 1.31). In Section 2.2.4 we discussed the point that although the denominator may be 0 or ∞, for a whole program, this almost-never happens. This can now be made precise:

$$\gamma(U_{0,\infty}) = 0$$

where $\gamma(V) = \int_D \int_\Omega [y \in V] \cdot likelihood(y, \omega)\, \mathrm{d}\omega\, \mathrm{d}y$ is the prior predictive measure, and $U_{0,\infty} = \{y \mid \int_\Omega likelihood(y, \omega)\, \mathrm{d}\omega \in \{0, \infty\}\}$.

We conclude by mentioning, as an aside, that in complex situations, the Bayesian requirement of a single base measure λ on D can be subtle. The density functions for the GPA problem in Figure 2.3 are densities with respect to the mixed measure (*lebesgue* $+ \delta_4 + \delta_{10}$). The theory of conditional probability densities requires a single common base measure for all the different parameters. The following program will only give the right result if we use the same base measure (*lebesgue* $+ \delta_4 + \delta_{10}$) on $\mathbb{R}$ for the likelihood functions for all the different if-then-else branches.

let *american* = sample(*bernoulli*(0.5)) in
let *brilliant* = sample(*bernoulli*(0.01)) in
if*american* then
    if*brilliant* then observe 4 from *dirac*(4) else observe 4 from *uniform*(0, 4)
else
    if*brilliant* then observe 4 from *dirac*(10) else observe 4 from *uniform*(0, 10)
return(*american*)

This is subtle because the density of the Indian distribution *uniform*(0, 10) with respect to the base *lebesgue* measure is the constant 0.1 function, but the density of *uniform*(0, 10) with respect to the base measure (*lebesgue* + δ_4 + δ_{10}) must take value 0 at 4, as in Figure 2.3. Overall, then, the program is a Dirac measure at *american* = true.

In summary, the meaning of a closed probabilistic program is an unnormalized measure, thought of as the nominator in Bayes' rule. For a program expression that has free variables, its interpretation should be measurable in the valuation of those variables.

- Sampling from a probability measure is a measure.
- An observation observe x from d is a one point measure whose value is the density of d at x.
- The sequencing let $x = t$ in u means, roughly, integration: $\int_t u \, dx$.
- The simple statement return(t) means the Dirac delta measure.

We make this precise in Section 2.4.

2.3.3 Obstacles to measurability

We now illustrate why measurability of programs is not entirely trivial. Our counterexamples are based on the counting measure on the real numbers. This is an unnormalized distribution that assigns 1 to every singleton set. It turns out that although some infinite measures are definable in a probabilistic programming language, the counting measure on $\mathbb{R}$ is not definable – we show this in Section 2.5.2. But for now let us suppose that we add it to our language, as a command *counting*, and see what chaos ensues. (For now, we retain an intuitive view of measurability; precise definitions are in Section 2.4, with a precise version of the arguments in this section given in Section 2.5.2.)

As before, for any set U we can consider a function $[x \in U]$ which returns true if

$x \in U$ and false otherwise. For example, we might write $[x \in \{0, 1, 2, 3\}]$, $[x > 0]$, $[x = 42]$, and so on. The following lemma gives some intuition for the counting measure.

Lemma 2.4 *For any (measurable) set U, the program*

$$\text{let } r = counting \text{ in return}[r \in U]$$

gives weight #U to true *and* $\#(\mathbb{R} \setminus U)$ *to* false, *where #U is the cardinality of U if U is finite, or* ∞ *otherwise.*

In this extended language, the fundamental law of exchangeability is violated: the order of draws matters, as we now explain. Notice that let $s = counting$ in return$[r = s]$ has the same semantics as return(true), for all r, because there is exactly one s that is equal to any given r (Lemma 2.4). So

$$\text{let } r = uniform(0, 1) \text{ in let } s = counting \text{ in return}[r = s] \tag{2.7}$$

is an equivalent program to return(true). But

$$\text{let } r = uniform(0, 1) \text{ in return}[r = s]$$

has the same semantics return(false), for all s, because any r is almost surely different from a given s. So

$$\text{let } s = counting \text{ in let } r = uniform(0, 1) \text{ in return}[r = s] \tag{2.8}$$

has the same semantics as return(false). Comparing (2.8) to (2.7), we see that programs involving the counting measure cannot be reordered.

In fact, the measure-theoretic semantics of the language extended with *counting* is not always even fully defined. For an example of this, we recall that there exist Borel-measurable subsets U of the plane $\mathbb{R}^2$ for which the projection $\pi[U] \stackrel{\text{def}}{=} \{x \mid \exists y. (x, y) \in U\}$ is not Borel-measurable in $\mathbb{R}$. (In general $\pi[U]$ is called 'analytic'.) Now the program

$$\text{let } s = counting \text{ in return}[(r, s) \in U]$$

puts a non-zero weight on true if and only if $r \in \pi[U]$. So this program is not measurable in r, and so programs built from it, such as

$$\text{let } r = uniform(0, 1) \text{ in let } s = counting \text{ in return}[(r, s) \in U]$$

are not well defined.

As we will see in Section 2.4 (Lemma 2.7), this problem cannot arise in the language without the *counting* measure: every term is compositionally well-behaved.

2.4 Formal semantics of probabilistic programs as measures

We now turn to give a precise semantics of probabilistic programs. To this end we set up a typed language with a precise syntax.

In the previous section we have considered programs as Bayesian statistical models. However, this is only an intuition, and the semantics is given in terms of weighted simulations and measure theory. Moreover, some applications of weighted simulation are beyond the realms of Bayesian statistics.

For these reasons, the precise language that we now consider will have the keyword score(r), which weights the run by r, instead of the keyword observe. The two are inter-definable:

$$\text{observe } r \text{ from } p = \text{score}(f(r)), \quad \text{where } f \text{ is the density of } p$$
$$\text{score}(r) = \text{observe } 0 \text{ from } exponential(r)$$

2.4.1 Types

In what follows it is helpful to consider a typed programming language. We will consider types such as natural numbers, real numbers, tuples of real numbers, and lists of real numbers. In practice many probabilistic programming languages do not perform type checking, but having a type greatly simplifies the mathematical semantics. Moreover, types play an intuitive role, because a probabilistic program may describe a measure on the space of natural numbers, or the space of real numbers, or on the real plane. With this intuition, a type is just a syntactic description of a space. For instance, we can understand an expression of real type as a measure on the real line; an expression of integer type as a measure on the space of integers, and so on.

Our types are generated by the following grammar:

$$A, B ::= \mathbb{R} \mid P(A) \mid 1 \mid A \times B \mid \coprod_{i \in I} A_i$$

where I ranges over countable, non-empty sets. The type $\coprod_{i \in I} A_i$ is sometimes called a labelled variant or a tagged union. The type $P(A)$ is a type of distributions on A. Here are some examples of types in the grammar:

- The type $\mathbb{R}$ of the real line, and type $\mathbb{R} \times \mathbb{R}$ of the plane;
- The type $(1 + 1)$ of booleans (true/false), the type $\coprod_{i \in \mathbb{N}} 1$ of natural numbers;
- The type $\coprod_{i \in \mathbb{N}} \mathbb{R}^i$ of sequences of reals of arbitrary length;
- The type $P(1 + 1)$ of probability distributions over the booleans, and the type $P(\mathbb{R})$ of probability distributions on the reals.

To keep things simple we do include function types such as $(\mathbb{R} \to \mathbb{R})$ and $(\mathbb{R} \to \mathbb{R}) \to \mathbb{R}$. Also, this is not a type system that can be automatically checked in a

computer because we include infinite sum types rather than recursion schemes. We
do this primarily because countably infinite disjoint unions play such a crucial role
in classical measure theory, and constructive measure theory is an orthogonal issue
(but see e.g. (Ackerman et al., 2011)).

2.4.2 Types as measurable spaces

Types $\mathbb{A}$ are interpreted as measurable spaces $[\![\mathbb{A}]\!]$, by induction on their structure,
as follows. To be precise we distinguish between the syntactic name of the type $\mathbb{A}$
and the space $[\![\mathbb{A}]\!]$ which interprets it.

- $[\![\mathbb{R}]\!]$ is the measurable space of reals, with its Borel sets. The Borel sets are the
  smallest σ-algebra on $\mathbb{R}$ that contains the intervals. We will always consider $\mathbb{R}$
  with this σ-algebra.
- $[\![1]\!]$ is the unique measurable space with one point.
- $[\![\mathbb{A} \times \mathbb{B}]\!]$ is the product space $[\![\mathbb{A}]\!] \times [\![\mathbb{B}]\!]$. The σ-algebra $\Sigma_{[\![\mathbb{A} \times \mathbb{B}]\!]}$ is the least one
  containing the rectangles $(U \times V)$ with $U \in \Sigma_{[\![\mathbb{A}]\!]}$ and $V \in \Sigma_{[\![\mathbb{B}]\!]}$ (e.g. Pollard,
  2002, Def. 16)).
- $[\![\coprod_{i \in I} \mathbb{A}_i]\!]$ is the coproduct space $\biguplus_{i \in I} [\![\mathbb{A}_i]\!]$, the disjoint union. The σ-algebra
  $\Sigma_{[\![\coprod_{i \in I} \mathbb{A}_i]\!]}$ is least one containing the sets $\{(i, a) \mid a \in U\}$ for $U \in \Sigma_{[\![\mathbb{A}_i]\!]}$. For
  example, the type $\mathbb{N}$ is interpreted as the space $[\![\mathbb{N}]\!]$ of natural numbers with the
  discrete σ-algebra, where all sets are measurable.
- We let $[\![\mathsf{P}(\mathbb{A})]\!]$ be the set $P([\![\mathbb{A}]\!])$ of probability measures on $[\![\mathbb{A}]\!]$ together with the
  least σ-algebra containing the sets $\{\mu \mid \mu(U) < r\}$ for each $U \in \Sigma_X$ and $r \in [0, 1]$
  (the 'Giry monad' (Giry, 1982)).

2.4.3 Typed program expressions

We consider programs built from the following grammar:

$$t, t_0, t_1 ::= (i, t) \mid \mathsf{case}\ t\ \mathsf{of}\ \{(i, x) \Rightarrow u_i\}_{i \in I} \mid () \mid (t_0, t_1) \mid \mathsf{proj}_j(t) \mid f(t) \mid x$$
$$\mid \mathsf{return}(t) \mid \mathsf{let}\ x = t\ \mathsf{in}\ u \mid \mathsf{sample}(t) \mid \mathsf{score}(t) \mid \mathsf{normalize}(t)$$
(2.9)

The first line of (2.9) contains standard deterministic expressions, for example
destructing union and product types, with intended equations such as the following:

$$\left(\mathsf{case}\ (j, t)\ \mathsf{of}\ \{(i, x) \Rightarrow u_i\}\right) = u_j[t/x] \qquad \mathsf{proj}_j(t_0, t_1) = t_j.$$

We also include some basic functions f, and in fact, we may as well include all
measurable functions in our language, including arithmetic operations and constants
(e.g. $+$, $\times$, k_{10}), comparison predicates (e.g. $=$, $<$), and parameterized probability

measures (e.g. *normal, bernoulli*). There are also variables x that are bound by case and let.

In a real computer language, operations over infinite structures such as lists and numbers are given by induction or recursion. In this chapter, rather than worry about this, we simply allow the programmer to give a different case for every index into the infinite structure. This means that the case syntax is potentially infinite, since the set I might be (countably) infinite. It is routine to build a finite language with inductive primitives and translate it into this one.

The second line of (2.9) contains ways of combining programs (let) and sequencing, as well as the three crucial primitives of probabilistic programming: sample, score and normalize.

In this simple language, there is little syntactic sugar, and so the program about buses in Section 2.2.1 would be written:

1. normalize(
2.   let x = sample($bernoulli(\frac{2}{7})$) in
3.   let r = case x of $\{(1,\_) \Rightarrow \text{return}(k_3()), (2,\_) \Rightarrow \text{return}(k_{10}())\}$ in
4.   let $\_$ = score($\frac{1}{4!}r^4 e^{-r}$) in
5.   return(x))

$$(2.10)$$

where $k_3, k_{10} : 1 \rightarrow \mathbb{R}$ are the obvious constant functions, which are measurable.

Typed terms. We distinguish typing judgements: $\Gamma \vdash_d t: \mathbb{A}$ for deterministic terms, and $\Gamma \vdash_p t: \mathbb{A}$ for probabilistic terms. Here the context Γ is of the form $(x_1 : \mathbb{B}_1, \ldots, x_n : \mathbb{B}_n)$. The intuition is that if $\Gamma \vdash_d t: \mathbb{A}$ then the free variables of t are contained in $x_1 \ldots x_n$, and given values of the right type for each free variable, then the expression t will return something of type $\mathbb{A}$, either deterministically or probabilistically. For example, the entire program in (2.10) is a deterministic term returning a distribution, whereas lines 2–5 form a probabilistic term of type $(1 + 1)$. Neither have any free variables. The term score($\frac{1}{4!}r^4 e^{-r}$) is a probabilistic term with a real free variable r: real, so we write $r: \text{real} \vdash_p \text{score}(\frac{1}{4!}r^4 e^{-r}): 1$.

We have already explained that each type $\mathbb{A}$ is understood as a measurable space. Formally, a context $\Gamma = (x_1 : \mathbb{A}_1, \ldots, x_n : \mathbb{A}_n)$ is also interpreted as a measurable space $[\![\Gamma]\!] \stackrel{\text{def}}{=} \prod_{i=1}^{n} [\![\mathbb{A}_i]\!]$ of well-typed valuations for the variables. As will be seen in the next section, deterministic terms $\Gamma \vdash_d t: \mathbb{A}$ denote measurable functions from $[\![\Gamma]\!] \rightarrow [\![\mathbb{A}]\!]$, closed probabilistic terms $\vdash_p t': \mathbb{A}$ denote measures on $[\![\mathbb{A}]\!]$, and open probabilistic terms $\Gamma \vdash_p t': \mathbb{A}$ denote kernels $[\![\Gamma]\!] \rightsquigarrow [\![\mathbb{A}]\!]$. We give a syntax and type system here, and a semantics in Section 2.4.4.

We specify the valid judgements $\Gamma \vdash_d t: \mathbb{A}$ and $\Gamma \vdash_p t: \mathbb{A}$ as the least relations closed under the following rules.

Sums and products. The type system allows variables, and standard constructors and destructors for sum and product types.

$$\frac{}{\Gamma, x: A, \Gamma' \vdash_d x: A} \qquad \frac{\Gamma \vdash_d t: A_i}{\Gamma \vdash_d (i,t): \coprod_{i \in I} A_i}$$

$$\frac{\Gamma \vdash_d t: \coprod_{i \in I} A_i \quad (\Gamma, x: A_i \vdash_z u_i: B)_{i \in I}}{\Gamma \vdash_z \text{case } t \text{ of } \{(i,x) \Rightarrow u_i\}_{i \in I}: B} \quad (z \in \{d,p\})$$

$$\frac{}{\Gamma \vdash_d (): 1} \qquad \frac{\Gamma \vdash_d t_0: A_0 \quad \Gamma \vdash_d t_1: A_1}{\Gamma \vdash_d (t_0,t_1): A_0 \times A_1} \qquad \frac{\Gamma \vdash_d t: A_0 \times A_1}{\Gamma \vdash_d \text{proj}_j(t): A_j}$$

If the reader is not familiar with type systems, they might consult the early chapters of (Harper, 2016). We give an example of a typing derivation later, in (2.12). For instance, the rule for (t_0, t_1) says that "if term t_0 has type A_0 and term t_1 has type A_1 then the pair (t_0, t_1) has type $(A_0 \times A_1)$".

In the rules for sums, I may be infinite. In the last rule, j is 0 or 1. We use some standard syntactic sugar, such as false and true for the injections in the type bool = $1 + 1$, and if for case in that instance. The continuations of case expressions may be either deterministic or probabilistic, as indicated.

Sequencing. We include the standard constructs for sequencing (e.g. Levy et al., 2003; Moggi, 1991).

$$\frac{\Gamma \vdash_d t: A}{\Gamma \vdash_p \text{return}(t): A} \qquad \frac{\Gamma \vdash_p t: A \quad \Gamma, x: A \vdash_p u: B}{\Gamma \vdash_p \text{let } x = t \text{ in } u: B}$$

Notice that, in this simple language, everything probabilistic must be explicitly sequenced. For example, if $\Gamma \vdash_p t_0: A_0$ and $\Gamma \vdash_p t_1: A_1$, we cannot conclude that $\Gamma \vdash_p (t_0, t_1): A_0 \times A_1$. Rather, we have to explicitly write

$$\Gamma \vdash_p \text{let } x_0 = t_0 \text{ in let } x_1 = t_1 \text{ in return}(x_0, x_1): A_0 \times A_1$$
$$\text{or} \quad \Gamma \vdash_p \text{let } x_1 = t_1 \text{ in let } x_0 = t_0 \text{ in return}(x_0, x_1): A_0 \times A_1$$

Later (§2.5.1) we will show that the order of evaluation doesn't matter, so we could use (t_0, t_1) as an unambiguous syntactic sugar, but it makes the formal semantics simpler to insist that the order of evaluation is given explicitly.

Language-specific constructs. We also include constant terms for all measurable functions. Recall that a function $f: X \to Y$ between measurable spaces is itself measurable if the inverse image of a measurable set is again measurable.

$$\frac{\Gamma \vdash_d t: A}{\Gamma \vdash_d f(t): B} \quad (f: [\![A]\!] \to [\![B]\!] \text{ measurable}) \tag{2.11}$$

Thus we assign suitable types to the arithmetic operations and constants (e.g. $+$: $\mathbb{R} \times \mathbb{R} \to \mathbb{R}$, $k_{10} : 1 \to \mathbb{R}$), predicates (e.g. $(=) : \mathbb{R} \times \mathbb{R} \to$ bool) and probability measures (e.g. *normal* : $\mathbb{R} \times \mathbb{R} \to P(\mathbb{R})$). For instance, we have a judgement $\mu : \mathbb{R}, \sigma : \mathbb{R} \vdash_{\natural} normal(\mu, \sigma) \colon \mathsf{P}(\mathbb{R})$. (Some families are not defined for all parameters, e.g. the standard deviation should be positive, but we make ad-hoc safe choices throughout rather than using exceptions or subtyping.)

For example, the expression (if x then 3 else 10) is shorthand for

$$(\text{case } x \text{ of } \{(1, \_) \Rightarrow k_3() \,;\, (2, \_) \Rightarrow k_{10}()\})$$

We derive that the expression has type $\mathbb{R}$ when x has type bool, by deriving it from the rules as follows.

$$
\cfrac{
\cfrac{-}{x : \text{bool} \vdash_{\natural} x : \text{bool}}
\qquad
\cfrac{\cfrac{-}{x : \text{bool}, z : 1 \vdash_{\natural} () : 1}}{x : \text{bool}, z : 1 \vdash_{\natural} k_3() : \mathbb{R}}
\qquad
\cfrac{\cfrac{-}{x : \text{bool}, z : 1 \vdash_{\natural} () : 1}}{x : \text{bool}, z : 1 \vdash_{\natural} k_{10}() : \mathbb{R}}
}{
x : \text{bool} \vdash_{\natural} \text{case } x \text{ of } \{(1, z) \Rightarrow k_3() \,;\, (2, z) \Rightarrow k_{10}()\} : \mathbb{R}
}
\qquad (2.12)
$$

The core of the language is the constructs corresponding to the terms in Bayes' law: sampling from prior distributions, recording likelihood scores,

$$
\cfrac{\Gamma \vdash_{\natural} t : \mathsf{P}(\mathbb{A})}{\Gamma \vdash_{\flat} \text{sample}(t) : \mathbb{A}}
\qquad\qquad
\cfrac{\Gamma \vdash_{\natural} t : \mathbb{R}}{\Gamma \vdash_{\flat} \text{score}(t) : 1}
$$

and calculating the normalizing constant and a normalized posterior.

$$
\cfrac{\Gamma \vdash_{\flat} t : \mathbb{A}}{\Gamma \vdash_{\natural} \text{normalize}(t) : \mathbb{R} \times \mathsf{P}(\mathbb{A}) + 1 + 1}
$$

As we discussed in Section 2.2.4, normalization will fail if the normalizing constant is zero or infinity; so it produces either a normalization constant together with a normalized posterior distribution ($\mathbb{R} \times \mathsf{P}(\mathbb{A})$), or exceptionally one of the two failure possibilities ($+1 + 1$). In a complex model the normalized posterior could subsequently be used as a prior and sampled from. This is sometimes called a 'nested query' (see for instance Stuhlmuller and Goodman, 2014), but it remains to be seen whether it is computationally practical (Rainforth et al., 2018).

2.4.4 Expressions as s-finite kernels, programs as measures

In this section we will give an interpretation of closed programs $\vdash_{\flat} t : \mathbb{A}$ as measures on $\mathbb{A}$. To do this, we must also interpret open programs $\Gamma \vdash_{\flat} t : \mathbb{A}$, which will be families of measures on $[\![\mathbb{A}]\!]$ that are indexed by the valuations of the context $[\![\Gamma]\!]$. These are called *kernels*. (Warning: the word kernel is over-used and has other meanings.)

s-Finite kernels

A kernel k from X to Y is a function $k : X \times \Sigma_Y \to [0, \infty]$ such that each $k(x, -) : \Sigma_Y \to [0, \infty]$ is a measure and each $k(-, U) : X \to [0, \infty]$ is measurable. Because each $k(x, -)$ is a measure, we can integrate any measurable function $f : Y \to [0, \infty]$ to get $\int_{k(x)} f(y) \, dy \in [0, \infty]$. We write $k : X \rightsquigarrow Y$ if k is a kernel. We say that k is a *probability kernel* if $k(x, Y) = 1$ for all $x \in X$.

We need to further refine the notion of kernels, because arbitrary kernels do not behave well. The following result is a step towards the central notion of *s-finite* kernel.

Proposition 2.5 *Let X, Y be measurable spaces. If $k_1 \ldots k_n \cdots : X \rightsquigarrow Y$ are kernels then the function $(\sum_{i=1}^{\infty} k_i) : X \times \Sigma_Y \to [0, \infty]$ given by*

$$(\textstyle\sum_{i=1}^{\infty} k_i)(x, U) \stackrel{\text{def}}{=} \sum_{i=1}^{\infty} (k_i(x, U))$$

is a kernel $X \rightsquigarrow Y$. Moreover, for any measurable function $f : Y \to [0, \infty]$,

$$\int_{(\sum_{i=1}^{\infty} k_i)(x)} f(y) \, dy = \sum_{i=1}^{\infty} \int_{k_i(x)} f(y) \, dy.$$

Definition 2.6 Let X, Y be measurable spaces. A kernel $k : X \rightsquigarrow Y$ is *finite* if there is finite $r \in [0, \infty)$ such that, for all x, $k(x, Y) < r$.

A kernel $k : X \rightsquigarrow Y$ is *s-finite* if there is a sequence $k_1 \ldots k_n \ldots$ of finite kernels and $\sum_{i=1}^{\infty} k_i = k$.

Note that the bound in the finiteness condition, and the choice of sequence in the s-finiteness condition, are uniform, across all arguments to the kernel.

If the reader is familiar with the notion of σ-finite measure, they will note that this is different. In fact, an s-finite measure is the same thing as the push-forward of a σ-finite measure (Getoor, 1990; Sharpe, 1988). The definition of s-finite kernel is not so common but appears in recent work by (Kallenberg, 2014) and Last and Penrose (2016, App. A). It was proposed as a foundation for probabilistic programming by the author (Staton, 2017), but it has since attracted further use and development (e.g. Bichsel et al., 2018; Ong and Vákár, 2018).

Composition of kernels

Before we give the semantics of our language, we need a lemma which is central to the interpretation of let.

Lemma 2.7 *Let X, Y, Z be measurable spaces, and let $k : X \times Y \rightsquigarrow Z$ and $l : X \rightsquigarrow Y$ be s-finite kernels (Def. 2.6). Then we can define a s-finite kernel*

$(k \star l) : X \rightsquigarrow Z$ by

$$(k \star l)(x, U) \stackrel{\text{def}}{=} \int_{l(x)} k(x, y, U) \, dy$$

so that

$$\int_{(k\star l)(x)} f(z) \, dz = \int_{l(x)} \int_{k(x,y)} f(z) \, dz \, dy$$

A proof is given in (Staton, 2017), building on a well-known fact that the the property holds for finite kernels (e.g. Pollard, 2002, Thm. 20(ii)). The example in Section 2.3.3 shows that if we generalize to arbitrary kernels, we cannot construct $k \star l$ in general. In detail, let $X = Y = \mathbb{R}$ and let $Z = 1 = \{*\}$. Pick a Borel subset $U \subseteq \mathbb{R} \times \mathbb{R}$ whose projection is not Borel. Let $k(x, y, \{*\}) = [(x, y) \in U]$, and let $l(x, -)$ be the counting measure on $\mathbb{R}$. Then $(k \star l)(x, \{*\})$ is non-zero if and only if $x \in \pi[U]$, and so it is not measurable in x, and so it is not a kernel.

Semantics

Recall that types $\mathbb{A}$ are interpreted as measurable spaces $[\![\mathbb{A}]\!]$. We now explain how to interpret a deterministic term in context, $\Gamma \vdash_d t : \mathbb{A}$, as a measurable function $[\![t]\!] : [\![\Gamma]\!] \to [\![\mathbb{A}]\!]$, and how to interpret a probabilistic term in context, $\Gamma \vdash_p t : \mathbb{A}$, as an s-finite kernel $[\![t]\!] : [\![\Gamma]\!] \rightsquigarrow [\![\mathbb{A}]\!]$.

The semantics of the language, beginning with variables, sums and products, is roughly the same as a set-theoretic semantics. For each typed term $\Gamma \vdash_d t : \mathbb{A}$, and each valuation $\gamma \in [\![\Gamma]\!]$ of values for variables, we define an element $[\![t]\!]_\gamma$ of $\mathbb{A}$, in such a way that the assignment is measurable in γ. We do this by induction on the structure of typing derivations:

$$[\![x]\!]_\gamma \stackrel{\text{def}}{=} \gamma x \qquad\qquad [\![(i, t)]\!]_\gamma \stackrel{\text{def}}{=} (i, [\![t]\!]_\gamma)$$

$$[\![\text{case } t \text{ of } \{(i, x) \Rightarrow u_i\}_{i \in I}]\!]_\gamma \stackrel{\text{def}}{=} [\![u_i]\!]_{\gamma, d} \quad \text{if } [\![t]\!]_\gamma = (i, d)$$

$$[\![()]\!]_\gamma \stackrel{\text{def}}{=} () \qquad [\![(t_0, t_1)]\!]_\gamma \stackrel{\text{def}}{=} ([\![t_0]\!]_\gamma, [\![t_1]\!]_\gamma) \qquad [\![\pi_j(t)]\!]_\gamma \stackrel{\text{def}}{=} d_j \quad \text{if } [\![t]\!]_\gamma = (d_0, d_1)$$

Here we have only treated the case expressions when the continuation u_i is deterministic; we return to the probabilistic case later.

For each typed probabilistic term $\Gamma \vdash_p t : \mathbb{A}$, and each valuation $\gamma \in [\![\Gamma]\!]$, and each measurable set $U \in \Sigma_{[\![\mathbb{A}]\!]}$, we define a measure $[\![t]\!]_{\gamma;U} \in [0, \infty]$, in such a way that $[\![t]\!]$ is an s-finite kernel $[\![\Gamma]\!] \rightsquigarrow [\![\mathbb{A}]\!]$ (Def. 2.6). The semantics of sequencing are perhaps the most interesting: return is the Dirac delta measure, and let is integration.

$$[\![\text{return}(t)]\!]_{\gamma;U} \stackrel{\text{def}}{=} \begin{cases} 1 & \text{if } [\![t]\!]_\gamma \in U \\ 0 & \text{otherwise} \end{cases} \qquad [\![\text{let } x = t \text{ in } u]\!]_{\gamma;U} \stackrel{\text{def}}{=} \int_{[\![t]\!]_\gamma} [\![u]\!]_{\gamma, x; U} \, dx$$

The interpretation $[\![\text{return}(t)]\!]$ is finite, hence s-finite. The fact that $[\![\text{let } x = t \text{ in } u]\!]$ is an s-finite kernel is Lemma 2.7: this is the most intricate part of the semantics.

We return to the case expression where the continuation is probabilistic:

$$\llbracket \text{case } t \text{ of } \{(i, x) \Rightarrow u_i\}_{i \in I}\rrbracket_{\gamma;U} \overset{\text{def}}{=} \llbracket u_i \rrbracket_{\gamma,d;U} \quad \text{if } \llbracket t \rrbracket_\gamma = (i, d).$$

We must show that this is an s-finite kernel. Recall that $\llbracket u_i \rrbracket : \llbracket \Gamma \times A_i \rrbracket \rightsquigarrow \llbracket B \rrbracket$, s-finite. We can also form $\overline{\llbracket u_i \rrbracket} : \llbracket \Gamma \rrbracket \times \biguplus_j \llbracket A_j \rrbracket \rightsquigarrow \llbracket B \rrbracket$ with

$$\overline{\llbracket u_i \rrbracket}_{\gamma,(j,a);U} \overset{\text{def}}{=} \begin{cases} \llbracket u_i \rrbracket_{\gamma,a;U} & i = j \\ 0 & \text{otherwise} \end{cases}$$

and it is easy to show that $\overline{\llbracket u_i \rrbracket}$ is an s-finite kernel. Another easy fact is that a countable sum of s-finite kernels is again an s-finite kernel, so we can build an s-finite kernel $(\sum_i \overline{\llbracket u_i \rrbracket}) : \llbracket \Gamma \rrbracket \times \biguplus_j \llbracket A_j \rrbracket \rightsquigarrow \llbracket B \rrbracket$. Finally, we use a simple instance of Lemma 2.7 to compose $(\sum_i \overline{\llbracket u_i \rrbracket})$ with $\llbracket t \rrbracket : \llbracket \Gamma \rrbracket \to \biguplus_j \llbracket A_j \rrbracket$ and conclude that $\llbracket \text{case } t \text{ of } \{(i, x) \Rightarrow u_i\}_{i \in I}\rrbracket$ is an s-finite kernel.

The language specific constructions are straightforward.

$$\llbracket \text{sample}(t) \rrbracket_{\gamma;U} \overset{\text{def}}{=} \llbracket t \rrbracket_\gamma(U) \qquad \llbracket \text{score}(t) \rrbracket_{\gamma;U} \overset{\text{def}}{=} \begin{cases} |\llbracket t \rrbracket_\gamma| & \text{if } U - \{()\} \\ 0 & \text{if } U = \emptyset. \end{cases}$$

In the semantics of sample, we are merely using the fact that to give a measurable function $X \to P(Y)$ is to give a probability kernel $X \rightsquigarrow Y$. Probability kernels are finite, hence s-finite.

The semantics of score is a one point space whose measure is the argument. (We take the absolute value of $\llbracket t \rrbracket_\gamma$ because measures should be non-negative. An alternative would be to somehow enforce this in the type system.) We need to show that $\llbracket \text{score}(t) \rrbracket$ is an s-finite kernel. Although $\llbracket \text{score}(t) \rrbracket_{\gamma;1}$ is always finite, $\llbracket \text{score}(t) \rrbracket$ is not necessarily a *finite kernel* because we cannot find a uniform bound. To show that it is *s-finite*, for each $i \in \mathbb{N}_0$, define a kernel $k_i : \llbracket \Gamma \rrbracket \rightsquigarrow 1$

$$k_i(\gamma, U) \overset{\text{def}}{=} \begin{cases} \llbracket \text{score}(t) \rrbracket_{\gamma;U} & \text{if } \llbracket \text{score}(t) \rrbracket_{\gamma;U} \in [i, i + 1) \\ 0 & \text{otherwise} \end{cases}$$

So each k_i is a finite kernel, bounded by $(i + 1)$, and $\llbracket \text{score}(t) \rrbracket = \sum_{i=0}^{\infty} k_i$, so it is s-finite.

We give a semantics to normalization by finding the normalizing constant and dividing by it, as follows. Consider $\Gamma \vdash t : A$ and let $\text{evidence}_{\gamma,t} \overset{\text{def}}{=} \llbracket t \rrbracket_{\gamma;\llbracket A \rrbracket}$.

$$\llbracket \text{normalize}(t) \rrbracket_\gamma \overset{\text{def}}{=} \begin{cases} (0, (\text{evidence}_{\gamma,t}, \frac{\llbracket t \rrbracket_{\gamma;(-)}}{\text{evidence}_{\gamma,t}})) & \text{evidence}_{\gamma,t} \in (0, \infty) \\ (1, ()) & \text{evidence}_{\gamma,t} = 0 \\ (2, ()) & \text{evidence}_{\gamma,t} = \infty \end{cases}$$

2.5 Reasoning with measures

Once a formal semantics of probabilistic programs as measures is given, one can reason about programs by reasoning about measures. Moreover, since the semantics is compositional, one can build up properties of programs in a compositional way. We consider two examples.

2.5.1 Reasoning example: Commutativity

We can quickly verify the following law

$$\text{let } x_0 = t_0 \text{ in let } x_1 = t_1 \text{ in return}(x_0, x_1)$$
$$= \quad \text{let } x_1 = t_1 \text{ in let } x_0 = t_0 \text{ in return}(x_0, x_1) \tag{2.13}$$

whenever $\Gamma \vdash t_0 : \mathbb{A}_0$ and $\Gamma \vdash t_1 : \mathbb{A}_1$. To do this we recall that $[\![t_0]\!]_{\gamma;-}$ and $[\![t_1]\!]_{\gamma;-}$ are measures on $\mathbb{A}_0$ and $\mathbb{A}_1$ respectively, and calculate that

$$[\![\text{let } x_0 = t_0 \text{ in let } x_1 = t_1 \text{ in return}(x_0, x_1)]\!]_{\gamma;U}$$
$$= \int_{[\![t_0]\!](\gamma)} \int_{[\![t_1]\!](\gamma)} [(x_0, x_1) \in U] \, dx_1 \, dx_0$$

is the definition of the product measure on $\mathbb{A}_0 \times \mathbb{A}_1$. Product measures are not well-defined in general, but they are well-defined for finite measures, and this extends to s-finite measures. Indeed to conclude (2.13), one would notice that for any s-finite measures μ_0, μ_1 on $\mathbb{A}_0$ and $\mathbb{A}_1$, the product measures on $\mathbb{A}_0 \times \mathbb{A}_1$ are equal:

$$\int_{\mu_0} \int_{\mu_1} [(x_0, x_1) \in U] \, dx_1 \, dx_0 = \int_{\mu_1} \int_{\mu_0} [(x_0, x_1) \in U] \, dx_0 \, dx_1$$

This is known as the Fubini-Tonelli theorem, which holds for s-finite measures (e.g. Sharpe, 1988; Staton, 2017).

2.5.2 Reasoning example: Non-definability

We have seen in Section 2.3.3 that the counting measure on $\mathbb{R}$, which assigns to each set its size, is problematic for a probabilistic programming language. We now show that it is not definable. It is sufficient to show that it is not s-finite, since every definable program describes an s-finite measure. To show this we show that for every s-finite measure μ, the set $\{r \mid \mu(\{r\}) > 0\}$ is countable. The counting measure violates this invariant. Since a countable union of countable sets is countable, it suffices to show that $\{r \mid \mu(\{r\}) > 0\}$ is countable when μ is a finite measure. To see this, notice that for each positive integer n the set $\{r \mid \mu(\{r\}) > \frac{1}{n}\}$ must be finite, and so $\{r \mid \mu(\{r\}) > 0\} = \bigcup_{n \in \mathbb{Z}^+} \{r \mid \mu(\{r\}) > \frac{1}{n}\}$ must be countable.

2.6 Other approaches to semantics and open questions

2.6.1 Different approaches to semantic definitions

In other work (Staton et al., 2016) we have considered a semantics based on a monad

$$X \mapsto P([0, \infty) \times X)$$

on the category of measurable spaces. This arises from combining the writer monad for the monoid $([0, \infty), +, 0)$ of scores with the probability monad P. This naturally matches the two constructions (score for $[0, \infty)$ and sample for P), and it fits the weighted simulation semantics: the meaning of a program is a distribution over runs, each of which has a weight and a result. This semantics distinguishes things that should arguably be considered equal. For example, the semantics will distinguish

let x = sample($bernoulli(0.5)$) in if x then score(4) else score(6); return(42)

from

score(5); return(42)

This semantics can be translated to the less discriminating semantics in this chapter as follows. Every measurable function

$$f : Y \to P([0, \infty) \times X)$$

can be translated to an s-finite kernel $f^{\sharp} : Y \rightsquigarrow X$ where

$$f^{\sharp}(y, U) = \int_{f(y)} r \cdot [x \in U] \, \mathrm{d}(r, x).$$

In fact, every s-finite kernel arises in this way. This translation preserves all the structure. Thus the monadic interpretation of the language can be translated into the s-finite semantics compositionally.

In Section 2.3 we considered an even more fine-grained approach, where a program $- \natural \, t : \mathbb{A}$ is interpreted as a measurable function $\Omega \to [\![\mathbb{A}]\!]$, i.e. a random variable on some basic probability space, together with a separate likelihood function $\Omega \to [0, \infty)$. (See also e.g. Holtzen et al., 2018; Hur et al., 2015). By considering the law of the pairing $\Omega \to [0, \infty) \times [\![\mathbb{A}]\!]$ we arrive at a probability measure in $P([0, \infty) \times [\![\mathbb{A}]\!])$, and every such probability measure arises as the law of some such pairing. Another way to include weightings is to consider Ω to be a subset of some plane $\mathbb{R}^n$ with an unnormalized Lebesgue measure. It turns out that an s-finite measure on a standard Borel space X is the same thing as the pushforward measure of a Lebesgue measure along a measurable function $\Omega \to X$, where $\Omega \subseteq \mathbb{R}^n$. So these different semantic methods all agree on what can be considered.

Although s-finite measures and kernels behave very well and have many characterizations, it is currently an open question whether the category of s-finite kernels is itself the Kleisli category for a monad. Recently we have proposed to use quasi-Borel spaces as generalized measurable spaces. S-finite kernels between quasi-Borel spaces do form the Kleisli category for a monad (Scibior et al., 2018).

2.6.2 Other semantic issues

In this chapter we have focused on giving a simple, measure-theoretic semantics to the programs in the simple first-order language through s-finite kernels. The semantics is clear, but subtle, because of issues of infinite normalization constants and measurability issues. But this simple semantics is only a very first step. Beyond:

- Statisticians and probabilists are interested in other issues such as convergence and relative entropy, which might also be analyzed in a compositional way, together with their relationships to computability (e.g. Ackerman et al., 2011; Huang and Morrisett, 2017).
- We might also add different modes of conditioning, such as conditioning by disintegration rather than density (e.g. Shan and Ramsey, 2016).
- We might add other typical language features such as higher order functions (e.g. Staton et al., 2016; Heunen et al., 2017), higher order recursion (e.g. Ehrhard et al., 2018; Vákár et al., 2019), and abstract types (e.g. Staton et al., 2018).
- Other languages have additional, non-functional primitives, based on logic programming (e.g. Nitti et al., 2016; Wu et al., 2018).

Acknowledgements.

I have benefited from discussing this topic with a great many people at various meetings over the last three years. I would particularly like to thank Chris Heunen, Ohad Kammar, Sean Moss, Matthijs Vákár, Frank Wood, Hongseok Yang. The examples in Sections 2.2 and 2.3 arose in preparing various invited talks lectures on the subject, including ICALP 2018 and OPLSS 2019, and I am grateful for these opportunities. The material in Section 2.4 is based on my paper in ESOP 2017 (Staton, 2017), and I am grateful to the reviewers of that article.

My research is supported by a Royal Society University Research Fellowship.

Dartboard image (Fig. 2.7) based on TikZ example by Roberto Bonvallet (Creative Commons attribution license), with changes made.

References

Ackerman, N L, Freer, Cameron E, and Roy, Daniel M. 2011. Noncomputable Conditional Distributions. In: *Proc. LICS 2011*.

Ackerman, Nathanael L., Freer, Cameron E., and Roy, Daniel M. 2015. *On computability and disintegration.*

Bhat, Sooraj, Borgström, Johannes, Gordon, Andrew D., and Russo, Claudio V. 2017. Deriving Probability Density Functions from Probabilistic Functional Programs. *Logical Methods in Computer Science*, **13**(2).

Bichsel, Benjamin, Gehr, Timon, and Vechev, Martin. 2018. Fine-Grained Semantics for Probabilistic Programs. In: *Proc. ESOP 2018.*

Ehrhard, Thomas, Pagani, Michele, and Tasson, Christine. 2018. Measurable cones and stable, measurable functions: a model for probabilistic higher-order programming. In: *Proc. POPL 2018.*

Gehr, Timon, Misailovic, Sasa, and Vechev, Martin T. 2016. PSI: Exact Symbolic Inference for Probabilistic Programs. Pages 62–83 of: *Proc. CAV 2016.*

Getoor, R K. 1990. *Excessive Measures.* Birkhäuser.

Giry, M. 1982. A Categorical Approach to Probability Theory. *Categorical Aspects of Topology and Analysis*, **915**, 68–85.

Goodman, N. D., and Stuhlmüller, A. 2014. *The Design and Implementation of Probabilistic Programming Languages.*

Goodman, Noah, Mansinghka, Vikash, Roy, Daniel M, Bonawitz, Keith, and Tenenbaum, Joshua B. 2008. Church: a language for generative models. In: *UAI.*

Harper, Robert. 2016. *Practical Foundations for Programming Languages.* CUP.

Heunen, C, Kammar, O, Staton, S, and Yang, H. 2017. *A convenient category for higher-order probability theory.* arXiv:1701.02547.

Holtzen, Steven, den Broeck, Guy Van, and Millstein, Todd D. 2018. Sound Abstraction and Decomposition of Probabilistic Programs. In: *Proc. ICML 2018.*

Huang, Daniel, and Morrisett, Greg. 2017. An application of computable distributions to the semantics of probabilistic programs: part 2. In: *Proc. PPS 2017.*

Hur, Chung-Kil, Nori, Aditya V., Rajamani, Sriram K., and Samuel, Selva. 2015. A Provably Correct Sampler for Probabilistic Programs. In: *FSTTCS.*

Ismail, Wazim Mohammed, and chieh Shan, Chung. 2016. Deriving a probability density calculator (functional pearl). In: *Proc. ICFP 2016.*

Kallenberg, O. 2014. Stationary and invariant densities and disintegration kernels. *Probab. Theory Relat. Fields*, **160**, 567–592.

Koehl, Albert, Rupasinghe, Kevin, and Lee, Rachel. 2017 (Sept.). *Bloor St. bike lane used by over 6,000 cyclists per day.* Press release. Available at https://bellsonbloor.wordpress.com.

Last, G, and Penrose, M. 2016. *Lectures on the Poisson process.* CUP.

Levy, Paul Blain, Power, John, and Thielecke, Hayo. 2003. Modelling environments in call-by-value programming languages. *Inf. Comput.*, **185**(2).

Mansinghka, Vikash K., Selsam, Daniel, and Perov, Yura N. 2014. Venture: a higher-order probabilistic programming platform with programmable inference.

Moggi, Eugenio. 1991. Notions of computation and monads. *Inf. Comput.*, **93**(1), 55–92.

Narayanan, P, Carette, J, Romano, W, Shan, C-C, and Zinkov, R. 2016. Probabilistic inference by program transformation in Hakaru (system description). In: *Proc. FLOPS 2016*.

Nitti, Davide, Laet, Tinne De, and Raedt, Luc De. 2016. Probabilistic logic programming for hybrid relational domains. *Mach. Learn.*, **103**, 407–449.

Ong, Luke, and Vákár, Matthijs. 2018. S-finite Kernels and Game Semantics for Probabilistic Programming. In: *Proc. PPS 2018*.

Pollard, D. 2002. *A user's guide to measure theoretic probability*. CUP.

Rainforth, Tom, Cornish, Robert, Yang, Hongseok, Warrington, Andrew, and Wood, Frank. 2018. On Nesting Monte Carlo Estimators. In: *Proc. ICML 2018*.

Robert, Christian P. 2007. *The Bayesian Choice: From Decision-Theoretic Foundations to Computational Implementation*. Springer.

Schervish, Mark J. 1995. *Theory of Statistics*. Springer.

Scibior, Adam, Kammar, Ohad, Vákár, Matthijs, Staton, Sam, Yang, Hongseok, Cai, Yufei, Ostermann, Klaus, Moss, Sean K., Heunen, Chris, and Ghahramani, Zoubin. 2018. Denotational validation of higher-order Bayesian inference. In: *Proc. POPL 2018*.

Shan, Chung-Chieh, and Ramsey, Norman. 2016. *Symbolic Bayesian Inference by Symbolic Disintegration*.

Sharpe, M. 1988. *General theory of Markov Processes*. Academic Press.

Staton, S., Yang, H., Heunen, C., Kammar, O., and Wood, F. 2016. Semantics for probabilistic programming: higher-order functions, continuous distributions, and soft constraints. In: *Proc. LICS 2016*.

Staton, Sam. 2017. Commutative semantics for probabilistic programming. In: *Proc. ESOP 2017*.

Staton, Sam, Stein, Dario, Yang, Hongseok, and Nathanael L.. Ackerman, Cameron Freer, Daniel M Roy. 2018. The Beta-Bernoulli Process and Algebraic Effects. In: *Proc. ICALP 2018*.

Stuhlmuller, Andreas, and Goodman, Noah D. 2014. Reasoning about reasoning by nested conditioning: Modeling theory of mind with probabilistic programs. *Cognitive Systems Research*, **28**, 80–99.

Tjur, Tue. 1980. *Probability based on Radon measures*. Wiley.

Vákár, Matthijs, Kammar, Ohad, and Staton, Sam. 2019. A domain theory for statistical probabilistic programming. In: *Proc. POPL 2019*.

van de Meent, Jan-Willem, Paige, Brooks, Yang, Hongseok, and Wood, Frank. 2018. *An Introduction to Probabilistic Programming*. arxiv:1809.10756.

Wood, Frank, van de Meent, Jan Willem, and Mansinghka, Vikash. 2014. A New Approach to Probabilistic Programming Inference. In: *AISTATS*.

Wu, Yi, Srivastava, Siddharth, Hay, Nicholas, Du, Simon, and Russell, Stuart J. 2018. Discrete-Continuous Mixtures in Probabilistic Programming: Generalized Semantics and Inference Algorithms. Pages 5339–5348 of: *Proc. ICML 2018*.

3

An Application of Computable Distributions to the Semantics of Probabilistic Programs

Daniel Huang
University of California, Berkeley
Greg Morrisett
Cornell University
Bas Spitters
Aarhus University

Abstract: In this chapter, we explore how (Type-2) computable distributions can be used to give both (algorithmic) sampling and distributional semantics to probabilistic programs with continuous distributions. Towards this end, we sketch an encoding of computable distributions in a fragment of Haskell and show how topological domains can be used to model the resulting PCF-like language. We also examine the implications that a (Type-2) computable semantics has for implementing conditioning. We hope to draw out the connection between an approach based on (Type-2) computability and ordinary programming throughout the chapter as well as highlight the relation with constructive mathematics (via realizability).

3.1 Overview

Probabilistic programs exhibit a tension between the *continuous* and the *discrete*. On one hand, we are interested in using probabilistic programs to model natural phenomena—phenomena that are often modeled well with *reals* and *continuous distributions* (*e.g.*, as in physics and biology). On the other hand, we are also bound by the fundamentally *discrete nature of computation*, which limits how we can (1) represent models as programs and then (2) compute the results of *queries* on the model. The aim of this chapter[1][2][3] is to keep this tension in the fore by using the notion of a *(Type-2) computable distribution* as a lens through which to understand probabilistic programs. We organize our exploration via a series of questions.

---

[a] From *Foundations of Probabilistic Programming*, edited by Gilles Barthe, Joost-Pieter Katoen and Alexandra Silva published 2020 by Cambridge University Press.

[1] This chapter contains material from Huang (2017) and Huang and Morrisett (2016).

[2] Daniel Huang was supported by DARPA FA8750-17-2-0091.

[3] Bas Spitters was partially supported by the Guarded homotopy type theory project, funded by the Villum Foundation, project number 12386 and partially by the AFOSR project 'Homotopy Type Theory and Probabilistic Computation', 12595060. Any opinions, findings and conclusions or recommendations expressed in this material are those of the authors and do not necessarily reflect the views of the AFOSR.

(i) *What is a (Type-2) computable distribution* (Section 3.2)? First, we review *Type-2 computability* (*e.g.*, see Weihrauch, 2000) and how it applies to reals and continuous distributions. The high-level idea is to represent continuum-sized objects as a sequence of discrete approximations that converge to the appropriate object instead of abstracting the representation of such an object.

(ii) *How do we implement continuous distributions as a library in a general-purpose programming language* (Section 3.3)? After we have seen the basic idea behind Type-2 computability, we sketch an implementation of reals and continuous distributions in a fragment of Haskell. We emphasize that the implementation does not assume any reals, continuous distributions, or operations on them as black-box primitives.

(iii) *What mathematical structures can we use to model such a library* (Section 3.4)? Our next step is to find mathematical structures that can be used to faithfully model the implementation. Towards this end, we review *topological domains* (*e.g.*, see Battenfeld et al., 2007; Battenfeld, 2008), which are an alternative to traditional structures used in denotational semantics. Topological domains support all the standard domain-theoretic constructions needed to model PCF-like[4] languages as well as capture the notion of (Type-2) computability. In particular, we can encode reals and continuous distributions as topological domains so that they are suitable for our purposes of giving semantics.

(iv) *What does a semantics for a core language look like* (Section 3.5)? In this section, we make the connection between the implementation and the mathematics more concrete by using the constructs described previously to give both (algorithmic) sampling and distributional semantics to a core PCF-like language extended with reals and continuous distributions (via a probability monad) called λ_{CD}.[5] The sampling semantics can be used to guide implementation while the distributional semantics can be used for equational reasoning.

(v) *What are the implications of taking a (Type-2) computable viewpoint for Bayesian inference* (Section 3.6)? Perhaps surprisingly, at least to those who employ Bayesian inference in practice, it can be shown that *conditioning* is not (Type-2) computable (see Ackerman et al., 2011). Hence, there is a sense in which a "Turing-complete" probabilistic programming language cannot support conditional queries for every expressible probabilistic model. Fortunately, we do not run into these pathologies in practice and can recover conditioning in sufficiently general settings.

We hope to draw out the connection between an approach based on (Type-2)

---

[4] Recall that the PCF (Programming Computable Functions) language is a core calculus that can be used to model typed functional languages such as Haskell.

[5] λ_{CD} also supports distributions on any countably based space. This means that λ_{CD} does not (in general) have distributions on function spaces, although the language itself contains higher-order functions.

computability with ordinary programming (*i.e.*, programming in a fragment of Haskell) throughout the chapter as well as highlight the relation with constructive mathematics via *realizability* (*e.g.*, see Streicher, 2008) (Section 3.4.4).

Prerequisites We assume basic knowledge of programming language semantics (*e.g.*, at the level of Gunter, 1992). For our purposes, this primarily includes (1) the application of category theory to programming language semantics and (2) the use of complete partial orders (CPOs) to model the semantics of PCF. As we will be giving examples in Haskell, familiarity with the Haskell programming language will also be assumed.[6] Finally, we assume basic knowledge of measure-theoretic probability (*e.g.*, see Durrett, 2010).

3.2 Computability Revisited

What is a computable distribution? One approach to studying computability is based on Turing machines (*e.g.*, see Sipser, 2012). Under this approach, we define (1) a *machine model* (*i.e.*, the Turing machine) and (2) conditions under which the machine model is said to *compute*. More concretely, a Turing machine is said to *compute* a (partial) function $f : \Sigma^* \rightharpoonup \Sigma^*$ if it halts with $f(w) \in \Sigma^*$ on the output tape given $w \in \Sigma^*$ on an input tape, where Σ is a finite set and $\Sigma^* \triangleq \{a_0 \ldots a_n \mid a_i \in \Sigma, 0 \leq i \leq n\}$ is a collection of words comprised of characters from Σ. The two element set $\mathbf{2} \triangleq \{0, 1\}$ for bits (or booleans) is a commonly used alphabet.

This definition of computability reveals that traditional computation is fundamentally *discrete*. We can see this directly in the definition of a computable function (with type $\Sigma^* \rightharpoonup \Sigma^*$), which maps elements of a discrete domain (*i.e.*, a set of finite words Σ^*) to elements of a discrete codomain (*i.e.*, a set of finite words Σ^* again). As Σ^* is countable, it cannot be put in bijection with the reals $\mathbb{R}$; hence, we cannot encode all the reals on a Turing machine.

One immediate issue that this highlights for probabilistic programs is how one should handle reals and continuous distributions while maintaining the connection back to computation. A pragmatic solution to this is to use floating point arithmetic, *i.e.*, discretize and finitize the reals. From this perspective, we can model the semantics of probabilistic programs using floating point numbers and finitely-supported discrete distributions (on floats) so that the semantics more faithfully models an actual implementation. Nevertheless, we sacrifice the correspondence between the program and the mathematics that we use on pencil-paper. An alternative to the situation above is to generalize the notion of computability to continuum-sized

---

[6] Familiarity with other typed functional languages such as ML should also suffice, although we should remind ourselves that Haskell has call-by-need semantics so that it has a lazy order-of-evaluation.

sets in such a way that the computations can still by implemented by a standard machine.

3.2.1 Type-2 Computability

Type-Two Theory of Effectivity (abbreviated TTE, see Weihrauch, 2000) changes the conditions under which a machine is said to compute an answer but keeps the machine model as is. In this setting, a machine is said to *compute* a function $f : \Sigma^\omega \rightharpoonup \Sigma^\omega$ if it can write any initial segment of $f(w) \in \Sigma^\omega$ on the output tape in finite time given $w \in \Sigma^*$ on an input tape, where $\Sigma^\omega \triangleq \{a_0 a_1 \ldots \mid a_i \in \Sigma, i \in \mathbb{N}\}$ is the set of streams composed of symbols from the finite set Σ. The set Σ^ω has continuum cardinality, and hence, can represent the reals and a class of distributions (Section 3.2.2). Once we *represent* continuum-sized objects on a machine, we have an avenue for studying which functions are Type-2 computable. Throughout the rest of the chapter, we will abbreviate Type-2 computable as computable[7] and use Type-2 computable for emphasis. We now review computable reals and distributions.

3.2.2 Computability, Reals and Distributions

Computability and reals Intuitively, we can represent a real on a machine by encoding its binary expansion. More formally, we represent a real $x \in \mathbb{R}$ on a machine by encoding a fast Cauchy sequence of rationals that converges to x. Recall that a sequence $(q_n)_{n \in \mathbb{N}}$ where each $q_n \in \mathbb{Q}$ is *Cauchy* if for every $\epsilon > 0$, there is an N such that $|q_n - q_m| < \epsilon$ for every $n, m > N$. Thus, the elements of a Cauchy sequence become closer and closer to one another as we traverse the sequence. When $|q_n - q_{n+1}| < 2^{-n}$ for all n, we call $(q_n)_{n \in \mathbb{N}}$ a *fast Cauchy sequence*. Hence, the representation of a real as a fast Cauchy sequence evokes the idea of enumerating its binary expansion. A real $x \in \mathbb{R}$ is *computable* if we can enumerate (uniformly in an enumeration of rationals) a fast Cauchy sequence that converges to x.

We give some examples of reals encoded as fast Cauchy sequences now.

Example 3.1 (Rational)   Consider two encodings of 0 as a fast Cauchy sequence below.

(Constant) Let $(x_n)_{n \in \mathbb{N}}$ where $x_n \triangleq 0$ for $n \in \mathbb{N}$.
(Thrashing) Let $(y_n)_{n \in \mathbb{N}}$ where $y_n \triangleq \frac{1}{(-2)^{n+1}}$ for $n \in \mathbb{N}$.

As 0 itself is also a rational number, we can simply represent it as a constant 0 sequence given by $(x_n)_{n \in \mathbb{N}}$. We can also represent 0 as the sequence $(y_n)_{n \in \mathbb{N}}$, where

---

[7] Computability in the ordinary sense refers to Type-1 computability.

the sequence jumps back and forth between positive and negative fractional powers of two as it converges towards 0. 0 is clearly a computable real.

Example 3.2 (Irrational)   Let $x_n \triangleq 2 + \sum_{k=2}^{2+n} \frac{1}{k!}$. Then $(x_n)_{n \in \mathbb{N}}$ is a fast Cauchy encoding of e. It is easy to see that e is a computable real.

Example 3.3 (Non-computable)   Every real can be expressed as a fast Cauchy sequence so there are necessarily non-computable reals as well. Let $(M_n)_{n \in \mathbb{N}}$ be some enumeration of Turing machines. Let $t_0 \triangleq 1$ and

$$t_{n+1} \triangleq \begin{cases} 2 \cdot t_n & M_n \text{ halts} \\ 1 + t_n & M_n \text{ does not halt.} \end{cases}$$

Then $(x_n)_{n \in \mathbb{N}}$ where $x_n \triangleq \sum_{i=0}^{n} \frac{1}{2^{t_i}}$ is a fast Cauchy sequence that is not computable because the Halting problem is not decidable.

A function $f : \mathbb{R} \to \mathbb{R}$ is *computable* if given a (fast Cauchy) sequence converging to $x \in \mathbb{R}$, there is an algorithm that outputs a (fast Cauchy) sequence converging to $f(x)$ [8] We emphasize that the algorithm must work generically for any input (fast Cauchy) sequence including the non-computable ones. we give some examples now.

Example 3.4 (Addition)   The function $+_0 : \mathbb{R} \to \mathbb{R}$ that adds 0 is computable because an algorithm can obtain a (fast Cauchy) output sequence by adding the (fast Cauchy) input sequence element-wise to a (fast Cauchy) sequence of 0.

Most familiar functions are computable (*e.g.*, subtraction, multiplication, inverses, exponentiation, logarithms on non-negative reals, and trigonometric functions such as sines and cosines) so that there is an algorithm that transforms (fast Cauchy) inputs into (fast Cauchy) outputs. Nevertheless, there are familiar functions that are not computable.

Example 3.5 (Non-computable)   Consider the function $=_0: \mathbb{R} \to \mathbf{2}$ that tests if the input is equal to 0 or not. Intuitively, this function is not computable because we need to check the entire input sequence. For example, to check that the constant sequence is equivalent to the thrashing sequence, we have to check the entirety of both sequences, which cannot be done in finite time.

Computable metric spaces   Topological spaces enable us to build a more general notion of computability on a space. [9] For the purposes of introducing reals and distributions, we consider topological spaces with a notion of distance, *i.e.*, *metric spaces*. As a reminder, a *metric space* (X, d) is a set X equipped with a *metric*

---

[8] A function $f : \mathbb{R}^n \to \mathbb{R}$ is computable if given (fast Cauchy) sequences converging to $x_1, \ldots, x_n \in \mathbb{R}$, there is an algorithm that outputs a (fast Cauchy) sequence converging to $f(x_1, \ldots, x_n)$.

[9] For more background on topology, we refer the reader to Munkres (2000).

$d : X \times X \to \mathbb{R}$. A metric induces a collection of sets called *(open) balls*, where a ball centered at $c \in X$ with radius $r \in R$ is the set of points within r of c, *i.e.*, $B(c,r) \triangleq \{x \in X \mid d(c,x) < r\}$. The topology $O(X)$ associated with a metric space X is the one induced by the collection of balls. Hence, the open balls of a metric space provide a notion of distance in addition to providing a notion of approximation.

Example 3.6 $(\mathbb{N}, d_{\text{Discrete}})$ endows the naturals $\mathbb{N}$ with the discrete topology (*i.e.*, $O(\mathbb{N}) = 2^{\mathbb{N}}$), where d_{Discrete} is the discrete metric (*i.e.*, $d(n,m) \triangleq 0$ if $n = m$ and $d(n,m) \triangleq 1$ otherwise for $n,m \in \mathbb{N}$).

Example 3.7 $(\mathbb{R}, d_{\text{Euclid}})$ endows the reals $\mathbb{R}$ with the familiar Euclidean topology, where d_{Euclid} is the standard Euclidean metric (*i.e.*, $d_{\text{Euclid}}(x, y) \triangleq |x - y|$).

Example 3.8 $(2^{\omega}, d_{\text{Cantor}})$ endows the set of bit-streams 2^{ω} with the Cantor topology, where d_{Cantor} is defined as

$$d_{\text{Cantor}}(x, y) \triangleq \inf\{\frac{1}{2^n} \mid x_n \neq y_n\}.$$

One can check that a basic open set of the Cantor topology is of the form $a_1 \ldots a_n 2^{\omega} \triangleq \{b_1 b_2 \cdots \in 2^{\omega} \mid b_i = a_i, 1 \leq i \leq n\}$. That is, basic open sets of Cantor space fix finite-prefixes.

A computable metric space imposes additional conditions on a metric space so that a machine can enumerate successively more accurate approximations (according to the metric) of a point in the metric space. We need two additional definitions before we can state the definition. First, we say S is *dense* in X if for every $x \in X$, there is a sequence $(s_n)_{n \in \mathbb{N}}$ that converges to x, where $s_n \in S$ for every n. Second, we say that (X, d) is *complete* if every Cauchy sequence comprised of elements from X also converges to a point in X.

Definition 3.9 A *computable metric space* is a tuple (X, d, S) such that (1) (X, d) is a complete metric space, (2) S is a countable, enumerable, and dense subset, and (3) the real $d(s_i, s_j)$ is computable for $s_i, s_j \in S$ (see Hoyrup and Rojas, 2009, Def. 2.4.1).

Example 3.10 $(\mathbb{R}, d_{\text{Euclid}}, \mathbb{Q})$ is a computable metric space for the reals where we use the rationals $\mathbb{Q}$ as the approximating elements. Note that we can equivalently use dyadic rationals as the approximating elements instead of $\mathbb{Q}$.

Computability and distributions A distribution over the computable metric space (X, d, S) can be formulated as a point of the computable metric space

$$(\mathcal{M}(X), d_\rho, \mathcal{D}(S)),$$

where $\mathcal{M}(X)$ is the set of Borel probability measures on a computable metric space (X, d, S), d_ρ is the Prokhorov metric (see Hoyrup and Rojas, 2009, Defn. 4.1.1), and $\mathcal{D}(S)$ is the class of distributions with finite support at ideal points S and rational masses (see Hoyrup and Rojas, 2009, Prop. 4.1.1). The Prokhorov metric is defined as

$$d_\rho(\mu, \nu) \triangleq \inf\{\epsilon > 0 \mid \mu(A) \leq \nu(A^\epsilon) + \epsilon \text{ for every Borel } A\} ,$$

where $A^\epsilon \triangleq \{x \in X \mid d(x, y) < \epsilon \text{ for some } y \in A\}$. One can check that the sequence below converges (with respect to the Prokhorov metric) to the (standard) uniform distribution $\mathcal{U}(0, 1)$.

$$\left\{0 \mapsto \frac{1}{2}, \frac{1}{2} \mapsto \frac{1}{2}\right\}, \left\{0 \mapsto \frac{1}{4}, \frac{1}{4} \mapsto \frac{1}{4}, \frac{1}{2} \mapsto \frac{2}{4}, \frac{1}{4} \mapsto \frac{3}{4}, \frac{1}{4} \mapsto \frac{1}{4}\right\}, \ldots,$$

Thus, a uniform distribution can be seen as the limit of a sequence of increasingly finer discrete, uniform distributions. As with a computable real, we say that a distribution $\mu \in \mathcal{M}(X)$ is *computable* if we can enumerate (uniformly in an enumeration of a basis and rationals) a fast Cauchy sequence that converges to μ.

Although the idea of constructing a (computable) distribution as a (computable) point is fairly intuitive for the standard uniform distribution, it may be more difficult to perform the construction for more complicated distributions. Fortunately, we can also think of a distribution on a computable metric space (X, d, S) in terms of sampling, *i.e.*, as a Type-2 computable function $2^\omega \rightharpoonup X$. To make this more concrete, we sketch an algorithm that samples from the standard uniform distribution given a stream of fair coin flips. The idea is to generate a value that can be queried for more precision instead of a sample x in its entirety.

Let $\mu_{\mathrm{iid}}(a_1 \ldots a_n 2^\omega) \triangleq 1/2^n$ be the distribution associated with a stream of fair coin flips where 0 corresponds to heads and 1 corresponds to tails. A sampling algorithm will interleave flipping coins with outputting an element to the desired precision, such that the sequence of outputs $(s_n)_{n \in \mathbb{N}}$ converges to a sample. For instance, one binary digit of precision for a standard uniform distribution corresponds to obtaining the point $1/2$ because it is within $1/2$ of any point in the unit interval. Demanding another digit of precision produces either $1/4$ or $3/4$ according to the result of a fair coin flip. This is encoded below using the function `bisect`[10], which recursively bisects an interval n times, starting with $(0, 1)$, using the random bit-stream u to select which interval to recurse on.

$$\text{uniform} : (\texttt{Nat} \to \texttt{Bool}) \to (\texttt{Nat} \to \texttt{Rat})$$

$$\text{uniform} \triangleq \lambda u. \, \lambda n. \; \texttt{bisect} \; u \; 0 \; 1 \; n$$

In the limit, we obtain a single point corresponding to the sample.

---

[10] See the implementation of `stdUniform` in Section 3.3.2 for the full definition.

The sampling view is (computably) equivalent to the view of a computable distribution as a point in an appropriate computable metric space. To state the equivalence, we need a few definitions. A *computable probability space* (X, μ) is a pair where X is a computable metric space and μ is a computable distribution (see Hoyrup and Rojas, 2009, Def. 5.0.1). We call a distribution μ on X *samplable* if there is a computable function $s : (2^\omega, \mu_{\text{iid}}) \rightharpoonup (X, \mu)$ such that s is computable on $\text{dom}(s)$ of full-measure (*i.e.*, $\mu(X) = 1$) and is measure-preserving (*i.e.*, $\mu = \mu_{\text{iid}} \circ s^{-1}$).

Proposition 3.11   (Computable iff samplable, see Freer and Roy, 2010, Lem. 2 and Lem. 3). *A distribution $\mu \in M(X)$ on computable metric space (X, d, S) is computable iff it is samplable.*

Thus we can equivalently specify computable distributions by writing sampling algorithms.

3.3 A Library for Computable Distributions

How do we implement continuous distributions as a library in a general-purpose programming language? Our goal in this section is to translate the concepts about reals and distributions we saw previously in Section 3.2 into code. Towards this end, we sketch a Haskell library (Figure 3.1) that encodes reals and the sampling view of distributions.[11] We emphasize that the library does not assume any reals, continuous distributions, or operations on them as black-box primitives.

3.3.1 Library

The library consists of three modules. The first module `ApproxLib` provides the interface for computable metric spaces. The second module `RealLib` implements reals using the operations in `ApproxLib` and the third module `CompDistLib` implements (continuous) distributions. We go over the modules in turn now.

As we mentioned previously, the module `ApproxLib` provides abstractions for expressing elements as a sequence of approximations in a computable metric space. The core type exposed by the module is `Approx` τ, which models an element of a computable metric space and can be read as an approximation by a sequence of values of type τ. For example, a real can be given the type `Real` $\triangleq$ `Approx Rat`, meaning it is a sequence of rationals (`Rat`) that converges to a real. We form values of type `Approx` τ using `mkApprox` :: (`Nat` $\rightarrow \alpha$) $\rightarrow$ `Approx` α, which requires us to check[12] that the function we are coercing describes a fast Cauchy sequence, and project out approximations using `nthApprox` :: `Approx` $\alpha \rightarrow$ `Nat` $\rightarrow \alpha$.

---

[11] The code is available at `https://github.com/danehuang/cdist-sketch`.
[12] We do not use the Haskell type system to enforce that the function to coerce contains a fast Cauchy sequence so the caller of `mkApprox` needs to perform this check manually.

```
module ApproxLib (Approx(..), CMetrizable(..), mkApprox,
    nthApprox) where

newtype Approx a = Approx { getApprox :: Nat -> a }

mkApprox  :: (Nat -> a) -> Approx a   -- fast Cauchy sequence
nthApprox :: Approx a -> Nat -> a     -- project n-th approx.

class CMetrizable a where
    enum   :: [a]                     -- countable, dense subset
    metric :: a -> a -> Approx Rat    -- computable metric


module CompDistLib (RandBits, Samp(..), mkSamp) where
import ApproxLib

type RandBits = Nat -> Bool
newtype Samp a = Samp { getSamp :: RandBits -> a }

mkSamp :: (CMetrizable a) => (RandBits -> Approx a) -> Samp (
    Approx a)
mkSamp = Samp

instance Monad Samp where
    ...                                      -- see text
```

Figure 3.1 A Haskell library interface for expressing approximations in a computable metric space (module `ApproxLib`) and encoding (continuous) distributions (module `CompDistLib`). The library interface for reals (module `RealLib`) is not shown.

In order to form the type `Approx` τ, values of type τ should support the operations required of a computable metric space. We can indicate the required operations using Haskell's type-class mechanism.

```
class CMetrizable a where
    enum   :: [a]
    metric :: a -> a -> Approx Rat
```

As a reminder, Haskell has lazy semantics so that the type $[\alpha]$ denotes a stream as opposed to a list. Thus `enum` corresponds to an enumeration of type α where α is the type of the dense subset. When we implement an instance of `CMetrizable` τ, we should check that the implementation of `enum` enumerates a dense subset and `metric` computes a metric as a computable metric space requires (see Section 3.2.2).

Below, we give an instance of `Approx Rat` for computable reals.

```
instance CMetrizable Rat where
    enum = 0 : [ toRational m / 2^n
               | n <- [1..]
```

```
                    , m <- [-2^n * n..2^n * n]
                    , odd m || abs m > 2^n * (n-1) ]
        metric x y = A (\_ -> abs (x - y))
```

This instance enumerates the dyadic rationals, which are a dense subset of the reals. Note that there are many other choices here for the dense enumeration.[13] In this instance, we can actually compute the metric as a dyadic rational, whereas a computable metric requires the weaker condition that we can compute the metric as a computable real.

Next, we can use the module `ApproxLib` to implement computable operations on commonly used types. For example, a library for computable reals will contain the `CMetrizable` τ instance implementation above and other computable functions. However, some operations are not realizable (*e.g.*, equality of reals) and so this module does not contain all operations one may want to perform on reals (*e.g.*, equality is defined on floats).

```
module RealLib (Real, pi, (+), ...) where
import ApproxLib

type Real = Approx Rat
instance CMetrizable Rat where
    ...

pi :: Real
(+) :: Real -> Real -> Real
-- etc.
```

The module `CompDistLib` contains the implementation of distributions. A sampler `Samp` α is a function from a bit-stream to values of type α.[14]

```
type RandBits = Nat -> Bool
newtype Samp a = Samp { getSamp :: RandBits -> a }
```

We can implement an instance of the sampling monad as below.

```
instance Monad Samp where
    return x = Samp (const x)
    (>>=) s f = Samp ((uncurry (getSamp . f)) . (pair (getSamp
        s . fst) snd) . split)
        where pair f g = \x -> (f x, g x)
              split = pair even odd
              even u = (\n -> u (2 * n))
              odd u = (\n -> u (2 * n + 1))
```

As expected, `return` corresponds to a constant sampler (`const`) that ignores its input randomness. The bind operator »= corresponds to a composition of samplers;

---

[13] Algorithms that operate on computable metric spaces compute by enumeration so the algorithm is sensitive to the choice of enumeration.

[14] The type `RandBits` is represented isomorphically as Nat → Bool instead of [Bool].

we first split (`split`) the input randomness into two independent streams (via `even` and `odd`), use one to sample from `s`, and continue with the other in `f`.

The module `CompDistLib` provides the function `mkSamp` to coerce an arbitrary Haskell function of the appropriate type into a value of type `Samp α`.

```
mkSamp :: (CMetrizable a) => (RandBits -> Approx a) -> Samp (
    Approx a)
mkSamp = Samp
```

We should call `mkSamp` only on sampling functions realizing Type-2 computable sampling algorithms.

3.3.2 Examples

We now encode discrete and continuous distributions using the constructs provided by library. These examples demonstrate how familiar distributions used in probabilistic modeling can be encoded in a Type-2 computable manner. As we walk through the examples, we will encounter some semantic issues that we would like a denotational semantics of probabilistic programs to handle. We will flag these in italics and revisit them after introducing a semantics for probabilistic programs (Section 3.5).

Discrete distribution Discrete distributions are much simpler compared to continuous distributions. Nevertheless, when paired with recursion, semantic issues do arise. For instance, consider the encoding of a geometric distribution with bias $1/2$, which returns the number of fair Bernoulli trials until a success. The distribution `stdBernoulli` denotes a Bernoulli distribution with bias $1/2$.

```
stdGeometric :: Samp Nat
stdGeometric = do
  b <- stdBernoulli
  if b then return 1
      else stdGeometric >>= return . (\n -> n + 1)
```

One possibility, although it occurs with zero probability, is for the draw from `stdBernoulli` to always be false. Consequently, `stdGeometric` diverges with probability zero. *A semantics should clarify the criterion for divergence and show that this recursive encoding actually denotes a geometric distribution.*

Continuous distributions Next, we fill in the sketch of the standard uniform distribution we presented earlier. As a reminder, we need to convert a random bit-stream into a sequence of (dyadic) rational approximations.

```
stdUniform :: Samp Real
stdUniform = mkSamp (\u -> mkApprox (\n -> bisect (n+1) u 0 1
    0))
```

```
where
  bisect n u (l :: Rat) (r :: Rat) m
    | m < n && u m        =
        bisect n u l (midpt l r) (m+1)
    | m < n && not (u m) =
        bisect n u (midpt l r) r (m+1)
    | otherwise           =
        midpt l r
  midpt l r = l + (r - l) / 2
```

The function `bisect` repeatedly bisects an interval specified by (l, r). By construction, the sampler produces a sequence of dyadic rationals. We can see that this sampling function is uniformly distributed because it inverts the binary expansion specified by the uniformly distributed input bit-stream. Once we have the standard uniform distribution, we can encode other primitive distributions (*e.g.*, normal, exponential, etc.) as transformations of the uniform distribution as in standard statistics using return and bind.

For example, we give an encoding of the standard normal distribution using the Marsaglia polar transformation.

```
stdNormal :: Samp Real
stdNormal = do
  u1 <- uniform (-1) 1
  u2 <- uniform (-1) 1
  let s = u1 * u1 + u2 * u2
  if s < 1 then return (u1 * sqrt (log s / s))
           else stdNormal
```

The distribution `uniform (−1) 1` is the uniform distribution on the interval $(-1, 1)$ and can be encoded by shifting and scaling a draw from `stdUniform`. One subtle issue here concerns the semantics of `<`. As a reminder, equality on reals is not decidable. *Consequently, although we have used `<` at the type* `Real` $\rightarrow$ `Real` $\rightarrow$ `Bool` *in the example, it cannot have the standard semantics of deciding between `<` and $\geq$.*

Singular distribution Next, we give an encoding of the Cantor distribution. The Cantor distribution is singular so it is not a mixture of a discrete component and a component with a density. Perhaps surprisingly, this distribution is computable. The distribution can be defined recursively. It starts by trisecting the unit interval, and placing half the mass on the leftmost interval and the other half on the rightmost interval, leaving no mass for the middle, continuing in the same manner with each remaining interval that has positive probability. We can encode the Cantor distribution by directly transforming a random bit-stream into a sequence of approximations.

```
cantor :: Samp Real
cantor = mkSamp (\u -> mkApprox (\n -> go u 0 1 0 n))
```

```
where
  go u (left :: Rat) (right :: Rat) n m
    | n < m && u n        =
      go u left (left + pow) (n + 1) m
    | n < m && not (u n) =
      go u (right - pow) right (n + 1) m
    | otherwise           =
      right - (1 / 2) * pow
    where pow = 3 ^^ (-n)
```

The sampling algorithm keeps track of which interval it is currently in specified by
`left` and `right`. If the current bit is 1, we trisect the left interval. Otherwise, we
trisect the rightmost interval. The number of trisections is bounded by the precision
we would like to generate the sample to. *Crucially, the encoding makes use of the
idea of generating a sample to arbitrary accuracy using a representation instead of
the sample in its entirety.*

Partiality and distributions The next series of examples explores issues concerning
distributions and partiality.

```
botSamp :: (CMetrizable a) => Samp (Approx a)
botSamp = botSamp

botSampBot :: (CMetrizable a) => Samp (Approx a)
botSampBot = mkSamp (\_ -> bot)
    where bot = bot
```

In the term `botSamp`, we define an infinite loop at the type of samplers. Intuitively,
this corresponds to the case where we fail to provide a sampler, *i.e.*, an error in
the worst possible way. In the term `botSampBot`, we produce a sampler that fails
to generate a sample to any precision. In other words, we provide a sampler that
is faulty in the worst possible way. We can try to observe the differences in the
implementation (if any).

```
alwaysDiv :: Samp Real          neverDiv :: Samp Real
alwaysDiv = do                  neverDiv = do
  _ <- botSamp ::                 _ <- botSampBot ::
        Samp Real                      Samp Real
  stdUniform                      stdUniform
```

If we run the term `alwaysDiv` on the left, we will see that the program always
diverges. When we run the term `neverDiv` on the right, we will draw from the
sampler `botSampBot` but discard the result. Due to Haskell's lazy semantics, this
computation is ignored and the entire term behaves as a standard uniform distribution.
*We would like a denotational semantics to reflect the differences in the operational
behavior between these two terms.*

Commutativity and independence We end by considering the difference between a sampling and distributional interpretation of probabilistic programs. Below, we give equivalent encodings of distributions by commuting the order of sampling from independent distributions, but leaving everything else fixed.

```
myNormal :: Samp Real              myNormal' :: Samp Real
myNormal = do                      myNormal' = do
  x <- normal (-1) 1                 y <- normal (1) 1
  y <- normal (1) 1                  x <- normal (-1) 1
  return (x + y)                     return (x + y)
```

From a sampling perspective, the two distributions are not strictly equivalent because the stream of random bits is consumed in a different order; consequently, the samples produced by `myNormal` and `myNormal'` may be different. *Thus, while a sampling semantics is easily implementable, we would also like a distributional semantics to enable reasoning about the distributional equivalence of programs. For instance, this would enable us to reason that two different sampling algorithms for the same distribution are equivalent.*

3.3.3 Notes

The implementation we have sketched is a proof of concept that shows that we can realize the interface by implementing computable distributions and operations on them as Haskell code. We note that there are multiple approaches to coding up Type-2 computability as a library. One prominent alternative is given by synthetic topology (Escardó, 2004), which assumes that the function space in the programming language used to code up topological results is continuous and derives the notion of an open set. These ideas can be used to help us structure an implementation.

One shortcoming of the library, and implementations of Type-2 computability more generally, is efficiency. We intend the presentation of the library as a means to sketch the connection of the computation with the mathematics. In practice, there are still reasons for using floating point arithmetic. First, inference algorithms are computationally intensive, even assuming operations on reals and distributions are constant-time, so one is willing to make tradeoffs for efficiency. Second, it is not necessary to compute answers to arbitrary accuracy for most applications. Notably, most inference algorithms already make approximations as the solutions to many interesting models are analytically intractable. Thus, there is still a (large) gap in practice between semantics and implementation. For ideas on how to implement Type-2 computability efficiently, we refer the reader to Bauer and Kavkler (2008) and Lambov (2007).

Lastly, in our description of the library, we have elided one important detail. One computable function we need to encode is the *modulus* of a computable function between computable metric spaces. The modulus $g : (X \to Y) \to \mathbb{N} \to \mathbb{N}$ of a computable function $f : X \to Y$ between computable metric spaces (X, d_X, S_X) and (Y, d_Y, S_Y) is a function that computes the number of input approximations consumed to produce an output approximation to a specified precision. For example, if the algorithm realizing f looks at $s_{i_0}^X, \ldots, s_{i_{41}}^X$ to compute an output $s_{i_n}^Y$ such that $d_Y(s_{i_n}^Y, f(x)) < 2^{-(n+1)}$ and $(s_{i_m}^X)_{m \in \mathbb{N}} \to x$, then the modulus $g(f)(n)$ is 42. Within a machine model, one can simply "look at the tape and head location" to obtain the modulus. However, one can show that the modulus of continuity is not expressible in a functionally-extensional language. This in essence follows from the fact that the modulus of two extensionally equivalent functions may not be equivalent. We can use Haskell's imprecise exceptions mechanism (see Peyton Jones et al., 1999), an impure feature, in a restricted manner to express the modulus.[15]

3.4 Mathematical Structures for Modeling the Library

What mathematical structures can we use to model such a library? Now that we have seen that we can implement reals and continuous distributions in code, our next task is to find mathematical structures that can be used to faithfully model the implementation. In doing so, we will set ourselves up for giving *denotational semantics* to probabilistic programs under the additional constraint that the model takes computability into account (Section 3.5).

Towards this end, we review *topological domains*, an alternative to traditional domain theory (Section 3.4.1). Topological domains support all the standard domain-theoretic constructions needed to model PCF-like languages as well as capture the notion of Type-2 computability, and hence, can form the basis of a semantics for PCF-like languages. Next, we encode distributions as topological domains. We do this for a sampling view (Section 3.4.2) and a distributional view (Section 3.4.3) based on *valuations*, a topological variant of a measure. We also construct a probability monad (Giry, 1982) on countably based topological (pre)domains, which includes computable metric spaces, so we can model the monadic implementation of distributions in the library.

Finally, we put the approach proposed here, which emphasizes Type-2 computability, in perspective. We begin by exploring an alternative approach to capturing Type-2 computability via *realizability* (Section 3.4.4). Roughly speaking, we can view a constructive logic as a "programming language" that we can use to program computable distributions. We end by reviewing alternative structures that can be used to model the semantics of probabilistic programs (Section 3.4.5).

---

[15] See http://math.andrej.com/2006/03/27/sometimes-all-functions-are-continuous.

3.4.1 Domains and Type-2 Computability

In this section, we review *topological domains*. Unlike a CPO, a topological domain in general does not carry the Scott topology, and hence, does not consider the partial order primary. Instead, topological domains start with the topology as primary and derive the order. For a complete treatment, we refer the reader to Battenfeld (2008) and the references within (*e.g.*, see Battenfeld, 2004; Battenfeld et al., 2006, 2007). Towards this end, we will follow the overview given by Battenfeld et al. (2007) to introduce the main ideas, which constructs topological domains in two steps: (1) connecting computability to topology and (2) relating topology to order. Most of this overview can be skimmed upon a first read, although the examples will be helpful. At the end, we will summarize the relevant structure that makes topological domains good candidates for modeling probabilistic programs. In Section 3.5, we will use this structure to give semantics to a core language.

Computability to topology Topological domain theory starts with the observation that topological spaces provide a good model of *datatypes*. In short, a point in a topological space corresponds to an inhabitant of a datatype and the open sets of the topology describe the observable properties of points. Consequently, one can test if an inhabitant of a datatype satisfies an observable property by performing a (potentially diverging) computation that tests if the point is contained in an open set. To make use of this observation, topological domain theory builds off of the Cartesian closed category of qcb_0 spaces[16] (*e.g.*, see Escardó et al., 2004), a subcategory of topological spaces that makes the connection between computation and topology precise. It is helpful to introduce a qcb_0 space by way of a *represented space* which starts with the idea of realizing computations on a machine model before adding back the topological structure.

Definition 3.12 A *represented space* (X, δ_X) is a pair of a set X with a partial surjective function $\delta_X : 2^\omega \rightharpoonup X$ called a *representation*.

We call $p \in 2^\omega$ a *name* of x when $\delta_X(p) = x$. Thus, a name encodes an element of the base set X as a bit-stream which in turn can be computed on by a Turing machine. A *realizer* for a function $f : (X, \delta_X) \to (Y, \delta_Y)$ is a (partial) function $F : 2^\omega \rightharpoonup 2^\omega$ such that $\delta_Y(F(p)) = f(\delta_X(p))$ for $p \in \text{dom}(f \circ \delta_X)$. A function $f : X \to Y$ between represented spaces is called *computable* if it has a computable realizer. It is called *continuous* if it has a continuous realizer (with respect to the Cantor topology).[17] Unfolding the definition of continuity of a (partial) function $f : 2^\omega \rightharpoonup 2^\omega$ on Cantor space shows that it encodes a *finite prefix property*—this means that a machine can

---

[16] qcb_0 stands for a T_0 quotient of a countably based space.

[17] Note that a continuous function $f : X \to Y$ between represented spaces does not mean that $f : X \to Y$ is a topologically continuous function with respect to the final topologies induced by the respective representations.

compute $f(p)$ to arbitrary precision after consuming a finite amount of bits of p in finite time when f is continuous.

In order to relate the machine-model view to a topology so we can define a qcb_0 space, we will need a notion of an *admissible representation*. A representation δ_X of X is *admissible* if for any other representation δ'_X of X, the identify function on X has a continuous realizer (Battenfeld et al., 2007, Defn. 3.10).

Definition 3.13 A qcb_0 *space* is a represented space (X, δ_X) with *admissible representation* δ_X.

The topology is the *quotient topology* (or *final topology*) induced by the representation δ_X. If X and Y are qcb_0 spaces, then the topologically continuous functions between them coincide with those that have continuous realizers (Battenfeld et al., 2007, Cor. 3.13), which gives the same characterization as an admissible represented space. We give two examples of qcb_0 spaces to illustrate the corresponding realizers and topologies.

Example 3.14 Define the set $\mathbb{S} \triangleq \{\bot, \top\}$ with representation $\delta_\mathbb{S}(\bot) \triangleq 00\ldots$ and $\delta_\mathbb{S}(\top) \triangleq p$ for $p \neq 00\ldots$. Then $(\mathbb{S}, \delta_\mathbb{S})$ is a qcb_0 space known as *Sierpinski* space. In particular, Sierpinski space encodes the notion of semi-decidability—a Turing machine semi-decides that a proposition holds (encoded as $\top$) only if it eventually outputs a non-zero bit.

Example 3.15 Let (X, d, S) be a computable metric space. Then $(X, \delta_{\text{Metric}})$ is a qcb_0 space with admissible representation δ_{metric} that uses fast Cauchy sequences as names. More concretely, $(\delta_\mathbb{Q}(w_n))_{n \in \mathbb{N}} \to \delta_{\text{metric}}(p)$ where $\delta(p) = \langle w_1, w_2, \ldots \rangle$. As a special case, $(\mathbb{R}, \delta_\mathbb{R})$ is a represented space, where $\delta_\mathbb{R}$ is a representation that uses fast Cauchy sequences of rationals as names.

Topology to order The next piece of structure topological domain theory imposes is the order-theoretic aspect. The idea is to use the standard interpretation of recursive functions as the least upper bound of an ascending chain of the approximate functions obtained by unfolding. Because topological domain theory takes the topology as primary and the order as secondary, this task requires some additional work.

Recall that we can convert a topological space into a preordered set via the *specialization preorder*, which orders $x \sqsubseteq y$ if every open set that contains x also contains y. We write S to convert a topological space into a preordered set. Intuitively, $x \sqsubseteq y$ if x contains less information than y. For a metric space, we can always find an open ball that separates two distinct points x and y (because the distance between two distinct points is positive). Hence, the specialization preorder of a metric space always gives the discrete order (*i.e.*, information ordering), and hence degenerately, a CPO.

Definition 3.16 (Battenfeld et al., 2007, Defn. 5.1). A qcb_0 space is called a *topological predomain* if every ascending chain $(x_i)_{i\in\mathbb{N}}$ (with respect to the specialization preorder $\sqsubseteq$) has an upper bound x such that $(x_i)_{i\in\mathbb{N}} \to x$ (with respect to its topology).

Thus, we see in the definition that a topological predomain (1) builds off of a qcb_0 space and (2) ensures that least upper bounds of increasing chains exist. The former condition provides the topology and theory of effectivity while the latter condition prepares us for modeling least fixed-points. The following provides a useful characterization of qcb_0 spaces that relates the topology back to the order.

Definition 3.17 (Battenfeld et al., 2007, Defn. 5.3). A topological space $(X, O(X))$ is a *monotone convergence space* if its specialization order is a CPO and every open is Scott open.

Proposition 3.18 (Battenfeld et al., 2007, Prop. 5.4). *A qcb_0 space is a topological predomain iff it is a monotone convergence space.*

Hence, we see that the Scott topology is in general finer than the topology associated with a topological predomain.

Analogous to standard domain theory, a topological predomain is called a *topological domain* if it has least element, written $\bot$, under its specialization order (Battenfeld et al., 2007, Defn. 5.6).

Proposition 3.19 (Battenfeld et al., 2007, Thm. 5.7). *Every continuous endofunction on a topological domain has a least fixed-point.*

We look at the relation between order and topology more closely through a series of examples below.

Example 3.20 Consider the *discrete* CPO $(\mathbb{N}, \sqsubseteq_{\text{discrete}})$ with *discrete ordering* $\sqsubseteq_{\text{discrete}}$, (*i.e.*, $n \sqsubseteq_{\text{discrete}} m$ if $n = m$). The Scott topology on this CPO gives the *discrete topology*, i.e., $O(\mathbb{N}) = \{\{n\} \mid n \in \mathbb{N}\}$. The specialization preorder applied to the resulting topology gives back the original CPO. Thus, we additionally see that the topological predomain coincides with the CPO.

Example 3.21 Consider the CPO $(\{[a, 1) \mid a \in \mathbb{R}\} \cup \{[0, 1]\}, \subseteq)$ with ordering given by set inclusion. The Scott topology on this CPO gives the *lower topology*, i.e., $O([0, 1]) = \{(a, 1] \mid a \in [0, 1)\} \cup \{[0, 1]\}$. Like the previous example, the specialization preorder applied to the resulting topology gives back the original CPO. Hence, the topological domain also coincides with the CPO.

In the two examples above, we saw instances where the order and topology coincide. In the next two examples, we will see cases where they differ, thus highlighting differences between CPOs and topological (pre)domains.

Construction	$D \times E$	$D \Rightarrow E$	$D + E$	$D \otimes E$	$D \Rrightarrow E$	$D \oplus E$	$D_\perp$
TP	✓+	✓+	✓+				✓
TD	✓+	✓+		✓	✓	✓	✓
TD!	✓+	✓		✓	✓+	✓+	✓

Figure 3.2 Summary of constructs on topological predomains (category **TP**), topological domains (category **TD**), and topological domains with strict morphisms (category **TD!**). (Compare this figure with one for CPOs (Abramsky and Jung, 1994, pg. 46).) The symbol ✓ indicates that the category is closed under that construct and the symbol + additionally indicates that it corresponds to the appropriate categorical construct.

Example 3.22 The reals $\mathbb{R}$ with Euclidean topology is a metric space, and hence, the specialization preorder gives a discrete CPO $(\mathbb{R}, \sqsubseteq_{\text{discrete}})$. However, the Scott topology of the resulting discrete CPO is the discrete topology. Hence, the topologies do not coincide.

Example 3.23 The Scott continuous functions from $\mathbb{R}$ to $\mathbb{R}$ contain all functions. However, the space of functions between the topological predomains $\mathbb{R}$ and $\mathbb{R}$ contain just the continuous ones.

The last example concerns modeling divergence for reals.

Example 3.24 The *partial reals* $\tilde{\mathbb{R}}$ (*e.g.*, see Escardó, 1996) can be modeled as (closed) intervals $[l, u]$ ordered by reverse inclusion where l is a lower-real and a u is an upper-real. The subspace of the maximal elements yields the familiar Euclidean topology. Note that $\tilde{\mathbb{R}}_\perp \neq \mathbb{R}_\perp$.

Categorical structure We end by summarizing the categorical structure of topological domains (Figure 3.2) applicable to giving semantics to probabilistic programs.[18] In short, topological (pre)domains possess essentially the same categorical structure as their CPO counterparts. Hence, we will be able to give semantics to programming languages using topological domains in much the same way that we use CPOs.

The relevant categories include **TP** (topological predomains and continuous functions),[19] **TD** (topological domains and continuous functions),[20] and **TD!** (topological domains and strict continuous functions).[21] We will use the notation below for categorical constructions with the usual semantics.

[18] We include sums ($D + E$) and coalesced sums ($D \oplus E$) for completeness. Similar to a smash product, a coalesced sum $D \oplus E$ identifies the least element of D with the least element of E.

[19] **TP** is a full reflective exponential ideal of **QCB** (category with qcb_0 spaces as objects and continuous functions as morphisms) (Battenfeld et al., 2007, Thm. 5.5).

[20] **TD** is an exponential ideal of **QCB** and is closed under countable products in **QCB** (Battenfeld et al., 2007, Thm. 5.9).

[21] **TD!** (1) is countably complete (limits inherited from **QCB**), (2) has countable coproducts, and (3) $\oplus$ and $\Rrightarrow$ (with $\mathbb{S}$ as unit) provides symmetry monoidal closed structure on **TD!** (Battenfeld et al., 2007, Thm. 6.1, Thm. 6.2, Prop. 6.4).

(*Function*) We write $D \Rightarrow E$ for continuous functions ($D \Rrightarrow E$ for strict continuous functions); the corresponding operation includes eval : $(D \Rightarrow E) \times D \Rightarrow E$, uncurry : $(D \Rightarrow E \Rightarrow F) \Rightarrow (D \times E \Rightarrow F)$, and curry : $(D \times E \Rightarrow F) \Rightarrow D \Rightarrow E \Rightarrow F$. We will subscript function space $\Rightarrow$ with the appropriate category when it is not clear from context which function space we are referring to, *e.g.*, $D \Rightarrow_{\mathbf{TD}} E$.

(*Product*) We write $D \times E$ for products ($D \otimes E$ for smash products);[22] the corresponding operations include first projection $\pi_1 : D \times E \Rightarrow D$, second projection $\pi_2 : D \times E \Rightarrow E$, and pairing $\langle \cdot, \cdot \rangle : (D \Rightarrow E) \times (D \Rightarrow F) \Rightarrow (D \Rightarrow E \times F)$.

(*Lift*) $D_{\perp}$ lifts a (*pre*)*domain*; the corresponding operations include lifting elements $\lfloor \cdot \rfloor : D \Rightarrow D_{\perp}$, lifting the domain of a function $\text{lift}_D : (D \Rightarrow E_{\perp}) \Rightarrow (D_{\perp} \Rightarrow E_{\perp})$, lifting the codomain of a function $\text{lift}_C : (D \Rightarrow E) \Rightarrow (D \Rightarrow E_{\perp})$, and unlifting elements $\lceil \cdot \rceil : D_{\perp} \Rightarrow D$ for D ($\lceil \lfloor d \rfloor \rceil = d$ and undefined otherwise). Given a morphism $f : D \Rightarrow E$, we write $f_{\perp} : D_{\perp} \Rightarrow E_{\perp}$ to refer to the morphism with lifted domain and codomain.

3.4.2 Sampling

As a reminder, the library implementation converts an input bit-stream into a sample in the desired space. Hence, we begin by encoding the sampling implementation of distributions from the library as a topological domain.

Define an (endo)functor S that sends a topological predomain D to a sampler on D and a morphism to one that composes with the underlying sampler. Then, the topological domain $S(D)$ is a sampler producing values in the lifted topological domain $D_{\perp}$.

Proposition 3.25 *The functor S defined as*

$$S(D : \mathbf{TP}) \triangleq 2^{\omega} \Rightarrow D_{\perp}$$
$$S(f : D \Rightarrow E) \triangleq s \mapsto f_{\perp} \circ s,$$

is well defined, where 2^{ω} is the topological predomain equipped with the Cantor topology.

The least element is one that maps all bit-streams to $\perp$. Next, we define three operations on samplers. The first operation creates a sampler that ignores its input bit-randomness and always returns d:

$$\text{det} : D \Rightarrow S(D)$$
$$\text{det}(d) \triangleq \text{const}(\lfloor d \rfloor)$$

---

[22] A smash product $D \otimes E$ identifies the least element of D with the least element of E.

where const : $D \Rightarrow (E \Rightarrow D)$ produces a constant function.

The second operation splits an input bit-stream u into the bit-streams indexed by the even indices u_e and the odd indices u_o:

$$\text{split} : \mathbf{2}^{\omega} \Rightarrow \mathbf{2}^{\omega} \times \mathbf{2}^{\omega}$$

$$\text{split}(u) \triangleq (u_e, u_o).$$

Note that if u is a sequence of independent and identically distributed bits, then both u_e and u_o will be as well.

The third operation sequences two samplers:

$$\text{samp} : S(D) \times (D \Rightarrow S(E)) \Rightarrow S(E)$$

$$\text{samp}(s, f) \triangleq \text{uncurry}(\text{lift}_D(f)) \circ \langle s \circ \pi_1, \pi_2 \rangle \circ \text{split}.$$

It splits the input bit-randomness and runs the sampler s on one of the bit-streams obtained by splitting to produce a value. That value is fed to f, which in turn produces a sampler that is run on the other bit-stream obtained by splitting.

3.4.3 Valuations and a Probability Monad

Our goal now is encode distributions as *valuations* in the framework of topological domains. Once we have done so, we can interpret distribution terms in the library as elements of the appropriate topological domain. Next, we define the probability monad, which will be restricted to countably based topological (pre)domains. Consequently, the probability monad in λ_{CD} will be restricted to distributions on countably based spaces, which includes commonly used spaces such as reals and products of countably based spaces (Section 3.5).

Valuations and measures A valuation shares many of the same properties as a measure, and hence, can be seen as a topological variation of distribution.

Definition 3.26 A *valuation* $v : O(X) \rightarrow [0, 1]$ is a function that assigns to each open set of a topological space X a probability such that it is (1) strict ($v(\emptyset) = 0$), (2) monotone ($v(U) \leq v(V)$ for $U \subseteq V$), and (3) modular ($v(U) + v(V) = v(U \cup V) + v(U \cap V)$ for every open U and V).

One key difference between valuations and measures is that valuations are not required to satisfy countable additivity. Indeed, countable additivity is perhaps one of the defining features of a measure. We can rectify this situation for valuations by restricting attention to the ω-*continuous valuations*. As a reminder, a valuation v is called ω-*continuous* if $v(\bigcup_{n \in \mathbb{N}} V_n) = \sup_{n \in \mathbb{N}} v(V_n)$ for $(V_n)_{n \in \mathbb{N}}$ an increasing sequence of opens. Hence, the countable additivity of μ encodes the ω-continuous property. Importantly, note that every Borel measure μ can be restricted to the lattice of opens, written $\mu|_{O(X)}$, resulting in an ω-continuous valuation. Every Borel measure μ on X can be restricted to an ω-continuous valuation $\mu|_{O(X)}$: $[O^{\subseteq}(X) \Rightarrow_{\mathbf{CPO}} [0,1]^{\uparrow}]$ (see Schröder, 2007, Sec. 3.1). Moreover, μ is uniquely determined by its restriction to the opens $\mu|_{O(X)}$.[23] In other words, we can identify distributions on topological spaces with ω-continuous valuations.

Encoding valuations The presence of topological and order-theoretic structure suggests two strategies for encoding valuations as topological domains. In the first approach, we would take a realizer point of view as every topological domain is also a qcb_0 space. Under this approach, we would (1) define an admissible representation of the space of opens $O(X)$, (2) define an admissible representation of the interval $[0, 1]$, and (3) verify that a representation of a valuation $O(X) \to [0, 1]$ using the canonical function space representation is admissible and properly encodes a valuation. In the second approach, we would take an order-theoretic point of view. Under this approach, we would (1) verify that the space of opens $O(X)$ is a topological domain, (2) verify that the interval $[0, 1]$ is a topological domain, and (3) verify that the continuous functions $O(X) \Rightarrow [0, 1]$ encodes a valuation correctly. In either strategy, a common thread is that we need to encode the opens $O(X)$ and the interval $[0, 1]$. We start with the realizer perspective.

Let $todo(X, \mathbb{S})$ be the space of continuous functions between the represented spaces X and $\mathbb{S}$. Let $[0, 1]_< \triangleq ([0, 1], \delta_<)$ be the represented space with representation $\delta_<$ that represents $r \in [0, 1]$ as all the rational lower bounds. Next, we define the opens $O(X)$ and the interval $[0, 1]$ for the order-theoretic perspective. Let $O^{\subseteq}(X) \triangleq (O(X), \subseteq)$ be the lattice of opens (and hence a CPO) of a topological space X ordered by subset inclusion. Let $[0, 1]^{\uparrow} \triangleq ([0, 1], \leq)$ be the interval $[0, 1]$ ordered by $\leq$. The next proposition shows that the realizer perspective and the order-theoretic perspective are equivalent.

Proposition 3.27
(i) $[0, 1]_< \cong [0, 1]^{\uparrow}$ and
(ii) $todo(X, \mathbb{S}) \cong O^{\subseteq}(X)$ when X is an admissible represented space.[24]

The next proposition shows that the realizer and order-theoretic views are equivalent under the additional assumption that the base topological space is countably based.

Proposition 3.28   *Let $(X, O(X))$ be a countably based topological space.*
(i) $[O^{\subseteq}(X) \Rightarrow_{CPO} [0,1]^{\uparrow}] \cong todo(O(X), [0,1]_<)$ *and*

---

[23] Note that the ω-continuous condition encodes what it means for a function to be ω-Scott continuous, *i.e.*, an ω-CPO continuous function.

[24] The second item is due to Schröder (2007, Thm. 3.3).

(ii) $[O^{\subseteq}(X) \Rightarrow_{CPO} [0,1]^{\uparrow}] \cong [O^{\subseteq}(X) \Rightarrow_{TD} [0,1]^{\uparrow}].$[25]

Proposition 3.28 gives three equivalent views of a valuation as (1) a CPO continuous function, (2) a continuous map between represented spaces, and (3) a continuous function between topological domains. View (2) indicates that there is an associated theory of effectivity on valuations. We will use this view to give semantics to probabilistic programs.

Integration Similar to how one can integrate a measurable function with respect to a measure, one can integrate a lower semi-continuous function with respect to a valuation. Let X be a represented space and $\mu \in M_1(X)$ where $M_1(X)$ is the collection of Borel measures on X that have total measure 1.

Proposition 3.29 *The integral of a lower semi-continuous function $f \in todo(X, [0,1]_<)$ with respect to a Borel measure μ*

$$\int : todo(X, [0,1]_<) \times M_1(X) \to [0,1]_<$$

is lower semi-continuous (see Schröder, 2007, Prop. 3.6). In fact, it is even lower semi-computable (Schröder, 2007, Prop. 3.6) (Hoyrup and Rojas, 2009, Prop. 4.3.1).

The integral is defined in an analogous manner to the Lebesgue integral, *i.e.*, as the limit of step functions on opens instead of measurable sets. The integral possesses many of the same properties, including Fubini and monotone convergence.

Probability monad Finally, we combine the results about valuations and integration to define a probability monad. Let $\mathbf{TP}_\omega$ be the full subcategory of $\mathbf{TP}$ where the objects are countably based. Define the (endo)functor P on countably based topological predomains that sends an object D to the space of valuations on D and a morphism to one that computes the pushforward.

Proposition 3.30 *The functor P defined as*

$$P(D : \mathbf{TP}_\omega) \triangleq O^{\subseteq}(D) \Rightarrow [0,1]^{\uparrow}$$
$$P(f : D \Rightarrow E) \triangleq \mu \mapsto \mu \circ f^{-1}$$

is well defined.

It is straightforward to check that P is a functor. We can construct a probability monad using the functor P.

---

[25] The first item is due to Schröder (2007, Sec. 3.1, Thm 3.5, Cor. 3.5). For the second item, recall that every ω-continuous pointed CPO with its Scott topology coincides with a topological domain (Battenfeld et al., 2007). The least element is the valuation that maps every open set to 0.

Proposition 3.31   *The triple $(P, \eta, >_\flat)$ is a monad, where*

$$\eta(x)(U) \triangleq \mathbb{1}_U(x)$$

$$(\mu >_\flat f)(U) \triangleq \int f_U \, d\mu \text{ where } f_U(x) = f(x)(U).$$

It is largely straightforward to check that $(P, \eta, >_\flat)$ is a monad.[26]

3.4.4 Realizability

Sections 3.4.1, 3.4.2, and 3.4.3 taken together provide enough structure for giving semantics to probabilistic programs with continuous distributions. Thus, the reader interested in seeing the semantics "in action" in a core language can skip ahead to Section 3.5.

In this section, we explore another approach to Type-2 computability based on realizability. The primary motivation for doing so is that we will obtain another perspective on computability (*i.e.*, in addition to the topological and order-theoretic ones) that highlights the connection with *constructive* mathematics. Intuitively, we have a constructive object if we can *realize* the object as a *program*. As another source of motivation, it is also possible to give semantics to programming languages directly using the realizability approach (*e.g.*, see Longley, 1995). Hence, we will gain another method of giving semantics in addition to the traditional order-theoretic one.

Under the realizability approach, we will approach Type-2 computability using an abstract machine model, *i.e.*, a *partial combinatory algebra* (PCA) as opposed to a concrete machine model (*i.e.*, a Turing machine). A PCA consists of an underlying set X and a partial application function $\cdot : X \times X \rightharpoonup X$ subject to certain laws that ensure *combinatorial completeness*, *i.e.*, that a PCA can simulate untyped lambda calculus. Hence, we can think of a PCA as an algebraic take on substitution. We obtain ordinary Type-1 computability by instantiating a PCA over the naturals $\mathbb{N}$; the partial application function of a PCA $\cdot : \mathbb{N} \times \mathbb{N} \rightharpoonup \mathbb{N}$ can be defined to simulate the computation of partial recursive functions. By extension, we obtain a Type-2 machine by instantiating a PCA over *Baire space* $\mathbb{B} \triangleq \mathbb{N} \rightarrow \mathbb{N}$; the partial application function of a PCA $\cdot : \mathbb{B} \times \mathbb{B} \rightharpoonup \mathbb{B}$ can be defined to simulate the computation over streams of naturals. In the rest of this section, our goal is to unpack the (well-known) connection between computability and constructive mathematics via realizability, and to show that the base spaces and constructions that are useful for giving semantics to probabilistic programs with continuous distributions can be realized appropriately.

---

[26] In the case of bind, we can check that the identities involving integrals holds via standard arguments (*e.g.*, see Jones, 1989).

Overview The phrase we have in mind is: "Computability is the realizability interpretation of constructive mathematics" (Bauer, 2005). The high-level idea is to encode familiar mathematical objects in an appropriate logic and derive computability as a consequence of having a sound interpretation. Programming up mathematical spaces and their operations will then correspond to encoding the space and their operations in the logic.

(*Logic*) The logic for our setting is *elementary analysis* (*e.g.*, see Lietz, 2004, Sec. 1.3.3) called EL. EL extends an intuitionistic predicate logic with (1) Heyting arithmetic, (2) a sort for Baire space `Baire` for encoding continuum-sized objects, and (3) primitive-recursion and associated operators.

(*Semantics*) The semantics for this setting includes the category $\mathbf{Asm}(\mathcal{K}_2)$ of assemblies over Kleene's second algebra $\mathcal{K}_2$ (*i.e.*, a PCA over Baire space) and the full subcategory $\mathbf{Mod}(\mathcal{K}_2)$ of modest sets over $\mathcal{K}_2$. For more details on assemblies and modest sets, we refer the reader to the relevant literature (*e.g.*, see Streicher, 2008; Bauer, 2000a; Birkedal, 1999). For our purposes, it suffices to recall that a modest set can be identified with a represented space and that an assembly is a represented space with a *multi-representation*. Hence, modest sets model datatypes and assemblies model intuitionistic logic.

Because we take a constructive vantage point, we will need to check that the semantics induced by the relevant encodings of familiar mathematical objects in the logic coincides with the usual interpretation. For our purposes, this means checking that encodings of objects such as reals and distributions in EL produce the expected semantics. Towards this end, recall that we can associate a theory of effectivity with a space by defining it as a quotient of Baire space $\mathbb{B}/\sim$ by a *partial equivalence relation* (PER) $\sim$. A quotient by a PER allows us to construct quotients and subsets of Baire space in one go. We recall the conditions required of the relation $\sim$ for the constructive encoding to coincide with the classical interpretation below.

Definition 3.32 (Lietz, 2004, Prop. 3.3.2). We write $\sim^*$ if

(*RF conservative class*) antecedents of implications contained in $\sim$ are almost negative;[27]
(*partial equivalence relation*) $EL \vdash \mathrm{sym}(\sim) \wedge \mathrm{trans}(\sim)$ where $\mathrm{sym}(\sim) \triangleq \forall \alpha \beta :$ `Baire`. $\alpha \sim \beta \leftrightarrow \beta \sim \alpha$ and $\mathrm{trans}(\sim) \triangleq \forall \alpha \beta \gamma :$ `Baire`. $\alpha \sim \beta \rightarrow \beta \sim \gamma \rightarrow \alpha \sim \gamma$; and
(*stability*) $EL \vdash \forall x\, y :$ `Baire`. $\neg\neg(x \sim y) \rightarrow x \sim y$.

---

[27] More formally, whenever $A \rightarrow B$ is a subformula of $\sim$, then the antecedent A is almost negative. As a reminder, a formula is *almost negative* if it only contains existential quantifiers in front of prime (*i.e.*, atomic) formulas.

Now we recall a sufficient condition for the constructive interpretation to coincide with the classical interpretation.

Proposition 3.33   (Lietz, 2004, Prop. 3.3.2). *If ~*, then the interpretations of* $\mathbb{B}/_\sim$ *in the categories* **Asm**$(\mathcal{K}_2)$ *and* **Asm**$_t(\mathcal{K}_2)$ *(i.e., the truth or classical interpretation) yield computably equivalent realizability structures.*

Encodings   Before proceeding to the encodings of the sets of interest in *EL*, we define two enumerations that will be useful for constructing the encodings. Let $\pi_1 \langle n, m \rangle = n$ and $\pi_2 \langle n, m \rangle = m$ so that they are pairing functions on naturals (e.g., Cantor pairing function). We also overload the notation $\langle \alpha, \beta \rangle$ to pair $\alpha \in \mathbb{B}$ and $\beta \in \mathbb{B}$.

(*Integers*)   Encode the integers as

$$\mathbb{Z} = \mathbb{N} \times \mathbb{N}/_{=_{\mathbb{N}}}$$

where $\langle a, b \rangle =_{\mathbb{N}} \langle c, d \rangle$ if $a - d = c - b$ (e.g., as in Bauer, 2000a, Sec. 5.5.1). In words, we can think of an integer as a difference of two naturals. We write Int to refer to the enumeration on $\mathbb{N} \times \mathbb{N}$.

(*Rationals*)   Encode the rationals as

$$\mathbb{Q} = \mathbb{Z} \times (\mathbb{N} \backslash \{0\})/_{=_{\mathbb{Q}}}$$

where $\langle p, q \rangle =_{\mathbb{Q}} \langle s, t \rangle$ if $p \cdot t = s \cdot q$ (e.g., as in Bauer, 2000a, Sec. 5.5.1). In words, we can think of a rational as a ratio of an integer and a non-negative natural. We write Rat to refer to the enumeration on $\mathbb{Z} \times (\mathbb{N} \backslash \{0\})$. We write $\leq_{\mathbb{Q}}$ and $<_{\mathbb{Q}}$ to implement $\leq$ and $<$ respectively on rationals.[28]

(*Non-negative rationals*)   Encode the non-negative rationals similarly to the rationals, where we replace $\mathbb{Z}$ with $\mathbb{N}$. We write NonNegRat to refer to the enumeration on $\mathbb{N} \times (\mathbb{N} \backslash \{0\})$. We write $<_{\mathbb{Q}^+}$ to implement $<$ on the non-negative rationals.

We now encode the base spaces as quotients of Baire space. In defining the quotient $\sim$, it is helpful to recall the encoding of the space first. For example, a *lower real* is an encoding of a real that enumerates all of its rational lower bounds. Hence, two lower reals will be related if their encodings enumerate the same lower bounds. As another example, we can encode reals as a fast Cauchy sequences. Hence, two reals will be related if their fast Cauchy sequences are suitably close to one another. We summarize useful quotient encodings of base spaces below.

Proposition 3.34

(*Sierpinski*) *Let* $\alpha \sim_{\mathbb{S}} \beta$ *if* $(\forall n : \mathtt{Nat}.\, \alpha\, n = 0) \leftrightarrow (\forall n : \mathtt{Nat}.\, \beta\, n = 0)$.

---

[28] Note that we have that $\langle p, q \rangle < \langle s, t \rangle$ if $p \cdot t < s \cdot q$ (e.g., as in Bauer, 2000a, Sec. 5.5.1).

(*Lower real*) *Let* $\alpha \sim_{\mathbb{R}_<} \beta$ *if* $\forall q : \texttt{Rat}. (\forall n : \texttt{Nat}. q <_{\mathbb{Q}} \alpha\, n) \leftrightarrow (\forall n : \texttt{Nat}. q <_{\mathbb{Q}} \beta\, n)$.

(*Lower non-negative real*) *Let* $\alpha \sim_{\mathbb{R}_<^+} \beta$ *if* $\forall q : \texttt{NonNegRat}. (\forall n : \texttt{Nat}. q <_{\mathbb{Q}^+} \alpha\, n) \leftrightarrow (\forall n : \texttt{Nat}. q <_{\mathbb{Q}^+} \beta\, n)$.

(*Upper real*) *Let* $\alpha \sim_{\mathbb{R}_>} \beta$ *if* $\forall q : \texttt{Rat}. (\forall n : \texttt{Nat}. \alpha\, n <_{\mathbb{Q}} q) \leftrightarrow (\forall n : \texttt{Nat}. \beta\, n <_{\mathbb{Q}} q)$.

(*Lifted partial real*) *Let* $\langle \alpha_l, \alpha_u, \alpha_<, \alpha_> \rangle \sim_{\tilde{\mathbb{R}}} \langle \beta_l, \beta_u, \beta_<, \beta_> \rangle$ *if* $\alpha_l \sim_{\mathbb{R}_<} \beta_l \wedge \alpha_u \sim_{\mathbb{R}_>} \beta_u \wedge \alpha_< \sim_{\mathbb{S}} \beta_< \wedge \alpha_> \sim_{\mathbb{S}} \beta_>$.

(*Real*) *Let* $\alpha \sim_{\mathbb{R}} \beta$ *if* $\forall n : \texttt{Nat}. |\alpha\, n - \beta\, n| \leq_{\mathbb{Q}} 2^{-n+2}$.

We have $\sim_{\mathbb{S}}^*$, $\sim_{\mathbb{R}_<}^*$, $\sim_{\mathbb{R}_<^+}^*$, $\sim_{\mathbb{R}_>}^*$, $\sim_{\tilde{\mathbb{R}}}^*$, *and* $\sim_{\mathbb{R}}^*$.

It is largely straightforward to check that $\sim^*$ holds for the $\sim$ defined above.[29] Next, we state that semantic constructs can be encoded as quotients of Baire space as well.

Proposition 3.35 *Suppose* $\sim_X^*$ *and* $\sim_Y^*$.

(*Lift*) *Let* $\langle \alpha_C, \alpha_X \rangle \sim_\perp \langle \beta_C, \beta_X \rangle$ *if* $\alpha_C \sim_{\mathbb{S}} \beta_C \wedge \alpha_X \sim_X \beta_X$.

(*Product*) *Let* $\langle \alpha_X, \alpha_Y \rangle \sim_{X \times Y} \langle \beta_X, \beta_Y \rangle$ *if* $\alpha_X \sim_Y \beta_Y \wedge \alpha_Y \sim_Y \beta_Y$

(*Function*) *Let* $\alpha \sim_{X \to Y} \beta$ *if* $\forall \gamma : \texttt{Baire}$, $\alpha \,|\, \gamma \sim_Y \beta \,|\, \gamma$ *where* $\alpha \,|\, \gamma$ *applies* α *to* γ (*in* $\mathcal{K}_2$).

We have $\sim_\perp^*$, $\sim_{X \times Y}^*$, *and* $\sim_{X \to Y}^*$.

It is straightforward to check that $\sim^*$ for the $\sim$ defined above.

We end by encoding valuations as quotients of Baire space. First, we need an enumeration of the open sets of a topological space. For a topological space $(X, O(X))$, we can encode the collection of open sets as the function space $X \to \mathbb{S}$. As the measure of an open set is lower-semi computable (Proposition 3.4.3), a valuation can be encoded as an enumeration of pairs of a basic open and a non-negative lower real. For a countably based topological space with basis $\mathcal{B}(X)$, we have $\mathcal{B}(X) \cong \mathbb{N}$; hence, we can code a valuation as a sequence of non-negative lower reals.

Proposition 3.36 *Let* $\langle \alpha_1, \alpha_2, \dots \rangle \sim_{\mathcal{V}(X)} \langle \beta_1, \beta_2, \dots \rangle$ *if* $\forall n : \texttt{Nat}. \alpha_n \sim_{\mathbb{R}_<^+} \beta_n$. *Then* $\sim_{\mathcal{V}(X)}^*$.

Summary In summary, one view of what we have just seen is that we can use *EL* as a "programming language" (*i.e.*, a constructive logic as opposed to Haskell) for coding up mathematical structures relevant for probabilistic programs that have a notion of effectivity associated with them. In particular, the witnesses in the semantics of *EL* are given by elements of a PCA and modest sets over $\mathcal{K}_2$ can be identified with represented spaces (see Battenfeld et al., 2007, Sec. 8).

---

[29] For Sierpinski, see Lietz (2004, Defn. 3.2.4). For reals, see Bauer (2000b, Sec. 5.5.2). It is also useful to recall the notion of a *negative formula* (Bauer, 2000b, pg. 92) for checking the stability of $\sim$.

3.4.5 Alternative Approaches

Probabilistic programs have a long history, and indeed, many structures have been proposed for modeling their semantics. Naturally, the choice of mathematical structure affects the language features that we can model. We close this section by reviewing a few of these alternative approaches as a point of comparison to the perspective given here that emphasizes Type-2 computability. We will focus on denotational approaches. There are also operational approaches to modeling the semantics of probabilistic programs (*e.g.*, see Park et al., 2005; Dal Lago and Zorzi, 2012).

One natural idea is to extend semantics based on CPOs to the probabilistic setting by putting distributions on CPOs. Saheb-Djahromi (1978) develops a probabilistic version of LCF by considering distributions on CPOs corresponding to base types (*i.e.*, booleans and naturals). Saheb-Djahromi also gives operational semantics as a Markov chain (described as a transition matrix) and shows that the operational semantics is equivalent to the denotational semantics. Jones (1989), in her seminal work, develops the theory of valuations on CPOs to further the study of distributions on CPOs via a *probabilistic powerdomain* $\mathcal{P}$. The probabilistic powerdomain is not closed under the function space; consequently, Jones interprets the function space $D \Rightarrow E$ probabilistically as $D \Rightarrow \mathcal{P}(E)$ (not $\mathcal{P}(D) \Rightarrow P(E)$).

Instead of taking order-theoretic structure as primary and extending it with probabilistic concepts, another idea is to take the probabilistic structure as primary and derive structure that models programming language constructs (*e.g.*, order-theoretic structure to model recursion). Kozen (1981) takes a structure amenable for modeling probability as primary (*i.e.*, Banach spaces) and imposes order-theoretic structure. This approach supports standard continuous distributions, although it does not support higher-order functions. In addition to the distributional semantics, Kozen also gives a sampling semantics and shows it equivalent to the distributional semantics. Danos and Ehrhard (2011) identify the category of probabilistic coherence spaces (PCSs) and use it to give denotational semantics to a probabilistic variant of PCF extended with (countable) choice. Hence, their approach supports discrete distributions. Ehrhard et al. (2014) show that PCSs provide a fully abstract model for probabilistic PCF so that the connection between the operational and denotational semantics is tight. Ehrhard et al. (2018) identify a Cartesian closed category of measurable cones and stable, measurable maps that is also order complete. They also provide an operational sampling semantics and show an adequacy result to link the denotational with operational semantics. This category can be used to model higher-order probabilistic languages with continuous distributions and recursion. Crubillé (2018) shows that the category of PCSs embeds into the (Cartesian closed) category of measurable cones with stable, measurable maps.

One can also use measure-theoretic structure directly, although the category of measurable spaces with measurable maps is not Cartesian closed so higher-order functions cannot be modeled. Panangaden (1999) identifies a category of stochastic relations and shows how to use it to give denotational semantics to Kozen's first-order while language. The category has measurable spaces as objects and probability kernels as morphisms. Panangaden identifies (partially) additive structure in this category and uses it to interpret fix-points for Kozen's while language. Borgström et al. (2011) also interpret a type as a measurable space and use it to give denotational semantics to a first-order language without recursion based on measure transformers. They also show how to compile this language into a factor graph, which supports inference as well as provides an operational semantics. Staton (2017) shows how the category of measurable spaces with s-finite kernels can be used to give commutative semantics to a first-order language.

Another interesting approach considers alternatives to a measure-theoretic treatment of probability, but still considers the probabilistic structure as primary. Heunen et al. (2017) develop the theory of quasi-Borel spaces, which importantly, form a Cartesian closed category and show how quasi-Borel spaces can be used to model a higher-order probabilistic language with continuous distributions but without recursion. Vákár et al. (2019) show how to extend quasi-Borel spaces with order-theoretic structure so they can be used to model languages with recursion.

3.5 A Semantics for a Core Language

What does a semantics for a core language look like? Our goal in this section is to use the mathematical structures (*i.e.*, topological domains) we reviewed in the previous section to model a PCF-like language extended with reals and continuous distributions (via a probability monad) called λ_{CD}. We begin by introducing the syntax and statics of λ_{CD} (Section 3.5.1). As we might expect, the language features that we can model are restricted to the structure of the relevant topological domains. For instance, as we only define a probability monad on countably based spaces, the probability monad in λ_{CD} will be restricted to supporting only distributions on countably based spaces. This includes distributions on reals and products of countably based spaces, but does not include function spaces (although the language itself contains higher-order functions). Next, we give both (algorithmic) sampling and distributional semantics to λ_{CD} (Section 3.5.2). This illustrates more concretely the connection between the semantics and the library implementation of computable distributions. The structure of the semantics follows the usual one for PCF. Finally, we can use the core language and its semantics to resolve the semantic issues we raised when we sketched a library for computable distributions (Section 3.5.3).

$$\tau ::= \mathtt{Nat} \mid \tau \to \tau \mid \tau \times \tau \mid \mathtt{Real} \mid \mathtt{Dist}\ \tau$$

$$
\begin{aligned}
M ::=&\ \mathtt{o} \mid \mathtt{succ} \mid \mathtt{pred} \mid \mathtt{ifo}\ M\ M\ M &\text{(PCF-1)}\\
&\mid x \mid \lambda x : \tau.\ M \mid M\ N \mid \mathtt{fix}\ M &\text{(PCF-2)}\\
&\mid (M,M) \mid \mathtt{fst}\ M \mid \mathtt{snd}\ M &\text{(products)}\\
&\mid r \mid rop &\text{(reals)}\\
&\mid dist \mid \mathtt{return}\ M \mid x \leftarrow M\ ;\ M &\text{(distributions)}
\end{aligned}
$$

Figure 3.3 λ_{CD} extends a PCF-like language with products, reals, and distributions using a probability monad. The constructs for reals and distributions are shaded.

3.5.1 Syntax and Statics

Syntax The language λ_{CD} extends a PCF-like language with reals and distributions (Figure 3.3). The terms on lines *PCF-1* and *PCF-2* are standard PCF terms. The terms on the line marked *products* extend PCF with the usual constructions for pairs; (M, N) forms a pair of terms M and N, $\mathtt{fst}\ M$ takes the first projection of the pair M, and $\mathtt{snd}\ M$ takes the second projection of the pair M. The terms on the line marked *reals* add syntax for (1) constant reals r and (2) the application of primitive real functions *rop*. The terms on the line marked *distributions* add syntax for (1) primitive distributions *dist* and (2) return $\mathtt{return}\ M$ and bind $x \leftarrow M\ ;\ N$ for an appropriate probability monad.

Statics Like PCF, λ_{CD} is a typed language. In addition to PCF types (*i.e.*, $\mathtt{Nat}$ and $\tau \to \tau$), λ_{CD} includes the type of products ($\tau \times \tau$), reals ($\mathtt{Real}$), and distributions ($\mathtt{Dist}\ \tau$). Figure 3.4 summarizes the type-system for λ_{CD}. The expression typing judgement $\Gamma \vdash M : \tau$ is parameterized by a context Ψ (omitted in the rules) that contains the types of primitive distributions and functions.[30] The typing rules for the fragments marked *PCF-1*, *PCF-2*, and *products* is standard. The typing rules for the fragments marked *reals* and *distributions* are not surprising; nevertheless, we go over them as the constructs are less standard.

As expected, constant reals r are assigned the type $\mathtt{Real}$. Primitive operations on reals *rop* (for real operation) have the type $\mathtt{Real}^n \to \mathtt{Real}$ where $\mathtt{Real}^n \triangleq \mathtt{Real} \times \cdots \times \mathtt{Real}$ (*n*-times).

For expressions that operate on distributions, the judgement $\vdash_D \tau$ additionally enforces that the involved types are well formed. The distribution type $\mathtt{Dist}\ \tau$ is well formed if the space denoted by τ is a computable metric space (Definition 3.9). This

---

[30] The full expression typing judgement would be written $\Psi; \Gamma \vdash M : \tau$. We omit Ψ because it is constant across typing rules.

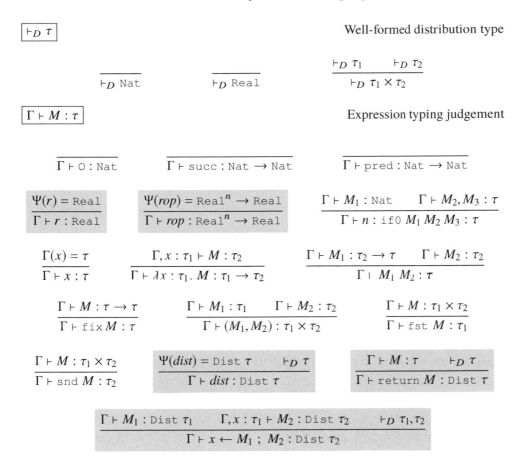

$\boxed{\vdash_D \tau}$ Well-formed distribution type

$$\frac{}{\vdash_D \mathtt{Nat}} \qquad \frac{}{\vdash_D \mathtt{Real}} \qquad \frac{\vdash_D \tau_1 \qquad \vdash_D \tau_2}{\vdash_D \tau_1 \times \tau_2}$$

$\boxed{\Gamma \vdash M : \tau}$ Expression typing judgement

$$\frac{}{\Gamma \vdash \mathtt{O} : \mathtt{Nat}} \qquad \frac{}{\Gamma \vdash \mathtt{succ} : \mathtt{Nat} \to \mathtt{Nat}} \qquad \frac{}{\Gamma \vdash \mathtt{pred} : \mathtt{Nat} \to \mathtt{Nat}}$$

$$\frac{\Psi(r) = \mathtt{Real}}{\Gamma \vdash r : \mathtt{Real}} \qquad \frac{\Psi(rop) = \mathtt{Real}^n \to \mathtt{Real}}{\Gamma \vdash rop : \mathtt{Real}^n \to \mathtt{Real}} \qquad \frac{\Gamma \vdash M_1 : \mathtt{Nat} \qquad \Gamma \vdash M_2, M_3 : \tau}{\Gamma \vdash n : \mathtt{if0}\ M_1\ M_2\ M_3 : \tau}$$

$$\frac{\Gamma(x) = \tau}{\Gamma \vdash x : \tau} \qquad \frac{\Gamma, x : \tau_1 \vdash M : \tau_2}{\Gamma \vdash \lambda x : \tau_1.\ M : \tau_1 \to \tau_2} \qquad \frac{\Gamma \vdash M_1 : \tau_2 \to \tau \qquad \Gamma \vdash M_2 : \tau_2}{\Gamma \vdash M_1\ M_2 : \tau}$$

$$\frac{\Gamma \vdash M : \tau \to \tau}{\Gamma \vdash \mathtt{fix}\ M : \tau} \qquad \frac{\Gamma \vdash M_1 : \tau_1 \qquad \Gamma \vdash M_2 : \tau_2}{\Gamma \vdash (M_1, M_2) : \tau_1 \times \tau_2} \qquad \frac{\Gamma \vdash M : \tau_1 \times \tau_2}{\Gamma \vdash \mathtt{fst}\ M : \tau_1}$$

$$\frac{\Gamma \vdash M : \tau_1 \times \tau_2}{\Gamma \vdash \mathtt{snd}\ M : \tau_2} \qquad \frac{\Psi(dist) = \mathtt{Dist}\ \tau \qquad \vdash_D \tau}{\Gamma \vdash dist : \mathtt{Dist}\ \tau} \qquad \frac{\Gamma \vdash M : \tau \qquad \vdash_D \tau}{\Gamma \vdash \mathtt{return}\ M : \mathtt{Dist}\ \tau}$$

$$\frac{\Gamma \vdash M_1 : \mathtt{Dist}\ \tau_1 \qquad \Gamma, x : \tau_1 \vdash M_2 : \mathtt{Dist}\ \tau_2 \qquad \vdash_D \tau_1, \tau_2}{\Gamma \vdash x \leftarrow M_1\ ;\ M_2 : \mathtt{Dist}\ \tau_2}$$

Figure 3.4 The type-system for λ_{CD}. The judgement $\vdash_D \tau$ checks that distribution types are well formed. The judgement $\Gamma \vdash M : \tau$ checks that expressions are well typed. The judgement is parameterized by a context Ψ (omitted), which contains that types of primitive distributions and functions. The typing rules for reals and distributions are shaded.

includes the type Nat, the type Real (Example 3.10), and products of well-formed types $\tau_1 \times \tau_2$.[31]

Given a term M that has a well-formed type, the construct return M corresponds to return in a probability monad and returns a point-mass centered at M. The typing rule for $x \leftarrow M\ ;\ N$ is the usual one for bind in a probability monad. The rule first checks that M has type Dist τ_1 and that τ_1 is well formed. Next, the rule checks that N under a typing context extended with $x : \tau_1$ has type Dist τ_2 and that τ_2 is well formed. The result is an expression of type Dist τ_2.

---

[31] As a reminder, we can also support distributions on any countably-based space (*e.g.*, distributions on distributions), but restrict our attention to these types for simplicity.

$$\mathcal{V}[\![\texttt{Nat}]\!] \triangleq \mathbb{N}_\perp$$

$$\mathcal{V}[\![\tau_1 \to \tau_2]\!] \triangleq (\mathcal{V}[\![\tau_1]\!] \Rightarrow \mathcal{V}[\![\tau_2]\!])_\perp$$

$$\mathcal{V}[\![\tau_1 \times \tau_2]\!] \triangleq (\mathcal{V}[\![\tau_1]\!] \times \mathcal{V}[\![\tau_2]\!])_\perp$$

$$\mathcal{V}[\![\texttt{Real}]\!] \triangleq \tilde{\mathbb{R}}_\perp$$

$$\mathcal{V}[\![\texttt{Dist }\tau]\!] \triangleq \{(s, \mathrm{psh}_{\mathcal{V}[\![\tau]\!]}(s)) \mid s \in S(\mathcal{V}[\![\tau]\!])\}$$

Figure 3.5 The interpretation of types $\mathcal{V}[\![\cdot]\!]$ denotes types as topological domains. We have shaded the interpretation of reals and distributions. Note that we are using a call-by-name interpretation.

3.5.2 Semantics

Interpretation of types The interpretation of types $\mathcal{V}[\![\tau]\!] \in \mathbf{TD}$ interprets a type τ as a topological domain and is defined by induction on types (Figure 3.5). The interpretation of types is similar to what one obtains from a standard CPO call-by-name interpretation.

For example, the interpretation of Nat lifts the topological domain $\mathbb{N}$. This is similar to the CPO interpretation of naturals as the lifted naturals. The interpretation of functions and products are the usual call-by-name interpretations, the difference being that we use the topological domain counterparts instead. The interpretation of the type of reals Real is a lifted partial real $\tilde{\mathbb{R}}_\perp$ (recall Example 3.24). The interpretation of the type of distributions Dist τ is a pair of a sampler and a distribution such that the sampler realizes the distribution. The (continuous) function $\mathrm{psh}_D : S(D) \Rightarrow P(D)$ computes the pushforward[32] and converts a sampler into its corresponding valuation. The well-formed distribution judgement $\vdash_D \tau$ ensures that the probability monad P is applied to only the countably based topological domains.

Denotation function The expression denotation function $\mathcal{E}[\![\Gamma \vdash M : \tau]\!] : \mathcal{V}[\![\Gamma]\!] \Rightarrow \mathcal{V}[\![\tau]\!]$ (see Proposition 3.38) is defined by induction on the typing derivation and is summarized in Figure 3.6. It is parameterized by a global environment Υ that interprets constant reals r, primitive functions rop, and primitive distributions $dist$. The global environment Υ should be well formed (defined shortly) with respect to the global context Ψ used in the expression typing judgement. After we introduce the notion of a well-formed global environment, we walk though the semantics and connect it with the library implementation, with a particular focus on the relation between a sampling and distributional view of probabilistic programs.

---

[32] We have that $\mathrm{psh}_D(s) \triangleq U \mapsto \int \mathbb{1}_U(\cdot) \, d\mu_s$ where $\mu_s \triangleq \mu_{\text{iid}} \circ s^{-1}$.

$$\mathcal{E}[\![\Gamma \vdash x : \tau]\!] \triangleq \pi_x$$

$$\mathcal{E}[\![\Gamma \vdash \mathtt{zero} : \mathtt{Nat}]\!] \triangleq \mathrm{lift}_C \circ \mathrm{const} \circ \Upsilon(\mathtt{zero})$$

$$\mathcal{E}[\![\Gamma \vdash \mathtt{succ} : \mathtt{Nat} \to \mathtt{Nat}]\!] \triangleq \mathrm{lift}_C \circ \mathrm{const} \circ \Upsilon(\mathtt{succ})$$

$$\mathcal{E}[\![\Gamma \vdash \mathtt{pred} : \mathtt{Nat} \to \mathtt{Nat}]\!] \triangleq \mathrm{lift}_C \circ \mathrm{const} \circ \Upsilon(\mathtt{pred})$$

$$\mathcal{E}[\![\Gamma \vdash \lambda x : \tau_1.\ M : \tau_1 \to \tau_2]\!] \triangleq \mathrm{lift}_C \circ \mathrm{curry}(\mathcal{E}[\![\Gamma, x : \tau_1 \vdash M : \tau_2]\!])$$

$$\mathcal{E}[\![\Gamma \vdash M_1\ M_2 : \tau_2]\!] \triangleq \mathrm{eval} \circ \langle \mathrm{unlift}(\mathcal{E}[\![\Gamma \vdash M_1 : \tau_1 \to \tau_2]\!]), \mathcal{E}[\![\Gamma \vdash M_2 : \tau_1]\!] \rangle$$

$$\mathcal{E}[\![\Gamma \vdash \mathtt{if0}\ M_1\ M_2\ M_3 : \tau]\!] \triangleq \mathrm{if0} \circ \langle \mathcal{E}[\![\Gamma \vdash M_1 : \mathtt{Nat}]\!], \mathcal{E}[\![\Gamma \vdash M_2 : \tau]\!], \mathcal{E}[\![\Gamma \vdash M_3 : \tau]\!] \rangle$$

$$\mathcal{E}[\![\Gamma \vdash \mathtt{fix}\ M : \tau]\!] \triangleq \mathrm{fix} \circ \mathrm{unlift}(\mathcal{E}[\![\Gamma \vdash M : \tau \to \tau]\!])$$

$$\mathcal{E}[\![\Gamma \vdash (M_1, M_2) : \tau_1 \times \tau_2]\!] \triangleq \mathrm{lift}_C \circ \langle \mathcal{E}[\![\Gamma \vdash M_1 : \tau_1]\!], \mathcal{E}[\![\Gamma \vdash M_2 : \tau_2]\!] \rangle \rangle$$

$$\mathcal{E}[\![\mathtt{fst}\ \Gamma \vdash M : \tau_1]\!] \triangleq \pi_1 \circ \mathrm{unlift} \circ \mathcal{E}[\![\Gamma \vdash M : \tau_1 \times \tau_2]\!]$$

$$\mathcal{E}[\![\mathtt{snd}\ \Gamma \vdash M : \tau_2]\!] \triangleq \pi_2 \circ \mathrm{unlift} \circ \mathcal{E}[\![\Gamma \vdash M : \tau_1 \times \tau_2]\!]$$

$$\mathcal{E}[\![\Gamma \vdash r : \mathtt{Real}]\!] \triangleq \mathrm{lift}_C \circ \mathrm{const} \circ \Upsilon(r)$$

$$\mathcal{E}[\![\Gamma \vdash rop : \mathtt{Real}^n \to \mathtt{Real}]\!] \triangleq \mathrm{lift}_C \circ \mathrm{const} \circ \Upsilon(rop)$$

$$\mathcal{E}[\![\Gamma \vdash dist : \mathtt{Dist}\ \tau]\!] \triangleq \mathrm{lift}_C \circ \mathrm{const} \circ \Upsilon(dist)$$

$$\mathcal{E}[\![\Gamma \vdash \mathtt{return}\ M : \mathtt{Dist}\ \tau]\!] \triangleq \langle \det \circ f, \eta \circ f \rangle \text{ where } f = \mathcal{E}[\![\Gamma \vdash M : \tau]\!]$$

$$\mathcal{E}[\![\Gamma \vdash x \leftarrow M_1\ ;\ M_2 : \mathtt{Dist}\ \tau_2]\!] \triangleq \langle \mathrm{samp} \circ \langle \pi_1 \circ f, \pi_1 \circ \mathrm{curry}(g) \rangle,$$

$$(\pi_2 \circ f) >_b (\pi_2 \circ g) \rangle$$

$$\text{where } f = \mathcal{E}[\![\Gamma \vdash M_1 : \mathtt{Dist}\ \tau_1]\!]$$

$$\text{where } g = \mathcal{E}[\![\Gamma, x : \tau_1 \vdash M_2 : \tau_2]\!]$$

Figure 3.6 The denotational semantics of λ_{CD} is given by induction on the typing derivation (semantics of additional constructs are shaded). The structure of the semantics is similar to one where we use CPOs. Υ is a global environment used to interpret constants. The function π_x projects the variable x from the environment.

Well-formed global environment To ensure that we do not introduce non-computable constants into λ_{CD} (*e.g.*, non-computable operations on reals *rop*) and that the constants have the appropriate types, the global environment Υ should be well formed with respect to the global context Ψ. To distinguish the semantic value obtained from a global environment lookup from the syntax, we will put a bar over the constant (*e.g.*, $\Upsilon(r) = \bar{r}$) to refer to the semantic value. We say that Υ is well formed with respect to Ψ, written $\Psi \vdash \Upsilon$, if the conditions below hold.

(*real-wf*) For any $r \in \mathrm{dom}(\Psi)$, $\Upsilon(r)$ is the realizer of a real $\bar{r}$ when $\Psi(r) = \mathtt{Real}$.
(*dist-wf*) For any $dist \in \mathrm{dom}(\Psi)$, $\Upsilon(dist)$ is the name of a pair $\overline{dist}$ that realizes a

sampler over values in $\mathcal{V}[\![\tau]\!]$ and the corresponding distribution when $\Psi(dist) =$ Dist τ.

(*rop-wf*) For any $rop \in \text{dom}(\Psi)$, the corresponding semantic function $\overline{rop}$ is strict, continuous on its domain, and a n-ary real-valued function on reals when $\Psi(rop) = $ Real$^n \rightarrow$ Real.

Denotation function and sampling The denotation of terms corresponding to the PCF fragment are standard. Hence, we will focus on the constructs λ_{CD} introduces. The denotation of a constant real r is a global environment lookup.

$$\mathcal{E}[\![\Gamma \vdash r : \text{Real}]\!] \triangleq \text{lift}_C \circ \text{const} \circ \Upsilon(r)$$

By the well-formedness of the global environment, $\Upsilon(r)$ will have a realizer. Likewise, the denotation of a primitive function on reals *rop* is a global environment lookup and corresponds to a representation of the code implementing the function.

$$\mathcal{E}[\![\Gamma \vdash rop : \text{Real}^n \rightarrow \text{Real}]\!] \triangleq \text{lift}_C \circ \text{const} \circ \Upsilon(rop)$$

The well-formedness of the global environment Υ enforces these conditions. Our next task is to explain the denotation of distribution constructs in λ_{CD}.

As a reminder, the interpretation of types is a pair of a sampler and the distribution that it realizes. As we will see shortly, the semantics of the sampling component and the semantics of the distribution component do not depend on one another (besides the fact that we want the distribution to be realized by the sampler). Hence, we could have given two different semantics and related them. Nevertheless, in this form, we will obtain that the valuation is the pushforward along the sampler, and consequently, make the connection between what is given by a distributional semantics and what was implemented in the sampling library. We walk through the distribution constructs now.

The denotation of a constant primitive distribution *dist* is a global environment lookup. Note that the interpretation of Dist τ is a pair of a sampler and valuation so the lookup should also produce a pair.

$$\mathcal{E}[\![\Gamma \vdash dist : \text{Dist } \tau]\!] \triangleq \text{lift}_C \circ \text{const} \circ \Upsilon(dist)$$

The denotation of return M produces a pair of a sampler that ignores the input bit-randomness and a point mass valuation centered at M.

$$\mathcal{E}[\![\Gamma \vdash \text{return } M : \text{Dist } \tau]\!] \triangleq \langle \det \circ f, \eta \circ f \rangle \text{ where } f = \mathcal{E}[\![\Gamma \vdash M : \tau]\!]$$

The meaning of $x \leftarrow M$; N also gives a sampler and a valuation.

$$\mathcal{E}[\![\Gamma \vdash x \leftarrow M_1 ; M_2 : \text{Dist } \tau_2]\!] \triangleq$$
$$\langle \text{samp} \circ \langle \pi_1 \circ f, \pi_1 \circ \text{curry}(g) \rangle, (\pi_2 \circ f) >_\flat (\pi_2 \circ g) \rangle$$

where $f = \mathcal{E}[\![\Gamma \vdash M_1 : \text{Dist } \tau_1]\!]$ and $g = \mathcal{E}[\![\Gamma, x : \tau_1 \vdash M_2 : \tau_2]\!]$. Under the sampling view, we use samp to compose the sampler obtained by $\pi_1 \circ f$ with the function $\pi_1 \circ g$. Under the valuation component, we reweigh $\pi_2 \circ g$ according to the valuation $\pi_2 \circ f$ using monad bind $\succ_\flat$ from $\boldsymbol{P}$. We can check that the valuation given by the semantics is indeed the pushforward along the sampler.

Proposition 3.37 (Push)   *Let D and E be countably based topological predomains* (qcb_0 *spaces more generally*).
(i) $\text{psh}_D(\det(d)) = \eta(d)$ *for any* $d \in D$.
(ii) $\text{psh}_E(\text{samp}(s)(f)) = \text{psh}_D(s) \succ_\flat v \mapsto \text{psh}_E(f(v))$ *for any* $s \in S(D)$ *and*
  $f : D \Rightarrow S(E)$.

In the case of bind (the second item), it is necessary that the split operation used in samp (Section 3.4.2) produces an independent stream of bits.

We end by checking that the expression denotation function is well defined.

Proposition 3.38 (Well defined)   *The expression denotation function* $\mathcal{E}[\![\cdot]\!]$ *is well defined, i.e.,* $\mathcal{E}[\![\Gamma \vdash M : \tau]\!] : \mathcal{V}[\![\Gamma]\!] \Rightarrow \mathcal{V}[\![\tau]\!]$ *for any well-typed term* $\Gamma \vdash M : \tau$ *and well-formed global environment* $\Psi \vdash \Upsilon$.

The structure of the argument showing that the expression denotation function is well defined is similar to the argument for showing that the CPO semantics of PCF is well defined. The interesting cases correspond to `return` M and $x \leftarrow M_1 ; M_2$ where we need to relate the sampling component with the valuation it denotes, which is given by Proposition 3.37.

3.5.3 Reasoning About Programs

We now return to resolving some semantic issues that were raised when we used the library to implement distributions. Throughout this section, we overload $\mathcal{E}[\![\Gamma \vdash M : \text{Dist } \tau]\!]$ to mean $\pi_2 \circ \mathcal{E}[\![\Gamma \vdash M : \text{Dist } \tau]\!]$ so that it just provides the distributional view. As shorthand, we write $\mathcal{E}[\![\cdot]\!]\rho$ instead of $\mathcal{E}[\![\cdot]\!](\rho)$ where the meta-variable ρ ranges over environments.

Reasoning about distributions   We first show that the encoding of the standard geometric distribution is correct. Let μ_B be an unbiased Bernoulli distribution and

μ^n correspond to n un-foldings of `stdGeometric`:

$$\mathcal{E}[\![\text{stdGeometric}]\!]\rho(U) = \sup_{n\in\mathbb{N}} \int \left(v \mapsto \begin{cases} \mathbb{1}_U(1) & v = t \\ \int w \mapsto \mathbb{1}_U(w+1)d\mu^n & v = f \end{cases} \right) d\mu_B$$

$$= \sup_{n\in\mathbb{N}}(\mathbb{1}_U(1)\frac{1}{2} + \sum_{w=0}^{\infty} \mathbb{1}_U(w+1)\mu^n(\{w\}))$$

$$= \mathbb{1}_U(1)\frac{1}{2} + \sum_{w=0}^{\infty} \mathbb{1}_U(w+1)(\sup_{n\in\mathbb{N}} \mu^n(\{w\})).$$

By induction on n, we can show that μ^n is the measure

$$\mu^n = \{0\} \mapsto 0, \{1\} \mapsto (1/2), \ldots, \{n\} \mapsto (1/2)^n .$$

Hence, we can conclude that $\sup_{n\in\mathbb{N}} \mu^n$ is a geometric distribution and that the encoding of `stdGeometric` is correct (for any environment ρ).

Primitive functions In our encoding of the standard normal distribution via the Marsaglia polar transformation, we used < as if it had a return type of `Bool` even though equality on reals is not computable. Indeed, the well-formedness conditions imposed on the global environment would disallow < at the current type. To resolve the semantics of <, we can think in terms of an implementation. In particular, we can encode < as dovetailing computations that semi-decides $x < y$ (*i.e.*, return () if $x < y$ and diverge otherwise) and semi-decides $x > y$ (*i.e.*, returns () if $x > y$ and diverge otherwise)). On the case of equality, which occurs with probability 0 in the Marsaglia polar transform, the function diverges.

Partiality and divergence We investigate the semantics of divergence more closely now. For convenience, we repeat the two expressions from Section 3.3 that provided two differing notions of divergence below.

```
botSamp :: (CMetrizable a) => Samp (Approx a)
botSamp = botSamp

botSampBot :: (CMetrizable a) => Samp (Approx a)
botSampBot = mkSamp (\_ -> bot)
     where bot = bot
```

In the former, we obtain the bottom valuation, which assigns 0 mass to every open set. This corresponds to the sampling function $u \in 2^\omega \mapsto \bot$ and can be interpreted as failing to provide a sampler. In the latter, we obtain the valuation that assigns 0 mass to every open set, except for the set $\{\lfloor X \rfloor \cup \bot\}$ which is assigned mass 1. This corresponds to the sampling function $u \in 2^\omega \mapsto \lfloor \bot \rfloor$ and can be interpreted as providing a sampling function that fails to produce a sample.

As before, we can check that laziness works in the appropriate manner by selectively ignoring the results of draws from the distributions above.

```
alwaysDiv :: Samp Real          neverDiv :: Samp Real
alwaysDiv = do                  neverDiv = do
  _ <- botSamp ::                 _ <- botSampBot ::
         Samp Real                      Samp Real
  stdUniform                      stdUniform
```

We can check that the denotation of the former is equivalent to that of `botSamp`:

$$\mathcal{E}[\![\texttt{alwaysDiv}]\!]\rho(U) = \int (\cdot \mapsto \mu_{\mathcal{U}}(U)) \, d\mathcal{E}[\![\texttt{botSamp}]\!]\rho$$
$$= 0$$

where $\mu_{\mathcal{U}}$ is the standard uniform distribution. Note that $\mathcal{E}[\![\texttt{botSamp}]\!]\rho$ maps every open set to 0 so the integral is 0 as well. However, the denotation of the latter is equivalent to that of `stdUniform`:

$$\mathcal{E}[\![\texttt{neverDiv}]\!]\rho(U) = \int (\cdot \mapsto \mu_{\mathcal{U}}(U)) \, d\mathcal{E}[\![\texttt{botSampBot}]\!]\rho$$
$$= \sup_{s \text{ simple}} \left\{ \int s \, d\mathcal{E}[\![\texttt{botSampBot}]\!]\rho \mid s \leq \cdot \mapsto \mu_{\mathcal{U}}(U) \right\}$$
$$= \mu_{\mathcal{U}}(U).$$

As a reminder, $\mathcal{E}[\![\texttt{botSampBot}]\!]\rho(U) = 1$ when $U = \mathcal{V}[\![\texttt{Real}]\!]$. Hence, the integral takes its largest value on the simple function[33] $\mu_{\mathcal{U}}(U) \, \mathbb{1}_{\mathcal{V}[\![\texttt{Real}]\!]}(\cdot)$.

As a final example, consider the program below that uses a coin flip to determine its diverging behavior.

```
maybeBot :: Samp Bool
maybeBot = do
  b <- stdBernoulli
  if b then return bot else stdBernoulli
```

Intuitively, this distribution returns a *sampler that always generates diverging samples* with probability 1/2 and returns an unbiased Bernoulli distribution with probability 1/2. If we changed `return bot` to `botSamp` as below

```
maybeBot' :: Samp Bool
maybeBot' = do
  b <- stdBernoulli
  if b then bot else stdBernoulli
```

then the semantics would change to a distribution that returns a *diverging sampler* with probability 1/2 and an unbiased Bernoulli distribution with probability 1/2.

---

[33] As a reminder, a simple function in our context is a linear combination of indicator functions on open sets.

Independence and commutativity In Section 3.3.2, we saw that we could not argue that two distributions that commuted the order in which we sampled independent normal distributions were equivalent. As a reminder, the issue was that commuting the order of sampling meant that the underlying random bit-stream was consumed in a different order. Consequently, the values produced by the two terms may be different. However, as the semantics we just saw relates the sampling view with the distributional view by construction, we can easily see that these two terms will be distributionally equivalent by Fubini.

3.6 Bayesian Inference

What are the implications of taking a computable viewpoint for Bayesian inference? In this section, we discuss the implications of taking a computable viewpoint for Bayesian inference. Perhaps surprisingly, one can show that conditioning is not computable in general. Nevertheless, conditioning in practical settings does not run into these pathologies. It will be important for probabilistic programming languages to support conditioning in these cases. Note that these results say nothing about the efficiency of inference. In practice, we will still need approximate inference algorithms to compute conditional distributions.

3.6.1 Conditioning is not Computable

Figure 3.7 gives an encoding in λ_{CD} of an example by Ackerman et al. (2011) that shows that conditioning is not always computable. Similar to other results

```
nonComp :: Samp (Nat, Real)
nonComp = do
  n <- geometric (1/2)
  c <- bernoulli (1/3)
  u <- uniform 0 1
  v <- uniform 0 1
  x <- return (mkApprox
              (\k -> select u v c k (tmHaltsIn n)))
  return (n, x)
    where select u v c k m
            | m > k  = nthApprox v k
            | m == k = if c then 1 else 0
            | m < k  = nthApprox u (k - m - 1)
```

Figure 3.7 A Haskell encoding of a counter-example given by Ackerman et al. (2011) that shows that conditioning is not always computable. The function `tmHaltsIn` in the code outputs the number of steps the n-th Turing machine halts in or ∞ (for diverges) if the n-th Turing machine does not halt. The idea is that an algorithm that could compute this conditional distribution would imply a decision procedure for the Halting problem.

in computability theory, the example demonstrates that an algorithm computing the conditional distribution would also solve the Halting problem. The function `tmHaltsIn` accepts a natural n specifying the n-th Turing machine and outputs the number of steps the n-th Turing machine halts in or ∞ (for diverges) if the n-the Turing machine does not halt. Upon inspection, we see the function `nthApprox` produces the binary expansion (as a dyadic rational) of a real, using `tmHaltsIn` to select different bits of the binary expansion of u or v, or the bit c depending on whether the n-th Turing machine halts within k steps or not.

Consider computing the conditional distribution $\mathbb{P}(\mathbf{N} \mid \mathbf{X})$, where the random variable $\mathbf{N}$ corresponds to the program variable n and $\mathbf{X}$ to x. Thus, computing the conditional distribution $\mathbb{P}(\mathbf{N} \mid \mathbf{X})$ corresponds to determining the value of the program variable n given the value of the program variable x. We informally discuss why this distribution is not computable now. Observe that (1) the value of x depends on the value of n—whether the n-th Turing machine halts within k steps or not for every k (hence whether the n-th Turing machine halts or not)—and (2) the geometric distribution is supported on $\mathbb{N} \backslash \{0\}$ so we need to consider every Turing machine. Consequently, we would require a decision procedure for the Halting problem in order to compute the posterior distribution on n. Thus, `nonComp` encodes a computable distribution $\mathbb{P}(\mathbf{N}, \mathbf{X})$ whose conditional $\mathbb{P}(\mathbf{N} \mid \mathbf{X})$ is not computable. We refer the reader to the full proof (see Ackerman et al., 2011) for more details.

3.6.2 Conditioning is Computable

Now, we add conditioning as a library to λ_{CD} (Figure 3.8). λ_{CD} provides only a restricted conditioning operation `obsDens`, which requires a conditional density. We will see that the computability of `obsDens` corresponds to an effective version of Bayes' rule. We have given only one conditioning primitive here, but it is possible to identify other situations where conditioning is computable and add those to the conditioning library. For example, conditioning on positive probability events is computable (see Galatolo et al., 2010, Prop. 3.1.2).

The library provides the conditioning operation `obsDens`, which enables us to condition on *continuous*-valued data when a bounded and computable conditional density is available.

Proposition 3.39 (Ackerman et al., 2011, Cor. 8.8). *Let U be a U-valued random variable, V be a V-valued random variable, and Y be Y-valued random variable, where Y is independent of V given U. Let U, V, and Y be computable. Moreover, let $p_{Y|U}(y \mid u)$ be a conditional density of Y given U that is bounded and computable. Then the conditional distribution $\mathbb{P}[(U, V) \mid Y]$ is computable.*

The bounded and computable conditional density enables the following integral

```
module CondLib (BndDens, obsDens) where
import ApproxLib
import CompDistLib
import RealLib

newtype BndDens a b =
    BndDens { getBndDens :: (Approx a -> Approx b -> Real, Rat)
        }

-- Requires bounded and computable density
obsDens :: forall u v y.
    (CMetrizable u, CMetrizable v, CMetrizable y) =>
    Samp (Approx (u, v)) -> BndDens u y -> Approx y -> Samp (
        Approx (u, v))

-- Extend with more conditioning operators below ...
```

Figure 3.8 An interface for conditioning (module `CondLib`). The function `obsDens` enables conditioning on continuous-valued data when a bounded and computable conditional density is available.

to be computed, which is in essence Bayes' rule. A version of the conditional distribution $\mathbb{P}((U,V) \mid Y)$ is

$$\kappa_{(U,V)|Y}(y,B) = \frac{\int_B p_{Y|U}(y \mid u) \, d\mu_{(U,V)}}{\int p_{Y|U}(y \mid u) \, d\mu_{(U,V)}}$$

where B is a Borel set in the space associated with $U \times V$ and $\mu_{(U,V)}$ is the joint distribution of U and V.[34]

Another interpretation of the restricted situation is that our observations have been corrupted by independent smooth noise (Ackerman et al., 2011, Cor. 8.9). To see this, consider the following generative model:

$$(U,V) \sim \mu_{(U,V)}$$
$$N \sim \mu_{\text{noise}}$$
$$Y = U + N$$

where μ_{noise} has density $p_N(\cdot)$. The random variable U can be interpreted as the ideal model of how the data was generated and the random variable V can be interpreted as the model parameters. The random variable Y can then be interpreted as the data we observe that is smoothed by the noise N so that $p_{Y|U}(y \mid u) = p_N(y - u)$. Notice that the model (U,V) is not required to have a density and can be an arbitrary

---

[34] As a reminder, $p_{Y|(U,V)}(y \mid u, v) = p_{Y|U}(y \mid u)$ due to the conditional independence of Y and V given U. Hence, the conditional density $p_{Y|U}(y \mid u)$ in the integral written more precisely is $(u, v) \mapsto p_{Y|U}(y \mid u)$.

computable distribution. The idea is that we condition on **Y** (*i.e.*, the smoothed data) as opposed to **U** (*i.e.*, the ideal data) when we compute the posterior distribution for the model parameters **V**.[35] Indeed, probabilistic programming systems proposed by the machine learning community impose a similar restriction (*e.g.*, see Goodman et al., 2008; Wood et al., 2014).

Now, we describe `obsDens`, starting with its type signature. Let the type `BndDens` τ σ represent a bounded computable density:

```
newtype BndDens a b =
    BndDens { getBndDens :: (Approx a -> Approx b -> Real, Rat)
            }
```

Conditioning thus takes a samplable distribution, a bounded computable density describing how observations have been corrupted, and returns a samplable distribution representing the conditional. In the context of Bayesian inference, it does not make sense to condition distributions such as `maybeBot` that diverge with positive probability. Hence, we do not give semantics to conditioning on those distributions.

The implementation of `obsDens` is in essence a λ_{CD} program that implements the proof that conditioning is computable in this restricted setting. This is possible because results in computability theory have computable realizers.[36]

```
obsDens :: forall u v y.
    (CMetrizable u, CMetrizable v, CMetrizable y) =>
    Samp (Approx (u, v)) -> BndDens u y -> Approx y -> Samp (
        Approx (u, v))
obsDens dist (BndDens (dens, bnd)) d =
    let f :: Approx (u, v) -> Real = \x -> dens (approxFst x) d
        mu :: Prob (u, v) = sampToComp dist
        nu :: Prob (u, v) = \bs ->
                let num   = integrateBndDom mu f bnd bs
                    denom = integrateBnd mu f bnd
                in map fst (cauchyToLU (num / denom))
    in
        compToSamp nu
```

The parameter `dist` corresponds to the joint distribution of the model (both model parameters and likelihood), `dens` corresponds to a bounded conditional density

---

[35] As an illustrative example, consider the following situation where we hope to model how a scene in an image is constructed so we can identify objects in the image (see Kulkarni et al., 2015, for a probabilistic programming language designed for scene perception). The model parameters **V** contain all the information describing the objects in the scene, including their optical properties and their positions. The resulting image **U** is then rendered by a graphics engine. The caveat is that the graphics engine uses an enumeration of the Halting set to add artifacts to the image so it is pathological. (Thus, this distribution is a version of `nonComp`.) Instead of attempting to compute the posterior distribution $\mathbb{P}(U \mid V)$, which is not computable, we smooth out the rendered image **U** with some noise given by $p_{Y|U}(y \mid u)$. In other words, we apply some filtering to the image **U** so we obtain an image **Y** free of artifacts introduced by the pathological graphics engine. The posterior $\mathbb{P}((U, V) \mid V)$ is then computable. In this example, the posterior would give the positions and optical properties of objects given an image so it could be used in computer vision applications.

[36] That is, we implement the Type-2 machine code as a Haskell program.

describing how observation of data has been corrupted by independent noise, and d is the observed data. Next, we informally describe the undefined functions in the sketch. The function `approxFst` projects out the first component of a product of approximations. The functions `sampToComp` and `compToSamp` witness the computable isomorphism between samplable and computable distributions.[37] The functions `integrateBndDom` and `integrateBnd` compute an integral (see Hoyrup and Rojas, 2009, Prop. 4.3.1), and correspond to an effective Lebesgue integral. `cauchyToLU` converts a Cauchy description of a computable real into an enumeration of lower and upper bounds.

Because `obsDens` works with conditional densities, we do not need to worry about the Borel paradox. The Borel paradox shows that we can obtain different conditional distributions when conditioning on probability zero events (*e.g.*, see Rao and Swift, 2006). To illustrate this, suppose that X and Y are two independent random variables with standard normal distributions. We can ask a (classic) question: "What is the conditional distribution of Y given that $X = Y$?"

In statistics, the appropriate response is to notice that the question as posed is ill-formed—one cannot condition on a measure zero event. The well-posed formulation is to define an auxiliary random variable Z and condition on a constant. For instance, $Z = X - Y$ conditioned on $Z = 0$, $Z = Y/X$ conditioned on $Z = 1$, and $Z = \mathbb{I}_{Y=X}$ conditioned on $Z = 1$. Remarkably, all three versions lead to different answers (Proschan and Presnell, 1998).

A probabilistic programming language that does not provide a notion of random variable such as λ_{CD} will need an alternative method of addressing this issue. Type-2 computability provides a straight-forward answer—it is not possible to create a boolean value that distinguishes two probability zero events in λ_{CD}. For instance, the operator == implementing equality on reals returns false if two reals are provably not-equal and diverges otherwise because equality is not decidable.

3.7 Summary and Further Directions

We hope to have shown that we do not need to sacrifice traditional notions of computation when modeling reals and continuous distributions by keeping their *representations* in mind. The simple observation is that we can "program" them in a general-purpose programming language. With this in mind, we can now ask a basic question: "What does it mean for a probabilistic programming language to be Turing-complete?" From the perspective of Type-2 computability, one answer is that such a language can express all *Type-2 computable distributions*, analogous to

---

[37] The computable isomorphism relies on the distributions being full-measure. The algorithm is undefined otherwise.

how a Turing-complete language can express all computable functions. Indeed, this resolution is somewhat tautological!

This answer raises another interesting question related to full-abstraction and universality[38] of probabilistic programs. In the standard setting of PCF, one approach to the full-abstraction problem is to add *parallel or* `por` to the language so that the operational behavior coincides with the denotational semantics. Additionally adding a searching operator `exists` means that all computable functions will be definable. One may wonder, if an analogous result holds for probabilistic programs. In particular, a universality result would crystallize the thought that Turing-complete probabilistic programming languages express Type-2 computable distributions.

As we are now back on familiar grounds with regards to computability, we can turn our attention to the *design* of probabilistic programming languages. The design of such languages will demand more from a semantics of probabilistic programs. For example, for the purposes of automating Bayesian inference, it is crucial that the inference procedure be *efficient* (and not simply computable). One direction is to find compilation strategies that can efficiently realize Type-2 computable distributions or approximate them (for some notion of approximation) using floating point numbers. Another direction is to consider alternative language designs (in addition to PCF with a probability monad) and the corresponding structures that we will need to model these languages.

Acknowledgments

We thank our anonymous reviewers for their helpful comments and feedback.

References

Abramsky, Samson, and Jung, Achim. 1994. Domain Theory. Pages 1–168 of: Abramsky, Samson, Gabbay, Dov M, and Maibaum, T S E (eds), *Handbook of Logic in Computer Science*, vol. 3. Oxford University Press.

Ackerman, Nathanael Leedom, Freer, Cameron E, and Roy, Daniel M. 2011. Noncomputable Conditional Distributions. Pages 107–116 of: *Proceedings of the 26th Annual Symposium on Logic in Computer Science*. IEEE.

Battenfeld, Ingo. 2004. *A Category of Topological Predomains*. M.Phil. thesis, TU Darmstadt.

Battenfeld, Ingo. 2008. *Topological Domain Theory*. Ph.D. thesis, University of Edinburgh.

Battenfeld, Ingo, Schröder, Matthias, and Simpson, Alex. 2006. Compactly generated domain theory. *Mathematical Structures in Computer Science*, **16**(2), 141–161.

---

[38] A programming language is universal if all computable elements in the domain of interpretation are definable.

Battenfeld, Ingo, Schröder, Matthias, and Simpson, Alex. 2007. A Convenient Category of Domains. *Electronic Notes in Theoretical Computer Science*, **172**, 69–99.

Bauer, Andrej. 2000a. *The Realizability Approach to Computable Analysis and Topology*. Ph.D. thesis, School of Computer Science, Carnegie Mellon University.

Bauer, Andrej. 2000b. *The Realizability Approach to Computable Analysis and Topology*. Ph.D. thesis, Carnegie Mellon University.

Bauer, Andrej. 2005. *Realizability as the connection between computable and constructive mathematics*. Unpublished lecture notes.

Bauer, Andrej, and Kavkler, Iztok. 2008. Implementing Real Numbers With RZ. *Electronic Notes in Theoretical Computer Science*, **202**, 365–384.

Birkedal, Lars. 1999. *Developing Theories of Types and Computability via Realizability*. Ph.D. thesis, School of Computer Science, Carnegie Mellon University.

Borgström, Johannes, Gordon, Andrew D, Greenberg, Michael, Margetson, James, and Van Gael, Jurgen. 2011. Measure Transformer Semantics for Bayesian Machine Learning. Pages 77–96 of: *Programming Languages and Systems*. Springer.

Crubillé, Raphaëlle. 2018. Probabilistic Stable Functions on Discrete Cones are Power Series. Pages 275–284 of: *Proceedings of the 33rd Annual ACM/IEEE Symposium on Logic in Computer Science*. ACM.

Dal Lago, Ugo, and Zorzi, Margherita. 2012. Probabilistic operational semantics for the lambda calculus. *RAIRO-Theoretical Informatics and Applications*, **46**(3), 413–450.

Danos, Vincent, and Ehrhard, Thomas. 2011. Probabilistic coherence spaces as a model of higher-order probabilistic computation. *Information and Computation*, **209**(6), 966–991.

Durrett, Rick. 2010. *Probability: Theory and Examples*. 4 edn. Cambridge University Press.

Ehrhard, Thomas, Tasson, Christine, and Pagani, Michele. 2014. Probabilistic Coherence Spaces are Fully Abstract for Probabilistic PCF. Pages 309–320 of: *ACM SIGPLAN Notices*, vol. 49. ACM.

Ehrhard, Thomas, Pagani, Michele, and Tasson, Christine. 2018. Measurable Cones and Stable, Measurable Functions: A Model for Probabilistic Higher-Order Programming. *Proceedings of the ACM on Programming Languages*, **2**(POPL), 59.

Escardó, Martín Hötzel. 1996. PCF extended with real numbers. *Theoretical Computer Science*, **162**(1), 79–115.

Escardó, Martín Hötzel. 2004. Synthetic topology: of data types and classical spaces. *Electronic Notes in Theoretical Computer Science*, **87**, 21–156.

Escardó, Martín Hötzel, Lawson, Jimmie, and Simpson, Alex. 2004. Comparing Cartesian closed categories of (core) compactly generated spaces. *Topology and its Applications*, **143**(1), 105–145.

Freer, Cameron E, and Roy, Daniel M. 2010. Posterior distributions are computable from predictive distributions. Pages 233–240 of: *Proceedings of the 13th International Conference on Artificial Intelligence and Statistics*. SAIS.

Galatolo, Stefano, Hoyrup, Mathieu, and Rojas, Cristóbal. 2010. Effective symbolic dynamics, random points, statistical behavior, complexity and entropy. *Information and Computation*, **208**(1), 23–41.

Giry, Michèle. 1982. A categorical approach to probability theory. Pages 68–85 of: *Categorical Aspects of Topology and Analysis*. Springer.

Goodman, Noah, Mansinghka, Vikash, Roy, Daniel M, Bonawitz, Keith, and Tenenbaum, Joshua B. 2008. Church: A language for generative models. Pages 220–229 of: *Proceedings of the 24th Conference on Uncertainty in Artificial Intelligence*. AUAI.

Gunter, Carl A. 1992. *Semantics of Programming Languages: Structures and Techniques*. Foundations of Computing. The MIT Press.

Heunen, Chris, Kammar, Ohad, Staton, Sam, and Yang, Hongseok. 2017. A Convenient Category for Higher-Order Probability Theory. Pages 1–12 of: *Logic in Computer Science (LICS), 2017 32nd Annual ACM/IEEE Symposium on*. IEEE.

Hoyrup, Mathieu, and Rojas, Cristóbal. 2009. Computability of probability measures and Martin-Löf randomness over metric spaces. *Information and Computation*, **207**(7), 830–847.

Huang, Daniel, and Morrisett, Greg. 2016. An Application of Computable Distributions to the Semantics of Probabilistic Programming Languages. Pages 337–363 of: *Programming Languages and Systems*.

Huang, Daniel Eachern. 2017. *On Programming Languages for Probabilistic Modeling*. Ph.D. thesis, Harvard University.

Jones, Claire. 1989. *Probabilistic Non-determinism*. Ph.D. thesis, University of Edinburgh.

Kozen, Dexter. 1981. Semantics of Probabilistic Programs. *Journal of Computer and System Sciences*, **22**(3), 328–350.

Kulkarni, Tejas D, Kohli, Pushmeet, Tenenbaum, Joshua B, and Mansinghka, Vikash. 2015. Picture: A Probabilistic Programming Language for Scene Perception. Pages 4390–4399 of: *Proceedings of the IEEE Conference on Computer Vision and Pattern Recognition*. IEEE.

Lambov, Branimir. 2007. RealLib: An Efficient Implementation of Exact Real Arithmetic. *Mathematical Structures in Computer Science*, **17**(1), 81–98.

Lietz, Peter. 2004. *From Constructive Mathematics to Computable Analysis via the Realizability Interpretation*. Ph.D. thesis, TU Darmstadt.

Longley, John R. 1995. *Realizability Toposes and Language Semantics*. Ph.D. thesis, University of Edinburgh.

Munkres, James R. 2000. *Topology*. 2 edn. Prentice Hall.

Panangaden, Prakash. 1999. The Category of Markov Kernels. *Electronic Notes in Theoretical Computer Science*, **22**, 171–187.

Park, Sungwoo, Pfenning, Frank, and Thrun, Sebastian. 2005. A Probabilistic Language Based Upon Sampling Functions. Pages 171–182 of: *Proceedings of the 32nd ACM SIGPLAN-SIGACT Symposium on Principles of Programming Languages*. ACM.

Peyton Jones, Simon, Reid, Alastair, Henderson, Fergus, Hoare, Tony, and Marlow, Simon. 1999. A Semantics for Imprecise Exceptions. Pages 25–36 of: *Proceedings of the 1999 ACM SIGPLAN Conference on Programming Language Design and Implementation*. ACM.

Proschan, Michael A, and Presnell, Brett. 1998. Expect the Unexpected from Conditional Expectation. *The American Statistician*, **52**(3), 248–252.

Rao, Malempati M, and Swift, Randall J. 2006. *Probability theory with applications*. 2 edn. Mathematics and Its Applications, vol. 582. Springer.

Saheb-Djahromi, Nasser. 1978. Probabilistic LCF. *Mathematical Foundations of Computer Science*, **64**, 442–451.

Schröder, Matthias. 2007. Admissible Representations of Probability Measures. *Electronic Notes in Theoretical Computer Science*, **167**, 61–78.

Sipser, Michael. 2012. *Introduction to the Theory of Computation*. 3 edn. Cengage Learning.

Staton, Sam. 2017. Commutative Semantics for Probabilistic Programming. Pages 855–879 of: *European Symposium on Programming*. Springer.

Streicher, Thomas. 2008. *Realizability*. http://www.mathematik.tu-darmstadt.de/~streicher/REAL/REAL.pdf. Course Lecture Notes.

Vákár, Matthijs, Kammar, Ohad, and Staton, Sam. 2019. A Domain Theory for Statistical Probabilistic Programming. *Proceedings of the ACM on Programming Languages*, **3**(POPL), 36.

Weihrauch, Klaus. 2000. *Computable Analysis: An Introduction*. 2000 edn. Texts in Theoretical Computer Science. An EATCS Series. Springer.

Wood, Frank, van de Meent, Jan Willem, and Mansinghka, Vikash. 2014. A new approach to probabilistic programming inference. Pages 2–46 of: *Proceedings of the 17th International Conference on Artificial Intelligence and Statistics*. SAIS.

4

On Probabilistic λ-Calculi

Ugo Dal Lago
University of Bologna & INRIA Sophia Antipolis

Abstract: This chapter is meant to be a gentle introduction to probabilistic λ-calculi in their two main variations, namely randomised λ-calculi and Bayesian λ-calculi. We focus our attention on the operational semantics, expressive power and termination properties of randomised λ-calculi, only giving some hints and references about denotational models and Bayesian λ-calculi.

4.1 Introduction

Probabilistic models are more and more pervasive in computer science and are among the most powerful modelling tools in many areas like computer vision (Prince, 2012), machine learning (Pearl, 1988) and natural language processing (Manning and Schütze, 1999). Since the early times of computation theory (De Leeuw et al., 1956), the concept of an algorithm has been generalised from a purely deterministic process to one in which certain elementary computation steps can have a probabilistic outcome, this way enabling efficient solutions to many computational problems (Motwani and Raghavan, 1995). More recently, programs have been employed as means to express probabilistic *models* rather than *algorithms*, with program *evaluation* replaced by a form of *inference* which does not aim at looking for the result of a computation, but rather at the probability of certain events in the model.

How can all this be taken advantage of in programming languages, and in particular in *higher-order* functional programming languages? How is the underlying meta-theory affected? This Chapter is an attempt to give a brief introduction to this topic, presenting some basic notions and results, and pointing to the relevant literature on the subject. Although probabilistic λ-calculi have been known from four decades now (Saheb-Djaromi, 1978; Jones and Plotkin, 1989), their study has been quite scattered until very recently, and a unified view of their theory is, as a consequence, still missing.

[a] From *Foundations of Probabilistic Programming*, edited by Gilles Barthe, Joost-Pieter Katoen and Alexandra Silva published 2020 by Cambridge University Press.

A universally accepted paradigm for functional programs is Church's λ-calculus (Barendregt, 1984), in which the processes of forming functions and of passing parameters to them are modelled by dedicated constructs, namely by the λ-binder and binary application. Probabilistic λ-calculi most often take the form of ordinary λ-calculi in which the language of terms is extended with one or more constructs allowing for a form of probabilistic evolution. There are at least two ways to do that, which give rise to two different styles of λ-calculi, depending on the additional operators they provide.

Randomised λ-calculi. Here, the only new operator provided by the underlying programming language is a form of probabilistic choice, whose evaluation can produce different outcomes, in a probabilistic fashion. Various choice operators can be considered, the simplest one is a form of binary, fair, probabilistic choice. By that, one can form terms such as $M \oplus N$, which evolves like M or N depending on the outcome of a probabilistic process, typically corresponding to the flipping of a coin. The outcome of such a coin flip is thus a probabilistic event and different coin flips are taken as *independent* events. This new operator alone is perfectly sufficient to model randomised algorithms (Motwani and Raghavan, 1995). We call λ-calculi built along these lines *randomised* λ-calculi. As already mentioned, randomised λ-calculi have been investigated since the seventies (Saheb-Djaromi, 1978; Jones and Plotkin, 1989), but scatteredly until very recently, when they have been the object of much work about denotational semantics (Jung and Tix, 1998; Danos and Harmer, 2002; Danos and Ehrhard, 2011), program equivalence (Dal Lago et al., 2014a; Crubillé and Dal Lago, 2014; Bizjak and Birkedal, 2015) and type systems (Dal Lago and Grellois, 2017; Breuvart and Dal Lago, 2018).

Bayesian λ-calculi. In Bayesian λ-calculi, programs are not seen as modelling *algorithms*, like in randomised λ-calculi, but rather as a way to describe a certain kind of probabilistic models, namely *bayesian networks* (Pearl, 1988; Koller and Friedman, 2009), also known as *probabilistic graphical models*. This paradigm has been adopted in concrete programming languages like ANGLICAN (Tolpin et al., 2015) and CHURCH (Goodman et al., 2008) and ultimately consists in endowing the class of terms with two new constructs, the first one modelling *sampling* and thus conceptually similar to the probabilistic choice operator from randomised λ-calculi, and the second one allowing to *condition* the underlying distribution based on external evidence, this way giving rise to both an *a priori* and an *a posteriori* distribution. Bayesian λ-calculi, contrarily to randomised λ-calculi, have been introduced only relatively recently (Borgström et al., 2016), and their metatheory is definitely not as stable as the one of randomised λ-calculi. Most often, but not always, the sampling and conditioning operators works on real numbers, this way allowing to build continuous probabilistic models.

These two kinds of λ-calculi certainly have some similarities, but deserve to be introduced and described independently. Randomised λ-calculi will be the subject of Section 4.3, while Bayesian λ-calculi will be introduced in Section 4.4. As a prologue to that, we will give an introduction to probabilistic λ-calculi by way of an example, in Section 4.2.

Endowing programs with probabilistic primitives (e.g. an operator which models sampling from a distribution) significantly changes the underlying theory. The reader is however invited to keep in mind that this domain is still under investigation by the programming language and logic in computer science communities, and is thus intrinsically unstable, in particular as for Bayesian λ-calculi. In the following, we give some hints as for the challenges one needs to face when analysing randomised and bayesian λ-calculi.

Operational Semantics and Contextual Equivalence. Formally describing the computational process implicit in a λ-term becomes strictly more challenging when the latter is allowed to flip coins, thus evolving probabilistically rather than deterministically. In particular, capturing the evaluation process in a finitary way, like in ordinary λ-calculus, is impossible. When conditioning is present, the task becomes even more difficult, since computation is replaced by learning. Another difficulty one encounters when dealing with the operational semantics of randomised and bayesian λ-calculi is the necessity of some (admittedly basic) measure theory, this of course only in presence of *continuous* rather than *discrete* distributions.

Expressive Power. Not much is known about the expressive power of *probabilistic* higher-order calculi, as opposed to the extensive literature on the same subject about *deterministic* calculi (see, e.g. (Statman, 1979; Sørensen and Urzyczyn, 2006; Longley and Normann, 2015)). What happens to the class of representable functions if one enriches, say, a deterministic λ-calculus X with certain probabilistic choice primitives? Are the expressive power or the good properties of X somehow preserved? These questions have been given answers in the case in which X is the pure, untyped, probabilistic λ-calculus (Dal Lago and Zorzi, 2012): in that case, Turing-completeness continues to hold, i.e., fair binary probabilistic choice is sufficient to encode of computable distributions. But what if one restricts the underlying calculus, e.g., by way of a type system?

Termination. Termination is a key property already in deterministic functional programs, but how should it be spelled out in probabilistic λ-calculi? There are at least *two* different ways to give an answer to this question, following a pioneering work on probabilistic λ-calculus (Saheb-Djaromi, 1978) and recent extensive work on probabilistic termination (McIver and Morgan, 2005; Bournez and Garnier, 2005). On the one hand, we can consider *almost sure termination*, by which we mean termination with maximal likelihood. On the other hand, we can go for the stronger *positive almost sure termination*, in which one requires the average number of evaluation steps to be finite. Are there ways to enforce either form of termination in probabilistic λ-calculi, similarly to what has been done in deterministic ones?

Denotational Semantics. Already for a simple, imperative probabilistic programming language, giving a denotational semantics is nontrivial (Kozen, 1981). When languages also have higher-order constructs, everything becomes even harder (Jung and Tix, 1998) to the point of disrupting much of the beautiful theory known in the deterministic case (Barendregt, 1984). This has stimulated research on denotational semantics of higher-order probabilistic programming languages, with some surprising positive results coming out recently (Ehrhard et al., 2014; Heunen et al., 2017).

In the rest of this Chapter, we focus on the first three aspects, leaving the task of delving into the denotational semantics of probabilistic λ-calculi to some future contribution. We are mainly interested in randomised λ-calculi, giving some hints about bayesian λ-calculi in Section 4.4.

4.2 A Bird's Eye View on Probabilistic Lambda Calculi

Consider a λ-term M such that for every real number r, the term $M\ r$ deterministically reduces to $r \oplus (M\ (r + 1))$, where $\oplus$ is the new operator for binary probabilistic choice mentioned in the previous section. After evolving deterministically, the term $M\ r$ thus flips a fair coin, and either terminates 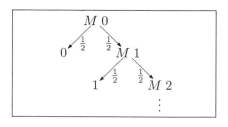 as r, with probability $\frac{1}{2}$ or proceeds as $M\ (r + 1)$, again with probability $\frac{1}{2}$. In Figure 4.2, the overall computational behaviour of the term $M\ 0$ is graphically represented as an infinite binary tree. This tree should not be confused with the reduction tree of an ordinary λ-term, in which branching models the *external* nondeterminism coming from the choice of the next redex to fire, rather than the *internal* nondeterminism coming from $\oplus$.

It should already be clear that some basic questions about the dynamics of term reduction are bound to receiving answers which are fundamentally different from the ones one gets in the ordinary λ-calculus. Let us consider some of them. First of all, *which value* does M 0 evaluate to? Clearly, the result of the evaluation process cannot just be *one* value, and must rather be a *distribution* of values. But which one? One is tempted to say that the distribution to which M 0 evaluates is the geometric distribution assigning probability $\frac{1}{2^{n+1}}$ to every natural number n. If this the correct answer, then how could we *prove* that this is the case? Finitary, inductively defined formal systems are bound *not* to be the right tool here, since such derivations can by construction only "prove" distributions having *finite support* to be those to which terms evaluate. Finitary derivations are however used to derive *approximations* to the operational semantics of the underlying term, as we will see in Section 4.3.2 below.

Another question then arises: should we consider M 0 as *terminating*? And *why?* Actually, termination becomes a probabilistic event in presence of probabilistic choices, and as such happens *with a certain probability*. The probability that the evaluation of M 0 terminates is easily seen to be $\sum_{i=0}^{\infty} \frac{1}{2^{n+1}}$, namely 1. As such, M 0 is an *almost surely terminating term*. This is not the end of the story, however: what if we are rather interested in checking that the *expected number of reduction steps* to termination for M 0 is finite? Again, the answer is positive, let us see why. The expected number of reduction steps can be computed by counting the number of *internal nodes* of the reduction tree of M 0 (again, see Figure 4.2), each node weighted by the probability of reaching it. This way every computation step is taken into account without having to deal directly with infinite traces and their probabilities, which requires measure theory. In the case at hand, internal nodes are those labelled with M n and each of them has probability $\frac{1}{2^n}$. As a consequence, the expected type to termination is $\sum_{n=0}^{\infty} \frac{1}{2^n} = 2$, and this witnesses the fact that M 0 is indeed *positively* almost surely terminating. Is there any relation between the two concepts we have just introduced? We will have something to say about that in Section 4.3.5 below.

One of the most interesting properties of the ordinary λ-calculus is *confluence*: the inherent nondeterminism induced by the presence of multiple redexes is of a very benign form, i.e., if M rewrites to both N and L, then there is P to which both N and L themselves rewrite. As consequence, the normal form of any term M if it exists, is unique. The choice of a strategy does not influence the actual final result of the computation, although not all strategies are guaranteed to lead to a normal form. Unfortunately, this nice picture is not there anymore if one endows the λ-calculus with the $\oplus$ operator. Consider the term M, defined as $(\lambda x.add_2(x,x))\ (0 \oplus 1)$ where add_2 is a operator computing addition modulo 2, which can be easily defined. Two redexes occur in M namely M itself and $0 \oplus 1$. Firing the latter first leads, independently on the outcome of the probabilistic choice, to 0. If M is fired first, instead, one obtains either 0 or 1, each with probability $\frac{1}{2}$. Please observe that the failure of confluence is *not* merely a consequence of the presence of probabilistic choice, but holds even if considering all possible outcomes.

4.3 A Typed λ-Calculus with Binary Probabilistic Choice

In this section, we introduce randomised λ-calculi in their simplest form, namely one in which the only probabilistic operator is one for binary probabilistic choice. We have chosen to go *typed* rather than *untyped*, because this way examples are easier to delineate. Most of the results we give here remain valid in an untyped setting, e.g. the setting considered in many relevant works on the subject (Ehrhard et al., 2011; Dal Lago and Zorzi, 2012; Dal Lago et al., 2014a). Going typed (Saheb-Djaromi, 1978; Jones and Plotkin, 1989; Danos and Harmer, 2002; Crubillé and Dal Lago, 2014; Bizjak and Birkedal, 2015) has also the advantage of allowing to present calculi and type systems guaranteeing termination without the need to significantly change the underlying notation. Bayesian λ-calculi are, by the way, naturally presented as typed calculi themselves (Culpepper and Cobb, 2017; Heunen et al., 2017; Wand et al., 2018; Vákár et al., 2019), and this is precisely what we are going to do in Section 4.4 below.

The calculus we introduce in the rest of Section 4.3, dubbed $\mathsf{PCF}_\oplus$, can be seen as being an extension of Plotkin's PCF in which an operator for binary probabilistic choice is available, while the rest of the system (including types and typing rules) remain essentially unaltered.

4.3.1 Types and Terms

The first notion we need is the one of a *type* which, as we already mentioned, is not different from the one of other typed λ-calculi:

Definition 4.1 ($\mathsf{PCF}_\oplus$: Types). The *types* of $\mathsf{PCF}_\oplus$ are the expressions derived by way of the following grammar:

$$\textbf{Types} \qquad \tau, \rho ::= \textsc{Unit} \mid \textsc{Num} \mid \tau \to \rho;$$

There are two type constants $\textsc{Unit}$ and $\textsc{Num}$, while type constructors only include the arrow, modelling function spaces, and do *not* include, e.g., products or coproducts. Including them in the calculus would be harmless, but would render the underlying metatheory unnecessarily more complicated. The ground type $\textsc{Unit}$ is to be interpreted as the singleton set, while the type of numbers $\textsc{Num}$ is interpreted as a monoid $(\mathbb{M}, +, 0_{\mathbb{M}})$. As an example, $\mathbb{M}$ could be the natural numbers or the real numbers. Taking real numbers as a ground type has the advantage of allowing a smooth integration of sampling from continuous distributions, as we will see in

Terms	$M, N ::= V \mid V\,W \mid \text{let } M = x \text{ in } N \mid M \oplus N$
	$\mid \text{if } V \text{ then } M \text{ else } N \mid f_n(V_1, \dots, V_n)$
Values	$V, W ::= \star \mid x \mid r \mid \lambda x.M \mid \text{fix } x.V$

Figure 4.1 Terms and Values

Section 4.4 below. All we say in this section holds independently on $\mathbb{M}$. In the following sections, however, sticking to one particular monoid $\mathbb{M}$ will sometimes be necessary. Whenever we want to insist on the underlying monoid to be $\mathbb{M}$, we write $\mathsf{PCF}_{\oplus}^{\mathbb{M}}$ instead of $\mathsf{PCF}_{\oplus}$.

We assume to reader to be familiar with the basic terminology and notation from usual, pure λ-calculus. Good references for that are Barendregt (1984) or Hindley and Seldin (2008), for example.

Definition 4.2 (PCF$_{\oplus}$: Terms and Values). *Terms* and *values* of PCF$_{\oplus}$ are both defined in Figure 4.1, where r ranges over $\mathbb{M}$, x ranges over a denumerable sets of variables $\mathcal{V}$, and f_n ranges over a class of function symbols $\mathcal{F}_n$, each of them interpreted as a total function $f_n^* : \mathbb{M}^n \to \mathbb{M}$. Both terms and values, as customary, are taken modulo α-equivalence. The set of all terms (respectively, all values) is indicated as $\mathbb{T}$ (respectively, as $\mathbb{V}$).

The calculus PCF$_{\oplus}$, is indeed a close relative of ordinary PCF. One difference is the fact that terms are written in so-called *A-normal form*: one cannot form the application MN of two *arbitrary* λ-terms M and N, but only of two *values* V and W. The generic form of an application can however be recovered as follows:

$$M\,N = \text{let } M = x \text{ in let } N = y \text{ in } (x\ y)$$

where x and y are fresh variables not occurring free in M nor in N. The other main difference, of course, is the presence of a binary choice operator $\oplus$, which models fair binary probabilistic choice. A slightly more general form of binary choice is sometimes used in the literature, namely one in which the left argument is chosen with probability p and the right argument is chosen with probability $1 - p$, the number p being any rational number between 0 and 1. Choice then becomes *biased*, and takes the form of a family of operators $\{\oplus_p\}_{p \in \mathbb{Q}_{[0,1]}}$. Fair binary choice is however perfectly sufficient for our purposes, including the one of guaranteeing the calculus to be universal as for its expressive power.

Value Typing Rules

$$\frac{}{\Gamma \vdash \star : \text{Unit}} \; \text{S} \qquad \frac{}{\Gamma, x : \tau \vdash x : \tau} \; \text{V} \qquad \frac{}{\Gamma \vdash r : \text{Num}} \; \text{R}$$

$$\frac{\Gamma, x : \tau \vdash M : \rho}{\Gamma \vdash \lambda x.M : \tau \to \rho} \; \lambda \qquad \frac{\Gamma, x : \tau \to \rho \vdash M : \tau \to \rho}{\Gamma \vdash \text{fix } x.M : \tau \to \rho} \; \text{X}$$

Term Typing Rules

$$\frac{\Gamma \vdash V : \tau \to \rho \quad \Gamma \vdash W : \tau}{\Gamma \vdash V\,W : \rho} \; @ \qquad \frac{\Gamma \vdash M : \tau \quad \Gamma, x : \tau \vdash N : \rho}{\Gamma \vdash \text{let } M = x \text{ in } N : \rho} \; \text{L}$$

$$\frac{\Gamma \vdash M : \tau \quad \Gamma \vdash N : \tau}{\Gamma \vdash M \oplus N : \tau} \; \oplus \qquad \frac{\Gamma \vdash V : \text{Num} \quad \Gamma \vdash M : \tau \quad \Gamma \vdash N : \tau}{\Gamma \vdash \text{if } V \text{ then } M \text{ else } N : \tau} \; \text{I}$$

$$\frac{\Gamma \vdash V_1 : \text{Num} \quad \cdots \quad \Gamma \vdash V_n : \text{Num}}{\Gamma \vdash f_n(V_1, \ldots, V_n) : \text{Num}} \; \text{F}$$

Figure 4.2 Type System Rules

The notions of free and bound occurrences of variables in terms are the usual ones from ordinary λ-calculus, and allow us to define the subsets $\mathbb{CT}$ and $\mathbb{CV}$ (of $\mathbb{T}$ and $\mathbb{V}$, respectively) of *closed terms* and *closed values*.

Definition 4.3 (PCF$_\oplus$: Type Judgments and Rules). A *type judgment* is an expression in the form $\Gamma \vdash M : \tau$, where M is a term, τ is a type, and Γ is an *environment*, namely a set $\{x_1 : \rho_1, \cdots, x_m : \rho_m\}$ of assignments of types to variables which is non-ambiguous: $x_i = x_j$ implies $i = j$. As customary, such an environment Γ is indicated as $x_1 : \rho_1, \cdots, x_m : \rho_m$, thus omitting parentheses. The *typing rules* for values and terms are in Figure 4.2.

The typing rules as we have introduced them are standard. Just some quick comments are needed about the rule typing binary choices. The way one types $M \oplus N$ is quite restrictive, but anyway very natural: we require M and N to *both* have type τ in order for $M \oplus N$ to have type τ. This constraint might be relaxed by way of a notion of *monadic* typing, which, together with affinity and sized types, enforces termination (Dal Lago and Grellois, 2017).

Example 4.4. As an example of a term, consider the following expression

$$GEO := (\text{fix } f.\lambda x.x \oplus (\text{let } succ_1(x) = y \text{ in } f\ y))\ 0$$

Actually, *GEO* is nothing more than a PCF$_\oplus$ term behaving like the hypothetical term $M\ 0$ we were talking about in Section 4.2. Observe how writing it requires

One-Step Reduction

$$(\lambda x.M)V \to \delta(M[V/x])$$
$$\texttt{let } V = x \texttt{ in } M \to \delta(M[V/x])$$
$$\texttt{if } 0 \texttt{ then } M \texttt{ else } N \to \delta(M)$$
$$\texttt{if } r \texttt{ then } M \texttt{ else } N \to \delta(N) \text{ if } r \neq 0$$
$$M \oplus N \to \left\{ M : \frac{1}{2}, N : \frac{1}{2} \right\}$$
$$f(r_1, \cdots, r_n) \to \delta(f^*(r_1 \ldots, r_n))$$

$$\frac{M \to \{L_i : p_i\}_{i \in I}}{\texttt{let } M = x \texttt{ in } N \to \{\texttt{let } L_i = x \texttt{ in } N : p_i\}_{i \in I}}$$

Step-Indexed Reduction

$$\frac{}{M \Rightarrow_0 \emptyset} \qquad \frac{}{V \Rightarrow_1 \delta(V)} \qquad \frac{}{V \Rightarrow_{n+1} \emptyset} \qquad \frac{M \to \mathcal{D} \quad \forall N \in \mathsf{SUPP}(\mathcal{D}).N \Rightarrow_n \mathcal{E}_N}{M \Rightarrow_{n+1} \sum_{N \in \mathsf{SUPP}(\mathcal{D})} \mathcal{D}(N) \cdot \mathcal{E}_N}$$

Figure 4.3 Small-Step Distribution Semantics

the presence of a term $succ_1$ among the functions in $\mathcal{F}_1$. As expected, $succ_1^*$ is the successor function. Another key ingredient for writing *GEO* is of course the fixed-point operator $\texttt{fix}$, without which the essentially infinitary behaviour of *GEO* could not be captured.

Typing induces a family $\{\mathbb{CT}_\tau\}_\iota$, where $\mathbb{CT}_\tau$ is the set of all closed terms which can be assigned type τ in the empty environment, i.e. those terms M such that $\emptyset \vdash M : \tau$. Similarly for $\{\mathbb{CV}_\tau\}_\tau$.

4.3.2 Operational Semantics

We are now going to define the operational semantics of the closed terms of $\mathsf{PCF}_\oplus$. We first define a family of *step-indexed reduction relations*, and then take the *operational semantics* of a term as the sum of all its step-indexed approximations. In turn, the step-indexed reduction relation is obtained by convolution from a *one-step reduction relation*. Both these relations rewrite terms into *subdistributions* of terms, which need to be defined formally:

Definition 4.5 (Distributions). Given any set X, a *distribution* on X is a function $\mathcal{D} : X \to \mathbb{R}_{[0,1]}$ such that $\mathcal{D}(x) > 0$ only for denumerably many elements of X and that $\sum_{x \in X} \mathcal{D}(x) \leq 1$. The *support* of a distribution $\mathcal{D}$ on X is the subset $\mathsf{SUPP}(\mathcal{D})$

of X defined as

$$\mathsf{SUPP}(\mathcal{D}) := \{x \in X \mid \mathcal{D}(x) > 0\}.$$

The set of all distributions over X is indicated as $\mathbf{D}(X)$. We indicate the distribution assigning probability 1 to the element $x \in X$ and 0 to any other element of X, the so-called *Dirac distribution on* x, as $\delta(x)$. The *null distribution* $\emptyset \in \mathbf{D}(X)$ assigns 0 to every element of X. The distribution $\mathcal{D}$ on X mapping x_i to p_i for every $i \in \{1,\ldots,n\}$ (and 0 to any other element of X) is indicated as $\{x_1 : p_1, \cdots, x_n : p_n\}$, similarly for the expression $\{x_i : p_i\}_{i \in I}$, where I is any countable index set. Given a distribution $\mathcal{D}$ on X, its *sum* $\|\mathcal{D}\|$ is simply $\sum_{x \in X} \mathcal{D}(x)$.

The one-step reduction relation $\to$ is a relation between closed terms and distributions over closed terms, i.e., a subset of $\mathbb{CT} \times \mathbf{D}(\mathbb{CT})$ The step-indexed reduction relations are instead a *family* of relations $\{\Rightarrow_n\}_{n \in \mathbb{N}}$, where each $\Rightarrow_n$ is a subset of $\mathbb{CT} \times \mathbf{D}(\mathbb{CV})$. As customary, we write $M \Rightarrow_n \mathcal{D}$ to indicate that $(M, \mathcal{D}) \in \Rightarrow_n$, and similarly for $\to$. The rules deriving the one-step and step-indexed reduction relations are given in Figure 4.3, and are to be interpreted inductively. Observe that the only rule for $\to$ allowing for a distribution *not* in the form $\delta(M)$ in the right-hand side is, expectedly, the one for the binary probabilistic choice $M \oplus N$.

Remark 4.6. A quick inspection at the rules in Figure 4.3 reveals that $\to$ and each of the $\Rightarrow_n$ are *partial functions*: for every $M \in \mathbb{CT}$ and for every $n \in \mathbb{N}$, there are at most one $\mathcal{D} \in \mathbf{D}(\mathbb{CT})$ such that $M \to \mathcal{D}$ and one $\mathcal{D} \in \mathbf{D}(\mathbb{CV})$ such that $M \Rightarrow_n \mathcal{D}$. This can be proved formally by easy inductions on the structure of M, and on n.

The following is an easy observation, that will be useful in some of the forthcoming sections:

Lemma 4.7. *If $M \Rightarrow_n \mathcal{D}$, then* $\mathsf{SUPP}(\mathcal{D})$ *is a finite set.*

If we consider reduction of *typed* closed terms rather than mere terms, classic results in the theory of λ-calculus continue to hold. On the one hand, reduction can only get stuck at values:

Proposition 4.8 (Progress). *For every $M \in \mathbb{CT}_\tau$, either M is a value or there is $\mathcal{D}$ with $M \to \mathcal{D}$.*

Proof   The proof is by induction on the structure of any type derivation for M, whose conclusion has to be in the form $\emptyset \vdash M : \tau$.   □

On the other hand, reduction preserves typing:

Proposition 4.9 (Subject Reduction). *For every $M \in \mathbb{CT}_\tau$ and for every $n \in \mathbb{N}$, if $M \to \mathcal{D}$ and $M \Rightarrow_n \mathcal{E}$, then $\mathcal{D} \in \mathbf{D}(\mathbb{CT}_\tau)$ and $\mathcal{E} \in \mathbf{D}(\mathbb{CV}_\tau)$.*

Proof The proof, as usual, consists in first proving a Substitution Lemma, followed by some case analysis on the rules used to derive that $M \rightarrow \mathcal{D}$. The generalisation to $\Rightarrow_n$ can be proved by an induction on n. □

Example 4.10. By applying the rules in Figure 4.3, one easily derives that

$$GEO \Rightarrow_3 \left\{ 0 : \frac{1}{2} \right\}; \qquad GEO \Rightarrow_8 \left\{ 1 : \frac{1}{4} \right\}; \qquad GEO \Rightarrow_{13} \left\{ 2 : \frac{1}{8} \right\}.$$

More generally, $GEO \Rightarrow_{3+5n} \left\{ n : \frac{1}{2^{n+1}} \right\}$ for every n, while $GEO \Rightarrow_m \emptyset$ whenever m cannot be written as $3 + 5n$.

An interesting consequence of Progress and Subject Reduction is that $\Rightarrow_n$ becomes a total function on closed typable terms:

Corollary 4.11. *For every $M \in \mathbb{CT}_\tau$ and for every $n \in \mathbb{N}$, there is exactly one distribution $\mathcal{D}_n$ such that $M \Rightarrow_n \mathcal{D}_n$*

The distribution $\mathcal{D}_n$ from Corollary 4.11 will sometimes be indicated as $\langle M \rangle_n$. Noticeably, not only $\langle M \rangle_n$ but also $\sum_{m=0}^{m} \langle M \rangle_m$ is a distribution, as can be easily proved by induction on n.

Definition 4.12 (Pointwise Order on Distributions). Given two distributions $\mathcal{D}, \mathcal{E} \in \mathbf{D}(X)$, we write $\mathcal{D} \leq \mathcal{E}$ iff $\mathcal{D}(x) \leq \mathcal{E}(x)$ for every $x \in X$. This relation endows $\mathbf{D}(X)$ with the structure of a partial order, which is actually an $\omega\mathbf{CPO}$: every ω-chain $\{\mathcal{D}_n\}_{n \in \mathbb{N}}$ of distributions has a least upper bound, which is defined pointwise:

$$\sup \{\mathcal{D}_n\}_{n \in \mathbb{N}} = x \mapsto \sup_{n \in \mathbb{N}} \mathcal{D}_n(x).$$

That this is a good definition ultimately descends from the fact that $\mathbb{R}_{[0,1]}$ is itself and $\omega\mathbf{CPO}$.

We are now ready to give the most important definition of this section:

Definition 4.13 (Operational Semantics of Closed Terms.). Given a closed term $M \in \mathbb{CT}_\tau$, the *operational semantics* of M is defined to be the distribution $\langle M \rangle \in \mathbf{D}(\mathbb{CV}_\tau)$ defined as $\sum_{n \in \mathbb{N}} \langle M \rangle_n = \sup_{m \in \mathbb{N}} \sum_{n=0}^{m} \langle M \rangle_n$. That this is a well-posed definition is a consequence of $\sum_{n=0}^{m} \langle M \rangle_n$ being an ω-chain in $\mathbf{D}(\mathbb{CV}_\tau)$.

Example 4.14. It is routine to check that

$$\langle GEO \rangle = \sum_{n \in \mathbb{N}} \langle GEO \rangle_n = \left\{ n : \frac{1}{2^{n+1}} \right\}_{n \in \mathbb{N}}.$$

In other words, the operational semantics of *GEO* is indeed the geometric distribution on the natural numbers.

Term Contexts	$C_T, D_T ::= C_V \mid [\cdot] \mid C_V\, V \mid V\, C_V$
	$\mid$ let $C_T = x$ in N
	$\mid$ let $M = x$ in $C_T \mid C_T \oplus D_T$
	$\mid$ if V then C_T else D_T
Value Contexts	$C_V, D_V ::= \lambda x.C_T \mid$ fix $x.C_V$

Figure 4.4 Value and Term Contexts

An easy corollary of Subject Reduction is that $\langle M \rangle \in \mathbf{D}(\mathbb{CV}_\tau)$ whenever $M \in \mathbb{CT}_\tau$. In other words, the operational semantics respects types.

4.3.3 Contextual Equivalence

Once an operational semantics is given, the next step to be taken towards building a metatheory for $\mathsf{PCF}_\oplus$ consists in endowing it with a notion of *program equivalence*: when is it reasonable to dub two programs to be equivalent, i.e., to have the same behaviour? A first answer to the question above consists in stipulating that equivalent programs should behave the same when placed in any context.

Definition 4.15 ($\mathsf{PCF}_\oplus$: Contexts). *Value and term contexts* are defined in Figure 4.4. Given a term context C_T and a term M, the expression $C_T[M]$ stands for the term obtained by substituting the (unique) occurrence of $[\cdot]$ in C_T with M. Similarly for $C_V[M]$, which is by construction a *value*. When we speak of a *context*, what we are referring to is a *term* context, a concept more general than the one of a value context. Metavariables like C or D refer to *term* contexts.

It is easy to generalise the type system as we presented it in Section 4.3 to a formal system capable of deriving judgments in the form

$$\Gamma \vdash C[\Delta \vdash \cdot : \tau] : \rho.$$

The judgment above, when provable, ensures that the ordinary type judgment $\Gamma \vdash C[M] : \rho$ is provable whenever $\Delta \vdash M : \tau$ is itself derivable.

We are now ready to give the most important definition of this section.

Definition 4.16 (Contextual Equivalence). Given two terms M, N such that $\Gamma \vdash M : \tau$ and $\Gamma \vdash N : \tau$, we say that M and N are (Γ, τ)-*equivalent*, and we write $M \equiv_\Gamma^\tau N$ iff whenever $\emptyset \vdash C[\Gamma \vdash \cdot : \tau] : \mathsf{U}\textsc{nit}$, it holds that $\|\langle C[M] \rangle\| = \|\langle C[N] \rangle\|$.

The way we have defined contextual equivalence turns it into a *typed relation*, i.e. a family $\{\mathcal{R}_\Gamma^\tau\}_{\Gamma,\tau}$ of relations such that $M\mathcal{R}_\Gamma^\tau N$ implies $\Gamma \vdash M : \tau$ and $\Gamma \vdash N : \tau$. We say that any typed relation $\{\mathcal{R}_\Gamma^\tau\}_{\Gamma,\tau}$ is:

- A *congruence* iff each $\mathcal{R}_\Gamma^\tau$ is an equivalence and whenever $M\mathcal{R}_\Gamma^\tau N$ and $\Delta \vdash C[\Gamma \vdash \cdot : \tau] : \rho$, it holds that $C[M]\mathcal{R}_\Delta^\rho C[N]$.
- *Adequate* iff whenever $M\mathcal{R}_\Gamma^\tau N$ and $\emptyset \vdash C[\Gamma \vdash \cdot : \tau] :$ Unit, it holds that $\|\langle C[M]\rangle\| = \|\langle C[N]\rangle\|$.

In fact contextual equivalence is an adequate congruence, and is the largest such typed relation, as witnessed by the following result, whose proof is easy, and whose deterministic counterpart has been known since the inception of contextual equivalence (Morris, 1969):

Proposition 4.17. *Contextual equivalence is the largest adequate congruence.*

Contextual equivalence is thus a very satisfactory notion of program equivalence. This does not mean, however, that proving pairs of terms to be contextually equivalent is easy: the universal quantification over all contexts Definition 4.16 relies on makes concrete proofs of equivalence hard. This has stimulated many investigations on alternative notions of equivalence, not only in presence of probabilistic choice, but also in the realm of usual, deterministic λ-calculi.

4.3.4 On the Expressive Power of PCF$_\oplus^\mathbb{N}$

It is well-known that the class of partial functions on the natural numbers Plotkin's PCF can represent is precisely the class of partial recursive functions (see (Longley and Normann, 2015) for a proof). But how about PCF$_\oplus$? First of all, is there any analogue to the class of partial recursive functions if the underlying computation model is probabilistic rather than deterministic?

There are two essentially different ways in which one can answer the question above. The first one consists in seeing any probabilistic computational model (e.g. probabilistic Turing machines (De Leeuw et al., 1956; Santos, 1969) as a device meant to solve *ordinary* computational problems seen as functions or languages. If one proceeds this way, one soon realises that, under mild conditions, any probabilistic computational model only decides partial recursive functions, capturing all of them when the underlying deterministic machinery is sufficiently powerful (Santos, 1969).

Another route consists in looking at probabilistic computational models as devices computing functions from the natural numbers to *distributions* of natural numbers, called a *probabilistic function*. This is the route followed by the author in his work with Gabbrielli and Zuppiroli (Dal Lago et al., 2014b), in which a variation on Kleene's function algebra is proved to capture *probabilistic computable functions*, namely those probabilistic functions which can be represented by probabilistic Turing machines. In the rest of this Section, we give an overview of this result, only taking the definition of a probabilistic Turing machine for granted.

Let us start by defining probabilistic functions and their computability:

Definition 4.18 (Computable Probabilistic Functions). Any function $f : \mathbb{N} \to \mathbf{D}(\mathbb{N})$ is said to be a *probabilistic function*. Such a probabilistic function f is said to be *Turing-computable* (or just *computable*) iff there is a probabilistic Turing machine $\mathscr{M}$ which, when fed with the encoding of $n \in \mathbb{N}$ terminates producing in output an encoding of $m \in \mathbb{N}$ with probability $f(n)(m)$.

A quite similar definition can be obtained by replacing Turing machines with $\mathsf{PCF}_\oplus$:

Definition 4.19. Let M be a $\mathsf{PCF}_\oplus^{\mathbb{N}}$ closed term of type NUM $\to$ NUM. Then M is said to *compute* a probabilistic function $f : \mathbb{N} \to \mathbf{D}(\mathbb{N})$ if and only if for every $n \in \mathbb{N}$, it holds that $\langle M\ n \rangle = f(n)$. Such a probabilistic function f is in this case said to be *computable by* $\mathsf{PCF}_\oplus^{\mathbb{N}}$.

One may wonder how endowing either Turing machines or PCF with an operation for probabilistic choice affects the underlying expressive power. In fact, the obtained computational models remain equivalent:

Theorem 4.20. *The class of computable probabilistic functions coincides with the class of probabilistic functions computable by* $\mathsf{PCF}_\oplus^{\mathbb{N}}$.

Proof Proving that probabilistic functions computable by $\mathsf{PCF}_\oplus^{\mathbb{N}}$ are also Turing computable is straightforward, since the operational semantics of $\mathsf{PCF}_\oplus^{\mathbb{N}}$ is effective, thus implementable by a Turing machine. The converse implication can be easily proved via the already mentioned characterisation of probabilistic computable functions via a slight variation of Kleene partial recursive functions (Dal Lago et al., 2014b), namely one in which a basic function modelling probabilistic choice is present. □

4.3.5 Termination in PCF$_\oplus$

As we mentioned in the Introduction, techniques ensuring termination of probabilistic programs have already been investigated, and at least *two* distinct notions of termination for probabilistic programs have been introduced, namely *almost sure* termination, and its strengthening *positive* almost sure termination. Let us first of all see how these notions can be formalised in our setting.

Definition 4.21 (Almost Sure Termination). Let M be any closed term. We say that M is *almost surely terminating* if $\|\langle M \rangle\| = 1$, namely if its probability of convergence is 1.

Example 4.22. An example of an almost surely terminating term is certainly *GEO* from Example 4.4. Not all $\mathsf{PCF}_{\oplus}^{\mathbb{N}}$ terms are almost surely terminating, however. As an example, the term $M = (\mathbf{fix}\ f.f)\ 0$ is clearly not terminating because $M \to \delta(M)$, and as a consequence $\langle M \rangle_n = \emptyset$ for every natural number n. There are subtler examples, like the following variation on *GEO*:

$$TWICE := (\mathbf{fix}\ f.\lambda x.x \oplus (\mathbf{let}\ succ_1(x) = y\ \mathbf{in}\ f\ (f\ y)))\ 0.$$

Please observe how the only difference between *GEO* and *TWICE* lies in the presence of *two* nested recursive calls to f (instead of one) in the right-hand-side of the probabilistic choice operator. The reader is invited to derive a value for $\|\langle TWICE \rangle\|$ as an exercise.

There is nothing in the definition of an almost surely terminating term which ensures the term's expected number of reduction steps to be *finite*. Enforcing it requires an additional, further, constraint. But before introducing it, let us first define the *expected reduction length* of any closed term M. As already mentioned in Section 4.2, a convenient way to define it is as

$$\sum_{m=0}^{\infty} \Pr(T > m),$$

where T is the random variable counting the number of steps M requires to be reduced to a value. Now, how can we define $\Pr(T > m)$ in terms of the operational semantics of M? Actually, an easy way to do it is to observe that $\Pr(T > m)$ is $1 - \sum_{n=0}^{m} \|\langle M \rangle_n\|$: the quantity $\sum_{n=0}^{m} \|\langle M \rangle_n\|$ precisely captures the probability for M to reduce to a value in *at most* m reduction steps. As a consequence, *the average number of reduction steps* $ExLen(M)$ for M is defined as follows:

$$ExLen(M) := \sum_{m=0}^{\infty} \left(1 - \sum_{n=0}^{m} \|\langle M \rangle_n\| \right).$$

Definition 4.23 (Positive Almost Sure Termination). Let M be any closed term. We say that M is *positively almost surely terminating* if $ExLen(M) < +\infty$.

The following is easy to prove, and is a standard result in the theory of Markov chains and processes:

Lemma 4.24. *Every positively almost-surely terminating term is almost-surely terminating.*

Proof   A necessary condition for *ExLen(M)* to be finite is that

$$\lim_{m\to+\infty} \sum_{n=0}^{m} \|\langle M\rangle_n\| = \lim_{m\to+\infty} \left\|\sum_{n=0}^{m} \langle M\rangle_n\right\| = 1,$$

which can hold only if $\|\langle M\rangle\| = 1$, namely only if M is almost surely terminating.   □

The converse implication does not hold however, as witnessed by the following example.

Example 4.25. Consider the following $\mathsf{PCF}^\mathbb{N}_\oplus$ term:

$$RW := (\mathtt{fix}\ f.\lambda x.\mathtt{if}\ gt_2(x,0)\ \mathtt{then}\ (N_\Uparrow \oplus N_\Downarrow)\ \mathtt{else}\ 0)1,$$

where

$$N_\Uparrow := \mathtt{let}\ succ_1(x) = y\ \mathtt{in}\ f\ y$$
$$N_\Downarrow := \mathtt{let}\ pred_1(x) = y\ \mathtt{in}\ f\ y$$

The recursive function on which the term is based first tests whether the argument x (of type $\mathrm{N}\textsc{um}$) is positive, and in case it is, makes a recursive call with argument either decreased or increased by 1, each with equal probability $\frac{1}{2}$. The term RW, then, can be seen as modelling an unbounded, fair, random walk. As such it is well known to be almost surely terminating, but not positively: the average number of steps which are necessary to reach the base case is *infinite*.

Is there any reasonable way to restrict, e.g., $\mathsf{PCF}^\mathbb{N}_\oplus$ in such a way as to *enforce* almost-sure termination? The answer is positive. As an example:

- Removing fixpoints from the class of terms, replacing them with primitive recursion, namely with a combinator $\mathtt{rec}$ having type

$$(\mathrm{N}\textsc{um} \to \tau \to \tau) \to \tau \to \mathrm{N}\textsc{um} \to \tau$$

  turns the calculus into a probabilistic variation on Gödel's T, that we call $\mathsf{T}_\oplus$. Terms of the calculus are not only positively almost-surely terminating, but satisfy an even stronger constraint: there is a global, uniform, bound on the length of any probabilistic branch, i.e., for every $M \in \mathbb{CT}_\tau$ there is $n \in \mathbb{N}$ such that $\langle M\rangle_m = \emptyset$ for every $m \geq n$. By Lemma 4.7, we can conclude that $\mathsf{SUPP}(\langle M\rangle)$ is finite, i.e. that $\mathsf{T}_\oplus$ is an essentially finitary calculus. Notice that such a uniform bound cannot be found for terms like *GEO* which, although being almost surely terminating, can possibly diverge (of course with null probability).

- $\mathsf{T}_\oplus$ can be made infinitary by endowing it with a primitive $\mathtt{geo}$ behaving exactly as *GEO*, and having type $\mathrm{N}\textsc{um}$. Remarkably, this apparently innocuous change has the effect of making the calculus almost surely terminating, but *not* positively so.

4.3.6 Further Reading

In the previous sections, a brief introduction to randomised λ-calculi has been given. This Section is meant to be a repository of pointers to the literature about this class of idioms, without any hope of being comprehensive.

We have specified the operational semantics of $\mathsf{PCF}_\oplus$ in small-step style, and by way of an inductively defined set of rules. This is not, however, the only option. Indeed, one could certainly go big-step, but also interpret reduction rules coinductively (Dal Lago and Zorzi, 2012). Another choice we have implicitly made when introducing $\mathsf{PCF}_\oplus$ is to consider *call-by-value* rather than *call-by-name* evaluation. This, again, does not mean that the latter is a route which cannot be followed (Dal Lago and Zorzi, 2012; Danos and Ehrhard, 2011). What makes call-by-value more appealing is the possibility of "implicitly memoizing" the result of probabilistic choices by way of sequencing, something which is not available in call-by-name. Consider, as an example, a term M in which some probabilistic choice $(\lambda x.N) \oplus (\lambda x.L)$ occurs. In call-by-value evaluation, this occurrence can be copied unevaluated, and once one copy of it is indeed evaluated (i.e. when it becomes the argument of a `let`), the outcome of the probabilistic choice *can itself be copied*. In call-by-name, at least if sequencing is not available, this is simply impossible: once (a copy of) a subterm is evaluated, the result of its evaluation cannot be spread around the term by way of copying. This, by the way, is the source of some discrepancies between the nature of contextual equivalence in call-by-name and call-by-value evaluation, which shows up when probabilistic choice is available (Crubillé and Dal Lago, 2014).

Contextual equivalence, as we have introduced it, is a very satisfactory definition of equivalence for probabilistic programs, being the largest compatible and adequate (equivalence) relation. Contextual equivalence relying on a universal quantification over all contexts, however, makes concrete proofs of equivalence quite hard. Alternative methodologies have been introduced for the purpose of making proofs of equivalence easier in a probabilistic setting, following the extended body of work about the same problem in the deterministic setting (e.g. (Plotkin, 1973; Abramsky, 1990; Mitchell, 1996)). For example, step-indexed logical relations have been adapted to an higher-order probabilistic λ-calculus, and proved not only sound for contextual equivalence, but also complete (Bizjak and Birkedal, 2015). As an another example, Abramsky's applicative bisimilarity has been itself generalised to randomised λ-calculi (Dal Lago et al., 2014a; Crubillé and Dal Lago, 2014) and proved fully-abstract, the latter holding only when call-by-*value* evaluation is considered. Finally, a variation on the notion of Böhm tree (Barendregt, 1984) has been recently defined for an untyped, randomised λ-calculus (Leventis, 2018); quite interestingly, the classic separability result continues to hold.

Another way of proving terms to be equivalent consists in comparing their meanings in any adequate model, along the lines of so-called denotational semantics. Following this path has proved remarkably hard in randomised λ-calculi. In particular, coming up with a completely satisfactory notion of probabilistic powerdomain, this way modelling probabilistic choice in monadic style has proved to be impossible (Jones and Plotkin, 1989; Jung and Tix, 1998). On the other hand, interpreting $PCF_\oplus$ by denotational models in the style of coherence spaces (Danos and Ehrhard, 2011) is indeed possible, and also leads to *full abstraction* results (Ehrhard et al., 2014). Very recently, another way of giving semantics to randomised λ-calculi and based on Boolean-Valued models has been proposed (Bacci et al., 2018).

The two notions of termination for probabilistic programs we introduced and discussed in this section have been studied in depth in the context of imperative programming languages (McIver and Morgan, 2005), and have been proved to be strictly more difficult than their deterministic counterparts, recursion-theoretically (Kaminski and Katoen, 2015). Various techniques for proving imperative programs to be terminating have been introduced, based on the notion of ranking martingale or Lyapunov function, the natural probabilistic analogues of the so-called ranking function (Bournez and Garnier, 2005). While the same technique has been shown to be applicable to term rewrite systems recently (Avanzini et al., 2018), not much is known about its applicability to *higher-order* functional programs. Up to now, the only works in this directions are based on type systems, and in particular on variations on either sized-types (Dal Lago and Grellois, 2017) or intersection types (Breuvart and Dal Lago, 2018).

4.4 Sampling and Conditioning

In randomised λ-calculi, only one form of probabilistic choice is available, which most often has a discrete nature. As we argued in the last section, this is perfectly adequate to model randomised computation. In recent years, starting from the pioneering works on languages like CHURCH and ANGLICAN, functional programming languages have also been employed as vehicles for the representation of probabilistic *models* rather than *algorithms*. This amounts to a different execution model, in which *inference* takes the place of *evaluation*.

In this Section, we give some hints about how this style of programming can be modelled in an extension of $PCF_\oplus$, that we call $PCF_{\texttt{sample,score}}$. The latter calculus can be derived from the former by:

- Replacing binary probabilistic choice with an operator `sample` which, when evaluated, samples a real number in $[0,1]$ uniformly at random. This implies, in particular, that the underlying monoid $\mathbb{M}$ needs to include $[0,1]$, and is often

$$\text{Terms} \qquad M, N ::= \texttt{sample} \mid \texttt{score}(V).$$

Typing Rules	$\dfrac{}{\Gamma \vdash \texttt{sample} : \text{Num}}$ A	$\dfrac{\Gamma \vdash V : \text{Num}}{\Gamma \vdash \texttt{score}(V) : \text{Unit}}$ C

Figure 4.5 Grammar and Typing Rules for `sample` and `score`.

taken as the additive monoid of real numbers. The type of the new term `sample` is Num.

- Endowing the class of terms with another operator, called `score`, which takes a positive real number r as a parameter, and modifies the *weight* of the current probabilistic branch by multiplying it by r. This serves as a way to take *observations* into account, by *conditioning* on them. The type of `score` is Unit, while its argument must of course have type Num.

Formally, the language of terms and the typing rules are extended as shown in Figure 4.5. From a purely syntactical point of view, then, formally defining Bayesian λ-calculi poses absolutely no problem.

What is nontrivial, however, is to give a *meaning* to those calculi, even in the form of an operational semantics. As already mentioned, terms are not meant to model *algorithms* but *probabilistic models*, on which inference is supposed to take place. This can be dealt with by defining a *sampling* operational semantics, following (Borgström et al., 2016), or by a *distribution* semantics which, however, requires some nontrivial measure theory. We will deal with them in the following section.

4.4.1 Operational Semantics

How could we give an operational semantics to $\mathsf{PCF}_{\texttt{sample,score}}$? As we already mentioned, there are at least two answers to this questions, which lead to formal systems which are related, although having distinct properties.

One may first of all wonder whether the distribution semantics we introduced for $\mathsf{PCF}_\oplus$ could be adapted to $\mathsf{PCF}_{\texttt{sample,score}}$. In fact this can be done, at the price of making the whole development nontrivial, due to the underlying measure theory. To understand why this is the case, let us consider how the evaluation rule for `sample` would look like. At the right-hand-side of it, what we expect is a distribution $\mathcal{D}$ on $\mathbb{R}$. The latter's support, however, is $\mathbb{R}_{[0,1]}$, and is thus not countable. As a consequence, one needs to switch to *measures* in the sense of measure theory, and assume the underlying set, namely $\mathbb{R}$ to have the structure of a measurable space. Adapting the rule for `let`-terms naturally leads to

$$\frac{M \to \mu}{\text{let } M = x \text{ in } N \to \text{let } \mu = x \text{ in } N}$$

where `let` $\mu = x$ in N should itself be a measure, meaning that not only *real numbers*, but also *terms* should be endowed with the structure of a measurable space. Finally, the last rule in step-indexed reduction needs to be adapted itself, the summation in its conclusion to be replaced by an integral:

$$\frac{M \to \mu \quad \forall N \in \text{SUPP}(\mu).N \Rightarrow_n \sigma_N}{M \Rightarrow_{n+1} A \mapsto \int \sigma_N(A)\mu(dN)}$$

For the integral above to be well defined, the underlying function must be measurable. It turns out that the appropriate invariant is even stronger: each $\Rightarrow_{n+1}$ can be seen as *finite* kernel, and the operational semantics of M thus becomes an s-finite kernel (Staton, 2017).

Measure-theoretic distribution semantics, however, is not the only way a calculus like $\text{PCF}_{\text{sample,score}}$ can be given a meaning. An alternative consists of going for the so-called *sampling-based* semantics, in which the process of sampling and scoring are made explicit.

Definition 4.26 (Trace). A *trace* is a possibly empty finite sequence of elements from $\mathbb{R}_{[0,1]}$ and is indicated with metavariables like s, t. The trace whose first element is $r \in \mathbb{R}_{[0,1]}$, and whose other elements form a trace t is indicated as $r :: t$. The set of all traces is $\mathbb{X}$.

In sampling-based semantics, *one-step reduction* and *multi-step reduction* are both subsets of $(\mathbb{CT} \times \mathbb{X}) \times \mathbb{R}_+ \times (\mathbb{CT} \times \mathbb{X})$, i.e. ternary rather than binary relations. They are indicated as $\twoheadrightarrow$ and $\Rightarrow$, respectively. We write $\langle M, s \rangle \overset{r}{\twoheadrightarrow} \langle N, t \rangle$ for $((M,s),r,(N,t)) \in \twoheadrightarrow$. Similarly for $\langle M, s \rangle \overset{r}{\Rightarrow} \langle N, t \rangle$. Rules for small-step sampling semantics can be found in Figure 4.6. Observe that if $\langle M, s \rangle \overset{r}{\twoheadrightarrow} \langle N, t \rangle$ and $r \neq 1$, then the redex fired in M must be of the form $\text{score}(r)$.

The two kinds of semantics can be proved equivalent, in the following sense: for every measurable set of real numbers A, the total probability of observing A when evaluating $\emptyset \vdash M : \text{NUM}$ in sampling-based and distribution-based are the same (see, e.g., (Borgström et al., 2016) for some more details).

4.4.2 Further Reading

The study of Bayesian λ-calculi is in its infancy , and the underlying metatheory, despite some breakthrough advances in the last ten years, is still underdeveloped compared to the one of randomised λ-calculi.

One-Step Reduction

$$\langle (\lambda x.M)V, s\rangle \xrightarrow{1} \langle M[V/x], s\rangle$$

$$\langle \texttt{let } V = x \texttt{ in } M, s\rangle \xrightarrow{1} \langle M[V/x], s\rangle$$

$$\langle \texttt{if } 0 \texttt{ then } M \texttt{ else } N, s\rangle \xrightarrow{1} \langle M, s\rangle$$

$$\langle \texttt{if } r \texttt{ then } M \texttt{ else } N, s\rangle \xrightarrow{1} \langle N, s\rangle \text{ if } r \neq 0$$

$$\langle \texttt{sample}, r :: s\rangle \xrightarrow{1} \langle r, s\rangle$$

$$\langle \texttt{score}(r), s\rangle \xrightarrow{r} \langle \star, s\rangle$$

$$\langle f(r_1, \cdots, r_n), s\rangle \xrightarrow{1} \langle f^*(r_1 \ldots, r_n), s\rangle$$

$$\frac{\langle M, s\rangle \xrightarrow{r} \langle I, t\rangle}{\langle \texttt{let } M = x \texttt{ in } N, s\rangle \xrightarrow{r} \langle \texttt{let } L = x \texttt{ in } N, s\rangle}$$

Multi-Step Reduction

$$\frac{}{\langle V, s\rangle \xRightarrow{1} \langle V, s\rangle} \qquad \frac{\langle M, s\rangle \xrightarrow{r} \langle N, t\rangle \quad \langle N, t\rangle \xRightarrow{s} \langle L, u\rangle}{\langle M, s\rangle \xRightarrow{r \cdot s} \langle L, u\rangle}$$

Figure 4.6 Small-Step Sampling Semantics

Calculi in which continuous distributions and sampling from them are available were introduced by Ramsey and Pfeffer (Ramsey and Pfeffer, 2002) and Park, Pfenning, and Thrun (Park et al., 2005). The first example of a λ-calculus in which these two features are both present is due to the author, together with Börgstrom, Gordon, and Szymczak (Borgström et al., 2016), who introduced trace and distribution semantics for an *untyped* bayesian λ-calculus with primitives for sampling and scoring, together with trace and distribution semantics, both in small-step *and* big-step styles.

Contextual equivalence and logical relations for a typed λ-calculus with sampling and scoring were introduced in Culpepper and Cobb (2017), and adapted to a calculus with full higher-order recursion in Wand et al. (2018).

Giving a satisfactory denotational semantics for bayesian λ-calculi has been proved to be quite challenging. Quasi-borel spaces (Heunen et al., 2017) provide both a closed structure and the machinery necessary to model sampling and conditioning, something which is provably impossible in the category of measurable spaces. Subsequently, quasi-borel spaces have also been shown to give rise to a category of domains, thus accounting for the presence of recursion in the underlying calculus (Vákár et al., 2019). Generalising probabilistic coherent spaces (Danos and Ehrhard, 2011) to a calculus allowing sampling from continuous distributions has proved to be possible, but highly nontrivial (Ehrhard et al., 2018). At the time of writing, it is not clear whether all this scales to a calculus in which a general form of conditioning (as embodied by the score operator) is available.

References

Abramsky, Samson. 1990. The lazy lambda calculus. Pages 65–117 of: Turner, D. (ed), *Research Topics in Functional Programming*. Addison Wesley.

Avanzini, Martin, Lago, Ugo Dal, and Yamada, Akihisa. 2018. On probabilistic term rewriting. Pages 132–148 of: *Proc. of FLOPS 2018*.

Bacci, Giorgio, Furber, Robert, Kozen, Dexter, Mardare, Radu, Panangaden, Prakash, and Scott, Dana. 2018. Boolean-valued semantics for the stochastic λ-calculus. Pages 669–678 of: *Proc. of LICS 2018*.

Barendregt, Henk P. 1984. *The Lambda Calculus, Its Syntax and Semantics*. Elsevier.

Bizjak, Ales, and Birkedal, Lars. 2015. Step-indexed logical relations for probability. Pages 279–294 of: *Proc. of FoSSaCS 2015*.

Borgström, Johannes, Dal Lago, Ugo, Gordon, Andrew D., and Szymczak, Marcin. 2016. A lambda-calculus foundation for universal probabilistic programming. Pages 33–46 of: *Proc. of ICFP 2016*.

Bournez, Olivier, and Garnier, Florent. 2005. Proving positive almost-sure termination. Pages 323–337 of: *Proc. of RTA 2005*.

Breuvart, Flavien, and Dal Lago, Ugo. 2018. On intersection types and probabilistic lambda calculi. Pages 8:1–8:13 of: *Proc. of PPDP 2018*.

Crubillé, Raphaëlle, and Dal Lago, Ugo. 2014. On Probabilistic applicative bisimulation and call-by-value λ-calculi. Pages 209–228 of: *Proc. of ESOP 2014*.

Culpepper, Ryan, and Cobb, Andrew. 2017. Contextual equivalence for probabilistic programs with continuous random variables and scoring. Pages 368–392 of: *Proc. of ESOP 2017*.

Dal Lago, Ugo, and Grellois, Charles. 2017. Probabilistic termination by monadic affine sized typing. Pages 393–419 of: *Proc. of ESOP 2017*.

Dal Lago, Ugo, and Zorzi, Margherita. 2012. Probabilistic operational semantics for the lambda calculus. *RAIRO – Theor. Inf. and Applic.*, **46**(3), 413–450.

Dal Lago, Ugo, Sangiorgi, Davide, and Alberti, Michele. 2014a. On coinductive equivalences for higher-order probabilistic functional programs. Pages 297–308 of: *Proc. of POPL 2014*.

Dal Lago, Ugo, Zuppiroli, Sara, and Gabbrielli, Maurizio. 2014b. Probabilistic recursion theory and implicit computational complexity. *Sci. Ann. Comp. Sci.*, **24**(2), 177–216.

Danos, Vincent, and Ehrhard, Thomas. 2011. Probabilistic coherence spaces as a model of higher-order probabilistic computation. *Inf. Comput.*, **209**(6), 966–991.

Danos, Vincent, and Harmer, Russell. 2002. Probabilistic game semantics. *ACM Trans. Comput. Log.*, **3**(3), 359–382.

De Leeuw, Karel, Moore, Edward F, Shannon, Claude E, and Shapiro, Norman. 1956. Computability by probabilistic machines. *Automata Studies*, **34**, 183–198.

Ehrhard, Thomas, Pagani, Michele, and Tasson, Christine. 2011. The computational meaning of probabilistic coherence spaces. Pages 87–96 of: *Proc. of LICS 2011*.

Ehrhard, Thomas, Pagani, Michele, and Tasson, Christine. 2014. Probabilistic coherence spaces are fully abstract for probabilistic PCF. Pages 309–320 of: *Proc. of POPL 2014*.

Ehrhard, Thomas, Pagani, Michele, and Tasson, Christine. 2018. Measurable cones and stable, measurable functions: a model for probabilistic higher-order programming. Pages 59:1–59:28 of: *Proc. of POPL 2018*.

Goodman, Noah D., Mansinghka, Vikash K., Roy, Daniel M., Bonawitz, Keith, and Tenenbaum, Joshua B. 2008. Church: a language for generative models. Pages 220–229 of: *Proc. of UAI 2008*.

Heunen, Chris, Kammar, Ohad, Staton, Sam, and Yang, Hongseok. 2017. A convenient category for higher-order probability theory. Pages 1–12 of: *Proc. of LICS 2017*.

Hindley, J. Roger, and Seldin, Jonathan P. 2008. *Lambda-Calculus and Combinators: An Introduction*. 2 edn. Cambridge University Press.

Jones, Claire, and Plotkin, Gordon D. 1989. A probabilistic powerdomain of evaluations. Pages 186–195 of: *Proc. of LICS 1989*.

Jung, Achim, and Tix, Regina. 1998. The troublesome probabilistic powerdomain. *Electr. Notes Theor. Comput. Sci.*, **13**, 70–91.

Kaminski, Benjamin Lucien, and Katoen, Joost-Pieter. 2015. On the Hardness of Almost-Sure Termination. Pages 307–318 of: *Proc. of MFCS 2015*.

Koller, Daphne, and Friedman, Nir. 2009. *Probabilistic Graphical Models: Principles and Techniques – Adaptive Computation and Machine Learning*. The MIT Press.

Kozen, Dexter. 1981. Semantics of Probabilistic Programs. *J. Comput. Syst. Sci.*, **22**(3), 328–350.

Leventis, Thomas. 2018. Probabilistic Böhm Trees and Probabilistic Separation. Pages 649–658 of: *Proc. of LICS 2018*.

Longley, John, and Normann, Dag. 2015. *Higher-order Computability*. Theory and Applications of Computability. Springer.

Manning, Christopher D, and Schütze, Hinrich. 1999. *Foundations of Statistical Natural Language Processing*. Vol. 999. MIT Press.

McIver, Annabelle, and Morgan, Carroll. 2005. *Abstraction, Refinement and Proof for Probabilistic Systems*. Monographs in Computer Science. Springer.

Mitchell, John C. 1996. *Foundations of Programming Languages.* Cambridge, MA, USA: MIT Press.

Morris, James. 1969. *Lambda Calculus Models of Programming Languages.* Ph.D. thesis, Massachusetts Institute of Technology, Alfred P. Sloan School of Management.

Motwani, Rajeev, and Raghavan, Prabhakar. 1995. *Randomized Algorithms.* Cambridge University Press.

Park, Sungwoo, Pfenning, Frank, and Thrun, Sebastian. 2005. A probabilistic language based upon sampling functions. Pages 171–182 of: *Proc. of POPL 2005.* ACM.

Pearl, Judea. 1988. *Probabilistic Reasoning in Intelligent Systems: Networks of Plausible Inference.* Morgan Kaufmann.

Plotkin, Gordon. 1973. *Lambda-definability and logical relations.* Tech. rept. SAI-RM-4. University of Edinburgh.

Prince, Simon J. D. 2012. *Computer Vision: Models, Learning, and Inference.* New York, NY, USA: Cambridge University Press.

Ramsey, Norman, and Pfeffer, Avi. 2002. Stochastic lambda calculus and monads of probability distributions. Pages 154–165 of: *Proc. of POPL 2002.* ACM.

Saheb-Djaromi, N. 1978. Probabilistic LCF. Pages 442–451 of: *Proc. of MFCS 1978.*

Santos, Eugene S. 1969. Probabilistic Turing machines and computability. *Proceedings of the American Mathematical Society*, **22**(3), 704–710.

Sørensen, Morten Heine, and Urzyczyn, Pawel. 2006. *Lectures on the Curry–Howard Isomorphism,.* New York, NY, USA: Elsevier Science Inc.

Statman, Richard. 1979. The typed lambda-calculus is not elementary recursive. *Theor. Comput. Sci.*, **9**, 73–81.

Staton, Sam. 2017. Commutative semantics for probabilistic programming. Pages 855–879 of: *Proc. of ESOP 2017.*

Tolpin, David, van de Meent, Jan-Willem, and Wood, Frank D. 2015. Probabilistic programming in Anglican. Pages 308–311 of: *Proc. of ECML PKDD 2015, Part III.*

Vákár, Matthijs, Kammar, Ohad, and Staton, Sam. 2019. A domain theory for statistical probabilistic programming. Pages 36:1–36:29 of: *Proc. of POPL 2019.*

Wand, Mitchell, Culpepper, Ryan, Giannakopoulos, Theophilos, and Cobb, Andrew. 2018. Contextual equivalence for a probabilistic language with continuous random variables and recursion, arXiv https://arxiv.org/abs/1807.02809.

5

Probabilistic Couplings from Program Logics

Gilles Barthe
MPI For Security and Privacy, Bochum & IMDEA Software Institute, Madrid
Justin Hsu
University of Wisconsin–Madison

Abstract: *Proof by coupling* is a powerful technique for proving properties about pairs of probabilistic processes. Originally developed by probability theorists, this proof technique has recently found surprising applications in formal verification, enabling clean proofs of probabilistic relational properties. We show that the probabilistic program logic pRHL is a formal logic for proofs by coupling, with logical proof rules capturing reasoning steps in traditional coupling proofs. This connection gives a new method to formally verify probabilistic properties.

5.1 Introduction

Formal verification of probabilistic programs is an active area of research which aims to reason about safety and liveness properties of probabilistic computations. Many important properties for probabilistic programs are naturally expressed in terms of two program executions; for this reason, such properties are called *relational*. While there exist established approaches to verify relational properties of deterministic programs, reasoning about relational properties of probabilistic programs is more challenging. In this chapter we explore a powerful method called *proof by coupling*. This technique—originally developed in probability theory for analyzing Markov Chains—is surprisingly useful for establishing a broad range of relational properties, including:

- **probabilistic equivalence** (also **differential privacy**): two programs produce distributions that are equivalent or suitably close from an observer's point of view. For instance, *differential privacy* requires that two similar inputs—say, the private database and a hypothetical version with one individual's data omitted—yield closely related output distributions;

[a] From *Foundations of Probabilistic Programming*, edited by Gilles Barthe, Joost-Pieter Katoen and Alexandra Silva published 2020 by Cambridge University Press.

- **stochastic domination**: one probabilistic program is more likely than another to produce large outputs;
- **convergence** (also **mixing**): the output distributions of two probabilistic loops approach each other as the loops execute more iterations;
- **truthfulness** (also **Nash equilibrium**): an agent's average utility is larger when reporting an honest value instead of deviating to a misleading value.

At first glance, relational properties appear to be even harder to establish than standard, non-relational properties—instead of analyzing a single probabilistic computation, we now need to deal with two. (Indeed, any property of a single program can be viewed as a relational property between the target program and the trivial, do-nothing program.) However, relational properties often relate two highly similar programs, even comparing the same program on two different inputs. In these cases, we can leverage a powerful abstraction and an associated proof technique from probability theory—*probabilistic coupling* and *proof by coupling*.

The fundamental observation is that probabilistic relational properties compare computations in two different worlds, assuming no particular correlation between random samples. Accordingly, we may freely assume any correlation we like for the purposes of the proof—a relational property holds (or does not hold) regardless of which one we pick. For instance, if two programs generate identical output distributions, this holds whether they share coin flips or take independent samples; relational properties do not require that the two programs use separate randomness. By carefully arranging the correlation, we can reason about two executions as if they were linked in some convenient way.

To take advantage of this freedom, we need some way to design specific correlations between program executions. In principle, this can be a highly challenging task. The two runs may take samples from different distributions, and it is unclear exactly how they can or should share randomness. When the two programs have similar shapes, however, we can link two computations in a step-by-step fashion. First, correlations between intermediate samples can be described by *probabilistic couplings*, joint distributions over pairs. For example, a valid coupling of two fair coin flips could specify that the draws take opposite values; the correlated distribution would produce "(heads, tails)" and "(tails, heads)" with equal probability. A coupling formalizes what it means to share randomness: a single source of randomness simulates draws from two distributions. Since randomness can be shared in different ways, two distributions typically support a variety of distinct couplings.

A *proof by coupling*, then, describes two correlated executions by piecing together couplings for corresponding pairs of sampling instructions. In the course of a proof, we can imagine stepping through the two programs in parallel, selecting couplings along the way. For instance, if we apply the opposite coupling to link a coin flip in one program with a coin flip in the other, we may assume the samples remain opposite when analyzing the rest of the programs. By flowing these relations forward from two initial inputs, a proof by coupling can focus on just pairs of similar executions as it builds up to a coupling between two output distributions. This is the main product of the proof: features of the final coupling imply properties about the output distributions, and hence relational properties about the original programs.

Working in tandem, couplings and proofs by couplings can significantly simplify probabilistic reasoning in several ways.

- **Reduce to one source of randomness.** By analyzing two runs as if they shared a single source of randomness, we can reason about two programs as if they were one.

- **Abstract away probabilities.** Proofs by coupling isolate probabilistic reasoning from the non-probabilistic parts of the proof, which are more straightforward. We only need to think about probabilistic aspects when we select couplings at the sampling instructions; throughout the rest of the programs, we can reason purely in terms of deterministic relations between the two runs.

- **Enable compositional, structured reasoning.** By focusing on each step of an algorithm individually and then smoothly combining the results, the coupling proof technique enables a highly modular style of reasoning guided by the code of the program.

Proofs by coupling are also surprisingly flexible—many probabilistic relational properties, including the examples listed above, can be proved in this style. Individual couplings can also be combined in subtle ways, giving rise to a rich diversity of coupling proofs.

After reviewing probability theory basics (Section 5.2), we introduce probabilistic couplings and their key properties (Section 5.3). Then, we present intuition behind proof by coupling (Section 5.4). To formalize these arguments, we draw a connection to the program logic pRHL (Barthe et al., 2009). Proofs in the pRHL are formal proofs by coupling: valid judgments imply the existence of a coupling, and logical rules describing how to combine couplings to construct new couplings (Section 5.5). We demonstrate several examples of coupling proofs in the logic (Section 5.6), and conclude by briefly discussing related lines of work (Section 5.7).

Bibliographic note. This chapter is an updated and expanded version of the first two chapters of the second author's PhD thesis (Hsu, 2017).

5.2 Preliminaries

A discrete probability distribution associates each element of a set with a number in the unit interval $[0, 1]$, representing its *probability*. In order to model programs that may not terminate, we work with a slightly more general notion called a *sub-distribution*.

Definition 5.1   A (discrete) *sub-distribution* over a countable set $\mathcal{A}$ is a map $\mu : \mathcal{A} \to [0, 1]$ taking each element of $\mathcal{A}$ to a numeric weight such that the weights sum to at most 1:

$$\sum_{a \in \mathcal{A}} \mu(a) \leq 1.$$

We write $\mathbf{SDistr}(\mathcal{A})$ for the set of all sub-distributions over $\mathcal{A}$. When the weights sum to 1, we call μ a *proper* distribution; we write $\mathbf{Distr}(\mathcal{A})$ for the set of all proper distributions over $\mathcal{A}$. The *empty* or *null sub-distribution* $\perp$ assigns weight 0 to all elements.

We work with discrete sub-distributions throughout. While this is certainly a restriction—excluding, for instance, some well-known distributions over the real numbers—many interesting coupling proofs can already be expressed in our setting. Our results should mostly carry over to the continuous setting, as couplings are frequently used on continuous distributions in probability theory, but the general case introduces measure-theoretic technicalities (e.g., working with integrals rather than sums, checking sets are measurable, etc.) that would distract from our primary focus.

We need several concepts and notations related to discrete distributions. First, the probability of a set $S \subseteq \mathcal{A}$ is given by a sum:

$$\mu(S) \triangleq \sum_{a \in S} \mu(a).$$

The *support* of a sub-distribution is the set of elements with positive probability:

$$\mathrm{supp}(\mu) \triangleq \{a \in \mathcal{A} \mid \mu(a) > 0\}.$$

The *weight* of a sub-distribution is the total probability of all elements:

$$|\mu| \triangleq \sum_{a \in \mathcal{A}} \mu(a).$$

Finally, the *expected value* of a real-valued function $f : \mathcal{A} \to \mathbb{R}$ over a sub-distribution μ is

$$\mathbb{E}_{\mu}[f] \triangleq \mathbb{E}_{a \sim \mu}[f(a)] \triangleq \sum_{a \in \mathcal{A}} f(a) \cdot \mu(a).$$

Under light assumptions, the expected value is guaranteed to exist (for instance, when f is a bounded function).

To transform sub-distributions, we can lift a function $f : \mathcal{A} \to \mathcal{B}$ on sets to a map $f^{\sharp} : \textbf{SDistr}(\mathcal{A}) \to \textbf{SDistr}(\mathcal{B})$ via $f^{\sharp}(\mu)(b) \triangleq \mu(f^{-1}(b))$. For example, let $p_1 : \mathcal{A}_1 \times \mathcal{A}_2 \to \mathcal{A}_1$ and $p_2 : \mathcal{A}_1 \times \mathcal{A}_2 \to \mathcal{A}_2$ be the first and second projections from a pair. The corresponding *probabilistic projections* $\pi_1 : \textbf{SDistr}(\mathcal{A}_1 \times \mathcal{A}_2) \to \textbf{SDistr}(\mathcal{A}_1)$ and $\pi_2 : \textbf{SDistr}(\mathcal{A}_1 \times \mathcal{A}_2) \to \textbf{SDistr}(\mathcal{A}_2)$ are defined by

$$\pi_1(\mu)(a_1) \triangleq p_1^{\sharp}(\mu)(a_1) = \sum_{a_2 \in \mathcal{A}_2} \mu(a_1, a_2)$$

$$\pi_2(\mu)(a_2) \triangleq p_2^{\sharp}(\mu)(a_2) = \sum_{a_1 \in \mathcal{A}_1} \mu(a_1, a_2).$$

We call a sub-distribution μ over pairs a *joint sub-distribution*, and the projected sub-distributions $\pi_1(\mu)$ and $\pi_2(\mu)$ the *first* and *second marginals*, respectively.

5.3 Couplings and liftings: definitions and basic properties

A probabilistic coupling models two distributions with a single joint distribution.

Definition 5.2   Given μ_1, μ_2 sub-distributions over $\mathcal{A}_1$ and $\mathcal{A}_2$, a sub-distribution μ over pairs $\mathcal{A}_1 \times \mathcal{A}_2$ is a *coupling* for (μ_1, μ_2) if $\pi_1(\mu) = \mu_1$ and $\pi_2(\mu) = \mu_2$.

Generally, couplings are not unique—different witnesses represent different ways to share randomness between two distributions. To give a few examples, we first introduce some standard distributions.

Definition 5.3   Let $\mathcal{A}$ be a finite, non-empty set. The *uniform distribution* over $\mathcal{A}$, written **Unif**$(\mathcal{A})$, assigns probability $1/|\mathcal{A}|$ to each element. We write **Flip** for the uniform distribution over the set $\{0, 1\}$. This can be viewed as the distribution of a fair coin flip.

Example 5.4 (Couplings from bijections)   We can give two distinct couplings of (**Flip, Flip**):

Identity coupling:

$$\mu_{\text{id}}(a_1, a_2) \triangleq \begin{cases} 1/2 & : a_1 = a_2 \\ 0 & : \text{otherwise.} \end{cases}$$

Negation coupling:

$$\mu_{\neg}(a_1, a_2) \triangleq \begin{cases} 1/2 & : a_1 = 1 - a_2 \\ 0 & : \text{otherwise.} \end{cases}$$

More generally, any bijection $f : \mathcal{A} \to \mathcal{A}$ yields a coupling of $(\mathbf{Unif}(\mathcal{A}), \mathbf{Unif}(\mathcal{A}))$:

$$\mu_f(a_1, a_2) \triangleq \begin{cases} 1/|\mathcal{A}| & : f(a_1) = a_2 \\ 0 & : \text{otherwise.} \end{cases}$$

This coupling matches samples: each sample a from the first distribution is paired with a corresponding sample $f(a)$ from the second distribution. To take two correlated samples from this coupling, we can imagine first sampling from the first distribution, and then applying f to produce a sample for the second distribution. When f is a bijection, this gives a valid coupling for two uniform distributions: viewed separately, both the first and second correlated samples are distributed uniformly.

For more general distributions, if a_1 and a_2 have different probabilities under μ_1 and μ_2 then the correlated distribution cannot return $(a_1, -)$ and $(-, a_2)$ with equal probabilities; for instance, a bijection with $f(a_1) = a_2$ would not give a valid coupling. However, general distributions can be coupled in other ways.

Example 5.5 Let μ be a sub-distribution over $\mathcal{A}$. The *identity coupling* of (μ, μ) is

$$\mu_{\text{id}}(a_1, a_2) \triangleq \begin{cases} \mu(a) & : a_1 = a_2 = a \\ 0 & : \text{otherwise.} \end{cases}$$

Sampling from this coupling yields a pair of equal values.

Example 5.6 Let μ_1, μ_2 be sub-distributions over $\mathcal{A}_1$ and $\mathcal{A}_2$. The *independent* or *trivial* coupling is

$$\mu_\times(a_1, a_2) \triangleq \mu_1(a_1) \cdot \mu_2(a_2).$$

This coupling models μ_1 and μ_2 as independent distributions: sampling from this coupling is equivalent to first sampling from μ_1 and then pairing with an independent draw from μ_2. The coupled distributions must be proper in order to ensure the marginal conditions.

Since any two proper distributions can be coupled by the trivial coupling, the mere existence of a coupling yields little information. Couplings are more useful when the joint distribution satisfies additional conditions, for instance when all elements in the support satisfy some property.

Definition 5.7 (Lifting) Let μ_1, μ_2 be sub-distributions over $\mathcal{A}_1$ and $\mathcal{A}_2$, and let $\mathcal{R} \subseteq \mathcal{A}_1 \times \mathcal{A}_2$ be a relation. A sub-distribution μ over pairs $\mathcal{A}_1 \times \mathcal{A}_2$ is a *witness* for the $\mathcal{R}$-*lifting* of (μ_1, μ_2) if:
(i) μ is a coupling for (μ_1, μ_2), and
(ii) $\text{supp}(\mu) \subseteq \mathcal{R}$.

If there exists μ satisfying these two conditions, we say μ_1 and μ_2 are related by the *lifting of* $\mathcal{R}$ and write

$$\mu_1 \; \mathcal{R}^\sharp \; \mu_2.$$

We typically express $\mathcal{R}$ using set notation, i.e.,

$$\mathcal{R} = \{(a_1, a_2) \in \mathcal{A}_1 \times \mathcal{A}_2 \mid \Phi(a_1, a_2)\}$$

where Φ is some logical formula. When the sets $\mathcal{A}_1$ and $\mathcal{A}_2$ are clear from the context, we leave them implicit and just write Φ, sometimes enclosed by parentheses (Φ) for clarity.

Example 5.8 Many of the couplings we saw before are more precisely described as liftings.

Bijection coupling. For a bijection $f : \mathcal{A} \to \mathcal{A}$, the coupling in Theorem 5.4 witnesses the lifting

$$\mathbf{Unif}(\mathcal{A}) \; G_f^\sharp \; \mathbf{Unif}(\mathcal{A}).$$

where the relation $G_f \triangleq \{(a_1, a_2) \mid f(a_1) = a_2\}$ models the graph of f.
Identity coupling. The coupling in Theorem 5.5 witnesses the lifting

$$\mu \; (=)^\sharp \; \mu.$$

Trivial coupling. The coupling in Theorem 5.6 witnesses the lifting

$$\mu_1 \; \top^\sharp \; \mu_2,$$

where $\top \triangleq \mathcal{A}_1 \times \mathcal{A}_2$ is the trivial relation relating all pairs of elements.

5.3.1 Useful consequences of couplings and liftings

A coupling μ between (μ_1, μ_2) can be used for proving probabilistic properties about μ_1 and μ_2. Surprisingly, many properties already follow from the *existence* of a lifting from some relation R—no analysis of the coupling distribution μ is required. First of all, two coupled distributions have equal weight.

Proposition 5.9 (Equality of weight) *Suppose μ_1 and μ_2 are sub-distributions over $\mathcal{A}$ such that there exists a coupling μ of μ_1 and μ_2. Then $|\mu_1| = |\mu_2|$.*

This follows because μ_1 and μ_2 are both projections of μ, and projections preserve weight. Couplings can also show that two distributions are equal.

Proposition 5.10 (Equality of distributions) *Suppose μ_1 and μ_2 are two sub-distributions over $\mathcal{A}$. Then $\mu_1 = \mu_2$ if and only if $\mu_1 \; (=)^\sharp \; \mu_2$.*

Proof   For the forward direction, define $\mu(a, a) \triangleq \mu_1(a) = \mu_2(a)$ and $\mu(a_1, a_2) \triangleq 0$ otherwise. Evidently, μ has support in the equality relation $(=)$ and also has the desired marginals: $\pi_1(\mu) = \mu_1$ and $\pi_2(\mu) = \mu_2$. Thus μ is a witness to the desired lifting.

For the reverse direction, let the witness be μ. By the support condition, $\pi_1(\mu)(a) = \pi_2(\mu)(a)$ for every $a \in \mathcal{A}$. Since the left and right sides are equal to $\mu_1(a)$ and $\mu_2(a)$ respectively by the marginal conditions, $\mu_1(a) = \mu_2(a)$ for every a. So, μ_1 and μ_2 are equal. □

In some cases we can show results in the converse direction: if a property of two distributions holds, then there exists a particular lifting. To give some examples, we first introduce a powerful equivalence due to Strassen (1965).

Theorem 5.11   *Let μ_1, μ_2 be sub-distributions over $\mathcal{A}_1$ and $\mathcal{A}_2$, and let $\mathcal{R}$ be a binary relation over $\mathcal{A}_1$ and $\mathcal{A}_2$. Then $\mu_1 \ \mathcal{R}^\sharp \ \mu_2$ implies $\mu_1(\mathcal{S}_1) \leq \mu_2(\mathcal{R}(\mathcal{S}_1))$ for every subset $\mathcal{S}_1 \subseteq \mathcal{A}_1$, where $\mathcal{R}(\mathcal{S}_1) \subseteq \mathcal{A}_2$ is the image of $\mathcal{S}_1$ under $\mathcal{R}$:*

$$\mathcal{R}(\mathcal{S}_1) \triangleq \{a_2 \in \mathcal{A}_2 \mid \exists a_1 \in \mathcal{A}_1, \ (a_1, a_2) \in \mathcal{R}\}.$$

(For instance, if $\mathcal{A}_1 = \mathcal{A}_2 = \mathbb{N}$ and $\mathcal{R}$ is the relation $\leq$, then $\mathcal{R}(\mathcal{S})$ is the set of all natural numbers larger than $\min \mathcal{S}$.) The converse holds if μ_1 and μ_2 have equal weight.

Strassen proved Theorem 5.11 for continuous (proper) distributions using deep results from probability theory. In our discrete setting, there is an elementary proof by the maximum flow-minimum cut theorem (see, e.g., (Kleinberg and Tardos, 2005)). For now, we use this theorem to illustrate a few more useful consequences of liftings. First, couplings can bound the probability of an event in the first distribution by the probability of an event in the second distribution.

Proposition 5.12   *Suppose μ_1, μ_2 are sub-distributions over $\mathcal{A}_1$ and $\mathcal{A}_2$ respectively, and consider two subsets $\mathcal{S}_1 \subseteq \mathcal{A}_1$ and $\mathcal{S}_2 \subseteq \mathcal{A}_2$. Then,*

$$\mu_1 \ \{(a_1, a_2) \mid a_1 \in \mathcal{S}_1 \rightarrow a_2 \in \mathcal{S}_2\}^\sharp \ \mu_2$$

implies $\mu_1(\mathcal{S}_1) \leq \mu_2(\mathcal{S}_2)$. The converse holds when μ_1 and μ_2 have equal weight.

Proof   Let $\mathcal{R}$ be the relation $\{(a_1, a_2) \mid a_1 \in \mathcal{S}_1 \rightarrow a_2 \in \mathcal{S}_2\}$. The forward direction is immediate by Theorem 5.11, taking the subset $\mathcal{S}_1$. For the reverse direction, consider any non-empty subset $\mathcal{T}_1 \subseteq \mathcal{A}_1$. If $\mathcal{T}_1$ is not contained in $\mathcal{S}_1$, then $\mathcal{R}(\mathcal{T}_1) = \mathcal{A}_2$ and $\mu_1(\mathcal{T}_1) \leq \mu_2(\mathcal{R}(\mathcal{T}_1))$ since μ_1 and μ_2 have equal weight. Otherwise $\mathcal{R}(\mathcal{T}_1) = \mathcal{S}_2$, so

$$\mu_1(\mathcal{T}_1) \leq \mu_1(\mathcal{S}_1) \leq \mu_2(\mathcal{S}_2) = \mu_2(\mathcal{R}(\mathcal{T}_1)).$$

Theorem 5.11 gives the desired lifting:

$$\mu_1 \; \{(a_1, a_2) \mid a_1 \in \mathcal{S}_1 \to a_2 \in \mathcal{S}_2\}^{\sharp} \; \mu_2. \qquad \qquad \square$$

A slightly more subtle consequence is *stochastic domination*, an order on distributions over an ordered set.

Definition 5.13 Let $(\mathcal{A}, \leq_{\mathcal{A}})$ be a partially ordered set. For every $k \in \mathcal{A}$, let $k \uparrow \triangleq \{a \in \mathcal{A} \mid k \leq_{\mathcal{A}} a\}$. Suppose μ_1, μ_2 are sub-distributions over $\mathcal{A}$. We say μ_2 *stochastically dominates* μ_1, denoted $\mu_1 \leq_{sd} \mu_2$, if

$$\mu_1(k \uparrow) \leq \mu_2(k \uparrow)$$

for every $k \in \mathcal{A}$.

For an example of stochastic domination, take distributions over the natural numbers $\mathbb{N}$ with the usual order and μ_1 places weight 1 on 0 while μ_2 places weight 1 on 1.

Stochastic domination is precisely the probabilistic lifting of the order relation.

Proposition 5.14 *Suppose μ_1, μ_2 are sub-distributions over a set $\mathcal{A}$ with a partial order $\leq_{\mathcal{A}}$. Then $\mu_1 \; (\leq_{\mathcal{A}})^{\sharp} \; \mu_2$ implies $\mu_1 \leq_{sd} \mu_2$. The converse also holds when μ_1 and μ_2 have equal weight, as long as the upwards closed subsets of $\mathcal{A}$ are $\emptyset$, $\mathcal{A}$ and $k \uparrow$ with $k \in \mathcal{A}$ (e.g., $\mathcal{A} = \mathbb{N}$ or $\mathbb{Z}$ with the usual order).*

Proof Let $\mathcal{R} \triangleq (\leq_{\mathcal{A}})$. For the forward direction, Theorem 5.11 gives

$$\mu_1(k \uparrow) \leq \mu_2(\mathcal{R}(k \uparrow)) = \mu_2(k \uparrow).$$

This holds for all $k \in \mathcal{A}$, establishing $\mu_1 \leq_{sd} \mu_2$.

For the converse, suppose $\mu_1 \leq_{sd} \mu_2$ and μ_1 and μ_2 have equal weights, and let $\mathcal{S} \subseteq \mathcal{A}$ be any subset. Note that $\mathcal{R}(\mathcal{S})$ is upwards closed so we proceed by case analysis on $\mathcal{R}(\mathcal{S})$. If $\mathcal{R}(\mathcal{S}) = \emptyset$, then $\mathcal{S}$ is also empty and $\mu_1(\mathcal{S}) \leq \mu_2(\mathcal{R}(\mathcal{S}))$. If $\mathcal{R}(\mathcal{S}) = \mathcal{A}$, then $\mu_1(\mathcal{S}) \leq \mu_2(\mathcal{R}(\mathcal{S}))$ since μ_1 and μ_2 have equal weights. Finally, if $\mathcal{R}(\mathcal{S})$ is $k \uparrow$, and we have

$$\mu_1(\mathcal{S}) \leq \mu_1(\mathcal{R}(\mathcal{S})) = \mu_1(k \uparrow) \leq \mu_2(k \uparrow) = \mu_2(\mathcal{R}(\mathcal{S})),$$

where the middle inequality is by stochastic domination. Theorem 5.11 implies $\mu_1 \; (\leq_{\mathcal{A}})^{\sharp} \; \mu_2$. $\qquad \square$

Finally, a typical application of coupling proofs is showing that two distributions are close together.

Definition 5.15 Let μ_1, μ_2 be sub-distributions over $\mathcal{A}$. The *total variation distance* (also known as *TV-distance* or *statistical distance*) between μ_1 and μ_2 is defined as

$$d_{\text{tv}}(\mu_1, \mu_2) \triangleq \frac{1}{2} \sum_{a \in \mathcal{A}} |\mu_1(a) - \mu_2(a)| = \max_{S \subseteq \mathcal{A}} |\mu_1(S) - \mu_2(S)|.$$

In particular, the total variation distance bounds the difference in probabilities of any event.

Couplings are closely related to TV-distance, as captured by the following theorem. Theorem 5.16 is the fundamental result behind the so-called *coupling method* (Aldous, 1983), a technique to show two probabilistic processes converge by constructing a coupling that causes the processes to become equal with high probability. Unlike the previous facts, the target property about μ_1 and μ_2 does not directly follow from the existence of a lifting—we need more detailed information about the coupling μ.

Theorem 5.16 (see, e.g., Lindvall (2002); Levin et al. (2009))   *Let μ_1 and μ_2 be sub-distributions over $\mathcal{A}$ and let μ be a coupling. Then*

$$d_{tv}(\mu_1, \mu_2) \leq \Pr_{(a_1,a_2) \sim \mu} [a_1 \neq a_2].$$

In particular, if $S \subseteq \mathcal{A} \times \mathcal{A}$ and μ witnesses

$$\mu_1 \ \{(a_1, a_2) \in \mathcal{A} \times \mathcal{A} \mid (a_1, a_2) \in S \rightarrow a_1 = a_2\}^{\sharp} \ \mu_2,$$

then their TV-distance is bounded by the probability of the complement of S w.r.t. μ:

$$d_{tv}(\mu_1, \mu_2) \leq \Pr_{(a_1,a_2) \sim \mu} [(a_1, a_2) \notin S].$$

Moreover, there exists a coupling μ, called maximal coupling, *such that*

$$d_{tv}(\mu_1, \mu_2) = \Pr_{(a_1,a_2) \sim \mu} [a_1 \neq a_2].$$

Proof   We only prove the inequality. Let μ be a coupling of μ_1 and μ_2. We have:

$$d_{\text{tv}}(\mu_1, \mu_2)$$

$$= \max_P \left| \Pr_{a_1 \sim \mu_1} [a_1 \in P] - \Pr_{a_2 \sim \mu_2} [a_2 \in P] \right|$$

$$= \max_P \left| \Pr_{(a_1,a_2) \sim \mu} [a_1 \in P] - \Pr_{(a_1,a_2) \sim \mu} [a_2 \in P] \right|$$

$$= \max_P \left| \Pr_{(a_1,a_2) \sim \mu} [a_1 \in P \wedge a_1 = a_2] + \Pr_{(a_1,a_2) \sim \mu} [a_1 \in P \wedge a_1 \neq a_2] \right.$$

$$\left. - \Pr_{(a_1,a_2) \sim \mu} [a_2 \in P \wedge a_1 = a_2] - \Pr_{(a_1,a_2) \sim \mu} [a_2 \in P \wedge a_1 \neq a_2] \right|$$

$$= \max_{P} \left| \Pr_{(a_1,a_2)\sim\mu} [a_1 \in P \wedge a_1 \neq a_2] - \Pr_{(a_1,a_2)\sim\mu} [a_2 \in P \wedge a_1 \neq a_2] \right|$$

$$\leq \max_{P}(\max(\Pr_{(a_1,a_2)\sim\mu} [a_1 \in P \wedge a_1 \neq a_2], \Pr_{(a_1,a_2)\sim\mu} [a_2 \in P \wedge a_1 \neq a_2]))$$

$$\leq \Pr_{(a_1,a_2)\sim\mu} [a_1 \neq a_2]$$

The proof is similar when μ witnesses

$$\mu_1 \{(a_1,a_2) \in \mathcal{A} \times \mathcal{A} \mid (a_1,a_2) \in S \to a_1 = a_2\}^\sharp \mu_2$$

by case analysis on $(a_1,a_2) \in S$ rather than $a_1 = a_2$. $\qquad\qquad\qquad\square$

5.3.2 Composition properties

Couplings and liftings are closed under various notions of composition. Most important for our purposes will be sequential composition.

Theorem 5.17 *Let $\mu \in \mathbf{Distr}(\mathcal{A}_1 \times \mathcal{A}_2)$ witness $\mu_1 \; R^\sharp \; \mu_2$, where $\mu_1 \in \mathbf{Distr}(\mathcal{A}_1)$ and $\mu_2 \in \mathbf{Distr}(\mathcal{A}_2)$ and $R \subseteq \mathcal{A}_1 \times \mathcal{A}_2$. Let $M : \mathcal{A}_1 \times \mathcal{A}_2 \to \mathbf{Distr}(\mathcal{B}_1 \times \mathcal{B}_2)$ such that $M(a_1,a_2)$ witnesses for $M_1(a_1) \; S^\sharp \; M_2(a_2)$ for every $(a_1,a_2) \in R$. Then $\mathbf{bind}(\mu,M)$ witnesses*

$$\mathbf{bind}(\mu_1,M_1) \; S^\sharp \; \mathbf{bind}(\mu_2,M_2).$$

While this theorem may appear a bit cryptic at this point, it will play a key role in later developments—informally, this result enables us to build a coupling for a sequential composition of two processes by constructing a coupling for each piece.

5.3.3 Couplings and liftings for Markov chains

The previous results suggest an approach to proving properties of two distributions: demonstrate there exists a coupling of a particular form. This approach is indirect, but surprisingly fruitful, when employed to prove properties about probabilistic processes modelled as discrete-time Markov chains. Recall that a discrete-time Markov chain is given by a state space $\mathcal{A}$, which we assume to be discrete, by an initial distribution $\mu \in \mathbf{Distr}(\mathcal{A})$ and by a transition map $t : \mathcal{A} \to \mathbf{Distr}(\mathcal{A})$.

Couplings and R-liftings naturally extend to (discrete-time) Markov chains.

Definition 5.18 A coupling between two Markov chains given by initial sub-distributions μ_1 and μ_2 and transition functions t_1 and t_2 is a Markov chain given by an initial sub-distributions μ and a joint transition function $t : (\mathcal{A} \times \mathcal{A}) \to \mathbf{Distr}(\mathcal{A} \times \mathcal{A})$ such that:

- μ is a coupling for μ_1 and μ_2;

- for every x_1 and x_2, $t(x_1, x_2)$ is a coupling for $t_1(x_1)$ and $t_2(x_2)$.

The notion of $\mathcal{R}$-lifting extends similarly.

Definition 5.19   Let $\mathcal{R} \subseteq \mathcal{A}_1 \times \mathcal{A}_2$ be a relation. A $\mathcal{R}$-lifting between two Markov chains given by initial sub-distributions μ_1 and μ_2 and transition functions t_1 and t_2 is a Markov chain given by an initial sub-distributions μ and a joint transition function $t : (\mathcal{A} \times \mathcal{A}) \rightarrow \mathbf{Distr}(\mathcal{A} \times \mathcal{A})$ such that:

- μ is a $\mathcal{R}$-lifting for μ_1 and μ_2;
- for every $(x_1, x_2) \in \mathcal{R}$, $t(x_1, x_2)$ is a $\mathcal{R}$-lifting for $t_1(x_1)$ and $t_2(x_2)$.

The definition of $\mathcal{R}$-lifting naturally extends to families of relations $(\mathcal{R}_i)_{i \in \mathbb{N}}$. In this case one requires that the sub-distributions obtained by iterating k times the transition functions on the initial sub-distributions are related by $\mathcal{R}_k$. Other definitions relax these conditions; for instance, in shift couplings the relation needs not be pointwise, i.e. one can relate the two processes at different steps k_1 and k_2.

5.4 Proof by coupling

Finding appropriate couplings requires ingenuity and is often the main intellectual challenge when carrying out a proof by coupling. Given a conjecture, how are we supposed to find a witness distribution with the desired properties? To address this challenge, probability theorists have developed a powerful proof technique called *proof by coupling*. We close this section with an informal explanation and an example of the proof technique in action.

Given two probabilistic processes, a proof by coupling builds a coupling for the output distributions by coupling intermediate samples. In a bit more detail, we imagine stepping through the processes in parallel, one step at a time, starting from two inputs, and decoupling the transition function into a random sampling and a deterministic computation. For the samplings, we pick a valid coupling for the sampled distributions. The selected couplings induce a relation on samples, which we can assume when analyzing the rest of the computation (i.e. the deterministic part). For instance, by selecting couplings for earlier samples carefully, we may be able to assume the samplings yield equal values.

Example 5.20   Consider a probabilistic process that tosses a fair coin T times and returns the number of heads. If μ_1, μ_2 are the output distributions from running this process for $T = T_1, T_2$ iterations respectively and $T_1 \leq T_2$, then $\mu_1 \leq_{sd} \mu_2$.

Proof by coupling   For the first T_1 iterations, couple the coin flips to be equal—this ensures that after the first T_1 iterations, the coupled counts are equal. The remaining $T_2 - T_1$ coin flips in the second run can only increase the second count, while preserving the first count. Therefore under the coupling, the first count is no more than the second count at termination, establishing $\mu_1 \leq_{sd} \mu_2$. □

For readers unfamiliar with these proofs, this argument may appear bewildering. The coupling is constructed implicitly, and some of the steps are mysterious. To clarify such proofs, a natural idea is to design a formal logic describing coupling proofs. Somewhat surprisingly, the logic we are looking for was already proposed in the formal verification literature, originally for verifying security of cryptographic constructions.

5.5 A formal logic for coupling proofs

We will work with the logic PRHL (probabilistic Relational Hoare Logic) proposed by Barthe et al. (2009). Before detailing its connection to coupling proofs, we provide a brief introduction to program logics.

5.5.1 Program logics: A brief primer

A *logic* consists of a collection of formulas, also known as *judgments*, and an interpretation describing what it means—in typical, standard mathematics—for judgments to be true (*valid*). While it is possible to prove judgments valid directly by using regular mathematical arguments, this is often inconvenient as the interpretation may be quite complicated. Instead, many logics provide a *proof system*, a set of *logical rules* describing how to combine known judgments (the *premises*) to prove a new judgment (the *conclusion*). Each rule represents a single step in a formal proof. Starting from judgments given by rules with no premises (*axioms*), we can successively apply rules to prove new judgments, building a tree-shaped *derivation* culminating in a single judgment. To ensure that this final judgment is valid, each logical rule should be *sound*: if the premises are valid, then so is the conclusion. Soundness is a basic property, typically one of the first results to be proved about a logic.

Program logics were first introduced by Hoare (1969), building on earlier ideas by Floyd (1967); they are also called *Floyd-Hoare logics*. These logics are really two logics in one: the *assertion logic*, where formulas describe program states, and the program logic proper, where judgments describe program behavior. A judgment in the program logic consists of three parts: a program c and two *assertions* Φ and Ψ from the assertion logic. The *pre-condition* Φ describes the initial conditions before executing c (for instance, assumptions about the input), while the *post-condition* Ψ describes the final conditions after executing c (for instance, properties of the output). Hoare (1969) proposed the original logical rules, which construct a judgment for a program by combining judgments for its sub-programs. This compositional style of reasoning is a hallmark of program logics.

By varying the interpretation of judgments, the assertion logic, and the logical rules, Floyd-Hoare logics can establish a variety of properties about different kinds of imperative programs. Notable extensions reason about non-determinism (Dijkstra, 1976), pointers and memory allocation (O'Hearn et al., 2001; Reynolds, 2001, 2002), concurrency (O'Hearn, 2007), and more. (Readers should consult a survey for a more comprehensive account of Floyd-Hoare logic (Apt, 1981, 1983; Jones, 2003).)

In this tradition, Barthe et al. (2009) introduced the logic pRHL targeting security properties in cryptography. Compared to standard program logics, there are two twists: each judgment describes *two* programs,[1] and programs can use random sampling. In short, pRHL is a *probabilistic Relational Hoare Logic*. Judgments encode probabilistic relational properties of two programs, where a post-condition describes a probabilistic liftings between two output distributions. More importantly, the proof rules represent different ways to combine liftings, formalizing various steps in coupling proofs. Accordingly, we will interpret pRHL as a formal logic for proofs by coupling.

To build up to this connection, we first provide a brief overview of a core version of pRHL, reviewing the programming language, the judgments and their interpretation, and the logical rules.

5.5.2 *The logic pRHL: the programming language*

Programs in pRHL are defined in terms of *expressions* $\mathcal{E}$ including constants, like the integers and booleans, as well as combinations of constants and variables with primitive operations, like addition and subtraction. We suppose $\mathcal{E}$ also includes terms for basic datatypes, like tuples and lists. Concretely, $\mathcal{E}$ is inductively defined by the following grammar:

$$
\begin{array}{llll}
\mathcal{E} & ::= & \mathcal{X} \mid \mathcal{L} & \text{(variables)} \\
& \mid & \mathbb{Z} \mid \mathcal{E} + \mathcal{E} \mid \mathcal{E} - \mathcal{E} \mid \mathcal{E} \cdot \mathcal{E} & \text{(numbers)} \\
& \mid & \mathbb{B} \mid \mathcal{E} \wedge \mathcal{E} \mid \mathcal{E} \vee \mathcal{E} \mid \neg \mathcal{E} \mid \mathcal{E} = \mathcal{E} \mid \mathcal{E} < \mathcal{E} & \text{(booleans)} \\
& \mid & (\mathcal{E}, \ldots, \mathcal{E}) \mid \pi_i(\mathcal{E}) \mid [] \mid \mathcal{E} :: \mathcal{E} \mid O(\mathcal{E}) & \text{(tuples, lists, operations)}
\end{array}
$$

Expressions can mention two classes of variables: a countable set $\mathcal{X}$ of *program variables*, which can be modified by the program, and a set $\mathcal{L}$ of *logical variables*,

---

[1] Logics reasoning about two programs are known as *relational program logics* and were first considered by Benton (2004); see Section 5.7 for a discussion of other prior systems.

which model fixed parameters. Expressions are typed as numbers, booleans, tuples, or lists, and primitive operations O have typed signatures; we consider only well-typed expressions throughout. The expressions $(\mathcal{E}, \ldots, \mathcal{E})$ and $\pi_i(\mathcal{E})$ construct and project from a tuple, respectively; [] is the empty list, and $\mathcal{E} :: \mathcal{E}$ adds an element to the head of a list. We typically use the letter e for expressions, $x, y, z, \ldots$ for program variables, and lower-case Greek letters $(\alpha, \beta, \ldots)$ and capital Roman letters $(N, M, \ldots)$ for logical variables.

We write $\mathcal{V}$ for the countable set of *values*, including integers, booleans, tuples, finite lists, etc. We can interpret expressions given maps from variables and logical variables to values.

Definition 5.21 Program states are *memories*, maps $\mathcal{X} \to \mathcal{V}$; we usually write m for a memory and **State** for the set of memories. *Logical contexts* are maps $\mathcal{L} \to \mathcal{V}$; we usually write ρ for a logical context.

We interpret an expression e as a function $[\![e]\!]_\rho : \textbf{State} \to \mathcal{V}$ in the usual way, for instance:

$$[\![e_1 + e_2]\!]_\rho m \triangleq [\![e_1]\!]_\rho m + [\![e_2]\!]_\rho m.$$

Likewise, we interpret primitive operations o as functions $[\![o]\!]_\rho : \mathcal{V} \to \mathcal{V}$, so that

$$[\![o(e)]\!]_\rho m \triangleq [\![o]\!]_\rho([\![e]\!]_\rho m).$$

We fix a set $\mathcal{DE}$ of *distribution expressions* to model primitive distributions that our programs can sample from. For simplicity, we suppose for now that each distribution expression d is interpreted as a uniform distribution over a finite set. So, we have the coin flip and uniform distributions:

$$\mathcal{DE} := \textbf{Flip} \quad | \quad \textbf{Unif}(\mathcal{E})$$

where $\mathcal{E}$ is a list, representing the space of samples. We will introduce other primitive distributions as needed. To interpret distribution expressions, we define $[\![d]\!]_\rho : \textbf{State} \to \textbf{Distr}(\mathcal{V})$; for instance,

$$[\![\textbf{Unif}(e)]\!]_\rho m \triangleq \mathcal{U}([\![e]\!]_\rho m)$$

where $\mathcal{U}(\mathcal{S})$ is the mathematical uniform distribution over a set $\mathcal{S}$.

Now let's see the programming language. We work with a standard imperative language with random sampling. The programs, also called *commands* or *statements*, are defined inductively:

$$
\begin{array}{llll}
C & := & \textbf{skip} & \text{(no-op)} \\
  & | & \mathcal{X} \leftarrow \mathcal{E} & \text{(assignment)} \\
  & | & \mathcal{X} \xleftarrow{\$} \mathcal{DE} & \text{(sampling)}
\end{array}
$$

$C; C$	(sequencing)
if $\mathcal{E}$ **then** C **else** C	(conditional)
while $\mathcal{E}$ **do** C	(loop)

We assume throughout that programs are well-typed; for instance, the guard expressions in conditionals and loops must be boolean.

We interpret each command as a mathematical function from states to sub-distributions over output states; this function is known as the *semantics* of a command. Since the set of program variables and the set of values are countable, the set of states is also countable so sub-distributions over states are discrete. To interpret commands, we use two basic constructions on sub-distributions.

Definition 5.22   The function **unit** : $\mathcal{A} \to \mathbf{SDistr}(\mathcal{A})$ maps every element $a \in \mathcal{A}$ to the sub-distribution that places probability 1 on a. The function **bind** : $\mathbf{SDistr}(\mathcal{A}) \times (\mathcal{A} \to \mathbf{SDistr}(\mathcal{B})) \to \mathbf{SDistr}(\mathcal{B})$ is defined by

$$\mathbf{bind}(\mu, f)(b) \triangleq \sum_{a \in \mathcal{A}} \mu(a) \cdot f(a)(b).$$

Intuitively, **bind** applies a randomized function on a distribution over inputs.

We use a discrete version of the semantics considered by Kozen (1981), presented in Fig. 5.1; we write $m[x \mapsto v]$ for the memory m with variable x updated to hold v, and $a \mapsto b(a)$ for the function mapping a to $b(a)$. The most complicated case is for loops. The sub-distribution $\mu^{(i)}(m)$ models executions that exit after entering the loop body at most i times, starting from initial memory m. For the base case $i = 0$, the sub-distribution either returns m with probability 1 when the guard is false and the loop exits immediately, or returns the null sub-distribution $\bot$ when the guard is true. The cases $i > 0$ are defined recursively, by unrolling the loop.

Note that $\mu^{(i)}$ are increasing in i: $\mu^{(i)}(m) \leq \mu^{(j)}(m)$ for all $m \in \mathbf{State}$ and $i \leq j$. In particular, the weights of the sub-distributions are increasing. Since the weights are at most 1, the approximants converge to a sub-distribution as i tends to infinity by the monotone convergence theorem (see, e.g., Rudin (1976, Theorem 11.28), taking the discrete counting measure over **State**).

5.5.3 The logic PRHL: judgments and validity

The program logic PRHL features judgments of the following form:

$$c_1 \sim c_2 : \Phi \implies \Psi$$

Here, c_1 and c_2 are commands and Φ and Ψ are predicates on pairs of memories. To describe the inputs and outputs of c_1 and c_2, each predicate can mention two copies

$$[\![\mathbf{skip}]\!]_\rho m \triangleq \mathbf{unit}(m)$$

$$[\![x \leftarrow e]\!]_\rho m \triangleq \mathbf{unit}(m[x \mapsto [\![e]\!]_\rho m])$$

$$[\![x \xleftarrow{\$} d]\!]_\rho m \triangleq \mathbf{bind}([\![d]\!]_\rho m, v \mapsto \mathbf{unit}(m[x \mapsto v]))$$

$$[\![c; c']\!]_\rho m \triangleq \mathbf{bind}([\![c]\!]_\rho m, [\![c']\!]_\rho)$$

$$[\![\mathbf{if} \ e \ \mathbf{then} \ c \ \mathbf{else} \ c']\!]_\rho m \triangleq \begin{cases} [\![c]\!]_\rho m & : [\![e]\!]_\rho m = \mathbf{true} \\ [\![c']\!]_\rho m & : [\![e]\!]_\rho m = \mathbf{false} \end{cases}$$

$$[\![\mathbf{while} \ e \ \mathbf{do} \ c]\!]_\rho m \triangleq \lim_{i \to \infty} \mu^{(i)}(m)$$

$$\mu^{(i)}(m) \triangleq \begin{cases} \bot & : i = 0 \wedge [\![e]\!]_\rho m = \mathbf{true} \\ \mathbf{unit}(m) & : i = 0 \wedge [\![e]\!]_\rho m = \mathbf{false} \\ \mathbf{bind}([\![\mathbf{if} \ e \ \mathbf{then} \ c]\!]_\rho m, \mu^{(i-1)}) & : i > 0 \end{cases}$$

Figure 5.1 Semantics of programs

$x\langle 1 \rangle$, $x\langle 2 \rangle$ of each program variable x; these *tagged* variables refer to the value of x in the executions of c_1 and c_2 respectively.

Definition 5.23 Let $X\langle 1 \rangle$ and $X\langle 2 \rangle$ be the sets of *tagged variables*, finite sets of variable names tagged with $\langle 1 \rangle$ or $\langle 2 \rangle$ respectively:

$$X\langle 1 \rangle \triangleq \{x\langle 1 \rangle \mid x \in X\} \quad \text{and} \quad X\langle 2 \rangle \triangleq \{x\langle 2 \rangle \mid x \in X\}.$$

Let **State**$\langle 1 \rangle$ and **State**$\langle 2 \rangle$ be the sets of *tagged memories*, maps from tagged variables to values:

$$\mathbf{State}\langle 1 \rangle \triangleq X\langle 1 \rangle \to \mathcal{V} \quad \text{and} \quad \mathbf{State}\langle 2 \rangle \triangleq X\langle 2 \rangle \to \mathcal{V}.$$

Let **State**$_\times$ be the set of *product memories*, which combine two tagged memories:

$$\mathbf{State}_\times \triangleq X\langle 1 \rangle \uplus X\langle 2 \rangle \to \mathcal{V}.$$

For notational convenience we identify **State**$_\times$ with pairs of memories **State**$\langle 1 \rangle \times$ **State**$\langle 2 \rangle$; for $m_1 \in$ **State**$\langle 1 \rangle$ and $m_2 \in$ **State**$\langle 2 \rangle$, we write (m_1, m_2) for the product memory and we use the usual projections on pairs to extract untagged memories from the product memory:

$$p_1(m_1, m_2) \triangleq |m_1| \quad \text{and} \quad p_2(m_1, m_2) \triangleq |m_2|,$$

where the memory $|m| \in$ **State** has all variables in X. For commands c and expressions e with variables in X, we write $c\langle 1 \rangle$, $c\langle 2 \rangle$ and $e\langle 1 \rangle$, $e\langle 2 \rangle$ for the corresponding *tagged commands* and *tagged expressions* with variables in $X\langle 1 \rangle$ and $X\langle 2 \rangle$.

We consider a set $\mathcal{P}$ of *predicates* (*assertions*) from first-order logic defined by the following grammar:

$$\mathcal{P} := \quad \mathcal{E}\langle 1/2 \rangle = \mathcal{E}\langle 1/2 \rangle \quad | \quad \mathcal{E}\langle 1/2 \rangle < \mathcal{E}\langle 1/2 \rangle \quad | \quad \mathcal{E}\langle 1/2 \rangle \in \mathcal{E}\langle 1/2 \rangle$$
$$| \quad \top \quad | \quad \bot \quad | \quad O(\mathcal{E}\langle 1/2 \rangle, \ldots, \mathcal{E}\langle 1/2 \rangle) \qquad \text{(predicates)}$$
$$| \quad \mathcal{P} \wedge \mathcal{P} \quad | \quad \mathcal{P} \vee \mathcal{P} \quad | \quad \neg \mathcal{P} \quad | \quad \mathcal{P} \to \mathcal{P} \quad | \quad \forall \mathcal{L} \in \mathbb{Z}, \mathcal{P} \quad | \quad \exists \mathcal{L} \in \mathbb{Z}, \mathcal{P}$$
$$\text{(first-order formulas)}$$

We typically use capital Greek letters $(\Phi, \Psi, \Theta, \Xi, \ldots)$ for predicates. $\mathcal{E}\langle 1/2 \rangle$ denotes an expression where program variables are tagged with $\langle 1 \rangle$ or $\langle 2 \rangle$; tags may be mixed within an expression. We consider the usual binary predicates $\{=, <, \in, \ldots\}$ where $e \in e'$ means e is a member of the list e', and we take the always-true and always-false predicates $\top$ and $\bot$, and a set O of other predicates. Predicates can be combined using the usual connectives $\{\wedge, \vee, \neg, \to\}$ and can quantify over first-order types (e.g., the integers, tuples, etc.). We will often interpret a boolean expression e as the predicate $e = \textbf{true}$.

Predicates are interpreted as sets of product memories.

Definition 5.24   Let Φ be a predicate. Given a logical context ρ, Φ is interpreted as a set $[\![\Phi]\!]_\rho \subseteq \textbf{State}_\times$ in the expected way, e.g.,

$$[\![e_1\langle 1 \rangle < e_2\langle 2 \rangle]\!]_\rho \triangleq \{(m_1, m_2) \in \textbf{State}_\times \mid [\![e_1]\!]_\rho m_1 < [\![e_2]\!]_\rho m_2\}.$$

We can inject a predicate on single memories into a predicate on product memories; we call the resulting predicate *one-sided* since it constrains just one of two memories.

Definition 5.25   Let Φ be a predicate on **State**. We define formulas $\Phi\langle 1 \rangle$ and $\Phi\langle 2 \rangle$ by replacing all program variables x in Φ with $x\langle 1 \rangle$ and $x\langle 2 \rangle$, respectively, and we define

$$[\![\Phi\langle 1 \rangle]\!]_\rho \triangleq \{(m_1, m_2) \mid m_1 \in [\![\Phi]\!]_\rho\} \quad \text{and} \quad [\![\Phi\langle 2 \rangle]\!]_\rho \triangleq \{(m_1, m_2) \mid m_2 \in [\![\Phi]\!]_\rho\}.$$

Valid judgments in PRHL relate two output distributions by lifting the post-condition.

Definition 5.26 (Barthe et al. (2009))   A judgment is *valid* in logical context ρ, written $\rho \models c_1 \sim c_2 : \Phi \implies \Psi$, if for any two memories $(m_1, m_2) \in [\![\Phi]\!]_\rho$ there exists a lifting of Ψ relating the output distributions:

$$[\![c_1]\!]_\rho m_1 \; [\![\Psi]\!]_\rho^\sharp \; [\![c_2]\!]_\rho m_2.$$

For example, a valid judgment

$$\models c_1 \sim c_2 : \Phi \implies (=),$$

states that for any two input memories (m_1, m_2) satisfying Φ, the resulting output distributions from running c_1 and c_2 are related by lifted equality; by Theorem 5.10, these output distributions must be equal.

5.5.4 The logic PRHL: the proof rules

Valid judgments in PRHL state that the output distributions of two programs are related in a specific way. However, it is generally not possible to directly prove validity—even simple probabilistic programs with loops can produce highly complex output distributions, and we typically do not have a description of the output distribution that is more precise than the probabilistic program itself.

To make reasoning about probabilistic programs more tractable, PRHL includes a collection of logical rules to inductively build up a proof of a new judgment from known judgments, combining proofs about sub-programs into proofs about larger programs. The rules are superficially similar to those from standard Hoare logic. However, the interpretation of judgments in terms of liftings means some rules in PRHL are not valid in Hoare logic, and vice versa.

Before describing the rules, we introduce some necessary notation. A system of logical rules inductively defines a set of *derivable* formulas; we use the head symbol ⊢ to mark such formulas. As is standard in logic, the premises in each logical rule are written above the horizontal line, and the single conclusion is written below the line; for easy reference, the name of each rule is given to the left of the line.

The main premises are judgments in the program logic, but rules may also use other *side-conditions*. For instance, many rules require an assertion logic formula to be valid in all memories. Other side-conditions state that a program is terminating, or that certain variables are not modified by the program. We use the head symbol ⊨ to mark valid side-conditions; while we could give a separate proof system for these premises, in practice they are simple enough to check directly.

We also use notation for substitution in assertions. We write $\Phi\{e/x\}$ for the formula Φ with every occurrence of the variable x replaced by e. Similarly, $\Phi\{v_1, v_2/x_1\langle 1\rangle, x_2\langle 2\rangle\}$ is the formula Φ where occurrences of the tagged variables $x_1\langle 1\rangle, x_2\langle 2\rangle$ are replaced by v_1, v_2 respectively.

Now, we take a tour through the logical rules of PRHL. While most of these rules were proposed in prior works, we use the coupling interpretation to give a new way of thinking about what the rules mean. It turns out that certain steps of the informal coupling proofs we saw in Section 5.4 correspond to specific logical rules in PRHL, seen from the right perspective. We summarize this reading in Section 5.5.

One important feature of coupling proofs can already be seen in the form of the proof rules: though the notion of validity and target properties are probabilisitic—i.e., they describe pairs of probability *distributions*—assertions describe individual *mem-*

$$\textsc{Skip} \ \frac{}{\vdash \mathbf{skip} \sim \mathbf{skip} : \Phi \implies \Phi}$$

$$\textsc{Assn} \ \frac{}{\vdash x_1 \leftarrow e_1 \sim x_2 \leftarrow e_2 : \Psi \{e_1\langle 1\rangle, e_2\langle 2\rangle / x_1\langle 1\rangle, x_2\langle 2\rangle\} \implies \Psi}$$

$$\textsc{Sample} \ \frac{f : \mathrm{supp}(d_1) \to \mathrm{supp}(d_2) \text{ is a bijection}}{\vdash x_1 \xleftarrow{\$} d_1 \sim x_2 \xleftarrow{\$} d_2 : \forall v \in \mathrm{supp}(d_1), \ \Psi \{v, f(v)/x_1\langle 1\rangle, x_2\langle 2\rangle\} \implies \Psi}$$

$$\textsc{Seq} \ \frac{\vdash c_1 \sim c_2 : \Phi \implies \Psi \qquad \vdash c_1' \sim c_2' : \Psi \implies \Theta}{\vdash c_1; c_1' \sim c_2; c_2' : \Phi \implies \Theta}$$

$$\textsc{Cond} \ \frac{\models \Phi \to e_1\langle 1\rangle = e_2\langle 2\rangle \quad \vdash c_1 \sim c_2 : \Phi \wedge e_1\langle 1\rangle \implies \Psi \quad \vdash c_1' \sim c_2' : \Phi \wedge \neg e_1\langle 1\rangle \implies \Psi}{\vdash \mathbf{if} \ e_1 \ \mathbf{then} \ c_1 \ \mathbf{else} \ c_1' \sim \mathbf{if} \ e_2 \ \mathbf{then} \ c_2 \ \mathbf{else} \ c_2' : \Phi \implies \Psi}$$

$$\textsc{While} \ \frac{\models \Phi \to e_1\langle 1\rangle = e_2\langle 2\rangle \qquad \vdash c_1 \sim c_2 : \Phi \wedge e_1\langle 1\rangle \implies \Phi}{\vdash \mathbf{while} \ e_1 \ \mathbf{do} \ c_1 \sim \mathbf{while} \ e_2 \ \mathbf{do} \ c_2 : \Phi \implies \Phi \wedge \neg e_1\langle 1\rangle}$$

Figure 5.2 Two-sided pRHL rules

ories, rather than distributions over memories. Abstracting away from probabilistic aspect of the program makes probabilistic reasoning significantly easier, and is a key reason why the coupling proof technique is so powerful.

The rules of pRHL can be divided into three groups: *two-sided* rules, *one-sided* rules, and *structural* rules. All judgments are parameterized by a logical context ρ, but since this context is assumed to be a fixed assignment of logical variables—constant throughout the proof—we omit it from the rules. The two-sided rules in Fig. 5.2 apply when the two programs in the conclusion judgment have the same top-level shape.

The rule [Skip] simply states that **skip** instructions preserve the pre-condition. The rule [Assn] handles assignment instructions. It is the usual Hoare-style rule: if Ψ holds initially with $e_1\langle 1\rangle$ and $e_2\langle 2\rangle$ substituted for $x_1\langle 1\rangle$ and $x_2\langle 2\rangle$, then Ψ holds after the respective assignment instructions.

The rule [Sample] is more subtle. In some ways it is the key rule in pRHL, allowing us to select a coupling for a pair of sampling instructions. To gain intuition, the following rule is a special case:

$$\textsc{Sample*} \ \frac{f : \mathrm{supp}(d) \to \mathrm{supp}(d) \text{ is a bijection}}{\vdash x \xleftarrow{\$} d \sim x \xleftarrow{\$} d : \top \implies f(x\langle 1\rangle) = x\langle 2\rangle}$$

In terms of couplings, the conclusion states that there exists a coupling of a distribution d with itself such that each sample x from d is related to $f(x)$. Soundness of this rule crucially relies on d being *uniform*—as we have seen, any bijection f induces a coupling of uniform distributions (cf. Theorem 5.4). It is possible to support more general distributions at the cost of a more complicated side-condition,[2] but we will not need this generality. The full rule [SAMPLE] can prove a post-condition of any shape: a post-condition holds after sampling if it holds before sampling, where $x\langle 1 \rangle$ and $x\langle 2 \rangle$ are replaced by any two coupled samples $(v, f(v))$.

More generally, a key feature of coupling proofs can be seen in the rule [SAMPLE]: reducing two separate sources of randomness into a single source of randomness. A priori, two sampling instructions in the two programs are completely independent— we have no reason to think that the results of their random draws are related in any way. The sampling rule shows that for the purpose of the proof, it is sound to *assume* that the results from the two sampling statements are related by a bijection. In this way, we may analyze the two programs with their separate sources of randomness as if they shared a single, common source of randomness. When the original programs have similar shapes—as is the typical case in relational verification—this coordination enables us to limit our attention to pairs of highly similar program executions.

The rule [SEQ] resembles the normal rule for sequential composition in Hoare logic, but this superficial similarity hides some complexity. In particular, note that the intermediate assertion Ψ is interpreted differently in the two premises: in the first judgment it is a post-condition and interpreted as a relation between *distributions over memories* via lifting, while in the second judgment it is a pre-condition and interpreted as a relation between *memories*, not distributions over memories.

The next two rules deal with branching commands. Rule [COND] requires that the guards $e_1\langle 1 \rangle$ and $e_2\langle 2 \rangle$ are equal assuming the pre-condition Φ. The rule is otherwise similar to the standard Hoare logic rule: if we can prove the post-condition Ψ when the guard is initially true and when the guard is initially false, then we can prove Ψ as a post-condition of the conditional.

Rule [WHILE] uses a similar idea for loops. We again assume that the guards are initially equal, and we also assume that they are equal in the post-condition of the loop body. Since the judgments are interpreted in terms of couplings, this second condition is a bit subtle. For one thing, the rule does *not* require $e_1\langle 1 \rangle = e_2\langle 2 \rangle$ in all possible executions of the two programs—this would be a rather severe restriction, for instance ruling out programs where $e_1\langle 1 \rangle$ and $e_2\langle 2 \rangle$ are probabilistic. Rather, the guards only need to be equal *under the coupling of the two programs given by the premise*. The upshot is that by selecting appropriate couplings in the loop body,

---

[2] Roughly speaking, the probability of any set S under d should be equal to the probability of $f(S)$ under d.

$$\text{Assn-L} \quad \frac{}{\vdash x_1 \leftarrow e_1 \sim \textbf{skip} : \Psi\{e_1\langle 1\rangle / x_1\langle 1\rangle\} \Longrightarrow \Psi}$$

$$\text{Assn-R} \quad \frac{}{\vdash \textbf{skip} \sim x_2 \leftarrow e_2 : \Psi\{e_2\langle 2\rangle / x_2\langle 2\rangle\} \Longrightarrow \Psi}$$

$$\text{Sample-L} \quad \frac{}{\vdash x_1 \xleftarrow{\$} d_1 \sim \textbf{skip} : \forall v \in \text{supp}(d_1),\ \Psi\{v/x_1\langle 1\rangle\} \Longrightarrow \Psi}$$

$$\text{Sample-R} \quad \frac{}{\vdash \textbf{skip} \sim x_2 \xleftarrow{\$} d_2 : \forall v \in \text{supp}(d_2),\ \Psi\{v/x_2\langle 2\rangle\} \Longrightarrow \Psi}$$

$$\text{Cond-L} \quad \frac{\vdash c_1 \sim c : \Phi \land e_1\langle 1\rangle \Longrightarrow \Psi \qquad \vdash c_1' \sim c : \Phi \land \neg e_1\langle 1\rangle \Longrightarrow \Psi}{\vdash \textbf{if } e_1 \textbf{ then } c_1 \textbf{ else } c_1' \sim c : \Phi \Longrightarrow \Psi}$$

$$\text{Cond-R} \quad \frac{\vdash c \sim c_2 : \Phi \land e_2\langle 2\rangle \Longrightarrow \Psi \qquad \vdash c \sim c_2' : \Phi \land \neg e_2\langle 2\rangle \Longrightarrow \Psi}{\vdash c \sim \textbf{if } e_2 \textbf{ then } c_2 \textbf{ else } c_2' : \Phi \Longrightarrow \Psi}$$

$$\text{While-L} \quad \frac{\vdash c_1 \sim \textbf{skip} : \Phi \land e_1\langle 1\rangle \Longrightarrow \Phi \quad \models \Phi \rightarrow \Phi_1\langle 1\rangle \qquad \Phi_1 \models \textbf{while } e_1 \textbf{ do } c_1 \text{ lossless}}{\vdash \textbf{while } e_1 \textbf{ do } c_1 \sim \textbf{skip} : \Phi \Longrightarrow \Phi \land \neg e_1\langle 1\rangle}$$

$$\text{While-R} \quad \frac{\vdash \textbf{skip} \sim c_2 : \Phi \land e_2\langle 2\rangle \Longrightarrow \Phi \quad \models \Phi \rightarrow \Phi_2\langle 2\rangle \qquad \Phi_2 \models \textbf{while } e_2 \textbf{ do } c_2 \text{ lossless}}{\vdash \textbf{skip} \sim \textbf{while } e_2 \textbf{ do } c_2 : \Phi \Longrightarrow \Phi \land \neg e_2\langle 2\rangle}$$

Figure 5.3 One-sided PRHL rules

we can assume the guards are equal when analyzing loops with probabilistic guards. The rule is otherwise similar to the usual Hoare logic rule, where Φ is the loop invariant.

So far, we have seen rules that relate two programs of the same shape. These are the most commonly used rules in PRHL, as relational reasoning is most powerful when comparing two highly similar (or even the same) programs. However, in some cases we may need to reason about two programs with different shapes, even if the two top-level commands are the same. For instance, if we can't guarantee two executions of a program follow the same path at a conditional statement under a coupling, we must relate the two different branches. For this kind of reasoning, we can fall back on the *one-sided* rules in Fig. 5.3. These rules relate a command of a particular shape with **skip** or an arbitrary command. Each rule comes in a left- and a right-side version.

The assignment rules, [ASSN-L] and [ASSN-R], relate an assignment instruction to **skip** using the usual Hoare rule for assignment instructions. The sampling rules, [SAMPLE-L] and [SAMPLE-R], are similar; they relate a sampling instruction to **skip** if the post-condition holds for all possible values of the sample. These rules represent couplings where fresh randomness is used, i.e., where randomness is not shared between the two programs.

The conditional rules, [COND-L] and [COND-R], are similar to the two-sided conditional rule except there is no assumption of synchronized guards—the other command c might not even be a conditional. If we can relate the general command c to the true branch when the guard is true and relate c to the false branch when the guard is false, then we can relate c to the whole conditional.

The rules for loops, [WHILE-L] and [WHILE-R], can only relate loops to the **skip**; a loop that executes multiple iterations cannot be directly related to an arbitrary command that executes only once. These rules mimic the usual loop rule from Hoare logic, with a critical side-condition: *losslessness*.

Definition 5.27 A command c is Φ-*lossless* if for any memory m satisfying Φ and every logical context ρ, the output $[\![c]\!]_\rho m$ is a proper distribution (i.e., it has total probability 1). We write Φ-lossless as the following judgment:

$$\Phi \models c \text{ lossless}$$

Losslessness is needed for soundness: **skip** produces a proper distribution on any input and liftings can only relate sub-distributions with equal weights (Theorem 5.9), so the loop must also produce a proper distribution to have any hope of coupling the output distributions. For the examples we will consider, losslessness is easy to show since loops execute for a finite number of iterations; when there is no finite bound, proving losslessness may require more sophisticated techniques (e.g., Barthe et al. (2018a); Ferrer Fioriti and Hermanns (2015); Chatterjee et al. (2016b,a, 2017); McIver et al. (2018)).

Finally, PRHL includes a handful of *structural* rules which apply to programs of any shape. The first rule [CONSEQ] is the usual rule of consequence, allowing us to strengthen the pre-condition and weaken the post-condition—assuming more about the input and proving less about the output, respectively.

The rule [EQUIV] replaces programs by equivalent programs. This rule is particularly useful for reasoning about programs of different shapes. Instead of using one-sided rules, which are often less convenient, we can sometimes replace a program with an equivalent version and then apply two-sided rules. For simplicity, we use a strong notion of equivalence:

$$c_1 \equiv c_2 \triangleq [\![c_1]\!]_\rho = [\![c_2]\!]_\rho$$

$$\text{Conseq} \frac{\vdash c_1 \sim c_2 : \Phi' \Longrightarrow \Psi' \qquad \models \Phi \to \Phi' \qquad \models \Psi' \to \Psi}{\vdash c_1 \sim c_2 : \Phi \Longrightarrow \Psi}$$

$$\text{Equiv} \frac{\vdash c_1' \sim c_2' : \Phi \Longrightarrow \Psi \qquad c_1 \equiv c_1' \qquad c_2 \equiv c_2'}{\vdash c_1 \sim c_2 : \Phi \Longrightarrow \Psi}$$

$$\text{Case} \frac{\vdash c_1 \sim c_2 : \Phi \wedge \Theta \Longrightarrow \Psi \qquad \vdash c_1 \sim c_2 : \Phi \wedge \neg\Theta \Longrightarrow \Psi}{\vdash c_1 \sim c_2 : \Phi \Longrightarrow \Psi}$$

$$\text{Trans} \frac{\vdash c_1 \sim c_2 : \Phi \Longrightarrow \Psi \qquad \vdash c_2 \sim c_3 : \Phi' \Longrightarrow \Psi'}{\vdash c_1 \sim c_3 : \Phi' \circ \Phi \Longrightarrow \Psi' \circ \Psi}$$

$$\text{Frame} \frac{\vdash c_1 \sim c_2 : \Phi \Longrightarrow \Psi \qquad \mathrm{FV}(\Theta) \cap \mathrm{MV}(c_1, c_2) = \varnothing}{\vdash c_1 \sim c_2 : \Phi \wedge \Theta \Longrightarrow \Psi \wedge \Theta}$$

Figure 5.4 Structural PRHL rules

for every logical context ρ; more refined notions of equivalence are also possible, but will not be needed for our purposes. For our examples, we just use a handful of basic program equivalences, e.g., $c; \textbf{skip} \equiv c$ and $\textbf{skip}; c \equiv c$.

The rule [CASE] performs a case analysis on the input. If we can prove a judgment when Θ holds initially and a judgment when Θ does not hold initially, then we can combine the two judgments provided they have the same post-condition.

The rule [TRANS] is the transitivity rule: given a judgment relating $c_1 \sim c_2$ and a judgment relating $c_2 \sim c_3$, we can glue these judgments together to relate $c_1 \sim c_3$. The pre- and post-conditions of the conclusion are given by composing the pre- and post-conditions of the premises; for binary relations $\mathcal{R}$ and $\mathcal{S}$, relation composition is defined by

$$\mathcal{R} \circ \mathcal{S} \triangleq \{(x_1, x_3) \mid \exists x_2. \ (x_1, x_2) \in \mathcal{S} \wedge (x_2, x_3) \in \mathcal{R}\}.$$

The last rule [FRAME] is the frame rule (also called the *rule of constancy*): it states that an assertion Θ can be carried from the pre-condition through to the post-condition as long as the variables $\mathrm{MV}(c_1, c_2)$ that may be modified by the programs c_1 and c_2 don't include any of the variables $\mathrm{FV}(\Theta)$ appearing free in Θ; as usual, MV and FV are defined syntactically by collecting the variables that occur in programs and assertions.

As expected, the proof system of PRHL is sound.

Theorem 5.28 (Barthe et al. (2009))   *Let ρ be a logical context. If a judgment is* *derivable*

$$\rho \vdash c_1 \sim c_2 : \Phi \Longrightarrow \Psi,$$

then it is valid:

$$\rho \models c_1 \sim c_2 : \Phi \Longrightarrow \Psi.$$

5.5.5 *The coupling interpretation*

Now that we have seen the core logical rules of PRHL, we revisit the connection with couplings. Not only do valid judgments assert the existence of a coupling between two output distributions, the proof system itself is a formalization of proofs by coupling, which we saw in Section 5.4. This perspective gives a better, more precise understanding of what proofs by coupling are, and how they work.

In more detail, a valid judgment $\rho \models c_1 \sim c_2 : \Phi \Longrightarrow \Psi$ implies that for any two input memories related by Φ, there exists a coupling with support in Ψ between the two output distributions. By applying the results in Section 5.3, valid judgments imply relational properties of programs.

Moreover, we can identify common steps in standard coupling proofs in the form of specific logical rules. For instance, [SAMPLE] selects a coupling for corresponding sampling statements; the function f lets us choose among different bijection couplings. The rule [SEQ] formalizes the sequential composition principle for couplings; when two processes produce samples related by Ψ under a particular coupling, we can continue to assume this relation when analyzing the remainder of the program. The structural rule [CASE] shows we can select between two possible couplings depending on whether a predicate Θ holds. In short, not only is PRHL a logic for verifying cryptographic constructions, it is also a formal logic for proofs by coupling.

5.6 Constructing couplings, formally

The coupling proof technique has been applied to a variety of probabilistic properties, using the same basic pattern: construct a coupling of a specific form between the output distributions of two programs, then use the existence of this coupling to conclude a relational property using known consequences of couplings (cf. Section 5.3). Given the close connection between coupling proofs and our logic, we carry out this proof pattern in PRHL to build formal proofs of three classical properties: equivalence, stochastic domination, and convergence.

Remark 5.29 There are some inherent challenges in presenting formal proofs on paper. Fundamentally, our proofs are branching derivation trees. When such a proof is linearized, it becomes more difficult to follow which part of the derivation tree the paper proof corresponds to. To help organize the proof, we generally proceed in a top-down fashion, giving proofs and judgments for the most deeply nested parts of the program first and then gradually zooming out to consider larger and larger parts of the whole program.

Applications of sequential composition are also natural places to signpost the proof. We typically consider the commands in order, unless the second command is much more complex than the first. Finally, for space reasons we will gloss over applications of the assignment rule [Assn] and minor uses of the rule of consequence [Conseq]; a completely formal proof would necessarily include these details.

5.6.1 Probabilistic equivalence

To warm up, we prove two programs to be probabilistically equivalent. Our example models perhaps the most basic encryption scheme: the XOR cipher. Given a boolean s representing the secret message, the XOR cipher flips a fair coin to draw the secret key k and then returns $k \oplus s$ as the encrypted message. A receiving party who knows the secret key can decrypt the message by computing $k \oplus (k \oplus s) = s$.

To prove secrecy of this scheme, we consider the following two programs:

$$k \xleftarrow{\$} \textbf{Flip};$$
$$r \leftarrow k \oplus s$$

$$k \xleftarrow{\$} \textbf{Flip};$$
$$r \leftarrow k$$

The first program xor_1 implements the encryption function, storing the encrypted message into r. The second program xor_2 simply stores a random value into r. If we can show the distribution of r is the same in both programs, then the XOR cipher is secure: the distribution on outputs is completely random, leaking no information about the secret message s. In terms of PRHL, it suffices to prove the following judgment:

$$\vdash xor_1 \sim xor_2 : \top \implies r\langle 1 \rangle = r\langle 2 \rangle$$

By validity of the logic, this judgment implies that for any two memories m_1, m_2, the output distributions are related by a coupling that always returns outputs with equal values of r; by reasoning similar to Theorem 5.10, this implies that the output distributions over $r\langle 1 \rangle$ and $r\langle 2 \rangle$ are equal.[3]

Before proving this judgment in the logic, we sketch the proof by coupling. If $s\langle 1 \rangle$ is true, then we couple k to take opposite values in the two runs. If $s\langle 1 \rangle$ is false, then we couple k to be equal in the two runs. In both cases, we conclude that the results $r\langle 1 \rangle, r\langle 2 \rangle$ are equal under the coupling.

---

[3] To be completely precise, Theorem 5.10 assumes that we have lifted equality, while here we only have a lifting where the variables r are equal. An analogous argument shows that the marginal distributions of variable r must be equal.

To formalize this argument in PRHL, we use the [CASE] rule:

$$\text{CASE} \frac{\begin{array}{l} \vdash xor_1 \sim xor_2 : s\langle 1 \rangle = \textbf{true} \Longrightarrow r\langle 1 \rangle = r\langle 2 \rangle \\ \vdash xor_1 \sim xor_2 : s\langle 1 \rangle \neq \textbf{true} \Longrightarrow r\langle 1 \rangle = r\langle 2 \rangle \end{array}}{\vdash xor_1 \sim xor_2 : \top \Longrightarrow r\langle 1 \rangle = r\langle 2 \rangle} \ .$$

For the first premise we select the negation coupling using the bijection $f = \neg$ in [SAMPLE], apply the assignment rule [ASSN], and combine with the sequencing rule [SEQ]. Concretely, we have

$$\text{SAMPLE} \frac{f = \neg}{\vdash k \xleftarrow{\$} \textbf{Flip} \sim k \xleftarrow{\$} \textbf{Flip} : s\langle 1 \rangle = \textbf{true} \Longrightarrow k\langle 1 \rangle = \neg k\langle 2 \rangle \wedge s\langle 1 \rangle = \textbf{true}}$$

$$\text{ASSN} \frac{}{\vdash r \leftarrow k \oplus s \sim r \leftarrow k : k\langle 1 \rangle = \neg k\langle 2 \rangle \wedge s\langle 1 \rangle = \textbf{true} \Longrightarrow r\langle 1 \rangle = r\langle 2 \rangle}$$

and we combine the two judgments to give:

$$\text{SEQ} \frac{\begin{array}{l} \vdash k \xleftarrow{\$} \textbf{Flip} \sim k \xleftarrow{\$} \textbf{Flip} : s\langle 1 \rangle = \textbf{true} \Longrightarrow k\langle 1 \rangle = \neg k\langle 2 \rangle \wedge s\langle 1 \rangle = \textbf{true} \\ \vdash r \leftarrow k \oplus s \sim r \leftarrow k : k\langle 1 \rangle = \neg k\langle 2 \rangle \wedge s\langle 1 \rangle = \textbf{true} \Longrightarrow r\langle 1 \rangle = r\langle 2 \rangle \end{array}}{\vdash xor_1 \sim xor_2 : s\langle 1 \rangle = \textbf{true} \Longrightarrow r\langle 1 \rangle = r\langle 2 \rangle} \ .$$

For the other case $s\langle 1 \rangle \neq \textbf{true}$, we give the same proof except with the identity coupling in [SAMPLE]:

$$\text{SAMPLE} \frac{f = \text{id}}{\vdash k \xleftarrow{\$} \textbf{Flip} \sim k \xleftarrow{\$} \textbf{Flip} : s\langle 1 \rangle \neq \textbf{true} \Longrightarrow k\langle 1 \rangle = k\langle 2 \rangle \wedge s\langle 1 \rangle \neq \textbf{true}}$$

and the assignment rule, we have

$$\text{ASSN} \frac{}{\vdash r \leftarrow k \oplus s \sim r \leftarrow k : k\langle 1 \rangle = k\langle 2 \rangle \wedge s\langle 1 \rangle \neq \textbf{true} \Longrightarrow r\langle 1 \rangle = r\langle 2 \rangle} \ .$$

Combining the conclusions, we get

$$\text{SEQ} \frac{\begin{array}{l} \vdash k \xleftarrow{\$} \textbf{Flip} \sim k \xleftarrow{\$} \textbf{Flip} : s\langle 1 \rangle \neq \textbf{true} \Longrightarrow k\langle 1 \rangle = \neg k\langle 2 \rangle \wedge s\langle 1 \rangle \neq \textbf{true} \\ \vdash r \leftarrow k \oplus s \sim r \leftarrow k : k\langle 1 \rangle = k\langle 2 \rangle \wedge s\langle 1 \rangle \neq \textbf{true} \Longrightarrow r\langle 1 \rangle = r\langle 2 \rangle \end{array}}{\vdash xor_1 \sim xor_2 : s\langle 1 \rangle \neq \textbf{true} \Longrightarrow r\langle 1 \rangle = r\langle 2 \rangle} \ .$$

By [CASE], we conclude the desired post-condition $r\langle 1 \rangle = r\langle 2 \rangle$.

5.6.2 Stochastic domination

For our second example, we revisit Theorem 5.20 and replicate the proof in PRHL. The following program *sdom* flips a coin T times and returns the number of coin flips that come up true:

$$i \leftarrow 0; ct \leftarrow 0;$$
$$\textbf{while } i < T \textbf{ do}$$
$$\quad i \leftarrow i + 1;$$
$$\quad s \xleftarrow{\$} \textbf{Flip};$$
$$\quad ct \leftarrow s \mathbin{?} ct + 1 : ct$$

(The last line uses the *ternary conditional operator*—$s \mathbin{?} ct + 1 : ct$ is equal to $ct + 1$ if s is true, otherwise equal to ct.)

We consider two runs of this program executing T_1 and T_2 iterations, where $T_1 \leq T_2$ are logical variables; call the two programs $sdom_1$ and $sdom_2$. By soundness of the logic and Theorem 5.14, the distribution of ct in the second run stochastically dominates the distribution of ct in the first run if we can prove the judgment

$$\vdash sdom_1 \sim sdom_2 : \top \implies ct\langle 1 \rangle \leq ct\langle 2 \rangle.$$

Encoding the argument from Theorem 5.20 in PRHL requires a bit of work. The main obstacle is that the two-sided loop rule in PRHL can only analyze loops in a synchronized fashion, but this is not possible here: when $T_1 < T_2$ the two loops run for different numbers of iterations, no matter how we couple the samples. To get around this problem, we use the equivalence rule [EQUIV] to transform *sdom* into a more convenient form using the following equivalence:

$$\textbf{while } e \textbf{ do } c \equiv \textbf{while } e \wedge e' \textbf{ do } c; \textbf{while } e \textbf{ do } c$$

This transformation, known in the compilers literature as *loop splitting* (Callahan and Kennedy, 1988), separates out the first iterations where e' holds, and then runs the original loop to completion. We transform $sdom_2$ as follows:

$$sdom'_{2a} \triangleq \left\{ \begin{array}{l} i \leftarrow 0; ct \leftarrow 0; \\ \textbf{while } i < T_2 \wedge i < T_1 \textbf{ do} \\ \quad i \leftarrow i + 1; \\ \quad s \xleftarrow{\$} \textbf{Flip}; \\ \quad ct \leftarrow s \mathbin{?} ct + 1 : ct; \end{array} \right. \left. \begin{array}{l} i \leftarrow 0; ct \leftarrow 0; \\ \textbf{while } i < T_1 \textbf{ do} \\ \quad i \leftarrow i + 1; \\ \quad s \xleftarrow{\$} \textbf{Flip}; \\ \quad ct \leftarrow s \mathbin{?} ct + 1 : ct; \end{array} \right\} \triangleq sdom_1$$

$$sdom'_{2b} \triangleq \left\{ \begin{array}{l} \textbf{while } i < T_2 \textbf{ do} \\ \quad i \leftarrow i + 1; \\ \quad s \xleftarrow{\$} \textbf{Flip}; \\ \quad ct \leftarrow s \mathbin{?} ct + 1 : ct \end{array} \right.$$

We aim to relate $sdom'_{2a}; sdom'_{2b}$ to $sdom_1$. First, we apply the two-sided rule

[WHILE] to relate $sdom_1$ to $sdom'_{2a}$. Taking the identity coupling with $f = \mathrm{id}$ in [SAMPLE], we relate the sampling in the loop body via

$$\text{SAMPLE} \ \frac{f = \mathrm{id}}{\vdash s \xleftarrow{\$} \textbf{Flip} \sim s \xleftarrow{\$} \textbf{Flip} : \top \implies s\langle 1 \rangle = s\langle 2 \rangle}$$

and establish the loop invariant

$$\Theta \triangleq i\langle 1 \rangle = i\langle 2 \rangle \wedge ct\langle 1 \rangle = ct\langle 2 \rangle,$$

proving the judgment

$$\vdash sdom_1 \sim sdom'_{2a} : \top \implies \Theta.$$

Then we use the one-sided rule [WHILE-R] for the loop $sdom'_{2b}$ with loop invariant $ct\langle 1 \rangle \leq ct\langle 2 \rangle$:

$$\vdash \textbf{skip} \sim sdom'_{2b} : \Theta \implies ct\langle 1 \rangle < ct\langle 2 \rangle.$$

Composing these two judgments with [SEQ] and applying [EQUIV] gives the desired judgment:

$$\text{EQUIV} \ \frac{\vdash sdom_1; \textbf{skip} \sim sdom'_{2a}; sdom'_{2b} : \top \implies ct\langle 1 \rangle \leq ct\langle 2 \rangle}{\vdash sdom_1 \sim sdom_2 : \top \implies ct\langle 1 \rangle \leq ct\langle 2 \rangle}$$

using the equivalence $sdom_1; \textbf{skip} \equiv sdom_1$.

5.6.3 Probabilistic convergence

In our final example, we build a coupling witnessing convergence of two *random walks*. Each process begins at an integer starting point *start*, and proceeds for T steps. At each step it flips a fair coin. If true, it increases the current position by 1; otherwise, it decreases the position by 1. Given two random walks starting at different initial locations, we want to bound the distance between the two resulting output distributions in terms of T. Intuitively, the position distributions spread out as the random walks proceed, tending towards the uniform distribution on the even integers or the uniform distribution over the odd integers depending on the parity of the initial position and the number of steps. If two walks initially have the same parity (i.e., their starting positions differ by an even integer), then their distributions after taking the same number of steps T should approach one another in total variation distance.

We model a single random walk with the following program *rwalk*:

$$pos \leftarrow start; i \leftarrow 0; hist \leftarrow [start];$$
while $i < T$ **do**
$\quad i \leftarrow i + 1;$
$\quad r \xleftarrow{\$} \textbf{Flip};$
$\quad pos \leftarrow pos + (r \; ? \; 1 : -1);$
$\quad hist \leftarrow pos :: hist$

The last command records the history of the walk in *hist*; this *ghost variable* does not affect the final output value, but will be useful for our assertions.

By Theorem 5.16, we can bound the TV-distance between the position distributions by constructing a coupling where the probability of $pos\langle 1\rangle \neq pos\langle 2\rangle$ tends to 0 as T increases. We don't have the tools yet to reason about this probability (we will revisit this point in the next chapter), but for now we can build the coupling and prove the judgment

$$\vdash rwalk \sim rwalk : start\langle 2\rangle - start\langle 1\rangle = 2K$$
$$\implies K + start\langle 1\rangle \in hist\langle 1\rangle \rightarrow pos\langle 1\rangle = pos\langle 2\rangle$$

where K is an integer logical variable. The pre-condition states that the initial positions are an even distance apart. To read the post-condition, the predicate $K + start\langle 1\rangle \in hist\langle 1\rangle$ holds if and only if the first walk has moved to position $K + start\langle 1\rangle$ at some time in the past; if this has happened, then the two coupled positions must be equal.

Our coupling mirrors the two walks. Each step, we have the walks make symmetric moves by arranging opposite samples. Once the walks meet, we have the walks match each other by coupling the samples to be equal. In this way, if the first walk reaches $start\langle 1\rangle + K$, then the second walk must be at $start\langle 2\rangle - K$ since both walks are coupled to move symmetrically. In this case, the initial condition $start\langle 2\rangle - start\langle 1\rangle = 2K$ gives

$$pos\langle 1\rangle = start\langle 1\rangle + K = start\langle 2\rangle - K = pos\langle 2\rangle$$

so the walks meet and continue to share the same position thereafter. This argument requires the starting positions to be an even distance apart so the positions in the two walks always have the same parity; if the two starting positions are an odd distance apart, then the two distributions after T steps have disjoint support and the coupled walks can never meet.

To formalize this argument in PRHL, we handle the loop with the two-sided rule

[WHILE] and invariant

$$\Theta \triangleq \begin{cases} |hist\langle 1\rangle| > 0 \wedge |hist\langle 2\rangle| > 0 \\ K + start\langle 1\rangle \in hist\langle 1\rangle \rightarrow pos\langle 1\rangle = pos\langle 2\rangle \\ K + start\langle 1\rangle \notin hist\langle 1\rangle \rightarrow pos\langle 2\rangle - pos\langle 1\rangle = \\ \qquad 2(K - (hd(hist\langle 1\rangle)) - start\langle 1\rangle)), \end{cases}$$

where $hd(hist)$ is the first element (the *head*) of the non-empty list *hist*. The last two conditions model the two cases. If the first walk has already visited $K + start\langle 1\rangle$, the walks have already met under the coupling and they must have the same position. Otherwise, the walks have not met. If $d \triangleq hd(hist\langle 1\rangle) - start\langle 1\rangle$ is the (signed) distance the first walk has moved away from its starting location and the two walks are initially $2K$ apart, then the current distance between coupled positions must be $2(K - d)$.

To show the invariant is preserved, we perform a case analysis with [CASE]. If $K + start\langle 1\rangle \in hist\langle 1\rangle$ holds then the walks have already met in the past and currently have the same position (by Θ). So, we select the identity coupling in [SAMPLE]:

$$\text{SAMPLE} \frac{f = \text{id}}{\vdash r \xleftarrow{\$} \textbf{Flip} \sim r \xleftarrow{\$} \textbf{Flip} : K + start\langle 1\rangle \in hist\langle 1\rangle \implies r\langle 1\rangle = r\langle 2\rangle} .$$

Since $K + start\langle 1\rangle \in hist\langle 1\rangle \rightarrow pos\langle 1\rangle = pos\langle 2\rangle$ holds at the start of the loop, we know $pos\langle 1\rangle = pos\langle 2\rangle$ at the end of the loop; since $K + start\langle 1\rangle \in hist\langle 1\rangle$ is preserved by the loop body, the invariant Θ holds.

Otherwise if $K + start\langle 1\rangle \notin h\langle 1\rangle$, then the walks have not yet met and should be mirrored. So, we select the negation coupling with $f = \neg$ in [SAMPLE]:

$$\text{SAMPLE} \frac{f = \neg}{\vdash r \xleftarrow{\$} \textbf{Flip} \sim r \xleftarrow{\$} \textbf{Flip} : K + start\langle 1\rangle \notin hist\langle 1\rangle \implies \neg r\langle 1\rangle = r\langle 2\rangle}$$

To show the loop invariant, there are two cases. If $K + start\langle 1\rangle \in h\langle 1\rangle$ holds after the body, the two walks have just met for the first time and $pos\langle 1\rangle = pos\langle 2\rangle$ holds. Otherwise, the walks remain mirrored: $pos\langle 1\rangle$ increased by $r\langle 1\rangle$ and $pos\langle 2\rangle$ decreased by $r\langle 1\rangle$, so $pos\langle 2\rangle - pos\langle 1\rangle = 2(K + (hd(hist\langle 1\rangle)) - start\langle 1\rangle))$ and the invariant Θ is preserved.

Putting it all together, we have the desired judgment:

$$\vdash rwalk \sim rwalk : start\langle 2\rangle - start\langle 1\rangle = 2K \implies K + start\langle 1\rangle \in h\langle 1\rangle \rightarrow pos\langle 1\rangle = pos\langle 2\rangle.$$

While this judgment describes a coupling between the position distributions, we need to analyze finer properties of the coupling distribution to apply Theorem 5.16 – namely, we must bound the probability that $pos\langle 1\rangle$ is not equal to $pos\langle 2\rangle$. We will consider how to extract this information in the next chapter.

5.6.4 *Verifying non-relational properties: independence and uniformity*

As we have seen, couplings are a natural fit for probabilistic relational properties. Properties describing a single program can also be viewed relationally in some cases, enabling cleaner proofs by coupling. Barthe et al. (2017b) develop this idea to prove *uniformity*, *probabilistic independence*, and *conditional independence*, examples of probabilistic non-relational properties. We briefly sketch their main reductions.

A uniform distribution places equal probability on every value in some range. Given a distribution μ over **State** and an expression e with finite range S (say, the booleans), e is *uniform* in μ if for all a and a' in S, we have

$$\Pr_{m \sim \mu} [[\![e]\!]m = a] = \Pr_{m \sim \mu} [[\![e]\!]m = a'].$$

When μ is the output distribution of a program c, uniformity follows from the PRHL judgment

$$\forall a, a' \in S, \vdash c \sim c : (=) \implies e\langle 1 \rangle = a \leftrightarrow e\langle 2 \rangle = a'.$$

This reduction is a direct consequence of Theorem 5.12. Moreover, the resulting judgment is ideally suited to relational verification since it relates two copies of the same program c.

Handling independence is only a bit more involved. Given a distribution μ and expressions e, e' with ranges S and S', we say e and e' are *probabilistically independent* if for all $a \in S$ and $a' \in S'$, we have

$$\Pr_{m \sim \mu} [[\![e]\!]m = a \wedge [\![e']\!]m = a'] = \Pr_{m \sim \mu} [[\![e]\!]m = a] \cdot \Pr_{m \sim \mu} [[\![e']\!]m = a'].$$

This useful property roughly implies that properties involving e and e' can be analyzed by focusing on e and e' separately. When e and e' are uniformly distributed, independence follows from uniformity of the tuple (e, e') over the product set $S \times S'$ so the previous reduction applies. In general, we can compare the distributions of e and e' in two experiments: when both are drawn from the output distribution of a single execution, and when they are drawn from two independent executions composed sequentially. If the expressions are independent, these two experiments should look the same. Concretely, independence follows from the relational judgment

$$\forall a \in S, a' \in S', \vdash c \sim c^{(1)}; c^{(2)} : \Phi \implies e\langle 1 \rangle = a \wedge e'\langle 1 \rangle = a' \leftrightarrow$$
$$e^{(1)}\langle 2 \rangle = a \wedge e'^{(2)}\langle 2 \rangle = a',$$

where $c^{(1)}$ and $c^{(2)}$ are copies of c with variables x renamed to $x^{(1)}$ and $x^{(2)}$ respectively; this construction is also called *self-composition* since it sequentially composes c with itself (Barthe et al., 2011). The pre-condition Φ states that the three copies of each variable are initially equal: $x\langle 1 \rangle = x^{(1)}\langle 2 \rangle = x^{(2)}\langle 2 \rangle$. Handling conditional independence requires a slightly more complex encoding, but the general pattern remains the same: encode products of probabilities by self-composition and equalities by lifted equivalence $(\leftrightarrow)^{\sharp}$.

These reductions give a simple method to prove uniformity and independence. Other non-relational properties could benefit from a similar approach, especially in conjunction with more sophisticated program transformations in PRHL to relate different copies of the same sampling instruction. Albarghouthi and Hsu (2018a) consider how to automatically construct such coupling proofs by program synthesis and verification techniques.

5.7 Related work

Relational Hoare logics and probabilistic couplings have been extensively studied and (re)discovered in various research communities.

5.7.1 Relational Hoare logics

The logic PRHL is a prime example of a *relational* program logic, which extend standard Floyd-Hoare logics to prove properties about two programs. Benton (2004) first designed a relational version of Hoare logic called RHL to prove equivalence between two (deterministic) programs. Benton used his logic to verify compiler transformations, showing the original program is equivalent to the transformed program. Relational versions of other program logics have also been considered, including an extension of separation logic by Yang (2007) to prove relational properties of pointer-manipulating programs. There is nothing particularly special about relating exactly *two* programs; recently, Sousa and Dillig (2016) give a Hoare logic for proving properties of k executions of the same program for arbitrary k. Barthe et al. (2017a) give an extended logic $\times$PRHL where judgments also include probabilistic product program simulating two coupled runs of the related programs; in a sense, coupling proofs are probabilistic product programs.

Barthe et al. (2009) extended Benton's work to prove relational properties of probabilistic programs, leading to the logic PRHL. As we have seen, the key technical insight is to interpret the relational post-condition as a probabilistic lifting between two output distributions. Barthe et al. (2009) used PRHL to verify security properties for a variety of cryptographic constructions by mimicking the so-called *game-hopping* proof technique (Shoup, 2004; Bellare and Rogaway, 2006), where the original program is transformed step-by-step to an obviously secure version (e.g., a program returning a random number). Security follows if each transformation approximately preserves the program semantics. Our analysis of the XOR cipher is a very simple example of this technique; more sophisticated proofs chain together dozens of transformations.

5.7.2 *Probabilistic couplings and liftings*

Couplings are a well-studied tool in probability theory; readers can consult the lecture notes by Lindvall (2002) or the textbooks by Thorisson (2000) and Levin et al. (2009) for entry points into this vast literature.

Probabilistic liftings were also considered in connection with *probabilistic bisimulation*, a powerful technique for proving equivalence of probabilistic transition systems. Larsen and Skou (1991) were the first to consider a probabilistic notion of bisimulation. Roughly speaking, their definition considers an equivalence relation E on states and requires that any two states in the same equivalence class have the same probability of stepping to any other equivalence class. The construction for arbitrary relations arose soon after, when researchers generalized probabilistic bisimulation to probabilistic simulation; Jonsson and Larsen (1991, Definition 4.3) proposes a *satisfaction relation* using witness distributions, similar to the definition used in pRHL. Desharnais (1999, Definition 3.6.2) and Segala and Lynch (1995, Definition 12) give an alternative characterization without witness distributions, similar to Strassen's theorem (Strassen, 1965); Desharnais (1999, Theorem 7.3.4) observed that both definitions are equivalent in the finite case via the max flow-min cut theorem. Probabilistic (bi)simulation can be characterized logically, i.e., two systems are (bi)similar if and only if they satisfy the same formulas in some modal logic (Larsen and Skou, 1991; Desharnais et al., 2002, 2003; Fijalkow et al., 2017). Deng and Du (2011) survey logical, metric, and algorithmic characterizations of these relations.

While proofs by bisimulation and proofs by coupling are founded on the same mathematical concept, they have been applied to different kinds of target properties. Verification techniques based on bisimulation, for instance, typically focus on possibly large, but finite state systems. In this setting, there are many algorithmic techniques known for constructing these proofs. On the other hand, the main strength of proofs by coupling is that by describing a binary relation between states using a logical formula, the proof technique directly extends to infinite state systems and systems with unknown parameters. At the same time, it appears that the coupling proof technique requires enough structure on the states in order to express possibly infinite relations with a compact logical formula. In contrast to the well-established algorithmic techniques for bisimulation, there has been little research to date on automating proofs of coupling (Albarghouthi and Hsu, 2018a,b). This direction deserves further exploration.

5.7.3 *Approximate couplings and differential privacy*

Differential privacy is a recent, statistical notion of privacy for database queries, proposed by Dwork et al. (2006). This property is essentially a form of sensitivity: pairs of similar input databases should lead to pairs of indistinguishable output distributions. Inspired by pRHL, Barthe et al. (2013) developed an approximate version of the program logic called apRHL to verify this property. The logic apRHL relies on a probabilistic notion of relation lifting but unlike pRHL, this lifting is approximate in a quantitative sense—it approximately models two given distributions with a joint distribution.[4] Much like for probabilistic couplings, the existence of an approximate lifting with a particular support relating two distributions can imply relational properties about the two distributions. For instance, the approximate lifting of the equality relation relates pairs of indistinguishable distributions.

Approximate liftings can be fruitfully viewed as an approximate generalization of probabilistic coupling. Moreover, the proof rules in apRHL immediately suggest a clean method to build approximate couplings. Informally, we can construct approximate couplings much like regular probabilistic couplings, while keeping track of two numeric approximation parameters (ϵ, δ) on the side. To reason about pairs of sampling instructions, we can apply any approximate coupling of the two primitive distributions if we increment (ϵ, δ) by the parameters of the selected coupling; in this way, we can think of (ϵ, δ) as kind of a *cost* that must be paid in order to apply approximate couplings. This idea enables new proofs of differential privacy by coupling, conceptually simpler and more amenable to formal verification than existing arguments (Barthe et al., 2016b,a). The interested reader can consult the thesis (Hsu, 2017) for more on the theory and applications of approximate couplings.

5.7.4 *Expectation couplings and the Kantorovich metric*

Probabilistic couplings and approximate probabilistic couplings apply to distributions over sets. In some cases, the ground sets may naturally come with a notion of distance. For instance, programs may generate distributions over the real numbers (or vectors) with the Euclidean distance. A classical way of comparing such distributions is with the *Kantorovich metric*, which lifts a distance on the ground space to a distance on distributions over the ground space. This metric is closely related to probabilistic couplings—one way to define the Kantorovich metric is as the minimum average distance over all couplings of the two given distributions. By constructing specific couplings and reasoning about the expected distance, we can upper-bound the

---

[4] There are several definitions of approximate relation lifting (Barthe and Olmedo, 2013; Olmedo, 2014; Sato, 2016; Albarghouthi and Hsu, 2018b); many of which can be shown equivalent (Barthe et al., 2017c).

Kantorovich metric between two output distributions and derive finer relational properties of probabilistic programs. Barthe et al. (2018b) develop a program logic EpRHL extending pRHL to carry out this kind of reasoning, and establish quantitative relational properties including algorithmic stability of machine learning algorithms and rapid mixing of Markov chains.

References

Albarghouthi, Aws, and Hsu, Justin. 2018a. Constraint-Based Synthesis of Coupling Proofs. In: *International Conference on Computer Aided Verification (CAV), Oxford, England.* To appear.

Albarghouthi, Aws, and Hsu, Justin. 2018b. Synthesizing Coupling Proofs of Differential Privacy. *Proceedings of the ACM on Programming Languages,* **2**(POPL). Appeared at ACM SIGPLAN–SIGACT Symposium on Principles of Programming Languages (POPL), Los Angeles, California.

Aldous, David. 1983. Random Walks on Finite Groups and Rapidly Mixing Markov Chains. Pages 243–297 of: *Séminaire de Probabilités XVII 1981/82.* Lecture Notes in Mathematics, vol. 986. Springer-Verlag.

Apt, Krzysztof R. 1981. Ten Years of Hoare's Logic: A Survey–Part I. *ACM Transactions on Programming Languages and Systems,* **3**(4), 431–483.

Apt, Krzysztof R. 1983. Ten years of Hoare's logic: A survey–Part II: Nondeterminism. *Theoretical Computer Science,* **28**(1), 83–109.

Barthe, Gilles, and Olmedo, Federico. 2013. Beyond Differential Privacy: Composition Theorems and Relational Logic for f-Divergences between Probabilistic Programs. Pages 49–60 of: *International Colloquium on Automata, Languages and Programming (ICALP), Riga, Latvia.* Lecture Notes in Computer Science, vol. 7966. Springer-Verlag.

Barthe, Gilles, Grégoire, Benjamin, and Zanella-Béguelin, Santiago. 2009. Formal Certification of Code-Based Cryptographic Proofs. Pages 90–101 of: *ACM SIGPLAN–SIGACT Symposium on Principles of Programming Languages (POPL), Savannah, Georgia.*

Barthe, Gilles, D'Argenio, Pedro R., and Rezk, Tamara. 2011. Secure Information Flow by Self-Composition. *Mathematical Structures in Computer Science,* **21**(06), 1207–1252.

Barthe, Gilles, Köpf, Boris, Olmedo, Federico, and Zanella-Béguelin, Santiago. 2013. Probabilistic Relational Reasoning for Differential Privacy. *ACM Transactions on Programming Languages and Systems,* **35**(3), 9:1–9:49.

Barthe, Gilles, Fong, Noémie, Gaboardi, Marco, Grégoire, Benjamin, Hsu, Justin, and Strub, Pierre-Yves. 2016a. Advanced Probabilistic Couplings for Differential Privacy. Pages 55–67 of: *ACM SIGSAC Conference on Computer and Communications Security (CCS), Vienna, Austria.* There is an error in the treatment of advanced composition; please see my thesis for the correction.

Barthe, Gilles, Gaboardi, Marco, Grégoire, Benjamin, Hsu, Justin, and Strub, Pierre-Yves. 2016b. Proving Differential Privacy via Probabilistic Couplings. Pages 749–758 of: *IEEE Symposium on Logic in Computer Science (LICS), New York, New York*.

Barthe, Gilles, Grégoire, Benjamin, Hsu, Justin, and Strub, Pierre-Yves. 2017a. Coupling Proofs Are Probabilistic Product Programs. Pages 161–174 of: *ACM SIGPLAN–SIGACT Symposium on Principles of Programming Languages (POPL), Paris, France*.

Barthe, Gilles, Espitau, Thomas, Grégoire, Benjamin, Hsu, Justin, and Strub, Pierre-Yves. 2017b. Proving Uniformity and Independence by Self-Composition and Coupling. Pages 385–403 of: *International Conference on Logic for Programming, Artificial Intelligence and Reasoning (LPAR), Maun, Botswana*. EPiC Series in Computing, vol. 46.

Barthe, Gilles, Espitau, Thomas, Hsu, Justin, Sato, Tetsuya, and Strub, Pierre-Yves. 2017c. ⋆-Liftings for Differential Privacy. Pages 102:1–102:12 of: *International Colloquium on Automata, Languages and Programming (ICALP), Warsaw, Poland*. Leibniz International Proceedings in Informatics, vol. 80. Schloss Dagstuhl–Leibniz Center for Informatics.

Barthe, Gilles, Espitau, Thomas, Gaboardi, Marco, Grégoire, Benjamin, Hsu, Justin, and Strub, Pierre-Yves. 2018a. An Assertion-Based Program Logic for Probabilistic Programs. In: *European Symposium on Programming (ESOP), Thessaloniki, Greece*.

Barthe, Gilles, Espitau, Thomas, Grégoire, Benjamin, Hsu, Justin, and Strub, Pierre-Yves. 2018b. Proving Expected Sensitivity of Probabilistic Programs. *Proceedings of the ACM on Programming Languages*, **2**(POPL). Appeared at ACM SIGPLAN–SIGACT Symposium on Principles of Programming Languages (POPL), Los Angeles, California.

Bellare, Mihir, and Rogaway, Phillip. 2006. The Security of Triple Encryption and a Framework for Code-Based Game-Playing Proofs. Pages 409–426 of: *IACR International Conference on the Theory and Applications of Cryptographic Techniques (EUROCRYPT), Saint Petersburg, Russia*. Lecture Notes in Computer Science, vol. 4004. Springer-Verlag.

Benton, Nick. 2004. Simple Relational Correctness Proofs for Static Analyses and Program Transformations. Pages 14–25 of: *ACM SIGPLAN–SIGACT Symposium on Principles of Programming Languages (POPL), Venice, Italy*.

Callahan, David, and Kennedy, Ken. 1988. Compiling Programs for Distributed-Memory Multiprocessors. *The Journal of Supercomputing*, **2**(2), 151–169.

Chatterjee, Krishnendu, Fu, Hongfei, Novotný, Petr, and Hasheminezhad, Rouzbeh. 2016a. Algorithmic Analysis of Qualitative and Quantitative Termination Problems for Affine Probabilistic Programs. Pages 327–342 of: *ACM SIGPLAN–SIGACT Symposium on Principles of Programming Languages (POPL), Saint Petersburg, Florida*.

Chatterjee, Krishnendu, Fu, Hongfei, and Goharshady, Amir Kafshdar. 2016b. Termination Analysis of Probabilistic Programs through Positivstellensatz's. Pages 3–22 of: *International Conference on Computer Aided Verification (CAV), Toronto, Ontario*. Lecture Notes in Computer Science, vol. 9779. Springer-Verlag.

Chatterjee, Krishnendu, Novotný, Petr, and Žikelić, D. 2017. Stochastic Invariants for Probabilistic Termination. Pages 145–160 of: *ACM SIGPLAN–SIGACT Symposium on Principles of Programming Languages (POPL), Paris, France*.

Deng, Yuxin, and Du, Wenjie. 2011 (March). *Logical, Metric, and Algorithmic Characterisations of Probabilistic Bisimulation*. Tech. rept. CMU-CS-11-110. Carnegie Mellon University.

Desharnais, Josée. 1999. *Labelled Markov Processes*. Ph.D. thesis, McGill University.

Desharnais, Josée, Edalat, Abbas, and Panangaden, Prakash. 2002. Bisimulation for Labelled Markov Processes. *Information and Computation*, **179**(2), 163–193.

Desharnais, Josée, Gupta, Vineet, Jagadeesan, Radha, and Panangaden, Prakash. 2003. Approximating Labelled Markov Processes. *Information and Computation*, **184**(1), 160–200.

Dijkstra, Edsger W. 1976. *A Discipline of Programming*. Series in Automatic Computation. Prentice Hall.

Dwork, Cynthia, McSherry, Frank, Nissim, Kobbi, and Smith, Adam D. 2006. Calibrating Noise to Sensitivity in Private Data Analysis. Pages 265–284 of: *IACR Theory of Cryptography Conference (TCC), New York, New York*. Lecture Notes in Computer Science, vol. 3876. Springer-Verlag.

Ferrer Fioriti, Luis María, and Hermanns, Holger. 2015. Probabilistic Termination: Soundness, Completeness, and Compositionality. Pages 489–501 of: *ACM SIGPLAN–SIGACT Symposium on Principles of Programming Languages (POPL), Mumbai, India*.

Fijalkow, Nathanaël, Klin, Bartek, and Panangaden, Prakash. 2017. Expressiveness of Probabilistic Modal Logics, Revisited. Pages 105:1–105:12 of: Chatzigiannakis, Ioannis, Indyk, Piotr, Kuhn, Fabian, and Muscholl, Anca (eds), *International Colloquium on Automata, Languages and Programming (ICALP), Warsaw, Poland*. Leibniz International Proceedings in Informatics, vol. 80. Dagstuhl, Germany: Schloss Dagstuhl–Leibniz Center for Informatics.

Floyd, Robert W. 1967. Assigning Meanings to Programs. In: *Symposium on Applied Mathematics*. American Mathematical Society.

Hoare, Charles A. R. 1969. An Axiomatic Basis for Computer Programming. *Communications of the ACM*, **12**(10), 576–580.

Hsu, Justin. 2017. *Probabilistic Couplings for Probabilistic Reasoning*. Ph.D. thesis, University of Pennsylvania.

Jones, Cliff B. 2003. The Early Search for Tractable Ways of Reasoning about Programs. *Annals of the History of Computing*, **25**(2), 26–49.

Jonsson, Bengt, and Larsen, Kim Guldstrand. 1991. Specification and Refinement of Probabilistic Processes. Pages 266–277 of: *IEEE Symposium on Logic in Computer Science (LICS), Amsterdam, The Netherlands.*

Kleinberg, Jon, and Tardos, Eva. 2005. *Algorithm Design.* Addison-Wesley.

Kozen, Dexter. 1981. Semantics of Probabilistic Programs. *Journal of Computer and System Sciences*, **22**(3), 328–350.

Larsen, Kim Guldstrand, and Skou, Arne. 1991. Bisimulation through Probabilistic Testing. *Information and Computation*, **94**(1), 1–28.

Levin, David A., Peres, Yuval, and Wilmer, Elizabeth L. 2009. *Markov Chains and Mixing Times.* American Mathematical Society.

Lindvall, Torgny. 2002. *Lectures on the Coupling Method.* Courier Corporation.

McIver, Annabelle, Morgan, Carroll, Kaminski, Benjamin Lucien, and Katoen, Joost-Pieter. 2018. A new proof rule for almost-sure termination. *Proceedings of the ACM on Programming Languages*, **2**(POPL), 33:1–33:28.

O'Hearn, Peter W. 2007. Resources, Concurrency, and Local Reasoning. *Theoretical Computer Science*, **375**(1), 271–307. Festschrift for John C. Reynolds's 70th birthday.

O'Hearn, Peter W., Reynolds, John C., and Yang, Hongseok. 2001. Local Reasoning about Programs That Alter Data Structures. Pages 1–19 of: *International Workshop on Computer Science Logic (CSL), Paris, France.* Lecture Notes in Computer Science, vol. 2142. Springer-Verlag.

Olmedo, Federico. 2014. *Approximate Relational Reasoning for Probabilistic Programs.* Ph.D. thesis, Universidad Politécnica de Madrid.

Reynolds, John C. 2001. Intuitionistic Reasoning about Shared Mutable Data Structure. *Millennial Perspectives in Computer Science*, **2**(1), 303–321.

Reynolds, John C. 2002. Separation Logic: A Logic for Shared Mutable Data Structures. Pages 55–74 of: *IEEE Symposium on Logic in Computer Science (LICS), Copenhagen, Denmark.*

Rudin, Walter. 1976. *Principles of Mathematical Analysis.* Third edn. International Series in Pure and Applied Mathematics. McGraw-Hill.

Sato, Tetsuya. 2016. Approximate Relational Hoare Logic for Continuous Random Samplings. In: *Conference on the Mathematical Foundations of Programming Semantics (MFPS), Pittsburgh, Pennsylvania.*

Segala, Roberto, and Lynch, Nancy A. 1995. Probabilistic Simulations for Probabilistic Processes. *Nordic Journal of Computing*, **2**(2), 250–273.

Shoup, Victor. 2004. *Sequences of Games: A Tool for Taming Complexity in Security Proofs.* Cryptology ePrint Archive, Report 2004/332.

Sousa, Marcelo, and Dillig, Isil. 2016. Cartesian Hoare Logic for Verifying k-Safety Properties. Pages 57–69 of: *ACM SIGPLAN Conference on Programming Language Design and Implementation (PLDI), Santa Barbara, California.*

Strassen, Volker. 1965. The Existence of Probability Measures with Given Marginals. *The Annals of Mathematical Statistics*, 423–439.

Thorisson, Hermann. 2000. *Coupling, Stationarity, and Regeneration.* Springer-Verlag.

Yang, Hongseok. 2007. Relational Separation Logic. *Theoretical Computer Science*, **375**(1), 308–334. Festschrift for John C. Reynolds's 70th birthday.

6

Expected Runtime Analysis
by Program Verification

Benjamin Lucien Kaminski, Joost-Pieter Katoen and Christoph Matheja
RWTH Aachen University

Abstract: This chapter is concerned with analysing the expected runtime of probabilistic programs by exploiting program verification techniques. We introduce a weakest pre-conditioning framework à la Dijkstra that enables to determine the expected runtime in a compositional manner. Like weakest pre-conditions, it is a reasoning framework at the syntax level of programs. Applications of the weakest pre-conditioning framework include determining the expected runtime of randomised algorithms, as well as determining whether a program is positive almost-surely terminatiing, i.e., whether the expected number of computation steps until termination is finite for every possible input. For Bayesian networks, a restricted class of probabilistic programs, we show that the expected runtime analysis can be fully automated. In this way, the simulation time under rejection sampling can be determined. This is in particular useful for ill-conditioned inference queries.

6.1 Introduction

In 1976, Michael Rabin published his paper titled *Randomized Algorithms* in which he describes a method for solving the *closest-pair problem* in computational geometry (Rabin, 1976). This work is today considered *the* seminal paper on randomized algorithms (Smid, 2000). While a naïve deterministic brute-force approach takes quadratic time, Rabin's randomized algorithm solves the closest-pair problem in *expected linear time*.

One year later, in 1977, Robert Solovay and Volker Strassen presented a randomized primality test that decides in *polynomial time* whether a given number is either composite or probably prime, thus proving that primality testing is in the complexity class coRP (Solovay and Strassen, 1977). In 1992, Leonard Adleman and Ming-Deh Huang further reduced the complexity of primality testing

[a] From *Foundations of Probabilistic Programming*, edited by Gilles Barthe, Joost-Pieter Katoen and Alexandra Silva published 2020 by Cambridge University Press.

to ZPP, thus proving that primality testing can be solved efficiently in expectation (Adleman and Huang, 1992). Turning an inefficient deterministic algorithm into a randomized algorithm that is – in expectation – more efficient (possibly at the cost of incorrect results, though with low probability) is a principal motivation of introducing randomization into the computation. Prime examples are Freivalds' matrix multiplication verification (Freivalds, 1979) or Hoare's variant of quicksort with random pivot selection (Hoare, 1962). Some problems even inherently require randomized solutions such as various self-stabilization algorithms in anonymous distributed systems.

Probabilistic programs are, however, not limited to randomized algorithms. In fact, they are a powerful modeling formalism for describing, amongst others, graphical models, such as Bayesian networks or Markov random fields (Koller and Friedman, 2009). This lead to the emergence of *probabilistic programming* (Gordon et al., 2014) as a new paradigm for probabilistic modeling. A key feature of probabilistic programming languages is that they decouple individual models from algorithms for their analysis, e.g. Bayesian inference techniques. For example, one of the first approaches to perform inference on probabilistic programs first compiles a program into a Bayesian network and then applies standard techniques for graphical models (Minka and Winn, 2017). Probabilistic programming also enables to resort to established program analysis techniques, such as slicing (Hur et al., 2014), to optimize probabilistic models. In this context, analyzing expected runtimes, i.e. the expected time required for sampling from a complex probability distribution described by a probabilistic program, to speed up inference algorithms is of paramount importance, too.

Reasoning about expected runtimes of probabilistic programs is surprisingly subtle and full of nuances as we will discuss in detail in this chapter. Thus, there is a desire for *a formal verification technique* suited for reasoning about expected runtimes. The main objective of this chapter is to provide a gentle introduction to one particular formal method for analyzing expected runtimes of probabilistic programs: The *expected runtime calculus*. This approach was originally developed in Kaminski et al. (2016) and was further studied in Olmedo et al. (2016); Batz et al. (2018); Kaminski et al. (2018b); Kaminski (2019). The calculus is a weakest-precondition style calculus à la Dijkstra (see Dijkstra, 1976) to derive runtime assertions. In a similar vein to Dijkstra's predicate transformers, our calculus uses *runtime transformers*. Its core is the expected runtime transformer ert:

$$\mathsf{ert}[c](t)(\sigma)$$

captures the expected runtime of program c when started in initial state σ. The t appearing above is the so-called *postruntime*: t is a function mapping program states to non-negative reals and captures the expected runtime of the computation following program c. It is hence evaluated in the *final* states reached after termination of c on σ. In particular, this subsumes the plain expected runtime of program c on initial state σ if t is the constantly zero runtime. For most control structures, ert is defined in a straightforward compositional manner. The action of the transformer on loops is given using fixed-point techniques. To avoid the tedious reasoning about such fixed points and to enhance the calculus' usability, we provide *invariant-based proof rules* that establish bounds on the expected runtime of loops.

A notable feature of the ert-calculus is that it firmly builds upon standard techniques from formal semantics and program verification – in particular denotational semantics, fixed point theory, and invariants. It provides a useful abstraction from the semantical intricacies of probabilistic programs and the underlying probability theory. ert thus enables writing elegant and *compositional* proofs to bound expected runtimes (from above and below) *on source code level*. Furthermore, the reliance on standard techniques makes ert amenable to a large degree of automation. The ert-calculus yields *comprehensible* proofs for the expected runtime of complex randomized algorithms. For instance, it has been successfully applied to analyze the Coupon Collector's problem (Kaminski et al., 2016), a Sherwood binary search (Olmedo et al., 2016), and expected sampling times in Bayesian networks (Batz et al., 2018). The latter can be derived fully automatically.

Ngo et al. (2018) have developed an automatic approach for deriving polynomial runtime bounds, using our ert calculus as an underlying theoretical framework for proving soundness of their approach. The ert calculus has also been mechanized in the interactive theorem prover Isabelle/HOL by Hölzl (2016). In particular, Hölzl proved that our calculus is indeed sound and complete and that our proof rules for deriving runtime bounds are correct.

A second asset is that ert enables determining whether the expected runtime of a randomized algorithm (for all possible inputs) is finite or not. To the best of our knowledge, this is the first formal verification framework that can handle both almost-sure termination (does a program terminate with probability one?) and positive almost-sure termination (does a program terminate within finite expected time?). The universal positive almost-sure termination problem is complete for level Π_3^0 of the arithmetical hierarchy (Kaminski and Katoen, 2015) and hence strictly harder to decide than the universal halting problem for deterministic programs (which is Π_2^0-complete).

Organization of this chapter. We describe a simple probabilistic programming language in Section 6.2. In Section 6.3, we then present challenges and phenomena encountered when reasoning about expected runtimes. The expected runtime calculus and our proof rules for loops are presented in Section 6.4. An application of our calculus to the automated analysis of expected sampling times of Bayesian networks is presented in Section 6.6. Finally, in Section 6.7, we conclude with a discussion of recent research directions.

6.2 Probabilistic Programs

In this chapter, we consider probabilistic programs written in a simple probabilistic extension of Dijkstra's Guarded Command Language (GCL) (Dijkstra, 1976). To that end, we extend GCL with *random assignments*. Let us briefly go over the statements in the resulting *probabilistic* Guarded Command Language (pGCL) by means of small examples. Furthermore, since we want to reason about (expected) runtimes of pGCL programs, we also discuss our underlying runtime model, i.e. the time consumed by each pGCL statement. Our pGCL programs adhere to the grammar

$$C \quad \longrightarrow \quad \texttt{empty} \mid x :\approx \mu \mid C; C$$
$$\mid \texttt{if}\,(\varphi)\,\{C\}\,\texttt{else}\,\{C\}$$
$$\mid \{c_1\} \,\square\, \{c_2\}$$
$$\mid \texttt{while}\,(\varphi)\,\{C\}$$

where empty is a program that has no effect and consumes no time, x is a program variable, μ represents a (discrete) probability distribution, and φ a Boolean expression. We now go over the language constructs and the runtime model. For more details, in particular on an operational semantics capturing our runtime model, please refer toKaminski et al. (2016).

Random assignments. The key feature of pGCL is the ability to sample values from a (discrete) probability distribution, say μ, and assign the sampled value to a program variable, say x. The corresponding pGCL statement is a *random assignment* of the form

$$x :\approx \mu \,.$$

For example, the random assignment

$$heads :\approx {}^1\!/_3 \cdot \langle \mathsf{true} \rangle + {}^2\!/_3 \cdot \langle \mathsf{false} \rangle$$

simulates a biased coin flip: With probability $^1\!/_3$ the value true is assigned to variable *heads* and with the remaining probability, i.e. $^2\!/_3$, the value false is assigned, respectively. The right-hand side of a random assignment may be any (computable) discrete probability distribution over the set of possible values of a variable. In particular, we allow probability distributions to depend on the current program state, i.e. an evaluation of all program variables. For instance, the random assignment

$y :\approx \texttt{uniform}(0, x)$ samples from a (discrete) uniform distribution over the range from 0 to the current value stored in variable x and assigns the thereby obtained value to variable y. Notice that deterministic assignments, such as $x :\approx x + 1$, are a special case in which a probability of one is assigned to a single value.

In our runtime model, every random assignment consumes *one* unit of time. Note that this is a design choice in order to keep the calculus we are going to present as clean and simple as possible. It is unproblematic to assume a more nuanced runtime model for random assignments. The same holds for the runtimes we associate with the other language constructs below.

Control flow. pGCL is equipped with standard control flow constructs for sequential composition, conditional choices, and loops:

- The *sequential composition* $c_1; c_2$ first executes program c_1 and then executes program c_2. The composition operation itself consumes *no* time.
- The *conditional choice* $\texttt{if}\,(\varphi)\,\{c_1\}\,\texttt{else}\,\{c_2\}$ executes c_1 if the (deterministic) guard φ evaluates to true and c_2 if φ evaluates to false, respectively. The guard evaluation consumes *one* unit of time.
- The *loop* $\texttt{while}\,(\varphi)\,\{c\}$ keeps executing the loop body c as long as the guard φ evaluates to true at the loop head. If the guard evaluates to false, the loop terminates. *Every* guard evaluation consumes *one* unit of time.

Let us consider the following probabilistic program inspired by Chakarov and Sankaranarayanan (2013):

$$
\begin{aligned}
&h :\approx 0;\ t :\approx 30;\\
&\texttt{while}\,(h \leq t)\,\{\\
&\qquad c :\approx {}^1\!/_2 \cdot \langle \text{true} \rangle + {}^1\!/_2 \cdot \langle \text{false} \rangle;\\
&\qquad \texttt{if}\,(c = \text{true})\,\{\\
&\qquad\qquad h :\approx h + \texttt{uniform}[0 \ldots 10]\\
&\qquad \}\,\texttt{else}\,\{\texttt{empty}\};\\
&\qquad t :\approx t + 1\\
&\}\,.
\end{aligned}
$$

Here, $\texttt{empty}$ is a pGCL statement representing the empty program, i.e. the statement has *no effect* and consumes *no time*. The example models a race between a tortoise and a hare; the variables t and h represent their respective positions. The tortoise starts with a lead of 30 and advances one step in each round, i.e. each loop iteration. The hare with probability $^1\!/_2$ advances a random number of steps between 0 and 10 (governed by a uniform distribution) and with the remaining probability remains still. The race ends when the hare passes the tortoise.

Regarding the runtime, the program requires two units of time for the initial assignments. In every loop iteration, the program consumes either four or five units of time: It always takes one unit of time to evaluate the loop guard, flip a coin, evaluate the conditional, and to update variable t, respectively. If the conditional is evaluated to true, an additional unit of time is consumed to update the value of variable h.

Nondeterminism. Apart from sampling from a known distribution, pGCL also supports true nondeterminism: The statement $\{c_1\} \ \square \ \{c_2\}$ represents a nondeterministic choice between programs c_1 and c_2, i.e. either c_1 or c_2 is executed, but there is no probability distribution underlying the choice between the two programs. Similarly to sequential composition, a nondeterministic choice itself consumes no additional time in our runtime model.

As an example, consider the program

$$\{x :\approx 3\} \ \square \ \{x :\approx 5\}\,;$$
$$\texttt{while}\,(x > 0)\,\{$$
$$x :\approx x - 1$$
$$\}\,.$$

This program has two possible executions: One execution initially assigns 3 to x and has a runtime of 8 units of time. The other execution initially assigns 5 to x and has a runtime of 12 units of time. When reasoning about *the* expected runtime of a pGCL program, we resolve nondeterminism by a *demonic* scheduler (cf. McIver and Morgan, 2004; Dijkstra, 1976). That is, nondeterministic choices are resolved in a way that *maximizes* the runtime. In the above example, this means that the nondeterministic choice is resolved such that 5 is assigned to x. Strictly speaking, we thus reason about *worst-case* expected runtimes.

Remark on the runtime model. We stress that the runtime model presented in this section is one particular design choice for the sake of concreteness. It is straightforward to adapt our approach to alternative runtime models, where, for example, only loop iterations or assignments are considered relevant. The same holds for alternative resolutions of nondeterminism such as using an angelic scheduler. Furthermore, more fine-grained models that take, for instance, the size of expressions and distributions that appear in the random assignments into account can easily be incorporated.

6.3 Semantic Intricacies

Reasoning about expected runtimes of probabilistic programs is full of nuances. Let us illustrate this by discussing a few phenomena. To this end, we consider a fundamental property of ordinary, i.e. non-probabilistic, programs: *An ordinary program terminates, meaning all of its runs are finite, if and only if it has a finite runtime.* What is a probabilistic analog of this property when considering *expected* runtimes?

Termination is too strong. A single diverging run of an ordinary program causes its runtime to be infinite. This is not the case for probabilistic programs. They may admit *arbitrarily long* and even *infinite* runs while still having a *finite* expected runtime. For example, the program

$$c_{geo}: \quad b :\approx 1;$$
$$\texttt{while}(b = 1)\{$$
$$b :\approx \; {}^1\!/_2 \cdot \langle 0 \rangle + {}^1\!/_2 \cdot \langle 1 \rangle$$
$$\}.$$

keeps flipping a fair coin until observing the first heads (represented by 0). It admits arbitrarily long runs, since – for every natural number n – the probability of not seeing a heads in the first n trials is non-zero. It even admits a non-terminating run, namely the one in which the outcome of all coin flips is tails. The runtime of program c_{geo}, however, is geometrically distributed and therefore its expected runtime is finite, even constant: On average, it terminates after two loop iterations.

The classical notion of termination for ordinary programs – all program runs have to be finite – is thus too strong for probabilistic programs (with respect to the considered property). In the above example, we observe that the only infinite run of program c_{geo} has probability zero. A more sensible notion of termination might thus require that all infinite runs of a program have probability zero. Conversely: The probability of termination is one. This is referred to as *almost-sure termination* (Hart et al., 1983). Does almost-sure termination – instead of classical termination – capture finite expected runtimes?

Almost-sure termination is too weak. For ordinary programs, termination always implies finite runtime. For probabilistic programs this is not always true – even if we consider almost-surely terminating programs only. For example, consider the program

$$c_{rw}: \quad x :\approx 10;$$
$$\texttt{while}\,(x > 0)\{$$

$$x :\approx {}^1\!/_2 \cdot \langle x{-}1 \rangle + {}^1\!/_2 \cdot \langle x{+}1 \rangle$$
$$\} \, ,$$

which models a one-dimensional random walk of a particle: Starting from position 10, in each step the particle moves randomly one step to the left or one step to the right, until reaching position 0. The particle reaches position 0 with probability one. The program c_{rw} thus terminates almost-surely. However, doing so requires infinitely many steps on average (cf. Ibe, 2013, Chapter 3.7.3). The expected runtime of c_{rw} is thus infinite.

Since an almost-surely terminating program might run – in expectation – infinitely long, a better probabilistic analog of classical termination might be to require that a program's expected runtime is finite. This is referred to as *positive* almost-sure termination (Bournez and Garnier, 2005). In fact, having a finite expected runtime implies almost-sure termination (Olmedo et al., 2016, Theorem 5.3). However, there are subtle differences between classical termination and positive almost-sure termination. From a complexity-theoretic view, it is noteworthy that the decision problem "does a program terminate in finite expected time (on all inputs)?" is Π_3^0-complete in the arithmetical hierarchy, and thus strictly harder than the universal halting problem for ordinary programs (Kaminski and Katoen, 2015; Kaminski et al., 2018a).

Positive almost-sure termination is not compositional. Running two ordinary terminating programs in sequence yields again a terminating program. Termination is thus closed under sequential composition. This is not true for probabilistic programs when considering positive almost-sure termination. Consider the pair of programs

```
c₁:  x :≈ 1; b :≈ 1;                    c₂:  while(x > 0){
         while(b = 1){                              x :≈ x − 1
             b :≈ ¹/₂·⟨0⟩ + ¹/₂·⟨1⟩;          · }
             x :≈ 2x
     }
```

Both programs terminate positive almost-surely: As the loop in C_1 terminates on average in two iterations, it has a finite expected runtime. Furthermore, program c_2 performs at most $\lceil x \rceil$ iterations for any initial value of x, i.e. its expected runtime is finite, too. However, the composed program $c_1 ; c_2$ has an *infinite* expected runtime – even though it almost-surely terminates. This is intuitively due to the fact that the expected value of x after termination of c_1 is infinite and c_2 needs x steps to terminate.

6.4 The Expected Runtime Calculus

We now present a sound and complete calculus that enables rigorous reasoning about expected runtimes of probabilistic programs. Apart from programs, the two central objects used within our calculus are program states and runtimes. A *program state* σ is an evaluation of program variables, i.e. a mapping from variables – collected in the set Var – to possible values, such as integers or rationals, which are collected in the set Val. A *runtime* is a function mapping every program state σ to a non-negative real number or infinity. Formally, the sets of program states and runtimes are given by

$$\Sigma = \{\sigma : \text{Var} \to \text{Val}\} \quad \text{and} \quad \mathbb{T} = \{t : \Sigma \to \mathbb{R}_{\geq 0}^{\infty}\} .$$

Our goal is to associate with every program c a runtime t mapping every program state σ to the average or expected runtime of executing program c on initial state σ. To this end, we express the expected runtime of programs in a continuation-passing style by means of the runtime transformer

$$\text{ert}[\,\cdot\,] : \text{pGCL} \to (\mathbb{T} \to \mathbb{T}) .$$

The number $\text{ert}[c](t)(\sigma)$ is the expected runtime of executing program c on initial state σ assuming that t captures the runtime of the computation *following* c. The ert-transformer thus applies backward reasoning. The runtime t is usually referred to as the *continuation* (or postruntime) and we can think of it as being evaluated in the final states that are reached upon termination of c. Thus, the plain expected runtime of executing c on initial state σ is $\text{ert}[c](0)(\sigma)$, where 0 is a shortcut for the constant runtime $\lambda\sigma.\,0$.[1] In general, we write k to denote the constant runtime $\lambda\sigma.\,k$ for $k \in \mathbb{R}_{\geq 0}^{\infty}$.

The ert-transformer is defined by induction on the structure of pGCL programs and adheres to our simple runtime model described in Section 6.2. That is, $\text{ert}[c](0)$ captures the expected number of assignments and guard evaluations. A summary of the ert definitions is found in Table 6.1. Let us briefly go over the definitions for each pGCL statement.

Empty program. Since the empty program `empty` has no effect on the program state and consumes no time, the expected runtime of `empty` with respect to continuation t corresponds to the identity, i.e.

$$\text{ert}[\texttt{empty}](t) = t .$$

---

[1] We use λ-expressions to denote functions: Function $\lambda X.\,f$ applied to an argument α evaluates to f in which every free occurrence of X is replaced by α.

Table 6.1 *Rules for defining the expected runtime transformer* ert.

c	$\text{ert}[c](t)$
`empty`	t
$x :\approx \mu$	$1 + \lambda\sigma.\ \sum_{v\in\text{Val}} \Pr_{[\![\mu]\!](\sigma)}(v) \cdot t[x/v](\sigma)$
$c_1;\ c_2$	$\text{ert}[c_1](\text{ert}[c_2](t))$
`if` $(\varphi)\ \{c_1\}$ `else` $\{c_2\}$	$1 + [\varphi]\cdot\text{ert}[c_1](t) + [\neg\varphi]\cdot\text{ert}[c_2](t)$
$\{c_1\}\ \square\ \{c_2\}$	$\max\{\text{ert}[c_1](t),\text{ert}[c_2](t)\}$
`while` $(\varphi)\ \{c'\}$	lfp F_t, where
	$F_t(X) = 1 + [\varphi]\cdot\text{ert}[c'](X) + [\neg\varphi]\cdot t$

Random assignment. For the random assignment $x :\approx \mu$, one unit of time is consumed. Moreover, the remaining expected runtime represented by continuation t has to be considered after updating t to take the possible new values of variable x – weighted according to their probabilities – into account. Formally, we define

$$\text{ert}[x :\approx \mu](t)(\sigma) = 1 + \sum_{v\in\text{Val}} \Pr_{[\![\mu]\!](\sigma)}(v) \cdot t\big(\sigma[x/v]\big),$$

where $\Pr_{[\![\mu]\!](\sigma)}(v)$ is the probability that – for state σ – distribution expression μ evaluates to value v. Moreover, $\sigma[x/v]$ is the program state σ in which the value assigned to variable x is updated to v. The above definition does, unfortunately, depend on the program state σ. If the distribution expression μ is agnostic of the program state, we can obtain a simpler definition. To this end, we define the "syntactic replacement" of a variable x in a runtime t by value v as $t[x/v] = \lambda\sigma.\ t(\sigma[x/v])$. Then, since the probability distribution μ is independent of σ, we can write the expected runtime of the random assignment without referring explicitly to a program state:

$$\text{ert}[x :\approx \mu](t) = 1 + \sum_{v\in\text{Val}} \Pr_{[\![\mu]\!]}(v) \cdot t[x/v]$$

For example, consider a biased coin flip $x :\approx \frac{1}{3}\cdot\langle 0\rangle + \frac{2}{3}\cdot\langle x+1\rangle$. Since the probability distribution does not depend on the program state, we have

$$\text{ert}\big[x :\approx \tfrac{1}{3}\cdot\langle 0\rangle + \tfrac{2}{3}\cdot\langle x+1\rangle\big](t) = 1 + \tfrac{1}{3}\cdot t[x/0] + \tfrac{2}{3}\cdot t[x/x+1].$$

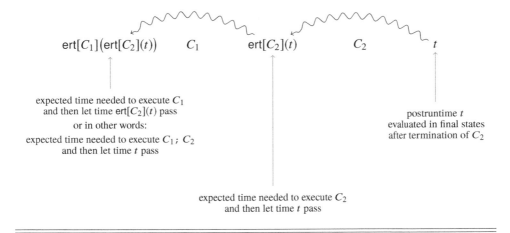

Figure 6.1 Continuation-passing style expected runtime transformer.

Sequential composition. For the composition $c_1;\ c_2$ of pGCL programs c_1 and c_2, it becomes evident that we reason backwards: We first determine the expected runtime of c_2 with respect to continuation t, i.e. $\text{ert}[c_2](t)$. Afterwards, we determine the expected runtime of c_1 with respect to continuation $\text{ert}[c_2](t)$. As a diagram, the intuition behind this is depicted in Figure 6.1. Formally, we define the ert of sequential composition as

$$\text{ert}[c_1;\ c_2](t)\ =\ \text{ert}[c_1](\text{ert}[c_2](t))\,.$$

Conditional choice. For the conditional $\text{if}\,(\varphi)\,\{c_1\}\ \text{else}\ \{c_2\}$, one unit of time is consumed to account for the guard evaluation. Furthermore, the expected runtime of c_1 (with respect to continuation t) is added if guard φ evaluates to true. Otherwise, the expected runtime of c_2 is added. The truth value of a Boolean expression ξ is captured by the indicator function, also called *Iverson bracket*,

$$[\xi]:\Sigma\rightarrow\{0,1\}\,,$$

which, for a given state σ, evaluates to 1 if ξ evaluates to true in state σ. Otherwise, it evaluates to 0. Using Iverson brackets, the ert of the conditional choice statement is given by

$$\text{ert}\big[\text{if}\,(\varphi)\,\{c_1\}\ \text{else}\ \{c_2\}\big](t)\ =\ 1\ +\ [\varphi]\cdot\text{ert}[c_1](t)\ +\ [\neg\varphi]\cdot\text{ert}[c_2](t)\,.$$

Nondeterminism. For the *nondeterministic choice* $\{c_1\}\ \square\ \{c_2\}$, either c_1 or c_2 is executed. In particular, no probability distribution guiding which of the two programs is executed is known. Since the choice itself consumes no time, the expected runtime of $\{c_1\} \; \Box \; \{c_2\}$ is either the expected runtime of c_1 or the expected runtime of c_2. Following the "demonic nondeterminism" school of thought (cf. McIver and Morgan, 2004; Dijkstra, 1976), we assume that the program with the worst expected runtime will be executed, i.e. we take the maximum of both expected runtimes. Formally, we define

$$\mathsf{ert}\big[\,\{c_1\} \; \Box \; \{c_2\}\,\big](t) \;=\; \max\big\{\mathsf{ert}[c_1](t), \mathsf{ert}[c_2](t)\big\} \;.$$

Loops. For the loop `while ($\varphi$) {c}`, we exploit the fact that the expected runtime of the loop coincides with the expected runtime of its unrolling

$$\texttt{if } (\varphi) \; \big\{c; \, \texttt{while } (\varphi)\, \{c\}\big\} \; \texttt{else } \{\texttt{empty}\} \;.$$

Applying ert to this program then yields (for a fixed continuation t):

$$
\begin{aligned}
&\mathsf{ert}[\texttt{while } (\varphi)\, \{c\}](t) \\
=\;& \mathsf{ert}[\texttt{if } (\varphi) \; \{c; \, \texttt{while } (\varphi)\, \{c\}\} \; \texttt{else } \{\texttt{empty}\}](t) \\
=\;& 1 + [\varphi] \cdot \mathsf{ert}[c; \, \texttt{while } (\varphi)\, \{c\}](t) && \text{(Definition of ert)} \\
& + [\neg\varphi] \cdot \mathsf{ert}[\texttt{empty}](t) \\
=\;& 1 + [\varphi] \cdot \mathsf{ert}[c]\big(\mathsf{ert}\big[\texttt{while } (\varphi)\, \{c\}\big](t)\big) + [\neg\varphi] \cdot t \;. && \text{(Definition of ert)}
\end{aligned}
$$

Every solution of this equation is a fixed point of the transformer

$$F_t: \qquad \mathbb{T} \to \mathbb{T}, \quad X \mapsto 1 + [\varphi] \cdot \mathsf{ert}[c](X) + [\neg\varphi] \cdot t \;,$$

in which we substituted $\mathsf{ert}[\texttt{while } (\varphi)\, \{c\}](t)$ by X. In fact, as is standard in denotational semantics, we are interested in the *least* fixed point. The underlying intuition is that, for every natural number n,

$$F_t^n(0) \;=\; F_t(F_t(\ldots (0)\ldots))$$

precisely captures the expected runtime when allowing at most n loop iterations. Consequently, we approximate the expected runtime of the loop from below and take the first solution capturing the expected runtime for all loop iterations, i.e. the least fixed point of F_t. The least fixed point of the characteristic functional F_t is guaranteed to exist for every loop `while ($\varphi$) {c}` and every continuation t, because $\mathbb{T}$ (with pointwise ordering of runtimes) is a complete lattice and F_t is continuous (and hence also monotonic). The Kleene Fixed Point Theorem (Kleene, 1952) then ensures by continuity that the least fixed point of F_t, which we denote by $\mathsf{lfp}\, F_t$, exists and coincides with the limit of $F_t^n(0)$ for $n \to \infty$. Hence, we define the expected runtime of loop `while ($\varphi$) {c}` with respect to continuation t as

$$\mathsf{ert}[\texttt{while } (\varphi)\, \{c\}](t) \;=\; \mathsf{lfp}\, F_t \;=\; \lim_{n \to \infty} F_t^n(0) \;.$$

Remark on soundness. Our expected runtime calculus is sound with respect to a simple operational semantics based on Markov Decision Processes, where each state corresponds to a program statement and each transition corresponds to one execution step. The time consumed by a statement is modeled using state rewards. More precisely, one can show that for every pGCL program c, every continuation t and every program state σ, the expected runtime $\text{ert}[c](t)(\sigma)$ coincides with the maximal expected reward (assuming demonic nondeterminism) of the unique Markov Decision Process corresponding to $c, t,$ and σ as defined by the operational semantics. We refer the interested reader to Kaminski et al. (2016) for further details.

A loop-free example. Consider the program c_{trunc}:

c_1: $x :\approx {}^1\!/_2 \cdot \langle\text{true}\rangle + {}^1\!/_2 \cdot \langle\text{false}\rangle$;

c_2: $\texttt{if}(x = \text{true})\{$

c_3: $x :\approx {}^1\!/_2 \cdot \langle\text{true}\rangle + {}^1\!/_2 \cdot \langle\text{false}\rangle$

c_4: $\texttt{if}(x = \text{true})\{$

c_5: $x :\approx {}^1\!/_2 \cdot \langle\text{true}\rangle + {}^1\!/_2 \cdot \langle\text{false}\rangle$

            $\}\,\texttt{else}\,\{\texttt{empty}\}$

        $\}\,\texttt{else}\,\{\texttt{empty}\}$

It simulates a geometric distribution that is truncated after the third coin flip. To determine its expected runtime, i.e. $\text{ert}[c_{\text{trunc}}](0)$, it suffices to apply the rules of the ert-transformer (see Table 6.1). Throughout this chapter, we will use the notation

$$\begin{array}{l}\text{/\!/\!/}\ s' \\ \text{/\!/\!/}\ s \\ c \\ \text{/\!/\!/}\ t\end{array}$$

to express the fact that $s = \text{ert}[c](t)$ and moreover that $s' = s$. It is thus more intuitive to read annotated programs from *bottom to top*, just like the ert-transformer moves from the back to the front. Using this notation, we can annotate the program c_{trunc} simply by applying the ert rules from Table 6.1 as shown below in Figure 6.2. Hence, on average, running program c_{trunc} takes ${}^{13}\!/_4$ units of time.

6.5 Proof Rules for Loops

Reasoning about the runtime of loop-free programs, such as the program c_{trunc} in the above example, amounts mostly to syntactic reasoning. The runtime of a loop, however, is defined as the least fixed point of its characteristic functional F_t. It can

/// $\frac{13}{4}$

/// $\cdots$

/// $1 + \frac{1}{2} \cdot \left(1 + [x = \text{true}] \cdot \frac{5}{2}\right)[x/\text{true}]$
$\qquad + \frac{1}{2} \cdot \left(1 + [x = \text{true}] \cdot \frac{5}{2}\right)[x/\text{false}]$

$x :\approx {}^{1}/_{2} \cdot \langle \text{true} \rangle + {}^{1}/_{2} \cdot \langle \text{false} \rangle;$

/// $1 + [x = \text{true}] \cdot \frac{5}{2}$

/// $1 + [x = \text{true}] \cdot \frac{5}{2} + [x = \text{false}] \cdot 0$

if$(x = \text{true})\{$

 /// $\frac{5}{2}$

 /// $1 + \frac{1}{2} \cdot \left(1 + 1\right) + \frac{1}{2} \cdot \left(1 + 0\right)$

 /// $1 + \frac{1}{2} \cdot \left(1 + [\text{true} = \text{true}]\right) + \frac{1}{2} \cdot \left(1 + [\text{false} = \text{true}]\right)$

 /// $1 + \frac{1}{2} \cdot \left(1 + [x = \text{true}]\right)[x/\text{true}]$
 $\qquad + \frac{1}{2} \cdot \left(1 + [x = \text{true}]\right)[x/\text{false}]$

 $x :\approx {}^{1}/_{2} \cdot \langle \text{true} \rangle + {}^{1}/_{2} \cdot \langle \text{false} \rangle$

 /// $1 + [x = \text{true}]$

 /// $1 + [x = \text{true}] \cdot 1 + [x = \text{false}] \cdot 0$

 if$(x = \text{true})\{$

  /// 1

  /// $1 + \frac{1}{2} \cdot 0[x/\text{true}] + \frac{1}{2} \cdot 0[x/\text{false}]$

  $x :\approx {}^{1}/_{2} \cdot \langle \text{true} \rangle + {}^{1}/_{2} \cdot \langle \text{false} \rangle$

  /// 0

 $\} \text{else}\{$

  /// 0

  empty

  /// 0

 $\}$

 /// 0

$\} \text{else}\{$

 /// 0

 empty

 /// 0

$\}$

/// 0

Figure 6.2 Runtime annotations for the program c_{trunc}. It is more intuitive to read the annotations from bottom to top. The postruntime after executing the whole program is 0; the a priori expected runtime of executing the whole program is $^{13}/_{4}$.

thus be obtained by fixed point iteration using Kleene's fixed point theorem (Kleene, 1952), i.e.

$$\mathsf{lfp}\, F_t \;=\; \sup_{n \in \mathbb{N}} F_t^n(0)\,,$$

where $F_t^n(X)$ denotes n-fold application of F_t to X. However, the fixed point is not necessarily reached within a finite number of iterations. We thus study various proof rules for approximating the expected runtime of loops.

6.5.1 Proof Rule for Upper Bounds

We first present a simple, yet powerful, proof rule for determining upper bounds on expected runtimes of loops. This rule is based on an alternative characterization of the least fixed point due to Tarski and Knaster (see Tarski *et al.*, 1955): Any X that satisfies $F(X) \leq X$ is called a *pre-fixed point* of the function F. The least fixed point of F can be characterized as its smallest pre-fixed point, i.e. the smallest X such that $F(X) \leq X$. Consequently, *every* pre-fixed point is greater than or equal to the least fixed point of F.

How does this lead us to a proof rule? Let F_t be the characteristic functional of some loop $\texttt{while}\,(\varphi)\,\{c\}$ with respect to a continuation $t \in \mathbb{T}$. In the context of runtimes, we refer to a pre-fixed point $I \in \mathbb{T}$ of F_t as an *upper invariant* of loop $\texttt{while}\,(\varphi)\,\{c\}$ and continuation t. By the above observation, we can then formulate our first proof rule as follows:

$$\underbrace{F_t(I) \leq I}_{I \text{ is an upper invariant}} \qquad \text{implies} \qquad \underbrace{\mathsf{ert}[\texttt{while}\,(\varphi)\,\{c\}](t) \;=\; \mathsf{lfp}\, F_t \leq I}_{I \text{ is an upper bound of the expected runtime}}\,.$$

In particular, since the exact expected runtime of a loop itself is an upper invariant, completeness of the above proof rule is immediate.

Example: The geometric distribution. Let us consider an application of our proof rule. The loop c_{geo} below has a geometrically distributed runtime as it keeps flipping a fair coin until it hits tails ($c = 0$).

$$c_{\mathsf{geo}}: \qquad \begin{aligned} &\texttt{while}\,(c = 1)\,\{ \\ &\qquad c :\approx {}^1\!/_2 \cdot \langle 0 \rangle + {}^1\!/_2 \cdot \langle 1 \rangle \\ &\} \end{aligned}$$

How can we apply our proof rule to verify an upper bound on the expected runtime of c_{geo}? The corresponding characteristic functional with respect to postruntime $t = 0$ is:

$$F_0(X) = 1 + [c \neq 1] \cdot 0 + [c = 1] \cdot \text{ert}[c :\approx \frac{1}{2} \cdot \langle 0 \rangle + \frac{1}{2} \cdot \langle 1 \rangle](X)$$
$$= 1 + [c = 1] \cdot \left(1 + \frac{1}{2} \cdot (X[c/0] + X[c/1])\right).$$

By the calculations below we verify that $I = 1 + [c = 1] \cdot 4$ is an upper invariant of the loop (with respect to 0):

$$F_0(I) = 1 + [c = 1] \cdot \left(1 + \frac{1}{2} \cdot (I[c/0] + I[c/1])\right)$$
$$= 1 + [c = 1] \cdot \left(1 + \frac{1}{2} \cdot (\underbrace{1 + [0 = 1] \cdot 4}_{= 1} + \underbrace{1 + [1 = 1] \cdot 4}_{= 5})\right)$$
$$= 1 + [c = 1] \cdot 4$$
$$= I \leq I.$$

Hence, I is an upper invariant. By our proof rule, we then obtain

$$\text{ert}\big[c_{\text{geo}}\big](0) \leq 1 + [c = 1] \cdot 4.$$

In words, the expected runtime of c_{geo} is at most $1 + 4 = 5$ from any initial state where $c = 1$ and at most $1 + 0 = 1$ from any other state. Notice that if the loop body is itself loop-free, as in the above example, verifying that some runtime I is an upper invariant is usually fairly easy. Inferring the invariant, in contrast, is one of the most involved part of the verification effort.

6.5.2 Proof Rule for Lower Bounds

It is tempting to use the converse version of our proof rule based on upper invariants to reason about lower bounds on the expected runtime. That is, one would like to check $I \leq F_t(I)$ for some runtime $I \in \mathbb{T}$ in order to verify that $I \leq \text{ert}[\texttt{while}\,(\varphi)\,\{c\}](0)$. Such a rule is unfortunately *not sound* as is, but we can add further premises to make it sound.

Metering Functions

We would like first to point out that it is not self-evident that the simple lower bound rule suggested above must necessarily fail: For *non-probabilistic* programs, Frohn et al. (2016) have shown that this very lower bound rule is indeed sound. They call an I, such that $I \leq F_t(I)$, a *metering function*. Whenever I is a metering function, I is a lower bound on the runtime of a *non-probabilistic loop*, just as I being an upper invariant implies that I is an upper bound on the (expected) runtime of a loop – be it probabilistic or not.

The intuition behind the soundness of the metering function rule is that for non-probabilistic programs there exists some $n \in \mathbb{N}$ such that

$$\bigl(\mathsf{lfp}\ F_t\bigr)(\sigma) \;=\; \bigl(F_t^n(0)\bigr)(\sigma)\,,$$

in case that the loop terminates on σ (this is not true if the loop diverges, but then any lower bound is a lower bound). Existence of n allows for proving soundness of the metering function rule by induction on n. This is *not true* for probabilistic programs: We may well have the situation that we need to take the limit for n, so that

$$\bigl(\mathsf{lfp}\ F_t\bigr)(\sigma) \;=\; \sup_{n \in \mathbb{N}}\bigl(F_t^n(0)\bigr)(\sigma)\,,$$

but for all $n \in \mathbb{N}$

$$\bigl(\mathsf{lfp}\ F_t\bigr)(\sigma) \;>\; \bigl(F_t^n(0)\bigr)(\sigma)\,,$$

even for a fixed initial state σ. Indeed, for probabilistic programs, the metering function approach is unfortunately unsound, as the following counterexample shows: Consider the loop c, given by

```
while (y = 1) {
    y :≈ 1/2 · ⟨0⟩ + 1/2 · ⟨1⟩;
    x :≈ x + 1
},
```

where we assume that x ranges over $\mathbb{N}$ for simplicity. Suppose we want to reason about a lower bound on the expected runtime of c by a metering function. The characteristic functional of the while loop with respect to postruntime 0 is given by

$$F_0(X) \;=\; 1 \;+\; [y = 1] \cdot \Bigl(2 + \tfrac{1}{2}\bigl(X[x/x + 1][y/0] + X[x/x + 1][y/1]\bigr)\Bigr)\,.$$

We now propose *two* fixed points of F_0, namely

$$I_1 \;=\; 1 + [y = 1]\,6 \qquad \text{and} \qquad I_2 \;=\; 1 + [y = 1]\bigl(6 + 2^{x+a}\bigr)\,,$$

for any constant $a \geq 0$, are both a fixed point of F_0 and hence also a metering function. I_1 is in fact the least fixed point of F_0 and we clearly have $I_1 \lneq I_2$. Thus, if we prove $I_2 \leq F_0(I_2)$, we cannot possibly have proven that I_2 is a lower bound on the least fixed point of F_0, since I_1 is a fixed point strictly smaller than I_2. The intuitive reason is that the expected runtime of c is completely independent of x but x has an influence on the value that I_2 assumes. For more details on the connections between the ert calculus and metering functions, we refer the interested reader Kaminski (2019, Sections 7.6.3 and 7.6.4).

Table 6.2 *Rules for obtaining upper or lower bounds on the (expected) runtime of a loop* while (φ) $\{c\}$ *with respect to postruntime t.*

	$\mathsf{ert}[\text{while}\,(\varphi)\,\{c\}](t) \leq I$	$I \leq \mathsf{ert}[\text{while}\,(\varphi)\,\{c\}](t)$
c **non-probabilistic**	$F_t(I) \leq I$	$I \leq F_t(I)$
c **probabilistic**	$F_t(I) \leq I$	$I \leq F_t(I)$ and $\lambda\sigma\centerdot\,\mathsf{ert}[c]\bigl(|I(\sigma) - I|\bigr)(\sigma) \leq c$

Probabilistic Metering Functions

We call a runtime I that satisfies $I \leq F_t(I)$ a *lower invariant*. We have learned above that I being a lower invariant is not enough of a premise to ensure that I is a lower bound on $\mathsf{ert}[\text{while}\,(\varphi)\,\{c\}](t)$. The additional premise that we have to add is that the *expected change of I* after performing one iteration of the loop body is *bounded by a constant*, i.e. for every initial state σ_{init}, we have

$$\mathsf{Exp}\Bigl(\bigl|I(\sigma_{\text{init}}) - I(\sigma_{\text{final}})\bigr|\Bigr) \;\leq\; c\,,$$

for some positive constant c (Hark et al., 2020). This property is called *conditional difference boundedness*. It is easy to show that the above expected value is upper bounded by $\lambda\sigma\centerdot\,\mathsf{ert}[c]\bigl(|I(\sigma) - I|\bigr)(\sigma)$ and hence we can add

$$\lambda\sigma\centerdot\,\mathsf{ert}[c]\bigl(|I(\sigma) - I|\bigr)(\sigma) \;\leq\; c\,, \quad \text{for some constant } c \geq 0$$

as a premise (additionally to $I \leq F_t(I)$), to ensure that I is a lower bound on $\mathsf{ert}[\text{while}\,(\varphi)\,\{c\}](t)$.[2] The overall situation is summarized in Table 6.2.

Example: The geometric distribution revisited. Let us consider an application of the lower bound proof rule by revisiting the loop c_{geo}:

$$c_{\mathsf{geo}}: \qquad \text{while}\,(c = 1)\,\{$$
$$c :\approx {}^1\!/_2 \cdot \langle 0 \rangle + {}^1\!/_2 \cdot \langle 1 \rangle$$
$$\}$$

We have already shown that $I = 1 + [c = 1] \cdot 4$ is not only a prefixed point of the corresponding characteristic function

$$F_0(X) \;=\; 1 \;+\; [c = 1] \cdot \Bigl(1 + \tfrac{1}{2} \cdot \bigl(X[c/0] + X[c/1]\bigr)\Bigr),$$

---

[2] Technically, we have to check a few finiteness conditions too, but those are easy to check.

and thus an upper bound on the expected runtime of the loop, but indeed a true fixed point. Thus, if we show that there exists a constant c, such that

$$\lambda\sigma. \, \text{ert}[body]\big(|I(\sigma) - I|\big)(\sigma) \leq c \, ,$$

then I is also a lower bound and hence the *exact* expected runtime. We can check the above condition as follows:

$$\lambda\sigma. \, \text{ert}[c :\approx \text{\textonehalf} \cdot \langle 0 \rangle + \text{\textonehalf} \cdot \langle 1 \rangle]\big(|I(\sigma) - I|\big)(\sigma)$$

$$= \lambda\sigma. \, \left(1 + \tfrac{1}{2} \cdot \Big(\big|I(\sigma) - I[c/0]\big| + \big|I(\sigma) - I[c/1]\big| \Big) \right)(\sigma)$$

$$= 1 + \tfrac{1}{2} \cdot \Big(\big|I - I[c/0]\big| + \big|I - I[c/1]\big| \Big)$$

$$= 1 + \tfrac{1}{2} \cdot \Big(\big|1 + [c = 1] \cdot 4 - 1 - [0 = 1] \cdot 4\big|$$

$$+ \, \big|1 + [c = 1] \cdot 4 - 1 - [1 = 1] \cdot 4\big| \Big)$$

$$= 1 + \tfrac{1}{2} \cdot \Big(\big|[c = 1] \cdot 4\big| + \big|[c = 1] \cdot 4 - 4\big| \Big)$$

$$\leq 1 + \tfrac{1}{2} \cdot (4 + 4)$$

$$= 5$$

Thus we have established that

$$\text{ert}\big[c_{\text{geo}}\big](0) = I = 1 + [c = 1] \cdot 4 \, .$$

6.5.3 Another Proof Rule for Lower Bounds

One can show that the lower bound rule we presented in the previous section is incomplete in the sense that there exist lower bounds which are not conditionally difference bounded. Furthermore, that proof rule is incapable of verifying *infinite* expected runtimes. We present in this section a third proof rule, which is more difficult to apply but in turn *complete* for verifying lower bounds on expected runtimes, in particular infinite expected runtimes.

Recall that, by Kleene's fixed point theorem (Kleene, 1952), the least fixed point characterizing the expected runtime of a loop with characteristic functional F_t is given by

$$\text{lfp} \, F_t = \sup_{n \in \mathbb{N}} F_t^n(0) \, .$$

It can thus be obtained by fixed point iteration: Starting at 0, we iteratively apply the characteristic functional and take the limit of this iteration process. We now under-approximate each step of this fixed point iteration. To this end, we use a

$$0 \;\leq\; F_t(0) \;\leq\; F_t^2(0) \;\leq\; F_t^3(0) \;\leq\; \ldots \;\leq\; \sup_{n \in \mathbb{N}} F_t^n(0) \;=\; \mathsf{lfp}\, F_t$$

	IV		IV		IV			IV

$$I_1 \qquad\qquad F_t(I_1) \qquad\qquad F_t(I_2) \qquad\qquad \ldots \qquad\qquad \lim_{n \to \infty} F_t(I_n)$$

	IV		IV			IV

$$I_2 \qquad\qquad I_3 \qquad\qquad \ldots \qquad\qquad \lim_{n \to \infty} I_n$$

Figure 6.3 Illustration of approximating each step of a fixed point iteration of F_t on initial value 0 with a lower ω-invariant I_n. The chain $0 \leq F_t(0) \leq F_t^2(0) \leq \ldots$ on top is a consequence of the monotonicity of F_t which in turn is a consequence of its continuity.

runtime $I_n \in \mathbb{T}$ that is parameterized in a natural number n. Then, I_n is called a *lower ω-invariant* of while $(\varphi)\,\{c\}$ with respect to runtime t if and only if

$$I_1 \;\leq\; F_t(0) \qquad \text{and} \qquad \forall\, n \geq 1: \quad I_{n+1} \;\leq\; F_t(I_n)\,.$$

Intuitively, a lower ω-invariant I_n under-approximates the n-th step of a fixed point iteration that determines the exact expected runtime of a loop. It thus represents a lower bound on the expected runtime of those executions that finish within n loop iterations, weighted according to their probabilities. Intuitively, the limit of I_n consequently represents a lower bound on the expected runtime for any number of loop iterations. More formally, we can show by induction that

$$I_{n+1} \;\leq\; F_t(I_n) \;\leq\; F_t^{n+1}(0)\,.$$

An illustration of a fixed point iteration approximated by I_n is given in Figure 6.3. Formally, we obtain the following proof rule based on ω-invariants: If I_n is a lower ω-invariant of loop while $(\varphi)\,\{c\}$ with respect to runtime t and the limit of I_n exists then

$$\lim_{n \to \infty} I_n \;\leq\; \mathsf{ert}[\text{while}\,(\varphi)\,\{c\}](t)\,.$$

This rule is obviously complete as we can always choose the exact fixed point iteration sequence $I_n = F_t^n(0)$ as lower ω-invariant.

It is worthwhile to note that for upper bounds there is no need for ω-invariants, even though a dual rule exists: I_n is called an *upper ω-invariant* of while $(\varphi)\,\{c\}$ with respect to runtime t if and only if

$$F_t(0) \;\leq\; I_1 \qquad \text{and} \qquad \forall\, n \geq 1: \quad F_t(I_n) \;\leq\; I_{n+1}\,.$$

If I_n is an upper ω-invariant of loop while $(\varphi)\,\{c\}$ with respect to runtime t and the limit of I_n exists, then indeed

$$\mathsf{ert}[\mathtt{while}\ (\varphi)\ \{c\}](t) \ \leq \ \lim_{n \to \infty} I_n \ .$$

However, one can show that in this case $\lim_{n \to \infty} I_n$ itself is already an upper (global) invariant, i.e.

$$F_t \left(\lim_{n \to \infty} I_n \right) \ \leq \ \lim_{n \to \infty} I_n$$

and thus, there is no need to guess such a sequence and then find the limit. Instead, we can just immediately guess a limit and check whether this limit is an upper invariant, without having to perform an additional induction on n.

Example: Disproving positive almost-sure termination. The expected runtime transformer ert enables proving positive almost-sure termination by verifying a finite upper bound on the expected runtime of a program. With the help of ω-invariants, it can also be employed to prove that infinity is a *lower bound* on the expected runtime. In other words, we can verify that a given program does *not* terminate positively almost-surely. As an example, let us verify that the concatenation of two positively almost-surely terminating programs may itself not terminate positively almost-surely. We already presented a counterexample, but without proof, namely the program

$$
\begin{aligned}
C_{\mathsf{cex}}: \quad & \text{1:}\ \ x := 1;\ b := 1; \\
& \text{2:}\ \ \mathtt{while}\ (b = 1)\ \{b :\approx \ ^1\!/_2\langle 0 \rangle + \ ^1\!/_2\langle 1 \rangle;\ x := 2x\}; \\
& \text{3:}\ \ \mathtt{while}\ (x > 0)\ \{x := x - 1\}\ .
\end{aligned}
$$

Our goal is to formally prove that C_{cex} has an infinite expected runtime, i.e. $\infty \leq \mathsf{ert}[C_{\mathsf{cex}}](0)$. To this end, let us denote the program in the i-th line of C_{cex} by c_i. By the rule for sequential composition, we then obtain

$$\mathsf{ert}[C_{\mathsf{cex}}](0) \ = \ \mathsf{ert}[c_1](\mathsf{ert}[c_2](\mathsf{ert}[c_3](0))) \ .$$

Let us thus start by analyzing the second loop, i.e. program c_3. Its characteristic functional with respect to continuation 0 is given by

$$F_0(X) \ = \ 1 + [x > 0] \cdot \big(1 + X[x/x - 1]\big) \ .$$

Since the variable x is decremented in each loop iteration and every iteration consumes two units of time (one for the guard evaluation and one for the assignment), we use the lower ω-invariant

$$I_n \ = \ 1 + [0 < x < n - 1] \cdot 2x + [x \geq n - 1] \cdot (2n - 3)$$

of the loop c_3 to conclude that

$$\text{ert}[c_3](0) \geq \lim_{n \to \infty} I_n = 1 + [x > 0] \cdot 2x .$$

We now have an under-approximation of the expected runtime of c_3. We can continue reasoning about c_2 using this under-approximation because the ert-transformer satisfies a fundamental property: it is *monotonic*. Hence,

$$\text{ert}[c_3](0) \geq 1 + [x > 0] \cdot 2x \qquad \text{implies}$$

$$\text{ert}[c_2 \,;\, c_3](0) = \text{ert}[c_2]\big(\text{ert}[c_3](0)\big) \geq \text{ert}[c_2](1 + [x > 0] \cdot 2x) .$$

Our next step is therefore to analyze the expected runtime of the first loop, i.e. c_2, with respect to continuation $t = 1 + [x > 0] \cdot 2x$. The corresponding characteristic functional is given by

$$
\begin{aligned}
G_t(X) = {} & 1 + [b \neq 1] \cdot (1 + [x > 0] \cdot 2x) \\
& + [b = 1] \cdot \left(2 + \tfrac{1}{2} \cdot X[x/2x][b/0] + \tfrac{1}{2} \cdot X[x/2x][b/1]\right) .
\end{aligned}
$$

As a lower ω-invariant of c_2, we propose

$$
\begin{aligned}
J_n = {} & 1 + [b \neq 1] \cdot (1 + [x > 0] \cdot 2x) \\
& + [b = 1] \cdot \left(7 - \tfrac{5}{2^{n-1}} + (n - 1) \cdot [x > 0] \cdot 2x\right) .
\end{aligned}
$$

The calculations establishing that J_n is a lower ω-invariant go as follows:

$$
\begin{aligned}
G_t(0) = {} & 1 + [b \neq 1] \cdot \left(1 + [x > 0] \cdot 2x\right) \\
& + [b = 1] \cdot \left(2 + \tfrac{1}{2} \cdot 0[x/2x][b/0] + \tfrac{1}{2} \cdot 0[x/2x][b/1]\right) \\
= {} & 1 + [b \neq 1] \cdot \left(1 + [x > 0] \cdot 2x\right) + [b = 1] \cdot 2 \\
= {} & I_1 \geq I_1 \;\checkmark
\end{aligned}
$$

$$
\begin{aligned}
G_t(J_n) = {} & 1 + [b \neq 1] \cdot \left(1 + [x > 0] \cdot 2x\right) \\
& + [b = 1] \cdot \left(2 + \tfrac{1}{2} \cdot J_n[x/2x][b/0] + \tfrac{1}{2} \cdot J_n[x/2x][b/1]\right) \\
= {} & 1 + [b \neq 1] \cdot \left(1 + [x > 0] \cdot 2x\right) \\
& + [b = 1] \cdot \left(2 + \tfrac{1}{2} \cdot (2 + [2x > 0] \cdot 4x) \right. \\
& \qquad\qquad \left. + \tfrac{1}{2} \cdot \left(8 - \tfrac{5}{2^{n-1}} + (n - 1) \cdot \underbrace{[2x > 0]}_{=\, [x>0]} \cdot 4x\right)\right) \\
= {} & 1 + [b \neq 1] \cdot \left(1 + [x > 0] \cdot 2x\right) \\
& + [b = 1] \cdot \left(7 - \tfrac{5}{2^{n+1-1}} + (n + 1 - 1) \cdot [x > 0] \cdot 2x\right)
\end{aligned}
$$

$$= I_{n+1} \geq I_{n+1} \checkmark$$

Hence, our proof rule for lower ω-invariants yields

$$\text{ert}[c_2](1 + [x > 0] \cdot 2x) \geq \lim_{n \to \infty} J_n$$
$$= 1 + [b \neq 1] \cdot \left(1 + [x > 0] \cdot 2x\right)$$
$$+ [b = 1] \cdot (7 + [x > 0] \cdot \infty) .$$

Again appealing to monotonicity of the ert-transformer, we can complete the run-time analysis of program c_{cex}:

$$\text{ert}[c_{\text{cex}}](0) = \text{ert}[c_1](\text{ert}[c_2](\text{ert}[c_3](0)))$$
$$\geq \text{ert}[c_1](\text{ert}[c_2](1 + [x > 0] \cdot 2x))$$
$$\geq \text{ert}[c_1]\Big(1 + [b \neq 1] \cdot \left(1 + [x > 0] \cdot 2x\right)$$
$$+ [b = 1] \cdot (7 + [x > 0] \cdot \infty)\Big)$$
$$- \text{ort}[x \; \shortmid - \; 1]\Big(\text{ort}[b \; \shortmid - \; 1]\Big($$
$$1 + [b \neq 1] \cdot \left(1 + [x > 0] \cdot 2x\right)$$
$$+ [b = 1] \cdot (7 + [x > 0] \cdot \infty)\Big)\Big)$$
$$= \text{ert}[x := 1](1 + 8 + [x > 0] \cdot \infty)$$
$$= 1 + 1 + 8 + [1 > 0] \cdot \infty$$
$$= \infty$$

Overall, we obtain that the expected runtime of program c_{cex} is infinite even though it terminates with probability one. In other words, c_{cex} terminates almost-surely, but not positively almost-surely. Furthermore, notice that both sub-programs c_2 and c_3 for themselves have finite expected runtimes, since

$$\text{ert}[c_2](0) = 1 + [b = 1] \cdot 4 \quad \text{and} \quad \text{ert}[c_3](0) = 1 + [x > 0] \cdot 2x .$$

We emphasize that the ert-calculus allows for reasoning about positive almost-sure termination (PAST) although PAST itself is not compositional.

6.5.4 *Independent and Identically Distributed Loops*

So far, we have studied two classes of complete proof rules. However, both rules rely on finding invariants, which is usually the hardest part of the verification process. We now consider a restricted class of loops whose *exact* expected runtime can be analyzed without invariants or other user-supplied artifacts. That class thus offers

```
while((x − 5)² + (y − 5)² ≤ 25) {
    x :≈ uniform[0 ... 10];
    y :≈ uniform[0 ... 10]
}
```

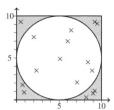

Figure 6.4 A probabilistic program sampling a point within a circle uniformly at random using rejection sampling. The picture on the right-hand side visualizes the procedure: In each iteration a point (×) is sampled. If we obtain a point within the white area inside the square, we terminate. Otherwise, we resample.

a high degree of automation. Intuitively, the key concept underlying our next proof rule are loops without data flow across different loop iterations. For deterministic programs, such loops are not very interesting: They either terminate after exactly one iteration or never. This is not the case for probabilistic programs. Consider, for example, the probabilistic program depicted in Figure 6.4. It samples a point within a circle with center $(5, 5)$ and radius 5 uniformly at random by means of rejection sampling: In each loop iteration, we sample a point $(x, y) \in [0, 10]^2$ with some fixed precision. If the sampled point lies within the circle, we terminate; otherwise, we resample. Although our program admits arbitrarily long runs, the program terminates within finite expected time. Moreover, there is no data flow across loop iterations. This is an example of an *independent and identically distributed (i.i.d.) loop*. In the remainder of this section we develop a proof rule to determine exact expected runtimes of i.i.d. loops.

Towards a rigorous proof rule, let us first formally characterize i.i.d. loops. Let $\mathsf{Var}(f)$ denote the set of all variables that "occur in" runtime $f \in \mathbb{T}$, i.e.

$$x \in \mathsf{Var}(f) \qquad \text{iff} \qquad \exists \sigma \, \exists v, v' : \quad f\big(\sigma[x/v]\big) \neq f\big(\sigma[x/v']\big) .$$

Furthermore, let the set $\mathsf{Mod}(c)$ be the collection of all variables that occur on the left-hand side of an assignment in a program c. We then call a runtime f *unaffected* by program c, denoted

$$f \, \text{⑭} \, c$$

if and only if $\mathsf{Var}(f) \cap \mathsf{Mod}(c) = \emptyset$. Moreover, let us denote by

$$\wp c(f)$$

the expected value of f after executing program c. This value can be computed similarly to expected runtimes with our ert-calculus by assuming that the time consumed by each statement is zero (this corresponds to the weakest preexpectation calculus of McIver and Morgan, 2004). With these notions at hand, a loop `while` (φ) $\{c\}$ is *f-i.i.d.* for some postruntime $f \in \mathbb{T}$ if and only if

(i) the probability of loop guard φ being true after one execution of loop body c is unaffected by c, i.e.

$$\wp c([\varphi]) \text{ 𝕗 } c \,,$$

(ii) the probability of violating the loop guard and continuing with runtime f after one execution of loop body c is unaffected by c, i.e.

$$\wp c([\neg\varphi] \cdot f) \text{ 𝕗 } c \,, \qquad \text{and}$$

(iii) every loop iteration runs in the same expected time, i.e.

$$\mathsf{ert}[c](0) \text{ 𝕗 } c \,.$$

For example, the program in Figure 6.4 that samples a point in a circle is *f*-i.i.d. for every postruntime $f \in \mathbb{T}$. How does the fact that a loop is *f*-i.i.d. help us when analyzing the expected runtime of a program? Intuitively, since each loop iteration has the same expected runtime, we can characterize the expected runtime of the whole loop as the expected runtime of a single loop iteration divided by the probability of termination, i.e. 1 minus the probability of satisfying the loop guard after execution the loop body. Formally, we additionally have to take the time consumed by guard evaluations and the possibility that the loop guard is never satisfied into account. This leads us to the following proof rule (Batz et al., 2018):

Proof rule for *f*-i.i.d. loops. Let `while` (φ) $\{c\}$ be an *f*-i.i.d. loop such that the loop body c terminates almost-surely, i.e. $\wp c(1) = 1$. Then, the expected runtime of `while` (φ) $\{c\}$ with respect to postruntime $f \in \mathbb{T}$ is

$$\mathsf{ert}[\texttt{while}\,(\varphi)\,\{c\}](f) = 1 + [\varphi] \cdot \frac{1 + \mathsf{ert}[c]([\neg\varphi] \cdot f)}{1 - \mathrm{Pr}[c]([\varphi])} + [\neg\varphi] \cdot f \,,$$

where we define $^0\!/\!_0 = 0$ and $^a\!/\!_0 = \infty$ for $a \neq 0$.

6.6 Application: Bayesian networks

The notion of *f*-i.i.d. loops prevents data flow across loop iterations. While this might seem like a severe restriction, it naturally applies to certain classes of probabilistic models. In particular, Bayesian networks (Koller and Friedman, 2009) are probabilistic graphical models representing joint probability distributions of sets of random variables with conditional dependencies. Graphical models are popular as they allow to succinctly represent complex distributions in a human-readable way. For example, Bayesian networks have applications in machine learning (Heckerman,

2008), speech recognition (Zweig and Russell, 1998), sports betting (Constantinou et al., 2012), gene regulatory networks (Friedman et al., 2000), medicine (Jiang and Cooper, 2010), and finance (Neapolitan and Jiang, 2010).

The central problem for Bayesian networks is *probabilistic inference*, i.e. determining the probability of an event given observed evidence. This problem is often approached using sampling-based techniques, such as rejection sampling: Repeatedly sample from the joint distribution of the network until the obtained sample complies with all observed evidence. However, a major problem with rejection sampling is that for poorly conditioned data, many samples have to be rejected to obtain a single compliant sample. In fact, Gordon et al. (2014) point out that "the main challenge in this setting [i.e. sampling based approaches] is that many samples that are generated during execution are ultimately rejected for not satisfying the observations." If too many samples are rejected, the expected sampling time grows so large that sampling becomes infeasible. The expected sampling time of a Bayesian network is therefore a key figure for deciding whether sampling based inference is the method of choice. In other words, we are concerned with the question:

"Given a Bayesian network with observed evidence, how long does it take to obtain a single sample that satisfies the observations?"

In this section, we present how this question can be addressed fully automatically: We translate a Bayesian network into an equivalent pGCL program such that the expected runtime of the resulting program corresponds to the expected sampling time of the network. The expected runtime is then determined using the ert-calculus and our proof rule for f-i.i.d. loops.

6.6.1 From Bayesian Networks to Probabilistic Programs

Let us briefly introduce Bayesian networks by means of an example. Further details – including formal definitions – are found in Batz et al. (2018); Koller and Friedman (2009). A Bayesian network is a directed acyclic graph in which every node is a random variable and every edge between two nodes represents a probabilistic dependency between these nodes. As a running example, consider the network depicted in Figure 6.5 (inspired by Koller and Friedman, 2009) that models the mood of students after taking an exam. The network contains four random variables. They represent the difficulty of the exam (D), the level of preparation of a student (P), the achieved grade (G), and the resulting mood (M). For simplicity, let us suppose that each random variable assumes either value 0 or 1. The underlying dependencies express that the mood of a student depends on the achieved grade which, in turn, depends on the difficulty of the exam and the amount of preparation before taking it. Every node is accompanied by a conditional probability table that

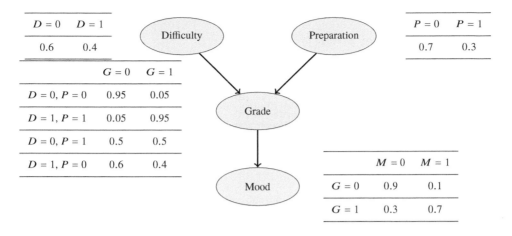

D = 0	D = 1
0.6	0.4

	G = 0	G = 1
D = 0, P = 0	0.95	0.05
D = 1, P = 1	0.05	0.95
D = 0, P = 1	0.5	0.5
D = 1, P = 0	0.6	0.4

P = 0	P = 1
0.7	0.3

	M = 0	M = 1
G = 0	0.9	0.1
G = 1	0.3	0.7

Figure 6.5 A Bayesian network

provides the probabilities of a node given the values of all the nodes it depends upon. We can then use the Bayesian network to answer queries such as "What is the probability that a student is well-prepared for an exam ($P = 1$), but ends up with a bad mood ($M = 0$)?"

It can be shown that every Bayesian network with observed evidence can be translated into an equivalent pGCL program, i.e. a program describing the same conditional probability distribution (Batz et al., 2018). For instance, Figure 6.6 shows the probabilistic program corresponding to the Bayesian network in Figure 6.5 and observation $P = 1$. Here, the statement `repeat { c } until` (φ) is a shortcut for c; `while` (φ) $\{c\}$. Essentially, every node in a network corresponds to a variable. It is then straightforward to encode the (discrete) conditional probability table of every node using conditional branching and random assignments.

To deal with observations, one could syntactically enrich the programming language to allow for `observe`-statements. This approach is taken in, for example,Katoen et al. (2015); Olmedo et al. (2018); Bichsel et al. (2018). However, taking that approach would not give us an insight on how long it would take to obtain an execution trace that complies with the observations. Instead, we wrap around the original program a global loop that implements rejection sampling. That is, the whole program is re-run until all observations are satisfied. Since no variable inside the loop body of such a program is accessed before it is set by a probabilistic assignment, there is no data flow across loop iterations. In other words, all loops that model Bayesian networks are f-i.i.d. for every postruntime $f \in \mathbb{T}$.

```
1   repeat {                                10        } else {
2       xD :≈ 0.6 · ⟨0⟩ + 0.4 · ⟨1⟩;        11            xG :≈ 0.6 · ⟨0⟩ + 0.4 · ⟨1⟩
3       xP :≈ 0.7 · ⟨0⟩ + 0.3 · ⟨1⟩         12        };
4       if (xD = 0 ∧ xP = 0) {              13        if (xG = 0) {
5           xG :≈ 0.95 · ⟨0⟩ + 0.05 · ⟨1⟩   14            xM :≈ 0.9 · ⟨0⟩ + 0.1 · ⟨1⟩
6       } else if (xD = 1 ∧ xP = 1) {       15        } else {
7           xG :≈ 0.05 · ⟨0⟩ + 0.95 · ⟨1⟩   16            xM :≈ 0.3 · ⟨0⟩ + 0.7 · ⟨1⟩
8       } else if (xD = 0 ∧ xP = 1) {       17        }
9           xG :≈ 0.5 · ⟨0⟩ + 0.5 · ⟨1⟩     18    } until (xP = 1)
```

Figure 6.6 The probabilistic program obtained from the network in Figure 6.5.

Consequently, the expected runtime of programs obtained from Bayesian networks can be analyzed fully automatically by applying the rules of the ert-calculus.

6.6.2 Implementation

We implemented a prototype to analyze expected sampling times of Bayesian networks (cf. Batz et al., 2018). More concretely, our tool takes as input a Bayesian network together with observations in the popular Bayesian Network Interchange Format.[3] The network is first translated into a probabilistic program. The expected runtime of the resulting program is then determined fully automatically by applying our ert-calculus together with our proof rule for f-i.i.d. loops.

The size of the resulting program is linear in the total number of rows of all conditional probability tables in the network. The program size is thus *not* the bottleneck of our analysis. As we are dealing with an NP-hard problem (Cooper, 1990; Dagum and Luby, 1993), it is not surprising that our algorithm has a worst-case exponential time complexity. However, also the space complexity of our algorithm is exponential in the worst case: As an expectation is propagated backwards through an `if`-clause of the program, the size of the expectation is potentially multiplied. This is also the reason that our analysis runs out of memory on some benchmarks.

We evaluated our implementation on the *largest* Bayesian networks in the Bayesian Network Repository (Scutari, 2017) that consists – to a large extent – of real-world Bayesian networks including expert systems for, e.g., electromyography (`munin`) (Andreassen et al., 1989), hematopathology diagnosis (`hepar2`) (Onisko et al., 1998), weather forecasting (`hailfinder`) (Abramson et al., 1996), and printer troubleshooting in the Windows 95 operating system (`win95pts`) (Ramanna et al., 2013, Section 5.6.2). All experiments were performed on an HP BL685C G7.

---

[3] http://www.cs.cmu.edu/ fgcozman/Research/InterchangeFormat/

Although up to 48 cores with 2.0GHz were available, only one core was used apart from Java's garbage collection. The Java virtual machine was limited to 8GB of RAM.

Our experimental results are shown in Table 6.3. The number of nodes of the considered networks ranges from 56 to 1041. For each Bayesian network, we computed the expected sampling time (EST) for different collections of observed nodes (#obs). EST = ∞ means that our implementation automatically infers that the expected sampling time is in fact infinite, which is the case if and only if the probability of complying with all observed evidence is precisely 0. #obs = 0 means that no evidence is observed; the repeat-until loop would thus be executed exactly once. For #obs > 0, observations were picked at random. Note that the time required by our prototype varies depending on both the number of observed nodes and the actual observations. Thus, there are cases in which we run out of memory although the total number of observations is small. Furthermore, Table 6.3 provides the *average Markov Blanket size*, i.e. the average number of parents, children and children's parents of nodes in the Bayesian network (Pearl, 1985), as an indicator measuring how independent nodes in the network are.

In order to obtain an understanding of what the EST corresponds to in actual execution times on a real machine, we also performed simulations for the `win95pts` network. More precisely, we generated Java programs from this network analogously to the translation from Bayesian networks into pGCL programs. This allowed us to approximate that our Java setup can execute $9.714 \cdot 10^6$ steps (in terms of EST) per second. For the `win95pts` with 17 observations, an EST of $1.11 \cdot 10^{15}$ then corresponds to an expected time of approximately 3.6 *years* in order to obtain a *single* valid sample. We were additionally able to find a case with 13 observed nodes where our tool discovered within 0.32 seconds an EST that corresponds to approximately 4.3 *million years*. In contrast, exact inference using variable elimination was almost instantaneous. This demonstrates that knowing expected sampling times upfront can indeed be beneficial when selecting an inference method.

6.7 Conclusion and Future Directions

We presented a weakest-precondition-style calculus for reasoning about the expected runtime of probabilistic programs. Our calculus demonstrates how standard techniques from program verification – in particular denotational semantics and invariants – enable elegant proofs of (non)positive-almost sure termination. Furthermore, both lower and upper bounds on the expected runtime can be determined. We studied the restricted class of independently and identically distributed loops, which enable a fully automated runtime analysis. In particular, Bayesian networks

Table 6.3 *Experimental results. Time is in seconds. MO denotes out of memory.*
#obs refers to the number of observed nodes.

Network	#obs	Time	EST	#obs	Time	EST	#obs	Time	EST
earthquake	#nodes: 5, #edges: 4, avg. Markov Blanket: 2.00								
	0	0.09	$8.000 \cdot 10^0$	2	0.23	$9.276 \cdot 10^1$	4	0.24	$1.857 \cdot 10^2$
cancer	#nodes: 5, #edges: 4, avg. Markov Blanket: 2.00								
	0	0.09	$8.000 \cdot 10^0$	2	0.22	$1.839 \cdot 10^1$	5	0.20	$5.639 \cdot 10^2$
survey	#nodes: 6, #edges: 6, avg. Markov Blanket: 2.67								
	0	0.09	$1.000 \cdot 10^1$	2	0.21	$2.846 \cdot 10^2$	5	0.22	$9.113 \cdot 10^3$
asia	#nodes: 8, #edges: 8, avg. Markov Blanket: 2.50								
	0	0.26	$1.400 \cdot 10^1$	2	0.25	$3.368 \cdot 10^2$	6	0.25	$8.419 \cdot 10^4$
sachs	#nodes: 11, #edges: 17, avg. Markov Blanket: 3.09								
	0	0.13	$2.000 \cdot 10^1$	3	0.24	$7.428 \cdot 10^2$	6	2.72	$5.533 \cdot 10^7$
insurance	#nodes: 27, #edges: 52, avg. Markov Blanket: 5.19								
	0	0.17	$5.200 \cdot 10^1$	3	0.31	$5.096 \cdot 10^3$	5	0.91	$1.373 \cdot 10^5$
alarm	#nodes: 37, #edges: 46, avg. Markov Blanket: 3.51								
	0	0.14	$6.200 \cdot 10^1$	2	MO	—	6	40.47	$3.799 \cdot 10^5$
barley	#nodes: 48, #edges: 84, avg. Markov Blanket: 5.25								
	0	0.46	$8.600 \cdot 10^1$	2	0.53	$5.246 \cdot 10^4$	5	MO	—
hailfinder	#nodes: 56, #edges: 66, avg. Markov Blanket: 3.54								
	0	0.23	$9.500 \cdot 10^1$	5	0.63	$5.016 \cdot 10^5$	9	0.46	$9.048 \cdot 10^6$
hepar2	#nodes: 70, #edges: 123, avg. Markov Blanket: 4.51								
	0	0.22	$1.310 \cdot 10^2$	1	1.84	$1.579 \cdot 10^2$	2	MO	—
win95pts	#nodes: 76, #edges: 112, avg. Markov Blanket: 5.92								
	0	0.20	$1.180 \cdot 10^2$	1	0.36	$2.284 \cdot 10^3$	3	0.36	$4.296 \cdot 10^5$
	7	0.91	$1.876 \cdot 10^6$	12	0.42	$3.973 \cdot 10^7$	17	61.73	$1.110 \cdot 10^{15}$
pathfinder	#nodes: 135, #edges: 200, avg. Markov Blanket: 3.04								
	0	0.37	217	1	0.53	$1.050 \cdot 10^4$	3	31.31	$2.872 \cdot 10^4$
	5	MO	—	7	5.44	∞	7	480.83	∞
andes	#nodes: 223, #edges: 338, avg. Markov Blanket: 5.61								
	0	0.46	$3.570 \cdot 10^2$	1	MO	—	3	1.66	$5.251 \cdot 10^3$
	5	1.41	$9.862 \cdot 10^3$	7	0.99	$8.904 \cdot 10^4$	9	0.90	$6.637 \cdot 10^5$
pigs	#nodes: 441, #edges: 592, avg. Markov Blanket: 3.66								
	0	0.57	$7.370 \cdot 10^2$	1	0.74	$2.952 \cdot 10^3$	3	0.88	$2.362 \cdot 10^3$
	5	0.85	$1.260 \cdot 10^5$	7	1.02	$1.511 \cdot 10^6$	8	MO	—
munin	#nodes: 1041, #edges: 1397, avg. Markov Blanket: 3.54								
	0	1.29	$1.823 \cdot 10^3$	1	1.47	$3.648 \cdot 10^4$	3	1.37	$1.824 \cdot 10^7$
	5	1.43	∞	9	1.79	$1.824 \cdot 10^{16}$	10	65.64	$1.153 \cdot 10^{18}$

– if interpreted as probabilistic programs – are covered by this class. Hence, exact expected sampling times of Bayesian networks can be determined automatically.

Since the original development of the expected runtime calculus (Kaminski et al., 2016), there has been ongoing research into several further directions. We conclude with a brief discussion of recent developments.

Applications. The main application of our calculus is the analysis of *randomized algorithms*. However, many randomized algorithms rely on advanced programming features that are not supported by the simplistic language considered in this chapter. There have been various extensions of weakest-precondition-style calculi for probabilistic programs that attempt to support additional features while maintaining elegant and applicable proof rules. In particular, recursion (Olmedo et al., 2016) and dynamic data structures (Batz et al., 2019) have been incorporated into our probabilistic guarded command language. An important feature that is still missing is support for concurrent randomized algorithms.

Automation. While finding invariants is a challenging task, we were usually able to find correct invariants by considering a few loop unrollings. Hence, there is hope that the proof rules presented in this chapter provide a foundation for automated reasoning about expected runtimes. As a first step, our calculus has been mechanized in the theorem prover IsABELLE (Hölzl, 2016). Furthermore, the class of i.i.d. loops is a further step towards automation for a restricted class of programs. More recently, Ngo et al. (2018) extended work on automated amortized resource analysis to automatically reason about bounds on the expected runtime of a larger class of probabilistic programs. They reduce inference of upper bounds to a linear programming problem. In fact, their work can be considered an extension of our ert-calculus by specialized rules. In particular, soundness of their approach explicitly relies on the soundness of the expected runtime transformer presented here.

Almost-sure termination. Our calculus allows for proving positive almost-sure termination, i.e. finite expected runtimes. A weaker notion is plain almost-sure termination, i.e. termination with probability 1. Powerful rules for proving almost-sure termination of a large class of programs have been developed (McIver et al., 2018), and for certain subclasses of probabilistic programs even automated approaches for proving almost-sure termination exist (Esparza et al., 2012; Chatterjee et al., 2016, 2017; Agrawal et al., 2017).

Acknowledgements

Kaminski and Katoen have been supported by the ERC Advanced Grant FRAP-PANT (project number 787914) and the DFG-funded Research Training Group 2236 UnRAVeL. Matheja was supported by the DFG Project ATTESTOR. The authors thank Kevin Batz and Federico Olmedo; joint work with them provided the basis for this chapter.

References

Abramson, Bruce, Brown, John, Edwards, Ward, Murphy, Allan, and Winkler, Robert L. 1996. Hailfinder: A Bayesian system for forecasting severe weather. *International Journal of Forecasting*, **12**(1), 57–71.

Adleman, Leonard Max, and Huang, Ming-Deh. 1992. *Primality Testing and Abelian Varieties over Finite Fields. Lecture Notes in Mathematics*, **1512**.

Agrawal, Sheshansh, Chatterjee, Krishnendu, and Novotný, Petr. 2017. Lexicographic ranking supermartingales: an efficient approach to termination of probabilistic programs. *Proceedings of the ACM on Programming Languages*, **2**(POPL), 1–32.

Andreassen, Steen, Jensen, Finn V, Andersen, Stig Kjær, Falck, B, Kjærulff, U, Woldbye, M, Sørensen, AR, Rosenfalck, A, and Jensen, F. 1989. MUNIN: an expert EMG assistant. Pages 255–277 of: *Computer-aided Electromyography and Expert Systems*. Pergamon Press.

Batz, Kevin, Kaminski, Benjamin Lucien, Katoen, Joost-Pieter, and Matheja, Christoph. 2018. How long, O Bayesian network, will I sample thee? – A program analysis perspective on expected sampling times. Pages 186–213 of: *European Symposium on Programming (ESOP)*. Lecture Notes in Computer Science, vol. 10801. Springer.

Batz, Kevin, Kaminski, Benjamin Lucien, Katoen, Joost-Pieter, Matheja, Christoph, and Noll, Thomas. 2019. Quantitative separation logic: a logic for reasoning about probabilistic pointer programs. *Proceedings of the ACM on Programming Languages*, **3** (POPL), 1–29.

Bichsel, Benjamin, Gehr, Timon, and Vechev, Martin T. 2018. Fine-grained semantics for probabilistic programs. Pages 145–185 of: *European Symposium on Programming (ESOP)*. Lecture Notes in Computer Science, vol. 10801. Springer.

Bournez, Olivier, and Garnier, Florent. 2005. Proving positive almost-sure termination. Pages 323–337 of: *International Conference on Rewriting Techniques and Applications (RTA)*. Lecture Notes in Computer Science, vol. 3467. Springer.

Chakarov, Aleksandar, and Sankaranarayanan, Sriram. 2013. Probabilistic program analysis with martingales. Pages 511–526 of: *Computer Aided Verification (CAV)*. Lecture Notes in Computer Science, vol. 8044. Springer.

Chatterjee, Krishnendu, Fu, Hongfei, Novotný, Petr, and Hasheminezhad, Rouzbeh. 2016. Algorithmic analysis of qualitative and quantitative termination problems for affine probabilistic programs. Pages 327–342 of: *Principles of Programming Languages (POPL)*. ACM.

Chatterjee, Krishnendu, Novotný, Petr, and Zikelic, Dorde. 2017. Stochastic invariants for probabilistic termination. Pages 145–160 of: *Principles of Programming Languages (POPL)*. ACM.

Constantinou, Anthony C., Fenton, Norman E., and Neil, Martin. 2012. pi-football: a Bayesian network model for forecasting Association Football match outcomes. *Knowledge-Based Systems*, **36**, 322–339.

Cooper, Gregory F. 1990. The computational complexity of probabilistic inference using Bayesian Belief Networks. *Artificial intelligence*, **42**(2-3), 393–405.

Dagum, Paul, and Luby, Michael. 1993. Approximating probabilistic inference in Bayesian Belief Networks is NP-hard. *Artificial intelligence*, **60**(1), 141–153.

Dijkstra, Edgser W. 1976. *A Discipline of Programming*. Prentice Hall.

Esparza, Javier, Gaiser, Andreas, and Kiefer, Stefan. 2012. Proving termination of probabilistic programs using patterns. Pages 123–138 of: *Computer Aided Verification (CAV)*. Lecture Notes in Computer Science, vol. 7358. Springer.

Freivalds, Rūsiņš Mārtiņš. 1979. Fast probabilistic algorithms. Pages 57–69 of: *Mathematical Foundations of Computer Science (MFCS)*. Lecture Notes in Computer Science, vol. 74. Springer.

Friedman, Nir, Linial, Michal, Nachman, Iftach, and Pe'er, Dana. 2000. Using Bayesian networks to analyze expression data. Pages 127–135 of: *Computational Molecular Biology (RECOMB)*. ACM.

Frohn, Florian, Naaf, Matthias, Hensel, Jera, Brockschmidt, Marc, and Giesl, Jürgen. 2016. Lower runtime bounds for integer programs. Pages 550–567 of: *International Joint Conference on Automated Reasoning (IJCAR)*. Lecture Notes in Computer Science, vol. 9706. Springer.

Gordon, Andrew D., Henzinger, Thomas A., Nori, Aditya V., and Rajamani, Sriram K. 2014. Probabilistic programming. Pages 167–181 of: *Future of Software Engineering (FOSE)*. ACM.

Hark, Marcel, Kaminski, Benjamin Lucien, Giesl, Jürgen, and Katoen, Joost-Pieter. 2020. Aiming low Is harder – inductive proof rules for lower bounds on weakest pre-expectations in probabilistic program verification. *Proceedings of the ACM on Programming Languages*, **4**(POPL), 37:1–37:28.

Hart, Sergiu, Sharir, Micha, and Pnueli, Amir. 1983. Termination of probabilistic concurrent programs. *ACM Transactions on Programming Languages and Systems*, **5**(3), 356–380.

Heckerman, David. 2008. A tutorial on learning with Bayesian networks. Pages 33–82 of: *Innovations in Bayesian Networks*. Studies in Computational Intelligence, vol. 156. Springer.

Hoare, Charles Antony Richard. 1962. Quicksort. *The Computer Journal*, **5**(1), 10–15.

Hölzl, Johannes. 2016. Formalising semantics for expected running time of probabilistic programs. Pages 475–482 of: *Interactive Theorem Proving (ITP)*. Lecture Notes in Computer Science, vol. 9807. Springer.

Hur, Chung-Kil, Nori, Aditya V, Rajamani, Sriram K, and Samuel, Selva. 2014. Slicing probabilistic programs. Pages 133–144 of: *ACM SIGPLAN Notices*, vol. 49. ACM.

Ibe, Oliver C. 2013. *Elements of Random Walk and Diffusion Processes*. John Wiley & Sons.

Jiang, Xia, and Cooper, Gregory F. 2010. A Bayesian spatio-temporal method for disease outbreak detection. *Journal of the American Medical Informatics Association*, **17**(4), 462–471.

Kaminski, Benjamin Lucien. 2019. *Advanced Weakest Precondition Calculi for Probabilistic Programs*. Ph.D. thesis, RWTH Aachen University, Germany.

Kaminski, Benjamin Lucien, and Katoen, Joost-Pieter. 2015. On the hardness of almost-sure termination. Pages 307–318 of: *Mathematical Foundations of Computer Science (MFCS), Part I*. Lecture Notes in Computer Science, vol. 9234. Springer.

Kaminski, Benjamin Lucien, Katoen, Joost-Pieter, Matheja, Christoph, and Olmedo, Federico. 2016. Weakest precondition reasoning for expected runtimes of probabilistic programs. Pages 364–389 of: *European Symposium on Programming (ESOP)*. Lecture Notes in Computer Science, vol. 9632. Springer.

Kaminski, Benjamin Lucien, Katoen, Joost-Pieter, and Matheja, Christoph. 2018a. On the hardness of analyzing probabilistic programs. *Acta Informatica*, 1–31.

Kaminski, Benjamin Lucien, Katoen, Joost-Pieter, Matheja, Christoph, and Olmedo, Federico. 2018b. Weakest precondition reasoning for expected runtimes of randomized Algorithms. *Journal of the ACM*, **65**(5), 30:1–30:68.

Katoen, Joost-Pieter, Gretz, Friedrich, Jansen, Nils, Kaminski, Benjamin Lucien, and Olmedo, Federico. 2015. Understanding probabilistic programs. Pages 15–32 of: *Correct System Design – Symposium in Honor of Ernst-Rüdiger Olderog on the Occasion of His 60th Birthday*. Lecture Notes in Computer Science, vol. 9360. Springer.

Kleene, Stephen Cole. 1952. *Introduction to Metamathematics*. North-Holland.

Koller, Daphne, and Friedman, Nir. 2009. *Probabilistic Graphical Models – Principles and Techniques*. MIT Press.

McIver, Annabelle, and Morgan, Carroll. 2004. *Abstraction, Refinement and Proof for Probabilistic Systems*. Springer.

McIver, Annabelle, Morgan, Carroll, Kaminski, Benjamin Lucien, and Katoen, Joost-Pieter. 2018. A new proof rule for almost-sure termination. *Proceedings of the ACM on Programming Languages*, **2**(POPL), 33:1–33:28.

Minka, Tom, and Winn, John. 2017. *Infer.NET*. Accessed online at http://infernet.azurewebsites.net July 30, 2018.

Neapolitan, Richard E, and Jiang, Xia. 2010. *Probabilistic Methods for Financial and Marketing Informatics*. Morgan Kaufmann.

Ngo, Van Chan, Carbonneaux, Quentin, and Hoffmann, Jan. 2018. Bounded expectations: resource analysis for probabilistic programs. Pages 496–512 of: *Proceedings of the Conference on Programming Language Design and Implementation (PLDI)*. ACM.

Olmedo, Federico, Kaminski, Benjamin Lucien, Katoen, Joost-Pieter, and Matheja, Christoph. 2016. Reasoning about recursive probabilistic programs. Pages 672–681 of: *Logic in Computer Science (LICS)*. ACM.

Olmedo, Federico, Gretz, Friedrich, Jansen, Nils, Kaminski, Benjamin Lucien, Katoen, Joost-Pieter, and McIver, Annabelle. 2018. Conditioning in probabilistic programming. *ACM Transactions on Programming Languages and Systems*, **40**(1), 4:1–4:50.

Onisko, Agnieszka, Druzdzel, Marek J, and Wasyluk, Hanna. 1998. A probabilistic causal model for diagnosis of liver disorders. Pages 379–387 of: *Intelligent Information Systems (IIS)*.

Pearl, Judea. 1985. Bayesian networks: a model of self-activated memory for evidential reasoning. Pages 329–334 of: *Conference of the Cognitive Science Society*.

Rabin, Michael Oser. 1976. Probabilistic algorithms. Pages 21–39 of: Traub, Joseph Frederick (ed), *Algorithms and Complexity: New Directions and Recent Results*. Academic Press.

Ramanna, Sheela, Jain, Lakhmi C, and Howlett, Robert J. 2013. *Emerging Paradigms in Machine Learning*. Springer.

Scutari, Marco. 2017. *Bayesian Network Repository*. Accessed online at http://www.bnlearn.com July 30, 2018.

Smid, Michiel. 2000. Closest-point problems in computational geometry. Pages 877–935 of: Sack, Jörg-Rüdiger, and Urrutia, Jorge (eds), *Handbook of Computational Geometry*. North–Holland.

Solovay, Robert, and Strassen, Volker. 1977. A fast Monte-Carlo test for primality. *SIAM Journal on Computing*, **6**(1), 84–85.

Tarski, Alfred, et al. 1955. A lattice-theoretical fixpoint theorem and its applications. *Pacific Journal of Mathematics*, **5**(2), 285–309.

Zweig, Geoffrey, and Russell, Stuart J. 1998. Speech recognition with dynamic Bayesian networks. Pages 173–180 of: *AAAI/IAAI*. AAAI Press / The MIT Press.

7

Termination Analysis of Probabilistic Programs with Martingales

Krishnendu Chatterjee
IST Austria
Hongfei Fu
Shanghai Jiao Tong University
Petr Novotný
Masaryk University

Abstract: Probabilistic programs extend classical imperative programs with random-value generators. For classical non-probabilistic programs, termination is a key question in static analysis of programs, that given a program and an initial condition asks whether it terminates. In the presence of probabilistic behavior there are two fundamental extensions of the termination question, namely, (a) the *almost-sure* termination question that asks whether the termination probability is 1; and (b) the *bounded-time* termination question that asks whether the expected termination time is bounded. While there are many active research directions to address the above problems, one important research direction is the use of martingale theory for termination analysis. We will survey the main techniques related to martingale-based approach for termination analysis of probabilistic programs.

7.1 Introduction

Stochastic models and probabilistic programs. The analysis of stochastic models is a fundamental problem, and randomness plays a crucial role in several disciplines across computer science. Some prominent examples are (a) randomized algorithms (Motwani and Raghavan, 1995); (b) stochastic network protocols (Baier and Katoen, 2008; Kwiatkowska et al., 2011); (c) systems that interact with uncertainty in artificial intelligence (Kaelbling et al., 1996, 1998; Ghahramani, 2015). Programming language support for analysis of such models requires extending the classical non-probabilistic programming models, and the extension of classical imperative programs with *random value generators* that produce random values according to some desired probability distribution gives rise to the class of probabilistic programs (Gordon et al., 2014). The formal analysis of probabilistic systems and probabilistic programs is an active research topic across different disciplines,

[a] From *Foundations of Probabilistic Programming*, edited by Gilles Barthe, Joost-Pieter Katoen and Alexandra Silva published 2020 by Cambridge University Press.

such as probability theory and statistics (Durrett, 1996; Howard, 1960; Kemeny et al., 1966; Rabin, 1963; Paz, 1971), formal methods (Baier and Katoen, 2008; Kwiatkowska et al., 2011), artificial intelligence (Kaelbling et al., 1996, 1998), and programming languages (Chakarov and Sankaranarayanan, 2013; Fioriti and Hermanns, 2015; Sankaranarayanan et al., 2013; Esparza et al., 2012; Chatterjee et al., 2016a).

Termination questions. One of the most basic, yet fundamental, question in analysis of reactive systems or programs is the *termination* problem. For non-probabilistic program the termination problem asks whether a given program always terminates. The termination problem represents the fundamental notion of liveness for programs, and corresponds to the classical halting problem of Turing machines. While for general programs the termination problem is undecidable, static analysis methods for program analysis aim to develop techniques that can answer the question for subclasses of programs. For non-probabilistic programs, the proof of termination coincides with the construction of *ranking functions* (Floyd, 1967), and many different approaches exist for such construction (Bradley et al., 2005a; Colón and Sipma, 2001; Podelski and Rybalchenko, 2004; Sohn and Gelder, 1991). For probabilistic programs, the presence of randomness requires that the termination questions are extended to handle stochastic aspects. The most natural and basic extensions of the termination problem are as follows: First, the *almost-sure* termination question asks whether the program terminates with probability 1. Second, the *bounded* termination question asks whether the expected termination time is bounded. While the bounded termination implies almost-sure termination, the converse is not true in general. Section 7.2.4 illustrates the concepts on several examples.

Non-determinism. Besides stochastic aspects, another fundamental modeling concept is the notion of *non-determinism*. A classic example of non-determinism in program analysis is *abstraction*: for efficient static analysis of large programs, it is infeasible to track all variables of the program. Abstraction ignores certain variables and replaces them with worst-case behavior modeled as non-determinism. Moreover, non-determinism can be used to replace large portions of a program by overapproximating their effect on variables.

Martingales for probabilistic programs. While there are various different approaches for analyzing probabilistic programs (see Section 7.6 for further discussion), the focus of this chapter is to consider martingale-based approaches. This approach considers martingales (a special type of stochastic processes) and how they can be used to develop algorithmic analysis techniques for analysis of probabilistic programs. The approach brings together various different disciplines, namely, probability theory, algorithmic aspects, and program analysis techniques. Below we present a glimpse of the main results, and then the organization of the chapter.

Glimpse of main results. We present a brief description of main results related to the martingale-based approach.

- *Finite probabilistic choices.* First, for probabilistic programs with non-determinism, but restricted to finite probabilistic choices, quantitative invariants were used to establish termination in McIver and Morgan (2004, 2005).
- *Infinite probabilistic choices without non-determinism.* The approach presented in McIver and Morgan (2004, 2005) was extended in Chakarov and Sankaranarayanan (2013) to *ranking* supermartingales to obtain a sound (but not complete, see Chakarov and Sankaranarayanan (2013, page 10) for a counterexample) approach for almost-sure termination for infinite-state probabilistic programs without non-determinism, but with infinite-domain random variables. The connection between termination of probabilistic programs without non-determinism and *Lyapunov ranking functions* was considered in Bournez and Garnier (2005). For probabilistic programs with countable state space and without non-determinism, Lyapunov ranking functions provide a sound and complete method to prove bounded termination (Bournez and Garnier, 2005; Foster, 1953).
- *Infinite probabilistic choices with non-determinism.* The interaction of non-determinism and infinite probabilistic choice is quite tricky as illustrated in Fioriti and Hermanns (2015). For bounded termination, the ranking supermartingale based approach is sound and complete (Chatterjee and Fu, 2017; Fu and Chatterjee, 2019). As mentioned above, a key goal is to obtain algorithmic methods for automated analysis. Automated approaches for synthesis of linear and polynomial ranking supermartingales have been studied in Chatterjee et al. (2016a,b). Moreover, recently parametric supermartingales, rather than ranking supermartingales, (McIver et al., 2018; Chatterjee and Fu, 2017; Huang et al., 2018) and lexicographic ranking supermartingales (Agrawal et al., 2018) have been considered for proving almost-sure termination of probabilistic programs. The martingale-based approach has also been studied to prove high-probability termination and non-termination of probabilistic programs (Chatterjee et al., 2017).
- *Undecidability characterization.* The problem of deciding termination (almost-sure termination and bounded termination) of probabilistic programs is undecidable, and its precise undecidability characterization has been studied in Kaminski and Katoen (2015).

Organization. The chapter is organized as follows: In Section 7.2 we present the preliminaries (syntax, semantics, and the formal definition of termination problems). In Section 7.3 we present the results related to the theoretical foundations of ranking supermartingales and bounded termination. In Section 7.4 we discuss algorithmic approaches for synthesis of linear and polynomial ranking supermaritngales. In Section 7.5 we consider the martingale-based approach beyond bounded termination: we first consider almost-sure termination and discuss the parametric supermartingale and lexicographic ranking supermartingale based approach, then discuss the approach for high-probability termination. Finally, we discuss related works (Section 7.6), and conclude with future perspective (Section 7.7).

7.2 Preliminaries

7.2.1 Syntax of Probabilistic Programs

We consider a mathematically clean formulation of a simple imperative probabilistic programming language with real-valued numerical variables. An abstract grammar of our probabilistic language is presented in Figure 7.1. There, $\langle pvar \rangle$ stands for program variables, while $\langle expr \rangle$ and $\langle boolexpr \rangle$ represent arithmetic expressions and boolean predicates, respectively.

Expressions and Predicates. We assume that the expressions used in each program satisfy the following: (1) for each expression E over variables $\{x_1, \ldots, x_n\}$ and each n-dimensional vector $\mathbf{x}$ the value $E(\mathbf{x})$ is well defined; and (2) the function defined by each expression E is Borel-measurable (for definition of Borel-measurability, see, e.g. Billingsley (1995)). This holds in particular for expressions built using standard arithmetic operators $(+, -, *, /)$, provided that expressions evaluating to zero are not allowed as divisors. A *predicate* is a boolean combination of *atomic predicates* of the form $E \leq E'$, where E, E' are expressions. We denote by $\mathbf{x} \models \psi$ the fact that the predicate ψ is satisfied by substituting values from of $\mathbf{x}$ for the corresponding variables in ψ.

Probability and Non-Determinism. Apart from the classical programming constructs, our probabilistic programs also have constructs introducing *probabilistic* and *non-deterministic* behaviour. The former include probabilistic branching (e.g. 'if $\mathbf{prob}(\frac{1}{3})$ then...') and sampling of a variable value from a probability distribution (e.g. $x := \mathbf{sample}(\text{Uniform}[-2, 1])$). We allow both discrete and continuous distributions and we also permit sampling instructions to appear in place of variables within expressions. For the purpose of our analysis, we require that for each distribution d appearing in the program we know the following characteristics: the expected value $\mathbb{E}[d]$ and a set SP_d containing the *support* of d (the support of d is the smallest closed set of real numbers whose complement has probability zero under d). We also allow (demonic) non-deterministic branching represented by $\star$ in the conditional guard. The techniques presented in this chapter can be extended also to

$$\langle stmt \rangle ::= \langle assgn \rangle \mid \textbf{skip} \mid \langle stmt \rangle \, ; \, \langle stmt \rangle$$
$$\mid \textbf{if } \langle ndboolexpr \rangle \textbf{ then } \langle stmt \rangle \textbf{ else } \langle stmt \rangle \textbf{ fi}$$
$$\mid \textbf{while } \langle boolexpr \rangle \textbf{ do } \langle stmt \rangle \textbf{ od}$$
$$\langle assgn \rangle ::= \langle pvar \rangle := \langle expr \rangle \mid \langle pvar \rangle := \textbf{sample}(\langle dist \rangle)$$
$$\langle ndboolexpr \rangle ::= \star \mid \textbf{prob}(p) \mid \langle boolexpr \rangle$$

Figure 7.1 Abstract grammar of imperative probabilistic programs.

programs with non-deterministic assignments, but we omit this feature for the sake of simplicity.

Affine Probabilistic Programs. The mathematical techniques presented in this chapter are applicable to a rather general class of probabilistic programs. When considering *automation* of these methods, we restrict our attention to *affine* programs. A probabilistic program $\mathcal{P}$ is affine if each arithmetic expression occurring in $\mathcal{P}$ (i.e. in its loop guards, conditionals, and right-hand sides of assignments) is an *affine expression,* i.e. an expression of the form $b + \sum_{i=1}^{n} a_i x_i$, where $b, a_1, \ldots, a_n$ are real-valued constants.

7.2.2 Semantics of Probabilistic Programs

We now sketch our definition of semantics of PPs with non-determinism. We use the standard operational semantics presented in more detail in (Agrawal et al., 2018).

Basics of Probability Theory. We assume some familiarity with basic concepts of probability theory. A *probability space* is a triple $(\Omega, \mathcal{F}, \mathbb{P})$, where Ω is a non-empty set (so called *sample space*), $\mathcal{F}$ is a *sigma-algebra* of measurable sets over Ω, i.e. a collection of subsets of Ω that contains the empty set $\emptyset$, and that is closed under complementation and countable unions, and $\mathbb{P}$ is a *probability measure* on $\mathcal{F}$, i.e., a function $\mathbb{P} \colon \mathcal{F} \to [0, 1]$ such that: (1) $\mathbb{P}(\emptyset) = 0$, (2) for all $A \in \mathcal{F}$ it holds $\mathbb{P}(\Omega \smallsetminus A) = 1 - \mathbb{P}(A)$, and (3) for all pairwise disjoint countable set sequences $A_1, A_2, \cdots \in \mathcal{F}$ (i.e., $A_i \cap A_j = \emptyset$ for all $i \neq j$) we have $\sum_{i=1}^{\infty} \mathbb{P}(A_i) = \mathbb{P}(\bigcup_{i=1}^{\infty} A_i)$.

A *random variable* in a probability space $(\Omega, \mathcal{F}, \mathbb{P})$ is an $\mathcal{F}$-measurable function $R \colon \Omega \to \mathbb{R} \cup \{\infty\}$, i.e., a function such that for every $a \in \mathbb{R} \cup \{\infty\}$ the set $\{\omega \in \Omega \mid R(\omega) \le a\}$ belongs to $\mathcal{F}$. We denote by $\mathbb{E}[R]$ the *expected value* of a random variable R (see (Billingsley, 1995, Chapter 5) for a formal definition). A *random vector* in $(\Omega, \mathcal{F}, \mathbb{P})$ is a vector whose every component is a random variable in this probability space. We denote by $\mathbf{X}[j]$ the j-component of a vector $\mathbf{X}$. A *stochastic process* in a probability space $(\Omega, \mathcal{F}, \mathbb{P})$ is an infinite sequence of random vectors in this space. A *filtration* in the probability space is an infinite non-decreasing sequence of sigma-algebras $\mathcal{F}_0 \subseteq \mathcal{F}_1 \subseteq \mathcal{F}_2 \subseteq \cdots \mathcal{F}$ characterizing an increase of available information over time (see (Williams, 1991, Chapter 10)). A process $\{X_n\}_{n \in \mathbb{N}_0}$ is *adapted* to the filtration $\{\mathcal{F}_n\}_{n \in \mathbb{N}_0}$, if X_n is $\mathcal{F}_n$-measurable for each $n \in \mathbb{N}_0$. We will also use random variables of the form $R: \Omega \to S$ for some finite set S, which easily translates to the variables above.

Configurations and Runs. For a program $\mathcal{P}$ we denote by $V_{\mathcal{P}}$ the set of programs variables used in $\mathcal{P}$ (we routinely drop the subscript when $\mathcal{P}$ is known from the context). A *configuration* of a PP $\mathcal{P}$ is a tuple $(\ell, \mathbf{x})$, where ℓ is a program location (a line of the source code carrying a command) and $\mathbf{x}$ is *valuation*, i.e. a $|V_{\mathcal{P}}|$-dimensional vector s.t. $\mathbf{x}[t]$ is the current value of variable $t \in V_{\mathcal{P}}$. A *run* is a finite or infinite sequence of configurations corresponding to a possible execution of the program. A finite run which does not end in the program's terminal location is also called an *execution fragment*.

Schedulers. Non-determinism in a program is resolved via a *scheduler*. Formally, a scheduler is a function σ assigning to every execution fragment that ends in a location containing a command **if ⋆ then... else...** a probability distribution over the if- and else branches. We impose an additional *measurability* condition on schedulers, so as to ensure that the semantics of probabilistic non-deterministic programs is defined in a mathematically sound way. The definition of a measurable scheduler that we use is the standard one used when dealing with systems that exhibit both probabilistic and non-deterministic behaviour over a continuous state space (Neuhäußer et al., 2009; Neuhäußer and Katoen, 2007). In the rest of this work, we refer to measurable schedulers simply as "schedulers."

From a Program to a Stochastic process. A program $\mathcal{P}$ together with a scheduler σ and initial variable valuation $\mathbf{x}_0$ define a stochastic process which produces a random run $(\ell_0, \mathbf{x}_0)(\ell_1, \mathbf{x}_1)(\ell_2, \mathbf{x}_2) \cdots$. The evolution of this process can be informally described as follows: we start in the initial configuration, i.e. $(\ell_0, \mathbf{x}_0)$, where ℓ_0 corresponds to the first command of $\mathcal{P}$ and ℓ_0 is the initial valuation of variables (from now on, we assume that each program is accompanied by some initial variable valuation denoted $\mathbf{x}_{init}$). Now assume that i steps have elapsed and the program has not yet terminated, and let $\pi_i = (\ell_0, \mathbf{x}_0)(\ell_1, \mathbf{x}_1) \cdots (\ell_i, \mathbf{x}_i)$ be the execution fragment produced so far. Then the next configuration $(\ell_{i+1}, \mathbf{x}_{i+1})$ is chosen as follows:

- If ℓ_i corresponds to a deterministic assignment, the assignment is performed and the program location advances to the next command, which yields the new configuration.
- If ℓ_i corresponds to a probabilistic assignment, the value to assign is first sampled from a given distribution, after which the assignment of the sampled value is performed as above.

- If ℓ_i corresponds to a command **if ⋆ then...**, then a branch to execute is sampled according to scheduler σ, i.e. from the distribution $\sigma(\pi_i)$. The valuation remains unchanged, but ℓ_{i+1} advances to the first command of the sampled branch.
- If ℓ_i corresponds to a command **if prob(p) then...**, then we select the if branch with probability p and the else branch with probability $1 - p$. The selected branch is then executed as above.
- Otherwise, ℓ_i contains a standard deterministic conditional (branching or loop guard). We evaluate the truth value of the conditional under the current valuation $\mathbf{x}_i$ to select the correct branch, which is then executed as above.

The above intuition can be formalized by showing that each probabilistic program $\mathcal{P}$ together with a scheduler σ and initial valuation $\mathbf{x}_0$ uniquely determine a certain probability space $(\Omega_{Run}, \mathcal{R}, \mathbb{P}_{\mathbf{x}_0}^{\sigma})$ in which Ω_{Run} is a set of all runs in $\mathcal{P}$, and a stochastic process $C^{\sigma} = \{C_i^{\sigma}\}_{i=0}^{\infty}$ in this space such that for each run $\varrho \in \Omega_{Run}$ we have that $\mathbf{C}_i^{\sigma}(\varrho)$ is the i-th configuration on ϱ. The formal construction of $\mathcal{R}$ and $\mathbb{P}_{\mathbf{x}_0}^{\sigma}$ proceeds via the standard *cylinder construction* (Ash and Doléans-Dade, 2000, Theorem 2.7.2). We denote by $\mathbb{E}_{\mathbf{x}_0}^{\sigma}$ the expectation operator in the probability space $(\Omega_{Run}, \mathcal{R}, \mathbb{P}_{\mathbf{x}_0}^{\sigma})$.

7.2.3 Termination

Each program $\mathcal{P}$ has a special location ℓ_{out} corresponding to the value of the program counter after finishing the execution of $\mathcal{P}$. We say that a run *terminates* if it reaches a configuration whose first component is ℓ_{out}; such configurations are called *terminal*.

Analysing program termination is one of the fundamental questions already in non-probabilistic program analysis. The question whether (every execution of) a program terminates is really just a re-statement of the classical Halting problem for Turing machines, which is, per one of the first fundamental results in computer science, undecidable (Turing, 1937). While we cannot *decide* whether a given program terminates, we can still aim to *prove* program termination via automated means, i.e. construct an algorithm which proves termination of as many terminating programs as possible, and reports a failure when it is unable to find such a proof (note that failure to find a termination proof does not, per se, prove the program's non-termination).

A classical technique for proving termination of non-probabilistic programs is the synthesis of an appropriate *ranking function* (Floyd, 1967). A ranking function maps program configurations to rational numbers, satisfying the following two properties: (1) each step of the program's execution strictly decreases the value of the ranking function by a value bounded away from zero, say at least by one; and (2) non-terminal configurations are mapped to positive numbers. Due to this strict decrease, the value of the function cannot stay positive *ad infinitum*; hence, the existence of a ranking function shows that the program terminates. Conversely, if we restrict to non-probabilistic programs with *bounded non-determinism* (where the number of non-deterministic choices in every step is bounded by some constant, such as in our syntax), then each such terminating program possesses a ranking function which maps a configuration $(\ell, \mathbf{x})$ to the maximal number of steps the program needs to reach a terminal configuration from $(\ell, \mathbf{x})$. Since termination is undecidable, we cannot have a sound and complete algorithm for synthesis of such ranking functions. We can however employ techniques that are sound and *conditionally complete* in the sense that they search for ranking functions of a restricted form (such as linear ranking functions) and are guaranteed to find such a restricted ranking function whenever it exists (Bradley et al., 2005a; Colón and Sipma, 2001; Podelski and Rybalchenko, 2004).

7.2.4 Termination Questions for Probabilistic Programs

Termination and Termination Time. Recall that ℓ_{out} is a location to a terminated program execution. We define a random variable *Term* such that for each run ϱ the value *Term*(ϱ) represents the first point in time when the current location is ℓ_{out}. If a run ϱ does *not* terminate, then *Term*$(\varrho) = \infty$. We call *Term* the *termination time* of $\mathcal{P}$.

We consider the following fundamental computational problems regarding termination:

* *Almost-sure termination:* A probabilistic program $\mathcal{P}$ is almost-surely (a.s.) terminating if under each scheduler σ it holds that $\mathbb{P}^{\sigma}_{\mathbf{x}_{init}}(\{\varrho \in \Omega_{Run} \mid \varrho \text{ terminates}\}) = 1$, or equivalently, if for each σ it holds $\mathbb{P}^{\sigma}_{\mathbf{x}_{init}}(Term < \infty) = 1$.
* *Finite and bounded termination:* A probabilistic program $\mathcal{P}$ is said to be *finitely* (aka *positive almost-surely* (Fioriti and Hermanns, 2015)) terminating if under each σ it holds that $\mathbb{E}^{\sigma}_{\mathbf{x}_{init}}[Term] < \infty$. Furthermore, the program $\mathcal{P}$ is *boundedly* terminating if we have $\sup_{\sigma} \mathbb{E}^{\sigma}_{\mathbf{x}_{init}}[Term] < \infty$.
* *Probabilistic termination:* In this generalization of the a.s. termination problem, we aim to compute a non-trivial lower bound $p \in [0, 1]$ on termination probability, i.e. p s.t. for each σ we have $\mathbb{P}^{\sigma}_{\mathbf{x}_{init}}(\{\varrho \in \Omega_{Run} \mid \varrho \text{ terminates}\}) \geq p$. In particular, here we also aim to analyse programs that are not necessarily a.s. terminating.

Remark 7.1 We present some remarks about the above definitions.

* First, finite termination implies almost-sure termination as $\mathbb{E}^{\sigma}_{\mathbf{x}_{init}}[Term] < \infty$ implies $\mathbb{P}^{\sigma}_{\mathbf{x}_{init}}(Term) = 1$; however, the converse does not hold (see Example 7.2 below).
* Second, there is subtle but important conceptual difference between finite and bounded termination. While the first asks for the expected termination time to be

finite for all schedulers, the expected termination time can still grow unbounded with different schedulers. In contrast, the bounded termination asks for the expected termination time to be bounded for all schedulers (but can depend on initial configuration). For probabilistic programs without non-determinism they coincide, since there is no quantification over schedulers. In general bounded termination implies finite termination; however, the converse does not hold (see Example 7.3 below).

It follows that bounded termination provides the strongest termination guarantee among the above questions, and we will focus on bounded termination.

Example 7.2 We present an example program that is almost-sure terminating, but not finite terminating. Consider the probabilistic program depicted in Figure 7.2. The loop models the classical symmetric random walk that hits zero almost-surely, but in infinite expected termination time (see Williams, 1991, Chapter 10). Hence, the loop is a.s. terminating but not finitely terminating.

Example 7.3 We present, in Figure 7.3, an example program that is finitely terminating, but not boundedly terminating. A scheduler for the program can be characterized by how many times the scheduler chooses the program counter 6 from the non-deterministic branch at the program counter 5 (finitely or infinitely), as once the scheduler chooses the program counter 10, the program then jumps out of the while loop at the program counter 4 and terminates after the execution of the while loop at the program counter 12. Under each such scheduler, the expected termination time is finite, so we have that the program is finitely terminating. However, since we have 3^n at the right-hand-side of the program counter 10 and the probability to jump out of the while loop at the non-deterministic branch 4 is 0.5 by the Bernoulli distribution, the expected termination time under a scheduler can be arbitrarily large when the number of times to choose the program counter 6 at the program counter 5 increases. Hence, there is no upper bound on the expected termination time for all schedulers, i.e., the probabilistic program is not boundedly terminating. See Fioriti and Hermanns (2015, Page 2) for details.

We now argue that termination analysis for probabilistic programs is more complex than for non-probabilistic programs.

First, note that the classical ranking functions do not suffice to prove even almost-sure termination. Since ranking functions are designed for non-probabilistic programs, applying them to probabilistic programs would necessitate replacing probabilistic choices and assignments with non-determinism. But Figure 7.2 shows a program which terminates almost-surely in the probabilistic setting, but does not necessarily terminate when the choice on line 3 is replaced by non-determinism (the non-deterministic choice might e.g. alternate between the if- and the else-branch, preventing x from decreasing to 0).

Second, there are deeper theoretical reasons for the hardness of probabilistic termination. The termination of classical programs, i.e. the halting problem, is undecidable but recursively enumerable. As shown by (Kaminski and Katoen, 2015), the problems of deciding almost sure and positive termination in probabilistic programs are complete for the 2nd level of the arithmetic hierarchy.

Hence, the classical analysis is not applicable and new approaches to probabilistic termination are needed.

7.3 Theoretical Foundations for Bounded Termination

In this section, we establish theoretical foundations for proving bounded termination of probabilistic programs. First, we consider probabilistic programs without non-determinism and demonstrate mathematical approaches for proving bounded termination over such programs. Second, we extend the approach to probabilistic programs with non-determinism. Third, we show that our approach is sound and complete for proving bounded termination of non-deterministic probabilistic programs. Finally, we describe algorithms for proving bounded termination.

7.3.1 Probabilistic Programs without Non-determinism

For probabilistic programs without non-determinism, Chakarov and Sankaranarayanan (2013) first proposed a sound approach for proving bounded termination. (Recall that in the absence of non-determinism, finite and bounded termination coincide.) The approach can be described as follows.

- First, a general result on bounded termination of a special class of stochastic processes called *ranking supermartingales* (RSMs) is established.
- Second, program executions are translated into stochastic processes through a notion of *RSM-maps*.
- Third, the existence of RSM-maps that ensure bounded termination of probabilistic programs without non-determinism is established. The central idea of the proof is a construction of RSMs from RSM-maps.

We begin with the notion of *ranking supermartingales* which is the key to the approach. We take the original definition in Chakarov and Sankaranarayanan (2013).

Definition 7.4 (Ranking Supermartingales)   A discrete-time stochastic process $\Gamma = \{X_n\}_{n \in \mathbb{N}_0}$ adapted to a filtration $\{\mathcal{F}_n\}_{n \in \mathbb{N}_0}$ is a *ranking supermartingale* (RSM) if there exist real numbers $\epsilon > 0$ and $K \leq 0$ such that for all $n \in \mathbb{N}_0$, the following conditions hold:

- (integrability) $\mathbb{E}[|X_n|] < \infty$;
- (lower-bound) it holds a.s. that $X_n \geq K$;

```
1:  x := 100;
2:  while  x ≥ 0  do
3:      if  prob(0.5)  then
4:          x := x + 1
        else
5:          x := x - 1
        fi ;
    od
6:
```

Figure 7.2 An a.s. (but not finitely) terminating example

```
1:  n := 0;  2:  i := 0;  3:  c := 0;
4:  while  c = 0  do
5:      if  ⋆  then
6:          c := sample(Bernoulli (0.5));
7:          if  c = 0  then
8:              n := n + 1
            else
9:              i := n
            fi
        else
10:         i := 3^n ;
11:         c := 1
        fi
    od ;
12: while  i > 0  do
13:     i := i - 1
    od
14:
```

Figure 7.3 A finitely (but not boundedly) terminating example

- (ranking) it holds a.s. that $\mathbb{E}[X_{n+1}|\mathcal{F}_n] \leq X_n - \epsilon \cdot \mathbf{1}_{X_n \geq 0}$, where the random variable $\mathbb{E}[X_{n+1}|\mathcal{F}_n]$ is the conditional expectation of X_{n+1} given the sigma-algebra $\mathcal{F}_n$ (see Williams, 1991, Chapter 9 for details), and the random variable $\mathbf{1}_{X_n \geq 0}$ takes value 1 if the event $X_n \geq 0$ holds and 0 otherwise.

Informally, an RSM is a stochastic process whose values have a lower bound and decrease in expectation when the step increases.

The random variable Z_Γ.   Given an RSM $\Gamma = \{X_n\}_{n \in \mathbb{N}_0}$ adapted to a filtration $\{\mathcal{F}_n\}_{n \in \mathbb{N}_0}$, we define the random variable Z_Γ by $Z_\Gamma(\omega) := \min\{n \mid X_n(\omega) < 0\}$ where $\min \emptyset := \infty$. By definition, the random variable Z_Γ measures the amount of steps before the value of the stochastic process Γ drops below zero for the first time.

The following theorem from illustrates the relationship between an RSM Γ and its termination time Z_Γ. There are several versions for the theorem. The original version is Chakarov and Sankaranarayanan (2013) which only asserts almost-sure termination. (Recall that bounded termination implies almost-sure termination, but not vice versa.) Then in Fioriti and Hermanns (2015, Lemma 5.5), the theorem was extended to bounded termination with an explicit upper bound on expected termination time. The version in Fioriti and Hermanns (2015, Lemma 5.5) restricts K to be zero. Here we follow the version in Chatterjee et al. (2018a) that relaxes K to be a non-positive number while deriving an upper bound on the expected termination time.

Proposition 7.5   *Let $\Gamma = \{X_n\}_{n \in \mathbb{N}_0}$ be an RSM adapted to a filtration $\{\mathcal{F}_n\}_{n \in \mathbb{N}_0}$ with ϵ, K given as in Definition 7.4. Then $\mathbb{P}(Z_\Gamma < \infty) = 1$ and $\mathbb{E}[Z_\Gamma] \leq \frac{\mathbb{E}(X_0) - K}{\epsilon}$.*

Proof Sketch   Using the ranking condition in Definition 7.4, we first prove by induction on $n \geq 0$ that $\mathbb{E}[X_n] \leq \mathbb{E}[X_0] - \epsilon \cdot \sum_{k=0}^{n-1} \mathbb{P}(X_k \geq 0)$. Moreover, we have from the lower-bound condition in Definition 7.4 that $\mathbb{E}[X_n] \geq K$, for all n. Then we obtain that for all n, it holds that

$$\sum_{k=0}^{n} \mathbb{P}(X_k \geq 0) \leq \frac{\mathbb{E}[X_0] - \mathbb{E}[X_{n+1}]}{\epsilon} \leq \frac{\mathbb{E}[X_0] - K}{\epsilon}.$$

Hence, the series $\sum_{k=0}^{\infty} \mathbb{P}(X_k \geq 0)$ converges and is no greater than $\frac{\mathbb{E}[X_0] - K}{\epsilon}$. It follows from $Z_\Gamma(\omega) > k \Rightarrow X_k(\omega) \geq 0$ (for all k, ω) that

- $\mathbb{P}(Z_\Gamma = \infty) = \lim_{k \to \infty} \mathbb{P}(Z_\Gamma > k) = 0$, and
- $\mathbb{E}[Z_\Gamma] = \sum_{k=0}^{\infty} \mathbb{P}(k < Z_\Gamma < \infty) \leq \sum_{k=0}^{\infty} \mathbb{P}(X_k \geq 0) \leq \frac{\mathbb{E}[X_0] - K}{\epsilon}$.

Then the desired result follows. See Fioriti and Hermanns (2015, Lemma 5.5) and Chatterjee et al. (2018a, Proposition 3.2) for details.   □

Theorem 7.5 established the first step of the approach. In the next step, we need to relate RSMs with probabilistic programs. To accomplish this, the notion of RSM-maps plays a key role. We first introduce the notion of *pre-expectation*, then that of *RSM-maps*.

Below we fix a non-deterministic probabilistic program P with the set L of locations (values of the program counter), the set V of program variables and the set $\mathcal{D}$ of probability distributions appearing in P. Then the set of variable valuations is $\mathbb{R}^{|V|}$ and the set of configurations is $L \times \mathbb{R}^{|V|}$. Moreover, we say that a *sampling* valuation is a real vector in $\mathbb{R}^{|\mathcal{D}|}$ that represents a vector of sampled values from all probability distributions. Then for each assignment statement in P at a location ℓ, regardless of whether the assignment statement is deterministic or a sampling, we have a function F_ℓ which maps each current variable valuation $\mathbf{x}$ and current sampling valuation $\mathbf{r}$ to the next variable valuation $F_\ell(\mathbf{x}, \mathbf{r})$ after the execution of the assignment statement.

The following definition introduces the notion of *pre-expectation* (Chatterjee et al., 2018a; Chakarov and Sankaranarayanan, 2013; McIver and Morgan, 2005).

Definition 7.6 (Pre-expectation) Let $\eta : L \times \mathbb{R}^{|V|} \to \mathbb{R}$ be a function which maps every configuration to a real number. We define the *pre-expectation* of η as the function $\mathrm{pre}_\eta : L \times \mathbb{R}^{|V|} \to \mathbb{R}$ by:

- $\mathrm{pre}_\eta(\ell, \mathbf{x}) := \sum_{\ell' \in L} p_{\ell,\ell'} \cdot \eta(\ell', \mathbf{x})$ if ℓ corresponds to a probabilistic branch and $p_{\ell,\ell'}$ is the probability that the next location is ℓ';
- $\mathrm{pre}_\eta(\ell, \mathbf{x}) := \eta(\ell', \mathbf{x})$ if ℓ corresponds to either an if-branch or a while-loop and ℓ' is the next location determined by the current variable valuation $\mathbf{x}$ and the boolean predicate associated with ℓ;
- $\mathrm{pre}_\eta(\ell, \mathbf{x}) := \eta(\ell', \mathbb{E}_\mathbf{r}(F_\ell(\mathbf{x}, \mathbf{r})))$ if ℓ corresponds to an assignment statement, where ℓ' is the location after the assignment statement and the expectation $\mathbb{E}_\mathbf{r}(-)$ is considered when $\mathbf{x}$ is fixed and $\mathbf{r}$ observes the corresponding probability distributions in $\mathcal{D}$.

Intuitively, $\mathrm{pre}_\eta(\ell, \mathbf{x})$ is the expected value of η after the execution of the statement at ℓ with the current configuration $(\ell, \mathbf{x})$.

Remark 7.7 The pre-expectation here is taken from Chatterjee et al. (2018a), and is a *small-step* version that only considers the execution of one individual statement. A *big-step* version is given in Chakarov and Sankaranarayanan (2013) and McIver and Morgan (2005) that consider the execution of a block of statements. The big-step version can be obtained by iterating the small-step version statement by statement in the block.

Invariants. To introduce the notion of ranking-supermartingale maps, we further need the notion of *invariants*. Formally, given an initial configuration $(\ell_0, \mathbf{x}_0)$, an invariant I is a function that assigns to each location ℓ a subset of variable valuations $I(\ell)$ such that in any program execution from the initial configuration and for all configurations $(\ell, \mathbf{x})$ visited in the execution, we have that $\mathbf{x} \in I(\ell)$. Intuitively, an invariant is an over-approximation of the reachable configurations from a specified initial configuration. A trivial invariant is the one that assigns to all locations the set $\mathbb{R}^{|V|}$ of all variable valuations. Usually, we can obtain more precise invariants that tightly approximate the reachable configurations through well-established techniques such as abstract interpretation (Cousot and Cousot, 1977).

Now we introduce the notion of ranking-supermartingale maps.

Definition 7.8 (Ranking-supermartingale Maps) A *ranking-supermartingale map* (RSM-map) wrt an invariant I is a function $\eta : L \times \mathbb{R}^{|V|} \to \mathbb{R}$ such that there exist real numbers $\epsilon > 0$ and $K, K' < 0$ such that for all configurations $(\ell, \mathbf{x})$, the following conditions hold:

(C1) if $\ell \neq \ell_{out}$ and $\mathbf{x} \in I(\ell)$, then $\eta(\ell, \mathbf{x}) \geq 0$;
(C2) if $\ell = \ell_{out}$ and $\mathbf{x} \in I(\ell)$, then $K \leq \eta(\ell, \mathbf{x}) \leq K'$;
(C3) if $\ell \neq \ell_{out}$ and $\mathbf{x} \in I(\ell)$, then $\mathrm{pre}_\eta(\ell, \mathbf{x}) \leq \eta(\ell, \mathbf{x}) - \epsilon$.

Intuitively, the condition (C1) specifies that when the program does not terminate then the value of the RSM-map should be non-negative. The condition (C2) specifies that when the program terminates, then the value should be negative and bounded from below. Note that (C1) and (C2) together guarantees that the program terminates iff the value of the RSM-map is negative. Finally, the condition (C3) specifies that the pre-expectation at non-terminal locations should decrease at least by some fixed positive amount, which is related to the ranking condition in the RSM definition (cf. Definition 7.4).

The key role played by RSM-maps is that if we have an RSM-map, then we can assert the bounded termination of the program and an explicit upper bound. In other words, RSM-maps are *sound* for proving bounded termination of probabilistic programs. This is demonstrated by the following proposition from (Chatterjee et al., 2018a, Theorem 3.8).

Proposition 7.9 (Soundness) *If there exists an RSM-map η wrt some invariant I, then we have that* $\sup_\sigma \mathbb{E}^\sigma_{\mathbf{x}_{init}}[Term] \leq \frac{\eta(\ell_0, \mathbf{x}_{init}) - K}{\epsilon}$.

Proof Sketch Suppose that there is an RSM-map η. Let the stochastic process $\Gamma = \{X_n\}_{n \in \mathbb{N}_0}$ be given by: $X_n := \eta(\mathbf{C}_n)$. (Recall that $\mathbf{C}_n$ is the vector of random variables that represents the configuration at the n-th step in a program execution.) Then from (C2) and (C3), we have that Γ is an RSM with the same ϵ, K. Thus we obtain from Proposition 7.5 that $\mathbb{E}[Z_\Gamma] \leq \frac{\mathbb{E}[X_0] - K}{\epsilon}$. Furthermore, from (C1) and (C2), we have that $Term = Z_\Gamma$. It follows that $\mathbb{E}^\sigma_{\mathbf{x}_{init}}[Z_\Gamma] \leq \frac{\mathbb{E}[X_0] - K}{\epsilon}$ for all schedulers σ. See Chatterjee et al. (2018a, Theorem 3.8) for details. □

Below we illustrate the approach of RSM-maps for proving bounded termination of probabilistic programs through a simple example. The example is taken from Chakarov and Sankaranarayanan (2013, Example 2).

Example 7.10 (A Tortoise-Hare Race) Consider a scenario where a tortoise and a hare race against each other. The program representation for such a race is depicted in the left part of Figure 7.4. At the beginning, the hare starts at the position 0

```
1:  h := 0;
2:  t := 30;
3:  while h ≤ t do
4:      if prob(0.5) then
5:          r := sample(Uniform(0, 10));
6:          h := h + r
        else
7:          skip
        fi;
8:      t := t + 1
    od
9:
```

ℓ	Invariant I	RSM-map η
1	true	119
2	$h = 0$	118
3	$h \le t + 9$	$3 \cdot (t - h) + 27$
4	$h \le t$	$3 \cdot (t - h) + 26$
5	$h \le t$	$3 \cdot (t - h) + 18$
6	$h \le t$ $\wedge$ $0 \le r \le 10$	$3 \cdot (t - h - r) + 32$
7	$h \le t$	$3 \cdot (t - h) + 32$
8	$h \le t + 10$	$3 \cdot (t - h) + 31$
9	$t \le h$	-1

Figure 7.4 **Left**: The Probabilistic Program for a Tortoise-Hare Race **Right**: An RSM-map for the Program

(location 1), while the tortoise starts at the position 30 (location 2). Then in each round (an iteration of the loop body from the location 4 to location 8), the hare either stops (location 7) or proceeds with a random distance that observes the uniform distribution over $[0, 10]$ (location 6), both with probability $\frac{1}{2}$, while the tortoise always proceeds with a unit distance (location 8). It is intuitively clear that the hare will eventually catch the tortoise and the program will enter the terminal location $\ell_{out} = 9$ in finite expected time.

The right part of Figure 7.4 illustrates an RSM-map η w.r.t an invariant I for the program, where "ℓ" stands for "location", the invariant I is specified through conditions on program variables for each location (e.g., $I(3)$ is the set of all variable valuations $\mathbf{x}$ where $\mathbf{x}[h] \le \mathbf{x}[t] + 9$), and the RSM-map η is also specified for each location (e.g., $\eta(3, \mathbf{x}) = 3 \cdot (\mathbf{x}[t] - \mathbf{x}[h]) + 27$).

The function η is an RSM-map with $\epsilon = 1, K = K' = -1$ since it satisfies (C1)–(C3). For example, the condition (C1) is satisfied at the location 3 since $\mathbf{x}[h] \le \mathbf{x}[t]+9$ implies that $3 \cdot (\mathbf{x}[t] - \mathbf{x}[h]) + 27 \ge 0$; the condition (C2) is straightforwardly satisfied at the location 9; finally, the condition (C3) at the location 5 is satisfied as we have $\mathbb{E}[\text{uniform}(0, 10)] = 5$ and $3 \cdot (t - h - \mathbb{E}(r)) + 32 \le 3 \cdot (t - h) + 18 - 1$. As a consequence, we obtain that $\mathbb{E}_{\mathbf{x}_{init}}[Term] \le \frac{\eta(1, \mathbf{x}_{init}) - K}{\epsilon} = 120$. □

7.3.2 Probabilistic Programs with Non-determinism

The approach of ranking supermartingales can be directly extended to non-determinism. However, before we illustrate the extension, an important issue to resolve is the operational semantics with non-determinism. There is a diversity in the operational semantics for probabilistic programs with non-determinism. The semantics can be either directly based on random samplings (Fioriti and Hermanns, 2015) or Markov decision processes (MDPs). Below we first describe the result with random-sampling semantics (Fioriti and Hermanns, 2015), then the results with the MDP semantics (Chatterjee et al., 2018a).

Sampling-Based Semantics.   In Fioriti and Hermanns (2015), a semantics directly based on samplings is proposed. Under this semantics, a sample point (in the sample space) is an infinite sequence of sampled values from corresponding probability distributions in the program. Then for each scheduler σ, there is a termination-time random variable $Term^{\sigma}$. The advantage of this semantics is that there is only one probability space (i.e., the set of all infinite sequences of sampled values). However, the cost is that there are many random variables $Term^{\sigma}$, and one needs to define a "supremum" random variable $Term^{*} := \sup_{\sigma} Term^{\sigma}$ where σ ranges over all schedulers. As a result, a relative completeness result under such semantics is established in Fioriti and Hermanns (2015, Theorem 5.8) which states that if $\mathbb{E}(Term^{*}) < \infty$ then there exists a ranking supermartingale. As the semantics takes the supremum over all termination-time random variables, it is infeasible to explore the internal effect of an individual scheduler. As a consequence, it is difficult to develop algorithmic approaches based on this semantics.

MDP-Based Semantics.   In Chatterjee et al. (2018a), the MDP-semantics is adopted. MDPs are a standard operational model for probabilistic systems with non-determinism. Under the MDP-semantics, a state is a configuration of the program, while the probabilistic transitions between configurations are determined by the imperative semantics of each individual statement. Compared with the sampling-based semantics, there is only one termination-time random variable $Term$ and each scheduler determines a probabilistic space. Since the behaviour of an individual scheduler can be manipulated under this semantics, algorithmic approaches can be developed (which will be further illustrated in Section 7.4).

We follow the MDP-based semantics and demonstrate the extension of ranking supermartingales to non-determinism. To introduce the notion of RSM-maps in the context of non-determinism, we first extend the notion of pre-expectation.

Below we fix a non-deterministic probabilistic program P with the set L of locations, the set V of program variables and the set $\mathcal{D}$ of probability distributions appearing in P.

Definition 7.11 (Pre-expectation)   Let $\eta : L \times \mathbb{R}^{|V|} \to \mathbb{R}$ be a function which maps every configuration to a real number. We define the *pre-expectation* of η as the function $\mathrm{pre}_\eta : L \times \mathbb{R}^{|V|} \to \mathbb{R}$ by:

- $\mathrm{pre}_\eta(\ell, \mathbf{x}) := \sum_{\ell' \in L} p_{\ell,\ell'} \cdot \eta(\ell', \mathbf{x})$ if ℓ corresponds to a probabilistic branch and $p_{\ell,\ell'}$ is the probability that the next location is ℓ';
- $\mathrm{pre}_\eta(\ell, \mathbf{x}) := \eta(\ell', \mathbf{x})$ if ℓ corresponds to either an if-branch or a while-loop and ℓ' is the next location given the current variable valuation $\mathbf{x}$;
- $\mathrm{pre}_\eta(\ell, \mathbf{x}) := \eta(\ell', \mathbb{E}_{\mathbf{r}}[F_\ell(\mathbf{x}, \mathbf{r})])$ if the location ℓ corresponds to an assignment statement, where ℓ' is the location after the assignment statement and the expectation $\mathbb{E}_{\mathbf{r}}(-)$ is considered when $\mathbf{x}$ is fixed and $\mathbf{r}$ observes the corresponding probability distributions in $\mathcal{D}$;
- $\mathrm{pre}_\eta(\ell, \mathbf{x}) := \max\{\eta(\ell_{\mathrm{th}}, \mathbf{x}), \eta(\ell_{\mathrm{el}}, \mathbf{x})\}$ if ℓ corresponds to a non-deterministic branch where ℓ_{th} and ℓ_{el} are the locations for respectively the then- and else-branch.

Compared with Definition 7.6, the current definition is extended with non-determinism. In the last item of Definition 7.11, the pre-expectation at a non-deterministic branch are defined as the maximum over its then- and else-branches. The reason to have maximum is that the non-deterministic branch in our programming language can be resolved arbitrarily by any scheduler, so we need to consider the worst case at non-deterministic branches regardless of the choice of the scheduler.

Soundness Result. Once we extend pre-expectation with non-determinism, we can keep the definition for RSM-maps the same as in Definition 7.8. Then with similar proofs, the statement of Proposition 7.9 still holds with non-determinism. Thus, RSM-maps are sound for proving bounded termination of probabilistic programs with non-determinism.

Proposition 7.12 (Soundness) *RSM-maps are sound for proving bounded termination of probabilistic programs with non-determinism.*

Completeness Result. In Fu and Chatterjee (2019, Theorem 2), a completeness result is established for RSM-maps and probabilistic programs with integer-valued variables. The result states that if the expected termination time of the probabilistic program is bounded for all schedulers, then there exists an RSM-map. The formal statement is as follows.

Proposition 7.13 (Completeness) *If all program variables in a probabilistic program P are integer-valued and $\sup_\sigma \mathbb{E}^\sigma_{\mathbf{x}_{init}}[\mathit{Term}] < \infty$, then there exists an RSM-map w.r.t some invariant I for P.*

From Proposition 7.12 and Proposition 7.13, we obtain that the approach of RSMs is sound and complete (through RSM-maps).

Theorem 7.14   *RSM-maps are sound and complete for proving bounded termination of probabilistic programs.*

Remark 7.15   Note that the termination problems for probabilistic programs generalize the termination problems for non-probabilistic programs (i.e., the halting problem of Turing machines) and is undecidable (for detailed complexity characterization see Kaminski and Katoen (2015)). The above soundness and completeness result does not imply that program termination is decidable, as it only ensures the existence of an RSM-map in general form which is not always computable. Thus the completeness result is orthogonal to the decidability results, however, special classes of RSM-maps can be obtained algorithmically which we consider in the following section.

7.4 Algorithms for Proving Bounded Termination

In the previous sections, we have illustrated that the existence of an RSM-map leads to bounded termination of probabilistic programs. Thus, in order to develop an algorithmic approach to prove bounded termination of probabilistic programs, it suffices to synthesize an RSM-map. Furthermore, since it is infeasible to synthesize an RSM-map in general form, in an algorithmic approach one needs to restrict the form of an RSM-map so as to make the approach feasible. In this section, we illustrate algorithmic approaches that can synthesize linear and polynomial RSM-maps given an input invariant (also in special form). Since the class of linear/polynomial RSM-maps is quite general, the corresponding algorithmic approaches can be applied to typical probabilistic programs such as gambler's ruin, random walks, robot navigation, etc. (see the experimental results in Chakarov and Sankaranarayanan (2013), Chatterjee et al. (2018a) and Chatterjee et al. (2016b) for details).

We first describe the algorithmic approach for synthesizing linear RSM-maps over *affine* probabilistic programs where the right-hand-side of each assignment statement is affine in program variables. A *linear* RSM-map is an RSM-map η such that for each location ℓ, the function $\eta(\ell, -)$ is affine in the program variables of P. For example, the RSM-map at the right part of Figure 7.4 is linear.

To illustrate the algorithm, we need the well-known Farkas' Lemma that characterizes the inclusion of a polyhedron in a halfspace.

Theorem 7.16 (Farkas' Lemma (Farkas, 1894; Schrijver, 2003))   *Let $\mathbf{A} \in \mathbb{R}^{m \times n}$, $\mathbf{b} \in \mathbb{R}^m$, $\mathbf{c} \in \mathbb{R}^n$ and $d \in \mathbb{R}$. Assume that $\{\mathbf{x} \in \mathbb{R}^n \mid \mathbf{A}\mathbf{x} \leq \mathbf{b}\} \neq \emptyset$. Then we have that*

$$\{\mathbf{x} \in \mathbb{R}^n \mid \mathbf{A}\mathbf{x} \leq \mathbf{b}\} \subseteq \{\mathbf{x} \in \mathbb{R}^n \mid \mathbf{c}^{\mathsf{T}}\mathbf{x} \leq d\}$$

iff there exists $\mathbf{y} \in \mathbb{R}^m$ *such that* $\mathbf{y} \geq \mathbf{0}$, $\mathbf{A}^T\mathbf{y} = \mathbf{c}$ *and* $\mathbf{b}^T\mathbf{y} \leq d$, *where* $\mathbf{y} \geq \mathbf{0}$ *means that every coordinate of* $\mathbf{y}$ *is non-negative.*

The Farkas' Linear Assertions Φ. Farkas' Lemma transforms the inclusion testing of systems of linear inequalities into an emptiness problem. Given a polyhedron $H = \{\mathbf{x} \in \mathbb{R}^n \mid \mathbf{A}\mathbf{x} \leq \mathbf{b}\}$ as in the statement of Farkas' Lemma (Theorem 7.16), we define the predicate $\Phi[H, \mathbf{c}, d](\xi)$ (which is called a Farkas' linear assertion) for Farkas' Lemma by

$$\Phi[H, \mathbf{c}, d](\xi) := (\xi \geq \mathbf{0}) \wedge \left(\mathbf{A}^T\xi = \mathbf{c}\right) \wedge \left(\mathbf{b}^T\xi \leq d\right)$$

where ξ is a variable representing a column vector of dimension m. Then by Farkas' Lemma, we have that $H \subseteq \{\mathbf{x} \mid \mathbf{c}^T\mathbf{x} \leq d\}$ iff there exists a column vector $\mathbf{y}$ such that $\Phi[H, \mathbf{c}, d](\mathbf{y})$ holds.

Linear Invariants. We also need the notion of linear invariants. Informally, A *linear invariant* is an invariant I such that for all locations ℓ we have that $I(\ell)$ is a finite union of polyhedra.

Now we illustrate the algorithm for synthesizing linear RSM-maps w.r.t a given linear invariant. The description of the algorithm is as follows.

(i) First, the algorithm establishes a linear template for an RSM map. The linear template specifies that at each location, the function is affine in program variables with unknown coefficients. Besides, the algorithm also sets up three unknown parameters ϵ, K, K' which correspond to the counterparts in the definition of RSM-maps (cf Definition 7.8).

(ii) Second, the algorithm transforms the conditions (C1)–(C3) equivalently into Farkas' linear assertions through Farkas' Lemma.

(iii) Third, since the Farkas' linear assertions refer to the emptiness problem over polyhedra, we can use linear programming to solve those assertions. If a linear programming solver eventually finds the concrete values for the unknown coefficients in the template, then the algorithm finds a linear RSM-map that witnesses the bounded termination of the input program. Otherwise, the algorithm outputs "fail", meaning that the algorithm does not know whether the input program is boundedly terminating or not.

Since linear programming can be solved in polynomial time, our algorithm also runs in polynomial time, as is illustrated by the following theorem.

Theorem 7.17 (Chatterjee et al., 2018a, Theorem 4.1) *The problem to synthesize a linear RSM-map over non-deterministic affine probabilistic programs where all loop guards are in disjunctive normal form can be solved in polynomial time.*

Below we illustrate the details on how the algorithm works on Example 7.10.

Example 7.18   We illustrate our algorithm on Example 7.10, where the input invariant is the same as given by the right part of Figure 7.4.

(i) First, the algorithm establishes a template η for a linear RSM-map so that $\eta(i,-) = a_i \cdot h + b_i \cdot t + c_i \cdot r + d_i$ for $1 \le i \le 9$, where a_i, b_i, c_i, d_i are unknown coefficients. The algorithm also sets up the three unknown parameters ϵ, K, K'.

(ii) Second, the algorithm transforms the conditions (C1)–(C3) at all locations into Farkas' linear assertions. We present two examples for such transformation.

- The condition (C1) at location 6 says that $\eta(6,-)$ should be non-negative over the polyhedron $H' := \{\mathbf{x} \mid \mathbf{x}[h] \le \mathbf{x}[t] \wedge 0 \le \mathbf{x}[r] \le 10\}$. Then from Farkas' Lemma, we construct the Farkas' linear assertion $\Phi[H', (-a_6, -b_6, -c_6)^{\mathsf{T}}, d_6](\xi)$ where ξ is a column vector of fresh variables.

- The condition (C3) at location 4 says that $0.5 \cdot \eta(5,-) + 0.5 \cdot \eta(7,-) + \epsilon \le \eta(4,-)$ holds over the polyhedron $H'' := \{\mathbf{x} \mid \mathbf{x}[h] \le \mathbf{x}[t]\}$. Note that $0.5 \cdot \eta(5,-) + 0.5 \cdot \eta(7,-) + \epsilon - \eta(4,-) = (\mathbf{c}') \cdot (h,t,r)^{\mathsf{T}} - d'$ where $\mathbf{c}' = (0.5 \cdot (a_5 + a_7) - a_4, 0.5 \cdot (b_5 + b_7) - b_4, 0.5 \cdot (c_5 + c_7) - c_4)$ and $d' = -0.5 \cdot (d_5 + d_7) + d_4 - \epsilon$. So we construct the Farkas' linear assertion $\Phi[H'', \mathbf{c}', d'](\xi')$ with fresh variables in ξ'. Note that this assertion is linear in both the unknown coefficients (i.e., a_i, b_i, c_i, d_i's), the unknown parameters ϵ, K, K' and the variables in ξ'.

(iii) Third, the algorithm collects all the Farkas' linear assertions constructed from the second step in the conjunctive fashion. Then, together with the constraint $\epsilon \ge 1$ and $K, K \le -1$ (which is equivalent to $\epsilon > 0$ and $K, K < 0$ as we can always multiply them with a large enough factor), the algorithm calls a linear programming solver (e.g. Cplex, 2010, Lpsolve, 2016) to get the solution to the unknown coefficients in the template.

Remark 7.19 (Synthesis of Polynomial RSM-maps)   In several situations, linear RSM-maps do not suffice to prove bounded termination of probabilistic programs. To extend the applicability of RSM-maps, Chatterjee et al. (2016b) proposed an efficient sound approach to synthesize polynomial RSM-maps. The approach is through Positivstellensatz's (Scheiderer, 2008), an extension of Farkas' Lemma to polynomial case, and linear/semidefinite programming. This sound approach gives polynomial-time algorithms. Moreover, it is shown in Chatterjee et al. (2016b) that the existence of polynomial RSM-maps is decidable through the first-order theory of reals.

Remark 7.20 (Angelic Non-determinism)   In this chapter, all non-deterministic branches are *demonic* in the sense that they cannot be controlled and we need to consider the worst-case. In contrast to demonic non-deterministic branches, *angelic* non-deterministic branches are branches that can be controlled in order to fulfill a prescribed aim. Similar to the demonic case, theoretical and algorithmic approaches for angelic branches have been considered. The differences for angelic non-determinism as compared to demonic non-determinism are follows: (i) Motzkin's Transposition Theorem is used instead of Farkas' Lemma in the algorithm, and (ii) the problem to decide the existence of a linear RSM-map over affine probabilistic programs with angelic non-determinism is NP-hard and in PSPACE (see Chatterjee et al. (2018a) for details).

Remark 7.21 (Concentration Bound)   A key advantage of martingales is that with additional conditions sharp concentration results can be obtained. For example, in Chatterjee et al. (2018a), it is shown that the existence of a *difference-bounded* RSM can derive a *concentration bound* beyond which the probability of non-termination within a given number of steps decreases exponentially. Informally, an RSM is difference-bounded if its change of value is bounded from the current step to the next step. The key techniques for such concentration bounds are Azuma's or Hoeffding's inequality; for a detailed discussion see Chapter 8 of this book.

7.5 Beyond Bounded Termination

As shown above, ranking supermartingales provide a sound and complete method of proving bounded termination. In this section, we present several martingale techniques capable of proving *a.s.* termination of programs that do not necessarily terminate in bounded or even finite expected time. Moreover, already for programs that *do* terminate boundedly, some of the techniques we present here provide a computationally more efficient approach to termination proving. For succinctness, we will from now on omit displaying the terminal location when presenting program examples.

7.5.1 Zero Trend and Zeno Behaviour

Consider a program modelling a symmetric random walk (Figure 7.5, here in a discrete variant where the change in each step is either -1 or $+1$, with equal probability). It is well-known that such a program is a.s. terminating. At the same time it does not admit any ranking supermartingale. This is because ranking supermartingales require that the "distance" to termination strictly decreases (in expectation) in every step, while the expected one-step change of the symmetric random walk is zero. Another scenario in which the standard ranking supermartingales are not applicable is when there is a progress towards termination, but the magnitude of this progress decreases over the runtime of the program, as is the case in Figure 7.6.

McIver et al. (2018) give a martingale-based proof rule which can handle the above issues. Here we present a re-formulation of the rule within the scope of our

```
1:    while  x ≥ 1  do
2:            x := x + sample(Uniform{−1, 1})
      od
```

Figure 7.5 Symmetric random walk.

```
1:    while  x ≥ 1  do
2:        p := 1/(x + 1)
3:        t := sample(Uniform[0, 1])
4:        if  t ≤ p  then
5:                x := 0
          else
6:                x := x + 1
          fi  od
```

Figure 7.6 Escaping spline program from (McIver et al., 2018).

syntax and semantics of PPs. In the following, we say that a real function f is *antitone* (or, alternatively, *non-increasing*) if $f(x) \leq f(y) \Leftrightarrow y \leq x$.

Definition 7.22   A non-negative discrete-time stochastic process $\Gamma = \{X_n\}_{n \in \mathbb{N}_0}$ adapted to a filtration $\{\mathcal{F}_n\}_{n \in \mathbb{N}_0}$ is a *parametric ranking supermartingale* (PRSM) if there exist functions d (for "decrease") of type $d \colon \mathbb{R} \to \mathbb{R}_{\geq 0}$, and p (for "probability") of type $\mathbb{R} \to [0, 1]$, both of them antitone and strictly positive on positive reals, such that the following conditions hold:

(i) for each $n \in \mathbb{N}_0$, $\mathbb{E}[X_{n+1} \mid \mathcal{F}_n] \leq X_n$; and
(ii) for each $n \in \mathbb{N}_0$, $\mathbb{P}(X_{n+1} \leq X_n - d(X_n) \mid \mathcal{F}_n) \geq p(X_n)$.

In PRSMs, the constraint on expected change is relaxed so that we prohibit an expected increase of the value (i.e., Γ has to be a supermartingale). On the other hand, in each step, there is a positive probability of a strict decrease, and this probability as well as the magnitude of the decrease can only get larger as the value of the process approaches zero (this is to avoid a possible "Zeno behaviour", when the process would approach zero but never reach it).

Theorem 7.23   *Let $\Gamma = \{X_n\}_{n \in \mathbb{N}_0}$ be a PRSM adapted to some filtration. Then $\mathbb{P}(Z_\Gamma < \infty) = 1$, i.e. with probability 1 the process reaches a zero value.*

Proof (sketch).   Let $H \in \mathbb{N}$ be arbitrary, and and let T_H be a random variable returning the first point in time in which Γ jumps out of the interval $(0, H]$. Then has $\mathbb{P}(T_H < \infty) = 1$. This is because within the interval $(0, H]$ both the probability and magnitude of decrease of Γ are bounded away from zero (as p and d are antitone on positive reals), so Γ cannot stay within this interval forever with positive probability. Hence, we can apply the optional stopping theorem for non-negative supermartingales Williams (1991, Section 10.10 d)), which says that the expected value $\mathbb{E}[X_{T_H}]$ of Γ at time T_H satisfies $\mathbb{E}[X_{T_H}] \leq \mathbb{E}[X_0]$. But at the same time $\mathbb{E}[X_{T_H}] \geq H \cdot \mathbb{P}(X_{T_H} \geq H)$, so $\mathbb{P}(X_{T_H} \geq H) \leq E[X_0]/H$. Hence, the probability that Γ "escapes" through the upper boundary of $(0, H]$ decreases as H increases. It follows that, denoting ℓ_H the probability that Γ escapes through the lower boundary, we have $\ell_H \rightarrow 1$ as $H \rightarrow \infty$. But each ℓ_H is a lower bound on $\mathbb{P}(Z_\Gamma < \infty)$, from which the result follows. $\qquad\square$

One way to apply this theorem to a concrete program $\mathcal{P}$ equipped with an invariant I is to find positive antitone functions p_ℓ, d_ℓ (one per each location) along with a function η mapping $\mathcal{P}$'s configurations to non-negative real numbers, such that the following holds whenever $\mathbf{x} \in I(\ell)$: $\eta(\ell, \mathbf{x}) > 0$ if ℓ is not the terminal configuration; $\mathrm{pre}_\eta(\ell, \mathbf{x}) \leq \eta(\ell, \mathbf{x})$; and, denoting $P_{\eta, \mathbf{x}, \ell}$ the function mapping $(\ell', \mathbf{y})$ to 0 if $\eta(\ell', \mathbf{y}) \leq \eta(\ell, \mathbf{x}) - d_\ell(\eta(\ell, \mathbf{x}))$, and to 1 otherwise, we have $\mathrm{pre}_{P_{\eta, \mathbf{x}, \ell}}(\ell, \mathbf{x}) \leq 1 - p_\ell(\eta(\ell, \mathbf{x}))$. We call such a function η a *PRSM map*. Existence of such a PRSM map guarantees that the program terminates almost-surely. (Note that allowing separate d and p functions for each location is acceptable, since there are only finitely many locations and a minimum of finitely many positive antitone functions is again positive and antitone.) However, finding PRSM maps might be an intricate process. To illustrate this, consider the symmetric random walk in Figure 7.5. Looking at a definition of a PRSM, it would seem natural to choose x itself as the required function, since its expected change is non-positive and with probability $\frac{1}{2}$ the value of x decreases by 1 in every loop iteration. However, a mapping η assigning x to each of the two program locations is not a PRSM map, since at the beginning of each loop iteration, when transitioning from location 1 to location 2, there is not a positive probability of decrease of x. Indeed, a simple computation shows that there is no linear PRSM map for the program. Nevertheless, a PRSM map exists, as the following example shows.

Example 7.24 Take η such that $\eta(1, x) = \sqrt{x + 1}$ and $\eta(2, x) = \frac{1}{2} \cdot \sqrt{x} + \frac{1}{2} \cdot \sqrt{x + 2}$. Indeed, such η only takes positive values for $x \geq 0$ and furthermore, $\mathrm{pre}_\eta(2, \mathbf{x}) = \eta(2, \mathbf{x})$ (by definition) and $\mathrm{pre}_\eta(1, \mathbf{x}) = \frac{1}{2} \cdot \sqrt{x} + \frac{1}{2} \cdot \sqrt{x + 2} \leq \sqrt{x + 1}$ the last inequality following by a straightforward application of calculus. As for the decrease function, when making a step from 2 to 1, there is a $p_2 = \frac{1}{2}$ probability of the value decreasing by $d_2(\eta(2, x)) = \frac{1}{2}\sqrt{x + 2} - \frac{1}{2}\sqrt{x}$; while a step from 1 to 2 entails decrease by $d_1(\eta(1, x)) = \sqrt{x + 1} - \frac{1}{2}\sqrt{x + 2} - \frac{1}{2}\sqrt{x}$ with probability $p_1 = 1$. A straightforward analysis reveals that both d_1 and d_2 are positive and antitone on positive reals.

An alternative "loop-based" approach to usage of PRSMs was proposed in (McIver et al., 2018). Imagine that our aim is to prove almost-sure termination of a probabilistic loop 1 : **while** ψ **do** $\mathcal{P}$ **od**, and that we are provided with an invariant $I(1)$ for the head of the loop. Assume that for each configuration $\mathbf{x}$ such that $\mathbf{x} \in I(1)$ and $\mathbf{x} \models \psi$, the body $\mathcal{P}$ of the loop terminates when started with variables set according to $\mathbf{x}$. (Such a guarantee might be obtained by recursively analysing $\mathcal{P}$. If $\mathcal{P}$ is loopless, the guarantee holds trivially.) Let f be a non-negative function mapping variable valuations to real numbers. Since $\mathcal{P}$ is guaranteed to terminate a.s., we can define a stochastic process $\{X_i^f\}_{i \in \mathbb{N}_0}$ such that for a run ϱ, $X_i^f(\varrho)$ returns the value $f(\tilde{\mathbf{x}}_i)$, where $\tilde{\mathbf{x}}_i$ is the valuation of variables immediately after the i-th iteration of the loop along ϱ (if ϱ traverses the loop less than i times, we put $X_i^f(\varrho) = 0$). If the process $\{X_i^f\}_{i \in \mathbb{N}_0}$ is a PRSM, then with the help of Theorem 7.23 it can be easily shown that the loop indeed terminates almost surely.

Example 7.25   Returning to the symmetric random walk (Figure 7.5), let $f(x) = x$. In each iteration of the loop, the value of x has zero expected change, and with probability $p = \frac{1}{2}$ it decreases by $d = 1$. Hence, $\{X_i^f\}_{i \in \mathbb{N}_0}$ is a PRSM and the walk terminates a.s.

Example 7.26   Consider the escaping spline in Figure 7.6 and set $f(x, p) = x$. Fix any point in which the program's execution passes through the loop head and let a be the value of x at this moment. Then the expected value of x after performing one loop iteration is $0 \cdot \frac{1}{a+1} + (a + 1) \cdot \frac{a}{a+1} = a$, so the expected change of x in each loop iteration is zero. Moreover, in each iteration the value of x decreases by at least 1 with probability $p = \frac{1}{x+1}$. Since p is antitone, it follows that $\{X_i^f\}_{i \in \mathbb{N}_0}$ is a PRSM, and hence the program terminates a.s.

This loop-based use of PRSMs is non-local: we have to analyse the behaviour of f along one whole loop iteration, as opposed to single computational steps. For complex loops, finding the right f and checking its properties might be an intricate process. In McIver et al. (2018), the authors propose proving required properties of f in the *weakest pre-expectation logic,* a formal calculus which extends the classical weakest-precondition reasoning to probabilistic programs. While falling short of automated termination analysis, formalizing the proofs in the formal logic makes use of interactive proof assistants possible, with a potential to achieve provably correct results with significantly decreased human workload.

Remark 7.27   A similar martingale-based approach for proving almost-sure termination of probabilistic while loops is proposed in Huang et al. (2018). Compared with McIver et al. (2018), the martingale-based approach in Huang et al. (2018) can derive asymptotically optimal bounds on *tail probabilities* of program non-termination within a given number of steps, while McIver et al. (2018) cannot derive such probabilities. On the other hand, the approach in McIver et al. (2018)

```
1:  while  x ≥ 1  and  y ≥ 1  do
2:       if  ⋆  then
3:               x := x + sample(Uniform{−3, 1})
         else
4:               y := y − 1
5:               x := 2x + sample(Uniform{−1, 1})
         fi
```

Figure 7.7 A program without a linear RSM but admitting a LexRSM.

refines that in Huang et al. and can prove the almost-sure termination of probabilistic programs that Huang et al. cannot. Another related approach in Huang et al. (2018) uses Central Limit Theorem to prove almost-sure termination.

7.5.2 Lexicographic Ranking Supermartingales

For some programs (even for those that do terminate in finite expected time), it might be difficult to find an RSM because of a complex control flow structure, which makes the computation go through several phases, each with a different program behaviour.

Example 7.28 Consider the program in Figure 7.7 with an invariant I s.t. $I(1) = \{(x, y) \mid x \geq -2 \wedge y \geq 0\}$, $I(2) = I(3) = I(4) = \{(x, y) \mid x \geq 1 \wedge y \geq 1\}$ and $I(5) = \{(x, y) \mid x \geq 1 \wedge y \geq 0\}$. The program terminates in bounded expected time, as shown by the existence of the following (non-linear) RSM map η: $\eta(i) = (x + 2) \cdot 2^y \cdot y - \frac{(i-1)}{2}$ for $i \in \{1, \ldots, 4\}$ and $\eta(5) = (x + 2) \cdot 2^{y+1} \cdot y + 1$. Next, it is easy to verify, that there is no *linear* RSM map for the program. Intuitively, in the else branch, executing the decrement of y can decrease the value of a linear function only by some constant, and this cannot compensate for the possibly unbounded increase of x caused by doubling.

The absence of a termination certificate within the scope of linear arithmetic is somewhat bothersome, as non-linear reasoning can become computationally hard. In non-probabilistic setting, similar issues were addressed by considering *multi-dimensional* termination certificates. The crucial idea is to consider functions that map the program configurations to real-valued vectors instead of just numbers, such that the value of the vector-valued function strictly decreases in every step w.r.t. some well-founded ordering of the vectors. This in essence entails a certain "decomposition" of the termination certificate: it might happen that a program admits a multi-dimensional certificate where each component is linear, even when no one-dimensional linear certificates exist. Such certificates can often be found via fully automated linear-arithmetic reasoning. A prime example of this concept are *lexicographic* ranking functions (Cook et al., 2013), where the well-founded ordering used is typically the lexicographic ordering on non-negative real vectors.

In the context of probabilistic programs, the lexicographic extension of ranking supermartingales was introduced in Agrawal et al. (2018). We again start with a general mathematical definition and a correctness theorem. In the following, an n-dimensional stochastic process is a sequence $\{\mathbf{X}_i\}_{i=0}^{\infty}$ of n-dimensional random vectors, i.e. each $\mathbf{X}_i$ is a vector whose component is a random variable. We denote by $\mathbf{X}_i[j]$ the j-component of $\mathbf{X}_i$.

Definition 7.29   An n-dimensional real-valued stochastic process $\{\mathbf{X}_i\}_{i=0}^{\infty}$ is a *lexicographic ϵ-ranking supermartingale (ϵ-LexRSM)* adapted to a filtration $\{\mathcal{F}_i\}_{i=0}^{\infty}$ if the following conditions hold:

(i) For each $1 \le j \le n$ the 1-dimensional stochastic process $\{\mathbf{X}_i[j]\}_{i=0}^{\infty}$ is adapted to $\{\mathcal{F}_i\}_{i=0}^{\infty}$.

(ii) For each $i \in \mathbb{N}_0$ and $1 \le j \le n$ it holds $\mathbf{X}_i[j] \ge 0$, i.e. the process takes values in non-negative real vectors.

(iii) For each $i \in \mathbb{N}_0$ there exists a partition of the set $\{\omega \in \Omega \mid \forall 1 \le j \le n, \mathbf{X}_i[j](\omega) > 0\}$ into n subsets $L_1^i, \ldots, L_n^i$, all of them $\mathcal{F}_i$-measurable, such that for each $1 \le j \le n$:

  - $\mathbb{E}[\mathbf{X}_{i+1}[j] \mid \mathcal{F}_i](\omega) \le \mathbf{X}_i[j](\omega) - \epsilon$ for each $\omega \in L_j^i$;
  - for all $1 \le j' < j$ we have $\mathbb{E}[\mathbf{X}_{i+1}[j'] \mid \mathcal{F}_i](\omega) \le \mathbf{X}_i[j'](\omega)$ for each $\omega \in L_j^i$.

Note that we dropped the integrability condition from Definition 7.4. This is because integrability is only needed to ensure that the conditional expectations in the definiton of a (Lex)RSM exist and are well-defined. However, the existence of conditional expectations is also guaranteed for random variables that are real-valued and non-negative, see Agrawal et al. (2018) for details. This is exactly the case in LexRSMs. Waiving the integrability condition might simplify application of LexRSMs to programs with non-linear arithmetic, where, as already shown in Fioriti and Hermanns (2015), integrability of program variables is not guaranteed.

The full proof of the following theorem is provided in Agrawal et al. (2018).

Theorem 7.30   *Let $\{\mathbf{X}_i\}_{i=0}^{\infty}$ be a LexRSM adapted to some filtration. Then with probability 1 at least one component of the process eventually attains a zero value.*

To apply LexRSMs to a.s. termination proving, let $\mathcal{P}$ be a program and I be an invariant for $\mathcal{P}$.

Definition 7.31 (Lexicographic Ranking Supermartingale Map)   Let $\epsilon > 0$. An n-dimensional *lexicographic ϵ-ranking supermartingale map (ϵ-LexRSM map)* for a program $\mathcal{P}$ with an invariant I is a vector function $\overrightarrow{\eta} = (\eta_1, \ldots, \eta_n)$, where each

η_i maps configurations of $\mathcal{P}$ to real numbers, such that for each configuration $(\ell, \mathbf{x})$ where $\mathbf{x} \in I(\ell)$ the following conditions are satisfied:

- for all $1 \le j \le n$: $\eta_j(\ell, \mathbf{x}) \ge 0$, and if $\ell \ne \ell_{out}$, then $\eta_j(\ell, \mathbf{x}) > 0$; and
- if $\ell \ne \ell_{out}$ and ℓ does not contain a non-deterministic choice, then there exists $1 \le j \le n$ such that
  - $\text{pre}_{\eta_j}(\ell, \mathbf{x}) \le \eta_j(\ell, \mathbf{x}) - \epsilon$, and
  - for all $1 \le j' < j$ we have $\text{pre}_{\eta_{j'}}(\ell, \mathbf{x}) \le \eta_{j'}(\ell, \mathbf{x})$;
- $\ell \ne \ell_{out}$ and ℓ contains a non-deterministic choice, then for each $\tilde{\ell} \in \{\ell_{th}, \ell_{el}\}$ (where ℓ_{th}, ℓ_{el} are the successor locations in the corresponding branches) there is $1 \le j \le n$ such that
  - $\eta_j(\tilde{\ell}, \mathbf{x}) \le \eta_j(\ell, \mathbf{x}) - \epsilon$, and
  - for all $1 \le j' < j$ we have $\eta_{j'}(\tilde{\ell}, \mathbf{x}) \le \eta_{j'}(\ell, \mathbf{x})$.

If additionally each η_i is a linear expression map, then we call $\overrightarrow{\eta}$ a linear ϵ-LexRSM map (ϵ-LinLexRSM).

Using Theorem 7.30, we get the following.

Theorem 7.32 *Let $\mathcal{P}$ be a probabilistic program and I its invariant. Assume that there exists an $\epsilon > 0$ and an n-dimensional ϵ-LexRSM map for $\mathcal{P}$ and I. Then $\mathcal{P}$ terminates almost surely.*

Example 7.33 Consider again the program in Figure 7.7, together with the invariant I from Example 7.28. Then the following 3-dimensional 1-LexRSM map $\overrightarrow{\eta}$ proves that the program terminates a.s.: $\overrightarrow{\eta}(1, \mathbf{x}) = (y+1, x+3, 4)$, $\overrightarrow{\eta}(2, \mathbf{x}) = (y+1, x+3, 3)$, $\overrightarrow{\eta}(3, \mathbf{x}) = \overrightarrow{\eta}(4, \mathbf{x}) = (y+1, x+3, 2)$, $\overrightarrow{\eta}(5, \mathbf{x}) = (y+2, x+3, 1)$, and $\overrightarrow{\eta}(\ell_{out}, \mathbf{x}) = (0, 0, 0)$.

(Agrawal et al., 2018) presented an algorithm for synthesis of linear LexRSM maps in affine probabilistic programs with pre-computed invariants. The algorithm is based on a method for finding lexicographic ranking functions presented in Alias et al. (2010). The method attempts to find a LinLexRSM map by computing one component at a time, iteratively employing the algorithm for synthesis of 1-dimensional RSMs (Section 7.4) as a sub-procedure. The method is complete in the sense that if there exists a LinLexRSM map for a program $\mathcal{P}$ with a given invariant I, then the algorithm finds such a map. If guards of all conditional statements and loops in the program are linear assertions (i.e. conjunctions of linear inequalities), then the algorithm runs in time polynomial in the size of $\mathcal{P}$ and I.

We now show that LexRSMs are indeed capable of proving a.s. termination of programs that terminate in infinite expected number of steps.

Example 7.34 Consider the program in Figure 7.8, together with an invariant I such that $I(1) = \{(x, c) \mid x \ge 1 \wedge c \ge 0\}$, $I(2) = I(3) = I(4) = \{(x, c) \mid x \ge 1 \wedge c \ge 1\}$,

```
1:     while  c ≥ 1  and  x ≥ 1  do
2:         if  prob(0.5)  then
3:             x := 2 · x
           else
4:             c := 0
           fi
       od ;
5:     while  x ≥ 1  do
6:         x := x − 1
       od
```

Figure 7.8 An example program that is a.s. terminating but with infinite expected termination time.

$I(5) = \{(x, c) \mid x \geq 0\}$, and $I(6) = \{(x, c) \mid x \geq 1\}$. The a.s. termination of the program is witnessed by a linear 1-LexRSM map $\overrightarrow{\eta}$ such that $\overrightarrow{\eta}(1, \mathbf{x}) = (6c+5, 2x+2)$, $\overrightarrow{\eta}(2, \mathbf{x}) = (6c + 4, 2x + 2)$, $\overrightarrow{\eta}(3, \mathbf{x}) = (6c + 6, 2x + 2)$, $\overrightarrow{\eta}(4, \mathbf{x}) = (6c, 2x + 2)$, $\overrightarrow{\eta}(5, \mathbf{x}) = (1, 2x + 2)$, and $\overrightarrow{\eta}(5, \mathbf{x}) = (1, 2x + 1)$. However, the program terminates in an infinite expected number of steps: to see this, note that that the expected value of variable x upon reaching the second loop is $\frac{1}{2} \cdot 1 + \frac{1}{4} \cdot 2 + \frac{1}{8} \cdot 4 + \cdots = \infty$, and that the time needed to get out of the second loop is equal to the value of x upon entering the loop.

Finally, we remark that (Agrawal et al., 2018) introduced further uses of LexRSMs, such as compositional termination proving (where we prove a.s. termination one loop at a time, proceeding from the innermost ones) and the use of special type of linear LexRSMs for obtaining polynomial bounds on expected termination time.

7.5.3 Quantitative Termination and Safety

Consider the program in Figure 7.9. Due to lines 5–6, the program does not terminate a.s., because there is a positive probability that x hits zero before y falls below 1. However, a closer look shows that such an event, while possible, is unlikely, since x tends to increase and y tends to decrease on average. (Chatterjee et al., 2017) studied martingale-based techniques that can provide lower bounds on termination probabilities of such programs.

First, the paper introduced the concept of *stochastic invariants*.

Definition 7.35   Let (PI, p) be a tuple such that PI is a function mapping each program location to a set of variable valuations and $p \in [0, 1]$ is a probability. The tuple (PI, p) is a *stochastic invariant* for a program $\mathcal{P}$ if the following holds: if we

```
1:  x := 150, y := 100
2:  while  y ≥ 1  do
3:      x := x + sample(Uniform[−¼, 1])
4:      y := y + sample(Uniform[−1, ¼])
5:      while  x ≤ 0  do
6:          skip  od
    od
```

Figure 7.9 A program with infinitely many reachable configurations which terminates with high probability, but not almost surely, together with a sketch of its pCFG.

denote by *Fail(PI)* the set of all runs that reach a configuration of the form $(\ell, \mathbf{x})$ with $\mathbf{x} \notin PI(\ell)$, then for all schedulers σ it holds $\mathbb{P}^\sigma(Fail(PI)) \leq 1 - p$.

Example 7.36 Consider the example in Figure 7.9 and a tuple (PI, p) for the program such that $PI(5) = \{(x, y) \mid x \geq \frac{1}{9}\}$, $PI(\ell) = \mathbb{R}^2$ for all the other locations, and $p = 10^{-5}$. Using techniques for analysis of random walks, one can prove that (PI, p) is a stochastic invariant for the program. Below, we will sketch a martingale-based technique that can be used to prove this formally (and automatically).

Intuitively, unlike their classical counterparts, stochastic invariants are not over-approximations of the set of reachable configurations. However, for small p, they can be viewed as good probabilistic approximations of this set, in the sense that the probability of reaching a configuration not belonging to this approximation is small (smaller than p). The following theorem illustrates a possible use of stochastic invariants in probabilistic termination analysis.

Theorem 7.37 *Let $\mathcal{P}$ be a probabilistic program, I a (classical) invariant, and (PI, p) a stochastic invariant for $\mathcal{P}$. Further, let $\eta \colon L \times \mathbb{R}^{|V|} \to \mathbb{R}$ be a mapping such that there exists $\epsilon > 0$ for which the following holds in each configuration $(\ell, \mathbf{x})$ of $\mathcal{P}$:*
- *if $\mathbf{x} \in I(\ell)$, then $\eta(\ell, \mathbf{x}) \geq 0$, and*
- *if $\ell \neq \ell_{out}$ and $\mathbf{x} \in I(\ell) \cap PI(\ell)$, then $pre_\eta(\ell, \mathbf{x}) \leq \eta(\ell, \mathbf{x}) - \epsilon$.*

Then, under each scheduler σ, the program $\mathcal{P}$ terminates with probability at least $1 - p$.

Proof (Sketch). The map η can be viewed as an RSM map for a modified version of $\mathcal{P}$ which immediately terminates whenever PI is violated. Such a modified program therefore terminates with probability 1. Since (PI, p) is a stochastic invariant, violations of PI can occur with probability at most p, so with probability at least $1 - p$ the modified (and thus also the original) program terminates in an orderly way. □

Example 7.38   Let $(PI, 10^{-5})$ be the stochastic invariant from Example 7.36 (concerning Figure 7.9). For the corresponding program we have a classical invariant I such that $I(1) = \{(30, 20)\}$, $I(2) = \{(x, y) \mid x \geq 0 \wedge y \geq 0\}$, $I(3) = \{(x, y) \mid x \geq 0 \wedge y \geq 1\}$, $I(4) = \{(x, y) \mid x \geq -\frac{1}{4} \wedge y \geq 1\}$, $I(5) = \{(x, y) \mid x \geq -\frac{1}{4} \wedge y \geq 0\}$, and $I(6) = \{(x, y) \mid 0 \geq x \geq -\frac{1}{4} \wedge y \geq 0\}$. Consider a map η defined as follows: $\eta(1) = \eta(5) = 16y + 3$, $\eta(2) = 16y + 2$, $\eta(3) = 16y + 1$, $\eta(4) = 16y$, and $\eta(6) = 16y + 4$. Then η satisfies the conditions of Theorem 7.37, from which it follows that the program terminates with probability at least 0.99999.

Given an affine probabilistic program and its classical and stochastic invariants, I and (PI, p) (both I and PI being linear), we can check whether there exists a linear RSM map satisfying Theorem 7.37 using virtually the same linear system as in Section 7.4. We just need to take the location-wise intersection I' of I and PI as the input invariant used to construct the linear constraints. Although I' is not a classical invariant, the linear RSM map obtained from solving the constraints satisfies the requirements of Theorem 7.37.

The question, then, is how to prove that a tuple (PI,p) is a stochastic invariant. In (Chatterjee et al., 2017), a concept of *repulsing supermartingales* (RepSMs) was introduced, which can be used to compute upper bounds on the probability of violating PI. RepSMs are inspired by use of martingale techniques in the analysis of one-counter probabilistic systems (Brázdil et al., 2013), and they are in some sense dual to RSMs: they show that a computation is probabilistically *repulsed* away from (rather than attracted to) some set of configurations. As was the case in the preceding martingale-based concepts, RepSMs are defined abstractly as a certain class of stochastic processes, and then applied to program analysis via the notion of *RepSM maps*. For the sake of succinctness, we present here only the latter concept.

Definition 7.39 (Linear repulsing supermartingales)   Let $\mathcal{P}$ be a PP with an initial configuration $(\ell_{init}, \mathbf{x}_{init})$, I its invariant, and $C \subseteq L \times \mathbb{R}^{|V|}$ some set of configurations of $\mathcal{P}$. An ϵ-repulsing supermartingale (ϵ-RepSM) map for C supported by I is a mapping $\eta \colon L \times \mathbb{R}^{|V|} \to V$ such that for all configurations $(\ell, \mathbf{x})$ of $\mathcal{P}$ the following holds:

- if $(\ell, \mathbf{x}) \in C$ and $\mathbf{x} \in I(\ell)$, then $\eta(\ell, \mathbf{x}) \geq 0$
- if $(\ell, \mathbf{x}) \notin C$ and $\mathbf{x} \in I(\ell)$, then $pre_\eta(\ell, \mathbf{x}) \leq \eta(\ell, \mathbf{x}) - \epsilon$,
- $\eta(\ell_{init}, \mathbf{x}_{init}) < 0$.

An ϵ-RepSM map supported by I has c-bounded differences if for each pair of locations ℓ, ℓ' and each pair of configurations $(\ell, \mathbf{x})$, $(\ell', \mathbf{x}')$ such that $\mathbf{x} \in I(\ell)$ and $(\ell', \mathbf{x}')$ can be produced by performing a step of computation from $(\ell, \mathbf{x})$ it holds $|\eta(\ell, \mathbf{x}) - \eta(\ell', \mathbf{x}')| \leq c$.

The following theorem is proved using Azuma's inequality, a concentration bound from martingale theory.

Theorem 7.40 *Let C be a set of configurations of a PP $\mathcal{P}$. Suppose that there exist $\epsilon > 0$, $c > 0$, and a linear ϵ-RepSM map η for C supported by some invariant I such that η has c-bounded differences. Then under each scheduler σ, the probability p_C that the program reaches a configuration from C satisfies*

$$p_C \leq \alpha \cdot \frac{\gamma^{\lceil |\eta(\ell_{init}, \mathbf{x}_{init})|/c \rceil}}{1 - \gamma}, \tag{7.1}$$

where $\gamma = \exp\left(-\frac{\epsilon^2}{2(c+\epsilon)^2}\right)$ and $\alpha = \exp\left(\frac{\epsilon \cdot |\eta(\ell_{init}, \mathbf{x}_{init})|}{(c+\epsilon)^2}\right)$.

Example 7.41 Consider again the program in Figure 7.9, with the same invariant I as in Example 7.36. Let $C = \{(\ell, (x, y)) \mid \ell = 5 \wedge x \leq \frac{1}{8}\}$. Then the following map η is a 13-bounded 1-RepSM map for C: $\eta(1) = \eta(5) = -16x + 2$, $\eta(2) = 16x + 1$, $\eta(3) = -16x$, and $\eta(4) = \eta(6) = -16x + 3$. Applying Theorem 7.40 yields that C is reached with probbaility at most $\exp\left(\frac{-116154}{392} - \frac{1}{392} \cdot \lceil \frac{116154}{14} \rceil\right) / (1 - \exp(-1/392)) \approx 1.2 \cdot 10^{-6} \leq 10^{-5}$. Now for the map PI in Example 7.36 it holds that violating PI entails reaching C, which shows that $(PI, 10^{-5})$ is indeed a stochastic invariant.

Checking whether there is a linear RepSM map (supported by a given linear invariant) for a set of configurations defined by a given system of linear constraints can be again performed by linear constraint solving, using techniques analogous to Section 7.4.

Finally, we mention that RepSM maps can be used to *refute* almost-sure and finite termination.

Theorem 7.42 *Let C be a set of terminal configurations of a program $\mathcal{P}$, i.e. of those configurations where the corresponding location is terminal. Suppose that there exist $\epsilon \geq 0$, $c > 0$, and a linear ϵ-RepSM map η for C supported by some invariant I such that η has c-bounded differences. Then, no matter which scheduler is used, $\mathcal{P}$ does not terminate in finite expected time. Moreover, if $\epsilon > 0$, then $\mathcal{P}$ terminates with probability less than 1 under every scheduler.*

Example 7.43 Consider the symmetric random walk (Figure 7.5) together with an invariant $x \geq 0$ in every location. Assuming that initially $x > 1$, the mapping which to each non-terminal configuration (ℓ, x) assigns the number $-x + 1$, while each terminal configuration is assigned zero, is a 0-RepSM for the set of terminal configurations, with 1-bounded differences. Hence, the symmetric random walk indeed does not terminate in finite expected time.

7.6 Related Works

Termination approaches. In Sharir et al. (1984) the termination of concurrent probabilistic programs with finite-state space was considered as a fairness problem, and the precise probabilities did not play a role in termination. A sound and complete method for proving termination of finite state programs was given in Esparza et al. (2012). The above approaches do not apply to programs with countable state space in general. For countable state space and almost-sure termination a characterization through fixed-point theory was presented in Hart and Sharir (1985). The analysis of non-probabilistic program and the termination problem has also been extensively studied (Bradley et al., 2005a; Colón and Sipma, 2001; Podelski and Rybalchenko, 2004; Sohn and Gelder, 1991; Bradley et al., 2005b; Cook et al., 2013; Lee et al., 2001). The focus of this chapter was to present the key aspects of martingale-based approaches for termination of infinite-state probabilistic programs.

Proof-rule based approach. In this work we consider the supermartingale based approach for probabilistic programs, and an alternative approach is based on the notion of proof rules (Kaminski et al., 2016; Hesselink, 1993; Olmedo et al., 2016). These two approaches complement each other, and have their own advantages. The proof-rule based approach itself does not depend on classical invariants (see for exampleColón et al., 2003; Cousot, 2005) and is capable of establishing quantitative invariants, whereas the supermartingale approach usually requires classical invariants to achieve automation (Chakarov and Sankaranarayanan, 2013; Chatterjee et al., 2016b,a). In contrast, the advantages of the supermartingale-based approach are: (a) the supermartingale based approach leads to automated and algorithmic approaches; (b) tail bounds can be obtained through supermartingales using the mathematical results such as Azuma's inequality or Hoeffding's inequality (Chatterjee et al., 2016a), and (c) in presence of conditioning, proof-rules cannot be applied to non-deterministic programs as the schedulers are not necessarily local, whereas ranking supermartingales can consider non-determinism as the semantics is through general MDPs and general schedulers.

Other results. Martingales can also be used for analysis of properties other than termination over probabilistic programs (e.g., probabilistic invariants (Barthe et al., 2016b) or proving recurrence/persistence/reactivity properties (Chakarov et al., 2016; Dimitrova et al., 2016; Chatterjee et al., 2017)). Other prominent approaches for analyzing probabilistic programs include: (a) techniques based on coupling proofs and their applications in analysis of differential privacy and probabilistic sensitivity (Barthe et al., 2017, 2018, 2016a); (b) static-analysis based approaches (Sankaranarayanan et al., 2013; Cusumano-Towner et al., 2018; Wang et al., 2018); (c) potential-function based approaches for cost analysis (Chatterjee et al., 2018b; Ngo et al., 2018). Moreover, the semantics of probabilistic programs is studied in Bichsel et al. (2018) and Staton et al. (2016).

7.7 Conclusion and Future Directions

In this chapter we present the main results related to martingale-based approach for termination analysis of probabilistic programs. There are several interesting directions of future work. First, for analysis of probabilistic programs with angelic non-determinism there is a complexity gap for linear RSMs and an interesting theoretical question is to close the complexity gap. Second, while the martingale-based approach and other approaches such as proof-rule based approach each has its own advantages, techniques for combining them is another interesting direction of future work. Finally, practical directions of building scalable tools using algorithmic results for martingales in conjunction with other methods such as compositional analysis are also largely unexplored.

Acknowledgements

Krishnendu Chatterjee is supported by the Austrian Science Fund (FWF) NFN Grant No. S11407-N23 (RiSE/SHiNE), and COST Action GAMENET. Hongfei Fu is supported by the National Natural Science Foundation of China (NSFC) Grant No. 61802254. Petr Novotný is supported by the Czech Science Foundation grant No. GJ19-15134Y.

References

Agrawal, S., Chatterjee, K., and Novotný, P. 2018. Lexicographic ranking super-martingales: an efficient approach to termination of probabilistic programs. *PACMPL*, **2**(POPL), 34:1–34:32.

Alias, Christophe, Darte, Alain, Feautrier, Paul, and Gonnord, Laure. 2010. Multi-dimensional Rankings, Program Termination, and Complexity Bounds of Flowchart Programs. Pages 117–133 of: *Proceedings of the 17th International Conference on Static Analysis*. SAS'10. Berlin, Heidelberg: Springer-Verlag.

Ash, R.B., and Doléans-Dade, C. 2000. *Probability and Measure Theory*. Harcourt/Academic Press.

Baier, C., and Katoen, J.-P. 2008. *Principles of Model Checking*. MIT Press.

Barthe, Gilles, Gaboardi, Marco, Grégoire, Benjamin, Hsu, Justin, and Strub, Pierre-Yves. 2016a. Proving Differential Privacy via Probabilistic Couplings. *In:* Grohe et al. (2016).

Barthe, Gilles, Espitau, Thomas, Fioriti, Luis María Ferrer, and Hsu, Justin. 2016b. Synthesizing Probabilistic Invariants via Doob's Decomposition. Pages 43–61 of: Chaudhuri, Swarat, and Farzan, Azadeh (eds), *Computer Aided Verification - 28th International Conference, CAV 2016, Toronto, ON, Canada, July 17-23, 2016, Proceedings, Part I.* Lecture Notes in Computer Science, vol. 9779. Springer.

Barthe, Gilles, Grégoire, Benjamin, Hsu, Justin, and Strub, Pierre-Yves. 2017. Coupling proofs are probabilistic product programs. Pages 161–174 of: Castagna, Giuseppe, and Gordon, Andrew D. (eds), *Proceedings of the 44th ACM SIGPLAN Symposium on Principles of Programming Languages, POPL 2017, Paris, France, January 18-20, 2017.* ACM.

Barthe, Gilles, Espitau, Thomas, Grégoire, Benjamin, Hsu, Justin, and Strub, Pierre-Yves. 2018. Proving expected sensitivity of probabilistic programs. *PACMPL*, **2**(POPL), 57:1–57:29.

Bichsel, Benjamin, Gehr, Timon, and Vechev, Martin T. 2018. Fine-Grained Semantics for Probabilistic Programs. Pages 145–185 of: Ahmed, Amal (ed), *Programming Languages and Systems - 27th European Symposium on Programming, ESOP 2018, Held as Part of the European Joint Conferences on Theory and Practice of Software, ETAPS 2018, Thessaloniki, Greece, April 14-20, 2018, Proceedings.* Lecture Notes in Computer Science, vol. 10801. Springer.

Billingsley, P. 1995. *Probability and Measure.* 3rd edn. Wiley.

Bournez, O., and Garnier, F. 2005. Proving Positive Almost-Sure Termination. Pages 323–337 of: *International Conference on Rewriting Techniques and Applications, RTA'05.* Springer.

Bradley, A. R., Manna, Z., and Sipma, H. B. 2005a. Linear Ranking with Reachability. Pages 491–504 of: *International Conference on Computer Aided Verification, CAV'05.* Springer.

Bradley, A. R., Manna, Z., and Sipma, H. B. 2005b. The Polyranking Principle. Pages 1349–1361 of: *International Colloquium on Automata, Languages, and Programming, ICALP'05.* Springer.

Brázdil, Tomáš, Brožek, Václav, Etessami, Kousha, and Kučera, Antonín. 2013. Approximating the termination value of one-counter MDPs and stochastic games. *Information and Computation*, **222**, 121–138.

Chakarov, A., and Sankaranarayanan, S. 2013. Probabilistic Program Analysis with Martingales. Pages 511–526 of: *CAV*.

Chakarov, Aleksandar, Voronin, Yuen-Lam, and Sankaranarayanan, Sriram. 2016. Deductive proofs of almost sure persistence and recurrence properties. Pages 260–279 of: *International Conference on Tools and Algorithms for the Construction and Analysis of Systems, TACAS'16.* Springer.

Chatterjee, K., Fu, H., Novotný, P., and Hasheminezhad, R. 2016a. Algorithmic analysis of qualitative and quantitative termination problems for affine probabilistic programs. Pages 327–342 of: *POPL*.

Chatterjee, K., Fu, H., and Goharshady, A. K. 2016b. Termination Analysis of Probabilistic Programs Through Positivstellensatz's. Pages 3–22 of: *CAV*.

Chatterjee, K., Novotný, P., and Žikelić, Đ. 2017. Stochastic Invariants for Probabilistic Termination. Pages 145–160 of: *POPL*.

Chatterjee, Krishnendu, and Fu, Hongfei. 2017. Termination of Nondeterministic Recursive Probabilistic Programs. *CoRR*, **abs/1701.02944**.

Chatterjee, Krishnendu, Fu, Hongfei, Novotný, Petr, and Hasheminezhad, Rouzbeh. 2018a. Algorithmic Analysis of Qualitative and Quantitative Termination Problems for Affine Probabilistic Programs. *ACM Trans. Program. Lang. Syst.*, **40**(2), 7:1–7:45.

Chatterjee, Krishnendu, Fu, Hongfei, Goharshady, Amir Kafshdar, and Okati, Nastaran. 2018b. Computational Approaches for Stochastic Shortest Path on Succinct MDPs. Pages 4700–4707 of: Lang, Jérôme (ed), *Proceedings of the Twenty-Seventh International Joint Conference on Artificial Intelligence, IJCAI 2018, July 13-19, 2018, Stockholm, Sweden*. ijcai.org.

Colón, M., and Sipma, H. 2001. Synthesis of Linear Ranking Functions. Pages 67–81 of: *TACAS*.

Colón, M., Sankaranarayanan, S., and Sipma, H. 2003. Linear Invariant Generation Using Non-linear Constraint Solving. Pages 420–432 of: *CAV*.

Cook, B., See, A., and Zuleger, F. 2013. Ramsey vs. Lexicographic Termination Proving. Pages 47–61 of: *TACAS*.

Cousot, P. 2005. Proving Program Invariance and Termination by Parametric Abstraction, Lagrangian Relaxation and Semidefinite Programming. Pages 1–24 of: *VMCAI*.

Cousot, Patrick, and Cousot, Radhia. 1977. Abstract Interpretation: A Unified Lattice Model for Static Analysis of Programs by Construction or Approximation of Fixpoints. Pages 238–252 of: Graham, Robert M., Harrison, Michael A., and Sethi, Ravi (eds), *POPL*. ACM.

Cplex. 2010. *IBM ILOG CPLEX Optimizer Interactive Optimizer Community Edition 12.6.3.0*. http://www-01.ibm.com/software/integration/optimization/cplex-optimizer/.

Cusumano-Towner, Marco, Bichsel, Benjamin, Gehr, Timon, Vechev, Martin T., and Mansinghka, Vikash K. 2018. Incremental inference for probabilistic programs. *In*: Foster and Grossman (2018).

Dimitrova, Rayna, Fioriti, Luis María Ferrer, Hermanns, Holger, and Majumdar, Rupak. 2016. Probabilistic CTL*: The Deductive Way. Pages 280–296 of: *International Conference on Tools and Algorithms for the Construction and Analysis of Systems, TACAS'16*. Springer.

Durrett, R. 1996. *Probability: Theory and Examples (Second Edition)*. Duxbury Press.

Esparza, J., Gaiser, A., and Kiefer, S. 2012. Proving Termination of Probabilistic Programs Using Patterns. Pages 123–138 of: *CAV*.

Farkas, J. 1894. A Fourier-féle mechanikai elv alkalmazásai (Hungarian). *Mathematikaiés Természettudományi Értesitö*, **12**, 457–472.

Fioriti, L. M. F., and Hermanns, H. 2015. Probabilistic Termination: Soundness, Completeness, and Compositionality. Pages 489–501 of: *POPL*.

Floyd, R. W. 1967. Assigning meanings to programs. *Mathematical Aspects of Computer Science*, **19**, 19–33.

Foster, F. G. 1953. On the Stochastic Matrices Associated with Certain Queuing Processes. *The Annals of Mathematical Statistics*, **24**(3), 355–360.

Foster, Jeffrey S., and Grossman, Dan (eds). 2018. *Proceedings of the 39th ACM SIGPLAN Conference on Programming Language Design and Implementation, PLDI 2018, Philadelphia, PA, USA, June 18-22, 2018*. ACM.

Fu, Hongfei, and Chatterjee, Krishnendu. 2019. Termination of Nondeterministic Probabilistic Programs. Pages 468–490 of: Enea, Constantin, and Piskac, Ruzica (eds), *Verification, Model Checking, and Abstract Interpretation - 20th International Conference, VMCAI 2019, Cascais, Portugal, January 13-15, 2019, Proceedings*. Lecture Notes in Computer Science, vol. 11388. Springer.

Ghahramani, Z. 2015. Probabilistic machine learning and artificial intelligence. *Nature*, **521**(7553), 452–459.

Gordon, A. D., Henzinger, T. A., Nori, A. V., and Rajamani, S. K. 2014. Probabilistic programming. Pages 167–181 of: *FOSE*.

Grohe, Martin, Koskinen, Eric, and Shankar, Natarajan (eds). 2016. *Proceedings of the 31st Annual ACM/IEEE Symposium on Logic in Computer Science, LICS '16, New York, NY, USA, July 5-8, 2016*. ACM.

Hart, S., and Sharir, M. 1985. Concurrent Probabilistic Programs, Or: How to Schedule if You Must. *SIAM J. Comput.*, **14**(4), 991–1012.

Hesselink, W. H. 1993. Proof Rules for Recursive Procedures. *Formal Asp. Comput.*, **5**(6), 554–570.

Howard, H. 1960. *Dynamic Programming and Markov Processes*. MIT Press.

Huang, Mingzhang, Fu, Hongfei, and Chatterjee, Krishnendu. 2018. New Approaches for Almost-Sure Termination of Probabilistic Programs. Pages 181–201 of: Ryu, Sukyoung (ed), *Programming Languages and Systems - 16th Asian Symposium, APLAS 2018, Wellington, New Zealand, December 2-6, 2018, Proceedings*. Lecture Notes in Computer Science, vol. 11275. Springer.

Kaelbling, L. P., Littman, M. L., and Moore, A. W. 1996. Reinforcement learning: A survey. *JAIR*, **4**, 237–285.

Kaelbling, L. P., Littman, M. L., and Cassandra, A. R. 1998. Planning and acting in partially observable stochastic domains. *Artificial intelligence*, **101**(1), 99–134.

Kaminski, B. L., and Katoen, J.-P. 2015. On the Hardness of Almost-Sure Termination. Pages 307–318 of: *MFCS*.

Kaminski, B. L., Katoen, J.-P., Matheja, C., and Olmedo, F. 2016. Weakest Precondition Reasoning for Expected Run-Times of Probabilistic Programs. Pages 364–389 of: *ESOP*.

Kemeny, J.G., Snell, J.L., and Knapp, A.W. 1966. *Denumerable Markov Chains*. D. Van Nostrand Company.

Kwiatkowska, M. Z., Norman, G., and Parker, D. 2011. PRISM 4.0: Verification of Probabilistic Real-Time Systems. Pages 585–591 of: *CAV*. LNCS 6806.

Lee, C. S., Jones, N. D., and Ben-Amram, A. M. 2001. The size-change principle for program termination. Pages 81–92 of: *POPL*.

Lpsolve. 2016. *lp_solve 5.5.2.3*. http://lpsolve.sourceforge.net/5.5/.

McIver, A., and Morgan, C. 2004. Developing and Reasoning About Probabilistic Programs in *pGCL*. Pages 123–155 of: *PSSE*.

McIver, A., and Morgan, C. 2005. *Abstraction, Refinement and Proof for Probabilistic Systems*. Monographs in Computer Science. Springer.

McIver, A., Morgan, C., Kaminski, B. L., and Katoen, J.-P. 2018. A new proof rule for almost-sure termination. *PACMPL*, **2**(POPL), 33:1–33:28.

Motwani, Rajeev, and Raghavan, Prabhakar. 1995. *Randomized Algorithms*. New York, NY, USA: Cambridge University Press.

Neuhäußer, M., Stoelinga, M., and Katoen, J.-P.. 2009. Delayed Nondeterminism in Continuous-Time Markov Decision Processes. Pages 364–379 of: *Foundations of Software Science and Computational Structures (FOSSACS 2009)*. Lecture Notes in Computer Science, vol. 5504. Springer.

Neuhäußer, Martin R, and Katoen, Joost-Pieter. 2007. Bisimulation and logical preservation for continuous-time Markov decision processes. Pages 412–427 of: *International Conference on Concurrency Theory (CONCUR 2007)*. Springer.

Ngo, Van Chan, Carbonneaux, Quentin, and Hoffmann, Jan. 2018. Bounded expectations: resource analysis for probabilistic programs. *In:* Foster and Grossman (2018).

Olmedo, F., Kaminski, B. L., Katoen, J.-P., and Matheja, C. 2016. Reasoning about Recursive Probabilistic Programs. Pages 672–681 of: *LICS*.

Paz, A. 1971. *Introduction to probabilistic automata (Computer science and applied mathematics)*. Academic Press.

Podelski, A., and Rybalchenko, A. 2004. A Complete Method for the Synthesis of Linear Ranking Functions. Pages 239–251 of: *VMCAI*.

Rabin, M.O. 1963. Probabilistic automata. *Inf. & Control*, **6**, 230–245.

Sankaranarayanan, S., Chakarov, A., and Gulwani, S. 2013. Static analysis for probabilistic programs: inferring whole program properties from finitely many paths. Pages 447–458 of: *PLDI*.

Scheiderer, Claus. 2008. Positivity and Sums of Squares: A Guide to Recent Results. *The IMA Volumes in Mathematics and its Applications*, **149**, 271–324.

Schrijver, Alexander. 2003. *Combinatorial Optimization - Polyhedra and Efficiency*. Springer.

Sharir, M., Pnueli, A., and Hart, S. 1984. Verification of Probabilistic Programs. *SIAM J. Comput.*, **13**(2), 292–314.

Sohn, K., and Gelder, A. V. 1991. Termination Detection in Logic Programs using Argument Sizes. Pages 216–226 of: *PODS*.

Staton, Sam, Yang, Hongseok, Wood, Frank D., Heunen, Chris, and Kammar, Ohad. 2016. Semantics for probabilistic programming: higher-order functions, continuous distributions, and soft constraints. *In:* Grohe et al. (2016).

Turing, Alan Mathison. 1937. On computable numbers, with an application to the Entscheidungsproblem. *Proceedings of the London mathematical society*, **2**(1), 230–265.

Wang, Di, Hoffmann, Jan, and Reps, Thomas W. 2018. PMAF: an algebraic framework for static analysis of probabilistic programs. *In:* Foster and Grossman (2018).

Williams, D. 1991. *Probability with Martingales*. Cambridge University Press.

Quantitative Analysis of Programs with Probabilities and Concentration of Measure Inequalities

Sriram Sankaranarayanan
University of Colorado, Boulder

Abstract: The quantitative analysis of probabilistic programs answers queries involving the expected values of program variables and expressions involving them, as well as bounds on the probabilities of assertions. In this chapter, we will present the use of concentration of measure inequalities to reason about such bounds. First, we will briefly present and motivate standard concentration of measure inequalities. Next, we survey approaches to reason about quantitative properties using concentration of measure inequalities, illustrating these on numerous motivating examples. Finally, we discuss currently open challenges in this area for future work.

8.1 Introduction

In this chapter, we present the use of concentration of measure inequalities for the quantitative analysis of probabilistic programs. A variety of approaches have focused on qualitative properties that involve the almost-sure satisfaction of temporal formulas involving the behaviors of programs with special attention towards the analysis of almost sure termination, recurrence and persistence (McIver and Morgan, 2004; Esparza et al., 2012; Bournez and Garnier, 2005; Chakarov and Sankaranarayanan, 2013; Fioriti and Hermanns, 2015; Kaminski et al., 2016; Chakarov et al., 2016; Dimitrova et al., 2016; Chatterjee et al., 2017, 2018; McIver et al., 2018). On the other hand, quantitative properties include reasoning about probabilities of assertions involving conditions over the program state, expectations involving the program variables, and expected time to program termination (Kaminski et al., 2016; Chatterjee et al., 2018).

A critical difficulty of quantitative analysis is the need to integrate over a potentially large number of random variables generated in a typical run of a probabilistic program in order to calculate the quantity of interest. Often, these variables are manipulated

---

[a] From *Foundations of Probabilistic Programming*, edited by Gilles Barthe, Joost-Pieter Katoen and Alexandra Silva published 2020 by Cambridge University Press.

using nonlinear functions over the course of long running loops that calculate the result of the program. Thus, the result is quite often a nonlinear function involving a large number of random variables. To make matters worse, the function is represented only indirectly as the computer program itself. Reasoning about such functions can be quite challenging and is normally performed in a case-by-case fashion, one program at a time, to ease the understanding of the behavior. Mechanizing this process to yield a more automated analysis approach can be quite challenging.

There are many approaches to tackle the challenge of quantitative reasoning over programs with probabilistic statements. One approach pioneered by McIver and Morgan annotates the program with assertions and *expectations* that serve the same role as loop invariants (see McIver and Morgan, 2004). This approach effectively represents the distributions over the intermediate states encountered during the execution at a sufficient level of abstraction to establish the property of interest for the program as a whole. The approach has also been mechanized using ideas from loop invariant synthesis (see Katoen et al., 2010), and extended to programs with distributions over continuous state variables (see Chakarov and Sankaranarayanan, 2013; Fioriti and Hermanns, 2015; Chatterjee et al., 2018).

In this chapter, we survey a related approach that uses concentration of measure inequalities – a set of elegant mathematical ideas that characterize how functions of random variables deviate from their expected value. More importantly, these inequalities place upper bounds on the probabilities of deviations of a particular magnitude. Paradoxically, they avoid the need for expensive integration and thus, become quite effective when deviations over a large number of random variables are considered. Most well known inequalities such as the Chernoff–Hoeffding bounds, however, suffer a number of limitations that prevent them from being directly applicable to the analysis of probabilistic programs. They require *independence* of the random variables involved, work only for random variables over *bounded sets of support*, and finally, prove concentrations over *sums* rather than more general functions of random variables. We show in this chapter how these limitations can be partly overcome through a series of increasingly more sophisticated inequalities and the *tricks* involved in applying them to specific situations.

The survey is based on previously published papers involving the author: see Chakarov and Sankaranarayanan (2013) and Bouissou et al. (2016). We present concentration of measure inequalities motivated by a set of interesting numerical examples. We show applications to probabilistic programs starting with control deterministic computations that are handled through approximations known as probabilistic affine forms, whereas, more general loops are handled through the use of super-martingale approaches. Our presentation is inspired by the excellent monograph on this topic by Dubhashi and Panconesi (2009). We recommend this

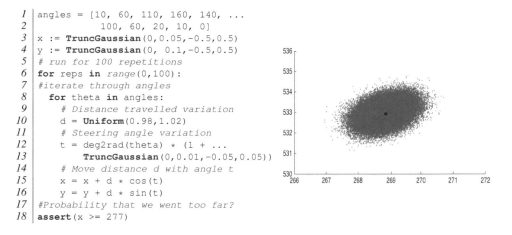

```
1   angles = [10, 60, 110, 160, 140, ...
2             100, 60, 20, 10, 0]
3   x := TruncGaussian(0,0.05,-0.5,0.5)
4   y := TruncGaussian(0, 0.1,-0.5,0.5)
5   # run for 100 repetitions
6   for reps in range(0,100):
7   #iterate through angles
8     for theta in angles:
9       # Distance travelled variation
10      d = Uniform(0.98,1.02)
11      # Steering angle variation
12      t = deg2rad(theta) * (1 + ...
13          TruncGaussian(0,0.01,-0.05,0.05))
14      # Move distance d with angle t
15      x = x + d * cos(t)
16      y = y + d * sin(t)
17  #Probability that we went too far?
18  assert(x >= 277)
```

Figure 8.1 **Left**: A probabilistic program capturing the final position of 2D robotic end effector. **Right:** Scatter plot showing the final (x, y) values. Note that TruncGaussian(m, s, l, u) generates a truncated Gaussian random variable with mean m, standard deviation s, lower bound l and upper bound u.

book as a starting point towards more mathematically detailed presentations that include Williams (1991) and Boucheron et al. (2016).

8.1.1 Motivating Examples

In this section, we present motivating examples involving a robotic end effector, an anesthesia infusion process and a linear aircraft model under wind disturbances.

Example 8.1 (2D robotic end effector). Consider the repetitive motion of a 2D end effector used for tasks such as soldering printed circuit boards for manufacturing applications. The end effector makes a series of cyclic repetitive movements for each widget, ending each cycle at the starting position for soldering the subsequent widget. At each step, small calibration errors can be introduced in its movement and these errors accumulate throughout the operation of the unit.

Figure 8.1 (left) shows the program that models the position of the end effector. Let (x, y) denote the position of the end effector. The initial position is defined by random variables (x_0, y_0) which are distributed as zero mean truncated Gaussian random variables over the set of support $[-0.5, 0.5]$ (see Figure 8.1, lines 3, 4). The program itself runs a for loop in line 6 for $N = 100$ iterations that represent 100 different repetitions of the same sequence of actions by the robot. Each iteration j consists of a $k = 10$ different geometric transformations of the robot's position that result in a sequence of coordinates $(x_{0,j}, y_{0,j}) \ldots, (x_{k+1,j}, y_{k+1,j}))$, wherein,

$$(x_{i+1,j}, y_{i+1,j}) = (x_{i,j} + d_{i,j} \cos(\theta_{i,j}), y_{i,j} + d_{i,j} \sin(\theta_{i,j})),$$

for $i = 1, \ldots, k$. Here $d_{i,j}$ is defined as a uniform random variable over $[0.98, 1.02]$. The mean values of $\theta_{i,j}$ are defined in degrees using the array `angles` in Figure 8.1 (line 2), with the uncertainties modeled in line 13. The starting position for iteration $j + 1$ is the end position at iteration j.

$$(x_{0,j+1}, y_{0,j+1}) = (x_{k+1,j}, y_{k+1,j}).$$

We are interested in the probability that the value of $x_{N,k+1} \geq 277$ (line 18), for $N = 100$ and $k = 10$. The value of $x_{N,k+1}$ is shown for 10^5 different runs of the program in the scatter plot in Figure 8.1(right) and none of these simulations violate the assertion of interest. Thus, we seek an upper bound on the probability of violating this assertion of the form:

$$\mathbb{P}(x \geq 277) \leq ?.$$

The challenge lies in obtaining nontrivial bounds for this program given that (a) it involves nonlinear transformations of random variables and (b) roughly 2000 independent random variables are involved in $N = 100$ iterations.

Example 8.2 (Anesthesia Infusion Model). The anesthesia model consists of a four-chamber pharmacokinetic model of the anesthetic Fentanyl that is administered to a surgical patient using an infusion pump (see McClain and Hug, 1980). This model has been used as part of automated anesthesia delivery systems (see Shafer et al., 1988; Yousefi et al., 2017). We model an erroneous infusion that results in varying amounts of anesthesia infused over time as a truncated Gaussian random noise. The state of the model at time t is a vector of concentrations of anesthesia in various "chambers" of the body:

$$\mathbf{x}(t) : (x_1(t), x_2(t), x_3(t), x_4(t))$$

The target state variable $x_4(t)$ measures the concentration of anesthesia in the blood plasma. Variable $u(t)$ denotes the rate of anesthesia infusion at time t, and is an input to the model.

At each step, the model evolves as

$$\mathbf{x}(t + 1) = A\mathbf{x}(t) + Bu(t)(1 + w(t))$$

The matrices A, B are specified as follows:

$$A: \begin{bmatrix} 0.9012 & 0.0304 & 0.0031 & 0 \\ 0.0139 & 0.9857 & 0 & 0 \\ 0.0015 & 0 & 0.9985 & 0 \\ 0.0838 & 0.0014 & 0.0001 & 0.9117 \end{bmatrix} \quad B: \begin{pmatrix} 0.2676 \\ 0.002 \\ 0.0002 \\ 0.0012 \end{pmatrix}$$

The disturbance $w(t)$ is a truncated Gaussian variable over the range $[-0.4, 0.4]$ with mean 0 and standard deviation $\sigma = 0.08$. These model the error in the infused anesthesia rate as a percentage of the commanded rate $u(t)$. This rate $u(t)$ is specified as the following fixed set of infusion rates and times:

t(100 seconds)	[0, 8]	[8, 14]	[14, 20]	[20, 26]	[26, 32]	[32, 38]	[38, 56]
$u(t)$(μmol/s)	60	64	66	68	64	62	60

The control inputs in this example are chosen for illustrative purposes, and do not carry medical significance. The goal is to check the probability that the infusion errors result either in too much anesthesia $x_4(5600) \geq 300ng/mL$ potentially causing loss of breathing or too little anesthesia $x_4(5600) \leq 150ng/mL$ causing consciousness during surgery.

Example 8.3 (Fixed-Wing UAV Collision). Fixed wing small UAVs are quite prone to wind disturbances. Thus, it is important to predict if a collision is imminent using short term forecast models based on a series of positions and velocities of the system.

Auto-regressive moving average state-space (ARMAX) models are an important class of data-driven time series models that enable such forecasts to be obtained over short time periods (Brockwell and Davis, 2009). Figure 8.2 shows such a forecast model for a small fixed wing UAV inferred using ridge regression from data collected during test flights. The data reports GPS positions (x, y, z) and velocities (v_n, v_e, v_d), respectively, in the north, east and downward directions every $h = 0.18$ seconds for a period of 3 hours. Once the model is inferred, the residual errors between the model prediction and actual results are histogrammed. Often these residuals are modeled using Gaussian distributions with some statistical analysis. Here, we simply model them as unknown distributions whose means and standard deviations are given.

Using the model in Figure 8.2, we seek to build a *predictive monitor* that given the current history of positions, velocities and deviations

$$(x(t), x(t - h), y(t), y(t - h), \cdots, e_z(t), e_z(t - h)),$$

estimates a bound on the probability:

$$\mathbb{P}((x(t + Nh), y(t + Nh), z(t + Nh)) \in U) \leq ?$$

where U represents unsafe regions in the airspace denoted by proximity to buildings, grounds and designated no fly zones.

$$
\begin{aligned}
x(t+h) &= x(t) + hv_e(t) + e_x(t+h) \\
y(t+h) &= y(t) + hv_n(t) + e_y(t+h) \\
z(t+h) &= z(t) + hv_d(t) + e_z(t+h) \\
v_n(t+h) &= 2.035v_n(t) - 1.11v_n(t-h) + 0.075v_n(t-2h) + w_1 && \leftarrow \sigma_1 : 0.055 \\
v_e(t+h) &= 1.923v_e(t) - 0.923v_e(t-h) + w_2 && \leftarrow \sigma_2 : 0.057 \\
v_d(t+h) &= 1.626v_d(t) - 0.778v_d(t-h) + 0.109v_d(t-2h) + w_3 && \leftarrow \sigma_3 : 0.16 \\
e_x(t+h) &= 0.567e_x(t) + 0.388e_x(t-h) + w_4 && \leftarrow \sigma_4 : 0.13 \\
e_y(t+h) &= 0.491e_y(t) + 0.27e_y(t-h) + 0.201e_y(t-2h) + w_5 && \leftarrow \sigma_5 : 0.14 \\
e_z(t+h) &= 1.35e_z(t) - 0.39e_z(t-h) + w_6 && \leftarrow \sigma_6 : 0.053
\end{aligned}
$$

Figure 8.2 Data-driven ARMAX model for predicting the future position of a UAV from its past positions and velocities. The time step h is 0.18 seconds in our model, x, y, z represent the position of the UAV, v_n, v_e, v_d represent the velocities in the north, east and downward directions, respectively, $e_x(t) : x(t) - x(t-h) - hv_e(t-h)$ is the deviation along the x direction, and similarly e_y, e_z denote deviations from y, z directions. $w_1, \ldots, w_6$ are residual errors that have been modeled using distributions with 0 mean and empirically estimated standard deviations σ_i shown alongside.

8.2 Quantitative Analysis: Problem and Approaches

In this section, we formally define the overall problem of quantitative analysis of probabilistic programs, focusing on (a) the type of systems that can be addressed, (b) the type of properties, and (c) sets of approaches that have been developed to reason about quantitative properties of probabilistic programs.

8.2.1 Programs and Properties

Given a "purely" probabilistic program P that computes a function $\mathbf{y} := F_P(X)$ over some random variables X, quantitative questions can be of two types: (a) bounds on the probability of an assertion φ involving $\mathbf{y}$: $\mathbb{P}(\varphi(\mathbf{y})) \bowtie c$? and (b) bounds on the expectation of some function $g(\mathbf{y})$: $\mathbb{E}(g(\mathbf{y})) \bowtie c$? wherein $\bowtie \in \{\geq, \leq, =\}$ and c is a constant? Some of these questions are illustrated by our motivating examples from Section 8.1.1. As mentioned earlier, quantitative reasoning about the running time of programs is addressed elsewhere (see also Chapter 6 in this volume), although the approaches mentioned in the present chapter remain generally applicable.

Beyond purely probabilistic programs, we may consider programs P that involve a combination of random variables X, *demonic* variables $\mathbf{w}$ controlled by the adversary, and angelic variables $\mathbf{u}$ controlled by a cooperative player. In such a situation, the program itself can be viewed as computing a joint function $\mathbf{y} := F_P(X, \mathbf{w}, \mathbf{u})$, wherein $\mathbf{y}$ denotes the outputs of the program. Interpreting $\varphi(\mathbf{y})$ as a *failure* condition, we wish to know if

$$
(\exists\, \mathbf{u}) \, (\forall\, \mathbf{w}) \, \mathbb{P}_X(\varphi(\mathbf{y})) \leq c,
$$

wherein c denotes a constant that is a desired failure threshold. We will focus our initial discussions on the case of purely probabilistic programs.

Furthermore, the probabilistic program will be assumed to be free of conditioning operation through `observe` or `assume` statements. Conditioning remains an open challenge for quantitative analysis and somewhat orthogonal to the purposes of quantitative reasoning considered in this chapter. Conditioning can simply be eliminated in restricted cases by computing the posterior distributions explicitly in the case of conjugate prior/posterior, or wherever symbolic integration approaches can tell us about the form of the posterior distribution (Narayanan et al., 2016; McElreath, 2015). Another approach involves the use of variational inference that can substitute prior probabilities by approximate posteriors from a predefined family of posterior distributions (Wingate and Weber, 2013).

Approaches to quantitative reasoning in probabilistic programs can be broadly classified into two: (a) simulation-based approaches and (b) symbolic approaches.

8.2.2 Simulation-Based Quantitative Reasoning

Simulation-based approaches execute the given program by sampling from the probability distributions generated in order to evaluate the property at hand. These approaches have been tied to statistical reasoning through hypothesis testing, starting with the work of Younes and Simmons (2006), leading to so-called *statistical model checking* approaches (Clarke et al., 2009; Agha and Palmskog, 2018; Jha et al., 2009).

Consider a probabilistic program P whose output variables are denoted as $\mathbf{y}$ and a quantitative property $\mathbb{P}(\varphi(\mathbf{y})) \leq c$. A simulation based approach consists of two components: (a) generate samples $\mathbf{y}_1, \ldots, \mathbf{y}_N$ and (b) perform a statistical hypothesis test between two competing hypotheses:

$$\mathcal{H}_0 := \mathbb{P}(\varphi(\mathbf{y}) \leq c) \text{ versus } \mathcal{H}_1 := \mathbb{P}(\varphi(\mathbf{y}) > c).$$

In particular, the hypothesis test works in a *sequential* fashion by examining how each added sample contributes towards the goal of accepting one hypothesis and rejecting another, with a new batch of samples generated *on-demand*.

To this end, the two most frequently used hypothesis tests include the sequential probability ratio test (SPRT) first proposed by Wald (1945) and the Bayes factor test proposed by Jeffries (Kass and Raftery, 1995). Details of these statistical tests are available from standard references, including the recent survey by Agha and Palmskog (2018). For instance, the Bayes factor test computes the so-called Bayes factor which is given by

$$\text{BayesFactor} := \frac{\mathbb{P}(\text{Observations } \mathbf{y}_1, \ldots, \mathbf{y}_N \mid \mathcal{H}_1)\mathbb{P}(\mathcal{H}_1)}{\mathbb{P}(\text{Observations } \mathbf{y}_1, \ldots, \mathbf{y}_N \mid \mathcal{H}_0)\mathbb{P}(\mathcal{H}_0)}$$

as a measure of the evidence in favor of hypothesis $\mathcal{H}_1$ against that in favor of $\mathcal{H}_0$. Here, $\mathbb{P}(\mathcal{H}_j)$ refers to the prior probability of the hypothesis $\mathcal{H}_j$ for $j = 0, 1$. If the resulting BayesFactor exceeds a given upper bound threshold (see Kass and Raftery, 1995 for an interpretation of the Bayes factor), the hypothesis $\mathcal{H}_1$ is accepted. On the other hand, if the BayesFactor falls below a lower bound, $\mathcal{H}_0$ is accepted in favor of $\mathcal{H}_1$. If the BayesFactor remains between these two bounds more evidence is sought since the data has insufficient evidence.

Besides the use of statistical tests, the generation of samples is another key problem. Often, in verification problems, the event of interest is a "rare" failure whose probability needs to be bounded by a small number $c \sim 10^{-6}$. To this end, the number of simulations needed can be prohibitively expensive, in practice. Thus, approaches such as importance sampling are used to artificially inflate the probability of obtaining a failure (see Srinivasan, 2002; Bucklew, 2004; Rubinstein and Kroese, 2008). Importance sampling approach first modifies the probabilistic program by replacing the distribution of random variables using sampling distributions designed to increase the probability and hence the number of samples that satisfy the assertion $\varphi(\mathbf{y})$ (assuming that φ is a rare event). The new samples are weighted by the ratio of the likelihood score under the original distribution and the new sampling distribution. A key challenge lies in designing a sampling distribution that can increase the number of rare event observations. This requires a lot of insight on the part of the analyzer. Approaches such as the cross-entropy method can be employed to systematically optimize the parameters of a family of sampling distributions to make failures more likely (Jégourel et al., 2012; Sankaranarayanan and Fainekos, 2012).

8.2.3 Symbolic Approaches

In contrast to simulation-based approaches, symbolic techniques focus on reasoning about probabilities of assertions and expectations through a process of *abstraction*. Often this abstraction takes one of two forms (see Cousot and Monerau (2012) for a more refined classification): (a) *abstractions of intermediate probability distributions over program states* or (b) *abstractions of intermediate states as functions over the random variables generated by the program*. Both approaches rely on symbolic integration to compute bounds on the probabilities and expectations.

Abstractions of Probability Distributions: The probability distributions over program variables can be precisely represented for finite state programs. This is the basis for the tool PRISM, that handles probabilistic programs over finite state variables by compiling them into Markov chains or Markov decision processes, depending on whether demonic/angelic nondeterminism is present (Kwiatkowska et al., 2011). These approaches can be extended to infinite state systems using the idea of a game-based abstraction that allows us to treat some of the probabilistic choices as non-deterministic but controlled by a different player (see Parker et al., 2006).

Abstractions for infinite state probabilistic systems are more complicated since the intermediate joint probability distributions between the program variables can be arbitrarily complicated (Kozen, 1981). A variety of approaches have been employed to abstract the intermediate distributions through probabilistic abstract domains that associate upper/lower bounds on measures associated with sets of states (Monniaux, 2000, 2005; Cousot and Monerau, 2012). Whereas initial approaches focused on intervals and polyhedral sets annotated with bounds, it became clear that the probability bounds can often become too large to be useful or alternatively, the number of subdivisions of the state-space needed becomes too high to maintain a desired level of precision. An alternative approach by Bouissou et al. (2012) uses ideas from imprecise probabilities such as Dempster–Shafer structures (see Dempster, 1967; Shafer, 1976) and P-boxes(Ferson et al., 2003) to represent probabilities more precisely. This approach has the added advantage of representing correlations between program variables in a more precise manner. However, the process of computing probabilities or expectations involves integration, and therefore a summation over a large number of cells that tile the region of interest.

Probabilistic Symbolic Execution: A related and complementary approach uses symbolic execution to represent program states as functions over the input variables that involve random variables generated by the program (Geldenhuys et al., 2012; Mardziel et al., 2011; Sankaranarayanan et al., 2013) followed by the use of symbolic integration to calculate the probability of an assertion exactly or approximately as needed. Algorithms for computing volume of polyhedra (De Loera et al., 2011) or interval-based branch-and-bound schemes for approximating these volumes (Sankaranarayanan et al., 2013) can be employed to perform quantitative analysis. A key drawback remains the high complexity of volume computation in terms of the number of dimensions of the region. Here, the dimensionality equals the number of random variables involved in the computation, which can be prohibitively large, as seen in our motivating examples. Thus, the applications are limited to programs that use fewer random variables and carry out complex computations over these. Furthermore, the exact volume computation is often not needed since for many applications of interest an upper bound over the probabilities of failure suffices.

8.3 Concentration of Measure Inequalities: a Primer

In this section, we present basic facts about concentration of measure inequalities. An accessible and complete exposition of them, and their application to randomized algorithms, is Dubhashi and Panconesi (2009).

Concentration of measure inequalities allow us to reason about the behavior of certain functions of independent random variables. The most basic inequality remains the widely applied Chernoff–Hoeffding inequality. Let $X_1, \ldots, X_n$ be independent random variables taking on values in the set $\{0, 1\}$. Consider the sum $S_n = X_1 + \cdots + X_n$. Clearly, $\mathbb{E}(S_n) = \sum_{j=1}^{n} \mathbb{E}(X_j)$. The key question is how likely is it for the sum to satisfy $S_n \geq \mathbb{E}(S_n) + t$ for some positive deviation $t \geq 0$?

There are many ways of answering such a question. For the special case of $\{0, 1\}$-valued random variables that are identically distributed so that $\mathbb{E}(X_i) = p$ for all $i \in \{1, \ldots, n\}$, the answer can be obtained from an application of combinatorics, as shown below:

$$\mathbb{P}\,(S_n \geq \mathbb{E}(S_n) + t) = \sum_{j = \lceil np + t \rceil}^{n} \binom{n}{j} p^j (1 - p)^{n-j} \, .$$

The RHS expression provides an exact answer but is often cumbersome to compute. The expression can be approximated in many ways. For instance, the *Poisson approximation* is possible when n is large and p is small so that np is "small enough". However, such attempts produce a numerical approximation which cannot be used to establish guaranteed bounds, in general. Furthermore, we cannot deal with other common situations that involve: (a) the sum of random variables that are not necessarily identically distributed; (b) the sum of random variables whose distributions can be continuous; and finally (c) the sum of random variables that are not all independent.

Concentration of measure inequalities attempt to answer these questions by providing upper bounds on deviations of certain functions of random variables from their expected values. Let $f(X_1, \ldots, X_n)$ be a function of random variables having some fixed arity n (the arity of f does not need to be fixed, however). As an example: $f(X_1, \ldots, X_n) = X_1 + \cdots + X_n$. Let $\mathbb{E}(f)$ denote the expectation $\mathbb{E}(f(X_1, \ldots, X_n))$ computed over random choices of $X_1, \ldots, X_n$. A concentration of measure inequality typically has the form:

$$\mathbb{P}\,(f(X_1, \ldots, X_n) \geq \mathbb{E}(f) + t) \leq g(n, t),$$

wherein $t \geq 0$, and g is a function that decreases sharply as t increases. Inequalities are often "symmetric" providing similar bounds for lower tails as well:

$$\mathbb{P}(f(X_1, \ldots, X_n) \leq \mathbb{E}(f) - t) \leq g(n, t),$$

The inequality is *sub-gaussian* if the bound $g(n,t)$ is of the form $g(n,t) := C \exp\left(\frac{-ct^2}{n}\right)$ for known constants C, c that depend on the moments and set of support of the random variables $X_1, \ldots, X_n$. Most of the bounds we will explore will be sub-gaussian in nature. The simplest and most fundamental of these bounds is the well-known Chernoff–Hoeffding inequality.

Theorem 8.4 (Chernoff–Hoeffding). *Let X_i be independent random variables that lies in the range $[a_i, b_i]$ almost surely, for $i = 1, \ldots, n$, and let $S_n = \sum_{j=1}^{n} X_j$. For all $t \geq 0$,*

$$\mathbb{P}(S_n \geq \mathbb{E}(S_n) + t) \leq \exp\left(-\frac{2t^2}{\sum_{j=1}^{n}(b_j - a_j)^2}\right).$$

Using Chernoff–Hoeffding inequality, we may bound the upper tail of the sum of Bernoulli random variables as:

$$\mathbb{P}(S_n \geq \mathbb{E}(S_n) + t) \leq \exp\left(-\frac{2t^2}{n}\right).$$

However, there are two important limitations of Chernoff–Hoeffding inequality: (a) the random variables $X_1, \ldots, X_n$ must be independent and (b) X_i must lie within a bounded range $[a_i, b_i]$, almost surely.

Example 8.5. We will now illustrate the direct use of Chernoff–Hoeffding bounds to prove upper bounds on the probability of failure for the model described in Example 8.2. Note that our main object of concern in this example is the value of the state variable x_4 at time $t = 5600s$. Since at each step, the new state $\mathbf{x}(t+1)$ is related to the previous state: $\mathbf{x}(t+1) = A\mathbf{x}(t) + Bu(t)(1 + w(t))$, the value of $x_4(5600)$ is, in fact, written as a summation of the following form:

$$x_4(5600) = a_0 + \sum_{i=1}^{4} a_i x_i(0) + \sum_{j=1}^{5600} b_j w(j), \tag{8.1}$$

wherein the coefficients a_i, b_j are obtained by computing the matrices for $A^i B$ for $i = 0, \ldots, 5600$ and A^n for $n = 5600$. Furthermore, $w(j)$ for $j = 1, \ldots, 5600$, represent mutually independent random variables over the range $[-0.4, 0.4]$ with mean 0 and standard deviation $\sigma = 0.08$.

We may, therefore, apply Chernoff–Hoeffding bounds to compute bounds of the form:

$$\mathbb{P}(x_4(5600) \geq \mathbb{E}(x_4(5600)) + t) \leq \exp\left(\frac{-2t^2}{\sum_{i=1}^{5600} b_i(0.8)^2}\right),$$

and likewise,

$$\mathbb{P}(x_4(5600) \leq \mathbb{E}(x_4(5600)) - t) \leq \exp\left(\frac{-2t^2}{\sum_{i=1}^{5600} b_i(0.8)^2}\right).$$

Note that in applying these bounds, we consider the summation of random variables that include a_0, $a_i x_i(0)$ and $w(j)$ from Eq. (8.1). The value of $\mathbb{E}(x_4(5600))$ is calculated using linearity of expectation to be 246.7985 up to 4 significant digits. The denominator of the exponent term for the Chernoff–Hoeffding is calculated as follows:

$$\sum_{i=1}^{5600} b_i(0.8)^2 = 234.3159.$$

Thus, we may bound the probability of the Fentanyl concentration in the effect chamber exceeding 300ng/ml as follows:

$$\mathbb{P}(x_4(5600) \geq 300) \leq 3.05 \times 10^{-5}.$$

Likewise, we may bound the probability of Fentanyl concentration falling below 150ng/ml as follows:

$$\mathbb{P}(x_4(5600) \leq 150) \leq 2.4 \times 10^{-15}.$$

Chernoff–Hoeffding inequalities are widely used in numerous applications to the analysis of randomized algorithms for bounding away the probability of an undesirable behavior of the algorithm at hand. However, their use is constrained by many important factors:

(i) The inequality applies to random variables X_i whose set of support is bounded by a finite interval. Random variables with an unbounded set of support such as Gaussian random variables are not handled.

(ii) The inequality uses only the range and first moment of each X_i. Further information such as the second or higher moments $\mathbb{E}(X_i^2)$ could be more useful in obtaining sharper bounds.

(iii) The inequality applies to sums of random variables. Programs often compute more complex functions of random variables than just sums.

(iv) The inequality applies to mutually independent random variables. Even if the random variables sampled by a program are mutually independent, the state variables become correlated as they depend on the same set of independent random variables.

We will now discuss how each of the limitations may be handled using other, more sophisticated concentration of measure inequalities and/or simply by adapting how the inequality is applied in the first place.

8.3.1 Inequalities Using Higher Moments

Numerous inequalities for the concentration of the sum $\sum_{i=1}^{n} X_i$ of independent random variables have been proposed that use higher moments such as the second moment $\mathbb{E}(X_i^2)$ of each random variable X_i in addition to $\mathbb{E}(X_i)$. Bernstein (1924) proposed a series of such inequalities.

Theorem 8.6 (Bernstein Inequality). *Let* $X_1, \ldots, X_n$ *be independent random variables such that (a) there exists a constant* $M > 0$ *such that* $|X_i - \mathbb{E}(X_i)| \leq M$ *for each* $i \in [1, n]$, *and (b) the variance of each* X_i *is* σ_i^2. *For any* $t \geq 0$:

$$\mathbb{P}(X - \mathbb{E}(X) \geq t) \leq exp\left(\frac{-t^2}{\frac{2}{3}Mt + 2\sum_{i=1}^{n}\sigma_i^2}\right) \tag{8.2}$$

For the left tail probability, we may derive an identical bound.

Note that if each random variable X_i ranges over a bounded interval, then condition (a) for Bernstein inequality is easily satisfied. Furthermore, if we let μ_i denote $\mathbb{E}(X_i)$, it is easy to show that if the interval $[\mu_i - \sigma_i, \mu_i + \sigma_i]$ for each random variable is small in comparison to the set of support $[a_i, b_i]$, this inequality will provide much tighter bounds when compared to Chernoff–Hoeffding bounds.

Example 8.7. Returning back to the analysis of the anesthesia model from Example 8.5, we will now apply Bernstein inequality to bound the probability that $x_4(5600) \geq 300$ng/ml. We can compute the sum of the variances $\sum_{i=1}^{5600}\sigma_i^2$ as 4.687. Similarly the value of M for Bernstein's inequality in (8.2) is calculated to be 2.362. These calculations are mechanized using the approach described in Section 8.4. Applying the inequality yields the bound:

$$\mathbb{P}(x_4(5600) \geq 300) \leq 7.1 \times 10^{-13}.$$

This is much more useful than the bound of 3.05×10^{-5} obtained using Chernoff–Hoeffding bounds. Similarly, the probability that the anesthesia level falls below the lower limit of 150ng/ml using Bernstein's inequality is obtained as 2.1×10^{-26}, once again a drastic improvement when compared to Chernoff–Hoeffding bounds.

Inequalities that use information from higher order moments beyond just the mean and the variance are also possible. In fact, these inequalities may be derived by using an expansion of the moment generating function $\mathbb{E}(e^{tX})$ for a random variable X whose set of support is bounded by $[a, b]$. The key lies in discovering useful bounds that can utilize as much information available about the random variables X_i as possible, while remaining computationally tractable. We see the use of such *designer inequalities* derived using computer algebra manipulations rather than using hand calculations as an important future step in mechanizing the application of concentration of measure inequalities.

8.3.2 Random Variables with Unbounded Support

All concentration of measure inequalities studied thus far, such as Chernoff–Hoeffding or Bernstein inequalities, rely on the random variables X_i having bounded set of support. However, this need not be the case for many commonly encountered distributions such as Gaussian or exponential random variables.

Let $X_1, \ldots, X_n$ be independent random variables whose support is unbounded (either $[-\infty, \infty]$, $[a, \infty)$ or $(-\infty, a]$, for some constant a). We say that a family of distributions is *Lévy stable* iff the linear combination of finitely many random variables belonging to the family, is also a random variable that belongs to the family. For instance, commonly occurring distributions such as Gaussian, exponential, gamma, and Poisson are Lévy stable. If the variables X_i are identically distributed and their distributions are Lévy stable, then it is possible to calculate the parameters for the distribution of the sum from the parameters of the original random variables. Likewise, questions such as $\mathbb{P}(X \geq \mathbb{E}(X) + t)$ can be handled by knowing the cumulative density functions of these variables.

However, appealing to stability property of the random variables will fail if the distributions are not stable or, more commonly, the variables $X_1, \ldots, X_n$ are not identically distributed. In this situation, a simple trick can enable us to successfully apply concentration of measure inequality as follows:

(i) For each X_i choose an interval $J_i := [a_i, b_i]$ and compute the probability p_i that $\mathbb{P}(X_i \notin J_i)$ (or compute an interval bounding p_i). Also define a random variable Y_i obtained by restricting the variable X_i to the interval J_i. Let $\mathbb{E}(Y_i)$ be its expectation.

(ii) To bound the probability that $\mathbb{P}(\sum X_i \geq t)$, we can consider two mutually exclusive events. $A := \bigwedge X_i \in J_i$ and $B := \bigvee X_i \notin J_i$. We have that

$$
\begin{aligned}
\mathbb{P}(\textstyle\sum X_i \geq t) &= \mathbb{P}(A)\mathbb{P}(\textstyle\sum X_i \geq t \mid A) + \mathbb{P}(B)\mathbb{P}(\textstyle\sum X_i \geq t \mid B) \\
&= \mathbb{P}(A)\mathbb{P}(\textstyle\sum Y_i \geq t) + \mathbb{P}(B)\mathbb{P}(\textstyle\sum X_i \geq t \mid B) \\
&\leq \mathbb{P}(A)\mathbb{P}(\textstyle\sum Y_i \geq t) + \mathbb{P}(B) \\
&\leq (\textstyle\prod_{i=1}^{n}(1 - p_i))\mathbb{P}(\textstyle\sum Y_i \geq t) + (1 - \textstyle\prod_{i=1}^{n}(1 - p_i))
\end{aligned}
$$

Note that we obtain $\mathbb{P}(A) = \prod_{i=1}^{n}(1 - p_i)$ through the independence of the random variables $X_1, \ldots, X_n$, and $\mathbb{P}(B) = 1 - \mathbb{P}(A)$. If independence of $X_1, \ldots, X_n$ is dropped (as we will see subsequently), we may instead use Fréchet bounds to conclude that $\mathbb{P}(A) \leq \min(1 - p_1, \ldots, 1 - p_n)$. Likewise, we may use a weaker bound $\mathbb{P}(B) \leq p_1 + \cdots + p_n$ through Boole's inequality (union bound) if the independence assumption is dropped. We may now estimate the probability $\mathbb{P}(\sum Y_i \geq t)$ using the Chernoff–Hoeffding bounds or Bernstein inequality (if the variance of Y_i is known).

The approach also presents an interesting trade-off between the size of the interval

J_i chosen for each random variable. A larger interval makes the probability $\mathbb{P}(B)$ vanishingly small. However, at the same time, the quality of the bounds depend on the width of the intervals J_i. For instance, the problem can be setup as an optimization to find the best bound that can be obtained by varying the width of J_i against the probability of event B.

Example 8.8. Returning to the anesthesia example (Ex. 8.2), we will consider the distribution of the noise to be a Gaussian random variable with mean 0 and variance 0.08. As a result, the concentration of measure inequalities are no longer applicable. However, if we consider $J_i := [-0.4, 0.4]$, we can estimate the probability $\mathbb{P}(w_i \notin J_i) \le 5.73 \times 10^{-7}$. The latter is obtained knowing the probability that the value of a normally distributed random variables lies $\pm 5\sigma$ away from the mean. As a result, the result from the Chernoff–Hoeffding bounds in Example 8.5 can be reused here to assert that

$$\mathbb{P}(x_4(5600) \ge 300) \le \underbrace{(1 - 5.73 \times 10^{-7})3.05 \times 10^{-5} + 5600 \times 5.73 \times 10^{-7}}_{=3.293 \times 10^{-3}}$$

On the other hand, We could use a larger interval $J_i := [-0.593, 0.593]$ that yields the probability $\mathbb{P}(w_i \notin J_i) \le 10^{-13}$. However, using this interval to truncate the random variable yields poorer results overall.

$$\mathbb{P}(x_4(5600) \ge 300) \le 0.0012 + 5600 \times 10^{-13} \le 0.0013.$$

The approach can also be used alongside Bernstein bounds provided the variance can be estimated for the truncated distribution. Here, we may use a formula for the variance of a truncated Gaussian distribution. In doing so with the larger interval $J_i := [-0.593, 0.593]$ we obtain a tighter bound:

$$\mathbb{P}(x_4(5600) \ge 300) \le 3.241 \times 10^{-8} + 5600 \times 10^{-13} \le 3.25 \times 10^{-8}.$$

8.3.3 Inequalities for Nonlinear Functions

Thus far, we have applied Chernoff–Hoeffding and Bernstein bounds for sums of independent random variables. However, more often, probabilistic programs yield nonlinear functions of random variables $f(X_1, \ldots, X_n)$. We are interested in tail bounds of the form

$$\mathbb{P}(f - \mathbb{E}(f) \ge t) \le \exp(-ct^2).$$

First, it is clear that not all functions will yield such a bound. It is important to understand properties of functions that are amenable to such a bound and check if the function computed by the program falls within such a class.

Example 8.9. Revisiting the 2D robotic end effector from Example 8.1, we note that the value of x at the end of the program in line 18 of Figure 8.1, is obtained as

$$x := x_0 + \sum_{i=0}^{99} \sum_{j=0}^{9} d_{i,j} \cos(\theta_{i,j}). \tag{8.3}$$

wherein x_0 is a truncated Gaussian random variable with mean 0 and standard deviation 0.05 over the range $[-0.5, 0.5]$ (see line 3), $d_{i,j}$ is a uniform random variable over the range $[0.98, 1.02]$ and $\theta_{i,j}$ is given by

$$\theta_{i,j} = \alpha_j (1 + w_{i,j})$$

wherein α_j is specified in the array `angles` in line 2 of the program shown in Figure 8.1 and $w_{i,j}$ is distributed as a truncated Gaussian random variable with mean 0, standard deviation $\sigma = 0.01$ and over the range $[-0.05, 0.05]$ (see line 13).

Definition 8.10 (Difference Bounded Functions). Let $f(x_1, \ldots, x_n)$ be a function from $S_1 \times \cdots \times S_n \rightarrow \mathbb{R}$ for sets $S_i \subseteq \mathbb{R}$. We say that f is *difference-bounded* iff there exists constants $c_1, \ldots, c_n$ such that

$$(\forall i \in \{1, 2, \cdots, n\})$$
$$(\forall\, x_1 \in S_1, \ldots, x_{i-1} \in S_{i-1}, x_{i+1} \in S_{i+1}, \ldots, x_n \in S_n)$$
$$(\forall x_i \in S_i, x_i' \in S_i)$$
$$|f(x_1, \ldots, \mathbf{x_i}, \ldots, x_n) - f(x_1, \ldots, \mathbf{x_i'}, \ldots, x_n)| \leq c_i.$$

In other words, varying just the ith argument while keeping the other arguments the same yields a bounded change in the value of the function. Dubhashi and Panconesi (2009) and many other authors sometimes use the terminology *Lipschitz* functions to refer to difference-bounded functions, above. Note that the notion of difference bounded is not the same as the standard notion of Lipschitz continuity that one encounters in calculus, wherein the right hand side of the inequality is $L|x_i - x_i'|$ rather than a fixed constant c_i. It is easy to see that a Lipschitz continuous function is difference-bounded provided the sets $S_1, \ldots, S_n$ are compact. On the other hand, the step function (a discontinuous function) is difference-bounded over $[-1, 1]$ but not Lipschitz continuous.

A well-known result known as McDiarmid's inequality (see McDiarmid, 1989) shows that a difference-bounded function of independent random variables concentrates around its mean.

Theorem 8.11 (McDiarmid's Inequality). *Let $X_1, \ldots, X_n$ be independent random variables and f be a difference-bounded function over the Cartesian product of the* *set of support of the random variables. We conclude that*

$$\mathbb{P}(f(X_1, \ldots, X_n) \leq \mathbb{E}(f) + t) \leq \exp\left(\frac{-2t^2}{\sum_{j=1}^{n} c_j^2}\right).$$

A similar inequality holds for the lower tail, as well.

Example 8.12. Continuing with the calculation for Example 8.9, we will first show that the function in Equation (8.3) is difference-bounded and derive the corresponding constants bounding the differences by hand:

Random Variable	Difference-Bound Constant
x_0	1
$d_{i,j}$	$0.04u_j$
$w_{i,j}$	$1.02(u_j - l_j)$

Here

$$u_j := \max(|\cos(0.95\alpha_j)|, |\cos(1.05\alpha_j)|)$$

and

$$l_j := \min(|\cos(0.95\alpha_j)|, |\cos(1.05\alpha_j)|).$$

Carrying out this calculation, the sum of the squares of the difference-bound constants is obtained as 13.68. Next we need to estimate $\mathbb{E}(f)$, which is challenging as it involves integrating a multivariate nonlinear function over the random variables. A systematic approach to doing so using a combination of affine forms, interval arithmetic and Taylor series expansions is described in our previous work (Bouissou et al., 2016). Using an implementation of our approach, we estimate an interval that bounds the value of $\mathbb{E}(x)$ as

$$\mathbb{E}(x) \in [268.6170484, 270.6914916].$$

Such a range is nevertheless useful in estimating tail probabilities. For instance, to bound upper tail probabilities $\mathbb{P}(f - \mathbb{E}(f) \geq t)$, we use the upper limit of the given range for $\mathbb{E}(f)$. Likewise, we use the the lower limit for the lower tail probabilities in order to obtain conservative bounds. Therefore, we conclude that

$$\mathbb{P}(x \geq 277) = \mathbb{P}(x - 270.69 \geq 6.31) \leq \exp\left(\frac{-2 * 6.31^2}{13.68}\right) = 2.96 \times 10^{-3}.$$

This bound is much improved using the systematic approach that incorporates variance information originally described in Bouissou et al. (2016), as will be discussed in the subsequent section.

8.3.4 Inequalities for Correlated Random Variables

We will now examine how concentration inequalities can be derived for dependent random variables $X_1, \ldots, X_n$. If the variables are correlated in some manner, it is hard to provide useful concentration bounds for the general case. However, in some cases, the "structure" of the correlation can be exploited to directly derive inequalities by adapting existing approaches such as Chernoff–Hoeffding or Bernstein inequalities.

Numerous cases have been studied such as *negatively dependent* random variables (Dubhashi and Panconesi, 2009; Dubhashi and Ranjan, 1998). We will focus our approach on sums of random variables with a given *correlation graph*. Let $X_1, \ldots, X_n$ be a set of random variables with an undirected graph $G := (\{X_1, \ldots, X_n\}, E)$ whose vertices correspond to the random variables $X_1, \ldots, X_n$. An edge between two random variables (X_i, X_j) signifies a dependency between the variables.

Example 8.13. Let X_1, X_2 and X_3 be three independent random variables and X_4 denote a function $f(X_1, X_2, X_3)$. The dependency graph has edges connecting X_4 with X_1, X_2 and X_3.

Naturally, existing approaches discussed thus far require the random variables to be independent. As a result, it is not possible to apply them in this context. We will describe an elegant "trick" due to Janson (2004), and in turn following ideas from Hoeffding's seminal paper (Hoeffding, 1963)) introducing the Chernoff–Hoeffding inequality.

First, we will introduce the notion of a weighted independent-set cover. Let A be the set of random variables $\{X_1, \ldots, X_n\}$. A subset $A_j \subseteq A$ is an independent set if any two variables in A_j are mutually independent, i.e, there are no edges between them in the graph G.

An *independent set cover* is a family of independent sets $A_1, \ldots, A_k$ such that $A_1 \cup \cdots \cup A_k = A$. A *weighted cover* is a family of independent sets with positive real-valued weights

$$(A_1, w_1), \ldots, (A_k, w_k),$$

such that (a) $A_1, \ldots, A_k$ form an independent set cover and (b) for each X_i, $\sum_{A_j \mid X_i \in A_j} w_j \geq 1$. In other words, for each element X_i, the sum of weights for all independent sets that contain X_i is greater than or equal to 1. Note that every independent set cover that partitions the set A is also a weighted cover by assigning the weights 1 to each set. The total weight of a cover is given by $w_1 + \cdots + w_k$. Given a graph G its chromatic number $\xi(G) = k$, for some $k \in \mathbb{N}$, is the smallest number of sets that form an independent set cover of A. Likewise, its *fractional chromatic number* $\xi^*(G)$ is the minimum weight $\sum_{j=1}^{k} w_j$ of some $A_1, \ldots, A_k$ such that $(A_1, w_1), \ldots, (A_k, w_k)$ forms a weighed cover.

Let $(A_1, w_1), \ldots, (A_k, w_k)$ be a weighted cover of the set of random variables A. Let $[a_i, b_i]$ represent the set of support for random variable X_i. Let $c_j := \sum_{X_i \in A_j} (b_i - a_i)^2$.

Theorem 8.14 (Janson, 2004). *Given a set of random variables $A := \{X_1, \ldots, X_n\}$ with correlations specified by graph G. Let $(A_1, w_1), \ldots, (A_j, w_j)$ be a weighted independent set cover of G. The following bound holds:*

$$\mathbb{P}(\sum X_j - \mathbb{E}(\sum X_j) \geq t) \leq \exp\left(\frac{-2t^2}{T^2}\right), \tag{8.4}$$

wherein $T^2 = \left(\sum_{j=1}^{k} w_j \sqrt{c_j}\right)^2$ and $c_j = \sum_{X_i \in A_j} (b_i - a_i)^2$.

With $\xi^*(G)$ as the fractional chromatic number of G, we obtain the bound

$$\mathbb{P}(\sum X_j - \mathbb{E}(\sum X_j) \geq t) \leq \exp\left(\frac{-2t^2}{\xi^*(G) \sum_{j=1}^{n} (b_j - a_j)^2}\right). \tag{8.5}$$

First we note that if all the variables are mutually independent, then the optimal weighted cover is simply $(A, 1)$ yielding $\xi^*(G) = 1$. Both Equations (8.4) and (8.5) yield the same answer as Chernoff–Hoeffding bounds. Applying the bound in (8.4) requires us to compute a weighted independent set cover of the graph G. A simple approach lies in using a greedy algorithm to partition the set A into subsets of independent sets, and using weights 1 to convert the cover into a weighted cover.

Example 8.15. Continuing with Example 8.13, an independent set cover is given by $\{X_1, X_2, X_3\}$ and $\{X_4\}$ which yields a weighted cover by assigning a weight 1 to each independent set.

Therefore, let $S := X_1 + X_2 + X_3 + X_4$ and $\lfloor a_i, b_i \rfloor$ denote the range of each random variable X_i. Applying Janson's inequality for any $t \geq 0$, we get:

$$\mathbb{P}(S \geq \mathbb{E}(S) + t) \leq \exp\left(\frac{-2t^2}{\left(\sqrt{(b_1 - a_1)^2 + (b_2 - a_2)^2 + (b_3 - a_3)^2} + (b_4 - a_4)\right)^2}\right).$$

Beyond Chernoff–Hoeffding bounds, Janson presents extensions of other inequalities such as Bernstein's inequality to the case of correlated random variables with known correlation structure.

Thus far, we have studied various concentration of measure inequalities and how they can be applied to reason about the probability of assertions for some specific programs. The bigger question, however, is to what extent can the process of choosing and applying the right inequality be mechanized for a given probabilistic program. To answer it, we examine the case of *control deterministic* programs and use the idea of affine forms to symbolically reason about the distribution of program variables during and after the program execution. This provides us a means to apply the inequalities we have discussed thus far in this section without requiring extensive manual calculations.

8.4 Control Deterministic Computations

In this section, we briefly touch upon how the concentration of measure inequalities presented in the previous sections can be systematically applied to reasoning about programs. We begin our discussion with a simple class of *control deterministic computations*. The material in this section is based upon joint work with Olivier Bouissou, Eric Goubault and Sylvie Putot (see Bouissou et al., 2016). Control determinism is an important property that is satisfied by many probabilistic programs that occur naturally in application domains such as cyber-physical systems (CPS), control theory, and motion planning, to name a few. In this section, we briefly summarize the notion of control determinism and examine how probability distributions of variables can be abstracted in a symbolic fashion, to enable reasoning using various concentration of measure inequalities.

8.4.1 *Control Deterministic Programs*

Put simply, a program is control deterministic if and only if the control flow of the program is unaffected by the stochastic or nondeterministic choices made during the program execution. In effect, the program does not have any if-then-else branches, and all loops in the program terminate after a pre-determined number of iterations. Furthermore, the "primitive" assignment statements of the program involve a continuous function as their RHS.

Formally, a control deterministic program over real-valued program variables $\mathbf{x}$ is constructed using the grammar shown below:

$$
\begin{aligned}
\text{program} \quad &\rightarrow \quad \text{statement}^* \\
\text{statement} \quad &\rightarrow \quad \text{assignment} \\
&\quad | \quad \textbf{repeat} < n > (\text{statement}^*) \\
\text{assignment} \quad &\rightarrow \quad x_i \leftarrow f(x_{i_1}, \ldots, x_{i_k}) \\
&\quad | \quad x_j \sim \mathcal{D} \\
x_1, \ldots, x_n \quad &\in \quad \text{Identifiers} \\
n \quad &\in \quad \mathbb{N} \\
f \quad &\in \quad \text{Continuous} \\
\mathcal{D} \quad &\in \quad \text{Distributions}
\end{aligned}
$$

The program consists of a set Identifiers of real-valued state variables $x_1, \ldots, x_n$ that are manipulated using a sequence of assignment statements and deterministic loops that repeat a set of statements a fixed number n of times. Further, each assignment involves a continuous function f applied to a subset of variables. The

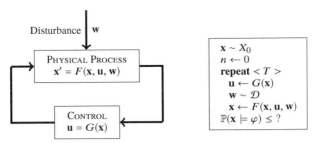

Figure 8.3 Discrete-time control of a physical process under uncertainties caused by external disturbances and a control deterministic probabilistic program that simulates it.

statement $x \sim \mathcal{D}$ denotes drawing a sample from a distribution $\mathcal{D}$ and assigning the value to variable x. The semantics of such a program can be defined in the usual manner (see Kozen, 1981), and are omitted for this discussion.

Despite the limitations on expressivity due to the absence of control branches, control deterministic computations form an important class of probabilistic programs. They arise naturally in the domain of cyber-physical systems, wherein it is important to reason about uncertainty in the physical state of the system due to external disturbances. For instance, all the motivating examples from Section 8.1.1 are all control deterministic.

Figure 8.3 shows a schematic diagram of a physical process whose internal state $\mathbf{x}$ is updated at each time step using the law $\mathbf{x}' = F(\mathbf{x}, \mathbf{u}, \mathbf{w})$ wherein $\mathbf{u}$ is the control applied externally by a controller and $\mathbf{w} \sim \mathcal{D}$ is a stochastic disturbance. We assume that F is a continuous, but possibly nonlinear function. Similarly, the feedback law G is a continuous and possibly nonlinear function $\mathbf{u} = G(\mathbf{x})$. Given the uncertainty in the initial state $\mathbf{x} \sim X_0$, our goal is to evaluate bounds on the probability that $\mathbf{x}(T) \models \varphi$ for some assertion φ specifying the unsafe set of states.

8.4.2 Symbolic Execution Using Affine Forms

In this section, we briefly describe an approach that symbolically executes a control deterministic program based on affine forms defined in previous work by Bouissou et al. (2012) and subsequently by Bouissou et al. (2016). Affine forms abstract how the variables in a computation depend as an affine function of the distributions that affect the program execution. However, many programs of interest are not affine. To handle these, affine forms are abstracted in two ways: (a) affine forms involve *abstract noise symbols* that represent a set of possible distributions; (b) the symbols in the affine form can be correlated.

Let us define a set of noise symbols $Y = \{y_1, y_2, \ldots\}$, wherein each symbol y_i has an associated set of support in the form of an interval $[\ell_i, u_i]$, intervals for expectation $\mathbb{E}(y_i) \in [a_i, b_i]$, and possibly, a list of intervals for its higher moments $\mathbb{E}(y_i^2), \mathbb{E}(y_i^3), \cdots, \mathbb{E}(y_i^k)$.

Definition 8.16 (Environment). An environment $\mathcal{E} := \langle Y, \mathsf{support}, \mathbb{E}(\cdot), G \rangle$ is given by a finite set of noise symbols $Y = \{y_1, \ldots, y_n\}$, a map support from each symbol y_j to an interval I_j indicating its set of support, a map that associates some select monomial terms $m := y_1^{k_1} \cdots y_n^{k_n}$ to intervals that bound their expectations $\mathbb{E}(m)$, and finally, a directed graph G whose vertices are the symbols in Y and edges (y_i, y_j) denote that the variable y_j is derived as a function of y_i (and possibly other variables in Y).

An environment $\mathcal{E}$ represents a set of distributions $\mathcal{D}$ over the noise symbols in Y such that the sets of support and expectations all lie in the intervals defined by the environment. The graph G defines the functional dependence or independence within pairs of random variables using the following definition.

Definition 8.17 (Probabilistic Dependence). Noise symbols y_i and y_j are *probabilistically dependent* random variables if there exists y_k such that there are paths from y_k to y_i and y_j to y_k in the graph G. Otherwise, y_i, y_j represent mutually independent random variables.

An environment $\mathcal{E}$ with noise symbols $\mathbf{y} := (y_1, \ldots, y_n)$ corresponds to a set of possible random vectors $Y := (Y_1, \ldots, Y_n)$ that conform to the following constraints: (a) $(Y_1, \ldots, Y_n)$ must range over the set of support $\mathsf{support}(y_1) \times \cdots \times \mathsf{support}(y_n)$; (b) the moment vectors lie in the appropriate ranges defined by the environment; and, (c) if noise symbols y_i, y_j are probabilistically independent according to the dependence graph G, the corresponding random variables Y_i, Y_j are mutually independent. Otherwise, they are "arbitrarily" correlated while still respecting the range and moment constraints above.

Given an environment $\mathcal{E}$, affine forms are affine expressions over its noise symbols.

Definition 8.18 (Affine Forms). An affine form over an environment $\mathcal{E}$ is an expression of the form

$$a_0 + a_1 y_1 + \cdots + a_n y_n$$

where $a_0, a_1, \ldots, a_n$ are interval coefficients, and $y_1, \ldots, y_n$ are the corresponding noise symbols.

We assume that $\mathsf{support}(y_j)$ is bounded for all $y_j \in Y$. We, however, handle variables with unbounded set of support through the truncation procedure described in section 8.3.2. Another important aspect is that of missing moment information. We may use interval arithmetic to estimate missing information given the information on the set of support and available moments.

Lemma 8.19. *Let X be a (univariate) random variable whose set of support is the interval $I \subseteq \mathbb{R}$. It follows that $\mathbb{E}(X) \in I$.*

Let X_1, X_2 be two random variables. The following inequality holds:

$$-\sqrt{\mathbb{E}(X_1^2)\mathbb{E}(X_2^2)} \le \mathbb{E}(X_1 X_2) \le \sqrt{\mathbb{E}(X_1^2)\mathbb{E}(X_2^2)}.$$

The inequality above follows from the Cauchy–Schwarz inequality. Further details on how missing moment information is inferred are explained in Bouissou et al. (2016).

Example 8.20. First we will provide an illustrative example of an environment $\mathcal{E}$. Let $Y = \{y_1, y_2, y_3\}$ be a set of noise symbols such that $\mathsf{support}(y_1) = [-1, 1]$, $\mathsf{support}(y_2) = [0, 2]$ and $\mathsf{support}(y_3) = [-2, 3]$. The corresponding expectations are

$$\mathbb{E}(y_1) = [-0.1, 0.1], \ \mathbb{E}(y_2) = [1.1, 1.3], \ \mathbb{E}(y_3) = [-0.5, -0.3].$$

Furthermore, assume we are provided the higher order moment information

$$\mathbb{E}(y_1^2) = [0.2, 0.5], \ \mathbb{E}(y_1 y_2) = [-0.4, 0.6], \ \mathbb{E}(y_3^2) = [0.4, 0.6].$$

The dependency graph has the edges (y_1, y_3) indicating that y_3 is functionally dependent on y_1, which in turn are both pairwise independent of y_2.

An example affine form in this environment $\mathcal{E}$ is

$$\eta_1 := [0.5, 1.5] + [2.0, 2.01]y_1 - [2.8, 3.2]y_3.$$

Semantically, an affine form $f(\mathbf{y}) := a_0 + \sum_{i=1}^n a_i y_i$ represents a set of linear expressions $\llbracket f(\mathbf{y}) \rrbracket$ over $\mathbf{y}$:

$$\llbracket f(\mathbf{y}) \rrbracket := \left\{ r_0 + \sum_{i=1}^n r_i Y_i \mid r_i \in a_i, (Y_1, \ldots, Y_n) \in \llbracket \mathcal{E} \rrbracket \right\}.$$

Given affine forms, we can define a calculus that describes how basic operations such as sums, differences, products and application of continuous (and k-times differentiable) functions are carried out over these affine forms.

Sums, Differences and Products: Let f_1, f_2 be affine forms in an environment $\mathcal{E}$ given by $f_1 := \mathbf{a}^t \mathbf{y} + a_0$ and $f_2 := \mathbf{b}^t \mathbf{y} + b_0$. We define the sum $f_1 \oplus f_2$ to be the affine form $(\mathbf{a} + \mathbf{b})^t \mathbf{y} + (a_0 + b_0)$. Likewise, let λ be a real number. The affine form λf_1 is given by $(\lambda \mathbf{a})^t \mathbf{y} + \lambda a_0$.

We now define the product of two forms $f_1 \otimes f_2$.

$$f_1 \otimes f_2 = a_0 b_0 + a_0 f_2 + b_0 f_1 + \mathsf{approx}\left(\sum_{i=1}^n \sum_{j=1}^n a_i a_j y_i y_j \right).$$

Note that $a_0 b_0, a_0 f_2, b_0 f_1$ and $a_i a_j$ denote the result of multiplying two intervals. The product of two intervals $[l_i, u_i][l_j, u_j]$ is defined as the interval

$$[\min(l_i l_j, u_i l_j, l_i u_j, u_i l_j), \max(l_i l_j, u_i l_j, l_i u_j, u_i l_j)]$$

(see Moore et al., 2009).

The product of two affine forms $f_1 \otimes f_2$ separates the affine and linear parts of this summation from the nonlinear part that must be approximated to preserve the affine form. To this end, we define a function approx that replaces the nonlinear terms by a collection of fresh random variables. In particular, we add a fresh random variable y_{ij} to approximate the product term $y_i y_j$.

Dependencies: We add the dependency edges (y_{ij}, y_i) and (y_{ij}, y_j) to the graph G to denote the newly defined functional dependences.

Set of Support: The set of support for y_{ij} is the interval product of the set of supports for y_i, y_j, respectively. In particular if $i = j$, we compute the set of support for y_i^2. Interval I_{ij} will represent the set of support for y_{ij}.

Moments: The moments of y_{ij} are derived from those of y_i and y_j, as follows.

Case-1 $(i = j)$. If $i = j$, we have that the $\mathbb{E}(y_{ij}^p) = \mathbb{E}(y_i^{2p})$. Therefore, the even moments of y_i are taken to provide the moments for y_{ij}. However, since we assume that only the first k moments of y_i are available, we have that the first $\frac{k}{2}$ moments of y_{ij} are available, in general. To fill in the remaining moments, we approximate using intervals as follows: $\mathbb{E}(y_{ij}^r) \in I_{ij}^r$. While this approximation is often crude, this is a tradeoff induced by our inability to store infinitely many moments for the noise symbols.

Case-2 $(i \neq j)$. If $i \neq j$, we have that $\mathbb{E}(y_{ij}^p) = \mathbb{E}(y_i^p y_j^p)$. If y_i, y_j form an independent pair, this reduces back to $\mathbb{E}(y_i^p)\mathbb{E}(y_j^p)$. Thus, in this instance, we can fill in all k moments directly as entry-wise products of the moments of y_i and y_j. Otherwise, they are dependent, so we use the Cauchy–Schwarz inequality (see Lemma 8.19): $-\sqrt{\mathbb{E}(y_i^{2p})\mathbb{E}(y_j^{2p})} \leq \mathbb{E}(y_{ij}^p) \leq \sqrt{\mathbb{E}(y_i^{2p})\mathbb{E}(y_j^{2p})}$, and the interval approximation $\mathbb{E}(y_{ij}^p) \in I_{ij}^p$.

Continuous Functions: Let $g(\mathbf{y})$ be a continuous and $(m + 1)$-times differentiable function of $\mathbf{y}$, where $\mathbf{y}$ belongs to a compact interval J. The Taylor expansion of g around a point $\mathbf{y}_0 \in \text{interior}(J)$ allows us to approximate g as a polynomial:

$$g(\mathbf{y}) = g(\mathbf{y}_0) + Dg(\mathbf{y}_0)(\mathbf{y} - \mathbf{y}_0) + \sum_{2 \leq |\alpha|_1 \leq m} \frac{D^\alpha g(\mathbf{y}_0)(\mathbf{y} - \mathbf{y}_0)^\alpha}{\alpha!} + R_g^{m+1},$$

wherein Dg denotes the vector of partial derivatives $(\frac{\partial g}{\partial y_j})_{j=1,\ldots,n}$; $\alpha := (d_1,\ldots,d_n)$ ranges over all vector of indices, where $d_i \in \mathbb{N}$ is a natural number; $|\alpha|_1 := \sum_{i=1}^{n} d_i$; $\alpha! = d_1! d_2! \cdots d_n!$; $D^\alpha g$ denotes the partial derivative $\frac{\partial^{d_1} g \cdots \partial^{d_n} g}{\partial y_1^{d_1} \cdots \partial y_n^{d_n}}$; and $(\mathbf{y} - \mathbf{y}_0)^\alpha :=$ $\prod_{j=1}^{n} (y_j - y_{0,j})^{d_j}$. Finally, R_g^{m+1} is an interval-valued *Lagrange remainder*:

$$R_g^{m+1} \in \left\{ \sum_{|\alpha|_1 = m+1} \frac{D^\alpha g(\mathbf{z})}{\alpha!} (\mathbf{z} - \mathbf{y}_0)^{m+1} \mid \mathbf{z} \in J \right\}.$$

This computation is automated in our implementation through a combination of standard ideas from automatic differentiation and interval arithmetic (see Moore et al., 2009).

Since we have discussed sums and products of affine forms, the Taylor approximation may be evaluated entirely using affine forms.

The remainder is handled using a fresh noise symbol $y_g^{(m+1)}$. Its set of support is R_g^{m+1} and moments are estimated based on this interval. The newly added noise symbol is functionally dependent on all variables $\mathbf{y}$ that appear in $g(\mathbf{y})$. These dependencies are added to the graph G.

The Taylor expansion allows us to approximate continuous functions including rational and trigonometric functions of these random variables.

Example 8.21. We illustrate this by computing the sine of an affine form. Let y_1 be a noise symbol over the interval $[-0.2, 0.2]$ with the moments

$$(\mathbb{E}(y_1) = 0, \quad \mathbb{E}(y_1^2) \in [0.004, 0.006], \quad \mathbb{E}(y_1^3) = 0,$$
$$\mathbb{E}(y_1^4) \in [6 \times 10^{-5}, 8 \times 10^{-5}], \quad \mathbb{E}(y_1^5) = 0).$$

We consider the form $\sin(y_1)$. Using a Taylor series expansion around $y_1 = 0$, we obtain

$$\sin(y_1) = y_1 - \frac{1}{3!} y_1^3 + [-1.3 \times 10^{-5}, 1.4 \times 10^{-5}].$$

We introduce a fresh variable y_2 to replace y_1^3 and a fresh variable y_3 for the remainder interval $I_3 := [-1.3 \times 10^{-5}, 1.4 \times 10^{-5}]$.

Dependencies: We add the edges (y_2, y_1) and (y_3, y_1) to G.

Sets of Support: $I_2 := [-0.008, 0.008]$ and $I_3 := [-1.3 \times 10^{-5}, 1.4 \times 10^{-5}]$.

Moments: $\mathbb{E}(y_2) = \mathbb{E}(y_1^3) = 0$. Further moments are computed using interval arithmetic. The moment vector $I(m_2)$ is $(0, [0, 64 \times 10^{-6}], [-512 \times 10^{-9}, 512 \times 10^{-9}], \ldots)$. For y_3, the moment vector

$$I(m_3) := (I_3, \text{square}(I_3), \text{cube}(I_3), \ldots).$$

The resulting affine form for $\sin(y_1)$ is $[1,1]y_1 - [0.16, 0.17]y_2 + [1,1]y_3$.

8.4.3 *Approximating Computations using Affine Forms*

Having developed a calculus of affine forms, we may directly apply it to propagate uncertainties across control deterministic computations. Let $X = \{x_1, \ldots, x_p\}$ be a set of *program variables* collectively written as $\mathbf{x}$ with an initial value $\mathbf{x}_0$. Our semantics consist of a tuple $(\mathcal{E}, \eta)$ wherein $\mathcal{E}$ is an environment and $\eta := X \rightarrow \mathsf{AffineForms}(\mathcal{E})$ maps each variable $x_i \in X$ to an affine form over $\mathcal{E}$. The initial environment $\mathcal{E}_0$ has no noise symbols and an empty dependence graph. The initial mapping η_0 associates each x_i with the constant $x_{i,0}$. The basic operations are of two types: (a) assignment to a fresh random variable, and (b) assignment to a function over existing variables.

Random Number Generation: This operation is of the form $x_i := \mathsf{rand}(I, \mathbf{m})$, wherein I denotes the set of support interval for the new random variable, and $\mathbf{m}$ denotes a vector of moments for the generated random variable. The operational rule is $(\mathcal{E}, \eta) \xrightarrow{x_i := \mathsf{rand}(I, \mathbf{m})} (\mathcal{E}', \eta')$, wherein the environment $\mathcal{E}'$ extends $\mathcal{E}$ by a fresh random variable y whose set of support is given by I and moments by $\mathbf{m}$. The dependence graph is extended by adding a new node corresponding to y but without any new edges since freshly generated random numbers are assumed independent. However, if the newly generated random variable is dependent on some previous symbols, such a dependency is also easily captured in our framework.

Assignment: The assignment operation is of the form $x_i \leftarrow g(\mathbf{x})$, assigning x_i to a continuous and $(j + 1)$-times differentiable function $g(\mathbf{x})$. The operational rule has the form $(\mathcal{E}, \eta) \xrightarrow{x_i \leftarrow g(\mathbf{x})} (\mathcal{E}', \eta')$. First, we compute an affine form f_g that approximates the function $g(\eta(x_1), \ldots, \eta(x_n))$. Let Y_g denote a set of fresh symbols generated by this approximation with new dependence edges E_g. The environment $\mathcal{E}'$ extends $\mathcal{E}$ with the addition of the new symbols Y_g and and new dependence edges E_g. The new map is $\eta' := \eta[x_i \mapsto f_g]$.

Let C be a computation defined by a sequence of random number generation and assignment operations. Starting from the initial environment $(\mathcal{E}_0, \eta_0)$ and applying the rules above, we obtain a final environment $(\mathcal{E}, \eta)$. However, our main goal is to answer *queries* such as $\mathbb{P}(x_j \in I_j)$ that seek the probability that a particular variable x_j belongs to an interval I_j. This directly translates to a query involving the affine form $\eta(x_j)$ which may involve a prohibitively large number of noise symbols that may be correlated according to the dependence graph G.

Example 8.22 (2D robotic end effector). Consider a simplified version of the 2D robotic end effector model presented in Example 8.1, yielding an affine form with 6900 noise symbols for the variable x that we care about. The computation required 15 seconds of computational time on a laptop with Intel 3.1 core i7 processor and 16GB RAM.

$$x = \begin{cases} [8.06365, 8.06441] + [1, 1] * y_0 + [0.984807, 0.984808] * y_2 + \\ [0.0303060, 0.0303069] * y_3 + [-1, -1] * y_4 + \\ [0.0303060, 0.0303069] * y_5 + [-1, -1] * y_6 + \\ [0.499997, 0.500026] * y_9 + \\ [0.90686, 0.906894] * y_{10} + \\ \cdots \\ [0.119382, 0.119386] * y_{6885} + [-1, -1] * y_{6886} + [0.984807, 0.984808] * y_{6889} \\ + [0.0303060, 0.0303069] * y_{6890} + [-1, -1] * y_{6891} + [0.0303060, 0.0303069] * y_{6892} + \\ [-1, -1] * y_{6893} + [1, 1] * y_{6896} + [-1, -1] * y_{6898} + [-1, -1] * y_{6899} \end{cases}$$

Based on the affine form, we can bound the support for $x \in [213.19, 326.12]$ and its expectation as $\mathbb{E}(x) \in [268.61, 270.7]$, and the second central moment (variance) in the range $[0.12, 0.28]$.

8.4.4 Applying Concentration of Measure Inequalities

We will now apply the results from section 8.3 to analyzing the affine forms generated from control deterministic programs. First, we note that each affine form is a sum of possibly dependent random variables with information about sets of support, first and possibly higher order moments available. Thus, many strategies for applying the results in the previous section are available. These are summarized in detail in Bouissou et al. (2016). In what follows, we will illustrate the application of these results directly to some of the motivating examples from Section 8.1 using a prototype implementation of the ideas mentioned thus far. The prototype implementation in the C++ language interprets a given program using a library of affine forms. Next, it mechanizes the process of answering queries by analyzing the dependency graph. The automatic analysis uses a series of approaches that include:

(i) The application of Chernoff–Hoeffding bounds by using a *compaction* procedure that combines multiple noise symbols into a single one, so that the affine forms are all summations over independent random variables. Similarly, Bernstein inequalities are used whenever second moments are consistently available.

(ii) The application of the chromatic number bound Janson (2004), using $1 + \Delta$ as an approximation for the fractional chromatic number, wherein Δ is the maximum degree of any node in the dependence graph.

Example 8.23 (2D end effector). Resuming the analysis in Ex. 8.22, we can automate the application of various approaches discussed thus far, starting with the Chernoff–Hoeffding bounds.

The original affine form has 6900 variables which are not all mutually independent. To obtain mutual independence, we analyze the strongly connected components of the undirected dependence graph yielding 3100 different components such that variables in distinct components are pairwise independent. Using this, we compact the affine form into one involving 3100 random variables and apply Chernoff–Hoeffding

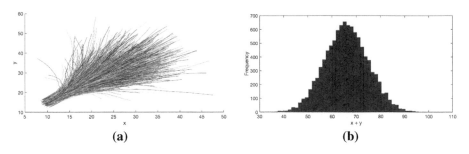

Figure 8.4 **(a)** Simulated (x, y) positions of UAV over the time horizon $[0, 3.6]$ seconds and **(b)** Histogram of final position $x(3.6) + y(3.6)$.

bounds. This is performed by computing the strongly connected components (SCC) of the dependency graph G, and taking the set of support and mean of the sum of random variables belonging to each SCC. Note that Chernoff–Hoeffding bounds can be applied since noise symbols belonging to different SCCs are mutually independent.

This yields

$$\mathbb{P}(x \geq 277) \leq \exp\left(\frac{-(268.6170484 - 277)^2}{7.486493141}\right) \leq 8.38 \times 10^{-5}.$$

Applying Bernstein's inequality yields:

$$\mathbb{P}(X \leq t) \leq \exp\left(\frac{-(268.6170484 - t)^2}{0.4868099186 + 0.3333 * (t - 286.6170484)}\right) \leq 5.18 \times 10^{-10}.$$

The chromatic number bound of Janson (2004) computes a weaker bound given by 0.106.

Now, we will consider the example of a fixed-wing UAV collision probability estimation from Ex. 8.3.

Example 8.24. Consider a prediction horizon of $t = 20 \times 0.18 = 3.6$ seconds. Our goal is to run the model twenty times, starting from a given initial state and query the probability that $x + y \geq 165$. We obtain an affine form for $x + y$ with 88 noise symbols. The mean value $\mathbb{E}(x + y) \in [65.85, 65.86]$ matches very well with the empirical estimate of 65.84 from 10,000 simulations. Furthermore, the variance is estimated in the range $[78.95, 78.96]$ which also matches quite well with the empirical variance of 78.76 obtained from 10,000 simulations. Some of the trajectories of the system and the scatter plot with 10000 end points are shown in Figure 8.4.

Using the Bernstein inequality, we obtain the estimate

$$\mathbb{P}(x + y \geq 165) \leq 9.6 \times 10^{-4}.$$

and more generally,

$$\mathbb{P}(x + y \geq 65.859 + t) \leq \exp\left(\frac{-t^2}{157.8869 + 12.57t}\right).$$

8.5 Super-martingales and Concentration of Measure

In the final section, we look at concentration of measure inequalities using super-martingales. A previous chapter in the same volume by Chatterjee et al adapts the concept of a super-martingales to prove termination. We will recall the definition and show that super-martingales are also useful for proving concentration. First let us recall conditional expectations. Let X, Y be two random variables. The conditional expectation $\mathbb{E}(X|Y)$ is defined as a function $f(y)$ defined over the support of the distribution Y such that

$$f(y) = \int_X x \, d\mathbb{P}(x|y)$$

In other words, for each value of y, the expectation integrates x over the conditional distribution of x given y.

Definition 8.25 (Martingales, Super- and Sub-Martingales). A sequence of random variables $X_0, X_1, \ldots, X_n$ is a *martingale* if and only if for each $i \geq 0$,

$$\mathbb{E}(X_{i+1} \mid X_i, \ldots, X_0) = X_i.$$

A super-martingale satisfies the condition

$$\mathbb{E}(X_{i+1} \mid X_i, \ldots, X_0) \leq X_i.$$

A *sub-martingale* satisfies the inequality:

$$\mathbb{E}(X_{i+1} \mid X_i, \ldots, X_0) \geq X_i.$$

A martingale is, therefore, both a super-martingale and a sub-martingale. Typically, the stochastic processes that are studied arise from Markovian models such as probabilistic programs wherein the next state distribution depends on just the current state. Thus, the conditional expectation $\mathbb{E}(X_{i+1} \mid X_i, \ldots, X_0)$ is written as $\mathbb{E}(X_{i+1} \mid X_i)$.

Example 8.26. Consider a random walk involving $x(t) \in \mathbb{Z}$ that is updated as

$$x(t + 1) = \begin{cases} x(t) + 1 & \text{with probability } \frac{1}{2} \\ x(t) - 1 & \text{with probability } \frac{1}{2} \end{cases}$$

It is easy to see that $x(t)$ is a martingale since

$$\mathbb{E}(x(t + 1) \mid x(t)) = \frac{1}{2}(x(t) + 1) + \frac{1}{2}(x(t) - 1) = x(t).$$

It is easy to see that a martingale is always a super-martingale, but not necessarily vice-versa. Another important observation is that often a stochastic process is not a (super-) martingale itself. However, another process built, for instance, by computing a function of the original process forms a (super-) martingale.

Example 8.27. Consider a different scenario wherein $x(t) \in \mathbb{R}$:

$$x(t + 1) = \begin{cases} 0.8x(t) & \text{with probability } \frac{1}{2} \\ 1.1x(t) & \text{with probability } \frac{1}{2} \end{cases}$$

Here, $x(t)$ is neither a martingale or a super-martingale. Note though that $y(t) = x(t)^2$ is a super-martingale:

$$\mathbb{E}(y(t + 1) \mid x(t)) = \frac{1}{2}0.8^2 y(t) + \frac{1}{2}1.1^2 y(t) = 0.925 y(t) \le y(t).$$

Some of the constructions that have been previously encountered such as the McDiarmid's Inequality (Theorem 8.11) involve a martingale under the hood.

Example 8.28 (Doob Martingale). Let $f(x_1, \ldots, x_n)$ be a function with n inputs which are drawn from independent random variables $X_1, \ldots, X_n$.

Consider the stochastic process

$$Y_i = \mathbb{E}_{X_{i+1}, \ldots, X_n}(f(X_1, \ldots, X_i, X_{i+1}, \ldots, X_n)),$$

for $i = 0, \ldots, n$. Note that each Y_i is a function of $X_1, \ldots, X_i$ while taking expectations over the remaining arguments. As a result Y_0 is the expected value of f under all its inputs, Y_i for $i > 0$ fixes random samples for the arguments indexed from 1 to i, and Y_n is the function f computed over some random sample of all the arguments.

Note that for every $i < n$, it is easy to show that

$$\mathbb{E}(Y_{i+1} \mid X_i, \ldots, X_1) = Y_i .$$

This construction can be achieved for any function f and is called Doob martingale. However, also note the independence requirements for the random variables $X_1, \ldots, X_n$.

Super-martingales from programs: As previously noted in chapter on termination, we seek expressions involving variables of the programs that form super-martingales.

Consider the program shown in Figure 8.5 (taken from our previous work (Chakarov and Sankaranarayanan, 2013)), wherein the position of an underwater vehicle (x, y) is updated at each step through a command that can be randomly chosen direction or just staying in one position. Based on this command, the actual position changes through a noisy execution of the command. However, at the same time, the estimation of the current position is updated. The question is how far the estimate deviates from

```
 1  x, y, estX, estY = 0, 0, 0, 0
 2  dx, dy, dxc, dyc = 0, 0, 0, 0
 3  N = 500
 4  for i in range(N):
 5      cmd = choice {N:0.1, S:0.1, E:0.1, W:0.1, NE:0.1, SE:0.1, NW: 0.1,
 6      SW: 0.1, Stay: 0.2}
 7      if (cmd == 'N'):
 8          dxc, dyc = 0, Uniform(1,2)
 9      elif (cmd == 'S'):
10          dxc, dyc = 0, Uniform(-2, -1)
11      elif (cmd == 'E'):
12          dxc, dyc = Uniform(1,2), 0
13      ...
14      else // cmd == 'Stay'
15          dxc, dyc = 0,0
16      dx = dxc + Uniform(-0.05, 0.05)
17      dy = dyc + Uniform(-0.05, 0.05)
18      x = x + dx
19      y = y + dy
20      estX = estX + dxc
21      estY = estY + dyc
22  assert( |x - estX| >= 3)
```

Figure 8.5 Program simulating a sequence of moves by a submarine, where (x, y) model the true position, dxc, dyc model the commanded change in position at any step, and $(estX, estY)$ model the estimates through dead-reckoning.

the true position after $N = 500$ steps? Note that for this program it is straightforward to establish that $x - estX$ and $y - estY$ are super-martingales.

Azuma–Hoeffding's Inequality: Let $\{X_n\}_{n=0}^N$ be a super-martingale that satisfies a bounded difference condition that $|X_{i+1} - X_i| \le c_i$ for each $i \in \{0, \ldots, N-1\}$. It follows that for any $j \in \{0, \ldots, N\}$,

$$\mathbb{P}(X_j - X_0 \ge t) \le \exp\left(\frac{-t^2}{2 \sum_{i=0}^{j-1} c_i^2}\right).$$

Furthermore, if X_n is a sub-martingale, we can conclude that

$$\mathbb{P}(X_j - X_0 \le -t) \le \exp\left(\frac{-t^2}{2 \sum_{i=0}^{j-1} c_i^2}\right).$$

Thus, for a martingale which is a super-martingale as well as a sub-martingale, both inequalities hold.

The Azuma–Hoeffding bound is a concentration of measure inequality much along the lines of previously encountered inequalities in this chapter. For a martingale, it bounds the probability of a large deviation on either side of its starting value. For a super-martingale, the inequality bounds the probability of a large deviation above the starting value. The martingale condition generalizes from the need for independent random variables that was seen for the case of Chernoff–Hoeffding inequalities.

Just as the latter inequalities are applied to random variables with bounded sets of support, we note the condition of bounded change on the (super-) martingale.

Example 8.29. Returning to the dead-reckoning example, we can use the martingale $x - estX$ to estimate the failure probability of the assertion at the end of the program. We note that every loop iteration, the absolute change in this expression is bounded by 0.05. Therefore, we obtain

$$\mathbb{P}(|x - estX| \geq 3) \leq 1.5 \times 10^{-3}.$$

Identical bounds are obtained for the deviation of y from $estY$, as well.

Super-martingales form very powerful approaches for quantitative reasoning. However, two major obstacles block their wider application:

(i) Automatically discovering super-martingale expressions remains a hard problem, especially for nonlinear expressions. However, a variety of approaches summarized in the termination chapter can be used in this regard. At the same time, the applications have been limited thus far.

(ii) The resulting bounds remain conservative since independent random variables are often treated as possibly dependent in the analysis for super-martingales. For instance, treating $x - estX$ as the sum of independent random variables for the dead-reckoning example above yields much more precise bounds.

However, super-martingales remain a promising approach for quantitative reasoning for more complex models that involve programs with branch conditions that cannot be treated with the approaches for control deterministic computations reviewed in the previous sections.

8.6 Conclusion

Thus far, we have examined situations where concentration of measure inequalities can be applied to analyze probabilistic programs. As the reader may have noticed, the key issue lies in mechanizing the process of inference, since even small programs can lead to cumbersome calculations that are hard to carry out by hand. However, there are numerous challenges that must be tackled before the full power of these approaches can be realized. First, most approaches are restricted to reasoning about programs that manipulate real values, whereas programs can exhibit a rich variety of structures ranging from Booleans, strings, lists, trees and graphs. Extending the concentration of measure approach to reason about a richer set of programs is an important area of future work.

Also, one notes that concentration of measure inequalities are often derived to uniformly exploit available moment information such as first moments, second moments and so on. It is easy to envision a process of customization that can derive inequalities based on the available moment information on a "per-problem" basis.

This approach of "designing" new inequalities on demand is yet another promising area of future investigation.

Finally, the broader area of analyzing probabilistic programs has been seemingly disconnected from the problem of Bayesian inference, which is an important concern for probabilistic programming. We note that the problem of model inference and analysis are important steps in the overall "analytics" pipeline. It is therefore natural, as a first step to study these problems separately. The problem of integrating Bayesian inference and subsequent analysis of the "posterior" model/program remains an important unsolved problem. Current approaches that combine Monte-Carlo techniques with their approximate convergence guarantees are not directly compatible with the use of concentration of measure or other symbolic approaches presented here. In this regard, the study of imprecise models of probability distributions, representing sets of distributions, along with concentration of measure inequalities on functions of samples drawn from such models is another promising area of future investigation.

Acknowledgments

The author gratefully acknowledges collaboration with Aleksandar Chakarov, Olivier Bouissou, Eric Goubault and Sylvie Putot that formed the basis for the ideas presented in this chapter. We acknowledge support from the US National Science Foundation (NSF) under awards 1320069, 1527075 and 1815983. All opinions expressed are those of the authors and not necessarily of the NSF.

References

Agha, Gul, and Palmskog, Karl. 2018. A Survey of Statistical Model Checking. *ACM Trans. Model. Comput. Simul.*, **28**(1), 6:1–6:39.

Bernstein, Sergei N. 1924. On a modification of Chebyshev's inequality and of the error formula of Laplace. *Ann. Sci. Inst. Sav. Ukraine, Sect. Math*, **1**.

Boucheron, Stephane, Lugosi, Gabor, and Massart, Pascal. 2016. *Concentration of Measure: An Asymptotic Theory of Independence*. Oxford University Press.

Bouissou, Olivier, Goubault, Eric, Goubault-Larrecq, Jean, and Putot, Sylvie. 2012. A generalization of P-Boxes to affine arithmetic. *Computing*.

Bouissou, Olivier, Goubault, Eric, Putot, Sylvie, Chakarov, Aleksandar, and Sankaranarayanan, Sriram. 2016. Uncertainty Propagation Using Probabilistic Affine Forms and Concentration of Measure Inequalities. Pages 225–243 of: Chechik, Marsha, and Raskin, Jean-François (eds), *Tools and Algorithms for the Construction and Analysis of Systems*. Springer.

Bournez, Olivier, and Garnier, Florent. 2005. Proving Positive Almost-Sure Termination. Pages 323–337 of: *RTA*. LNCS, vol. 3467. Springer.

Brockwell, P. J., and Davis, R. A. 2009. *Time Series: Theory and Methods*. Springer.

Bucklew, James Antonio. 2004. *Introduction to Rare-Event Simulations*. Springer.

Chakarov, Aleksandar, and Sankaranarayanan, Sriram. 2013. Probabilistic Program

Analysis using Martingales. Pages 511–526 of: *Computer-Aided Verification (CAV)*. LNCS, vol. 8044. Springer.

Chakarov, Aleksandar, Voronin, Yuen-Lam (Vris), and Sankaranarayanan, Sriram. 2016. Deductive Proofs of Almost Sure Persistence and Recurrence Properties. Pages 260–279 of: *Tools and Algorithms for Construction and Analysis of Systems (TACAS)*. LNCS, vol. 9636. Springer.

Chatterjee, Krishnendu, Novotný, Petr, and Zikelic, Dorde. 2017. Stochastic invariants for probabilistic termination. Pages 145–160 of: *ACM Principles of Programming Languages (POPL)*. ACM Press.

Chatterjee, Krishnendu, Fu, Hongfei, Novotný, Petr, and Hasheminezhad, Rouzbeh. 2018. Algorithmic Analysis of Qualitative and Quantitative Termination Problems for Affine Probabilistic Programs. *ACM Trans. Program. Lang. Syst.*, **40**(2), 7:1–7:45.

Clarke, Edmund, Donze, Alexandre, and Legay, Axel. 2009. Statistical Model Checking of Analog Mixed-Signal Circuits With An application to a third order $\Delta - \Sigma$ modulator. Pages 149–163 of: *Hardware and Software: Verification and Testing*. LNCS, vol. 5394/2009.

Cousot, Patrick, and Monerau, Michael. 2012. Probabilistic Abstract Interpretation. Pages 169–193 of: *ESOP*. LNCS, vol. 7211. Springer.

De Loera, J., Dutra, B., Koeppe, M., Moreinis, S., Pinto, G., and Wu, J. 2011. Software for Exact Integration of Polynomials over Polyhedra. *ArXiv e-prints*, July.

Dempster, A.P. 1967. Upper and Lower Probabilities Induced by a Multivalued Mapping. *The Annals of Mathematical Statistics*, **38**(2), 325–339.

Dimitrova, Rayna, Fioriti, Luis María Ferrer, Hermanns, Holger, and Majumdar, Rupak. 2016. Probabilistic CTL[*]: The Deductive Way. Pages 280–296 of: *Proc. TACAS*.

Dubhashi, Devdatt, and Ranjan, Desh. 1998. Balls and Bins: A Study in Negative Dependence. *Random Structures and Algorithms*, **13**(2), 99–124.

Dubhashi, Devdutt, and Panconesi, Alessandro. 2009. *Concentration of Measure for the Analysis of Randomized Algorithms*. Cambridge University Press.

Esparza, Javier, Gaiser, Andreas, and Kiefer, Stefan. 2012. Proving Termination of Probabilistic Programs Using Patterns. Pages 123–138 of: *CAV*. LNCS, vol. 7358. Springer.

Ferson, Scott, Kreinovich, Vladik, Ginzburg, Lev, Myers, David S., and Sentz, Kari. 2003 (January). *Constructing probability boxes and Dempster-Shafer structures*. Tech. rept. SAND2002-4015. Sandia Laboratories.

Fioriti, Luis María Ferrer, and Hermanns, Holger. 2015. Probabilistic Termination: Soundness, Completeness, and Compositionality. Pages 489–501 of: *Proc. Principles of Programming Languages, POPL*. ACM Press.

Geldenhuys, Jaco, Dwyer, Matthew B., and Visser, Willem. 2012. Probabilistic symbolic execution. Pages 166–176 of: *ISSTA*. ACM.

Hoeffding, Wassily. 1963. Probability Inequalities for Sums of Bounded Random Variables. *Journal of the American Statistical Association*, **58**(301), 13–30.

Janson, Svante. 2004. Large deviations for sums of partly dependent random variables. *Random Structures Algorithms*, **24**(3), 234–248.

Jégourel, Cyrille, Legay, Axel, and Sedwards, Sean. 2012. Cross-Entropy Optimisation of Importance Sampling Parameters for Statistical Model Checking. Pages 327–342 of: *CAV*. LNCS, vol. 7358. Springer.

Jha, Sumit Kumar, Clarke, Edmund M., Langmead, Christopher James, Legay, Axel, Platzer, André, and Zuliani, Paolo. 2009. A Bayesian Approach to Model Checking Biological Systems. Pages 218–234 of: *CMSB*. LNCS, vol. 5688. Springer.

Kaminski, Benjamin Lucien, Katoen, Joost-Pieter, Matheja, Christoph, and Olmedo, Federico. 2016. Weakest Precondition Reasoning for Expected Run-Times of Probabilistic Programs. Pages 364–389 of: *European Symposium on Programming (ESOP)*.

Kass, Robert E., and Raftery, Adrian E. 1995. Bayes Factors. *J. Amer. Stat. Assoc.*, **90**(430), 774–795.

Katoen, Joost-Pieter, McIver, Annabelle, Meinicke, Larissa, and Morgan, Carroll. 2010. Linear-Invariant Generation for Probabilistic Programs. Page 390–406 of: *Static Analysis Symposium (SAS)*. LNCS, vol. 6337. Springer.

Kozen, Dexter. 1981. Semantics of Probabilistic Programs. *J. Computer and System Sciences*, **22**, 328–350.

Kwiatkowska, M., Norman, G., and Parker, D. 2011. PRISM 4.0: Verification of Probabilistic Real-time Systems. Pages 585–591 of: *CAV*. LNCS, vol. 6806. Springer.

Mardziel, Piotr, Magill, Stephen, Hicks, Michael, and Srivatsa, Mudhakar. 2011. Dynamic Enforcement of Knowledge-based Security Policies. Pages 114–128 of: *Computer Security Foundations Symposium (CSF)*.

McClain, Deborah A., and Hug, Carl C. 1980. Intravenous Fentanyl Kinetics. *Clinical Pharmacology & Therapeutics*, **28**(1), 106–114.

McDiarmid, Colin. 1989. On the method of bounded differences. *Surveys in Combinatorics*, **141**(1), 148–188.

McElreath, Richard. 2015. *Statistical Rethinking: A Bayesian Course with Examples in R and Stan*. CRC Press.

McIver, Annabelle, and Morgan, Carroll. 2004. *Abstraction, Refinement and Proof for Probabilistic Systems*. Monographs in Computer Science. Springer.

McIver, Annabelle, Morgan, Carroll, Kaminski, Benjamin Lucien, and Katoen, Joost-Pieter. 2018. A new proof rule for almost-sure termination. *PACMPL*, **2**(POPL), 33:1–33:28.

Monniaux, David. 2000. Abstract Interpretation of Probabilistic Semantics. Pages 322–339 of: *Static Analysis Symposium (SAS)*. LNCS, vol. 1824. Springer.

Monniaux, David. 2005. Abstract interpretation of programs as Markov decision processes. *Sci. Comput. Program.*, **58**(1-2), 179–205.

Moore, R. E., Kearfott, R. B., and Cloud, M. J. 2009. *Introduction to Interval Analysis*. SIAM.

Narayanan, Praveen, Carette, Jacques, Romano, Wren, Shan, Chung-chieh, and Zinkov, Robert. 2016. Probabilistic inference by program transformation in Hakaru (system description). Pages 62–79 of: *FLOPS 2016*. Springer.

Parker, David, Norman, Gethin, and Kwiatkowska, Marta. 2006. Game-based Abstraction for Markov Decision Processes. Pages 157–166 of: *QEST'06*. IEEE Press.

Rubinstein, Reuven Y., and Kroese, Dirk P. 2008. *Simulation and the Monte Carlo Method*. Wiley Series in Probability and Mathematical Statistics.

Sankaranarayanan, Sriram, and Fainekos, Georgios E. 2012. Falsification of temporal properties of hybrid systems using the cross-entropy method. Pages 125–134 of: *HSCC*. ACM.

Sankaranarayanan, Sriram, Chakarov, Aleksandar, and Gulwani, Sumit. 2013. Static analysis for probabilistic programs: inferring whole program properties from finitely many paths. Pages 447–458 of: *PLDI*. ACM.

Shafer, Glenn. 1976. *A Mathematical Theory of Evidence*. Princeton University Press.

Shafer, Steven L., Siegel, Lawrence C., Cooke, James E., and Scott, James C. 1988. Testing Computer-controlled Infusion Pumps by Simulation. *Anesthesiology*, **68**, 261–266.

Srinivasan, Rajan. 2002. *Importance Sampling: Applications in Communications and Detection*. Springer.

Wald, A. 1945. Sequential Tests of Statistical Hypotheses. *The Annals of Mathematical Statistics*, **16**(2), 117–186.

Williams, David. 1991. *Probability with Martingales*. Cambridge University Press.

Wingate, David, and Weber, Theophane. 2013. Automated Variational Inference in Probabilistic Programming. *CoRR*, **abs/1301.1299**.

Younes, Håkan L. S., and Simmons, Reid G. 2006. Statistical Probabilistic Model Checking with a Focus on Time-Bounded Properties. *Information & Computation*, **204**(9), 1368–1409.

Yousefi, Mahdi, van Heusden, Klaske, M. Mitchell, Ian, Ansermino, Mark, and Dumont, Guy. 2017. A Formally-Verified Safety System for Closed-Loop Anesthesia. *IFAC-PapersOnLine*, **50**(1), 4424–4429.

9

The Logical Essentials of Bayesian Reasoning

Bart Jacobs
Radboud Universiteit, Nijmegen
Fabio Zanasi
University College London

Abstract: This chapter offers an accessible introduction to the channel-based approach to Bayesian probability theory. This framework rests on algebraic and logical foundations, inspired by the methodologies of programming language semantics. It offers a uniform, structured and expressive language for describing Bayesian phenomena in terms of familiar programming concepts, like channel, predicate transformation and state transformation. The introduction also covers inference in Bayesian networks, which will be modelled by a suitable calculus of string diagrams.

9.1 Introduction

In traditional imperative programming one interprets a program as a function that changes states. Intuitively, the notion of 'state' captures the state of affairs in a computer, as given for instance by the contents of the relevant parts of the computer's memory. More abstractly, a program is interpreted as a *state transformer*. An alternative, logical perspective is to interpret a program as a *predicate transformer*. In that case the program turns one predicate into a new predicate. This works in opposite direction: the program turns a predicate on the 'post-state' into a predicate on the 'pre-state', for instance via the weakest precondition computation. As discovered in the early days of programming semantics, basic relations exists between state transformation and predicate transformation, see for instance Dijkstra and Scholten (1990), Dijkstra (1997), and Proposition 9.11 below.

A similar theory of state and predicate transformation has been developed for probabilistic programming, see Kozen (1981, 1985). This approach has been generalised and re-formulated in recent years in categorical terms, typically using so-called Kleisli categories, in Jacobs (2017), and more generally via the notion of

[a] From *Foundations of Probabilistic Programming*, edited by Gilles Barthe, Joost-Pieter Katoen and Alexandra Silva published 2020 by Cambridge University Press.

effectus, in Cho et al. (2015). Category theory provides a fundamental language for the semantics of programming languages. This is clear in approaches based on domain theory. For instance, many constructions for types in programming languages have categorical counterparts, like (co)products, exponentials, and initial algebras (and final coalgebras) – where these (co)algebras are used for fixed points. These categorical notions come with universal properties that guide the design (syntax) and rules of programming languages.

This use of category theory is well-established in functional programming languages. However, it is less established in probabilistic programming. The description of some of the basic notions of probability theory in categorical terms goes back to the early 1980s (see Giry, 1982) and has seen a steady stream of activities since – see *e.g.* Jones and Plotkin (1989), Jung and Tix (1998), de Vink and Rutten (1999), Bartels et al. (2004), Tix et al. (2005), Varacca and Winskel (2006), Keimel (2008), Keimel and Plotkin (2009), Panangaden (2009), Sokolova (2011), Mislove (2012), Fong (2012), Culbertson and Sturtz (2014), Ścibior et al. (2015), Staton et al. (2016), Ścibior et al. (2018). This categorical perspective is not a goal in itself, but it does offer a structural, implementation-independent way of thinking which is natural for systematic programmers.

This chapter offers an introduction to this principled perspective on probability theory, especially for Bayesian probabilistic programming, based on earlier work of the authors' in this direction, see *e.g.* Jacobs (2011, 2013, 2018b), Jacobs and Zanasi (2016, 2017,?). Even though it is categorically-driven, our exposition does not require any categorical prerequisite. The reader interested in an explicitly categorical description of the framework may consult Jacobs and Zanasi (2016) or Cho and Jacobs (2019).

The fundamental concept will be called *channel*: all the basics of Bayesian probability theory (event, belief revision, Bayesian network, disintegration, ...) will be derived from this single primitive. In analogy with approaches in programming language semantics, channels are formally definable as arrows of a certain Kleisli category: depending on the category of choice, the derived notions instantiate to discrete or to continuous probability theory – and even to quantum probability too, although the quantum world is out of scope here (but see Jacobs and Zanasi, 2016 and Jacobs, 2018b). This setting does not only provide a completely *uniform* mathematical description for a variety of phenomena, but also introduces in Bayesian reasoning fundamental principles of programming theory, such as *compositionality*: channels are composable in a variety of ways, resulting in a structured and modular theory. Furthermore, we argue that the channel-based perspective improves traditional approaches. We will study scenarios in which the established language for describing probabilistic phenomena lacks in flexibility, expressiveness and rigour, while the new foundations disclose the underlying logical structure of phenomena, leading to new insights.

- Section 9.2 gives an informal overview of the channel-based view on probability theory in terms of a number of perspectives. These perspectives are stated explicitly, in imperative form, imposing how things are – or should be – seen from a channel-based perspective, in contrast to traditional approaches. These perspectives will already informally use the notions of 'state', 'predicate' and 'channel'.
- Section 9.3 commences the formal presentation of the ingredients of the channel-based framework, illustrating the concepts of state and predicate, as special forms of channels.
- Section 9.4 is devoted to conditioning, a key concept of Bayesian probability.
- Sections 9.5 and 9.6 are devoted to channel-based Bayesian inference. First, Section 9.5 explains the use of channels as predicate and state transformers. Then, Section 9.6 illustrates this setup to model inference in a Bayesian network, for the standard 'student' example from Koller and Friedman (2009). This section concludes with a clash of interpretations in an example taken from Barber (2012).
- Section 9.7 introduces a graphical calculus for channels – formally justified by their definition as arrows of a monoidal category. The calculus encompasses and enhances the diagrammatic language of Bayesian networks. It offers an intuitive, yet mathematically rigorous, description of basic phenomena of probability, including conditional independency.
- Section 9.8 uses the tools developed in the previous sections to study the relationship between joint distributions and their representation as Bayesian networks. First, we use the graphical calculus to give a channel-based account of disintegration. Second, we prove the equivalence of inference as performed on joint distributions and as performed in Bayesian networks (Theorem 9.16). The channel perspective explains the different dynamics at work in the two forms of inference, justifying our terminology of *crossover inference* and *transformer inference* respectively.

9.2 Perspectives

This section gives a first, informal view of the channel-based approach, through a series of perspectives. Each of them contains a prescription on how Bayesian phenomena appear in the channel-based perspective, and motivates how the channel language improves more traditional descriptions. These perspectives will informally use the notions of 'state', 'predicate' and 'channel'. To begin, we briefly explain what they are. A more systematic description is given later on.

- What is usually called a discrete probability distribution, we call a *state*. This terminology emphasises the role that distributions play in our programming-oriented framework: they express knowledge of a certain configuration (a state of affairs) that may be transformed by program execution (channels).

  A state/distribution is represented by a convex combination of elements from a set. For instance, on a set $A = \{a, b, c\}$ one can have a state $\frac{1}{3}|a\rangle + \frac{1}{2}|b\rangle + \frac{1}{6}|c\rangle$. The 'ket' notation $|\cdot\rangle$ is syntactic sugar: it has no mathematical meaning, but echoes how states are represented in quantum theory, where our theory may be also instantiated, see Jacobs and Zanasi (2016).

- A 'predicate' on a set A is a function $p\colon A \to 0, 1$. It assigns a probability $pa \in 0, 1$ to each element $a \in A$. Such predicates are often called 'fuzzy'. When $pa \in \{0, 1\}$, so that either $pa = 0$ or $pa = 1$, for each $a \in A$ the predicate is called sharp. A sharp predicate is traditionally called an event, and corresponds to a subset of A. For such a subset $E \subseteq A$ we write $\mathbf{1}_E\colon A \to 0, 1$ for the corresponding characteristic function (or sharp predicate), given by $\mathbf{1}_E a = 1$ if $a \in E$ and $\mathbf{1}_E a = 0$ if $a \notin E$. For the special case of a singleton set/event we write $\mathbf{1}_a$ instead of $\mathbf{1}_{\{a\}}$.

  Similarly to the case of states, our terminology draws an analogy with programming language semantics. There is a duality between states and predicates, which goes beyond the scope of this introduction – so the interested reader is referred to Jacobs (2017).

- A 'channel' $A \dashrightarrow B$ from a set A to another set B is an A-indexed collection $(\omega_a)_{a\in A}$ of states ω_a on the set B. Alternatively, it is a function $a \mapsto \omega_a$ that sends each element $a \in A$ to a distribution on B. For A and B finite, yet another equivalent description is as a stochastic matrix with $|A|$ columns and $|B|$ rows.

  Channels are the pivot of our theory: states, predicates, and – as we shall see in Section 9.6 – also Bayesian networks can be seen as particular cases of a channel. More specifically, a state ω on B can be seen as a channel $f\colon \{\star\} \dashrightarrow B$ with source the one-element set $\{\star\}$, defined by $f\star = \omega$. A predicate $p\colon A \to 0, 1$ can be seen as a channel $A \dashrightarrow \{0, 1\}$ that assigns to $a \in A$ the state $pa|1\rangle + 1 - pa|0\rangle$.

9.2.1 The state is made explicit

Our first perspective elaborates on the observation that, in traditional probability, it is custom to leave the probability distribution implicit, for instance in describing the probability $\mathrm{Pr}E$ of an event $E = \{a, c\} \subseteq A$. This is justified because this distribution, say $\omega = \frac{1}{3}|a\rangle + \frac{1}{2}|b\rangle + \frac{1}{6}|c\rangle$, is typically fixed, so that carrying it around explicitly, as in $\mathrm{Pr}_\omega E$, burdens the notation. In contrast, in probabilistic programming, programs act on distributions (states) and change them with every step. Hence in our framework it makes sense to use a richer notation, where states/distributions have a more prominent role.

First, pursuing a more abstract, logical viewpoint, we introduce notation $\models$ in place of Pr. For an arbitrary state ω on a set A and a predicate $p \colon A \to 0, 1$ on the same set A, the *validity* $\omega \models p$ of p in ω is the number in $0, 1$ given by:

$$\omega \models p := \sum_{a \in A} \omega a \cdot pa. \tag{9.1}$$

When we identify an event (sharp predicate) $E \subseteq A$ with its characteristic function $\mathbf{1}_E \colon A \to 0, 1$, we have $\omega \models \mathbf{1}_E = \mathrm{Pr}_\omega E = \frac{1}{2}$. The enhanced notation allows to distinguish this from the probability of E wrt. an alternative state $\psi = \frac{1}{4}|b\rangle + \frac{3}{4}|c\rangle$, written $\psi \models \mathbf{1}_E = \frac{3}{4}$.

Once we start treating states as explicit entities, we can give proper attention to basic operations on states, like parallel composition $\otimes$, marginalisation, and convex combination. These operations will be elaborated below in Section 9.3.

9.2.2 Conditional probability is state update with a predicate

Traditionally, conditional probability is described as $\mathrm{Pr}B \mid A$, capturing the probability of event B given event A. This notation is unfortunate, certainly in combination with the notation $\mathrm{Pr}B$ for the probability of event B. It suggests that conditioning $\mid$ is an operation on events, and that the probability $\mathrm{Pr} \cdot$ of the resulting event $B \mid A$ is computed. This perspective is sometimes called 'measure-free conditioning', see Dubois and Prade (1990). The fact that states are left implicit, see the previous point 9.2.1, further contributes to the confusion.

In the view advocated here, conditioning is an operation that updates a state ω in the light of evidence in the form of a predicate p. This is well-defined when ω and p have the same underlying set A, and when the validity $\omega \models p$ is non-zero. We shall then write $\omega|_p$ for the state "ω given p", see Section 9.4 for more details. We emphasise that the validity $\mathrm{Pr}B \mid A$ in state ω can now be expressed as $\omega|_{\mathbf{1}_A} \models \mathbf{1}_B$. It is the validity of B in the state where the evidence A is incorporated.

9.2.3 State/predicate transformation are basic operations

The following notation $\mathrm{Pr}X = a$ often occurs in traditional probability theory. What does it mean, and what is assumed? On close reading we find that the following data are involved.

- A set, often called sample space, Ω with a state/distribution ω on it; please note that ω is not an element of Ω but a probability distribution over elements of Ω;
- A stochastic (or random) variable, $X \colon \Omega \to A$, for some set A of outcomes;

- An element $a \in A$ with associated event $X^{-1}a = \{z \in \Omega \mid Xz = a\} \subseteq \Omega$;
- The probability $\mathrm{Pr}X = a$ is then the validity of the latter event in the state ω, that is, it is $\omega \models \mathbf{1}_{X^{-1}a}$.

A stochast is a special kind of channel (namely a deterministic one). The operation $X^{-1}a$ will be described more systematically as 'predicate transformation' $X \ll \mathbf{1}_a$ along the channel X. It turns the (singleton, sharp) predicate $\mathbf{1}_a$ on A into a predicate on Ω. In fact, $X \ll \mathbf{1}_a$ can be seen as just function composition $\Omega \to A \to 0,1$. Since $X \ll \mathbf{1}_a$ is now a predicate on Ω, the probability $\mathrm{Pr}X = a$ can be described more explicitly as validity: $\omega \models X \ll \mathbf{1}_a$. More generally, for an event E on A we would then determine the probability $\mathrm{Pr}X \in E$ as $\omega \models X \ll E$.

One can use the channel X also for 'state transformation'. In this way one transforms the state ω on Ω into a state $X \gg \omega$ on A. This operation $\gg$ is sometimes (aptly) called pushforward, and $X \gg \omega$ is the pushforward distribution. The probability $\mathrm{Pr}X = a$ can equivalently be described as validity $X \gg \omega \models \mathbf{1}_a$.

In Section 9.5 we elaborate on channels. One of our findings will be that the probabilities $\omega \models c \ll p$ and $c \gg \omega \models p$ are always the same – for a channel c from A to B, a state ω on A, and a predicate p on B.

Moreover, we can profitably combine predicate transformation $\ll$ and state transformation $\gg$ with conditioning of states from point 9.2.2. As will be elaborated later on, we can distinguish the following two basic combinations of conditioning and transformation, with the associated terminology.

notation	action	terminology
$\omega\vert_{c \ll q}$	first do predicate transformation $\ll$, then update the state	evidential reasoning, or explanation, or backward inference
$c \gg (\omega\vert_p)$	first update the state, then do state transformation $\gg$,	causal reasoning, or prediction, or forward inference

9.2.4 Channels are used as probabilistic functions

We have already mentioned the notation $c \colon A \rightsquigarrow B$ to describe a channel c from A to B. Recall that such a channel produces a state ca on B for each element $a \in A$. It turns out that there is a special way to compose channels: for $c \colon A \rightsquigarrow B$ and $d \colon B \rightsquigarrow C$ we can form a composite channel $d \circ c \colon A \rightsquigarrow C$, understood as "$d$ after c". We can define it via state transformation as $d \circ ca = d \gg ca$. It is not hard to check that $\circ$ is associative, and that there are identity maps id $: A \dashrightarrow A$, given by id$a = 1|a\rangle$. They form unit elements for channel composition $\circ$.

Abstractly, channels form morphisms in a 'category'. The concept of a category generalises the idea of sets and functions between them, to objects and morphisms between them. These morphisms in a category need not be actual functions, but they must be composable (and have units). Such morphisms can be used to capture different forms of computation, like non-deterministic, or probabilistic (via channels). Here we shall not use categorical machinery, but use the relevant properties in more concrete form. For instance, composition $\circ$ of channels interacts appropriately with state transformation and with predicate transformation, as in:

$$d \circ c \gg \omega = d \gg c \gg \omega \qquad \text{and} \qquad d \circ c \ll p = c \ll d \ll p.$$

In addition to sequential composition $\circ$ we shall also use parallel composition $\otimes$ of channels, with an associated calculus for combinining $\circ$ and $\otimes$.

9.2.5 Predicates are generally fuzzy

In the points above we have used *fuzzy* predicates, with outcomes in the unit interval $0, 1$, instead of the more usual *sharp* predicates, with outcomes in the two-element set $\{0, 1\}$ of Booleans. Why?

- The main technical reason is that fuzzy predicates are closed under probabilistic predicate transformation $\ll$, whereas sharp predicates are not. Thus, if we wish to do evidential (backward) reasoning $\omega|_{c \ll q}$, as described in point 9.2.3, we are forced to use fuzzy predicates.
- Fuzzy predicates are also closed under another operation, namely *scaling*: for each $p: A \to 0, 1$ and $s \in 0, 1$ we have a new, scaled predicate $s \cdot p: A \to 0, 1$, given by $s \cdot pa = s \cdot pa$. This scaling is less important than predicate transformation, but still it is a useful operation.
- Fuzzy predicates naturally fit in a probabilistic setting, where uncertainty is a leading concept. It thus makes sense to use this uncertainty also for evidence.
- Fuzzy predicates are simply more general than sharp predicates. Sharp predicates p can be recognised logically among all fuzzy predicates via the property $p \mathbin{\&} p = p$, where conjunction $\&$ is pointwise multiplication.

The traditional approach in probability theory focuses on sharp predicates, in the form of events. This is part of the notation, for instance in expressions like $\Pr X \in E$, as used earlier in point 9.2.2. It does not make much sense to replace this sharp E with a fuzzy p when writing $\Pr X \in E$. That is one more reason why we write validity via $\models$ and not via $\Pr$. Fuzzy predicates have actually surfaced in more recent research in Bayesian probability, see *e.g.* the concepts of 'soft' evidence in Valtorta et al. (2002) and 'uncertain' evidence in Mrad et al. (2015), see also Barber (2012).

Fuzzy predicates have a different algebraic structure than sharp predicates. The latter form Boolean algebras. Fuzzy predicates however form effect modules (see *e.g.* Jacobs, 2013). However, these algebraic/logical structures will not play a role in the current setting.

We shall later sketch how a fuzzy predicate can be replaced by an additional node in a Bayesian network, see Remark 9.4.

9.2.6 *Marginalisation and weakening are operations*

Marginalisation is the operation of turning a joint distribution ω on a product domain $X \times Y$ into a distribution on one of the components, say on X. Traditionally marginalisation is indicated by omitting one of the variables: if $\omega x, y$ is written for the joint distribution on $X \times Y$, then ωx is its (first) marginal, as a distribution on X. It is defined as $\omega x = \sum_y \omega x, y$.

We prefer to write marginalisation as an explicit operation, so that $\mathsf{M}_1\omega$ is the first marginal (on X), and $\mathsf{M}_2\omega$ is the second marginal (on Y). More generally, marginalisation can be performed on a state σ on a domain $X_1 \times \cdots \times X_n$ in 2^n many ways.

A seemingly different but closely related operation is weakening of predicates. If $p \in 0, 1^X$ is a predicate on a domain X, we may want to use it on a larger domain $X \times Y$ where we ignore the Y-part. In logic this called weakening; it involves moving a predicate to a larger context. One could also indicate this via variables, writing px for the predicate on X, and px, y for its extension to $X \times Y$, where y in px, y is a spurious variable. Instead we write $\mathsf{W}_1 p \in 0, 1^{X \times Y}$ for this weakened predicate. It maps x, y to px.

Marginalisation M and weakening W are each other's 'cousins'. As we shall see, they can both be expressed via projection maps $\pi_1 \colon X \times Y \to X$, namely as state transformation $\mathsf{M}_1\omega = \pi_1 \gg \omega$ and as predicate transformation $\mathsf{W}_1 p = \pi_1 \ll p$. As a result, the symbols M and W can be moved accross validity $\models$, as in (9.6) below. In what we call crossover inference later on, the combination of marginalisation and weakening plays a crucial role.

9.2.7 *States and predicates are clearly distinguished*

As just argued, marginalisation is an operation on states, whereas weakening acts on predicates (evidence). In general, certain operations only make sense on states (like convex sum) and others on predicates. This reflects the fact that states and predicates form very different algebraic structures: states on a given domain form a convex set (see *e.g.* Jacobs, 2013), whereas, as already mentioned in Section 9.2.5, predicates on a given domain form an effect module.

Despite the important conceptual differences, states and predicates are easily confused, also in the literature (see *e.g.* Example 9.14 below). The general rule of thumb is that states involve finitely many probabilities that add up to one – unlike for predicates. We elaborate formally on this distinction in Remark 9.3 below.

On a more conceptual level, one could spell out the difference by saying that states have an ontological flavour, whereas predicates play an epistemological role. That means, states describe factual reality, although in probabilistic form, via convex combinations of combined facts. In contrast, predicates capture just the likelihoods of individual facts as perceived by an agent. Thus probabilities in predicates do not need to add up to one, because our perception of reality (contrary to reality itself) is possibly inconsistent or incomplete.[1] We shall elaborate more on this perspective at the end of Example 9.14 below.

9.3 States and predicates

Section 9.2.1 claimed that states (finite probability distributions) and fuzzy predicates – and their different roles – should be given more prominence in probability theory. We now elaborate this point in greater detail. We thus retell the same story as in the beginning, but this time with more mathematical details, and with more examples.

States

A *state* (probability distribution) over a 'sample' set A is a formal weighted combination $r_1|a_1\rangle + \cdots + r_n|a_n\rangle$, where the a_i are elements of A and the r_i are elements of $0, 1$ with $_i\, r_i = 1$. We shall write $\mathcal{D}A$ for the set of states/distributions on a set A. We will sometimes treat $\omega \in \mathcal{D}A$ equivalently as a 'probability mass' function $\omega \colon A \to 0, 1$ with finite support $\mathrm{supp}\,\omega = \{a \in A \mid \omega a \neq 0\}$ and with $_{a \in A}\, \omega a = 1$. More explicitly, the formal convex combination $_i\, r_i|a_i\rangle$ corresponds to the function $\omega \colon A \to 0, 1$ with $\omega a_i = r_i$ and $\omega a = 0$ if $a \notin \{a_1, \ldots, a_n\}$. Then $\mathrm{supp}\,\omega = \{a_1, \ldots, a_n\}$, by construction.

For two states $\sigma_1 \in \mathcal{D}A_1$ and $\sigma_2 \in \mathcal{D}A_2$, we can form the joint 'product' state $\sigma_1 \otimes \sigma_2 \in \mathcal{D}A_1 \times A_2$ on the cartesian product $A_1 \times A_2$ of the underlying sets, namely as:

$$\sigma_1 \otimes \sigma_2 a_1, a_2 := \sigma_1 a_1 \cdot \sigma_2 a_2. \tag{9.2}$$

[1] Within this perspective, it is intriguing to read conditioning of a state by a predicate as adapting the facts according to the agent's beliefs. In Philosophy one would say that our notion of conditioning forces an "idealistic" view of reality; in more mundane terms, it yields the possibility of "alternative facts".

For instance, if $\sigma_1 = \frac{1}{3}|a\rangle + \frac{2}{3}|b\rangle$ and $\sigma_2 = \frac{1}{8}|1\rangle + \frac{5}{8}|2\rangle + \frac{1}{4}|3\rangle$, then their product is written with ket-notation as:

$$\sigma_1 \otimes \sigma_2 = \frac{1}{24}|a,1\rangle + \frac{5}{24}|a,2\rangle + \frac{1}{12}|a,3\rangle + \frac{1}{12}|b,1\rangle + \frac{5}{12}|b,2\rangle + \frac{1}{6}|b,3\rangle.$$

Marginalisation works in the opposite direction: it moves a 'joint' state on a product set to one of the components: for a state $\omega \in \mathcal{D}A_1 \times A_2$ we have first and second marginalisation $\mathsf{M}_i\omega \in \mathcal{D}A_i$ determined as:

$$\mathsf{M}_1\omega a_1 = \sum_{a_2 \in A_2} \omega a_1, a_2 \qquad \mathsf{M}_2\omega a_2 = \sum_{a_a \in A_1} \omega a_1, a_2. \qquad (9.3)$$

Here we use explicit operations M_1 and M_2 for taking the first and second marginal. The traditional way to write a marginal is to drop a variable: a joint distribution is written as $\Pr x, y$, and its marginals as $\Pr x$ and $\Pr y$, where $\Pr x = \sum_y \Pr x, y$ and $\Pr y = \sum_x \Pr x, y$.

The two original states σ_1 and σ_2 in a product state $\sigma_1 \otimes \sigma_2$ can be recovered as marginals of this product state: $\mathsf{M}_1\sigma_1 \otimes \sigma_2 = \sigma_1$ and $\mathsf{M}_2\sigma_1 \otimes \sigma_2 = \sigma_2$.

In general a joint state $\omega \in \mathcal{D}A_1 \times A_2$ does *not* equal the product $\mathsf{M}_1\omega \otimes \mathsf{M}_2\omega$ of its marginals, making the whole more than the sum of its parts. When we do have $\omega = \mathsf{M}_1\omega \otimes \mathsf{M}_2\omega$, we call ω *non-entwined*. Otherwise it is called *entwined*.

Example 9.1 Given sets $X = \{x, y\}$ and $A = \{a, b\}$, one can prove that a state $\omega = r_1|x, a\rangle + r_2|x, b\rangle + r_3|y, a\rangle + r_4|y, b\rangle \in \mathcal{D}X \times A$, where $r_1 + r_2 + r_3 + r_4 = 1$, is non-entwined if and only if $r_1 \cdot r_4 = r_2 \cdot r_3$. This fact also holds in the quantum case, see *e.g.* Mermin (2007, §1.5).

For instance, the following joint state is entwined:

$$\omega = \frac{1}{8}|x, a\rangle + \frac{1}{4}|x, b\rangle + \frac{3}{8}|y, a\rangle + \frac{1}{4}|y, b\rangle.$$

Indeed, ω has marginals $\mathsf{M}_1\omega \in \mathcal{D}X$ and $\mathsf{M}_2\omega \in \mathcal{D}A$, namely:

$$\mathsf{M}_1\omega = \frac{3}{8}|x\rangle + \frac{5}{8}|y\rangle \qquad \text{and} \qquad \mathsf{M}_2\omega = \frac{1}{2}|a\rangle + \frac{1}{2}|b\rangle.$$

The original state ω differs from the product of its marginals:

$$\mathsf{M}_1\omega \otimes \mathsf{M}_2\omega = \frac{3}{16}|x, a\rangle + \frac{3}{16}|x, b\rangle + \frac{5}{16}|y, a\rangle + \frac{5}{16}|y, b\rangle.$$

There is one more operation on states that occurs frequently, namely convex sum: if we have n states $\omega_i \in \mathcal{D}A$ on the same sets and n probabilities $r_i \in 0, 1$ with $\sum r_i = 1$, then $\sum r_i\omega_i$ is a state again.

Predicates

A *predicate* on a sample space (set) A is a function $p: A \to 0, 1$, taking values in the unit interval $0, 1$. We shall use the exponent notation $0, 1^A$ for the set of predicates on A. What in probability theory are usually called events (subsets of A) can be identified with *sharp* predicates, taking values in the subset of booleans $\{0, 1\} \subseteq 0, 1$. We write $1_E \in 0, 1^A$ for the sharp predicate associated with the event $E \subseteq A$, defined by $1_E a = 1$ if $a \in E$ and $1_E a = 0$ if $a \notin E$, where we recall that we simply write 1_a for $1_{\{a\}}$. Thus predicates are a more general, 'fuzzy' notion of event, which we prefer to work with for the reasons explained in Section 9.2.5. We write $1 = 1_A, 0 = 1_\emptyset$ for the truth and falsity predicates. They are the top and bottom elements in the set of predicates $0, 1^A$, with pointwise order. As special case, for an element $a \in A$ we write 1_a for the 'singleton' or 'point' predicate on A that is 1 only on input $a \in A$.

For predicates $p, q \in 0, 1^A$ and scalar $r \in 0, 1$ we define $p \,\&\, q \in 0, 1^A$ as $a \mapsto pa \cdot qa$ and $r \cdot p \in 0, 1^A$ as $a \mapsto r \cdot pa$. Moreover, there is an orthosupplement predicate $p^\perp \in 0, 1^A$ given by $p^\perp a = 1 - pa$. Then $p^{\perp\perp} = p$. Notice that $1_E \,\&\, 1_D = 1_{E\cap D}$ and $1_E^\perp = 1_{\neg E}$, where $\neg E \subseteq A$ is the set-theoretic complement of E.

Definition 9.2 Let $\omega \in \mathcal{D}A$ be a state and $p \in 0, 1^A$ be a predicate, both on the same set A. We write $\omega \models p$ for the *validity* or *expected value* of p in state ω. This validity is a number in the unit interval 0, 1. We recall its definition from (9.1):

$$\omega \models p := \sum_{a \in A} \omega a \cdot pa. \tag{9.4}$$

For an event (sharp predicate) E, the probability $\Pr E$ wrt. a state ω is defined as $\sum_{a \in E} \omega a$. Using the above validity notation (9.4) we write $\omega \models 1_E$ instead. As special case we have $\omega \models 1_x = \omega x$.

Notice that the validity $\omega \models 1$ of the truth predicate 1 is 1 in any state ω. Similarly, $\omega \models 0 = 0$. Additionally, $\omega \models p^\perp = 1 - \omega \models p$ and $\omega \models r \cdot p = r \cdot \omega \models p$.

There is also a parallel product $\otimes$ of predicates, like for states. Given two predicates $p_1 \in 0, 1^{A_1}$ and $p_2 \in 0, 1^{A_2}$ on sets A_1, A_2 we form the product predicate $p_1 \otimes p_2$ on $A_1 \times A_2$ via: $p_1 \otimes p_2 a_1, a_2 = p_1 a_1 \cdot p_2 a_2$. It is not hard to see that:

$$\omega_1 \otimes \omega_2 \models p_1 \otimes p_2 = (\omega_1 \models p_1) \cdot (\omega_2 \models p_2).$$

A product $p \otimes 1$ or $1 \otimes p$ with the truth predicate 1 corresponds to *weakening*, that is to moving a predicate p to a bigger set (or context). We also write:

$$\mathsf{W}_1 p := p \otimes 1 \qquad \text{and} \qquad \mathsf{W}_2 p := 1 \otimes p \tag{9.5}$$

for these first and second weakening operations, like in Section 9.2.6. We deliberately use 'dual' notation for marginalisation M and weakening W because these operations are closely related, as expressed by the following equations.

$$\mathsf{M}_1 \omega \models p = \omega \models \mathsf{W}_1 p \qquad \text{and} \qquad \mathsf{M}_2 \omega \models q = \omega \models \mathsf{W}_2 q. \tag{9.6}$$

As a result, $\sigma_1 \otimes \sigma_2 \models \mathsf{W}_1 p = \sigma_1 \models p$ and similarly $\sigma_1 \otimes \sigma_2 \models \mathsf{W}_2 q = \sigma_2 \models q$.

Remark 9.3   As already mentioned in Section 9.2.7, conceptually, it is important to keep states and predicates apart. They play different roles, but mathematically it is easy to confuse them. States describe a state of affairs, whereas predicates capture evidence. We explicitly emphasise the differences between a state $\omega \in \mathcal{D}A$ and a predicate $p \colon A \to 0, 1$ in several points.

(i) A state has finite support. Considered as function $\omega \colon A \to 0, 1$, there are only finitely many elements $a \in A$ with $\omega a \neq 0$. In contrast, there may be infinitely many elements $a \in A$ with $pa \neq 0$. This difference only makes sense when the underlying set A has infinitely many elements.

(ii) The finite sum $\sum_{a \in A} \omega a$ equals 1, since states involve a convex sum. In contrast there are no requirements about the sum of the probabilities $pa \in 0, 1$ for a predicate p. In fact, such a sum may not exist when A is an infinite set. We thus see that each state ω on A forms a predicate, when considered as a function $A \to 0, 1$. But a predicate in general does not form a state.

(iii) States and predicates are closed under completely different operations. As we have seen, for states we have parallel products $\otimes$, marginalisation M_i, and convex sum. In contrast, predicates are closed under orthosupplement $-^\perp$, conjunction $\&$, scalar multiplication $s \cdot -$ and parallel product $\otimes$ (with weakening as special case). The algebraic structures of states and of predicates is completely different: each set of states $\mathcal{D}A$ forms a convex set whereas each set of predicates $0, 1^A$ is an effect module, see *e.g.* Jacobs (2018b) for more details.

(iv) State transformation (along a channel) happens in a forward direction, whereas predicate transformation (along a channel) works in a backward direction. These directions are described with respect the direction of the channel. This will be elaborated in Section 9.5.

Remark 9.4   One possible reason why fuzzy predicates are not so common in (Bayesian) probability theory is that they can be mimicked via an extra node in a Bayesian network, together with a sharp predicate. We sketch how this works. Assume we have a set $X = \{a, b, c\}$ and we wish to consider a fuzzy predicate $p \colon X \to 0, 1$ on X, say with $pa = \frac{2}{3}$, $pb = \frac{1}{2}$ and $pc = \frac{1}{4}$. Then we can introduce an extra node $2 = \{t, f\}$ with a channel $h \colon X \rightsquigarrow 2$ given by:

$$ha = \tfrac{2}{3}|t\rangle + \tfrac{1}{3}|f\rangle \qquad hb = \tfrac{1}{2}|t\rangle + \tfrac{1}{2}|f\rangle \qquad hc = \tfrac{1}{4}|t\rangle + \tfrac{3}{4}|f\rangle.$$

The original predicate p on $X = \{a, b, c\}$ can now be reconstructed via predicate transformation along h as $h \ll 1_t$, where, recall, 1_t is the sharp predicate on 2 which is 1 at t and 0 at f.

As an aside: we have spelled out the general isomorphism between predicates on a set A and channels $A \rightsquigarrow 2$. Conceptually this is pleasant, but in practice we do not wish to extend our Bayesian network every time a fuzzy predicate pops up.

What this example also illustrates is that sharpness of predicates is not closed under predicate transformation.

9.4 Conditioning

Conditioning is one of the most fundamental operations in probability theory. It is the operation that updates a state in the light of certain evidence. This evidence is thus incorporated in a new, updated state, that reflects the new insight. For this reason conditioning is sometime called belief update or belief revision. It forms the basis of learning, training and inference, see also Section 9.6.

A conditional probability is usually written as $\Pr E \mid D$. It describes the probability of event E, given event D. In the current context we follow a more general path, using fuzzy predicates instead of events. Also, we explicitly carry the state around. From this perspective, the update of a state ω with a predicate p, leading to an updated state $\omega|_p$, is the fundamental operation. It allows us to retrieve probabilities $\Pr E \mid D$ as special case, as will be shown at the end of this section.

Definition 9.5 Let $\omega \in \mathcal{D}A$ be a state and $p \in 0, 1^A$ be a predicate, both on the same set A. If the validity $\omega \models p$ is non-zero, we write $\omega|_p$ for the conditional state "ω given p", defined as formal convex sum:

$$\omega|_p := \sum_{a \in A} \frac{\omega a \cdot pa}{\omega \models p} |a\rangle. \tag{9.7}$$

Example 9.6 Let's take the numbers of a dice as sample space: pips $= \{1, 2, 3, 4, 5, 6\}$, with a fair/uniform dice distribution dice $\in \mathcal{D}$pips.

$$\text{dice} = \tfrac{1}{6}|1\rangle + \tfrac{1}{6}|2\rangle + \tfrac{1}{6}|3\rangle + \tfrac{1}{6}|4\rangle + \tfrac{1}{6}|5\rangle + \tfrac{1}{6}|6\rangle.$$

We consider the predicate evenish $\in 0, 1^{\text{pips}}$ expressing that we are fairly certain of pips being even:

$$\text{evenish1} = \tfrac{1}{5} \qquad \text{evenish3} = \tfrac{1}{10} \qquad \text{evenish5} = \tfrac{1}{10}$$
$$\text{evenish2} = \tfrac{9}{10} \qquad \text{evenish4} = \tfrac{9}{10} \qquad \text{evenish6} = \tfrac{4}{5}$$

We first compute the validity of evenish for our fair dice:

$$\begin{aligned}
\text{dice} \models \text{evenish} &= \sum_x \text{dice} x \cdot \text{evenish} x \\
&= \tfrac{1}{6} \cdot \tfrac{1}{5} + \tfrac{1}{6} \cdot \tfrac{9}{10} + \tfrac{1}{6} \cdot \tfrac{1}{10} + \tfrac{1}{6} \cdot \tfrac{9}{10} + \tfrac{1}{6} \cdot \tfrac{1}{10} + \tfrac{1}{6} \cdot \tfrac{4}{5} \\
&= \tfrac{2+9+1+9+1+8}{60} = \tfrac{1}{2}.
\end{aligned}$$

If we take evenish as evidence, we can update our state and get:

$$\text{dice}|_{\text{evenish}}$$

$$= \sum_x \frac{\text{dice}x \cdot \text{evenish}x}{\text{dice} \models \text{evenish}} |x\rangle$$

$$= \tfrac{16 \cdot \frac{1}{5}}{12}|1\rangle + \tfrac{16 \cdot \frac{9}{10}}{12}|2\rangle + \tfrac{16 \cdot \frac{1}{10}}{12}|3\rangle + \tfrac{16 \cdot \frac{9}{10}}{12}|4\rangle + \tfrac{16 \cdot \frac{1}{10}}{12}|5\rangle + \tfrac{16 \cdot \frac{4}{5}}{12}|6\rangle$$

$$= \tfrac{1}{15}|1\rangle + \tfrac{3}{10}|2\rangle + \tfrac{1}{30}|3\rangle + \tfrac{3}{10}|4\rangle + \tfrac{1}{30}|5\rangle + \tfrac{4}{15}|6\rangle.$$

As expected, the probability of the even pips is now higher than the odd ones. The evidence has been factored into the state.

We collect some basic properties of conditioning.

Lemma 9.7 *Let $\omega \in \mathcal{D}A$ and $p, q \in 0, 1^A$ be a state with predicates on the same set A.*

(i) *Conditioning with truth does nothing: $\omega|_1 = \omega$.*

(ii) *Conditioning with a conjunction amounts to separate conditionings, that is:*
$\omega|_{p\&q} = (\omega|_p)|_q$.

(iii) *Conditioning with scalar product has no effect, when the scalar is non-zero:*
$\omega|_{r \cdot p} = \omega|_p$ *when $r \neq 0$.*

(iv) *Conditioning with a point predicate yields a point state: $\omega|_{\mathbf{1}_x} = 1|x\rangle$, when $\omega x \neq 0$.*

Now let $\sigma_i \in \mathcal{D}A_i$ and $p_i \in 0, 1^{A_i}$.

(v) $\sigma_1 \otimes \sigma_2|_{p_1 \otimes p_2} = \sigma_1|_{p_1} \otimes \sigma_2|_{p_2}$.

(vi) $\mathsf{M}_1(\sigma \otimes \tau|_{\mathsf{W}_1 p_1}) = \sigma|_{p_1}$ *and* $\mathsf{M}_2(\sigma \otimes \tau|_{\mathsf{W}_2 p_2}) = \tau|_{p_2}$.

Proof All these properties follow via straightforward computation. We shall do (ii) and (v).

For (ii) we use:

$$(\omega|_p|_q)a = \frac{\omega|_p a \cdot qa}{\omega|_p \models q} = \frac{\frac{\omega a \cdot pa}{\omega \models p} \cdot qa}{\sum_b \omega|_p b \cdot qb}$$

$$= \frac{\frac{\omega a \cdot pa}{\omega \models p} \cdot qa}{\sum_b \frac{\omega b \cdot pb}{\omega \models p} \cdot qb}$$

$$= \frac{\omega a \cdot pa \cdot qa}{\sum_b \omega b \cdot pb \cdot qb}$$

$$= \frac{\omega a \cdot p \& qa}{\omega \models p \& q}$$

$$= (\omega|_{p\&q})a.$$

Similarly, for (v) we use:

$$
\begin{aligned}
\sigma_1 \otimes \sigma_2\big|_{p_1 \otimes p_2} a_1, a_2 &= \frac{\sigma_1 \otimes \sigma_2 a_1, a_2 \cdot p_1 \otimes p_2 a_1, a_2}{\sigma_1 \otimes \sigma_2 \models p_1 \otimes p_2} \\
&= \frac{\sigma_1 a_1 \cdot \sigma_2 a_2 \cdot p_1 a_1 \cdot p_2 a}{\sigma_1 \models p_1 \cdot \sigma_2 \models p_2} \\
&= \frac{\sigma_1 a_1 \cdot p_1 a_1}{\sigma_1 \models p_1} \cdot \frac{\sigma_2 a_2 \cdot p_2 a}{\sigma_2 \models p_2} \\
&= \sigma_1\big|_{p_1} \otimes \sigma_2\big|_{p_2}. \qquad\qquad \square
\end{aligned}
$$

The following result gives the generalisation of Bayes' rule to the current setting with states and predicates.

Theorem 9.8 *Let $\omega \in \mathcal{D}A$ and $p, q \in 0, 1^A$ be a state and two predicates on the set A.*
(i) *The* product rule *holds:*

$$
\omega\big|_p \models q = \frac{\omega \models p \,\&\, q}{\omega \models p} \tag{9.8}
$$

(ii) Bayes' rule *holds:*

$$
\omega\big|_p \models q = \frac{\omega\big|_q \models p \cdot \omega \models q}{\omega \models p} \tag{9.9}
$$

Proof Point (ii) follows directly from (i) by using that $p \,\&\, q = q \,\&\, p$, so we concentrate on (i).

$$
\begin{aligned}
\omega\big|_p \models q = \sum_a \omega\big|_p a \cdot qa &= \sum_a \frac{\omega a \cdot pa}{\omega \models p} \cdot qa \\
&= \frac{\sum_a \omega a \cdot p \,\&\, qa}{\omega \models p} \\
&= \frac{\omega \models p \,\&\, q}{\omega \models p}. \qquad\qquad \square
\end{aligned}
$$

We now relate our state-and-predicate based approach to conditioning to the traditional one. Recall that for events $E, D \subseteq A$ one has, by definition:

$$
\mathrm{Pr}E \mid D = \frac{\mathrm{Pr}E \cap D}{\mathrm{Pr}D}.
$$

If these probabilities $\mathrm{Pr}\cdot$ are computed wrt. a distribution $\omega \in \mathcal{D}A$, we can continue as follows.

$$
\mathrm{Pr}E \mid D = \frac{\mathrm{Pr}E \cap D}{\mathrm{Pr}D} = \frac{\omega \models \mathbf{1}_{E \cap D}}{\omega \models \mathbf{1}_D} = \frac{\omega \models \mathbf{1}_E \,\&\, \mathbf{1}_D}{\omega \models \mathbf{1}_D} \overset{(9.8)}{=} \omega\big|_{\mathbf{1}_D} \models \mathbf{1}_E.
$$

Thus the probability $\mathrm{Pr}E \mid D$ can be expressed in our framework as the validity of the sharp predicate E in the state updated with the sharp predicate D. This is precisely the intended meaning.

9.5 Bayesian inference via state/predicate transformation

As mentioned in Section 9.2.4, a channel $c\colon A \rightsquigarrow B$ between two sets A, B is a probabilistic function from A to B. It maps an an element $a \in A$ to a state $ca \in \mathcal{D}B$ of B. Hence it is an actual function of the form $A \to \mathcal{D}B$. Such functions are often described as conditional probabilities $a \mapsto \mathrm{Pr}b \mid a$, or as stochastic matrices. We repeat that channels are fundamental – more so than states and predicates – since a state $\omega \in \mathcal{D}A$ can be identified with a channel $\omega\colon 1 \rightsquigarrow A$ for the singleton set $1 = \{0\}$. Similarly, a predicate $p \in 0, 1^A$ can be identified with a channel $p\colon A \rightsquigarrow 2$, where $2 = \{0, 1\}$; this uses that $\mathcal{D}2 \cong 0, 1$.

Channels are used for probabilistic state transformation $\gg$ and predicate transformation $\ll$, in the following manner.

Definition 9.9 Let $c\colon A \rightsquigarrow B$ be a channel, with a state $\omega \in \mathcal{D}A$ on its domain A and a predicate $q \in 0, 1^B$ on its codomain B.
(i) State transformation yields a state $c \gg \omega$ on B defined by:

$$(c \gg \omega)b := \sum_{a \in A} \omega a \cdot cab. \qquad (9.10)$$

(ii) Predicate transformation gives a predicate $c \ll q$ on A defined by:

$$(c \ll q)a := \sum_{b \in B} cab \cdot qb. \qquad (9.11)$$

The next example illustrates how state and predicate transformation can be used systematically to reason about probabilistic questions.

Example 9.10 In a medical context we distinguish patients with low (L), medium (M), and high (H) blood pressure. We thus use as 'blood' sample space $B = \{L, M, H\}$, say with initial ('prior' or 'base rate') distribution $\beta \in \mathcal{D}B$:

$$\beta = \tfrac{1}{8}|L\rangle + \tfrac{1}{2}|M\rangle + \tfrac{3}{8}|H\rangle.$$

We consider a particular disease, whose a priori occurrence in the population depends on the blood pressure, as given by the following table.

blood pressure	disease likelihood
Low	5%
Medium	10%
High	15%

We choose as sample space for the disease $D = \{d, d^{\perp}\}$ where the element d represents presence of the disease and $d^{\perp}$ represents absence. The above table is now naturally described as a 'sickness' channel $s\colon B \rightsquigarrow D$, given by:

$$sL = 0.05|d\rangle + 0.95|d^{\perp}\rangle$$
$$sM = 0.1|d\rangle + 0.9|d^{\perp}\rangle$$
$$sH = 0.15|d\rangle + 0.85|d^{\perp}\rangle.$$

We ask ourselves two basic questions.

(i) **What is the a priori probability of the disease?** The answer to this question is obtained by state transformation, namely by transforming the blood pressure distribution β on B to a disease distribution $s \gg \beta$ on D along the sickness channel s. Concretely:

$$
\begin{aligned}
\big(s \gg \beta d \overset{(9.10)}{=} \; &\textstyle\sum_{x \in B} \beta x \cdot sxd \\
= \; &\beta L \cdot sLd + \beta M \cdot sMd + \beta H \cdot sHd \\
= \; &\tfrac{1}{8} \cdot \tfrac{1}{20} + \tfrac{1}{2} \cdot \tfrac{1}{10} + \tfrac{3}{8} \cdot \tfrac{3}{20} \\
= \; &\tfrac{9}{80} \\
\big(s \gg \beta d^{\perp} \overset{(9.10)}{=} \; &\textstyle\sum_{x \in B} \beta x \cdot sxd^{\perp} \\
= \; &\beta L \cdot sLd^{\perp} + \beta M \cdot sMd^{\perp} + \beta H \cdot sHd^{\perp} \\
= \; &\tfrac{1}{8} \cdot \tfrac{19}{20} + \tfrac{1}{2} \cdot \tfrac{9}{10} + \tfrac{3}{8} \cdot \tfrac{17}{20} \\
= \; &\tfrac{71}{80}.
\end{aligned}
$$

Thus we obtain as a priori disease distribution $c \gg \beta = \tfrac{9}{80}|d\rangle + \tfrac{71}{80}|d^{\perp}\rangle = 0.1125|d\rangle + 0.8875|d^{\perp}\rangle$. A bit more than 11% of the population has the disease at hand.

(ii) **What is the likely blood pressure for people without the disease?** Before we calculate the updated ('a posteriori') blood pressure distribution, we reason intuitively. Since non-occurrence of the disease is most likely for people with low blood pressure, we expect that the updated blood pressure – after taking the evidence 'absence of disease' into account – will have a higher probability of low blood pressure than the orignal (a priori) value of $\frac{1}{8}$ in β.

The evidence that we have is the point predicate $\mathbf{1}_{d\perp}$ on D, representing absence of the disease. In order to update $\beta \in \mathcal{D}B$ we first apply predicate transformation $s \ll \mathbf{1}_{d\perp}$ to obtain a predicate on B. This transformed predicate in $0, 1^B$ is computed as follows.

$$
\begin{aligned}
\left(s \ll \mathbf{1}_{d\perp} L \right) &\overset{(9.11)}{=} \textstyle\sum_{y\in D} sLy \cdot \mathbf{1}_{d\perp}y \; = \; sLd^\perp \; = \; 0.95 \\
\left(s \ll \mathbf{1}_{d\perp} M \right) &\overset{(9.11)}{=} \textstyle\sum_{y\in D} sMy \cdot \mathbf{1}_{d\perp}y \; = \; sMd^\perp \; = \; 0.9 \\
\left(s \ll \mathbf{1}_{d\perp} H \right) &\overset{(9.11)}{=} \textstyle\sum_{y\in D} sHy \cdot \mathbf{1}_{d\perp}y \; = \; sHd^\perp \; = \; 0.85.
\end{aligned}
$$

Notice that although $\mathbf{1}_{d\perp}$ is a sharp predicate, the transformed predicate $s \ll \mathbf{1}_{d\perp}$ is not sharp. This shows that sharp predicates are not closed under predicate transformation – as mentioned earlier in Section 9.2.5.

We can now update the original blood pressure distribution β with the transformed evicence $s \ll \mathbf{1}_{d\perp}$. We first compute validity, and then perform conditioning:

$$
\begin{aligned}
\beta \models s \ll \mathbf{1}_{d\perp} \;\overset{(9.4)}{=}\;& \textstyle\sum_{x\in B} \beta x \cdot s \ll \mathbf{1}_{d\perp} x \\
=\;& \beta L \cdot s \ll \mathbf{1}_{d\perp} L \\
& + \beta M \cdot s \ll \mathbf{1}_{d\perp} M \\
& + \beta H \cdot s \ll \mathbf{1}_{d\perp} H \\
=\;& \tfrac{1}{8} \cdot \tfrac{19}{20} + \tfrac{1}{2} \cdot \tfrac{9}{10} + \tfrac{3}{8} \cdot \tfrac{17}{20} \\
=\;& \tfrac{71}{80}
\end{aligned}
$$

$$
\begin{aligned}
\beta|_{s \ll \mathbf{1}_{d\perp}} \;\overset{(9.7)}{=}\;& \textstyle\sum_{x\in B} \frac{\beta x \cdot s \ll \mathbf{1}_{d\perp} x}{\beta \models s \ll \mathbf{1}_{d\perp}} \big| x \big\rangle \\
=\;& \frac{\tfrac{1}{8} \cdot \tfrac{19}{20}}{\tfrac{71}{80}} |L\rangle + \frac{\tfrac{1}{2} \cdot \tfrac{9}{10}}{\tfrac{71}{80}} |M\rangle + \frac{\tfrac{3}{8} \cdot \tfrac{17}{20}}{\tfrac{71}{80}} |H\rangle \\
=\;& \tfrac{19}{142}|L\rangle + \tfrac{36}{71}|M\rangle + \tfrac{51}{142}|H\rangle \\
\sim\;& 0.134|L\rangle + 0.507|M\rangle + 0.359|H\rangle.
\end{aligned}
$$

As intuitively expected, a posteriori the probability of low blood pressure is higher than in the a priori distribution β – and the probability of high blood pressure is lower too.

These calculations with probabilities are relatively easy but may grow out of hand quickly. Therefore a library has been developed, called EFPROB see Cho and Jacobs (2017), that provides the relevant functions, for validity, state update, state and predicate transformation, *etc.*

It is natural to see a state β and a channel s, as used above, as stochastic matrices

M_β and M_s, of the form:

$$M_\beta = \begin{pmatrix} \frac{3}{8} \\ \frac{1}{2} \\ \frac{3}{8} \end{pmatrix} \qquad M_s = \begin{pmatrix} 0.05 & 0.1 & 0.15 \\ 0.95 & 0.9 & 0.85 \end{pmatrix}$$

These matrices are called stochastic because the columns add up to 1. The matrix of the state $s \gg \beta$ is then obtained by matrix multiplication $M_s M_\beta$. For predicate transformation $s \ll \mathbf{1}_{d^\perp}$ with $M_{\mathbf{1}_{d^\perp}} = \begin{pmatrix} 0 & 1 \end{pmatrix}$ one uses matrix multiplication in a different order:

$$M_{\mathbf{1}_{d^\perp}} M_s = \begin{pmatrix} 0 & 1 \end{pmatrix} \begin{pmatrix} 0.05 & 0.1 & 0.15 \\ 0.95 & 0.9 & 0.85 \end{pmatrix} = \begin{pmatrix} 0.95 & 0.9 & 0.85 \end{pmatrix}.$$

The diligent reader may have noticed in this example that the probability $s \gg \beta d^\perp = s \gg \beta \models \mathbf{1}_{d^\perp} = \frac{71}{80}$ in Example 9.10 coincides with the probability $\beta \models s \ll \mathbf{1}_{d^\perp} = \frac{71}{80}$. This in fact in an instance of the following general result, relating validity and transformations.

Proposition 9.11 *Let $c \colon A \rightarrow B$ be a channel, $\omega \in \mathcal{D}A$ be a state on its domain, and $q \in 0, 1^B$ a predicate on its codomain. Then:*

$$c \gg \omega \models q \ = \ \omega \models c \ll q. \tag{9.12}$$

Proof The result follows from a simple calculation:

$$
\begin{aligned}
c \gg \omega \models q \ &\overset{(9.4)}{=}\ \sum_{b \subset B} c \gg \omega b \cdot q b \\
&\overset{(9.10)}{=}\ \sum_{b \in B} \left(\sum_{a \in A} \omega a \cdot cab \right) \cdot q b \\
&=\ \sum_{a \in A, b \in B} \omega a \cdot cab \cdot q b \\
&=\ \sum_{a \in A} \omega a \cdot \left(\sum_{b \in B} cab \cdot q b \right) \\
&\overset{(9.11)}{=}\ \sum_{a \in A} \omega a \cdot c \ll qa \\
&\overset{(9.4)}{=}\ \omega \models c \ll q. \qquad \square
\end{aligned}
$$

There are two more operations on channels that we need to consider, namely sequential composition $\circ$ and parallel composition $\otimes$.

Definition 9.12 Consider channels $f \colon A \rightarrow B$, $g \colon C \rightarrow D$ and $h \colon X \rightarrow Y$. These channels can be composed sequentially and in parallel, yielding new channels:

$$g \circ f \colon A \rightarrow C \qquad \text{and} \qquad f \otimes h \colon A \times X \rightarrow B \times Y,$$

via the following definitions.

$$g \circ fa := g \gg fa \quad \text{so that} \quad g \circ fac = \sum_{b \in B} fab \cdot gbc.$$

The latter formula shows that channel composition is essentially matrix multiplication.

Next,

$$f \otimes ha, x := fa \otimes hx \quad \text{so that}$$

$$f \otimes ha, xb, y = fab \cdot hxy.$$

The product $\otimes$ on the right of $:=$ is the product of states, as described in (9.2). In terms of matrices, parallel composition of channels is given by the Kronecker product.

It is not hard to see that $\circ$ and $\otimes$ are well-behaved operations, satisfying for instance:

$$(g \otimes k) \circ (f \otimes h) = (g \circ f) \otimes (k \circ h).$$

They interact nicely with state and predicate transformation:

$$(g \circ f \gg \omega = g \gg (f \gg \omega$$
$$(g \circ f \ll q = f \ll (g \ll q$$
$$(f \otimes h \gg \sigma \otimes \tau = (f \gg \sigma) \otimes (h \gg \tau)$$
$$(f \otimes h \ll p \otimes q = (f \ll p) \otimes (g \ll q).$$

Moreover, for the identity channel id given by $\text{id}x = 1|x\rangle$ we have:

$$\text{id} \circ f = f = f \circ \text{id} \qquad \text{id} \otimes \text{id} = \text{id}.$$

We will see examples of parallel composition of channels in Section 9.7 when we discuss (the semantics of) Bayesian networks.

Remark 9.13   An ordinary function $f \colon A \to B$ can be turned into a 'deterministic' channel $\langle f \rangle \colon A \to B$ via:

$$\langle f \rangle a := 1|fa\rangle. \tag{9.13}$$

This operation $\langle \cdot \rangle$ sends function composition to channel composition: $\langle g \circ f \rangle = \langle g \rangle \circ \langle f \rangle$. The random variable $X \colon \Omega \to A$ that we used in Section 9.2.3 is an example of such a deterministic channel. Formally, we should now write $X^{-1}a = \langle X \rangle \ll 1_a$ for the event $X^{-1}a$ on Ω.

There are some further special cases of deterministic channels that we mention explicitly.

(i) For two sets A_1, A_2 we can form the cartesian product $A_1 \times A_2$ with its two projection functions $\pi_1 \colon A_1 \times A_2 \to A_1$ and $\pi_2 \colon A_1 \times A_2 \to A_2$. They can be turned into (deterministic) channels $\langle \pi_i \rangle \colon A_1 \times A_2 \to A_i$. One can then see that marginalisation and weakening are state transformation and predicate transformation along these projection channels:

$$\langle \pi_1 \rangle \gg \omega = \mathsf{M}_1 \omega \qquad \langle \pi_1 \rangle \ll p = \mathsf{W}_1 p = p \otimes 1$$

$$\langle \pi_2 \rangle \gg \omega = \mathsf{M}_2 \omega \qquad \langle \pi_2 \rangle \ll q = \mathsf{W}_2 q = 1 \otimes q$$

As a result, equation (9.6) is a special case of (9.12).

Moreover, these projection channels commute with parallel composition $\otimes$ of channels, in the sense that:

$$\langle \pi_1 \rangle \circ (f \otimes h) = f \circ \langle \pi_1 \rangle \qquad \langle \pi_2 \rangle \circ (f \otimes h) = h \circ \langle \pi_2 \rangle$$

(ii) For each set A there is a diagonal (or 'copy') function $\Delta \colon A \to A \times A$ with $\Delta a = a, a$. It can be turned into a channel too, as $\langle \Delta \rangle \colon A \to A \times A$. However, this copy channel does *not* interact well with parallel composition of channels, in the sense that in general:

$$\langle \Delta \rangle \circ f \neq (f \otimes f) \circ \langle \Delta \rangle.$$

This equation does hold when the channel f is deterministic. Via diagonals we can relate parallel products $\otimes$ and conjunctions $\&$ of predicates:

$$\langle \Delta \rangle \ll (p \otimes q) = p \,\&\, q.$$

In what follows we often omit the braces $\langle \cdot \rangle$ around projections and diagonals, and simply write projection and copy channels as $\pi_i \colon A_1 \times A_2 \to A_i$ and $\Delta \colon A \to A \times A$.

9.6 Inference in Bayesian networks

In this section we illustrate how channels can be used both to model Bayesian networks and to reason about them. We shall use a standard example from the literature, namely the 'student' network from Koller and Friedman (2009). The graph of the student network is described in original form in Figure 9.1. We see how a student's grade depends on the difficulty of a test and the student's intelligence. The SAT score only depends on intelligence; whether or not the student gets a strong (l^1) or weak (l^0) recommendation letter depends on the grade.

With each of the five nodes in the network a sample space is associated, namely:

$$D = \{d^0, d^1\}, \quad I = \{i^0, i^1\}, \quad G = \{g^1, g^2, g^3\}, \quad S = \{s^0, s^1\}, \quad L = \{l^0, l^1\}.$$

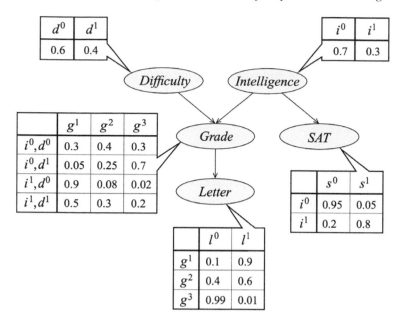

Figure 9.1 Picture of the student Bayesian network, copied from Koller and Friedman (2009), with conditional probability tables.

For the two inital nodes Difficulty (D) and Intelligence (I) we obtain two distributions/states ω_D and ω_I, whose probabilities are given in the two upper tables in Figure 9.1:

$$\omega_D = 0.6|d^0\rangle + 0.4|d^1\rangle \qquad \omega_I = 0.7|i^0\rangle + 0.3|i^1\rangle.$$

They capture the a priori state of affairs, with a 0.4 likelihood of a difficult test (d^1), and a 0.3 likelihood of an intelligent student (i^1).

The remaining three nodes Grade (G), Letter (L) and SAT (S) have incoming arrows from parent nodes, and are thus not initial. They correspond to three channels:

$$c_G \colon D \times I \dashrightarrow G, \qquad c_S \colon I \dashrightarrow S, \qquad c_L \colon G \dashrightarrow L.$$

The definitions of these channels can be read directly from the tables. The SAT channel $c_S \colon I \dashrightarrow S$ and the Letter channel $c_L \colon G \dashrightarrow L$ are thus of the form:

$$c_S i^0 = 0.95|s^0\rangle + 0.05|s^1\rangle$$
$$c_S i^1 = 0.2|s^0\rangle + 0.8|s^1\rangle$$

$$c_L g^1 = 0.1|l^0\rangle + 0.9|l^1\rangle$$
$$c_L g^2 = 0.4|l^0\rangle + 0.6|l^1\rangle$$
$$c_L g^3 = 0.99|l^0\rangle + 0.01|l^1\rangle$$

The Grade channel $c_G \colon D \times I \nrightarrow G$ looks as follows.

$$
\begin{aligned}
c_G d^0, i^0 &= 0.3|g^1\rangle + 0.4|g^2\rangle + 0.3|g^3\rangle \\
c_G d^0, i^1 &= 0.9|g^1\rangle + 0.08|g^2\rangle + 0.02|g^3\rangle \\
c_G d^1, i^0 &= 0.05|g^1\rangle + 0.25|g^2\rangle + 0.7|g^3\rangle \\
c_G d^1, i^1 &= 0.5|g^1\rangle + 0.3|g^2\rangle + 0.2|g^3\rangle
\end{aligned}
$$

(Notice that we switched the order of i and d wrt. the tables in Figure 9.1; we have done so in order to remain consistent with the order of the inputs D and I as suggested in the network in Figure 9.1. This is actually a subtle issue, because usually in graphs there is no order on the parents of a node, that is, the parents form a *set* and not a *list*.)

We now discuss a number of inference questions from Koller and Friedman (2009) and illustrate how they are answered systematically using our perspective with states, predicates and channels.

(i) **What are the a priori probabilities for the recommendation?** To answer this question we follow the graph in Figure 9.1 and see that the answer is given by twice using state transformation, namely:

$$
\begin{aligned}
c_L \gg (c_G \gg \omega_D \otimes \omega_I) &= 0.498|l^0\rangle + 0.502|l^1\rangle, \qquad \text{or, equivalently,} \\
&= (c_L \circ c_G) \gg \omega_D \otimes \omega_I.
\end{aligned}
$$

(ii) **What if we know that the student is not intelligent?** The non-intelligence translates into the point predicate $\mathbf{1}_{i^0}$ on the set I, which we use to update the intelligence state ω_I before doing the same state transformations:

$$
c_L \gg (c_G \gg \omega_D \otimes \omega_I|_{\mathbf{1}_{i^0}}) = 0.611|l^0\rangle + 0.389|l^1\rangle.
$$

(iii) **What if we additionally know that the test is easy?** The easiness evidence translates into the predicate $\mathbf{1}_{d^0}$ on D, which is used for updating the difficulty state:

$$
\begin{aligned}
c_L &\gg (c_G \gg \omega_D|_{\mathbf{1}_{d^0}} \otimes \omega_I|_{\mathbf{1}_{i^0}}) \\
&= 0.487|l^0\rangle + 0.513|l^1\rangle \\
&= (c_L \circ c_G) \gg (\omega_D \otimes \omega_I|_{\mathbf{1}_{d^0} \otimes \mathbf{1}_{i^0}}).
\end{aligned}
$$

The previous two outcomes are obtained by what is called 'causal reasoning' or 'prediction' or 'forward inference', see the table at the end of Section 9.2.3. We continue with 'backward inference', also called 'evidential reasoning' or 'explanation'.

(iv) **What is the intelligence given a C-grade (g^3)?** The evidence predicate $\mathbf{1}_{g^3}$ is a predicate on the set G. We like to learn about the revised intelligence. This is done as follows. Via predicate transformation we obtain a predicate $c_G \ll \mathbf{1}_{g^3}$ on $D \times I$. We can use it to update the product state $\omega_D \otimes \omega_I$. We then get the update intelligence by taking the second marginal, as in:

$$\mathsf{M}_2\big(\omega_D \otimes \omega_I|_{c_G \ll \mathbf{1}_{g^3}}\big) \;=\; 0.921|i^0\rangle + 0.0789|i^1\rangle.$$

We see that the new intelligence (i^1) is significantly lower than the a priori value of 0.3, once a low grade is observed. The updated difficulty (d^1) probability is higher than the original 0.4; it is obtained by taking the first marginal:

$$\mathsf{M}_1\big(\omega_D \otimes \omega_I|_{c_G \ll \mathbf{1}_{g^3}}\big) \;=\; 0.371|d^0\rangle + 0.629|d^1\rangle.$$

(v) **What is the intelligence given a weak recommendation?** We now have a point predicate $\mathbf{1}_{l^0}$ on the set L. Hence we have to do predicate transformation twice, along the channels c_L and c_G, in order to reach the initial states. This is done as:

$$\mathsf{M}_2\big(\omega_D \otimes \omega_I|_{c_G \ll c_L \ll \mathbf{1}_{l^0}}\big) \;=\; 0.86|i^0\rangle + 0.14|i^1\rangle, \qquad \text{or, equivalently,}$$
$$= \mathsf{M}_2\big(\omega_D \otimes \omega_I|_{c_L \circ c_G \ll \mathbf{1}_{l^0}}\big).$$

(vi) **What is the intelligence given a C-grade but a high SAT score?** We now have two forms of evidence, namely the point predicate $\mathbf{1}_{g^3}$ on G for the C-grade, and the point predicate $\mathbf{1}_{s^1}$ on S for the high SAT score. We can transform the latter to a predicate $c_S \ll \mathbf{1}_{s^1}$ on the set I and update the state ω_I with it. Then we can procede as in question (iv):

$$\mathsf{M}_2\big(\omega_D \otimes \omega_I|_{c_S \ll \mathbf{1}_{s^1}}|_{c_G \ll \mathbf{1}_{g^3}}\big) \;=\; 0.422|i^0\rangle + 0.578|i^1\rangle.$$

Thus the probability of high intelligence is 57.8% under these circumstances.

Using earlier calculation rules, see notably in Lemma 9.7, this intelligence distribution can also be computed by weakening the predicate $c_S \ll \mathbf{1}_{s^1}$ to $\mathsf{W}_2 c_S \ll \mathbf{1}_{s^1}$ on $D \times I$. Then we can take the conjunction with $c_G \ll \mathbf{1}_{g^3}$ and perform a single update, as in:

$$\mathsf{M}_2\big(\omega_D \otimes \omega_I|_{\mathsf{W}_2 c_S \ll \mathbf{1}_{s^1} \& c_G \ll \mathbf{1}_{g^3}}\big)$$

But one can also do the update with $c_S \ll \mathbf{1}_{s^1}$ at the very end, after the marginalisation, as in:

$$\mathsf{M}_2\big(\omega_D \otimes \omega_I|_{c_G \ll \mathbf{1}_{g^3}}\big)|_{c_S \ll \mathbf{1}_{s^1}}$$

The associated difficulty level is the first marginal:

$$\mathsf{M}_1\big(\omega_D \otimes \omega_I|_{\mathbf{1}_{s^1}}\big|_{c_G \ll \mathbf{1}_{g^3}}\big) = 0.24|d^0\rangle + 0.76|d^1\rangle.$$

The answers to the above questions hopefully convey the systematic thinking that is behind the use of channels – in forward or backward manner, following the network structure – in order to capture the essence of Bayesian networks. This systematics is elaborated further in subsequent sections. In the above 'student' example we have obtained the same outcomes as in traditional approaches. We conclude with an illustration where things differ.

Example 9.14 The power of the channel-based approach is that it provides a 'logic' for Bayesian inference, giving high-level expressions $c \gg \omega|_p$ and $\omega|_{c \ll q}$ for forward and backward inference. We include an illustration from Barber (2012) where our method produces a different outcome. The logical description may help to clarify the differences.

Consider the following Bayesian network, with nodes for burglary (B), earthquake (E), alarm (A) and radio (R).

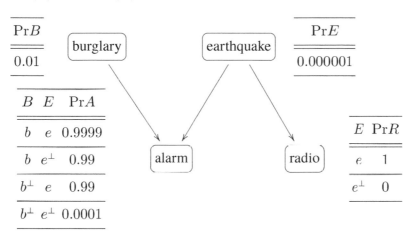

In this case we have binary sets $B = \{b, b^\perp\}$, $E = \{e, e^\perp\}$, $A = \{a, a^\perp\}$ and $R = \{r, r^\perp\}$ with initial states $\omega_B = 0.01|b\rangle + 0.99|b^\perp\rangle$ and $\omega_E = 0.000001|e\rangle + 0.999999|e^\perp\rangle$. There are two channels $c_A : B \times E \to A$ and $c_R : E \to R$ based on the above (two lower) tables. The predicted (a priori) alarm probability is 1%; it is computed as $c_A \gg \omega_B \otimes \omega_E = 0.01|a\rangle + 0.99|a^\perp\rangle$.

The following questions are asked in Barber (2012, Example 3.1 and 3.2).

(i) **What is the probability of a burglary given that the alarm sounds?** In this case we have evidence $\mathbf{1}_a$ on the set A, we pull it back to $B \times E$ along the channel c_A, and we update the joint state $\omega_B \otimes \omega_E$ and take the first marginal:

$$\mathsf{M}_1\big(\omega_B \otimes \omega_E|_{c_A \ll \mathbf{1}_a}\big) = 0.99000198|b\rangle + 0.00999802|b^\perp\rangle.$$

(ii) **What is this probability if we additionally hear a warning on the radio?** In that case we have additional evidence $\mathbf{1}_r$ on R, which is pulled back along the channel c_R and used to update the state ω_E. Then:

$$\mathsf{M}_1\big(\omega_B \otimes \omega_E|_{c_R \ll \mathbf{1}_r}|_{c_A \ll \mathbf{1}_a}\big) = 0.010099|b\rangle + 0.989901|b^\perp\rangle.$$

(iii) ... **"imagine that we are only 70% sure we heard the burglar alarm sounding"** In this situation we have a fuzzy predicate $q\colon A \to 0, 1$ with $qa = 0.7$ and $qa^\perp = 0.3$. We perform the same computation as in question (i), but now with evidence q instead of $\mathbf{1}_a$. This yields:

$$\mathsf{M}_1\big(\omega_B \otimes \omega_E|_{c_A \ll q}\big) = 0.0229|b\rangle + 0.9771|b^\perp\rangle. \tag{9.14}$$

However, in Barber (2012) a completely different computation is performed, following Jeffrey's rule. The assumption about the alarm is not interpreted as a predicate, but as a state $\sigma = 0.7|a\rangle + 0.3|a^\perp\rangle$. The result is computed via a corresponding convex combination of states:

$$0.7 \cdot (\text{update with evidence } a) \; + \; 0.3 \cdot (\text{update with evidence } a^\perp)$$
$$= 0.7 \cdot \mathsf{M}_1\big(\omega_B \otimes \omega_E|_{c_A \ll \mathbf{1}_a}\big) \; + \; 0.3 \cdot \mathsf{M}_1\big(\omega_B \otimes \omega_E|_{c_A \ll \mathbf{1}_{a^\perp}}\big) \tag{9.15}$$
$$= 0.693|b\rangle + 0.307|b^\perp\rangle.$$

For questions (i) and (ii) our calculations coincide with the ones in Barber (2012), but for question (iii) the answers clearly differ. We briefly analyse the situation. For a more extensive analysis in terms of Jeffrey's rule versus Pearl's for updating with soft/fuzzy evidence we refer to Jacobs (2019).

- The above computation (9.14) and the one (9.15) from Barber (2012) are based on different ways of understanding what soft evidence actually means. In Barber (2012) this notion, even though it is not made mathematically precise, appears to have an ontological interpretation: "the alarm was heard" is a new state of affairs, with 70% alarm probability, and is therefor used as a state (distribution). On the other hand, our fuzzy predicate interpretation has an epistemological flavour: it is new information about an agent's belief.

- In line with the previous point, different intuitive descriptions are developed in Jacobs (2019): the approach in (9.14) factors the soft evidence in, as improvement, using Bayesian rules. The approach (9.15) interprets the soft evidence as a 'surprising' state of affairs, that one has to adjust to – as correction – following Jeffrey's rule.

  The above formulation, quoted from Barber (2012), does not seem to suggest that the 70% certainty is a new, surprising state of affairs that we have to adjust to. Instead, it seems to be more like an improvement, so that the calculation (9.14) seems most appropriate.

We shall briefly return to these different was of computation in Example 9.17 where we show that the outcome in (9.14) also appears via 'crossover inference'.

9.7 String diagrams for Bayesian probability

Abstractly, channels are arrows of a category, which is *symmetric monoidal*: it has sequential $\circ$ and parallel $\otimes$ composition. This categorical structure enables the use of a graphical (yet completely formal) notation for channels in terms of *string diagrams* (Selinger, 2011). We have no intention of giving a complete account of the string diagrammatic calculus here, and refer instead to Fong (2012), Jacobs and Zanasi (2016, Sec. 3), and Jacobs et al. (2019, Sec. 3) for details. Nonetheless, it is worthwhile pointing similarities and differences between the graphical representation of channels as string diagrams and the usual Bayesian network notation, see also Jacobs et al. (2019). We shall also use string diagrams to give a pictorial account of the important notion of disintegration (in the next section).

Informally speaking, string diagrams for channels are similar to the kind of graphs that is used for Bayesian networks, see Figure 9.1, but there are important differences.

(i) Whereas flow in Bayesian networks is top-down, we will adopt the convention that in string diagrams the flow is bottom-up. This is an non-essential, but useful difference, because it makes immediately clear in the current context whether we are dealing with a Bayesian network or with a string diagram. Also, it makes our presentation uniform with previous work, see *e.g.* Cho and Jacobs (2019).

(ii) The category where channels are arrows has extra structure, which allows for the use of "special" string diagrams representing certain elementary operations. We will have explicit string diagrams for *copying* and *discarding* variables, namely:

There are some 'obvious' equations between diagrams involving such copy and discard, such as:

These equations represent the fact that copy is the multiplication and discard is the unit of a commutative monoid.

(iii) With string diagrams one can clearly express joint states, on product domains like $X_1 \times X_2$, or $X_1 \times \cdots \times X_n$. This is done by using multiple outgoing pins, coming out of a triangle shape – used for states – as for $\omega \in \mathcal{D}X_1 \times X_2$ and

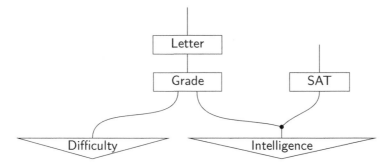

Figure 9.2 Student network from Figure 9.1 expressed as string diagram. Note that the two arrows coming out of Intelligence in Figure 9.1 are translated here into a single wire coming out the Intelligence state, followed by a copy.

$\sigma \in \mathcal{D}X_1 \times \cdots \times X_n$ in:

$$X_1 \quad X_2 \atop \omega \qquad\qquad X_1 \quad \cdots \quad X_n \atop \sigma$$

With this notation in place we can graphically express the marginals via discarding $\bar{\overline{\top}}$ of wires:

$$\mathsf{M}_1\omega \;=\; {X_1 \;\; \bar{\overline{\top}} \atop \omega} \qquad\qquad \text{and} \qquad\qquad \mathsf{M}_2\omega \;=\; {\bar{\overline{\top}} \;\; X_2 \atop \omega}$$

(iv) Channels are *causal* or *unitary* in the sense that discarding their output is the same as discarding their input:

$$\boxed{c} \;=\; \top$$

The Intelligence node in Figure 9.1 has two outgoing arrows, but this does not mean that Intelligence is a joint state. Instead, these two arrows indicate that the outgoing wire should be copied, with one copy going to the Grade node and one to the SAT node. In string diagram notation this copying is written explicitly as in the string-diagrammatic analogue of the student network in Figure 9.2.

Recall that we wrote $\omega_D = 0.6|d^0\rangle + 0.4|d^1\rangle$ and $\omega_I = 0.7|i^0\rangle + 0.3|i^1\rangle$ for the initial states of the student network. The product state

$$\omega_D \otimes \omega_I \;=\; 0.42|d^0, i^0\rangle + 0.18|d^0, i^1\rangle + 0.28|d^1, i^0\rangle + 0.12|d^1, i^1\rangle$$

is non-entwined, since it equals the product of its marginals ω_D and ω_I. A basic fact in probability is that conditioning can create entwinedness, see *e.g.* Jacobs and

Zanasi (2017) for more information. We can see this concretely when the above product state $\omega_D \otimes \omega_I$ is conditioned as in the fourth question in the previous section:

$$\omega_D \otimes \omega_I \big|_{c_G \ll 1_{g^3}}$$
$$= \tfrac{12600}{34636} | d^0, i^0 \rangle + \tfrac{36}{34636} | d^0, i^1 \rangle + \tfrac{19600}{34636} | d^1, i^0 \rangle + \tfrac{2400}{34636} | d^1, i^1 \rangle.$$

With some effort one can show that this state is *not* the product of its marginals: it is entwined. In the language of string diagrams we can express this difference by writing:

9.8 From joint states to Bayesian networks

Our framework allows to express states/distributions and Bayesian networks as entities of the same kind, namely as channels. It is natural to ask how the process of forming a Bayesian network from a distribution can be integrated in the picture.

In traditional probability theory, this procedure forms one of the original motivations for developing the notion of Bayesian network in the first place. Such networks allow for more efficient representation of probabilistic information (via probability tables, as in Figure 9.1) than joint states, which quickly become unmanageable via an exponential explosion. We quote from Koller and Friedman (2009): "... the explicit representation of the joint distribution is unmanageable from every perspective. Computationally, it is very expensive to manipulate and generally too large to store in memory" and from Russell and Norvig (2003): "... a Bayesian network can often be far more *compact* than the full joint distribution".

The procedure of forming a Bayesian network from a given state usually goes through a sub-routine called *disintegration*. For a channel-based definition of disintegration, suppose we have a state $\omega \in \mathcal{D}X$ and a channel $c \colon X \nrightarrow Y$. Then we can form a joint state $\sigma \in \mathcal{D}X \times Y$ as described by the following string diagram:

that is $\sigma x, y = \omega x \cdot c x y.$ (9.16)

The state ω is determined as the first marginal $\omega = \mathsf{M}_1 \sigma$ of σ. This can be seen by discarding $\bar{\top}$ the second wire – on the left and on the right in the above equation – and using that channels are causal, and that discarding one wire of a copy is the identity wire.

Disintegration is the process in the other direction, from a joint state to a channel.

Definition 9.15 Let $\sigma \in \mathcal{D}X \times Y$ be a joint state. A *disintegration* of σ is a channel $c \colon X \rightsquigarrow Y$ for which the equation (9.16) holds, where $\omega = \mathsf{M}_1\sigma$.

There is a standard formula for disintegration of a state $\sigma \in \mathcal{D}X \times Y$, namely:

$$cx := \mathsf{M}_2\big(\sigma|_{\mathbf{1}_x \otimes \mathbf{1}}\big) = \sum_y \frac{\sigma x, y}{\mathsf{M}_1\sigma x}|y\rangle. \tag{9.17}$$

We shall say that the channel c is 'extracted' from σ, or also that σ 'factorises' via c as in (9.16). Intuitively, channel c captures the conditional probabilities expressed in traditional notation as $\Pr_\sigma y \mid x$ via a distribution on Y indexed by elements $x \in X$.

Definition 9.15 gives the basic form of disintegration. There are several variations, which are explored in Cho and Jacobs (2019) as part of a more abstract account of this notion. For instance, by swapping the domains one can also extract a channel $Y \rightsquigarrow X$, in the other direction. Also, if σ is a joint state on n domains, there are in principle 2^n ways of extracting a channel, depending on which pins are marginalised out, and which (other) ones are reconstructed via the channel. For instance, a disintegration of $\omega \in \mathcal{D}X \times Y \times Z$ can also be a channel $c \colon Z \rightsquigarrow X \times Y$. This example suggests a digression on a channel-based definition of conditional independence: X and Y are conditionally independent in ω given Z, written as $X \perp Y \mid Z$, if any such disintegration c for ω can actually be decomposed into channels $c_1 \colon Z \rightsquigarrow X$ and $c_2 \colon Z \rightsquigarrow Y$. In string diagrams:

$$\tag{9.18}$$

where $\omega_3 = \mathsf{M}_3\omega = \Pr_\omega z$ is the third marginal. These channels c_1, c_2 may also be obtained by disintegration from the state $\mathsf{M}_{1,2}\omega = \Pr_\omega x, y$ obtained by marginalising out the third variable. In more traditional notation, one can intuitively read (9.18) as saying that $\Pr_\omega x, y, z = \Pr_\omega x \mid z \cdot \Pr_\omega y \mid z \cdot \Pr_\omega z$. We refer to Cho and Jacobs (2019) for the adequacy of this definition of conditional independence and its properties.

Another interesting observation is that disintegration forms a *modular* procedure. The formula (9.16) shows that disintegration yields a new decomposition of a given state: such a decomposition being a state itself, disintegration may be applied again. In fact, this repeated application is how a joint state on multiple domains gets represented as a Bayesian network. The channel-based approach understands this process uniformly as a step-by-step transformation of a given channel (a state) into another, equivalent channel (a Bayesian network). Once again, string diagrams are a useful formalism for visualising such correspondence. For instance, the joint state

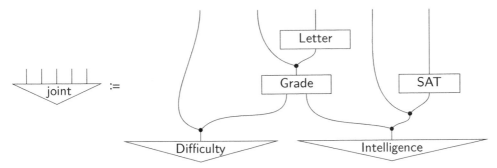

Figure 9.3 The joint distribution (9.19) for the student network from Figure 9.1 obtained as string diagram with additional copiers for non-final nodes.

associated with the Student network from Figures 9.1 and 9.2 can be expressed as in Figure 9.3. Notice that the diagram in Figure 9.3 is just the one in Figure 9.2 where each non-final node has been made externally accessible via additional copiers $\curlyvee$. Figure 9.3 has the type of a joint state. Its value can then be calculated via state transformation, via a composite channel that can be "read off" directly from the graph in Figure 9.3, namely:

joint

$$
:= \big(\mathrm{id}\otimes\mathrm{id}\otimes c_L\otimes\mathrm{id}\otimes\mathrm{id}\circ\mathrm{id}\otimes\Delta\otimes\mathrm{id}\otimes c_S\circ\mathrm{id}\otimes c_G\otimes\Delta\circ\Delta\otimes\Delta\big) \tag{9.19}
$$
$$
\gg (\omega_D\otimes\omega_I).
$$

The tool EⒻPʀᴏʙ, see Cho and Jacobs (2017), has been designed precisely to evaluate such systematic expressions.

Now that we have a formal description of the relationship between joint states and Bayesian networks, we turn to comparing Bayesian inference in these two settings. For reasons of simplicity, we concentrate on the binary case. Suppose we have a joint state $\sigma \in \mathcal{D}X \times Y$, now with *evidence* on X. In the present setting this evidence can be an arbitrary predicate $p \in 0, 1^X$ and not only a point predicate $\mathbf{1}_x$, as usual. We like to find out the distribution on Y, given the evidence p. Informally, this may be written as $\mathrm{Pr}Y \mid p$. More precisely, it is the second marginal of the state obtained by updating with the weakened version $\mathsf{W}_1 p = p \otimes 1$, as in:

$$
\mathsf{M}_2(\sigma|_{\mathsf{W}_1 p}).
$$

Now suppose we have factorised the joint state σ as a (mini) network (9.16) via the extracted state $c\colon X \rightsquigarrow Y$. We can also perform causal reasoning – *i.e.* forward inference – and obtain the state:

$$
c \gg \omega|_p \qquad \text{where} \qquad \omega = \mathsf{M}_1 \sigma.
$$

The *Bayesian inference theorem* says that these outcomes are the same, not only for forward reasoning, but also for backward reasoning.

Theorem 9.16   *Let $\sigma \in \mathcal{D}X \times Y$ be a joint state with extracted channel $c \colon X \rightarrowtail Y$ as in (9.16). For predicates $p \in 0, 1^X$ and $q \in 0, 1^Y$ one has:*

$$\mathsf{M}_2\bigl(\sigma|_{\mathsf{W}_1 p}\bigr) \;=\; c \gg (\mathsf{M}_1\sigma|_p) \quad \textit{and} \quad \mathsf{M}_1\bigl(\sigma|_{\mathsf{W}_2 q}\bigr) \;=\; \mathsf{M}_1\sigma|_{c \ll q}.$$

Before giving a proof, we comment on the significance of the statement. Inference with joint states, as on the left-hand-side of the equations in Theorem 9.16, involves weakening W of evidence in one coordinate and marginalisation M in another coordinate. It uses the entwinedness of the joint state σ, so that one coordinate can influence the other, see Jacobs and Zanasi (2017) where this is called *crossover influence*. Therefor we like to call this form of inference via joint states *crossover inference*.

In contrast, inference on the right-hand-side of the equations in Theorem 9.16 essentially uses state and predicate transformation $\gg$ and $\ll$. Therefor we refer to this form of inference as *transformer inference*. It consists of what we have called backward and forward inference in the table at the end of Section 9.2.3.

Thus the Bayesian inference theorem states the equivalence of crossover inference and transformer inference. Whereas crossover inference works well with small samples (see the examples below), it does not scale to larger networks, where transformations inference is preferable. The equivalence is widely known at some implicit level, but its formulation in this explicit form only arises within the current channel-based perspective on Bayesian networks.

We now provide a proof of the theorem. A purely diagrammatic argument is given in Cho and Jacobs (2019).

Proof of Theorem 9.16   We confine ourselves to proving the first equation in concrete form, using the definition of extracted channel from (9.17):

$$
\begin{aligned}
\bigl(c \gg \mathsf{M}_1\sigma|_p\bigr)y \\
&= \sum_x cxy \cdot \mathsf{M}_1\sigma|_p x \\
&\overset{(9.17)}{=} \sum_x \frac{\sigma x, y}{\mathsf{M}_1\sigma x} \cdot \frac{\mathsf{M}_1\sigma x \cdot px}{\mathsf{M}_1\sigma \models p} \\
&\overset{(9.6)}{=} \sum_x \frac{\sigma x, y \cdot px}{\sigma \models \mathsf{W}_1 p} \\
&= \sum_x \frac{\sigma x, y \cdot \mathsf{W}_1 px, y}{\sigma \models \mathsf{W}_1 p} \qquad \text{since } \mathsf{W}_1 px, y = p \otimes \mathbf{1}x, y = px \\
&= \sum_x \sigma|_{\mathsf{W}_1 p} x, y \\
&= \mathsf{M}_2\bigl(\sigma|_{\mathsf{W}_1 p}\bigr)y. \qquad\qquad\qquad\qquad\qquad \square
\end{aligned}
$$

We conclude this section by giving two demonstrations of the equivalence stated in Theorem 9.16. First, we answer once again the six questions about the student network in Section 9.6: whereas therein we applied transformer inference, we now compute using crossover inference. We shall write:

$$\mathsf{joint} \in \mathcal{D}(D \times G \times L \times I \times S)$$

for the joint state associated with the student network, obtained in formula (9.19), following Figure 9.3. We write M_i for the i-th marginal, obtained by summing out all domains which are not in the i-th position. For the sake of clarity we do not use the notation W for weakening, but use parallel product with the truth predicate $\mathbf{1}$ instead. In agreement with Theorem 9.16, the outcomes are the same as in Section 9.6, but they have been computed separately (in EFPROB).

(i) **What are the a priori probabilities for the recommendation?**

$$\mathsf{M}_3\mathsf{joint} = 0.498|l^0\rangle + 0.502|l^1\rangle.$$

(ii) **What if we know that the student is not intelligent?**

$$\mathsf{M}_3\big(\mathsf{joint}|_{\mathbf{1}\otimes\mathbf{1}\otimes\mathbf{1}\otimes\mathbf{1}_{i^0}\otimes\mathbf{1}}\big) = 0.611|l^0\rangle + 0.389|l^1\rangle.$$

(iii) **What if we additionally know that the test is easy?**

$$\mathsf{M}_3\big(\mathsf{joint}|_{\mathbf{1}_{d^0}\otimes\mathbf{1}\otimes\mathbf{1}\otimes\mathbf{1}_{i^0}\otimes\mathbf{1}}\big) = 0.487|l^0\rangle + 0.513|l^1\rangle.$$

(iv) **What is the intelligence given a C-grade (g^3)?**

$$\mathsf{M}_4\big(\mathsf{joint}|_{\mathbf{1}\otimes\mathbf{1}_{g^3}\otimes\mathbf{1}\otimes\mathbf{1}\otimes\mathbf{1}}\big) = 0.921|i^0\rangle + 0.0789|i^1\rangle.$$

(v) **What is the intelligence given a weak recommendation?**

$$\mathsf{M}_4\big(\mathsf{joint}|_{\mathbf{1}\otimes\mathbf{1}\otimes\mathbf{1}_{l^0}\otimes\mathbf{1}\otimes\mathbf{1}}\big) = 0.86|i^0\rangle + 0.14|i^1\rangle.$$

(vi) **What is the intelligence given a C-grade but a high SAT score?**

$$\mathsf{M}_4\big(\mathsf{joint}|_{\mathbf{1}\otimes\mathbf{1}_{g^3}\otimes\mathbf{1}\otimes\mathbf{1}\otimes\mathbf{1}_{s^1}}\big) = 0.422|i^0\rangle + 0.578|i^1\rangle.$$

As a second demonstration of the theorem, we briefly return to the controversy around inference with soft predicates in Example 9.14.

Example 9.17 We first re-arrange the Bayesian network from Example 9.14 in string diagrammatic form so that we can compute the joint state $\omega \in \mathcal{D}B \times A \times E \times R$

as:

$$\omega = \big(\text{id} \otimes \text{id} \otimes c_R \otimes \text{id}$$
$$\circ\, \text{id} \otimes c_A \otimes \Delta$$
$$\circ\, \Delta \otimes \Delta\big) \gg \omega_B \otimes \omega_E.$$

i.e.

Recall that we have soft/fuzzy evidence $qa = 0.7, qa^\perp = 0.3$ on A. Given this evidence, we want to know the burglar probability. Using crossover inference it is computed as:

$$\mathsf{M}_1\big(\omega|_{\mathbf{1}\otimes q\otimes\mathbf{1}\otimes\mathbf{1}}\big) = 0.0229|b\rangle + 0.9771|b^\perp\rangle.$$

We obtain the same outcome as via transformer inference in (9.14). Of course, the Bayesian Inference Theorem 9.16 tells that the outcomes should coincide in general. This additional computation just provides further support for the appropriateness of doing inference via forward and backward transformations along channels.

9.9 Conclusions

This chapter provides an introduction to an emerging area of channel-based probability theory. It uses standard compositional techniques from programming semantics in the area of Bayesian inference, giving a conceptual connection between forward and backward inference (or: causal and evidential reasoning) on the one hand, and crossover influence on the other.

Promising research directions within this framework include the development of channel-based algorithms for Bayesian reasoning, see Jacobs (2018a). Moreover, the abstract perspective offered by the channel approach may apply to probabilistic graphical models other than Bayesian networks, including models for machine learning such as neural networks (see Jacobs and Sprunger, 2019 for first steps). Paired with the mathematical language of string diagrams, this framework may eventually offer a unifying compositional perspective on the many different pictorial notations for probabilistic reasoning.

Acknowledgements

Fabio Zanasi acknowledges support from EPSRC grant nr. EP/R020604/1. Bart Jacobs' research has received funding from the European Research Council under the European Union's Seventh Framework Programme (FP7/2007-2013) / ERC grant agreement nr. 320571.

References

Barber, D. 2012. *Bayesian Reasoning and Machine Learning*. Cambridge Univ. Press. publicly available via `http://web4.cs.ucl.ac.uk/staff/D.Barber/pmwiki/pmwiki.php?n=Brml.HomePage`.

Bartels, F., Sokolova, A., and de Vink, E. 2004. A hierarchy of probabilistic system types. *Theoretical Computer Science*, **327(1-2)**, 3–22.

Cho, K., and Jacobs, B. 2017. The EfProb Library for Probabilistic Calculations. In: Bonchi, F., and König, B. (eds), *Conference on Algebra and Coalgebra in Computer Science (CALCO 2017)*. LIPIcs, vol. 72. Schloss Dagstuhl.

Cho, K., and Jacobs, B. 2019. Disintegration and Bayesian inversion via string diagrams. *Math. Struct. in Comp. Sci.*, **29(7)**, 938–971.

Cho, K., Jacobs, B., Westerbaan, A., and Westerbaan, B. 2015. *An Introduction to Effectus Theory*. see `arxiv.org/abs/1512.05813`.

Culbertson, J., and Sturtz, K. 2014. A Categorical Foundation for Bayesian Probability. *Appl. Categorical Struct.*, **22(4)**, 647–662.

de Vink, E., and Rutten, J. 1999. Bisimulation for probabilistic transition systems: a coalgebraic approach. *Theoretical Computer Science*, **221**, 271–293.

Dijkstra, E., and Scholten, C. 1990. *Predicate Calculus and Program Semantics*. Berlin: Springer.

Dijkstra, E. W. 1997. *A Discipline of Programming*. 1st edn. Upper Saddle River, NJ, USA: Prentice Hall PTR.

Dubois, D., and Prade, H. 1990. The Logical View of Conditioning and Its Application to Possibility and Evidence Theories. *Int. Journ. of Approximate Reasoning*, **4**, 23–46.

Fong, B. 2012. *Causal Theories: A Categorical Perspective on Bayesian Networks*. M.Phil. thesis, Univ. of Oxford. see `arxiv.org/abs/1301.6201`.

Giry, M. 1982. A categorical approach to probability theory. Pages 68–85 of: Banaschewski, B. (ed), *Categorical Aspects of Topology and Analysis*. Lect. Notes Math., no. 915. Springer, Berlin.

Jacobs, B. 2011. Probabilities, Distribution Monads, and Convex Categories. *Theoretical Computer Science*, **412(28)**, 3323–3336.

Jacobs, B. 2013. Measurable Spaces and their Effect Logic. In: *Logic in Computer Science*Computer Science Press, for IEEE.

Jacobs, B. 2017. A recipe for State and Effect Triangles. *Logical Methods in Comp. Sci.*, **13(2)**. See `https://lmcs.episciences.org/3660`.

Jacobs, B. 2018a. *A Channel-based Exact Inference Algorithm for Bayesian Networks*. See `arxiv.org/abs/1804.08032`.

Jacobs, B. 2018b. From Probability Monads to Commutative Effectuses. *Journ. of Logical and Algebraic Methods in Programming*, **94**, 200–237.

Jacobs, B. 2019. The Mathematics of Changing one's Mind, via Jeffrey's or via Pearl's update rule. *Journ. of Artif. Intelligence Res.*, **65**, 783–806.

Jacobs, B., and Sprunger, D. 2019, to appear. Neural Nets via Forward State Transformation and Backward Loss Transformation. In: König, B. (ed), *Math. Found. of Programming Semantics*. Elect. Notes in Theor. Comp. Sci. Elsevier, Amsterdam. See `arxiv.org/abs/1803.09356`.

Jacobs, B., and Zanasi, F. 2016. A predicate/state transformer semantics for Bayesian learning. Pages 185–200 of: Birkedal, L. (ed), *Math. Found. of Programming Semantics*. Elect. Notes in Theor. Comp. Sci., no. 325. Elsevier, Amsterdam.

Jacobs, B., and Zanasi, F. 2017. A Formal Semantics of Influence in Bayesian Reasoning. In: Larsen, K., Bodlaender, H., and Raskin, J.-F. (eds), *Math. Found. of Computer Science*. LIPIcs, vol. 83. Schloss Dagstuhl.

Jacobs, B., Kissinger, A., and Zanasi, F. 2019. Causal Inference by String Diagram Surgery. Pages 313–329 of: Bojańczyk, M., and Simpson, A. (eds), *Foundations of Software Science and Computation Structures*. Lect. Notes Comp. Sci., no. 11425. Springer, Berlin.

Jones, C., and Plotkin, G. 1989. A probabilistic powerdomain of evaluations. Pages 186–195 of: *Logic in Computer Science*Computer Science Press, for IEEE.

Jung, A., and Tix, R. 1998. The Troublesome Probabilistic Powerdomain. Pages 70–91 of: Edalat, A., Jung, A., Keimel, K., and Kwiatkowska, M. (eds), *Comprox III, Third Workshop on Computation and Approximation*. Elect. Notes in Theor. Comp. Sci., no. 13. Elsevier, Amsterdam.

Keimel, K. 2008. The monad of probability measures over compact ordered spaces and its Eilenberg-Moore algebras. *Topology and its Applications*, **156**, 227–239.

Keimel, K., and Plotkin, G. 2009. Predicate transformers for extended probability and non-determinism. *Math. Struct. in Comp. Sci.*, **19(3)**, 501–539.

Koller, D., and Friedman, N. 2009. *Probabilistic Graphical Models. Principles and Techniques*. Cambridge, MA: MIT Press.

Kozen, D. 1981. Semantics of probabilistic programs. *Journ. Comp. Syst. Sci*, **22(3)**, 328–350.

Kozen, D. 1985. A probabilistic PDL. *Journ. Comp. Syst. Sci*, **30(2)**, 162–178.

Mermin, N.D. 2007. *Quantum Computer Science: An Introduction*. Cambridge Univ. Press.

Mislove, M. 2012. Probabilistic Monads, Domains and Classical Information. Pages 87–100 of: Kashefi, E., Krivine, J., and van Raamsdonk, F. (eds), *Developments of Computational Methods (DCM 2011)*. Elect. Proc. in Theor. Comp. Sci., no. 88.

Mrad, A. Ben, Delcroix, V., Piechowiak, S., Leicester, P., and Abid, M. 2015. An explication of uncertain evidence in Bayesian networks: likelihood evidence and probabilistic evidence. *Applied Intelligence*, **23(4)**, 802–824.

Panangaden, P. 2009. *Labelled Markov Processes*. London: Imperial College Press.

Russell, S., and Norvig, P. 2003. *Artificial Intelligence. A Modern Approach*. Prentice Hall.

Ścibior, A., Ghahramani, Z., and Gordon, A. 2015. Practical Probabilistic Programming with Monads. Pages 165–176 of: *Proc. 2015 ACM SIGPLAN Symp. on Haskell*. ACM.

Ścibior, A., Kammar, O., Vákár, M., Staton, S., Yang, H., Cai, Y., Ostermann, K., Moss, S., Heunen, C., and Ghahramani, Z. 2018. Denotational Validation of Higher-order Bayesian Inference. Pages 60:1–60:29 of: *Princ. of Programming Languages*. ACM Press.

Selinger, P. 2011. A survey of graphical languages for monoidal categories. *Springer Lecture Notes in Physics*, **13**(813), 289–355.

Sokolova, A. 2011. Probabilistic systems coalgebraically: A survey. *Theoretical Computer Science*, **412(38)**, 5095–5110.

Staton, S., Yang, H., Heunen, C., Kammar, O., and Wood, F. 2016. Semantics for probabilistic programming: higher-order functions, continuous distributions, and soft constraints. In: *Logic in Computer Science* Computer Science Press, for IEEE.

Tix, R., Keimel, K., and Plotkin, G. 2005. *Semantic Domains for Combining Probability and Non-Determinism*. Elect. Notes in Theor. Comp. Sci., no. 129. Elsevier, Amsterdam.

Valtorta, M., Kim, Y.-G., and Vomlel, J. 2002. Soft evidential update for probabilistic multiagent systems. *Int. Journ. of Approximate Reasoning*, **29**(1), 71–106.

Varacca, D., and Winskel, G. 2006. Distributing probability over non-determinism. *Math. Struct. in Comp. Sci.*, **16**, 87–113.

10

Quantitative Equational Reasoning

Giorgio Bacci
Aalborg University
Radu Mardare
University of Stratchclyde
Prakash Panangaden
McGill University
Gordon Plotkin
University of Edinburgh

Abstract: Equational logic is central to reasoning about programs. What is the right equational setting for reasoning about probabilistic programs? It has been understood that instead of equivalence relations one should work with (pseudo)metrics in a probabilistic setting. However, it is not clear how this relates to equational reasoning. In recent work the notion of a *quantitative equational logic* was introduced and developed. This retains many of the features of ordinary logic but fits naturally with metric reasoning. The present chapter is an elementry introduction to this topic. In this setting one can define analogues of algebras and free algebras. It turns out that the Kantorovich (Wasserstein) metric emerges as a free construction from a simple quantitative equational theory. We give a couple of examples of quantitative analogues of familiar effects from programming language theory. We do not assume any background in equational logic or advanced category theory.

10.1 Introduction

Equational reasoning is at the heart of mathematics and theoretical computer science. In algebra, we define algebraic structures by giving (mostly) equational axioms. In analysis there are numerous equations linking concepts; of course, inequalities play a major role too but this just highlights the importance of equality. In programming language semantics one has equations capturing notions of behavioural equivalence of programs. The monadic approach, due to Moggi (1991), to incorporating effects in higher-order functional programming has been understood through the work of

[a] From *Foundations of Probabilistic Programming*, edited by Gilles Barthe, Joost-Pieter Katoen and Alexandra Silva published 2020 by Cambridge University Press.

Plotkin and Power (2004), Hyland et al. (2006), and Hyland and Power (2007) and others in terms of operations and equations.

With the emergence of probabilistic programming[1] a new emphasis on quantitative reasoning has become important. One thinks in terms of "how close are two programs?" rather than "are they completely indistinguishable?" This concept is captured by a *metric* and was first advocated in Giacalone et al. (1990). The idea here was that instead of using a behavioural equivalence relation like bisimulation one should use a pseudometric whose kernel is bisimulation. Such a metric was first defined in Desharnais et al. (1999). What we aim to do here is show how a version of equational reasoning, which we call *quantitative equational logic*, captures such metric reasoning principles. This work first appeared in Mardare et al. (2016, 2017) and Bacci et al. (2018).

The most compelling example of a programming language setting where quantitative reasoning is important is probabilistic programming; the subject of this book. While our work is not specifically adapted to this setting it does provide the general framework for such reasoning. In particular, one of the most important ways of comparing probability distributions is the Kantorovich (Wasserstein) metric and, for example, in machine learning it has recently been a source of much attention. In our quantitative equational framework this metric emerges naturally from simple quantitative equations.

The key idea is to introduce equations indexed by positive rational numbers:

$$s =_\varepsilon t$$

where s and t are terms of some language and ε is a (presumably small) positive real number. One reads this as "s is within ε of t". Certainly, the relation $=_\varepsilon$ is not an equivalence relation: transitivity does not hold, if $s =_\varepsilon t$ and $t =_\varepsilon u$ then there is no reason to think $s =_\varepsilon u$. Indeed, one can only say $s =_{2\varepsilon} u$.

In the usual notion of equational reasoning one has a trinity of ideas: equations, Lawvere theories, and monads on **Set**. The equational presentation of algebras was systematically worked out by universal algebraists. Lawvere showed how to give a cateorical presentation of algebraic theories which freed the subject from some of the awkwardness of dealing with different presentations of the same theory. In the 1950s it was understood that algebras arose as the "algebras of a monad" defined on the category **Set**. Essentially, the action of the monad is to construct the free algebras.

These concepts can be generalized to other settings, see, for example, Robinson (2002). In the present work we have quantitative equations and it turns out that one can get monads on **Met**, for some suitable category of metric spaces.

---

[1] To a lesser extent, real-time programming as well.

10.2 Equational Logic

In this section we review the standard familiar concepts of equational logic; where we mean equations in the usual sense of the word. The equality concept is one of the oldest abstract mathematical ideas and is well understood intuitively.

The basic syntax of equational logic starts with a *signature* of symbols

$$\Omega = \{f_j : \kappa_i \mid i \in I\},$$

consisting of a set of *function symbols* (or *operations*) f_i each having associated with it a cardinal number (finite or infinite) κ_i called its *arity*. The arity specifies how many arguments the function symbol takes. Some function symbols may have arity 0; these are the *constants* of the language. We have not restricted the collection of operations to be finite or countable, and one of our main examples will indeed have uncountably many operations. It is possible to consider operations which take infinitely many arguments and we will consider such an example later.

Terms are constructed inductively starting from a fixed countable set X of *variables*, ranged over by $x, y, z, \ldots$. Then the function symbols are applied to the appropriate number of previously constructed terms to give new terms. We can succinctly express the collection of terms through the following grammar:

$$t ::= x \mid f(t_i)_{i \in \kappa}, \qquad \text{for } x \in X \text{ and } f : \kappa \in \Omega$$

The set of terms constructed this way is denoted by $\mathbf{T}_\Omega X$. When the signature of operation symbols Ω is clear from from the context, the set of terms will be simply denoted as $\mathbf{T}X$.

A *substitution* is a function $\sigma : X \to \mathbf{T}X$: it defines what it means to substitute a variable for a term. It can be (homomorphically) extended to a function $\tilde{\sigma} : \mathbf{T}X \to \mathbf{T}X$ over terms as follows:

$$\tilde{\sigma}(x) = \sigma(x) \qquad \text{for } x \in X,$$
$$\tilde{\sigma}(f(t_l)_{l \in \kappa}) = f(\tilde{\sigma}(t_i))_{i \in \kappa} \qquad \text{for } f : \kappa \in \Omega.$$

In what follows we won't make any distinction between the substitution and its extension. We will denote by $\Sigma(X)$ the set of substitutions on $\mathbf{T}X$.

The basic formulas of equational logic are *equations* of the form

$$s = t, \qquad \text{for } s, t \in \mathbf{T}X.$$

There are no quantifiers or logical connectives. We use $\mathcal{E}(\mathbf{T}X)$ to denote the set of equations over $\mathbf{T}X$. Conjunction is implicit when one writes a sequence of equations, but there is no disjunction, nor negation or implication. A *judgement* is an expression of the form

$$\Gamma \vdash \phi,$$

where $\Gamma \subseteq \mathcal{E}(\mathbf{T}X)$ is an enumerable set of equations and $\phi \in \mathcal{E}(\mathbf{T}X)$. The judgment $\Gamma \vdash \phi$ is intended to mean that under the assumptions in Γ the equation ϕ holds. We refer to the elements of Γ as the *hypotheses* and to ϕ as the *conclusion* of the judgment; $\mathcal{J}(\mathbf{T}X)$ denotes the collection of judgments on $\mathbf{T}X$.

Judgments are used for reasoning; we now define the important concept of equational theory.

An *equational theory of type* Ω *over* X is a set $\mathcal{U}$ of judgements on $\mathbf{T}X$ such that, for arbitrary $s, t, u \in \mathbf{T}X$ and $\Gamma, \Theta \subseteq \mathcal{E}(\mathbf{T}X)$

> (**Refl**) $\emptyset \vdash t = t \in \mathcal{U}$,
>
> (**Symm**) $\{s = t\} \vdash t = s \in \mathcal{U}$,
>
> (**Trans**) $\{s = u, u = t\} \vdash s = t \in \mathcal{U}$,
>
> (**Cong**) $\{s_i = t_i \mid i \in \kappa\} \vdash f(s_i)_{i \in \kappa} = f(t_i)_{i \in \kappa} \in \mathcal{U}$, for any $f : \kappa \in \Omega$,
>
> (**Subst**) if $\Gamma \vdash s = t \in \mathcal{U}$, then $\sigma(\Gamma) \vdash \sigma(s) = \sigma(t) \in \mathcal{U}$, for any $\sigma \in \Sigma(X)$,
>
> (**Cut**) if $\Theta \vdash \Gamma \in \mathcal{U}$ and $\Theta \vdash s = t \in \mathcal{U}$, then $\Gamma \vdash s = t \in \mathcal{U}$,
>
> (**Assum**) if $s = t \in \Gamma$, then $\Gamma \vdash s = t \in \mathcal{U}$,

where we write $\Gamma \vdash \Theta \in \mathcal{U}$ to mean that $\Gamma \vdash \phi \in \mathcal{U}$ holds for all $\phi \in \Theta$; and $\sigma(\Gamma) = \{\sigma(s) = \sigma(t) \mid s = t \in \Gamma\}$.

The rules (**Refl**), (**Symm**), and (**Trans**) capture the idea that equality is indeed an equivalence relation. The congruence rule (**Cong**) describes how equality interacts with the term-forming operations of the underlying term language. Finally, the substitution rule (**Subst**) states that substitution preserve equality, while (**Cut**) and (**Assum**) are the usual cut and assumption rules of logical reasoning.

A trivial consequence of the cut rule is that $\emptyset \vdash s = t \in \mathcal{U}$ implies that $\Gamma \vdash s = t \in \mathcal{U}$, for any set of equations Γ. In other words, whatever can be proven in a theory $\mathcal{U}$ without using any hypothesis, can also be proven from any set of hypothesis. This is the familiar *weakening* rule.

Given an equational theory $\mathcal{U}$ and a set $S \subseteq \mathcal{U}$, we say that S is a set of axioms for $\mathcal{U}$, or S axiomatizes $\mathcal{U}$, if $\mathcal{U}$ is the smallest equational theory that contains S. An equational theory $\mathcal{U}$ is *inconsistent* if $\emptyset \vdash x = y \in \mathcal{U}$ for two distinct variables $x, y \in X$; $\mathcal{U}$ is *consistent* if it is not inconsistent. From the substitution rule, inconsistency implies that *every* equation is derivable.

10.2.1 Algebra

Equational logic is intimately tied to algebra. For most of the familiar algebraic structures one sees, the basic definition is given in terms of equations (although, there are a few notable exceptions). To describe the equations characterising algebraic structures like a group or monoid, e.g., the associativity equation, one starts with a set of variables X and signature of operations. This gives the *term algebra* over which the equational properties are described. For example, for monoids one can use the signature

$$\{e\colon 0, \ \cdot\colon 2\}$$

consisting of a 0-arity function symbol e (*i.e.*, a constant) for the identity element and an 2-arity function symbol "$\cdot$" (typically used as an infix operator). The terms for this language look like $x \cdot (y \cdot z), e \cdot x, \ldots$ [2].

The properties are spelled out as equations. For monoids, these are

$$e \cdot x = x, \qquad x \cdot e = x, \qquad (x \cdot y) \cdot z = x \cdot (y \cdot z),$$

for $x, y, z \in X$ variables.

Given a Ω-*algebra*, *i.e.*, an algebraic structure over the signature Ω, such as a monoid, we need to explain what it means for it to *satisfy* an equation, or more generally a judgement.

A particular instance of an Ω-algebra $\mathcal{A} = (A, \Omega_{\mathcal{A}})$ consists of a set A, called the *carrier*, containing the elements of the algebra, and a collection $\Omega_{\mathcal{A}}$ of *interpretations* for each function symbol in Ω. If $f\colon a \in \Omega$ is a function symbol of arity κ, then its interpretation is a function $f_{\mathcal{A}}\colon A^{\kappa} \to A$, where A^{κ} is the κ-fold cartesian product of A; for a constant symbol this corresponds to select a designated element of A. Thus a particular monoid $\mathcal{M}$ will be described by giving a set M of its elements, a designated element $e_{M} \in M$ to stand for e, and a binary operation $\cdot_{M}\colon M \times M \to M$.

Given the notion of algebra we can define a *subalgebra*. A subalgebra of $\mathcal{A}$ is another algebra with the same signature and whose elements form a subset of A. Given two algebras $\mathcal{A} = (A, \Omega_{\mathcal{A}})$, $\mathcal{B} = (B, \Omega_{\mathcal{B}})$ of the same signature, we can define a *homomorphism* h to be a set-theoretic function from A to B, which preserves the operations of the signature:

$$h(f_{\mathcal{A}}(a_i)_{i \in \kappa}) = f_{\mathcal{B}}(h(a_i))_{i \in \kappa}, \qquad \text{for all } f\colon \kappa \in \Omega,$$

where the equality symbol appearing in this equation means **identity** between elements in B.

If we fix a set of variables X and a signature Ω, the *term algebra* has the set of terms $\mathbf{T}X$ build over X as carrier and interpretation for the function symbols $f\colon \kappa \in \Omega$ canonically given by

$$(t_i)_{i \in \kappa} \in (\mathbf{T}X)^{\kappa} \mapsto f(t_i)_{i \in \kappa} \in \mathbf{T}X.$$

We denote as $\mathbf{T}X$ for this structure as well as its the underlying set of terms. Consider a Ω-algebra $\mathcal{A} = (A, \Omega_{\mathcal{A}})$ and a assignment function $\iota\colon X \to A$ from X to A,

---

[2] Actually, it is even more common to leave it out altogether and indicate the operation by mere juxtaposition.

interpreting variables as elements in $\mathcal{A}$; this extends inductively to a function, also written ι, from $\mathbf{T}X$ to A:

$$\iota(x) = \sigma(x) \qquad\qquad \text{for } x \in X,$$
$$\iota(f(t_i)_{i \in \kappa}) = f_{\mathcal{A}}(\iota(t_i))_{i \in \kappa} \qquad\qquad \text{for } f : \kappa \in \Omega.$$

It is immediate from this definition that ι is a homomorphism from $\mathbf{T}X$ to $\mathcal{A}$. It should also be clear that *every* homomorphism from $\mathbf{T}X$ to $\mathcal{A}$ arises in this way; we just have to restrict the homomorphism to X.

Definition 10.1. We say that a judgement $\Gamma \vdash s = t$ in $\mathcal{J}(\mathbf{T}X)$ is **satisfied** by $\mathcal{A}$, written $\mathcal{A} \models (\Gamma \vdash s = t)$, if for every assignment $\iota : X \to A$ the following implication holds:

$$\big(\text{for all } (s' = t') \in \Gamma, \iota(s') = \iota(t')\big) \text{ implies } \iota(s) = \iota(t).$$

The "term algebra" that we have defined so far is not really a proper algebra of the type we have in mind because it does not satisfy the equations that define the class of algebraic structures. We now repair this by an appropriate quotient construction.

Let S be a set of judgements and $\mathcal{U}_S$ the smallest equational theory that contains S. We define a relation between terms s, t by

$$s \sim_S t, \text{ if } (\emptyset \vdash s = t) \in \mathcal{U}_S.$$

Since $\mathcal{U}_S$ is closed under the rules of equational logic, in other words, it is closed under reflexivity, symmetry, transitivity, substitution, and congruence; this gives us a congruence[3] relation on $\mathbf{T}X$. We write $[t]$ for the equivalence class of t with respect to the congruence $\sim_S$. The quotient set $\mathbf{T}X/_{\sim_S}$ is the collection of such equivalence classes. It will be the underlying set of the term algebra. We define an interpretation, written f_S, for an operator $f : \kappa \in \Omega$ of the signature on $\mathbf{T}X/_{\sim_S}$ as follows:

$$f_S([t_i])_{i \in \kappa} = [f(t_i)_{i \in \kappa}].$$

This is well defined precisely because $\sim_S$ is a congruence. The set $\mathbf{T}X/_{\sim_S}$ is now a Ω-algebra; we denote it by $\mathbf{T}_S[X]$, or simply $\mathbf{T}[X]$ when S is clear from the context. It should be clear that by its construction, the algebra $\mathbf{T}_S[X]$ satisfies all the judgements in S (and $\mathcal{U}_S$).

Examples of familiar algebras that can be presented purely equationally are semigroups, monoids, groups, rings, lattices, and boolean algebras. Vector spaces have two sorts of elements, but the theory described above can readily be extended to this case and thus we include vector spaces as equationally defined algebras. Stacks as used in computer science are another familiar example. Some algebraic structures require a strictly more powerful construct, namely *Horn clauses* in

---

[3] We always implicitly include the notion of equivalence relation when we say "congruence."

their axiomatizations. These are judgements with a nonempty set of hypothesis representing a condition that must hold. For example, right-cancellative monoids are required to satisfy the judgement

$$\{x \cdot z = y \cdot z\} \vdash x = y.$$

A familiar example of a right-cancellative monoid is the set of words over an alphabet with the operation being concatenation of words.

Fields are not an example of equationally defined class of algebras. One of the field axioms says: "if $x \neq 0$ then there exist an element x^{-1} such that $x \cdot x^{-1} = x^{-1} \cdot x = 1$". Here 1 is the multiplicative identity element. It is clearly not an equation because of the side condition. It is not obvious to see that one cannot replace this with a bona-fide equation.

A very interesting example of an algebra that we will extensively discuss in the quantitative setting are *barycentric algebras*. The signature of barycentric algebras has uncountably many binary operations

$$\{+_e : 2 \mid e \in [0,1]\}$$

satisfying the following equations, due to Stone,

(B1) $\emptyset \vdash x +_1 y = x$,

(B2) $\emptyset \vdash x +_e x = x$,

(SC) $\emptyset \vdash x +_e y = y +_{1-e} x$,

(SA) $\emptyset \vdash (x +_{e_1} y) +_{e_2} z = x +_{e_1 e_2} (y +_{\frac{e_2 - e_1 e_2}{1 - e_1 e_2}} z)$, for $e_1, e_2 \in (0,1)$,

axiomatizing the notion of convex combination of a pair of elements. Any convex subset of a real vector space satisfies these axioms. Barycentric algebras can be axiomatized in other ways. For example, instead of binary convex combinations one can introduce n-ary convex combinations for all $n \in \mathbb{N}$. One of the most important examples of a barycentric algebra is the set of probability measures on a finite set or indeed on more complicated spaces. In Section 10.3.1 we review some probability theory on metric spaces.

10.2.2 General Results

Given an equational theory $\mathcal{U}$ and an algebra $\mathcal{A}$ over the same signature, we write $\mathcal{A} \models \mathcal{U}$ to mean that $\mathcal{A}$ satisfies all the judgements in $\mathcal{U}$. As is usual in model theory, we write $\mathcal{U} \models (\Gamma \vdash \phi)$ to mean that the judgement $\Gamma \vdash \phi$ is satisfied by any algebra $\mathcal{A}$ for which $\mathcal{A} \models \mathcal{U}$ holds.

The celebrated Birkhoff completeness theorem relates the semantic notion of satisfiability to deducibility (see, for example p. 95 of Burris and Sankappanavar, 1981).

Theorem 10.2 (Completeness). $\mathcal{U} \models (\Gamma \vdash \phi)$, *if and only if,* $(\Gamma \vdash \phi) \in \mathcal{U}$.

The proof is by construction of a suitable universal model: the algebra $\mathbf{T}_{\mathcal{U}}[X]$ over the quotient $\mathbf{T}X/_{\sim_{\mathcal{U}}}$ introduced in Section 10.2.1. We will see that an analogous result holds in the quantitative case.

Let $\mathbf{K}(\Omega, \mathcal{U})$ denote the collection of Ω-algebras satisfying all the judgements in $\mathcal{U}$, i.e., $\mathcal{A} \in \mathbf{K}(\Omega, \mathcal{U})$ if $\mathcal{A} \models \mathcal{U}$; $\mathbf{K}(\Omega, \mathcal{U})$ becomes a category if we take the morphisms to be Ω-homomorphisms. If we don't need to emphasize which signature we use will simply write $\mathbf{K}(\mathcal{U})$.

Let X be a set of variables. We have seen that $\mathbf{T}_{\mathcal{U}}[X]$ is an algebra in $\mathbf{K}(\mathcal{U})$. There is a map $\eta_X : X \to \mathbf{T}_{\mathcal{U}}[X]$ given by $\eta_X(x) = [x]$, which is *universal* in the following sense:

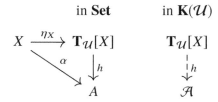

in **Set**   in $\mathbf{K}(\mathcal{U})$

for any algebra $\mathcal{A} \in \mathbf{K}(\mathcal{U})$ and function α from X to the underlying set A of $\mathcal{A}$, there exists a *unique* algebra homomorphism $h: \mathbf{T}_{\mathcal{U}}[X] \to \mathcal{A}$ such that $h \circ \eta_X = \alpha$. In other words any set theoretic function can be uniquely extended to an algebra homomorphism. This makes $\mathbf{T}_{\mathcal{U}}[X]$ the *free algebra* in $\mathbf{K}(\mathcal{U})$ generated from X.

The construction of $\mathbf{T}_{\mathcal{U}}[X]$ from the set X is functorial and such a functor is left adjoint to the forgetful functor from $\mathbf{K}(\mathcal{U})$ to **Set**. As usual with an adjunction, one gets a monad: the *term monad* $(\mathbf{T}_{\mathcal{U}}, \eta, \mu)$ on the category **Set**, with unit $\eta: Id \Rightarrow \mathbf{T}_{\mathcal{U}}$ assigning a variable x to the equivalence class $[x]$ of terms provably equal in $\mathcal{U}$, and multiplication $\mu: \mathbf{T}_{\mathcal{U}}^2 \Rightarrow \mathbf{T}_{\mathcal{U}}$ expressing term composition up to provable equivalence in $\mathcal{U}$.

Moreover, the (Eilenberg-Moore) algebras for the monad $\mathbf{T}_{\mathcal{U}}$ are in one-to-one correspondence with the algebras in $\mathbf{K}(\mathcal{U})$; actually this correspondence is and isomorphism of categories.

The collection of algebras defined by a set of equations is called a *variety of algebras*[4]. A famous theorem, also due to Birkhoff (1935) gives conditions under which a collection of algebras can be a variety.

Theorem 10.3. *A collection of algebras is a variety of algebras if and only if it is closed under homomorphic images, subalgebras, and products.*

---

[4] Please do not confuse this with the notion of algebraic variety which means something completely different.

There are analogous results for algebras defined by Horn clauses: these are called quasi-variety theorems. Consider $\mathbb{Z}_2 \times \mathbb{Z}_2$. It is not a field because, *e.g.* $(1,0) \times (0,1) = (0,0)$; fields are not supposed to have zero-divisors. Hence fields cannot be described by equations.

There is a quantitative analogue of this theorem (see Mardare et al., 2017) but we will not discuss it in this article as it is rather more technical than is appropriate for the present chapter.

10.3 Background

We assume that basic concepts of metric and topological spaces are well-known to the reader.

Definition 10.4. Apseudometric on a set X is a function $d \colon X \times X \to [0, \infty)$ satisfying

$$\forall x \in X, \qquad d(x,x) = 0,$$
$$\forall x, y \in X, \qquad d(x,y) - d(y,x),$$
$$\forall x, y, z \in X, \qquad d(x,y) \le d(x,z) + d(z,y).$$

Note that we do *not* require $d(x,y) = 0$ implies that $x = y$; if we impose this condition we get what is usually called a *metric*. In a pseudometric one can have distinct points at 0 distance. The relation of being at zero distance is easily seen to be an equivalence relation called the *kernel* of the pseudometric. If we take the quotient of the underlying space by the kernel there is a natural metric defined on the equivalence classes which will satisfy the additional axiom above. The concepts of induced topology, convergence, continuity, completeness all work equally well with pseudometrics as with metrics.

Let (X, d_X), (Y, d_Y) be two (pseudo)metric spaces. A function f from to X to Y is *non-expansive* if for all $x, x' \in X$, $d_X(x,x') \ge d_Y(f(x), f(x'))$.

Metric spaces with the non-expansive maps between them form a category, usually called **Met**. Although **Met** has finite products and, more generally, finite limits, it does not have countable products nor binary coproducts. A simple way to recover completeness of the category, is to work with *extended* metric spaces: these are spaces where the metric may take on infinite values.

We define **EMet** to be the category where the objects are extended metric spaces and the morphisms are non-expansiveness maps. In **EMet** the product of a collection of spaces, $\{(X_i, d_i)\}_{i \in I}$ as the cartesian product of the individual spaces $\prod_{i \in I} X_i$ and the metric between two points $(x_i)_{i \in I}, (y_i)_{i \in I}$ is $\sup_{i \in I} d_i(x_i, y_i)$. This supremum may, of course, be infinite; this is fine in **EMet** but not in **Met**. Coproducts is **EMet** are defined by taking the coproduct as sets, *i.e.*, the disjoint union; the distance between two points in the same component is just whatever it is in the original space, while the distance between two points in different components is ∞. Whenever one has an extended metric space (X, d), one can define an equivalence relation $\sim$ by $x \sim y$ iff $d(x, y) < \infty$. The equivalence classes are called components and in fact the original space is just the coproduct of the components. One can extend many standard results about ordinary metric spaces by using this decomposition. However, some things require extra caution: for example, Banach's fixed point theorem requires some care.

10.3.1 Measure Theory

Excellent sources for background on measure theory and probability are Billingsley (1995) or Dudley (1989). A quicker introduction is in Panangaden (2009).

It is a fact that on many familiar spaces, like $\mathbb{R}$, one cannot define a sensible measure on all the sets. For example, on the real line one would like a measure that that co-incides with the concept of length on intervals; but there is no such measure defined on *all* subsets of the real line. Accordingly, we have to choose "nice" families of sets on which one can hope to do measure theory properly. Being able to take countable unions and sums is the key.

Definition 10.5. A σ-**algebra** on a set X is a family of subsets of X which includes X itself and which is closed under complementation and countable unions.

A set equipped with a σ-algebra is called a *measurable space*. Given a topological space, we can define the σ-algebra generated by the open sets (or, equivalently, by the closed sets). Here, when we say that a σ-algebra is *generated* by some family of sets, say $\mathcal{F}$, we mean the smallest σ-algebra containing $\mathcal{F}$; which always exists and is unique. When the σ-algebra is generated by a topology it is usually referred to as *Borel* σ-*algebra*.

Definition 10.6. Given a σ-algebra (X, Σ), a **(subprobability) measure** on X is a ([0, 1]-valued) $[0, \infty]$-valued set function, μ, defined on Σ such that

- $\mu(\emptyset) = 0$,
- for a countable collection of pairwise disjoint sets, $\{A_i \mid i \in I\}$, in Σ, we require

$$\mu(\bigcup_{i \in I} A_i) = \sum_{i \in I} \mu(A_i).$$

In addition, for probability measures we require $\mu(X) = 1$, while for subprobability measures we require $\mu(X) \leq 1$.

There is a unique measure that one can construct defined on the Borel algebra of the real line which coincides with the notion of length of an interval: this is called *Lebesgue* measure.

It is worth clarifying how the word "measurable" is used in the literature. Given a σ-field Σ on a set X one says "measurable set" for a member of Σ. Suppose that one has a measure μ. One can have the following situation. There can be sets of measure zero which contain non-measurable subsets. Because these sets are not measurable one cannot say that they have measure zero. This happens with Lebesgue measure on the Borel sets in the real line, for example. There is a "completion" procedure[5] which produces a larger σ-algebra and an extension of the original measure in such a way that all subsets of sets of measure zero are measurable and have measure zero. The completion works by adding to the σ-algebra all sets X such that there exist Y, Z measurable sets with $Y \subseteq X \subseteq Z$ and with Y and Z having the same measure. When applied to the Borel subsets of the real line we get a much bigger σ-algebra called the Lebesgue measurable sets. One often uses the phrase "measurable set" to mean a set which belongs to the completed σ-field rather than the original σ-field.

Definition 10.7. A function $f\colon (X, \Sigma_X) \to (Y, \Sigma_Y)$ between measurable spaces is said to be **measurable** if $\forall B \in \Sigma_Y.\ f^{-1}(B) \in \Sigma_X$.

A very important class of spaces are the ones that come from metrics.

Definition 10.8. A **Polish** space is the topological space underlying a complete, separable metric space; *i.e.*, it has a countable dense subset.

Note that completeness is a metric concept but being Polish is a topological concept. A space like $(0, 1)$ is not complete in its usual metric, however, it is homeomorphic to the whole real line which is complete in its usual metric; thus, $(0, 1)$ is a Polish space.

10.3.2 The Giry Monad

A very important monad that arises in probabilistic semantics is the Giry monad described in Giry (1981). The idea was originally due to Lawvere (1962), who described a category of probabilistic mappings. Later Giry described the monad from which Lawvere's category emerges as the Kleisli category.

The underlying category is **Mes**: the objects are measurable spaces (X, Σ) and the morphisms $f\colon (X, \Sigma) \to (Y, \Lambda)$ are measurable functions. The monad is an endofunctor: $\mathcal{G}\colon \mathbf{Mes} \to \mathbf{Mes}$. The explicit definition is, on objects

$$\mathcal{G}(X, \Sigma) = \{p \mid p \text{ is a probability measure on } \Sigma\}.$$

We need to equip the set $\mathcal{G}(X, \Sigma)$ with a σ-algebra structure. For each $A \in \Sigma$, define $e_A\colon \mathcal{G}(X, \Sigma) \to [0, 1]$ by $e_A(p) = p(A)$. We equip $\mathcal{G}(X, \Sigma)$ with the smallest σ-algebra making all the e_A measurable.

---

[5] This is an unfortunate name because it gives the mistaken impression that the result cannot be further extended.

The action of G on morphisms $f : (X, \Sigma) \to (Y, \Lambda)$ is given by

$$G(f) \colon G(X, \Sigma) \to G(Y, \Lambda) : \qquad G(f)(p)(B \in \Lambda) = p(f^{-1}(B)).$$

Here p is a probability measure on (X, Σ). The effect of the functor is to push forward measures through the measurable function f.

Now we can define the monad structure as follows: $\eta_X : X \to G(X)$ is given by $\eta_X(x) = \delta_x$, where $\delta_x(A) = 1$ if $x \in A$ and 0 if $x \notin A$. The monad multiplication is

$$\mu_X(Q \in G^2(X))(A) = \int e_A \mathrm{d}Q.$$

One can think of this as an "averaging" over all the measures in $G(X)$ where we use Q as the weight for the averaging process.

Now we can present the Kleisli category as follows. The objects are the same as **Mes**; the morphisms from (X, Σ) to (Y, Λ) are measurable functions from (X, Σ) to $G(Y, \Lambda)$. Kleisli composition of $h \colon X \to G(Y)$ and $k \colon Y \to G(Z)$ is given by the formula:

$$(k \; \tilde{\circ} \; h) = \mu_Z \circ G(k) \circ h,$$

where $\tilde{\circ}$ denotes the Kleisli composition and $\circ$ is composition in **Mes**.

If we curry the definition of Kleisli morphism from (X, Σ) to (Y, Λ) as $h \colon X \times \Lambda \to [0, 1]$ we get what are called *Markov kernels*. We call this category **Ker**. One can think of these as the probabilistic analogue of relations just as ordinary relations are the Kleisli category of the powerset monad. Kleisli composition can be written in terms of kernels:

$$(k \; \tilde{\circ} \; h)(x, C) = \int_{y \in Y} k(y, C) \mathrm{d}h(x, \cdot),$$

for $x \in X$ and C a measurable subset in Z. In this form the analogy with relational composition is much clearer. One can also see this as the analogue of matrix multiplication; if the spaces were finite sets the kernels would be matrices and this composition formula would be matrix multiplication.

10.3.3 Metrics between Probability Distributions

Let p, q be probability distributions on a metric space (X, d) equipped with its Borel σ-algebra Σ. There are a number of important metrics one can place on the space of probability distributions $G(X, \Sigma)$.

The most basic is the *total variation metric*

$$TV(p, q) = \sup_{E \in \Sigma} |p(E) - q(E)|.$$

This measures how much p and q disagree on particular measurable sets.

A more subtle metric is the Kantorovich metric which measures how different are the integrals defined by the two measures being compared. The definition is

$$\mathbb{K}(p,q) = \sup_f \left| \int f\,\mathrm{d}p - \int f\,\mathrm{d}q \right|,$$

with supremum ranging over bounded and non-expansive (which implies continuous) $[0,1]$-valued functions f on X. If we allowed any measurable functions then we could exaggerate the value of the function being integrated on sets where the measures disagree and obtain an infinite sup every time. One can think of the total variation metric as a variant of the Kantorovich metric by considering only indicator functions. However, this is not quite right, as indicator functions are far from non-expansive.

There is an entirely different way of thinking of the Kantorovich metric in terms of transport theory. One thinks of the probability distribution as a "pile of sand" on the space X. Then one needs to move some sand around to change the shape of the pile from p to q. Moving a certain amount of sand has a cost associated with it: this cost is measured by the distance that one has to move the sand. In order to describe a specific "plan" for moving sand we introduce a measure on the product space $X \times X$. A *coupling* π between p, q is a probability distribution on $X \times X$ such that the marginals of π are p, q; in other words we have

$$\pi(A \times X) = p(A) \qquad \text{and} \qquad \pi(X \times B) = q(B).$$

Such a coupling describes a transport plan: $\pi(A \times B)$ describes how much of the probability mass was moved from A to B.

We write $C(p,q)$ for the space of couplings. Then we have the following theorem called *Kantorovich–Rubinstein duality*

$$\mathbb{K}(p,q) = \inf_{\pi \in C(p,q)} \int d(x,y)\mathrm{d}\pi(x,y).$$

In other words the same metric is given by the cost of the minimum-cost transport plan. The right hand side can also be taken to be the definition of the metric. This is usually *incorrectly* called the *Wasserstein metric*[6]

A small variation of the Kantorovich metric can be obtained as follows:

$$W^{(m)}(p,q) = \inf_{\pi \in C(p,q)} \left[\int d(x,y)^m \mathrm{d}\pi(x,y) \right]^{1/m}.$$

If we take $m = 1$ we get the usual Kantorovich metric. A fundamental fact is that

$$W^{(m)}(\delta_x, \delta_y) = d(x,y).$$

---

[6] Both versions of the metric were invented by Kantorovich. Years later Wasserstein used it in a minor way. Perhaps the fact that Kantorovich used the letter W in his paper added to the confusion. It is also called the "earth movers' distance" by people in the computer vision community and the Hutchinson metric by researchers working on fractals.

This says that the original space is *isometrically embedded* in the space of probability measures.

10.3.4 Markov Processes

Markov processes provide the basic operational semantics for probabilistic programming languages. A L-labelled Markov process (see Panangaden, 2009) is a quadruple:

$$(X, \Sigma, L, (\tau_a \colon X \times \Sigma \to [0,1])_{a \in L}),$$

where the τ_a are Markov kernels. One thinks of a labelled Markov process as a probabilistic labelled transition system with a state space that may be a general measurable space or a Polish space.

One can define a notion of bisimulation as was done by Larsen and Skou (1991) and later extended to the continuous case in Desharnais et al. (2002).

Definition 10.9. An equivalence relation $R \subseteq X \times X$ on the state space of a Markov Process as above is a **bisimulation** if whenever $x \mathrel{R} y$, then

$$\text{for all } a \in L, \quad \tau_a(x, C) = \tau_a(y, C)$$

where C is a measurable union of R-equivalence classes.

Two states x, y are bisimilar if there is *some* bisimulation relation relating them. There is a maximum bisimulation relation which we call simply bisimulation. There is a logical characterization of bisimulation proved in Desharnais et al. (1998, 2002, 2003).

Giacalone et al. (1990) suggested that one move from equality between processes to distances between processes. In Desharnais et al. (1999, 2004) a pseudometric was defined whose kernel was bisimulation. If two states are not bisimilar then some formula distinguishes them. The idea of the metric is: if the *smallest* formula separating two states is "big" the states are "close." Later Worrell and van Breugel (2001) developed a fixed-point definition of the metric and showed how ideas from transport theory could be used to compute the metric more efficiently.

10.4 Quantitative Equational Logic

As we mentioned in the introduction, the basic idea is to introduce approximate equations of the form: $s =_\varepsilon t$, which we understand to mean that s is within ε of t. Clearly, the phrase "within ε" is redolent of a metric but the theory has to be developed to the point where it becomes clear that it is indeed a metric in the precise technical sense.

At the outset it should be clear that, whatever else it might be, the binary relation denoted by $=_\varepsilon$ is not an equivalence relation. If we have $s =_\varepsilon t$ and $t =_\varepsilon u$ there is no reason to expect $s =_\varepsilon u$; indeed one might expect something more like $s =_{2\varepsilon} u$. The family of relations $\{=_\varepsilon | \ \varepsilon \in [0, \infty]\}$ defines a structure called a *uniformity* but we will not stress this aspect here. We need to formalize what it means to reason with the symbol $=_\varepsilon$ and see that it really corresponds to a quantitative analogue of equational reasoning. In order to do this we will state analogues of the results one has for ordinary equational logic: completeness results, universality of free algebras, Birkhoff-like variety theorem and monads arising from free algebras.

10.4.1 Quantitative Equations

We begin by following as closely as possible the presentation of ordinary equational logic. We have a signature Ω and a set of variables X; in the usual inductive way we get terms denoted by $\mathbf{T}X$. A *quantitative equation* over these terms is of the form:

$$s =_\varepsilon t, \qquad\qquad \text{for } s, t \in \mathbf{T}X \text{ and } \varepsilon \in \mathbb{Q}_+ .$$

We use $\mathcal{I}(\mathbf{T}X)$ to denote the set of quantitative equations over $\mathbf{T}X$. Note that $=_0$ represents ordinary equality $=$, and consequently, $\mathcal{E}(\mathbf{T}X) \subseteq \mathcal{I}(\mathbf{T}X)$.

Let $Q(\mathbf{T}X)$ be the class of *quantitative judgments* on $\mathbf{T}X$, which are expressions of the form

$$\Gamma \vdash \phi,$$

with as hypotheses is an enumerable set $\Gamma \subseteq \mathcal{I}(\mathbf{T}X)$ of quantitative equations and a quantitative equation $\phi \in \mathcal{I}(\mathbf{T}X)$ as conclusion. Since we are identifying $=$ with $=_0$, we observe that $\mathcal{J}(\mathbf{T}X) \subseteq Q(\mathbf{T}X)$.

Quantitative equations and quantitative judgments are used for reasoning, and to this end we define the concept of quantitative equational theory, which, as might be expected, will generalize the classical equational theory, in the sense that $=_0$ is ordinary term equality. However, for $\varepsilon \neq 0$, $=_\varepsilon$ is not an equivalence: the transitivity rule has to be replaced by a rule, (**Triang**) encoding the triangle inequality. We will also have an infinitary rule, (**Cont**), that reflects the density of rational numbers within the reals.

A *quantitative equational theory of type Ω over X* is a set $\mathcal{U}$ of quantitative judgements on $\mathbf{T}X$ such that for arbitrary terms $s, t, u \in \mathbf{T}X$, set of quantitative judgements $\Gamma, \Theta \subseteq \mathcal{I}(\mathbf{T}X)$, and positive rationals $\varepsilon, \varepsilon' \in \mathbb{Q}_+$

(Refl) $\emptyset \vdash t =_0 t \in \mathcal{U}$,

(Symm) $\{s =_\varepsilon t\} \vdash t =_\varepsilon s \in \mathcal{U}$,

(Triang) $\{s =_\varepsilon u, u =_{\varepsilon'} t\} \vdash s =_{\varepsilon+\varepsilon'} t \in \mathcal{U}$,

(Max) $\{s = t\} \vdash s =_{\varepsilon+\varepsilon'} t \in \mathcal{U}$,

(NExp) $\{s_i =_\varepsilon t_i \mid i \in \kappa\} \vdash f(s_i)_{i\in\kappa} =_\varepsilon f(t_i)_{i\in\kappa} \in \mathcal{U}$,   for any $f: \kappa \in \Omega$,

(Cont) $\{s =_{\varepsilon'} t \mid \varepsilon' > \varepsilon\} \vdash s =_\varepsilon t \in \mathcal{U}$,

(Subst) if $\Gamma \vdash s =_\varepsilon t \in \mathcal{U}$, then $\sigma(\Gamma) \vdash \sigma(s) =_\varepsilon \sigma(t) \in \mathcal{U}$, for any $\sigma \in \Sigma(X)$,

(Cut) if $\Theta \vdash \Gamma \in \mathcal{U}$ and $\Theta \vdash s =_\varepsilon t \in \mathcal{U}$, then $\Gamma \vdash s =_\varepsilon t \in \mathcal{U}$,

(Assum) if $s =_\varepsilon t \in \Gamma$, then $\Gamma \vdash s =_\varepsilon t \in \mathcal{U}$,

Given a quantitative equational theory $\mathcal{U}$ and a set $S \subseteq \mathcal{U}$, we say, as in the classical case, that S is a set of axioms for $\mathcal{U}$, or S axiomatizes $\mathcal{U}$, if $\mathcal{U}$ is the smallest quantitative equational theory that contains S. A quantitative equational theory $\mathcal{U}$ over $\mathbf{T}X$ is *inconsistent* if $\emptyset \vdash x =_0 y \in \mathcal{U}$, where $x, y \in X$ are two distinct variables; $\mathcal{U}$ is *consistent* if it is not inconsistent.

10.4.2 Quantitative Algebras

Now that we have quantitative equations we can turn to defining quantitative analogues of the concept of algebra. Essentially, one combines the algebraic structure from Section 10.2.1 with the concept of a metric space.

A *quantitative Ω-algebra* $\mathcal{A} = (A, d, \Omega_{\mathcal{A}})$ consists of an extended metric space (A, d) and a collection $\Omega_{\mathcal{A}}$ of non-expansive interpretations for each operation symbol in Ω. If $f: a \in \Omega$ is a function symbol of arity κ, then its interpretation is a non-expansive function $f_{\mathcal{A}}: A^\kappa \to A$, where A^κ is the κ-fold cartesian product[7] of the metric space A.

An *homomorphism* from $\mathcal{A} = (A, d_A, \Omega_{\mathcal{A}})$ to $\mathcal{B} = (B, d_B, \Omega_{\mathcal{B}})$ is a non-expansive homomorphism of Ω-algebras from $(A, \Omega_{\mathcal{A}})$ to $(B, \Omega_{\mathcal{B}})$.

Fixed a set of variables X and a signature Ω, we would like to define the quantitative analogue of the term algebra, but to do so we don't yet have a metric on $\mathbf{T}X$. To do that, we need to explain what it means for an algebra to satisfy a judgement.

Definition 10.10. We say that a quantitative Ω-algebra $\mathcal{A}$ **satisfies** a quantitative judgement $\Gamma \vdash s =_\varepsilon t$ in $Q(\mathbf{T}X)$, written $\mathcal{A} \models (\Gamma \vdash s =_\varepsilon t)$, if for every assignment $\iota: X \to A$ the following implication holds:

$$\left(\text{for all } (s' =_{\varepsilon'} t') \in \Gamma, \, d(\iota(s'), \iota(t')) \le \varepsilon'\right) \text{ implies } d(\iota(s), \iota(t)) \le \varepsilon.$$

---

[7] Note that extended metric spaces have all small products; this is not the case for metric spaces.

For a quantitative equational theory $\mathcal{U}$, we write $\mathcal{A} \models \mathcal{U}$ to mean that $\mathcal{A}$ satisfies all the judgements in $\mathcal{U}$. We write $\mathbf{K}(\mathcal{U}, \Omega)$ for the collection of Ω-algebras satisfying $\mathcal{U}$, or simply $\mathbf{K}(\Omega)$ when the signature is clear.

We can now define a metric on $\mathbf{T}X$ over the quantitative theory $\mathcal{U}$:

$$d^{\mathcal{U}}(s,t) = \inf\{\varepsilon \mid \emptyset \vdash s =_\varepsilon t \in \mathcal{U}\} \,.$$

The idea is that we look at the equations we can derive with the smallest possible ε. We allow only special judgements with empty set of hypotheses. Why not using the following?

$$d^{\mathcal{U}}(s,t) = \inf\{\varepsilon \mid \forall \Gamma \subseteq \mathcal{I}(X), \Gamma \vdash s =_\varepsilon t \in \mathcal{U}\} \,.$$

It turns out that it defines exactly the same metric. Two things are to be noted: first we only have a pseudometric and second, the metric can take on infinite values. To get a proper quantitative algebra on $\mathbf{T}_{\mathcal{U}}[X]$, we have to do the analogue of what we did in the case of ordinary equations: quotient by a suitable equivalence relation. The kernel of the pseudometric is a congruence for Ω. If we take the quotient we get an extended metric space.

We call the resulting quantitative algebra on $\mathbf{T}_{\mathcal{U}}[X]$, the *quantitative term algebra* generated from X; by construction is in $\mathbf{K}(\mathcal{U})$.

10.4.3 General Results

In this section we describe the quantitative analogues of the results mentioned in Section 10.2.2. The first is completeness which was proved in Mardare et al. (2016).

Theorem 10.11 (Completeness). $\mathcal{U} \models (\Gamma \vdash \phi)$, *if and only if,* $(\Gamma \vdash \phi) \in \mathcal{U}$.

This is the analogue of the usual completeness theorem for equational logic. From the right to the left is by definition. The reverse direction is also a model construction argument as in the ordinary case but the proof needs to deal with quantitative aspects and uses the infinitary limit rule (**Cont**) in a crucial way.

Just as in the ordinary case the construction of the term algebra provides us with free algebra. The difference this time is that we start from an *extended metric space* instead of just a set. Starting from an extended metric space (M, d) and a quantitative theory $\mathcal{U}$, we can construct the free quantitative Ω-algebra $\mathbf{T}_{\mathcal{U}}[X]$ generated from (M, d), by adding constants for each $m \in M$ and the judgements $\emptyset \vdash m =_\varepsilon n$ to the generating quantitative theory $\mathcal{U}$, for every rational $\varepsilon \in \mathbb{Q}_+$ such that $d(m, n) \leq \varepsilon$. Call this extended signature Ω_M and the extended theory $\mathcal{U}_M$. Clearly, any algebra in $\mathbf{K}(\Omega_M, \mathcal{U}_M)$ can be viewed as an algebra in $\mathbf{K}(\Omega, \mathcal{U})$ by forgetting the interpretations of the additional constants from M.

Again, we have a non-expansive map $\eta_M : (M, d) \to (\mathbf{T}_{\mathcal{U}}[M], d^{\mathcal{U}_M})$, defined as $\eta_M(m) = [m]$, which is *universal* in the following sense:

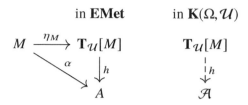

for any quantitative algebra $\mathcal{A} \in \mathbf{K}(\Omega, \mathcal{U})$ and function α from M to the underlying set A of $\mathcal{A}$, there exists a *unique* quantitative algebra homomorphism $h: \mathbf{T}_{\mathcal{U}}[M] \to \mathcal{A}$ such that $h \circ \eta_M = \alpha$. In other words, $\mathbf{T}_{\mathcal{U}}[M]$ is the *free algebra* in $\mathbf{K}(\Omega, \mathcal{U})$ generated from the space M.

The construction of $\mathbf{T}_{\mathcal{U}}[M]$ from the space (M, d) is functorial and gives the left adjoint to the forgetful functor from $\mathbf{K}(\mathcal{U})$ to $\mathbf{EMet}$, the category of extended metric spaces and non-expansive maps. As usual, this gives rise to a monad on $\mathbf{EMet}$, namely, the *quantitative term monad* $(\mathbf{T}_{\mathcal{U}}, \eta, \mu)$ with unit and multiplication defined as in the equational case.

Differently from the equational case, the (Eilenberg-Moore) algebras for the monad $\mathbf{T}_{\mathcal{U}}$ are not always in one-to-one correspondence with the algebras in $\mathbf{K}(\mathcal{U})$. However, the isomorphism of categories is recovered in the case the quantitative theory $\mathcal{U}$ is *basic*, *i.e.*, generated by judgements of the form

$$\{x_i =_{\varepsilon_i} y_i \mid i \in I\} \vdash s =_{\varepsilon} t$$

where x_i, y_i are variables in X (see Bacci et al., 2018).

10.5 Examples

The subject as we have presented it so far may seem like generalization for its own sake. In fact there are compelling examples that drove this investigation and these examples come from the world of probabilistic programming.

10.5.1 Axiomatizing the Total Variation Metric

First we return to the example of barycentric algebras from the end of Section 10.2.1. This time we present it as a quantitative algebra. Recall that the signature of barycentric algebras has uncountably many binary operations

$$\{+_e : 2 \mid e \in [0, 1]\},$$

satisfying the equations below (here given in the form of quantitative judgements) expressing that $+_e$ is the convex combination of pair of elements

(**B1**) $\emptyset \vdash x +_1 y =_0 x$,

(**B2**) $\emptyset \vdash x +_e x =_0 x$,

(**SC**) $\emptyset \vdash x +_e y =_0 y +_{1-e} x$,

(**SA**) $\emptyset \vdash (x +_{e_1} y) +_{e_2} z =_0 x +_{e_1 e_2} (y +_{\frac{e_2-e_1 e_2}{1-e_1 e_2}} z)$, for $e_1, e_2 \in (0,1)$,

To the above equations, which just use ordinary equality $=_0$, we add a new quantitative equation schema

(**LI**) $\emptyset \vdash x +_e z =_\varepsilon y +_e z$, for all $e \leq \varepsilon \in \mathbb{Q} \cap [0,1]$,

called the *left-invariant axiom schema*. Here we are using a nontrivial instance of a quantitative equation.

The barycentric algebras that satisfy (**LI**) are called *left-invariant barycentric algebras* or LIB algebras for short. Denote by $\mathcal{U}_{LI}$ the quantitative equational theory generated form the axioms above. Clearly, the objects in $\mathbf{K}(\mathcal{U}_{LI})$ are exactly the LIB algebras.

If one were to draw a picture of what this means it would violate one's geometric intuition; *it is not meant to be understood in terms of euclidean distance in the plane*. What does this axiomatize? Remarkably, this axiomatizes the total variation metric on probability distributions. This is striking because no mention was made of probability in the above axiomatization and of all the metrics that one can imagine there is nothing in the (**LI**) axiom schema that suggests the total variation metric. Here we sketch the ideas, a detailed proof can be found in Mardare et al. (2016).

We know from the general theory that there is a freely generated LIB algebra from an extended metric space (M, d). What is it concretely? Let us return to this question after constructing a specific LIB algebra.

We recall the definition of the total variation metric from Section 10.3.3:

$$TV(p,q) = \sup_{E \in \Sigma} |p(E) - q(E)|.$$

Here p and q are probability distributions on (M, d) with Borel σ-algebra Σ. There is a beautiful duality theorem for the total variation metric just as there is for the Kantorovich metric (see Lindvall, 2002) which is based on the notion of coupling (see Section 10.3.3 for the definition):

$$TV(p,q) = \min\{\pi(\neq) \mid \pi \in C(p,q)\}.$$

where $C(p,q)$ denote the space of couplings and $\neq$ is the inequality relation on M. Implicit in this statement is the claim that the minimum is attained.

It is easy to see that a convex combination of couplings is a coupling, hence

$C(p, q)$ can be turned into a barycentric algebra. Moreover, one can prove (see Mardare et al., 2016) that the following splitting lemma holds:

Lemma 10.12. *If* p, q *are Borel probability distributions and* $e = TV(p, q)$, *then there are Borel probability distributions* p', q', r *such that*

$$p = ep' + (1 - e)r \qquad and \qquad q = eq' + (1 - e)r .$$

With these tools in hand we investigate the space of Borel probability distributions on (M, d).

Let $\Pi[M]$ be the barycentric algebra obtained by taking the *finitely-supported* probability distributions on M and interpreting $+_e$ as convex combination; it is easy to verify that the barycentric axioms hold. Then we endow this algebra of distributions with the total-variation metric to make it a quantitative algebra. Using the convexity property of $C(p, q)$ one can prove the following theorem.

Theorem 10.13. $\Pi[M] \in \mathbf{K}(\mathcal{U}_{LI})$.

Moreover, by using the splitting lemma we can prove:

Theorem 10.14. $\Pi[M]$ *is the free algebra generated from* M *in* $\mathbf{K}(\mathcal{U}_{LI})$.

Since free algebras are unique up to isomorphism, $\Pi[M]$ and the term algebra $\mathbf{T}_{\mathcal{U}_{LI}}[M]$ generated over the left-invariant barycentric axioms are essentially the same algebra. In this sense, we say that the axioms of LIB algebras give rise to the total-variation metric.

10.5.2 Interpolative Barycentric Algebras

We consider a (seemingly) slight variation of the above construction. We have the same signature as barycentric algebras: we keep the axioms (**B1**), (**B2**), (**SC**), (**SA**) but we drop (**LI**). Instead we add the following quantitative equation schema

$$(\mathbf{IB}_m) \quad \{x =_{\varepsilon_1} y, x' =_{\varepsilon_2} y'\} \vdash x +_e x' =_\delta y +_e y',$$

for all $\delta \in \mathbb{Q}_+$ such that

$$(e\varepsilon_1^m + (1 - e)\varepsilon_2^m)^{1/m} \leq \delta .$$

Note that now we have assumptions in the equation so this axiom is a judgment with a nonempty left-hand side. We call this axiom (**IB**_m), which stands for *interpolative barycentric* and the m is a numerical parameter. The barycentric algebras satisfying (**IB**_m) are called *interpolative barycentric algebras* or IB algebras for short.

To better understand the axiom ($\mathbf{IB}_m$), it is more illuminating to look at the special case where $m = 1$:

$$\{x =_{\varepsilon_1} y, x' =_{\varepsilon_2} y'\} \vdash x +_e x' =_\delta y +_e y', \qquad \text{where } e\varepsilon_1 + (1 - e)\varepsilon_2 \leq \delta .$$

We can illustrate this with the picture shown in Figure 10.1.

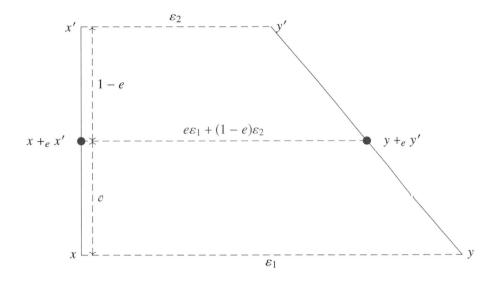

Figure 10.1 The interpolative axiom

We can ask the same questions as we asked for the LIB algebras. What are free IB algebras? We start with an extended metric space (M, d) and consider finitely-supported Borel distributions on it, and interpret them as a barycentric algebra as before. We endow it with the m-Kantorovich metric (see Section 10.3.3) and show that we get an IB algebra. This uses the definition of the $W^{(m)}$ metrics as an inf and convexity of couplings. Again, we can prove a splitting lemma for this case and show that the space of finitely-supported probability distributions with the m-Kantorovich metric is the free IB algebra. The arguments are similar to, but more involved than, the total variation case (see Mardare et al., 2016 for more details).

In fact one can do more. The finitely-supported measures are *weakly dense* in the space of all Borel probability measures. One can show that the space of all Borel probability measures on an extended metric space (M, d), call it $\mathcal{G}_m(M)$, endowed with the $W^{(m)}$ metric gives an IB algebra. One can show that if one constructs the free algebra from (M, d) and then performs *Cauchy completion* one gets a quantitative algebra isomorphic to $\mathcal{G}_m(M)$ by exploiting the weak denseness of the finitely-supported measures.

10.5.3 Quantitative Exceptions

In this and the next two subsections we discuss quantitative analogues of the well-known work by Plotkin and Power (2001, 2002, 2003, 2004).

The simplest example of an equational theory of effects is given by the algebraic theory of exceptions. We fix a set E of exceptions. For a given set of exception E, the signature is given by a nullary operation symbol $\mathsf{raise}_e : 0$ for each exception $e \in E$:

$$\Omega_E = \{\mathsf{raise}_e : 0 \mid e \in E\}.$$

The theory is simply the trivial one, that is the one that contains only identities $t = t$ between terms constructed over the signature.

The induced monad on **Set**, called the *exception monad*, maps a set A to the set $A + E$, the disjoint union of sets A and E.

In the quantitative case one is allowed to view the set of exceptions as an extended metric space with metric measuring the distance between exceptions. This interpretation can be useful, for example, in scenarios where exceptions carry the time-stamps of the moment they have been thrown. In this way one can compare program implementations by measuring the frequency of which exception are thrown.

For (E, d_E), an extended metric space of exceptions, we define the quantitative equational theory of exceptions over E by taking the same signature as above, namely Ω_E, and adding to the theory the quantitative equations

$$\emptyset \vdash \mathsf{raise}_{e_1} =_\varepsilon \mathsf{raise}_{e_2}, \qquad \text{for } \varepsilon \geq d_E(e_1, e_2)$$

for any pair of exceptions $e_1, e_2 \in E$ and positive rational ε. The role of this axiom is to lift to the set of terms the underlying metric of E.

The monad T_E on **EMet** induced by this quantitative equational theory is the one that maps an extended metric space M to the extended metric space $M + E$, i.e., the disjoint sum of the extended metric spaces M and E. This example is, admittedly, a trivial extension of the non-metric case.

10.5.4 Quantitative Interactive Input/Output

For representing interactive input and output using equational theories of effects, we typically assume a countable alphabet I of inputs and a set O of outputs; for a signature we take an operation symbol input of arity $|I|$ and a unary operation symbol output_o, for each output symbol $o \in O$

$$\Omega_{I/O} = \{\mathsf{input} : |I|\} \cup \{\mathsf{output}_o : 1 \mid o \in O\}.$$

The meaning behind the operation symbols is that $\mathsf{input}(t)_i$ represents a computation that waits for user's input and proceeds as t, if the user's entered input is i; while $\mathsf{output}_o(t)$ represents a computation that outputs o and proceeds as t. For example, given a mapping $f : I \to O$ from inputs to outputs, the term

$$\mathsf{input}(\mathsf{output}_{f(i)}(\mathsf{output}_{f(i)}(t)))_i, \qquad \text{for all } i \in I$$

represents a computation that waits for the user's input i, repeats the output $f(i)$ twice, and then proceeds as t. Above, the term $\mathsf{input}(t_i)_i$ abbreviates the countably branching term

$$\mathsf{input}(t_{i_1}, t_{i_2}, \dots),$$

where $i_1, i_2, \dots$ is an enumeration of input alphabet I.

The equational theory for interactive input/output is given by the trivial theory over the signature $\Omega_{I/O}$. The **Set**-monad $T_{I/O}$ for interactive I/O corresponding to this equational theory is the free monad on the signature functor $\Omega_{I/O}(Y) = Y^I + (O \times Y)$, which is given by the least fixed point

$$T_{I/O}(X) = \mu Y.(Y^I + (O \times Y) + X).$$

Now we consider the situation where the difference between the output symbols produced is measured by a metric. For example we may produce output streams and there are natural metrics between streams. We assume that (O, d_O) is a metric space of outputs and we define a quantitative equational theory to capture interactive input/output effects.

Recall that the general theory for quantitative equations requires every operation symbol to satisfy the following axiom of non-expansiveness:

$$\{x_i =_\varepsilon y_i \mid i \in I\} \vdash \mathsf{input}(x_i)_i =_\varepsilon \mathsf{input}(y_i)_i,$$
$$\{x =_\varepsilon y\} \vdash \mathsf{output}_o(x) =_\varepsilon \mathsf{output}_o(y) \qquad \text{for all } o \in O.$$

In order to obtain a quantitative theory of interactive input/output effects able to reflect the difference of two computations producing sequences of outputs symbols, in addition to the above quantitative equations we require the theory to have the following axioms:

$$\{x =_\varepsilon y\} \vdash \mathsf{output}_{o_1}(x) =_\delta \mathsf{output}_{o_2}(y), \qquad \text{for } \delta \geq \max(\varepsilon, d_O(o_1, o_2)),$$

for each pair $o_1, o_2 \in O$ of outputs symbols and positive rationals ε, δ.

As a consequence the theory will also contain the quantitative equation

$$\emptyset \vdash \mathsf{output}_{a_1, \dots, a_n}(x) =_\delta \mathsf{output}_{b_1, \dots, b_n}(x), \qquad \text{for } \delta \geq \max_{i=1}^{n} d_O(a_i, b_i),$$

where $\text{output}_{o_1,\dots,o_n}(t)$ abbreviates the term

$$\text{output}_{o_1}(\text{output}_{o_2}(\text{output}_{o_3}(\dots \text{output}_{o_n}(t)))),$$

representing a computation printing the word $o_1 \cdots o_n$ and proceeding as t. Hence the difference of printing two words of the same length is quantified as the maximal point-wise distance between their characters. There are, of course, other variations one can imagine.

This quantitative equational theory induces a monad $T_{I/O}$ for interactive input/output determined as the following least fixed point on **EMet**

$$T_{I/O}(X) = \mu Y.(Y^I + (O \times Y) + X).$$

10.5.5 Quantitative Side-Effects (State Monad)

To describe state with a finite set L of locations and a countable metric space (V, d_V) of data values, we take a signature containing an operation symbol lookup_l of arity $|V|$ for each location $l \in L$, and a unary operation symbol $\text{update}_{l,v}$ for each location $l \in L$ and data value $v \in V$.

$$\Omega_{\text{State}} = \{\text{lookup}_l : |V| \mid l \in L\} \cup \{\text{update}_{l,v} : 1 \mid l \in L \text{ and } v \in V\}.$$

The term $\text{lookup}_l(t)_v$ represents a computation that looks up the contents of location l and proceeds as t if the stored value is v. The term $\text{update}_{l,v}(t)$ represents a computation that updates the location l with v and proceeds as t. For example, the term

$$\text{lookup}_{l_1}(\text{update}_{l_2,v}(t))_v \qquad \text{for all } v \in V$$

represents a computation that copies the contents of l_1 into the location l_2 and proceeds as t. Note that, as for the case of the input operation in Section 10.5.4, the term $\text{lookup}_l(t_{v_i})_{v_i}$ is an abbreviation for the countably branching term

$$\text{lookup}_l(t_{v_1}, t_{v_2}, \dots),$$

where $v_1, v_2, \dots$ is an enumeration of the data values in V.

The quantitative theory of side-effects is given by the following axioms

$$\emptyset \vdash \mathsf{lookup}_l(\mathsf{update}_{l,v}(x))_v =_0 x,$$
$$\emptyset \vdash \mathsf{lookup}_l(\mathsf{lookup}_l(x)_{v_2})_{v_1} =_0 \mathsf{lookup}_l(y)_{v_1},$$
$$\emptyset \vdash \mathsf{update}_{l,v_1}(\mathsf{lookup}_l(x)_{v_2}) =_0 \mathsf{update}_{l,v_1}(y),$$
$$\emptyset \vdash \mathsf{update}_{l,v_1}(\mathsf{update}_{l,v_2}(x)) =_0 \mathsf{update}_{l,v_2}(x),$$
$$\emptyset \vdash \mathsf{lookup}_{l_1}(\mathsf{lookup}_{l_2}(x)_{v_2})_{v_1} =_0 \mathsf{lookup}_{l_2}(\mathsf{lookup}_{l_1}(x)_{v_1})_{v_2},$$
$$\emptyset \vdash \mathsf{update}_{l_1,v_1}(\mathsf{lookup}_{l_2}(x)_{v_2}) =_0 \mathsf{lookup}_{l_2}(\mathsf{update}_{l_1,v_1}(x))_{v_2},$$
$$\emptyset \vdash \mathsf{update}_{l_1,v_1}(\mathsf{update}_{l_2,v_2}(x)) =_0 \mathsf{update}_{l_2,v_2}(\mathsf{update}_{l_1,v_1}(x)),$$

$$\{x =_\varepsilon y\} \vdash \mathsf{update}_{l,v_1}(x) =_\delta \mathsf{update}_{l,v_2}(y), \qquad \text{for } \delta \geq \max(\varepsilon, d_V(v_1, v_2)),$$

where in the above, the locations l_1, l_2 are assumed to be distinct: $l_1 \neq l_2$.

The first four equations describe the behaviour of operations on a single location: the first one says that updating a location with its current contents has no effect; the second one that the state does not change between two consecutive lookups; the third one that the state is determined immediately after an update; and the fourth one that the second update overwrites the first one. The next three ordinary equations state that operations on different locations commute. The last equation, which is also the only truly quantitative one in the above list, states that the difference between side-effects depends on the distance of the values observed point-wise in each location.

The monad on **EMet** induced by the above axioms maps an extended metric space M to $(S \times M)^S$, where $S = V^L$.

Remark 10.15. If we took an *infinite* set L of locations, the induced monad would not be the standard one for state. Since the elements of the free model are built inductively from operations and represent computations that only update a finite number of locations at a time. In contrast, the elements of the standard monad represent computations that can perform an arbitrary modification of the state.

10.6 Conclusions

This chapter introduces a new approach to approximate reasoning. Metrics for probabilistic processes have been investigated for nearly twenty years by Desharnais et al. (1999, 2004) and van Breugel and Worrell (2001b,a) and of course the deBakker school has emphasized metric ideas in semantics for decades. Logics for reasoning quantitatively have essentially been modal logics that were particularly crafted for probabilistic systems but a *generic* way of capturing the notion of approximate equality has been missing.

The approach described in this chapter is just a beginning. We hope that the striking emergence of the Kantorovich metric as a free algebra from a fairly simple equational theory is a foretaste of what might be expected in the future. From the programming point of view we have just presented very simple obvious extensions to quantitative theories of effects. We are actively investigating a more comprehensive theory of effects specifically for probabilistic programming languages. In recent work (Bacci et al., 2018) we have shown how one can combine different monads to obtain, for example, an equational characterization of Markov processes.

The theory presented here has a number of restrictions introduced for ease of exposition. For example, nonexpansiveness can certainly be weakened. We know that we only require nonexpansiveness in each argument separately. However, we expect that yet weaker conditions are possible, perhaps at the price of complicating the underlying theory.

A number of other directions for future research are: (i) developing a quantitative term rewriting theory that meshes with quantitative equational logic, (ii) understanding better how much the bounds degrade as one manipulates sequences of equations and (iii) algorithms based on quantitative equations. To elaborate point (ii): in ordinary equational logic, a long series of equations comes without cost but in quantitative equational logic a long series of quantitative equational manipulations may well cause the ε's appearing to get larger and larger to the point of being uninformative. It would be useful to get a handle on the "ergonomics"[8] of quantitative equational reasoning.

Acknowledgements

We have benefitted from many discussions with colleagues. We mention William Boshuk, Florence Clerc, Vincent Danos, Nathanaël Fijalkow, Marcelo Fiore, Jeremy Gibbons, Bartek Klin, Dexter Kozen, Alexander Kurz, Bart Jacobs, Paul Levy, Michael Mislove, Marcin Sabok, Dana Scott and Alexandra Silva. This research has been supported by a grant from NSERC (Panangaden) and the Danish Research Council (Mardare, Bacci).

References

Bacci, Giorgio, Mardare, Radu, Panangaden, Prakash, and Plotkin, Gordon D. 2018. An Algebraic Theory of Markov Processes. Pages 679–688 of: *Proceedings of the 33rd Annual ACM/IEEE Symposium on Logic in Computer Science, LICS 2018, Oxford, UK, July 09-12, 2018.*

Billingsley, P. 1995. *Probability and Measure.* Wiley-Interscience.

---

[8] We thank Jeremy Gibbons for bringing this point to our attention as well as coining this phrase.

Birkhoff, G. 1935. On the structure of abstract algebras. *Proc. Cambridge Philos. Soc.*, **31**, 433–454.

Burris, Stanley, and Sankappanavar, Hanamantagouda P. 1981. *A course in universal algebra*. Graduate Texts in Mathematics, vol. 78. Springer-Verlag.

Desharnais, J., Edalat, A., and Panangaden, P. 1998. A Logical Characterization of Bisimulation for Labelled Markov Processes. Pages 478–489 of: *proceedings of the 13th IEEE Symposium On Logic In Computer Science, Indianapolis*. IEEE Press.

Desharnais, J., Gupta, V., Jagadeesan, R., and Panangaden, P. 1999. Metrics for Labeled Markov Systems. In: *Proceedings of CONCUR99*. Lecture Notes in Computer Science, no. 1664. Springer-Verlag.

Desharnais, J., Edalat, A., and Panangaden, P. 2002. Bisimulation for Labeled Markov Processes. *Information and Computation*, **179**(2), 163–193.

Desharnais, J., Gupta, V., Jagadeesan, R., and Panangaden, P. 2003. Approximating Labeled Markov Processes. *Information and Computation*, **184**(1), 160–200.

Desharnais, Josée, Gupta, Vineet, Jagadeesan, Radhakrishnan, and Panangaden, Prakash. 2004. A metric for labelled Markov processes. *Theoretical Computer Science*, **318**(3), 323–354.

Dudley, R. M. 1989. *Real Analysis and Probability*. Wadsworth and Brookes/Cole.

Giacalone, A., Jou, C., and Smolka, S. 1990. Algebraic Reasoning for Probabilistic Concurrent Systems. In: *Proceedings of the Working Conference on Programming Concepts and Methods*. IFIP TC2.

Giry, M. 1981. A Categorical Approach to Probability Theory. Pages 68–85 of: Banaschewski, B. (ed), *Categorical Aspects of Topology and Analysis*. Lecture Notes In Mathematics, no. 915. Springer-Verlag.

Hyland, Martin, and Power, John. 2007. The Category Theoretic Understanding of Universal Algebra: Lawvere Theories and Monads. *Electronic Notes in Theor. Comp. Sci.*, **172**, 437–458.

Hyland, Martin, Plotkin, Gordon, and Power, John. 2006. Combining effects: Sum and tensor. *Theoretical Computer Science*, **357**(1), 70–99.

Larsen, K. G., and Skou, A. 1991. Bisimulation through Probablistic Testing. *Information and Computation*, **94**, 1–28.

Lawvere, F. W. 1962. *The category of probabilistic mappings*. Unpublished typescript. Available at
`ncatlab.org/nlab/files/lawvereprobability1962.pdf`.

Lindvall, Torgny. 2002. *Lectures on the coupling method*. Courier Corporation.

Mardare, Radu, Panangaden, Prakash, and Plotkin, Gordon. 2016. Quantitative algebraic reasoning. Pages 700–709 of: *Proceedings of the 31st Annual ACM-IEEE Symposium on Logic in Computer Science*.

Mardare, Radu, Panangaden, Prakash, and Plotkin, Gordon. 2017. On the axiomatizability of quantitative algebras. In: *Proceedings of the 32nd Annual ACM-IEEE Symposium on Logic in Computer Science*.

Moggi, Eugenio. 1991. Notions of computation and monads. *Information and computation*, **93**(1), 55–92.

Panangaden, Prakash. 2009. *Labelled Markov Processes*. Imperial College Press.

Plotkin, Gordon, and Power, John. 2001. Semantics for algebraic operations. *Electronic Notes in Theoretical Computer Science*, **45**, 332–345.

Plotkin, Gordon, and Power, John. 2002. Notions of computation determine monads. Pages 342–356 of: *Foundations of Software Science and Computation Structures*. Springer.

Plotkin, Gordon, and Power, John. 2003. Algebraic operations and generic effects. *Applied Categorical Structures*, **11**(1), 69–94.

Plotkin, Gordon, and Power, John. 2004. Computational effects and operations: An overview. *Electronic Notes in Theoretical Computer Science*, **73**, 149–163.

Robinson, Edmund. 2002. Variations on Algebra:Monadicity and generalisations of equational theories. *Formal Aspects of Computing*, **13**, 308–326.

van Breugel, Franck. 2001. An introduction to metric semantics: operational and denotational models for programming and specification languages. *Theoretical Computer Science*, **258**(1), 1–98.

van Breugel, Franck, and Worrell, James. 2001a. An Algorithm for Quantitative Verification of Probabilistic Systems. Pages 336–350 of: Larsen, K. G., and Nielsen, M. (eds), *Proceedings of CONCUR'01*. Lecture Notes In Computer Science, no. 2154. Springer-Verlag.

van Breugel, Franck, and Worrell, James. 2001b. Towards Quantitative Verification of Probabilistic Systems. In: *Proceedings of the Twenty-eighth International Colloquium on Automata, Languages and Programming*. Springer-Verlag.

11

Probabilistic Abstract Interpretation: Sound Inference and Application to Privacy[a]

José Manuel Calderón Trilla
Galois, Inc.
Michael Hicks
University of Maryland, College Park
Stephen Magill
Galois, Inc.
Piotr Mardziel
Carnegie Mellon University
Ian Sweet
University of Maryland, College Park

Abstract: Bayesian probability models uncertain knowledge and learning from observations. As a defining feature of optimal adversarial behaviour, Bayesian reasoning forms the basis of safety properties in contexts such as privacy and fairness. Probabilistic programming is a convenient implementation of Bayesian reasoning but the adversarial setting imposes obstacles to its use: approximate inference can underestimate adversary knowledge and exact inference is impractical in cases covering large state spaces.

By abstracting distributions, the semantics of a probabilistic language, and inference, jointly termed *probabilistic abstract interpretation*, we demonstrate adversary models both approximate and sound.

We apply the techniques to build a privacy protecting monitor and describe how to trade off the precision and computational cost in its implementation all the while remaining sound with respect to privacy risk bounds.

11.1 Introduction

Bayesian probability is the de facto standard for modeling uncertainty and learning from observations. Adversaries with uncertain information will employ Bayesian reasoning if they wish to optimize the effectiveness of their attacks. Defenders

---

[a] This research was developed with funding from the Defense Advanced Research Projects Agency (DARPA). The views, opinions and/or findings expressed are those of the author and should not be interpreted as representing the official views or policies of the Department of Defense or the US Government.

[b] From *Foundations of Probabilistic Programming*, edited by Gilles Barthe and Joost-Pieter Katoen and Alexandra Silva published 2020 by Cambridge University Press.

must build systems assuming such canny attackers or else risk underestimating the knowledge an adversary can gain and the damage it may inflict.

Probabilistic programming, a mechanization of Bayesian reasoning, offers the requisite elements for doing so. It is a tool for describing adversary knowledge; for specifying the systems adversaries interact with, including the experiments or channels through which they make observations; and for defining and verifying guarantees such as those bounding the damage adversaries can inflict.

Unfortunately, using a practical probabilistic programming system may lead one to draw not entirely trustworthy conclusions about an adversary's bounds. Practical systems are necessarily approximate, for reasons of performance and expressiveness, and are often designed with the average or best case in mind, rather than the worst case. However, when sensitive information is at stake, i.e., in a conservative risk-averse analysis, an *over*-approximation of adversarial capabilities is acceptable but an under-approximation is not.

Probabilistic abstract interpretation is a technique addressing exactly this point: it is approximate and thus more practical than exact inference but it can be made approximate in a manner that adversarial risks can be checked soundly, that is, never underestimated. In our case *soundness* means simply that any likelihood is never underestimated. We leverage this guarantee to bound Bayes' vulnerability, a measure of adversary knowledge and privacy risk.

We begin in Section 11.2 with example privacy and algorithmic fairness properties that motivate the approach to follow. In Section 11.3 we describe a language and its probabilistic semantics suitable for defining and verifying those properties. In Section 11.4 we outline abstractions for probability and for probabilistic interpretation of programs which we then instantiate in Section 11.5 and develop in Section 11.6. We then apply abstract interpretation to implement a privacy monitor for limiting adversary knowledge in Section 11.7. In Section 11.8 we discuss closely related works and compare our approach with alternatives. We conclude with Section 11.9.

This chapter collects and expands on a progression of work on the development and use of probabilistic abstract interpretation to compute upper bounds on the likelihoods of outcomes of systems modeled using probabilistic languages (Mardziel et al., 2011, 2013; Sweet et al., 2018).

11.2 Quantitative Properties

Across domains from information security to algorithmic fairness, probability bounds impose limits on the likelihood of undesired outcomes. Consider, for example, disparate impact ratio and the 80-20 rule (Feldman et al., 2015):

Definition 11.1 (Disparate Impact Ratio)**.** Given a population random variable X

with domain X, a jointly distributed sub-population indicator Z, and a decision procedure $f : X \to \{+, -\}$, the *disparate impact ratio* is the likelihood of a positive outcome for a minority population as compared to the likelihood of a positive outcome for the majority population:

$$\text{DIR}(X, f) \overset{\text{def}}{=} \frac{\Pr[f(X) = + \mid Z = \text{minority}]}{\Pr[f(X) = + \mid Z = \text{majority}]}$$

The *80-20 rule* states that disparate impact ratio should not fall below 0.8 and is the basis of arguments of discrimination in the U.S. where legal restrictions limit the impact of gender, race, and other protected classes on decisions in hiring, housing, lending, and other areas. Example instantiations of this or similar rules are plentiful in the algorithmic fairness literature (Feldman et al., 2015).

Definition 11.2 (Posterior Bayes Vulnerability). Given a prior belief, or background knowledge, r.v. X about a secret, and a program $f : X \to Y$, the *Posterior Bayes vulnerability* is the probability of the most probable input upon observing a particular program output y.

$$V(X, f, y) \overset{\text{def}}{=} \max_{x} \Pr[X = x \mid f(X) = y]$$

Bounds on quantities such as Bayes vulnerability are, likewise, plentiful in the quantitative information flow literature. They aim to model the potential risk in an adversary learning the secret input and exploiting it in some manner (Alvim et al., 2012). In the case of Bayes vulnerability, risk measures the chance an adversary will guess the secret input in one try after making a particular observation on a given program (Smith, 2009).

A Privacy Monitor A key thrust throughout this chapter will be the development of a *privacy monitor* for a system that permits querying private information but wishes to enforce bounds on Bayes vulnerability. The setting is motivated by proposals to move personal private data from centralized services to individuals, allowing them tighter controls over their own personal data (Seong et al., 2010; Baden et al., 2009).

An online query interface with a privacy monitor allows interested parties to retrieve only the necessary data with the understanding that different parties will have interest in different aspect of the data. For example, consider an individual's full birth date, which has been shown to be privacy sensitive: along with zip-code[1] and gender, it suffices to uniquely identify 87% of Americans in the 1990 U.S. census (Sweeney, 2000) and 63% in the 2000 census (Golle, 2006). A horoscope application or "happy birthday" application might request only an individual's birth month and day while a different music recommendation application might instead request a

---

[1] Zip-code is the postal code in the United States.

$$\textit{Variables} \quad \textit{var} \; ::= X \mid Y \mid Z \mid \dots$$

$$\textit{Expressions exp} \; ::= \textit{var} \mid \textit{const} \mid \textit{op} \, (\textit{exp}_1, \textit{exp}_2)$$

$$\textit{Statements} \quad \textit{stmt} ::= \textit{var} := \textit{exp} \mid \quad .$$

$$\text{skip} \mid \textit{stmt}_1 \; ; \; \textit{stmt}_2 \mid$$

$$\text{while } \textit{exp} \text{ do } \textit{stmt} \mid$$

$$\text{if } \textit{exp} \text{ then } \textit{stmt}_1 \text{ else } \textit{stmt}_2 \mid$$

$$\text{prob } p \text{ then } \textit{stmt}_1 \text{ or } \textit{stmt}_2 \mid$$

$$\textit{var} := \text{uniform } \textit{const}_1 \; \textit{const}_2$$

Figure 11.1 `ImpWhile` with probability: syntax.

user's age (i.e., birth year). A traditional access control system might restrict one of these or the other, in order to hide the full date. But doing so excludes some reasonable applications. A privacy monitor using the Bayes vulnerability bound may allow services to query components of the birth date as they like as long as the full birth date is protected up to a given bound.

The privacy monitor is developed in detail in Section 11.7. It appeared originally in Mardziel et al. (2011), and was further developed in Mardziel et al. (2013) and Sweet et al. (2018). The monitor was also extended to consider individual privacy bounds on computations involving multiple parties, each with private inputs (Mardziel et al., 2012).

11.3 Distribution Semantics

This section presents a minimal, imperative probabilistic programming language and its formal, mathematical semantics. We will use the language to model systems of interest, and reason about their properties, including those noted in the prior section.

Figure 11.1 gives the syntax of the language. It is a simple imperative language, which we call `ImpWhile`, with (global) variables, (integer) constants, arithmetic and relational expressions, and statements, which include assignments, no-ops (skip), sequencing, iteration, and conditionals. `ImpWhile` programs manipulate *program states*, which are maps from variables to their current integer values; these values may be updated during execution, where the final state upon termination is termed the *output state*. The language also includes two probabilistic constructs: probabilistic choice and probabilistic uniform assignment. The former, written prob p then $\textit{stmt}_1$ or $\textit{stmt}_2$, has the following semantics: evaluate statement $\textit{stmt}_1$ with probability p (a ratio between 0 and 1) or otherwise evaluate statement $\textit{stmt}_2$.

X, Y, Z	Variable names.
x, y, z	Variable values.
$\Sigma \overset{\text{def}}{=} \text{Variables} \rightarrow \text{Integers}$	Set of all program states.
$\sigma, \tau \in \Sigma$	Program states.
$\Sigma \overset{\text{def}}{=} \Sigma \rightarrow [0, 1]$	Set of all program state distributions.
$\mathbf{X}, \mathbf{Y}, \mathbf{Z} \in \Sigma$	Program state distributions.
ϵ, ϵ	Initial program state, and the point distribution assigning probability 1 to only the initial state.
$\mathbf{X}(\sigma)$	Probability of state σ in distribution $\mathbf{X}$.
$\mathbf{X}(exp) \overset{\text{def}}{=}$	
$\quad \sum_{\sigma:exp \text{ is true for } \sigma} \mathbf{X}(\sigma)$	Marginal probability of exp being true in distribution $\mathbf{X}$.
$\mathbf{X}(exp_1 \mid exp_2) \overset{\text{def}}{=}$	
$\quad \mathbf{X}(exp_1 \wedge exp_2)/\mathbf{X}(exp_2)$	Marginal probability of exp_1 being true conditioned on exp_2 being true in distribution $\mathbf{X}$.
$[\![stmt]\!] : \Sigma \rightarrow \Sigma$	Concrete state semantics.
$[\![stmt]\!] : \Sigma \rightarrow \Sigma$	Concrete distribution semantics.
$a, b, c \in \mathbb{A}$	Regions; abstract program states of domain $\mathbb{A}$.
$\mathbf{a}, \mathbf{b}, \mathbf{c} \in \mathbb{A}$	Abstract distributions of domain $\mathbb{A}$.
$\langle\!\langle stmt \rangle\!\rangle : \mathbb{A} \rightarrow \mathbb{A}$	Abstract semantics for state domain $\mathbb{A}$.
$\langle\!\langle stmt \rangle\!\rangle : \mathbb{A} \rightarrow \mathbb{A}$	Abstract semantics for distribution domain $\mathbb{A}$.

Table 11.1 *Notations and conventions.*

Likewise, the uniform assignment $X :=$ uniform l u assigns to X an integer value uniformly at random from the range of integers between l and u inclusive. The probabilistic elements of this language and their semantics derive from foundational work on probabilistic programming (Kozen, 1981) and have appeared in a similar form in the quantitative information flow literature (Clarkson et al., 2009).

Before presenting the semantics of the language, we turn our attention to some notation, gathered in Table 11.3. This notation will help us talk about the properties of systems we are interested in. Non-bold capital letters, such as X, Y, and Z are variable names (as already mentioned). The lowercase counterparts, x, y, and z, are unspecified values attainable by variables. Lowercase Greek σ, τ denote program states, drawn from the set Σ. We write ϵ to denote the *initial state*, which is the state that maps all variables to 0. Bold capital letters, $\mathbf{X}$, $\mathbf{Y}$, and $\mathbf{Z}$, denote distributions[2] over program states from the set $\Sigma \overset{\text{def}}{=} \Sigma \rightarrow [0, 1]$.

Some of our conventions for the rest of this chapter depart from the standard probability conventions used in Definitions 11.1 and 11.2 due to the use of an imperative modeling language and the need to manipulate and distinguish distributions. First, we will no longer use random variables over values like $\mathcal{X}$. Instead, we use distributions like $\mathbf{X}$ and write $\mathbf{X}(\sigma)$ to designate the probability of the state σ according to the distribution $\mathbf{X}$. Second, we will no longer use $f(\mathcal{X})$ to designate the r.v. distributing output values of the function f given input values distributed according to r.v. $\mathcal{X}$. Instead we will write $[\![stmt]\!]\mathbf{X}$ to describe the distribution of output states after the evaluation of statement *stmt* starting from a distribution of input states $\mathbf{X}$.

We define two shorthands to make clear the connection between more familiar probabilistic notation and the distribution notations in this chapter. Given a boolean expression *exp*, we will write $\mathbf{X}(exp)$ to denote the marginal probability of the event that the variable *exp* is true. That is, $\mathbf{X}(exp) \overset{\text{def}}{=} \sum_{\sigma:exp \text{ is true for } \sigma} \mathbf{X}(\sigma)$. Given boolean expressions exp_1, exp_2, we will write $\mathbf{X}(exp_1 \mid exp_2)$ to denote the marginal probability of exp_1 being true given exp_2 being true. Formally, $\mathbf{X}(exp_1 \mid exp_2) \overset{\text{def}}{=} \mathbf{X}(exp_1 \wedge exp_2)/\mathbf{X}(exp_2)$. Probabilities such as $\Pr[f(\mathcal{X}) = + \mid \mathcal{Z} = \text{minority}]$ of Definition 11.1 will now be written as $([\![stmt]\!]\mathbf{X})(Y = + \mid Z = \text{minority})$. In this case we assumed *stmt* is the imperative implementation of f, the variable Y holds its sole output, and Z holds the minority status of the input individual.[3]

Now we present the mathematical semantics of the language in Figure 11.1. We call it the *concrete probabilistic semantics* $[\![stmt]\!]:\Sigma \rightarrow \Sigma$ (as distinct from abstract probabilistic semantics which will follow) and it describes the effect of statements on distributions (of states). It is presented in Figure 11.2. The meaning of a statement *stmt* evaluated on a distribution $\mathbf{X}$, written $[\![stmt]\!]\mathbf{X}$, captures informally the process of evaluating *stmt* on states sampled according to $\mathbf{X}$, and collecting the results in a distribution.[4] The probabilistic semantics described at the top of Figure 11.2 is defined in terms distribution operations and combinators in the bottom part. The two shorthand notations for marginal probability and marginal conditioned probability can likewise be defined in terms of these distribution operators. We note that distributions for the language are discrete. For space reasons, we omit many foundational probability theory details.

We can now rephrase our two example properties. Given a population of individuals $\mathbf{X}$ and a program (statement) *stmt* over some set of variables including protected class Z representing the individuals' attributes and producing its outcome in variable

---

[2] For simplicity, we often use the term *distribution* even when we are technically dealing with sub-distributions.

[3] When writing f in our language, the minority status { minority, majority } and outcome quality { +, - } would be encoded as integers.

[4] A formal treatment of distribution to distribution semantics first defines the intermediate state to distribution semantics to describe probabilistic statements and can be found in Clarkson et al. (2009).

$$[\![\text{skip}]\!]\mathbf{X} \stackrel{\text{def}}{=} \mathbf{X}$$

$$[\![X := exp]\!]\mathbf{X} \stackrel{\text{def}}{=} \mathbf{X}[X \to exp]$$

$$[\![stmt_1 \; ; \; stmt_2]\!]\mathbf{X} \stackrel{\text{def}}{=} [\![stmt_2]\!]([\![stmt_1]\!]\mathbf{X})$$

$$[\![\text{if } exp \text{ then } stmt_1 \text{ else } stmt_2]\!]\mathbf{X} \stackrel{\text{def}}{=} [\![stmt_1]\!]([\![exp]\!]\mathbf{X}) + [\![stmt_2]\!]([\![\neg exp]\!]\mathbf{X})$$

$$[\![stmt]\!]\mathbf{X} \stackrel{\text{def}}{=} [\![stmt]\!]([\![stmt_1]\!]([\![exp_1]\!]\mathbf{X})) + [\![\neg exp_1]\!]\mathbf{X}$$

where $stmt = \text{while } exp_1 \text{ do } stmt_1$

$$[\![\text{prob } q \text{ then } stmt_1 \text{ or } stmt_2]\!]\mathbf{X} \stackrel{\text{def}}{=} [\![stmt_1]\!](q \cdot \mathbf{X}) + [\![stmt_2]\!]((1-q) \cdot \mathbf{X})$$

$$[\![X := \text{uniform } l \; u]\!]\mathbf{X} \stackrel{\text{def}}{=} \sum_{x=l}^{u} \frac{1}{u-l+1} \cdot \mathbf{X}[X \to x]$$

$$\mathbf{X}[X \to exp] \stackrel{\text{def}}{=} \lambda\sigma. \; \sum_{\tau \mid \tau[X \to [\![exp]\!]\tau] = \sigma} \mathbf{X}(\tau)$$

$$\mathbf{X}_1 + \mathbf{X}_2 \quad \stackrel{\text{def}}{=} \lambda\sigma. \; \mathbf{X}_1(\sigma) + \mathbf{X}_2(\sigma)$$

$$[\![exp]\!]\mathbf{X} \quad \stackrel{\text{def}}{=} \lambda\sigma. \; \text{if } [\![exp]\!]\sigma \text{ then } \mathbf{X}(\sigma) \text{ else } 0$$

$$p \cdot \mathbf{X} \quad \stackrel{\text{def}}{=} \lambda\sigma. \; p \cdot \mathbf{X}(\sigma)$$

$$\|\mathbf{X}\| \quad \stackrel{\text{def}}{=} \sum_{\sigma} \mathbf{X}(\sigma)$$

$$\text{normal}(\mathbf{X}) \quad \stackrel{\text{def}}{=} \frac{1}{\|\mathbf{X}\|} \cdot \mathbf{X}$$

$$\mathbf{X} \mid exp \quad \stackrel{\text{def}}{=} \text{normal}([\![exp]\!]\mathbf{X})$$

Figure 11.2 `ImpWhile` with probability: probabilistic semantics (top) and distribution operators and combinators (bottom).

Y, we rewrite Definition 11.1 as below:

$$\frac{([\![stmt]\!]\mathbf{X})(Y = + \mid Z = \text{minority})}{([\![stmt]\!]\mathbf{X})(Y = + \mid Z = \text{majority})} \tag{11.1}$$

Likewise, given a program *stmt* processing variable X distributed according to prior states $\mathbf{X}$ to output Y, the posterior Bayes vulnerability given output y, as in Definition 11.2 is expressed as below:

$$\max_{x} \{([\![f]\!]\mathbf{X})(X = x \mid Y = y)\} \tag{11.2}$$

Example 11.3. The **Demographics**$_{stmt}$ program below computes a distribution for the demographics—just the birth year and day—of a population of individuals.

$$\textbf{Demographics}_{stmt} \stackrel{\text{def}}{=}$$
$$BDAY := \text{uniform } 0 \; 364;$$
$$BYEAR := \text{uniform } 1956 \; 1992$$

If $\mathbf{X}_0 = [\![\textbf{Demographics}_{stmt}]\!]\epsilon$ then $\mathbf{X}_0(\sigma) = \frac{1}{365*37}$ for states σ that have

$\sigma(BDAY) \in \{0, \cdots, 364\}$ and $\sigma(BYEAR) \in \{1956, \cdots, 1992\}$. $\mathbf{X}_0$ assigns probability 0 to all other states.

As the distribution is uniform it is not likely to represent a realistic population. More realistic distributions, informed from actual demographic reports such as the U.S. census, can be generated via combinations of the probabilistic choice prob and uniform assignment uniform statements. Such a distribution could then be used to represent an adversary's prior knowledge. Further, the abstraction described later in this chapter relaxes the need to exactly capture background knowledge. A discussion of background knowledge can be found in Section 11.8.

Example 11.4. The program $\mathbf{Birthday}_{stmt}$ below determines whether an individual's birth day (of the year) is within the week period starting from what is assumed to be today.

$$\mathbf{Birthday}_{stmt} \overset{\text{def}}{=}$$
$$\quad TODAY := 260;$$
$$\quad \text{if } BDAY \geq TODAY \land BDAY < (TODAY + 7) \text{ then}$$
$$\qquad OUTPUT := 1$$
$$\quad \text{else}$$
$$\qquad OUTPUT := 0$$

If $\mathbf{X}_1 = (\llbracket \mathbf{Birthday}_{stmt} \rrbracket \mathbf{X}_0) \mid (OUTPUT = 0)$ then $\mathbf{X}_1(\sigma) = \frac{1}{358*37}$ for states σ with $\sigma(BDAY) \in \{0, \cdots, 259, 267, \cdots, 364\}$ and $\sigma(BYEAR) \in \{1956, \cdots, 1992\}$. $\mathbf{X}_1$ assigns 0 probability to all other states.

Example 11.5. The program $\mathbf{Decennial}_{stmt}$ determines whether an individual is in a decennial year (their age is a multiple of 10), or otherwise gets lucky with a probabilistic draw.

$$\mathbf{Decennial}_{stmt} \overset{\text{def}}{=}$$
$$\quad AGE := 2011 - BYEAR;$$
$$\quad \text{if } AGE = 20 \lor AGE = 30 \lor ... \lor AGE = 60$$
$$\qquad \text{then}$$
$$\qquad\quad OUTPUT := 1$$
$$\qquad \text{else}$$
$$\qquad\quad OUTPUT := 0;$$
$$\quad \text{prob } 0.1 \text{ then } OUTPUT := 1 \text{ or skip}$$

Let $\mathbf{X}_2 = (\llbracket \mathbf{Decennial}_{stmt} \rrbracket \mathbf{X}_1)$, that is, before conditioning on any particular output. Then $\mathbf{X}_2$ has probability:

- $\mathbf{X}_2(\sigma) = \frac{1}{358*37}$ for states σ with $\sigma(OUTPUT) = 1$, $\sigma(BDAY) \in \{0, \cdots, 259, 267, \cdots, 364\}$, and $\sigma(BYEAR) \in \{1991, 1981, 1971, 1961\}$.

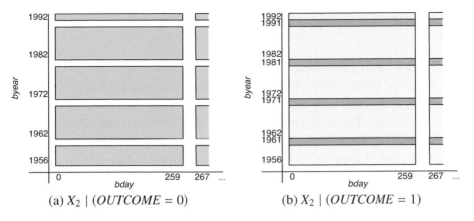

(a) $X_2 \mid (OUTCOME = 0)$ (b) $X_2 \mid (OUTCOME = 1)$

Figure 11.3 Posterior distributions given starting demographics according to **Demographics**$_{stmt}$, **Birthday**$_{stmt}$ outputs in the negative, and **Decennial**$_{stmt}$ outputs in the negative (a) or positive (b).

- $\mathbf{X}_2(\sigma) = \frac{1}{358*37} * \frac{1}{10}$ for states σ with $\sigma(OUTPUT) = 1$, $\sigma(BDAY) \in \{0, \cdots, 259, 267, \cdots, 364\}$, and $\sigma(BDAY) \in \{1956, \cdots, 1992\} \setminus \{1991, 1981, 1971, 1961\}$.

- $\mathbf{X}_2(\sigma) = \frac{1}{358*37} * \frac{9}{10}$ for states σ with $\sigma(OUTPUT) = 0$, $\sigma(BDAY) \in \{0, \cdots, 259, 267, \cdots 364\}$, and $\sigma(BYEAR) \in \{1956, \cdots, 1992\} \setminus \{1991, 1981, 1971, 1961\}$.

- $\mathbf{X}_2(\sigma) = 0$ for all other states σ.

The mass of the positive outcomes, $\|[\![OUTPUT = 1]\!]\mathbf{X}_2\|$, is $\frac{73}{370}$ while the mass of the negative outcomes, $\|[\![OUTPUT = 0]\!]\mathbf{X}_2\|$, is $\frac{297}{370}$. Combining the probabilities above with the masses, we let $X_2^+ = X_2 \mid (OUTCOME = 1)$ and $X_2^- \overset{\text{def}}{=} X_2 \mid (OUTPUT = 0)$ have probabilities as below:

- $\mathbf{X}_2^+(\sigma) = \frac{1}{358*37} / \frac{73}{370} = \frac{10}{358*73}$ for states σ with $\sigma(BDAY) \in \{0, \cdots, 259, 267, \cdots, 364\}$ and $\sigma(BYEAR) \in \{1991, 1981, 1971, 1961\}$.

- $\mathbf{X}_2^+(\sigma) = \frac{1}{358*37} * \frac{1}{10} / \frac{73}{370} = \frac{1}{358*73}$ for states σ with $\sigma(BDAY) \in \{0, \cdots, 259, 267, \cdots, 364\}$ and $\sigma(BYEAR) \in \{1991, 1981, 1971, 1961\} \setminus \{1991, 1981, 1971, 1961\}$.

- $\mathbf{X}_2^+(\sigma) = 0$ for all other states σ.

- $\mathbf{X}_2^-(\sigma) = \frac{1}{358*37} * \frac{9}{10} / \frac{297}{370} = \frac{1}{358*33}$ for states σ with $\sigma(BDAY) \in \{0, \cdots, 259, 267, \cdots, 364\}$ and $\sigma(BYEAR) \in \{1991, 1981, 1971, 1961\} \setminus \{1991, 1981, 1971, 1961\}$

- $\mathbf{X}_2^-(\sigma) = 0$ for all other states σ.

The two posterior distributions are visualized in Figure 11.3 with negative outcome on the left and positive outcome on the right. Darker regions correspond to higher probability.

As described and exemplified, the probabilistic semantics are exact. Computational issues, however, make it difficult to directly apply these semantics in practice. When the space of states becomes large, several aspects of the semantics and definitions become intractable. The assignment statement (see Figure 11.2) and the conditioning operator require sums to enumerate over potentially large number of states or even all possible states. Likewise, properties like Bayes vulnerability refer to all possible marginal states $(X = x)$. Finally, while loops may require potentially an infinite number of iterations to evaluate. In the next section we introduce abstractions that can overcome the state-space problems and conclude with a discussion on the problem of adapting abstract interpretation techniques for analyzing looping constructs to the probabilistic case.

11.4 Abstraction

Abstract interpretation is a technique for making tractable the verification of otherwise intractable program properties (Cousot and Cousot, 1977). As the term implies, abstraction is its main principle: instead of reasoning about potentially large sets of program states and behaviours, we abstract them and reason in terms of their abstract properties. We begin by describing the two principal aspects of abstract interpretation in general: an *abstract domain* and *abstract semantics* over that domain.

Definition 11.6 (Abstract Domain). Given a set of concrete objects C an *abstract domain* $\mathbb{A}$ is a set of corresponding abstract elements as defined by two functions:

- an *abstraction* function $\alpha : 2^C \to \mathbb{A}$, mapping sets of concrete elements to abstract elements, and
- a *concretization* function $\gamma : \mathbb{A} \to 2^C$, mapping abstract elements to sets of concrete elements.

In this chapter, C will be instantiated to either program states Σ or distributions $\overline{\Sigma}$ over program states. In either case, we assume that concrete program semantics for these elements are given. Because you can view a program's state as a point in a multidimensional space, we often refer specific sets or distributions of program states as *regions*.

We will ignore the abstraction function. For convenience we will consider abstract domains that can be defined as predicates over concrete states. I.e., $\gamma : a \mapsto \{c \in C : \varphi_a(c)\}$ where φ_a is a predicate parameterized by the abstract element a.

The second aspect of abstract interpretation is the *interpretation* part: an abstract

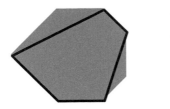 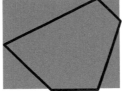

Figure 11.4 The (over)approximation of a polyhedron (black) using an octagon (shaded, left) and an interval (shaded, right).

semantics, written $\langle\!\langle stmt\rangle\!\rangle : \mathbb{A} \to \mathbb{A}$. We require that the abstract semantics be *sound* in that it over-approximates the concrete semantics.

Definition 11.7 (Sound Abstraction). Given an abstract domain $\mathbb{A}$ and its abstract semantics, the abstraction is *sound* if whenever $c \in \gamma(a)$ then $[\![stmt]\!]c \in \gamma(\langle\!\langle stmt\rangle\!\rangle a)$.

Abstractions generally sacrifice some precision: the abstraction of a set of elements C can be imprecise in that $\gamma(\alpha(C))$ contains strictly more than just C and likewise that $\gamma(\langle\!\langle stmt\rangle\!\rangle a)$ contains strictly more elements than $\{[\![stmt]\!]c : c \in \gamma(a)\}$. For this reason, an analysis satisfying Definition 11.7 is called a *may* analysis in that it contains the set of all states that may arise during program execution.

Numeric abstractions A large class of abstractions are designed specifically to model numeric values; in this chapter we restrict ourselves to integer-valued variables. The *interval domain* $\mathbb{I}$ represents "boxes" or non-relational bounded ranges of values for each variable X_i in a state (Cousot and Cousot, 1976):

$$\gamma : \{(l_i, u_i)\}_i \mapsto \{\sigma \in \Sigma : l_i \leq \sigma(X_i) \leq u_i \text{ for every } i\}$$

Abstract elements here are sets of bound pairs, l_i and u_i, forming the lower and upper bound, respectively, for every variable X_i. Intervals are efficient to compute, but imprecise, in that they cannot characterize invariants among variables. More precise, but less efficient numeric domains can be used.

More generally, an abstract domain can be defined in terms of a set of predicates over states, interpreted conjunctively:

$$\gamma : \{\phi_j\}_j \mapsto \{\sigma \in \Sigma : \phi_j(\sigma) \text{ for every } j\}$$

Restrictions on the types of predicates allowed define a family of abstractions. Examples include intervals $\mathbb{I}$ already mentioned, *polyhedra* $\mathbb{P}$ where ϕ_j are restricted to linear inequalities, and *octagons* (Miné, 2001) where the linear inequality coefficients are further restricted to the set $\{-1, 0, 1\}$. Polyhedra and octagons are relational in that they allow precise representations of states that constrain variables in terms of other variables (note this is not the case for intervals). In terms of tractability, intervals are faster to compute with than octagons which are faster than polyhedra. Precision follows the reverse ordering: polyhedra are more precise than octagons which are more precise than intervals. In other words, intervals can over-approximate the set of points represented by octagons which themselves can over-approximate the set of points represented by polyhedra. This relationship is visualized in Figure 11.4.

Other domains are specifically tailored to efficient analysis of particular types of systems. These include grids (Bagnara et al., 2006) for precisely handling modulo operations and domains designed for analysis of numeric values with overflow/underflow (Simon and King, 2007).

Abstract domains implement a set of standard operations including:

- *Meet*, $a \sqcap b$ is the smallest region containing the set of states in the intersection of $\gamma(a), \gamma(b)$. For convex linear domains this operation is least expensive and is exact.
- *Join*, $a \sqcup b$ is the smallest region containing both $\gamma(a)$ and $\gamma(b)$. For linear convex domains, this is supported by the convex hull operation.
- *Transform*, $a[x \rightarrow exp]$, computes an over-approximation of the state-wise assignment $x \mapsto exp$. In the case of invertible assignments, this operation is supported by linear domains via affine transformation. Non-invertible assignments require special consideration (Mardziel et al., 2011).

Abstraction combinators   Abstractions can also be extended disjunctively as in the *powerset* construction (Giacobazzi and Ranzato, 1998). For a base domain $\mathbb{A}$, the *powerset* $2^{\mathbb{A}}$ domain has concretization:

$$\gamma : \{a_j\}_j \mapsto \{\sigma \in \Sigma : \sigma \in \gamma(a_j) \text{ for some } j\} = \cup_j \gamma(a_j)$$

That is, an abstract element in $2^{\mathbb{A}}$ is itself a set of base elements from $\mathbb{A}$ and represents the set of states represented by at least one of its constituents base elements.

Abstraction in the manner outlined can also be applied to probability distributions which serve as the concrete elements. Earlier techniques (Monniaux, 2001) attached probability constraints to standard state domains. Given a state domain $\mathbb{A}$ we form the probabilistic (upper bound) domain $\overline{\mathbb{D}}(\mathbb{A})$ that adds a probability bound on all states represented by the base domain elements:

$$\gamma : (a, p) \mapsto \{\mathbf{X} \in \Sigma : \mathbf{X}(\sigma) \leq p \text{ for all } \sigma \in \gamma(a)\}$$

We can combine the probabilistic upper bound construction the powerset construction to define a domain for representing more complex distributions. A more expressive variant of powerset for probabilistic abstractions imposes a sum bound (as opposed to disjunction of bounds):

$$\gamma : \{(a_j, p_j)\}_j \mapsto \left\{ \mathbf{X} \in \Sigma : \mathbf{X}(\sigma) \le \sum_{j : \sigma \in \gamma(a_j)} p_j \text{ for every } \sigma \right\}$$

We emphasize in these abstractions the focus on the upper bounds of probability; such abstractions do not explicit track lower bounds (beyond the assumed trivial 0). That is, for any probabilistic abstraction a and any state σ, there exists $\mathbf{X} \in \gamma(a)$ such that $\mathbf{X}(\sigma) = 0$. Because of this, these upper bound abstractions lack sound definitions of conditioning. Recall Bayes' rule or the definition of conditioning in Figure 11.2 that involves a normalization by total mass of a (sub)distribution. Upper bounds alone cannot exclude the possibility of 0 as the total mass in the denominator. Posterior Bayes vulnerability of Definition 11.2 features conditioning by program output and disparate impact ratio of Definition 11.1 features probability in the denominator. Thus neither of these conditions can be soundly checked using purely upper-bound abstractions of probability described thus far.

11.5 Sound Domains with Conditioning

As suggested, sound inference needs to account for both lower and upper bounds on probability. The *dual-bounded probabilistic* construction does exactly this (Mardziel et al., 2011)[5]. In this Section we define this domain. In the next section we outline representative aspects of the implementation of its abstract semantics and outline soundness proofs.

The construction imposes probability bounds along with several other constraints used to preserve precision in the implementations of abstract operators to follow.

Definition 11.8. Given a state domain $\mathbb{A}$, the *dual-bounded probabilistic* domain $\mathbb{D}(\mathbb{A})$ is occupied by *probabilistic regions* defined by 4-tuples (a, s, p, m). A probabilistic region represent distributions satisfying 4 constraints: $a \in \mathbb{A}$ bounds their support, $s = (s^{min}, s^{max})$ bounds their number of support points, $p = (p^{min}, p^{max})$ bounds their probability mass per support point, and $m = (m^{min}, m^{max})$ bounds their total probability mass (recall we are working with sub-distributions). Formally these conditions define the concretization function:

$$\gamma(a, s, p, m) \mapsto \left\{ \begin{array}{l} \mathbf{X} \in \Sigma : support(\mathbf{X}) \subseteq \gamma(a), \\ \quad s^{min} \le \|support(\mathbf{X})\| \le s^{max}, \\ \quad m^{min} \le \|\mathbf{X}\| \le m^{max}, \\ \quad p^{min} \le \mathbf{X}(\sigma) \le p^{max} \text{ for every } \sigma \in support(\mathbf{X}) \end{array} \right\}$$

[5] This is a generalization of the *probabilistic polyhedra* domain from earlier work (Mardziel et al., 2011).

We will use non-bold lowercase a to denote abstract states and bold lowercase $\mathbf{a}$ to denote dual-bounded probabilistic regions. We will refer to the p parameters as the point bounds, the s parameters as size bounds, the m parameters as mass bounds, and the a parameter as the support bound.

This probabilistic construction applies to base domains that implement the standard set of abstract operations from the prior section in addition to the counting operation:

- Region size, written #(a), is the number of states (integer vectors in the case of integer-valued states being modeled) in the region, i.e., $\|\gamma(a)\|$. For some domains this is an expensive model counting operation and requires specialized tools such as Latte (De Loera et al., 2008). On the other hand, for other domains like intervals, this operation is trivial.

For convenience in the rest of this chapter, we use two additional operations that can be defined using the standard operations and size.

- Boolean expression conjunction on a region a, written $\langle\!\langle exp \rangle\!\rangle\, a$, returns a region containing at least the points in a that satisfy exp. This is the abstract equivalent of $[\![exp]\!]\sigma$ of Figure 11.2.
- Boolean expression count on a region a, written as $a\#exp$, is an upper bound on the number of points in a that satisfy exp.

Example 11.9. In the powerset of probabilistic polyhedra $\mathbb{D}(\mathbb{P})$, we can represent the negative outcome distributions of Figure 11.3(a), before normalization, with two probabilistic polyhedra $\mathbf{a}_1$ and $\mathbf{a}_2$ containing polyhedra a_1 and a_2 bounding regions $0 \leq BDAY \leq 259, 1956 \leq BYEAR \leq 1992$ and $267 \leq BDAY \leq 354, 1956 \leq BYEAR \leq 1992$, respectively. The other parameters for $\mathbf{a}_1$ would be as follows:

$$p_1^{\min} = p_1^{\max} = 9/135050 = \tfrac{1}{37*365} * \tfrac{9}{10}$$
$$s_1^{\min} = s_1^{\max} = 8580 = 260 * 33$$
$$m_1^{\min} = m_1^{\max} = 7722/13505 = p_1^{\min} * s_1^{\min}$$

Notice this over-approximation loses the fact that the states with $BYEAR \in \{1991, 1981, 1971, 1961\}$ have 0 probability in the concrete semantics. This is also evident in that $s_1^{\min} = s_1^{\max} = 8580 < \#(a_1) = 9620$, illustrating that the "bounding box" of the polyhedra covers more area than is strictly necessary for precision.

For the positive outcome of Figure 11.3(b), we can use the same two polyhedra a_1 and a_2 with the other parameters for a_1 as follows:

$$p_1^{\min} = 1/135050 = \tfrac{1}{37*365} * \tfrac{1}{10} \qquad p_1^{\max} = 10/135050 = \tfrac{1}{37*365}$$
$$s_1^{\min} = 9620 = 260 * 37 \qquad\qquad s_1^{\max} = 9620 = 260 * 37 \qquad (11.3)$$
$$m_1^{\min} = 26/185 \qquad\qquad\qquad m_1^{\max} = 26/185$$

In this case $s_1^{\min} = s_1^{\max} = \#(a_1)$, meaning that all covered points are possible, but $p_1^{min} \neq p_1^{max}$ as some points are more probable than others (i.e., those in the darker band). An astute reader might notice that here $m_1^{min} \neq p_1^{min} * s_1^{min}$ and $m_1^{max} \neq p_1^{max} * s_1^{max}$. The benefit of these seemingly redundant total mass quantities in the representation is that they can sometimes be computed precisely. In this case $m_1^{min} = m_1^{max} = \frac{4}{37} * \frac{260}{365} + \frac{1}{10} * \frac{33}{37} * \frac{260}{365}$. This quantity is the probability of **Decennial**$_{stmt}$ returning 1 composed of having a decennial (first term) plus not having a decennial (second term).

Notice that the exemplified representations are only some among many reasonable options. First, the use of polyhedra as a base domain was not necessary and intervals alone would have been sufficient. Second, more precise representations could have been constructed by using more than just two probabilistic polyhedra (or intervals). On the other hand, even less precise representations would use only a single probabilistic polyhedron (interval). Further nuances come into play for schemes with powerset abstractions that employ a dynamic number of probabilistic regions that can increase or decrease in the process of evaluating programs. How to best employ the representation power of powerset domains is not trivial remains an open problem.

11.6 Abstract Semantics

The abstract semantics for dual-bounded probabilistic regions is defined identically to concrete semantics in Figure 11.2(top) except with supplanting each of the concrete operations/combinators of Figure 11.2 (bottom) with abstract versions that operate on abstract distributions instead of concrete distributions. Soundness of the abstraction is then shown inductively on language statements from the soundness of the abstracted operations and combinators. We present some of these operations in this section; the full set of operations as well as the corresponding proofs can be found in Mardziel et al. (2013).

Abstract Conjunction The concrete conjunction operation restricts a distribution to states satisfying a boolean expression, nullifying probability mass of states that do not: $[\![exp]\!]\mathbf{X} \stackrel{\text{def}}{=} \lambda\sigma.$ if $[\![exp]\!]\sigma$ then $\mathbf{X}(\sigma)$ else 0. Using the expression conjunction and count for abstract states, we develop the abstract conjunction for probabilistic regions as follows.

Definition 11.10. Given a probabilistic region $\mathbf{a}_1 = (a_1, s_1, p_1, m_1)$ and boolean expression *exp*, let $n = a\#exp$ and $\bar{n} = a\#(\neg exp)$. That is, n is an over-approximation of the number of states in a that satisfy the condition *exp* and $\bar{n}$ is an over-approximation of the number of points in a that do not satisfy *exp*. Then, $\langle\!\langle exp \rangle\!\rangle \mathbf{a}_1$

is the probabilistic region $\mathbf{a}_2 = (a_2, s_2, p_2, m_2)$ defined by the parameters enumerated below.

$$
\begin{aligned}
p_2^{min} &= p_1^{min} & \quad s_2^{min} &= \max\left\{s_1^{min} - \bar{n}, 0\right\} \\
p_2^{max} &= p_1^{max} & \quad s_2^{max} &= \min\left\{s_1^{max}, n\right\} \\
m_2^{min} &= \max\left\{p_2^{min} \cdot s_2^{min}, \; m_1^{min} - p_1^{max} \cdot \min\left\{s_1^{max}, \bar{n}\right\}\right\} \\
m_2^{max} &= \min\left\{p_2^{max} \cdot s_2^{max}, \; m_1^{max} - p_1^{min} \cdot \max\left\{s_1^{min} - n, 0\right\}\right\} \\
a_2 &= \langle\!\langle exp \rangle\!\rangle \, a_1
\end{aligned}
$$

The soundness requirement for this and subsequent operations stipulates an inclusion relation between the concrete variant and the abstract variant. In the case of conjunction the statement is is thus: if $\mathbf{X} \in \gamma(\mathbf{a})$ then $[\![exp]\!]\mathbf{X} \in \gamma(\langle\!\langle exp \rangle\!\rangle \, \mathbf{a})$.

Abstract Plus The concrete plus operation combines mass of two given distributions: $\mathbf{X}_1 + \mathbf{X}_2 \stackrel{\text{def}}{=} \lambda\sigma.\ \mathbf{X}_1(\sigma) + \mathbf{X}_2(\sigma)$. The abstract counterpart over-approximates the result. Specifically, if $\mathbf{X}_1 \in \gamma(\mathbf{a}_1)$ and $\mathbf{X}_2 \in \gamma(\mathbf{a}_2)$ then $\mathbf{X}_1 + \mathbf{X}_2 \in \gamma(\mathbf{a}_1 + \mathbf{a}_2)$. For the remainder of the chapter, we will leave the association between a probabilistic region, $\mathbf{a}$, and its constituents, (a, s, p, m), implicit. When more than one probabilistic region is being discussed, the subscripts of the tuple elements will match the subscript of the region.

The abstract sum of two probabilistic regions is defined differently depending on whether their support regions overlap. In the case they do not overlap, the sum $\mathbf{a}_3$ has $a_3 = a_1 \sqcup a_2$ and parameters as below:

$$
\begin{aligned}
p_3^{min} &= \min\left\{p_1^{min}, p_2^{min}\right\} & \quad p_3^{max} &= \max\left\{p_1^{max}, p_2^{max}\right\} \\
s_3^{min} &= s_1^{min} + s_2^{min} & \quad s_3^{max} &= s_1^{max} + s_2^{max} \\
m_3^{min} &= m_1^{min} + m_2^{min} & \quad m_3^{max} &= m_1^{max} + m_2^{max}
\end{aligned}
$$

Otherwise, a_1 and a_2 overlap. We first determine the minimum and maximum number of points in the intersection that may be support points for both $\mathbf{a}$ and for $\mathbf{b}$. We refer to these counts as the *pessimistic overlap* and *optimistic overlap*, respectively.

Definition 11.11. Given two distributions $\mathbf{X}_1, \mathbf{X}_2$, we refer to the set of states that are in the support of both $\mathbf{X}_1$ and $\mathbf{X}_2$ as the *overlap* of $\mathbf{X}_1, \mathbf{X}_2$. The *pessimistic overlap* of $\mathbf{a}$ and $\mathbf{b}$, denoted $\mathbf{a} \odot \mathbf{b}$, is the cardinality of the smallest possible overlap between any two distributions $\mathbf{X}_1 \in \gamma(\mathbf{a})$ and $\mathbf{X}_2 \in \gamma(\mathbf{b})$ and the *optimistic overlap* $\mathbf{a} \odot \mathbf{b}$ is the cardinality of the largest possible overlap. They are computed as follows:

$$
\begin{aligned}
\mathbf{a} \odot \mathbf{b} &\stackrel{\text{def}}{=} \max\left\{s_1^{min} + s_2^{min} - \left(\#(a) + \#(b) - \#(a \sqcap b)\right), 0\right\} \\
\mathbf{a} \odot \mathbf{b} &\stackrel{\text{def}}{=} \min\left\{s_1^{max}, s_2^{max}, \#(a \sqcap b)\right\}
\end{aligned}
$$

The pessimistic overlap is derived from the inclusion-exclusion principle $\|A \cap B\| = \|A\| + \|B\| - \|A \cup B\|$ while the optimistic overlap cannot exceed the support size of either distribution or the size of the intersection.

Definition 11.12. The abstract sum of **a** and **b**, written **a** + **b**, is the probabilistic region **c** with parameters as follows:

$$
\begin{aligned}
c &= a \sqcup b \\[2mm]
p_3^{min} &= \begin{cases} p_1^{min} + p_2^{min} & \text{if } \mathbf{a} \odot \mathbf{b} = \#(c) \\ \min\{p_1^{min}, p_2^{min}\} & \text{otherwise} \end{cases} \\[2mm]
p_3^{max} &= \begin{cases} p_1^{max} + p_2^{max} & \text{if } \mathbf{a} \odot \mathbf{b} > 0 \\ \max\{p_1^{max}, p_2^{max}\} & \text{otherwise} \end{cases} \\[2mm]
s_3^{min} &= \max\{s_1^{min} + s_2^{min} - \mathbf{a} \odot \mathbf{b}, \ 0\} \\[2mm]
s_3^{max} &= \min\{s_1^{max} + s_2^{max} - \mathbf{a} \odot \mathbf{b}, \ \#(c)\} \\[2mm]
m_3^{min} &= m_1^{min} + m_2^{min} \quad | \quad m_3^{max} = m_1^{max} + m_2^{max}
\end{aligned}
$$

The setting of parameters in the sum is chosen to be as precise as possible while maintaining soundness: if $\mathbf{X}_1 \in \gamma(\mathbf{a})$ and $\mathbf{X}_2 \in \gamma(\mathbf{b})$ then $\mathbf{X}_1 + \mathbf{X}_2 \in \gamma(\mathbf{a} + \mathbf{b})$. The two cases for p_3^{min} derive from: (first case) the overlap between the operands is complete (the support of both is identical) and (second case) there is a possibility of a non-overlapping state that is in support of one of the operands but not the other. Likewise, the cases for p_3^{max} derive from: (first case) there is a possibility of support point overlap and (second case) there is no overlap possible between the operands. The size parameters follow from the inclusion-exclusion principle and the mass parameter is a mere sum that does not depend on where the operands distribute their probability mass.

Together the abstract operation soundness claims (see Mardziel et al. (2013) for the rest and their proofs) imply soundness of the abstract semantics:

Theorem 11.13 (Abstraction Semantics Soundness). *If* $\mathbf{X} \in \gamma(\mathbf{a})$ *then* $[\![stmt]\!]\mathbf{X} \in \gamma(\langle\!\langle\!\langle stmt \rangle\!\rangle\!\rangle \mathbf{a})$.

Abstract Normalization Critically, the dual-bounded probabilistic domain allows us to soundly define the conditioning operation which in turn is defined primarily via normalization operation. The normalization of a (sub) distribution produces a distribution whose total mass is equal to 1: $\operatorname{normal}(\mathbf{X}) \overset{\text{def}}{=} \frac{1}{\|\mathbf{X}\|} \cdot \mathbf{X}$. If a probabilistic region **a** has $m^{min} = 1$ and $m^{max} = 1$ then it represents a normalized distribution. We define below an abstract counterpart to distribution normalization for transforming an arbitrary probabilistic region into one containing only normalized distributions.

Definition 11.14. Assuming $m_1^{min} > 0$, normal($\mathbf{a}_1$) is the normalized region $\mathbf{a}_2$ with:

$$
\begin{array}{rcl|rcl}
p_2^{min} & = & p_1^{min}/m_1^{max} & s_2^{min} & = & s_1^{min} \\
p_2^{max} & = & p_1^{max}/m_1^{min} & s_2^{max} & = & s_1^{max} \\
m_2^{min} & = & m_2^{max} = 1 & a_2 & = & a_1
\end{array}
$$

The normalization operator illustrates the interaction between under and over approximation of probability in the abstraction: to ensure that the over-approximation of a state's probability (p^{max}) is sound, we must divide by the *under-approximation* of the total probability mass (m^{min}). This results in abstract normalization that is sound: If $\mathbf{X} \in \gamma(\mathbf{a})$ and $\mathbf{X}$ has non-zero mass, then normal($\mathbf{X}$) $\in \gamma$(normal($\mathbf{a}$)).

Together with soundness of abstract conjunction presented earlier in this section we arrive at the main goal of this work.

Theorem 11.15 (Soundness of Conditioning). *If $\mathbf{X} \in \gamma(\mathbf{a})$ and exp has non-zero marginal probability in $\mathbf{X}$ then $\mathbf{X} \mid exp \in \gamma(\mathbf{a} \mid exp)$.*

We can now show how to use our abstraction to soundly over-approximate quantities such as disparate impact ratio (Definition 11.1) and posterior Bayes vulnerability (Definition 11.2). We define upper and lower bounds on the probability of states as well as the marginal probability bounds for boolean expressions according to a dual-bounded probabilistic region.

Definition 11.16. Given probabilistic region $\mathbf{a}$ and a boolean expression *exp*, the *upper and lower bounds on the marginal probability of exp* are defined as $\mathbf{a}_{min}(exp) \stackrel{def}{=} m_1^{min}$ and $\mathbf{a}_{max}(exp) \stackrel{def}{=} m_1^{max}$ where the mass bound parameters are those of the probabilistic region $\mathbf{a}_1 = \langle\!\langle exp \rangle\!\rangle \mathbf{a}$. The *upper and lower state bounds* are the bounds on the probability of any single (possible) state and are defined $\mathbf{a}_{min} \stackrel{def}{=} p_1^{min}$ and $\mathbf{a}_{max} \stackrel{def}{=} p_1^{max}$.

Corollary 11.17. *The marginal and state probability bounds are sound. That is, for every $\mathbf{X} \in \gamma(\mathbf{a})$:*

$$\mathbf{a}_{min}(exp) \leq \mathbf{X}(exp) \leq \mathbf{a}_{max}(exp)$$

For every $\sigma \in support(\mathbf{X})$:

$$\mathbf{a}_{min} \leq \mathbf{X}(\sigma) \leq \mathbf{a}_{max}$$

Notice that the state bounds quantities $\mathbf{a}_{min}$ and $\mathbf{a}_{max}$ bound the probability of all support states (state with non-zero probability). Quantities such as vulnerability can thus be checked using state bounds without enumerating every possible state.

Returning to disparate impact ratio, let $\mathbf{X}$ be a distribution of individuals with variable Z referring to minority status and presume we have $\mathbf{X} \in \gamma(\mathbf{a})$. Let $\mathbf{a} \stackrel{def}{=} \langle\!\langle stmt \rangle\!\rangle (\mathbf{a} \mid Z = minority)$ and $\mathbf{b} \stackrel{def}{=} \langle\!\langle stmt \rangle\!\rangle (\mathbf{a} \mid Z = majority)$.

$$\frac{(\llbracket stmt \rrbracket \mathbf{X})\,(Y = + \mid Z = \text{minority})}{(\llbracket stmt \rrbracket \mathbf{X})\,(Y = + \mid Z = \text{majority})} \leq \frac{(\mathbf{a})_{\max}\,(Y = +)}{(\mathbf{b})_{\min}\,(Y = +)}$$

Note that though the abstraction, its semantics, and operations allow us to soundly check a disparate ratio bound, this check is outside the syntax and semantics of the language modeled. Though some languages support both probabilistic interpretation and subsequent manipulation of resulting distributions in the same host language, this is not a goal of our toy language and manipulations of distributions like those in the disparate impact ratio bound above have to be done in a separate language hosting the probabilistic interpreter.

In the next section we show how to use the state probability bound, an indicator of the probability of any support point in a distribution, to construct a vulnerability-based privacy monitor.

Powerset Bounds Single regions are firmly on the tractability side of the tractability/accuracy trade-off. Probabilistic regions can be additively combined using a probabilistic powerset construction of Section 11.4. There an abstract probability distribution is composed of a set of simpler abstract probability distributions (in our case dual-bounded probabilistic regions). The set represents all distributions equal to the distribution sum of the distributions represented by each of the abstract elements:

$$\gamma : \{\mathbf{a}_j\}_j \mapsto \left\{ \mathbf{X} \in \Sigma : \mathbf{X} = \sum_j \mathbf{X}_j \text{ where } \mathbf{X}_j \in \gamma\,(\mathbf{a}_j) \right\}$$

For sound base probabilistic abstractions as per Theorem 11.13 and with sound event probability bounds as per Corollary 11.17, the powerset construction provides similarly sound results. Details including the set operations taking part of the abstract interpretation, the probability bound definitions, and proofs can be found in Mardziel et al. (2013).

Widening A distinguishing aspect of abstract interpretation as compared to other static analysis techniques is its handling of looping programs. Recall the semantics of while:

$$\llbracket stmt \rrbracket \mathbf{X} \overset{\text{def}}{=} \qquad \llbracket stmt \rrbracket(\llbracket stmt_1 \rrbracket(\llbracket exp_1 \rrbracket \mathbf{X})) + \llbracket \neg exp_1 \rrbracket \mathbf{X}$$
$$\text{where } stmt = \text{while } exp_1 \text{ do } stmt_1$$

Notice the first term includes the evaluation of the same while statement as we are defining the semantics of. We rewrite this as a monotonic sequence $\mathbf{Y}_i$ via a recursive definition $\mathbf{X}_i$ (along with the abstract version of the same):

$$\mathbf{X}_0 \overset{\text{def}}{=} \mathbf{X} \qquad\qquad \mathbf{a}_0 \overset{\text{def}}{=} \mathbf{a}$$

$$\mathbf{X}_{i+1} \overset{\text{def}}{=} [\![stmt_1]\!]([\![exp_1]\!]\mathbf{X}_i) \qquad\qquad \mathbf{a}_{i+1} \overset{\text{def}}{=} \langle\!\langle stmt_1\rangle\!\rangle(\langle\!\langle\!\langle exp_1\rangle\!\rangle\mathbf{a}_i)$$

$$\mathbf{Y}_n \overset{\text{def}}{=} \sum_{i=0}^{n}[\![\neg exp_1]\!]\mathbf{X}_i \qquad\qquad \mathbf{b}_n \overset{\text{def}}{=} \sum_{i=0}^{n}\langle\!\langle\neg exp_1\rangle\!\rangle\mathbf{a}_i \qquad (11.4)$$

The result of $[\![stmt]\!]\mathbf{X}$ is the fixed-point of the sequence $\mathbf{Y}_i$, a point i at which $\mathbf{Y}_{i+1} = \mathbf{Y}_i$. The problem is that reaching the fixed-point may require large number of iterations. Given the motivation of large state spaces, it is plausible that the number of iterations in a loop is likewise large. Worse yet, in the abstract version of the semantics where abstractions may include concretely unrealizable distributions due to precision loss, the fixed-point may not be achieved in any finite number of steps even if the while loop terminates concretely.

Abstract interpretation employs the *widening* operator to make sure fixed-point computations take only a finite number of iterations. Let $\sqsubseteq$ be an ordering on abstractions respecting the subset relation in their concretizations ($\mathbf{a} \sqsubseteq \mathbf{b}$ implies $\gamma(\mathbf{a}) \subseteq \gamma(\mathbf{b})$).

Definition 11.18. A *widening* operator ∇ is a binary operator that defines for every ascending chain of abstractions $\mathbf{c}_i \sqsubseteq \mathbf{c}_{i+1}$, a chain $\mathbf{c}'_0 \overset{\text{def}}{=} \mathbf{c}_0$, $\mathbf{c}'_{i+1} \overset{\text{def}}{=} \mathbf{c}'_i \nabla \mathbf{c}_{i+1}$ that over-approximates the original chain ($\mathbf{c}'_i \sqsubseteq \mathbf{c}_i$) and has a finite fixed-point ($\mathbf{c}'_{i+1} = \mathbf{c}'_i$ for some finite i).

The abstract semantics of a while loop written as $\mathbf{b}_n$ of Equation 11.4 constitutes an ascending chain and it can thus be over-approximated with a chain having a finite fixed-point by employing widening. Practically, for a widening operator to be defined for an abstraction, it must come with an ordering and must be able to represent potentially infinite concrete states. For example, the interval domain constraints allows for variable bounds to be one-sided or even unbounded. That is, constraints for variables to ranges like $[c, +\infty]$, $[-\infty, c]$, and $[-\infty, +\infty]$, for constant c, are possible. The state abstractions discussed in this chapter all come with widening operators including the powerset constructions.

Widening for probabilistic abstractions, however, is another matter. For the integer-valued programs discussed, the techniques we described rely heavily on counting states. Merely admitting infinite state counts into the counting arguments of this section result in total loss of precision, distribution representations whose probability bounds are uselessly between 0 and 1. As a result, defining abstractions with non-trivial widening operators for probabilistic semantics with sound conditioning remains an open problem.

11.7 Privacy Monitor

In this section demonstrate an application of state bounds to an implementation of an online query privacy monitor. Such a monitor allows clients to query private information while owner can measure how much has been revealed by the queries and can decide to block queries that would otherwise reveal too much. Mardziel et al. (2011) motivate the use of such a system for retaining individual control over personal information while selling partial access to entities such as advertiser who might themselves derive full financial benefit from only limited access. A birthday cake merchant, for example, might be content with knowing that a user's birthday is within the next week in order to offer them a coupon (as in the program **Birthday**$_{stmt}$). An online query scheme allows the merchant to get the information they need and nothing else. On the other hand, repeated queries reveal additional information hence the proposed system tracks the knowledge of each querying party while interacting with the monitor.

The primary tool for monitor is the upper state probability bound with which posterior vulnerability can be soundly estimated. Given a program (the query) *stmt* processing variable X distributed according to prior states $\mathbf{X}$ to output Y and $\mathbf{X} \in \gamma(\mathbf{a})$, we bound the posterior Bayes vulnerability given output y:

$$\max_x \{(\llbracket f \rrbracket \mathbf{X})(X = x \mid Y = y)\} \leq (\langle\!\langle stmt \rangle\!\rangle \mathbf{a} \mid Y = y)_{\max} \overset{\text{def}}{=} \mathrm{V}(\mathbf{a}, stmt, y)$$

Specifically, the right hand inequality gives us a conservative overestimate of the risk in revealing the output y of the program *stmt* to an adversary whose prior knowledge is $\mathbf{X} \in \gamma(\mathbf{a})$ where risk is the likelihood that the adversary can guess value of the secret X correctly in one try. We will refer to the vulnerability bound based on the abstraction $\mathbf{a}$ as $\mathrm{V}(\mathbf{a}, stmt, y)$.

A common objection to privacy properties such as this is that they depend on having the right model of what potential adversaries know. Abstraction alleviates this problem. We need not know $\mathbf{X}$ exactly but only that whatever the adversary knowledge actually is, we capture it in the abstraction $\mathbf{a}$. We return to this point in Section 11.9.

A monitor serves as the gateway to the protected information and will, given a security parameter or vulnerability threshold t, make sure that the risk (in terms of vulnerability) never rises beyond t. This application presumes a querier only observes its interactions with the monitor (it does not infer anything about the secret from any other source).

Given a vulnerability threshold t, a secret state σ, prior adversary knowledge $\mathbf{a}$ with $\mathbf{X}(\sigma) > 0$ for some $\mathbf{X} \in \gamma(\mathbf{a})$, a query *stmt* whose output on the secret state is the value y of variable Y the dynamic monitor has three components: one to determine whether a query should be answered, one to determine what to return to the querier, and one to revise adversary knowledge:

$$\text{Allow}_t(stmt) : \mathbf{a} \mapsto \begin{cases} \text{true} & \text{if } V(\mathbf{a}, stmt, y) \le t \; \forall y \\ \text{false} & \text{otherwise} \end{cases}$$

$$\text{Observe}_t(stmt, y) : \mathbf{a} \mapsto \begin{cases} y & \text{if } \text{Allow}_t(stmt) \\ \text{deny} & \text{otherwise} \end{cases}$$

$$\text{Posterior}_t(stmt, y) : \mathbf{a} \mapsto \begin{cases} (\langle\!\langle\!\langle stmt \rangle\!\rangle\!\rangle \, \mathbf{a}) \mid (Y = y) & \text{if } \text{Allow}_t(stmt) \\ \mathbf{a} & \text{otherwise} \end{cases}$$

Note that in the Allow component, by way of a test for all possible outputs y, we are evaluating the "worst-case" posterior vulnerability (Köpf and Basin, 2007). Compared to making this check for conditional vulnerability given only the actual output y from *stmt* evaluated on secret σ, the worst-case has the benefit of being simulatable (Kenthapadi et al., 2005) in that it can be determined without knowledge of the secret value σ. The outcome of the vulnerability check in the Allow component, therefore, leaks no information about it beyond what is assumed to be known by the adversary.

Chaining applications of the monitor on a sequence of programs $stmt_i$ whose outputs are y_i, we define $\mathbf{a}_{i+1} = \text{Posterior}_t(stmt_i, y_i)(\mathbf{a}_i)$ as the sequence of knowledge revisions of a Bayesian adversary proposing queries $stmt_i$ and observing $\text{Observe}_t(stmt_i, y_i)$.

Theorem 11.19. *Assume a Bayesian adversary has prior knowledge $\mathbf{X} \in \gamma(\mathbf{a}_0)$ consistent with secret σ ($\mathbf{X}(\sigma) > 0$) and prior vulnerability bounded by threshold t ($\max_\sigma \mathbf{X}(\sigma) \le t$). Let y_i be a the set of query outputs sampled from $[\![stmt_i]\!]\sigma$. If the adversary observes nothing but the sequence $\text{Observe}_t(stmt_i, y_i)(\mathbf{a}_i)$, then at no stage will they have a likelihood of more than t of guessing the correct secret σ in a single try.*

We say that y_i are sampled in the theorem as *stmt* may contain probabilistic statements so more than one output value is possible. The theorem is principally based on the soundness of our abstraction for modeling probabilistic program semantics and conditioning. At each stage in the sequence, the abstraction $\mathbf{a}_i$ includes what the Bayesian adversary knows about the secret given their initial prior knowledge and the outputs of the queries before that point, noting query rejections do not reveal anything about the secret.

Example 11.20. Let us consider the sequence of queries, starting from prior according to **Demograhpics**$_{stmt}$, evaluating **Birthday**$_{stmt}$ which returns 0, and then evaluating **Birthday261**$_{stmt}$ which has $TODAY = 261$. In concrete interpretation we have distributions:

- $X_0 = [\![\textbf{Demograhpics}_{stmt}]\!]\epsilon$. At this point $X_0(\sigma) = \frac{1}{365*37}$, meaning we could reasonably employ the privacy monitor for any threshold t above $\frac{1}{365*37}$.
- $X_1 = ([\![\textbf{Birthday}_{stmt}]\!]X_0) \mid (OUTPUT = 0)$. At this point we have $X_1(\sigma) = \frac{1}{358}$ for states σ that have $\sigma(BDAY) \in \{0,\cdots,259,267,\cdots,364\}$ (and for some values of $BYEAR$). Thus if the threshold t was below $\frac{1}{358*37}$, the monitor would have already rejected this first query.
- $X_2' = ([\![\textbf{Birthday261}_{stmt}]\!]X_1)$.

The monitor now needs to determine whether to evaluate the report the output of the second birthday query. Were the output of this query to be 0, we would have posterior $X_2(\sigma) = \frac{1}{357*37}$ but if the query returned 1, we would instead have $X_2(\sigma) = \frac{1}{1*37}$, pinpointing the day of the year exactly. Thus for any threshold below $\frac{1}{37}$, the monitor must reject this query, regardless of whether it would return 0 or 1 on the true value of $BDAY$.

The example above is described in terms of concrete probabilistic semantics. Given soundness of the corresponding abstract semantics, the safe enforcement of the posterior vulnerability can also be done in the abstract (Theorem 11.19).

11.8 Related Work

The work presented in this chapter has connections to techniques for program analysis, notably abstraction interpretation, and methods for measuring and enforcing privacy. We briefly summarize the most related of these works. When considering privacy, we specifically consider works that do, and do not, require modeling prior knowledge when assessing information leakage.

Abstract Interpretation Static program analyses such as abstract interpretation(Cousot and Cousot, 1977) and symbolic execution (King, 1976; Cadar et al., 2008) model program behaviour over large sets of inputs or starting conditions with the goal of discovering or verifying the absence of undesirable conditions that would be difficult or close to impossible to verify with mere test cases or dynamic analyses. Static techniques employ forms of abstraction to explore the space of executions. The form of abstraction varies and has implications on the differences between the analyses both in terms of their tractability, precision, and soundness in modeling programs. The aspects of abstract interpretation that distinguish it from other static analysis techniques include its limits on the complexity of representation and the use of the widening operator to handle looping programs.

Abstract domains impose limits on the complexity of an analysis by abstract interpretation (recall domains of Section 11.4). Powerset domains typically restrict the number of disjuncts in a representation and the disjuncts themselves are limited by their underlying domain whose basic logical queries such as satisfiability are trivial or at least easy. This distinguishes abstract interpretation from analyses in which logical representation can grow ever more complex and employ more expressive theories, sometimes to the point where success of analysis depends primarily on an undecidable logical satisfiability test for an enormous formula employing potentially incomplete theories.

The abstract interpretation of probabilistic programs has been tackled by Monniaux (2001) who defined probabilistic program semantics based on over-approximating probabilities of program states. In other work, Di Pierro et al. (2005) described abstract interpretation for probabilistic lambda calculus, and Smith (2008) who used probabilistic abstract interpretation for verification of quantitative program properties. Such works are limited in their (lack of) sound handling of conditioning which is a necessary component of a wide variety of quantitative privacy notions. A theoretical investigation of probabilistic abstract interpretation as built atop traditional abstractions can be found in Cousot and Monerau (2012).

Dynamic Probabilistic Programming Dynamic analysis works characterizes properties of concrete program evaluations. Such an analysis has the benefit of not requiring an abstraction of semantics and hence can be easily adopted to full-featured languages. The analysis described in this chapter, on the other hand, works well for programs containing only linear expressions over integer-valued variables. Adapting such analyses to richer programs is possible but will invariably suffer in precision when modeling language features not specifically designed for in the abstraction.

In the context of this chapter's privacy application, the pertinent aspect of a probabilistic programming system is its ability to accurately or soundly approximate probability or a privacy criterion. Though generally lacking ability to derive exact probability or bounds, dynamic techniques and sampling have been used in privacy contexts. Köpf and Rybalchenko (2010), for example, use sampling to derive information flow bounds.

More recently, Sweet et al. (2018) have shown that sampling can be used to improve the precision of the abstract distribution representation discussed in this chapter. However, in this and other sampling techniques, the soundness guarantees become somewhat subtle. In the case of (Sweet et al., 2018), for example, the authors provide for a confidence bound (a probability over the sampling process) that the derived probability values (like posterior Vulnerability) are within a certain range.

Privacy with Background Knowledge Assumptions *Measurement* of adversary knowledge of private data as it is informed by a program's output has been a well-studied problem since Robling Denning (1982). Clark et al. (2005) define a static analysis that bounds the secret information a straight-line program can leak in terms of equivalence relations between the inputs and outputs. Backes et al. (2009) automate the synthesis of such equivalence relations and quantify leakage by computing the exact size of equivalence classes. Köpf and Rybalchenko (2010) extend this approach, improving its scalability by using sampling to identify equivalence classes and using under- and over-approximation to obtain bounds on their size. Mu and Clark (2009) present a similar analysis that uses over-approximation only. In all cases, the inferred equivalence classes can be used to compute entropy-based metrics of information leakage.

Along with tools, there is a growing number of quantitative information flow measures in the literature, varying according to the operational interpretation of risk. Instances include *Bayes vulnerability* (Smith, 2009) and *Bayes risk* (Chatzikokolakis et al., 2008), *Shannon entropy* (Shannon, 1948), and *guessing entropy* (Massey, 1994). The *g-vulnerability* framework (Alvim et al., 2012) is meant to encompass a more general set of operational interpretations.

Two important aspects of all of these works are (a) whether they deal with absolute or relative information and (b) whether they incorporate background knowledge.

For the first, an example absolute measure is posterior *vulnerability* discussed in this chapter. Relative measures compare the absolute measurements before and after an adversary makes an observation from some scrutinized system. Relative measurements of information further have variants which do not assume particular background knowledge on the adversary's part but instead quantify the worst-case difference in prior and posterior over all possible distributions. Channel capacity in FLOWCHECK (McCamant and Ernst, 2008) and various definitions of maximum leakage measures in the quantitative information flow literature are examples.

The reliance on having a sense of background knowledge of adversaries is the problematic assumption motivating other popular approaches such as *differential privacy* (Dwork, 2008). Unlike the approaches mentioned above, differential privacy lacks a clear connection to harms induced by privacy loss and attempts at connecting its privacy parameter to harms invariably make assumptions as problematic as those regarding background knowledge (Kifer and Machanavajjhala, 2011).

Though we make the assumption of having adversary background knowledge in our work, our use of probabilistic programming and abstract interpretation alleviates it. First, for cases where a secret is generated by a program which is known by the adversary, the distribution representing their background knowledge can be derived by probabilistic evaluation of said generating program. An over-approximation of the knowledge can likewise be generating using the techniques described in this chapter. Second, probabilistic programs can be viewed as tools for modeling background knowledge and can bring to bear their benefits specifically in terms of concisely describing distributions arising from generative processes. Finally, probabilistic abstract interpretation makes the process easier by not requiring the exact background knowledge of all adversaries to be known as long as it can be approximated in some abstraction. To this end, we can extend our toy probabilistic language with the "possibilistic" choice statement:

$$stmt ::= \text{poss } stmt_1 \text{ and } stmt_2 \mid \dots$$

The meaning of possibilistic choice is that either branch can occur. This cannot be modeled in the concrete semantics but can be approximated in the abstract semantics by making sure that when $\mathbf{b} = [\![\text{poss } stmt_1 \text{ and } stmt_2]\!]\mathbf{a}$ then $\gamma ([\![stmt_1]\!]\mathbf{a}) \subseteq \gamma (\mathbf{b})$ and $\gamma ([\![stmt_2]\!]\mathbf{a}) \subseteq \gamma (\mathbf{b})$. That is, the abstraction of possibility must include the abstractions of both branches. As an adversary modeling tool, this lets us remain uncertain which of the branches generates the true adversary knowledge, as long as one of them does.

The techniques described in this chapter can incorporate such a modeling tool by virtue of the imprecise but sound representations employed. The numeric abstractions, however, were not designed with this use-case in mind. Taking advantage of this feature of abstract interpretation for the purpose of modeling uncertainty in knowledge is an open problem.

11.9 Conclusions

In this chapter we have described a probabilistic programming approach with sound probability and inference bounds suitable for specifying fairness and privacy properties. Based on abstract interpretation, the technique allows one to trade off precision for speed of analysis all the while preserving a general soundness criterion. Probabilistic abstract interpretation therefore offers a unique set of benefits from among the probabilistic programming toolkit.

The field of abstract interpretation is an active area of research and offers many open problems. New domains, combinators, and algorithms for efficiently and accurately representing program states and reasoning about larger and more feature rich programs are proposed regularly. Considerations for probability, however, are not as thoroughly investigated. Fundamental aspects of abstraction such as widening remain unavailable for languages with sound conditioning and thus pose a hurdle to the wider adoption of the otherwise extremely successful program analysis technique to probabilistic applications.

References

Alvim, Mário S., Chatzikokolakis, Konstantinos, Palamidessi, Catuscia, and Smith, Geoffrey. 2012. Measuring Information Leakage Using Generalized Gain

Functions. In: *Proceedings of the IEEE Computer Security Foundations Symposium (CSF)*.

Backes, Michael, Köpf, Boris, and Rybalchenko, Andrey. 2009. Automatic Discovery and Quantification of Information Leaks. In: *Proceedings of the IEEE Symposium on Security and Privacy (S&P)*.

Baden, Randy, Bender, Adam, Spring, Neil, Bhattacharjee, Bobby, and Starin, Daniel. 2009. Persona: an online social network with user-defined privacy. In: *Proceedings of the ACM SIGCOMM Conference on Applications, Technologies, Architectures, and Protocols for Computer Communications (SIGCOMM)*.

Bagnara, Roberto, Dobson, Katy, Hill, Patricia M, Mundell, Matthew, and Zaffanella, Enea. 2006. Grids: A domain for analyzing the distribution of numerical values. Pages 219–235 of: *International Symposium on Logic-based Program Synthesis and Transformation*. Springer.

Cadar, Cristian, Ganesh, Vijay, Pawlowski, Peter M, Dill, David L, and Engler, Dawson R. 2008. EXE: automatically generating inputs of death. *ACM Transactions on Information and System Security (TISSEC)*, **12**(2), 10.

Chatzikokolakis, Konstantinos, Palamidessi, Catuscia, and Panangaden, Prakash. 2008. On the Bayes risk in information-hiding protocols. *Journal of Computer Security*, **16**(5).

Clark, David, Hunt, Sebastian, and Malacaria, Pasquale. 2005. Quantitative Information Flow, Relations and Polymorphic Types. *Journal of Logic and Computation*, **15**, 181–199.

Clarkson, Michael R., Myers, Andrew C., and Schneider, Fred B. 2009. Quantifying information flow with beliefs. *Journal of Computer Security*, **17**(5), 655–701.

Cousot, Patrick, and Cousot, Radhia. 1976. Static Determination of Dynamic Properties of Programs. In: *Proceedings of the Second International Symposium on Programming*.

Cousot, Patrick, and Cousot, Radhia. 1977. Abstract interpretation: a unified lattice model for static analysis of programs by construction or approximation of fixpoints. In: *Proceedings of the ACM SIGPLAN Conference on Principles of Programming Languages (POPL)*.

Cousot, Patrick, and Monerau, Michael. 2012. Probabilistic Abstract Interpretation. In: *Proceedings of the European Symposium on Programming (ESOP)*.

De Loera, Jesus A., Haws, David, Hemmecke, Raymond, Huggins, Peter, Tauzer, Jeremy, and Yoshida, Ruriko. 2008. *LattE*. http://www.math.ucdavis.edu/latte.

Di Pierro, Alessandra, Hankin, Chris, and Wiklicky, Herbert. 2005. Probabilistic Lambda-calculus and Quantitative Program Analysis. *Journal of Logic and Computation*, **15**(2), 159–179.

Dwork, Cynthia. 2008. Differential privacy: A survey of results. Pages 1–19 of: *International Conference on Theory and Applications of Models of Computation*. Springer.

Feldman, Michael, Friedler, Sorelle A., Moeller, John, Scheidegger, Carlos, and Venkatasubramanian, Suresh. 2015. Certifying and Removing Disparate Impact. Pages 259–268 of: *Proceedings of the 21th ACM SIGKDD International Conference on Knowledge Discovery and Data Mining*.

Giacobazzi, Roberto, and Ranzato, Francesco. 1998. Optimal domains for disjunctive abstract interpretation. *Science of Computer Programming*, **32**(1-3), 177–210.

Golle, Philippe. 2006. Revisiting the uniqueness of simple demographics in the US population. In: *Proceedings of the Workshop on Privacy in the Electronic Society (WPES)*.

Kenthapadi, Krishnaram, Mishra, Nina, and Nissim, Kobbi. 2005. Simulatable Auditing. In: *Proceedings of the ACM SIGMOD Symposium on Principles of Database Systems (PODS)*.

Kifer, Daniel, and Machanavajjhala, Ashwin. 2011. No free lunch in data privacy. Pages 193–204 of: *Proceedings of the 2011 ACM SIGMOD International Conference on Management of data*. ACM.

King, James C. 1976. Symbolic execution and program testing. *Communications of the ACM*, **19**(7), 385–394.

Köpf, Boris, and Basin, David. 2007. An Information-Theoretic Model for Adaptive Side-Channel Attacks. In: *Proceedings of the ACM Conference on Computer and Communications Security (CCS)*.

Köpf, Boris, and Rybalchenko, Andrey. 2010. Approximation and Randomization for Quantitative Information-Flow Analysis. In: *Proceedings of the IEEE Computer Security Foundations Symposium (CSF)*.

Kozen, Dexter. 1981. Semantics of probabilistic programs. *Journal of Computer and System Sciences*, **22**(3), 328–350.

Mardziel, Piotr, Magill, Stephen, Hicks, Michael, and Srivatsa, Mudhakar. 2011. Dynamic Enforcement of Knowledge-based Security Policies. In: *Proceedings of the IEEE Computer Security Foundations Symposium (CSF)*.

Mardziel, Piotr, Hicks, Michael, Katz, Jonathan, and Srivatsa, Mudhakar. 2012. Knowledge-Oriented Secure Multiparty Computation. In: *Proceedings of the ACM SIGPLAN Workshop on Programming Languages and Analysis for Security (PLAS)*.

Mardziel, Piotr, Magill, Stephen, Hicks, Michael, and Srivatsa, Mudhakar. 2013. Dynamic Enforcement of Knowledge-based Security Policies using Probabilistic Abstract Interpretation. *Journal of Computer Security*, Jan.

Massey, James L. 1994. Guessing and Entropy. In: *Proceedings of the IEEE International Symposium on Information Theory*.

McCamant, Stephen, and Ernst, Michael D. 2008. Quantitative information flow as network flow capacity. In: *Proceedings of the ACM SIGPLAN Conference on Programming Language Design and Implementation (PLDI)*.

Miné, Antoine. 2001. The Octagon Abstract Domain. In: *Proceedings of the Working Conference on Reverse Engineering (WCRE)*.

Monniaux, David. 2001. *Analyse de programmes probabilistes par interprétation abstraite*. Thèse de doctorat, Université Paris IX Dauphine.

Mu, Chunyan, and Clark, David. 2009. An Interval-based Abstraction for Quantifying Information Flow. *Elec. Notes in Theoretical Computer Science*, **253**(3), 119–141.

Robling Denning, Dorothy Elizabeth. 1982. *Cryptography and data security*. Addison-Wesley Longman Publishing Co., Inc.

Seong, Seok-Won, Seo, Jiwon, Nasielski, Matthew, Sengupta, Debangsu, Hangal, Sudheendra, Teh, Seng Keat, Chu, Ruven, Dodson, Ben, and Lam, Monica S. 2010. PrPl: a Decentralized Social Networking Infrastructure. In: *Proceedings of the Workshop on Mobile Cloud Computing & Services: Social Networks and Beyond*. Invited Paper.

Shannon, Claude. 1948. A Mathematical Theory of Communication. *Bell System Technical Journal*, **27**.

Simon, Axel, and King, Andy. 2007. Taming the wrapping of integer arithmetic. Pages 121–136 of: *International Static Analysis Symposium*. Springer.

Smith, Geoffrey. 2009. On the Foundations of Quantitative Information Flow. In: *Proceedings of the Conference on Foundations of Software Science and Computation Structures (FoSSaCS)*.

Smith, Michael J. A. 2008. Probabilistic Abstract Interpretation of Imperative Programs using Truncated Normal Distributions. *Electronic Notes in Theoretical Computer Science*, **220**(3), 43–59.

Sweeney, Latanya. 2000. *Simple Demographics Often Identify People Uniquely*. Tech. rept. LIDAP-WP4. Carnegie Mellon University, School of Computer Science, Data Privacy Laboratory.

Sweet, Ian, Trilla, José Manuel Calderón, Scherrer, Chad, Hicks, Michael, and Magill, Stephen. 2018. What's the Over/Under? Probabilistic Bounds on Information Leakage. Pages 3–27 of: Bauer, Lujo, and Küsters, Ralf (eds), *Principles of Security and Trust*. Cham: Springer International Publishing.

12

Quantitative Information Flow with Monads in Haskell

Jeremy Gibbons
University of Oxford
Annabelle McIver
Macquarie University
Carroll Morgan
University of New South Wales, and Data61 (CSIRO)
Tom Schrijvers
KU Leuven

Abstract: Monads are a popular feature of the programming language *Haskell* because they can model many different notions of computation in a uniform and purely functional way. Our particular interest here is the probability monad, which can be – and has been – used to synthesise models for probabilistic programming.

Quantitative Information Flow, or *QIF*, arises when security is combined with probability, and concerns the measurement of the *amount* of information that 'leaks' from a probabilistic program's state to a (usually) hostile observer: that is, not "whether" leaks occur but rather "how much?"

Recently it has been shown that *QIF* can be seen monadically, a 'lifting' of the probability monad from (simply) distributions to *distributions* of distributions – so called "hyper-distributions". Haskell's support for monads therefore suggests a synthesis of an executable model for *QIF*. Here we provide the first systematic and thorough account of doing that: using distributions of distributions to synthesise a model for Quantitative Information Flow in terms of monads in Haskell.

12.1 Introduction

In contexts where programs have access to or manipulate private information, assessing the control of how that information flows is an essential aspect of the verification task. In some, probably most cases *some* part of the secret must be released for the program to achieve anything useful at all – but it is the unintended leaks, which could be avoided by more careful programming, that concern us here. Preventing them is enormously challenging, and the idea of quantifying the

---

[a] From *Foundations of Probabilistic Programming*, edited by Gilles Barthe, Joost-Pieter Katoen and Alexandra Silva published 2020 by Cambridge University Press.

information that *does* flow was proposed by (Denning, 1982), (Millen, 1987), (Clark et al., 2005b) and others to provide a sound framework to enable the analysis of the severity and impact of such flows. Our model for Quantitative Information Flow, that is *QIF*, was originally expressed in terms of information-theoretic channels, even to the extent of measuring (change in) Shannon Entropy 'by default' as the method of choice (Millen, 1987); and as such it has been used successfully to assess flows related to confidentiality and privacy for relevant operational scenarios. More recently, however, this channel model has been generalised: more general entropies than Shannon's are applicable (Alvim et al., 2012), and flow can be defined for programs rather than just channels (McIver et al., 2010). (Programs can update the private information, whereas channels can only read it.) The key to this generalisation is hyper-distributions (McIver et al., 2010, 2014a) (§12.3 below) – based on 'hypers', *QIF* in computer programs can be given a monadic semantics that supports many different entropies.

This chapter combines the monadic semantics with a second idea: that monads (§12.2.1 below) abstract and unify common features of "notions of computation" (Moggi, 1991) and that monadic features can be, and have been built into (functional) programming languages (Wadler, 1992). Putting those two ideas together encourages the synthesis of an implementation of a '*QIF*-aware' programming language. We present a prototype of such a language, which we have called "Kuifje".[1] The synthesis also provides an important tool for experimentation with and analysis of how information flows in real programming.

A helpful guide to what we present is the analogous, but more straightforward synthesis that arises from a simpler combination: that simple probabilistic semantics (i.e. without flow) is also monadic (Lawvere, 1962; Giry, 1981). The result is easy implementations of functional probabilistic programming languages (Ramsey and Pfeffer, 2002; Erwig and Kollmansberger, 2006; Kiselyov and Shan, 2009). Our work here benefits from that, because *QIF*-aware programming languages are probabilistic – the 'quantities' in the information flow are derived from the probabilities occurring in the programs and in the probability distributions over the hidden state to which they are applied.

In the development of our functional implementation we use the notion of monoids as a guiding structure. Indeed, we can see both the syntactic- and the semantic domain of a simple programming language as a monoid, the former being free, so that its denotational semantics is then a monoid morphism. The initial-algebra representation of free monoids gives rise to a straightforward implementation of this denotational semantics as a functional-programming-style *fold*. Moreover, with 'fold fusion' (Malcolm, 1990; Hutton, 1999) we can easily derive an efficient implementation of the hyper-distribution semantics from its naïve specification.

---

[1] "Kuifje" is the Flemish/Dutch name of Hergé's Tintin, and refers to his hairstyle: a quiff.

12.2 Background

We begin by describing monads in general (briefly) as they are used in Computer Science (§12.2.1), how they relate to quantitative information flow (§12.2.2), how they are instantiated in the functional programming language Haskell (§12.2.3), and how their Haskell instantiation can be used to build the tools necessary for a probabilistic information-flow-aware programming-language implementation (§12.2.4). The Haskell-oriented reader may want to skip the theoretical background and jump straight to §12.2.3.

12.2.1 Monads

The mathematical structure of monads was introduced to Computer Science by Moggi in order to have a model of computation that was more general than the "gross simplification" of identifying programs with total functions from values to values, a view that "wipes out completely behaviours like non-termination, non-determinism or side effects..." (Moggi, 1991). Here we will be using that generality to capture the behaviour of programs that hide and, complementarily, leak information: and our particular focus will be on using the monadic facilities of the programming language Haskell (Peyton Jones, 2003) to illustrate our ideas (§12.2.3).

Moggi's insight was to model a "notion of computation" as a monad $\mathbb{T}$, in order to distinguish *plain* values of some type $\mathcal{A}$ from the computations $\mathbb{T}\mathcal{A}$ that *yield* such values. (Later, we will see $\mathbb{T}$ as a Haskell type-constructor.) Thus $\mathbb{T}$ might enrich sets $\mathcal{A}$ of values to $\mathcal{A}_\perp$ by adding an extra element $\perp$ denoting 'not a proper value', perhaps the simplest computational monad; or it might enrich $\mathcal{A}$ to $\mathbb{P}\mathcal{A}$, the subsets of $\mathcal{A}$, for modelling demonic choice; or it might enrich $\mathcal{A}$ to $\mathcal{W}^* \times \mathcal{A}$, pairing with a sequence of $\mathcal{W}$ values, for modelling 'writing' such as to a log file; or it might enrich $\mathcal{A}$ to $\mathbb{D}\mathcal{A}$, the discrete distributions on $\mathcal{A}$ which, below, will be our starting point here. We say "enrich" because in each case the original $\mathcal{A}$ can be found embedded within $\mathbb{T}\mathcal{A}$: a plain value can always be seen as a degenerate computation. Thus $\mathcal{A}$ is found: within $\mathcal{A}_\perp$ as that subset of computations yielding a proper value; within $\mathcal{W}^* \times \mathcal{A}$ as the computations $(\langle\,\rangle, a)$ in which no writes have yet occurred; within $\mathbb{P}\mathcal{A}$ as the singleton sets $\{a\}$ that represent the (degenerate) demonic choice of only one value, i.e. no choice at all (Hobson's Choice); and $\mathcal{A}$ is found within $\mathbb{D}\mathcal{A}$ as the point distribution $\langle a \rangle$, the probabilistic choice 'certainly a', this time no *probabilistic* choice at all.[2]

For a general monad $\mathbb{T}$, the embeddings illustrated above are all instances of the *unit function*, written η and of type $\mathcal{A} \rightarrow \mathbb{T}\mathcal{A}$, so that in the above four cases $\eta\,a$ is (the proper value) a, (the nothing-yet-written) $(\langle\,\rangle, a)$, (the singleton) $\{a\}$, and (the

---

[2] For $a \colon \mathcal{A}$ we write $\langle a \rangle$ for the *point distribution* in $\mathbb{D}\mathcal{A}$ which assigns probability 1 to a and probability 0 to all other elements of $\mathcal{A}$ (like a one-sided die).

point) $\langle a \rangle$, respectively. Whereas a pure function taking values from $\mathcal{A}$ to values in $\mathcal{B}$ has type $\mathcal{A} \rightarrow \mathcal{B}$, Moggi modelled an 'impure function' for a particular notion of computation $\mathbb{T}$ as a so-called *Kleisli arrow* $\mathcal{A} \rightarrow \mathbb{T}\mathcal{B}$ – that is, a pure function yielding a computation rather than a plain value. Thus partial functions are modelled as Kleisli arrows $\mathcal{A} \rightarrow \mathcal{B}_{\perp}$, 'writing functions' as Kleisli arrows $\mathcal{A} \rightarrow \mathcal{W}^* \times \mathcal{B}$, 'nondeterministic functions' as Kleisli arrows $\mathcal{A} \rightarrow \mathbb{P}\mathcal{B}$, and 'probabilistic functions' as Kleisli arrows $\mathcal{A} \rightarrow \mathbb{D}\mathcal{B}$.

If a monad $\mathbb{T}$ is to model a "notion of computation", then in particular it had better support sequential composition: if a program f takes a value $a : \mathcal{A}$ to some structure in $\mathbb{T}\mathcal{B}$, and it is followed by a compatible program g with the same notion $\mathbb{T}$ of computation, i.e. a Kleisli arrow of type $\mathcal{B} \rightarrow \mathbb{T}C$, then that second program g must *act* as if it has type $\mathbb{T}\mathcal{B} \rightarrow \mathbb{T}C$ if it is to be sequentially composed with f, since the input type of g, the second stage, must in some sense match the output type of the first stage f. This is achieved by defining a *Kleisli-lifting* $(-)^*$, which converts Kleisli arrow $g : \mathcal{B} \rightarrow \mathbb{T}C$ to a 'lifted' version g^*, a function of type $\mathbb{T}\mathcal{B} \rightarrow \mathbb{T}C$. Then the intuitive conclusion, that if f goes from $\mathcal{A}$ to $\mathcal{B}$ and g from $\mathcal{B}$ to C then their composition should go from $\mathcal{A}$ to C, is realised by the *Kleisli composition* $g \bullet f$ of $f : \mathcal{A} \rightarrow \mathbb{T}\mathcal{B}$ and $g : \mathcal{B} \rightarrow \mathbb{T}C$ defined as $g \bullet f = g^* \circ f$ having type $\mathcal{A} \rightarrow \mathbb{T}C$, using Kleisli-lifting $(-)^*$ and ordinary functional composition $(\circ)$ together.

A monad $\mathbb{T}$ can be seen as a *functor* which, among other things, means that for any function $h : \mathcal{A} \rightarrow \mathcal{B}$ there is another function $\mathbb{T}h : \mathbb{T}\mathcal{A} \rightarrow \mathbb{T}\mathcal{B}$ that behaves in a sensible way (in particular, respecting identity and composition). Then an alternative definition of Kleisli composition is to require that $\mathbb{T}$ have a *multiplication* operation $\mu : \mathbb{T}^2 C \rightarrow \mathbb{T}C$. In that case, for Kleisi arrow $g : \mathcal{B} \rightarrow \mathbb{T}C$ one can define g^* by $\mu \circ \mathbb{T}g$, and the Kleisli composition $g \bullet f$ of $f : \mathcal{A} \rightarrow \mathbb{T}\mathcal{B}$ and $g : \mathcal{B} \rightarrow \mathbb{T}C$ becomes $\mu \circ \mathbb{T}g \circ f$, thus achieving the same end. With suitable conditions on unit η and multiply μ, the two presentations, one in terms of Kleisli lifting and the other in terms of multiplication, are equivalent and we will use them interchangeably.

The precise conditions for operation $\mathbb{T}$ on sets $\mathcal{A}$ to be a monad are that $\mathbb{T}$ must act also on the functions between those sets, respecting typing (so that $\mathbb{T}f : \mathbb{T}\mathcal{A} \rightarrow \mathbb{T}\mathcal{B}$ when $f : \mathcal{A} \rightarrow \mathcal{B}$), and it must support families of functions $\eta_{\mathcal{A}} : \mathcal{A} \rightarrow \mathbb{T}\mathcal{A}$ and $\mu_{\mathcal{A}} : \mathbb{T}^2 \mathcal{A} \rightarrow \mathbb{T}\mathcal{A}$ that satisfy also the following algebraic identities (for $f : \mathcal{A} \rightarrow \mathcal{B}$ and $g : \mathcal{B} \rightarrow C$):

(a) $\mathbb{T}id_{\mathcal{A}} = id_{\mathbb{T}\mathcal{A}}$ — $\mathbb{T}$ respects identity.

(b) $\mathbb{T}g \circ \mathbb{T}f = \mathbb{T}(g \circ f)$ — $\mathbb{T}$ respects composition.

(c) $\eta_{\mathcal{B}} \circ f = \mathbb{T}f \circ \eta_{\mathcal{A}}$ — η is a natural transformation $1 \rightarrow \mathbb{T}$.

(d) $\mu_{\mathcal{B}} \circ \mathbb{T}^2 f = \mathbb{T}f \circ \mu_{\mathcal{A}}$ — μ is a natural transformation $\mathbb{T}^2 \rightarrow \mathbb{T}$.

(e) $\mu_{\mathcal{A}} \circ \mathbb{T}\mu_{\mathcal{A}} = \mu_{\mathcal{A}} \circ \mu_{\mathbb{T}\mathcal{A}}$ — μ is associative.

(f) $\mu_{\mathcal{A}} \circ \mathbb{T}\eta_{\mathcal{A}} = \mu_{\mathcal{A}} \circ \eta_{\mathbb{T}\mathcal{A}} = id_{\mathcal{A}}$ — η is unit of μ.

Identities (a,b) are the conditions for $\mathbb{T}$ to be a functor, and (c,d) require that the families η and μ form natural transformations, and finally (e,f) are the additional conditions for $(\mathbb{T}, \eta, \mu)$ to form a monad. In particular, it is a straightforward exercise to use these identities to verify that $(\bullet)$ and η form a monoid: we have $h \bullet (g \bullet f) = (h \bullet g) \bullet f$ and $\eta \bullet f = f = f \bullet \eta$.

To make those identities more concrete and familiar, we describe in words what the analogous identities would be for the powerset monad $\mathbb{P}$ used to model non-deterministic, i.e. 'demonic' programs. They are (in the same order)

(a) The image of a set X through the identity function *id* is X itself.
(b) The image of a set X through the composition $g \circ f$ is the image through g of the image through f of X.
(c) Making a singleton set $\{x\}$ from x, and then applying f to all elements of that set, is the same as applying f to x first and then making a singleton set from that: in both cases you get the singleton set $\{fx\}$.
(d) Applying f to the *elements of the elements* of a set of sets (that is, applying f 'twice deep'), and then taking the distributed union of the result, is the same as taking the distributed union of the set of sets first, and then applying f to its elements (i.e. once deep). Starting e.g. from $\{\{x_1\}, \{x_2, x_3\}\}$ you get $\{f\,x_1, f\,x_3, f\,x_3\}$ in both cases.
(e) Applying distributed union to each of the elements of a *set of sets of sets* (i.e. *three* nested braces), and then taking the distributed union of that, is the same as taking the distribution union twice. For example, starting from $\{\{\{x_1\}\}, \{\{x_2, x_3\}, \{x_4\}\}\}$ the former gives $\{\{x_1\}, \{x_2, x_3, x_4\}\}$ and then $\{x_1, x_2, x_3, x_4\}$, and the latter reaches the same result but via $\{\{x_1\}, \{x_2, x_3\}, \{x_4\}\}$ instead.
(f) Converting a set's elements to singleton sets, and then taking the distributed union, is the same as converting the set to a singleton set (of sets) and then taking the distributed union of that – and it is the identity in both cases. The former takes $\{x_1, x_2\}$ to $\{\{x_1\}, \{x_2\}\}$ and then (back) to $\{x_1, x_2\}$; and the latter goes via $\{\{x_1, x_2\}\}$.

12.2.2 Monads for probabilistic programming

Probabilistic computation is an instance of the more general monadic construction introduced in §12.2.1 just above, and it provides the essential 'numeric component' of moving from earlier, only qualitative descriptions of information flow (Cohen, 1977; Goguen and Meseguer, 1984) to *Quantitative Information Flow* (Denning, 1982; Millen, 1987; Gray, 1990; Clark et al., 2005b), abbreviated "*QIF*": the study of information leakage, typically from- or between computer programs, where –

crucially – the amount of information leaked can be measured and compared. Thus in this section we concentrate on probabilistic computation alone; we move on to information flow in §12.3.

A (discrete) probabilistic computation over some $\mathcal{A}$ takes an initial state $a: \mathcal{A}$ to a final distribution $\alpha: \mathbb{D}\mathcal{A}$ – thus it has type $\mathcal{A} \to \mathbb{D}\mathcal{A}$. For example with $\mathcal{A} = \{h, t\}$ for the head and tail faces of a coin, a computation P that 'seeks heads' might be

$$
\begin{aligned}
Ph &= \langle h \rangle && \text{if heads already, don't flip any more} \\
Pt &= \langle h, t \rangle && \text{if } t \text{ keep flipping}
\end{aligned}
$$

(12.1)

where in general we write $\langle a, b, \cdots, z \rangle$ for the uniform distribution over the elements listed inside $\langle \cdots \rangle$. As a special case $\langle a \rangle$ is the point distribution on a.

To seek heads twice we run P twice, i.e. we compose P with itself; but, as already noted more generally, the simple $P \circ P$ would be type-incorrect because the second-executed P (the left one) expects an $\mathcal{A}$ but the first P delivers a $\mathbb{D}\mathcal{A}$. Let us write a distribution list $\langle \cdots \rangle$ with superscripts summing to 1 for a discrete distribution with those probabilities (rather than uniform), so that omitted superscripts are assumed to be equal; and we write $\neg p$ for $1-p$. Then, following the Kleisli approach, we lift the second P to P^*, so that its argument is of type $\mathbb{D}\mathcal{A}$, and note that

$$
\begin{aligned}
&P^* \langle h^p, t^{\neg p} \rangle \\
=\quad& \{ \text{ definition } (-)^* \} \\
&(\mu \circ \mathbb{D}P) \langle h^p, t^{\neg p} \rangle \\
=\quad& \{ \text{ function composition } \} \\
&\mu(\mathbb{D}P \langle h^p, t^{\neg p} \rangle) \\
=\quad& \{ \text{ definition } \mathbb{D}P: \text{ see } \dagger \text{ below } \} \\
&\mu \langle \langle h \rangle^p, \langle h, t \rangle^{\neg p} \rangle \\
=\quad& \{ \text{ definition } \mu \text{ for monad } \mathbb{D}: \text{ see } \ddagger \text{ below } \} \\
&\langle h^{(1+p)/2}, t^{(1-p)/2} \rangle ,
\end{aligned}
$$

(12.2)

so that using P^* in its general form from (12.2) we can calculate

$$
P^2 h = P^*(Ph) = P^* \langle h \rangle = P^* \langle h^1, t^0 \rangle = \langle h^{(1+1)/2}, t^{(1-1)/2} \rangle = \langle h^1, t^0 \rangle = \langle h \rangle ,
$$

and again from (12.2) we have

$$
P^2 t = P^*(Pt) = P^* \langle h, t \rangle = P^* \langle h^{1/2}, t^{1/2} \rangle = \langle h^{(1+1/2)/2}, t^{(1-1/2)/2} \rangle = \langle h^{3/4}, t^{1/4} \rangle .
$$

For "see † below" we note that $\mathbb{D}P$ is in monadic terms the application of functor $\mathbb{D}$ to arrow h; in elementary probability this is the 'push forward' of h (Feller, 1971). For $f: \mathcal{A} \to \mathcal{B}$ and $\alpha: \mathbb{D}\mathcal{A}$ and $b: \mathcal{B}$ the *push forward* $\mathbb{D}f$ of f has type $\mathbb{D}\mathcal{A} \to \mathbb{D}\mathcal{B}$

and is defined

$$(\mathbb{D}f)\,\alpha\, b \quad = \quad \sum_{\substack{a:\mathcal{A} \\ fa=b}} \alpha\, a \quad = \quad \beta\, b \quad \text{say}, {}^3$$

i.e. so that the probability βb assigned by the $\mathbb{D}\mathcal{B}$-typed distribution $\beta = \mathbb{D}f\,\alpha$ to the element b of B is the total probability assigned by α in $\mathbb{D}\mathcal{A}$ to those a's in $\mathcal{A}$ such that $fa = b$.

For "see ‡ below" we have that the definition of multiply μ for $\mathbb{D}$ is the 'squash' or 'distributed average' that takes a distribution of distributions to a single distribution. With $\mathcal{D}$ as our base set, [4] we take some $\Delta:\mathbb{D}^2\mathcal{D}$ and $d:\mathcal{D}$ and have that $\mu\Delta \in \mathbb{D}\mathcal{D}$ and [5]

$$\mu\,\Delta\, d \quad = \quad \sum_{\delta:\Delta} \Delta\delta \times \delta d \quad .{}^6 \tag{12.3}$$

The above might seem quite general, particularly when there is a more conventional – and simpler – view of P in (12.1) above, the 'seek h' operation, as a Markov chain. We now look at that connection, strengthening the intuition for what the probability monad $\mathbb{D}$ and its η, μ are doing, and preparing ourselves for when their generality becomes more useful.

The Markov matrix for the head-seeking P is

$$\text{after } P$$

$$\text{before } P \quad \begin{pmatrix} 1 & 0 \\ {}^1\!/_2 & {}^1\!/_2 \end{pmatrix}$$

Such matrices are called *stochastic* because their rows sum to one: the rows above are (invisibly) labelled h above t, and the columns h before t; and each element of the matrix gives the probability that one application of P takes that row label to that column label. Thus for example h (upper row) is taken to h (left column) with probability 1; but t (lower row) is taken to h with probability only $^1\!/_2$. Now if the

---

[3] Here we follow the practice of avoiding parentheses as much as possible (because otherwise there would be so many). We don't write $((\mathbb{D}f)\,\alpha)\,b$, because function application associates to the left (and thus would allow even $\mathbb{D}f\,\alpha\,b$); and we don't write $\mathbb{D}(f)(\alpha)(b)$, because functional application is (in this area) usually indicated by juxtaposition without parentheses. Note also that we are using currying, where what might be seen as a multi-argument function is instead written as higher-order functions taking their single arguments one at a time from left to right.

[4] This is a temporary departure from $\mathcal{A}$, $\mathcal{B}$ as typical base sets, because we need to use "capital Greek D" as an element of $\mathbb{D}^2\mathcal{D}$.

[5] Concerning (:) vs. ($\in$) – we use the former to introduce a bound variable, both in text and in formulae. With for example $x \in X$ we are instead referring to x, X that are already defined.

[6] The definition of μ in the powerset monad $\mathbb{P}$ is analogous: it is a distributed union that takes a set of sets to a single set by removing one level of set braces. Specifically, if we think of a set as its characteristic predicate (a function from elements to booleans), then for a set of sets $X:\mathbb{P}^2\mathcal{A}$, we have $\mu\,X\,a = (\exists x:\mathbb{P}\mathcal{A}\,.\,X\,x \wedge x\,a)$ – that is, $a \in \mu\,X$ iff there exists some $x:X$ with $a \in x$.

initial distribution of the coin faces were $\langle h^p, t^{\neg p} \rangle$, then – as is well known – the final distribution of coin faces is given by the vector-matrix product

$$(p \;\; \neg p) \begin{pmatrix} 1 & 0 \\ 1/2 & 1/2 \end{pmatrix} \;\; = \;\; \left(\frac{1+p}{2} \;\; \frac{1-p}{2} \right) \;,$$

agreeing with what was calculated above at (12.2). And the effect of two P's in succession, that is $P(P\langle h^p, t^{\neg p} \rangle)$, is therefore given by the matrix product

$$\left((p \;\; \neg p) \begin{pmatrix} 1 & 0 \\ 1/2 & 1/2 \end{pmatrix} \right) \begin{pmatrix} 1 & 0 \\ 1/2 & 1/2 \end{pmatrix}$$

which, because of the associativity of matrix multiplication, can of course be written

$$(p \;\; \neg p) \;\; \left(\begin{pmatrix} 1 & 0 \\ 1/2 & 1/2 \end{pmatrix} \begin{pmatrix} 1 & 0 \\ 1/2 & 1/2 \end{pmatrix} \right) \;\; = \;\; (p \;\; \neg p) \begin{pmatrix} 1 & 0 \\ 3/4 & 1/4 \end{pmatrix} \;. \quad (12.4)$$

Now we can observe that although the type of P itself is $\mathcal{A} \rightarrow \mathbb{D}\mathcal{A}$, the type of 'multiply by the square matrix' in the examples above is $\mathbb{D}\mathcal{A} \rightarrow \mathbb{D}\mathcal{A}$ – that is, the matrix viewed 'row wise' is of type $\mathcal{A} \rightarrow \mathbb{D}\mathcal{A}$ but, viewed as a whole (and using the definition of matrix multiplication) it is of type $\mathbb{D}\mathcal{A} \rightarrow \mathbb{D}\mathcal{A}$. Thus the matrix as a whole corresponds to the Kleisli lifting P^* of its rows P. Then (12.4) goes on to show that $P^* \circ P$ corresponds in turn to the matrix multiplication with itself of the matrix corresponding to P^*. [7]

The wide applicability of matrix algebra comes in part from the fact (fortuitiously) that it has this monadic structure. In general, as Moggi explained, monads contribute to flexibility of general program-algebraic operations as well – and that flexibility is what we use here to explore – and implement – a program algebra for *QIF*.

Summary We will use the discrete-distribution monad $\mathbb{D}$ which takes a set $\mathcal{A}$ to the set $\mathbb{D}\mathcal{A}$ of its discrete distributions. The unit η of $\mathbb{D}$ takes an element of $\mathcal{A}$ to the point distribution $\langle a \rangle$ on a; the multiply μ takes a distribution-of-distributions $\Delta : \mathbb{D}^2 \mathcal{D}$ to its 'squash' as shown at (12.3) above, which is however equivalent to the 'smaller' summation over the support $\lceil \Delta \rceil$ of Δ only, thus

$$\mu \Delta d \;\; = \;\; \sum_{\delta : \lceil \Delta \rceil} \Delta\delta \times \delta d \;, \quad (12.5)$$

where the *support* of Δ is those $\delta : \mathbb{D}\mathcal{D}$ such that $\Delta\delta \neq 0$. (This is important in Haskell because we can then represent distributions as *finite* lists over their support, omitting the possibly infinitely many elements of probability zero.)

---

[7] This corresponds to the general Kleisli identity $(P^* \circ P)^* = P^* \circ P^*$.

12.2.3 Monads in Haskell

Monads were introduced into Haskell because their mathematical generality translates into expressive power. They are modelled as a type class *Functor* with a method *fmap*, and a subclass *Monad* of *Functor* providing two additional methods *return* and ($\gg=$); the latter is pronounced "bind". Their methods' types are

$$fmap \;\; :: (a \rightarrow b) \rightarrow m\,a \rightarrow m\,b$$
$$return :: a \rightarrow m\,a$$
$$(\gg=) \;\; :: m\,a \rightarrow (a \rightarrow m\,b) \rightarrow m\,b$$

where m and a,b correspond to the $\mathbb{T}$ and $\mathcal{A},\mathcal{B}$ of Section 12.2.1. Function *fmap* is the functorial action of monad m, and *return* is the unit η of monad m, and ($\gg=$) is Kleisli lifting (but with the two arguments swapped). The multiplication μ is modelled by

$$join :: m\,(m\,a) \rightarrow m\,a$$

As noted above, Kleisli lifting and monad multiplication are interdefinable: therefore we have the further identities

$$
\begin{aligned}
join\ x \;\; &= \;\; x \gg= id \\
x \gg= f \;\; &= \;\; join\ (fmap\ f\ x)
\end{aligned}
$$

All of those are just ordinary Haskell functions, defined in plain Haskell code, and it is straightforward to implement additional operations in terms of them. For example, Kleisli lifting with the arguments in the traditional order ($=\!\!\ll$) is defined in terms of bind by

$$
\begin{aligned}
(=\!\!\ll) &:: (a \rightarrow m\,b) \rightarrow (m\,a \rightarrow m\,b) \\
g =\!\!\ll x \;\; &= \;\; x \gg= g
\end{aligned}
$$

and backwards Kleisli composition ($<\!\!=\!\!<$) (written "$\bullet$" in Section 12.2.1) and its forwards version ($>\!\!=\!\!>$) are defined by

$$
\begin{aligned}
(<\!\!=\!\!<) &:: (b \rightarrow m\,c) \rightarrow (a \rightarrow m\,b) \rightarrow (a \rightarrow m\,c) \\
g <\!\!=\!\!< f \;\; &= \;\; join \circ fmap\ g \circ f \\
(>\!\!=\!\!>) &:: (a \rightarrow m\,b) \rightarrow (b \rightarrow m\,c) \rightarrow (a \rightarrow m\,c) \\
f >\!\!=\!\!> g \;\; &= \;\; join \circ fmap\ g \circ f
\end{aligned}
$$

Clearly they are equal, operationally performing f 'and then' g; it is solely a matter of convenience which way around to write it.

As a final link back to the familiar, we mimic our use of the powerset monad $\mathbb{P}$ in §12.2.1 to give a similar presentation here of the monad laws in Haskell, but using this time the list monad – call it $\mathbb{L}$. Then the functorial action of $\mathbb{L}$ on a function $f :: a \rightarrow b$ is to produce *map f* of type $[a] \rightarrow [b]$; unit η of $\mathbb{L}$ takes x to the one-element list $[x]$ containing just x, i.e. it is $(:[\,])$; and the multiply μ of $\mathbb{L}$ is the function *concat* that 'squashes' a list of lists into a single list. We now have

id	=	*map id*	— (a)
map g ∘ *map f*	=	*map* (*g* ∘ *f*)	— (b)
map f ∘ $(:[\,])$	=	$(:[\,])$ ∘ *f*	— (c)
concat ∘ *map* (*map f*)	=	*map f* ∘ *concat*	— (d)
concat ∘ *map concat*	=	*concat* ∘ *concat*	— (e)
concat ∘ *map* $(:[\,])$	=	*concat* ∘ $(:[\,])$ = *id*	— (f)

We will see see the benefit of all the above generality below, where these properties, and others, are exploited in a monadic treatment of *QIF* and the construction of a Haskell implementation of it.

12.2.4 Probabilistic programming in Haskell

With §12.2.2 and §12.2.3 as building blocks, we can model probabilistic programs in Haskell as Kleisli arrows for the distribution monad $\mathbb{D}$. Thus in this section we recall in more detail the previous work that shows how that is done (Ramsey and Pfeffer, 2002; Erwig and Kollmansberger, 2006; Kiselyov and Shan, 2009). (Note that we are still not addressing *QIF* itself.)

Representation   We limit probabilities to the rationals; and our distributions are discrete, represented as (finite) lists of pairs with each pair giving an element of the base type and the probability associated with that element. Usually (but not always) the representation will be *reduced* in the sense that the list includes only elements of the support of the distribution, and each of those exactly once, i.e. excluding both repeated elements and elements with probability zero.

> **type** *Prob* = *Rational*
>
> **newtype** *Dist a* = *D* {*runD* :: [(*a*, *Prob*)]}

The 'essence' of the representation is the type [(*a*, *Prob*)], i.e. lists of pairs. The *D* {*runD* :: ...} above is Haskell notation for defining *Dist a* as a record type, with a single field called *runD* that consists of a list of pairs, and introduces function *D* :: [(*a*, *Prob*)] → *Dist a* to wrap up such a list as a record value. The field-name *runD* can be used as a function, to extract the 'bare' list of pairs.

Monad instance   The make-probabilistic-monad functor is the type constructor *Dist* above, whose argument type *a* is the base type of the distribution. The unit *return* of the monad takes an element to the point distribution on that element. The bind operator ($\ggg=$) takes a distribution $d :: Dist\ a$ and a distribution-valued function $f :: a \rightarrow Dist\ b$ and computes effectively the application of the stochastic matrix f to the initial distribution d. [8]

> **instance** *Monad Dist* **where**
> $return\ x = D\ [(x, 1)]$
> $d \ggg= f\ = D\ [(y, p \times q) \mid (x, p) \leftarrow runD\ d, (y, q) \leftarrow runD\ (f\ x)]$

Note that ($\ggg=$) can produce representations that are not reduced, since values of y can be repeated between the supports of different distributions $f\ x$ as x itself varies over the support of d. We will arrange to reduce the representations where necessary.

Operations Function *uniform* constructs a discrete distribution from a non-empty list of elements, assigning the same probability to each element. (It is not defined on the empty list.)

> $uniform :: [a] \rightarrow Dist\ a$
> $uniform\ l = D\ [(x, 1\ /\ length\ l) \mid x \leftarrow l]$

The three-argument function $(-\ {}_{-}\oplus\ -)$ takes a probability p and two elements and from them constructs a distribution in which the first element has probability p and the second $1-p$.

> $-\ {}_{-}\oplus\ - :: Prob \rightarrow a \rightarrow a \rightarrow Dist\ a$
> $x\ {}_{p}\oplus\ y = D\ [(x, p), (y, 1 - p)]$

Again, the essence here is the two-element list $[(x, p), (y, \neg p)]$ of course. That is, the distribution $x\ {}_{p}\oplus\ y$ generally has two-element support – unless x and y coincide, in which case it is a point distribution (in unreduced form).

Reduction Function *reduction* removes duplicates and zeroes from the concrete representation of a distribution. That does not change the abstract distribution represented, but makes its handling more efficient. In the sequel it will be built-in to monadic compositions (such as ($\ggg=$) above, and ($\ggg=>$) etc.)

> $unpackD :: Ord\ a \Rightarrow Dist\ a \rightarrow [(a, Prob)]$
> $\qquad\qquad\qquad\qquad\qquad$ — Recover list representation, reduced.
> $unpackD = removeDups \circ removeZeroes \circ runD$
> $\quad$ **where**
> $\qquad removeZeroes = filter\ (\lambda(x, p) \rightarrow p \neq 0)$
> $\qquad removeDups = toList \circ fromListWith\ (+)$

---

[8] Think of f as taking a stochastic-matrix row-label to the distribution of column-label probabilities in that row.

output

0   1

channel: input $\left\{ \begin{matrix} 0 \\ 1 \end{matrix} \right.$ $\begin{pmatrix} .99 & .01 \\ .02 & .98 \end{pmatrix}$ ← sums to 1
← sums to 1

Figure 12.1 Channel matrix describing not-quite-perfect transmission

reduction :: *Ord a* ⇒ *Dist a* → *Dist a*
reduction = *D* ∘ *unpackD*   — Unpack and then repack.

Here (from right to left) function *runD* extracts the essence, namely the list of pairs; then *removeZeroes* and *removeDups* reduce the list; and finally *D* replaces the reduced list within the constructor, where it began. The Haskell library function *fromListWith* requires an ordering on the elements, so it can make use of a binary search tree in order to remove duplicates in $O(n \log n)$ time; one could instead require only element equality rather than ordering, at the cost of $O(n^2)$ time.

12.3 *QIF and hyper-distributions*

With the above preliminaries, we can now move to quantitative information flow.

12.3.1 *Background*

In the communication channels of (Shannon, 1948), information flows in at the source, is transmitted but possibly with errors introduced, and then flows out at the target. Typically the error-rate is described mathematically as a channel *matrix* that gives explicit probabilities for message corruption. For example, Fig. 12.1 shows a channel matrix representing correct transmission with high probability only – if a 0 is input, there is a 1% probability that a 1 will come out instead; and for a 1 input, the probability of error is 2%. As noted earlier, the matrix is called *stochastic* because its rows sum to one.

Analyses of channels like Fig. 12.1 assume a distribution over the inputs, and look at the correlation with the resulting output. For example, if we assume a uniform input distribution on $\{0, 1\}$, then the joint distribution matrix between inputs and outputs would be as in Fig. 12.2, obtained by multiplying the input probabilities ($^1/_2$ here) along the rows. Here it's the matrix as a whole that sums to 1, not the individual rows.

The 'information flow' due to such channel matrices is often expressed as the output

0   1

channel: uniform input $\left\{ \begin{array}{c} 0^{1/2} \\ 1^{1/2} \end{array} \right.$ $\begin{pmatrix} .495 & .005 \\ .01 & .49 \end{pmatrix}$ ← sums to 1 overall

Figure 12.2 Joint distribution between input and output, based on Fig. 12.1 and uniform input

output

0   1

channel: input $\left\{ \begin{array}{c} 0 \\ 1 \end{array} \right.$ $\begin{pmatrix} .51 & .49 \\ .49 & .51 \end{pmatrix}$ ← sums to 1
← sums to 1

Figure 12.3 Channel matrix describing a 1% success-rate

difference between the Shannon Entropy of the input before- and after the output is observed. [9] In this example the Shannon Entropy beforehand is the entropy of the prior distribution: simply 1 bit, because that distribution is uniform over two values. The Shannon Entropy *afterwards* is however the *conditional* Shannon Entropy obtained by averaging the Shannon Entropies of the posterior distributions, with the weights of that averaging being their probability of occurrence. In Fig. 12.2 for example, the marginal probability that a 0 is output is .495+.01 = .505 and the conditional distribution on the input is then the normalised column for that output, i.e. that it was 0 with probability $^{.495}/_{.505}$ = .980 and 1 with probability .020, which distribution has Shannon Entropy .140. Similarly, for output 1 the marginal probability is .495 and the conditional probability on the inputs is 0 with probability $^{.005}/_{.495}$ = .010 and output 1 with probability .990, with Shannon Entropy .081. The conditional Shannon Entropy overall is thus the weighted average of those two, that is .505×.140 + .495×.081 = .111, and the number of bits transmitted is the entropy-before vs. conditional-entropy-afterwards difference, that is 1−.111 = .889 bits in this case. It's a pretty good channel from the communication point of view.

When we look at this from the point of view of computer security however, it's a terrible channel: it has leaked almost all (0.889 bits) of the secret (1 bit). Far better for secrets would be the channel of Fig. 12.3 that has only a very slight bias induced on the output with respect to the input. A similar calculation for the above shows the conditional Shannon Entropy on the uniform input in this case to be 0.9997, so that

[9] The Shannon Entropy of a p vs. $1-p$ distribution is $-(p \lg(p) + (1-p) \lg(1-p))$.

this channel leaks only 0.0003 bits. This is more like what we want for our secure programs. (For communication, however, it's Fig. 12.3 that is a terrible channel.) Thus although the mathematics for flow of communications and for flow of secrets (leaks) from programs is the same, the interpretation is complementary.

In spite of that correspondence, it turns out that Shannon Entropy is sometimes (even often) very far from the best way to measure entropy where leaks from computer programs are concerned. (Smith, 2009) argued that in some cases it might be better to measure (in-)security by using instead the maximum probability that the secret could be guessed: an intelligent attacker would guess the secret(s) she knows to have the largest probability: this is called *Bayes Vulnerability*. As an entropy (but not *Shannon* entropy) this is expressed as a real-valued function that takes a distribution to $1 - maximum\ probability$, where the subtraction from one $(1-)$ is a technical device that ensures increasing disorder leads to increasing entropy: that function is called *Bayes Risk*. On a fixed state space X of size N, the maximum Bayes Risk is $1-1/N$ and – as for Shannon Entropy – occurs on the uniform distribution.

We illustrate the difference with an example of two possible distributions of passwords. In one distribution, people choose alphabetic passwords uniformly, but never use numbers or punctuation. In the other, people mostly choose their friends' names (which are alphabetic) but, among those who do not, the choice is uniform between all other passwords including other alphabetics and those with numbers and punctuation.

To keep the calculations simple, we will suppose the password space is the four-element set $\{A, a, 9, \%\}$ for names, alphabetics generally, numbers and, finally, other punctuation. Suppose that the first distribution has probabilities (in that order) of $(1/2, 1/2, 0, 0)$ and that the second distribution is $\{(2/3, 1/9, 1/9, 1/9)\}$. In Fig. 12.4 we see a tabulation of the Shannon Entropy H and Bayes Risk R for these two distributions.

Distribution π_1 has Shannon Entropy $H(\pi_1)=1$ and Bayes Risk $R(\pi_1)=1/2$. For π_2 we find $H(\pi_2) = 2/3 \lg(3/2) + 3 \cdot 1/9 \lg(9) \approx 1.45$, and $R(\pi_2) = 1-2/3 = 1/3$. Thus 'from Shannon's point of view' distribution π_2 is more secure than π_1 – that is $H(\pi_2) > H(\pi_1)$. But Bayes would say the opposite, because $R(\pi_2) < R(\pi_1)$ or, equivalently, we have $V(\pi_2) > V(\pi_1)$, indicating that π_2 is *more* vulnerable, not less. In summary, distribution π_2 has *more* Shannon Entropy, i.e. more information-theoretic disorder than π_1, but still is more vulnerable to a a one-guess attacker than π_1 is.

But it does not stop there: a later development (Alvim et al., 2012) was the further generalisation of entropies to not just two (Shannon, Bayes) but in fact an infinite family of them based on 'gain functions' that captured the economics of the attacker: How much is the secret worth to her? Both Shannon Entropy and Bayes Risk are

password →	A	a	9	%	Shannon Entropy $H()$	Bayes Risk $R()$	Bayes Vulnerability $V() = 1 - R()$
π_1 probability	$^1/_2$	$^1/_2$	0	0	1	$^1/_2$	$^1/_2$
π_2 probability	$^2/_3$	$^1/_9$	$^1/_9$	$^1/_9$	~1.45	$^1/_3$	$^2/_3$

Distribution π_2 has more Shannon Entropy than π_1, but still π_2 is an easier target than π_1 for the one-guess password hacker.

Figure 12.4 Entropies for two example password distributions

instances of these gain functions. [10] Then a final generalisation (McIver et al., 2015) (for now) was to recognise that, as functions, gain-function-determined entropies are characterised simply by being concave and continuous over distributions. [11]

Pulling back however from the brink of runaway generalisation, we simply note that, whatever entropy is being used, it is applied to the prior before the channel, and applied conditionally to the resulting joint distribution between input and output determined after the channel. In that latter case, the joint distribution is regarded as a distribution (the output marginal) over posterior distributions obtained by conditioning the input distribution on the event that each particular output has occurred (the normalised joint-matrix columns).

It is 'distributions on posterior distributions' that have been named *hyper-distributions* (McIver et al., 2014a, 2010), a conceptual artefact synthesised by asking "If we allow entropies from a general class of functions f on distributions (including Shannon Entropy and Bayes Risk as special cases), what operation do we carry out to determine the f-leakage of a channel with respect to a particular prior?" The answer is "Apply the entropy to the prior, and take the expected value of the same entropy over the hyper-distribution produced by the channel's acting on that prior; then compare the two numbers obtained." [12]

That is why we focus on hyper-distributions as a unifying concept for *QIF* – it is the common feature of determining leakage in the generalised setting explained above, where there are (infinitely) many possible entropies to consider. In other

[10] A technical detail for those familiar with (Alvim et al., 2012) – Shannon Entropy requires an infinitary gain funtion, and in fact is more neatly expressed with the complementary 'loss functions' that express how much the attacker has to lose.

[11] This generalisation was introduced in (McIver et al., 2015) as *loss* functions' determining 'uncertainty measures' that were continuous and *concave*.

[12] Popular comparisons include 'additive leakage', where you subtract the former from the latter, and 'multiplicative leakage' where you take the quotient.

$$\text{perfect channel:} \qquad \text{skewed input} \left\{ \begin{array}{c} 0^{0.9} \\ 1^{0.1} \end{array} \begin{array}{cc} \overbrace{\begin{array}{cc} 0 & 1 \end{array}}^{\text{output}} \\ \begin{pmatrix} 1 & 0 \\ 0 & 1 \end{pmatrix} \end{array} \right.$$

The resulting hyper is $0.9 \times (1,0) + 0.1 \times (0,1)$, indicating that with probability 0.9 the adversary will know the input was 0, and with probability 0.1 she will know that it was 1.

Figure 12.5 Perfect channel, 0-skewed input

$$\text{nearly perfect channel:} \qquad \text{skewed input} \left\{ \begin{array}{c} 0^{0.9} \\ 1^{0.1} \end{array} \begin{array}{cc} \overbrace{\begin{array}{cc} 0 & 1 \end{array}}^{\text{output}} \\ \begin{pmatrix} 1 & 0 \\ .01 & .99 \end{pmatrix} \end{array} \right.$$

Figure 12.6 Nearly perfect channel, 0-skewed input

work we discuss extensively how hyper-distributions lead to a robust notion of a program-refinement-like 'leakage ordering' ($\sqsubseteq$) on *QIF* programs (McIver et al., 2014a, 2010, 2015).

An example of that unification is the comparison of a perfect channel with a nearly perfect channel applied to the same non-uniform prior. We will appeal to two different entropies.

The point is not the precise numbers in the hypers, but rather that those hypers, as an abstraction, contain *all* the information needed to calculate the (conditional) Shannon Entropy, the Bayes Risk, and indeed any other well behaved entropy we require. For the perfect Fig. 12.5 the conditional Shannon Entropy is $0.9H(1,0) + 0.1H(0,1) = 0$, and the Bayes Risk is $0.9R(1,0) + 0.1R(0,1) = 0$. In both cases the observer is in no doubt about the input's value.

For the nearly perfect Fig. 12.6 however, the conditional Shannon Entropy is

$$0.901H(0.999, 0.001) + 0.099H(0,1) \qquad = \qquad 0.02 \quad ,$$

and the Bayes Risk is

$$0.901R(0.999, 0.001) + 0.099R(0,1) \qquad = \qquad 0.001 \quad .$$

In this case there is some residual doubt – but not much.

12.3.2 Hyper-distribution and generalised entropies seen monadically

We now bring our two conceptual threads together: monads and *QIF*.

In §12.2.1 we saw that monads capture a notion of computation $\mathbb{T}$ by lifting a base-type $\mathcal{A}$ to a type $\mathbb{T}\mathcal{A}$ of computations over $\mathcal{A}$; and in §12.2.2 we saw how in particular the distribution monad $\mathbb{D}$ lifted a type to the probabilistic computations on that type. Our approach to *QIF* is based on that; but to get the extra expressive power, i.e. to describe not only probability but information flow, we lift base-type $\mathbb{D}\mathcal{A}$, rather than $\mathcal{A}$ itself. The 'ordinary' probabilistic computations of type $\mathcal{A}{\rightarrow}\mathbb{D}\mathcal{A}$ are replaced by computations of type $\mathbb{D}\mathcal{A}{\rightarrow}\mathbb{D}(\mathbb{D}\mathcal{A})$, or $\mathbb{D}\mathcal{A}{\rightarrow}\mathbb{D}^2\mathcal{A}$ of 'information-flow aware' probabilistic computations on $\mathcal{A}$. For that we are using the same monad $\mathbb{D}$ as before, but we are starting 'one level up'. It is the $\mathbb{D}^2\mathcal{A}$ type that we have called the *hyper-distributions* on $\mathcal{A}$, or "hypers" for short.

The first application of $\mathbb{D}$ takes us, as we saw in §12.2.2 and have seen in other work in this area, to probabilistic computations – but with just the one $\mathbb{D}$ we have only the probabilistic computations that are information-flow *unaware*. For information-flow awareness we need the extra level that hypers provide, so that we can do the before-after comparisons described in §12.3.1 just above.

We will see that it is the unit η that takes say a distribution $\delta{:}\,\mathbb{D}\mathcal{A}$ to a particular hyper $\langle\delta\rangle$ that is information-flow *aware*, but in a degenerate sense, as before: it is aware of nothing. In fact it is only the point distribution on the original distribution δ, and so this hyper will in fact denote the (effect of) a probabilistic program that leaks nothing, just as η earlier gave us possibly improper programs that in fact are proper, sequence-writing programs that have not yet written, demonic programs that behave deterministically, and probabilistic programs that use only one-sided dice. This is indeed the kind of embedding that we mentioned before.

The multiplication μ, on the other hand, will now have a more interesting role beyond its technical use in defining Kleisli composition. Given a proper (i.e. not necessarily point) hyper Δ in $\mathbb{D}^2\mathcal{A}$, the squash $\mu\Delta$ of type $\mathbb{D}\mathcal{A}$ is the result of the 'simple' probabilistic program from which all information-flow properties have been removed. In §12.7.1 we discuss the antecedents of that approach.

Thus monadic *QIF* programs for us will have type $\mathbb{D}\mathcal{A}{\rightarrow}\mathbb{D}^2\mathcal{A}$. If we express a channel C that way, in the style of §12.3.1, and pick some uncertainty function f, then on a prior π the uncertainty beforehand is $f\pi$ – and after observing the output of channel C it is $(\mu{\circ}\mathbb{D}f)(C\pi)$. One then either subtracts or divides one from/by the other to obtain the additive- or multiplicative f-leakage of C applied to π.

But a further advantage of this extra structure, introduced by the 'second $\mathbb{D}$', is that we can represent –within the same type – both

Markov program steps that change the state probabilistically, but leak no information while they do that, and the complementary

Channel program steps that leak information but do not change the state while they
do that.

A (pure) Markov program M (for "Markov") will be of type $\mathbb{D}\mathcal{A} \rightarrow \mathbb{D}^2\mathcal{A}$ and has
the characteristic that for any initial distribution δ we find that $M\delta = \eta\delta'$ for some
δ', i.e. that the result of the M is always a *singleton* hyper. And indeed M as a matrix
would take row δ, encoding the initial distribution, to row δ' encoding the final
distribution. On the other hand, a (pure) channel C again has type $\mathbb{D}\mathcal{A} \rightarrow \mathbb{D}^2\mathcal{A}$ (the
same as a Markov program), but in addition has the characteristic that $\mu(C\delta) = \delta$,
i.e. that the state distribution is not changed: all that is possible is that information
can leak.

Recall that the trivial channel that leaks nothing, treating all inputs the same [13]
takes any prior to the singleton hyper on that prior: that is, its action is $\pi \mapsto \langle\pi\rangle$,
indicating that after the channel has run the adversary knows for sure that the
distribution on the input was... just π, which she knew before.

On the other hand, the channel that leaks everything (the identity matrix) takes input
π in general to a *non*-singleton hyper whose support is (only) point distributions: for
example the prior $(^2/_3, {}^1/_3)$ is taken by that channel to the hyper $^2/_3\langle(1,0)\rangle + {}^1/_3\langle(0,1)\rangle$,
indicating that with probability $^2/_3$ the adversary will know for sure that the input
was 0 and with probability $^1/_3$ she will know that it was 1. That is just what a 'leak
everything' channel should do.

With the above as a starting point, Kleisli composition of hyper programs allows
the two possibilities above to be combined sequentially, while still remaining within
the same type, even though we are now one level up at $\mathbb{D}\mathcal{A}$ rather than $\mathcal{A}$: that's
what the generality of Kleisli composition does for us automatically. That is, we
can *without any further definitions* write $C; M$ for a *QIF*-aware program that leaks
information *and then* changes the state; and similarly a program $M; C$ changes the
state first and then leaks that. [14] Either way, the result is a single function of type
$\mathbb{D}\mathcal{A} \rightarrow \mathbb{D}^2\mathcal{A}$. Further, the order-theoretic structure of the space $\mathbb{D}\mathcal{A}$, e.g. limits, allow
us to introduce smoothly all the apparatus of sequential programming, including
loops – with the probabilistic- and the *QIF* features added in 'for free' (McIver et al.,
2014b). [15]

---

[13] Concretely this is any channel matrix all of whose rows are equal: the nicest formulation is a 0-column matrix,
i.e. there is no output at all; but slightly less shocking is a one-column matrix of all 1's that gives the same
output for all inputs. With more than one column, there can clearly be more than one output: but since the rows
are the same, the relative frequencies of the outputs gives no information about which input produced them.

[14] Observe that the combination $C; M$ corresponds to a step of a Hidden Markov Model (Baum and Petrie, 1966):
in *HMM*'s first some information about the current state is released and then the state is probabilistically updated.
Here we arrange for those two effects to be conceptually separated, which allows them to be put together in any
combination.

[15] We do not discuss the *QIF* order theory in this chapter, however.

12.4 A concrete programming language *Kuifje*, and its semantics

In §12.3 we introduced Markov steps and channel steps as program fragments, but abstractly. Both are of type $\mathbb{D}\mathcal{A}{\rightarrow}\mathbb{D}^2\mathcal{A}$ but, as we saw, each has further specific and complementary properties: the Markov step releases no information, and the channel step makes no change to the state. In this section we give concrete notations for these program steps, together with constructions like conditional and iteration for making more substantial programs. The functional components from §12.2.4 above are used for that.

The presentation takes the form of a sequence of three small languages, of increasing expressivity. We start in §12.4.1 with a simple imperative command language CL consisting of assignment statements, conditionals, and loops; in §12.4.2 we add probabilistic assignment statements, yielding the probabilistic command language PCL (essentially *pGCL* of (McIver and Morgan, 2005)); and finally in §12.4.3 we add observations, yielding our complete *QIF* language Kuifje.

We use an initial-algebra representation for the syntax of these languages because it enables a straightforward implementation of their denotational semantics as *folds*. Moreover, the representation pays off in §12.5 where it allows us easily to derive an efficient implementation of the hyper-distribution semantics from its naïve specification.

12.4.1 Basic language CL

Concrete syntax We will start without probabilistic or *QIF* features, giving a basic *Command Language*, or CL for short, that is just the usual "toy imperative language" in which we can write programs like the following:

```
y := 0;
while (x > 0) {
   y := y + x;
   x := x - 1;
}
```

When this program is run with an initial state where $x = 3$, its final state has $x = 0$ and $y = 0 + 3 + 2 + 1 = 6$.

Abstract syntax The obvious representation of a CL program over a state space of type S is as the type $[\mathit{Instruction}\ S]$ of lists of instructions acting on S, where each instruction is either a state update, a conditional with a guard and two branches, or a loop with a guard and a body:

> **type** *CL s* = $[\mathit{Instruction}\ s]$

data *Instruction s*
  = *UpdateI* (*s* → *s*)
  | *IfI* (*s* → *Bool*) (*CL s*) (*CL s*)
  | *WhileI* (*s* → *Bool*) (*CL s*)

However, because the mutual recursion between instructions and programs would cause complications later on, we choose instead a 'continuation-style' representation that is directly recursive. Each of its constructors takes an additional argument representing 'the rest of the program', and there is an additional constructor *Skip* representing the 'empty' program:

data *CL s*
  = *Skip*
  | *Update* (*s* → *s*) (*CL s*)
  | *If* (*s* → *Bool*) (*CL s*) (*CL s*) (*CL s*)
  | *While* (*s* → *Bool*) (*CL s*) (*CL s*)   (12.6)

In particular, *CL S* is isomorphic to [*Instruction S*].

For instance, in the example program above we could use the state

data *S* = *S* {*x* :: *Int*, *y* :: *Int*}

(a record with two fields), which would allow us to render the above example as follows in Haskell: [16]

example$_1$ :: *CL S*
example$_1$ =
  Update (λ*s* → *s*.*y* := 0)
    (*While* (λ*s* → *s*.*x* > 0)
      (*Update* (λ*s* → *s*.*y* := (*s*.*y* + *s*.*x*))
        (*Update* (λ*s* → *s*.*x* := (*s*.*x* − 1))
          Skip))
  Skip)   (12.7)

We now discuss the constructions individually. *Skip* denotes the empty program. The program *Update f p* denotes the program that first transforms the state with *f* and then proceeds with program *p*. Program *If c p q r* checks whether the current state satisfies predicate *c*, and proceeds with *p* if it does and with *q* if it does not; in either case, it subsequently continues with *r*. Finally, the program *While c p q* checks whether the current state satisfies the predicate *c*; if it does, it executes *p* and then repeats the while loop, and if it does not, it continues with *q*.

---

[16] Note that notation like *s*.*y* := (*s*.*y* + *s*.*x*), with the obvious meaning, is not pseudo-code, but more familiar rendering of valid Haskell code based on `lens` library[17] operators. We refer the interested reader to this chapter's companion code for the details.

[17] https://hackage.haskell.org/package/lens

We now continue by using the abstract syntax to define several basic combinators that will allow us to write programs more compactly:

skip :: *CL s*
skip = *Skip*

update :: $(s \to s) \to CL\ s$
update f = *Update f skip*

cond :: $(s \to Bool) \to CL\ s \to CL\ s \to CL\ s$
cond c p q = *If c p q skip*

while :: $(s \to Bool) \to CL\ s \to CL\ s$
while c p = *While c p skip*

And we can define sequential composition:

$(\overset{\circ}{\circ})$ :: $CL\ s \to CL\ s \to CL\ s$
Skip $\overset{\circ}{\circ} k = k$
Update f p $\overset{\circ}{\circ} k$ = *Update f* $(p \overset{\circ}{\circ} k)$
If c p q r $\overset{\circ}{\circ} k$ = *If c p q* $(r \overset{\circ}{\circ} k)$
While c p q $\overset{\circ}{\circ} k$ = *While c p* $(q \overset{\circ}{\circ} k)$

Using the combinators and $(\overset{\circ}{\circ})$, the examples can be written equivalently as

$example_1$ =
  update $(\lambda s \to s.y := 0) \overset{\circ}{\circ}$
  while $(\lambda s \to s.x > 0)$
    (*update* $(\lambda s \to s.y := (s.y + s.x)) \overset{\circ}{\circ}$
      update $(\lambda s \to s.x := (s.x - 1)))$

Note that $\langle CL\ s, skip, (\overset{\circ}{\circ}) \rangle$ forms a monoid.

Semantics We can define a compositional semantics for CL programs over a state of type S as the carrier of a $(CL_F\ S)$-algebra for the functor $CL_F\ S$:

data $CL_F\ s\ a$
  = $Skip_F$
  | $Update_F\ (s \to s)\ a$
  | $If_F\ (s \to Bool)\ a\ a\ a$
  | $While_F\ (s \to Bool)\ a\ a$

Note that such a semantic definition, i.e. as a carrier of a syntactic algebra, is compositional by construction. A $(CL_F\ S)$-algebra is a pair (A, alg) consisting of a type A and a function $alg :: CL_F\ S\ A \to A$. In particular, $(CL\ S, c)$ is a $(CL_F\ S)$-algebra, where

$c :: CL_F\ s\ (CL\ s) \rightarrow CL\ s$
$c\ Skip_F \qquad\qquad = Skip$
$c\ (Update_F\ f\ p) \;= Update\ f\ p$
$c\ (If_F\ c\ p\ q\ r) \quad\; = If\ c\ p\ q\ r$
$c\ (While_F\ c\ p\ q) = While\ c\ p\ q$

Indeed, $(CL\ S, c)$ is the initial $(CL_F\ S)$-algebra; which is to say, for any other $(CL_F\ S)$-algebra (A, alg) there is a unique morphism of algebras $CL\ S \rightarrow A$; informally, this unique morphism 'propagates alg through the abstract syntax tree'. Since this unique morphism is determined by the algebra alg, we introduce a notation $(\!|alg|\!)$ for it. Concretely, $(\!|alg|\!)$ is defined as follows:

$(\!|-|\!) :: (CL_F\ s\ a \rightarrow a) \rightarrow (CL\ s \rightarrow a)$
$(\!|alg|\!)\ Skip \qquad\qquad = alg\ Skip_F$
$(\!|alg|\!)\ (Update\ f\ p) \;= alg\ (Update_F\ f\ ((\!|alg|\!)\ p))$
$(\!|alg|\!)\ (If\ c\ p\ q\ r) \quad = alg\ (If_F\ c\ ((\!|alg|\!)\ p)\ ((\!|alg|\!)\ q)\ ((\!|alg|\!)\ r))$
$(\!|alg|\!)\ (While\ c\ p\ q) = alg\ (While_F\ c\ ((\!|alg|\!)\ p)\ ((\!|alg|\!)\ q))$

which propagates alg through the abstract syntax of a given program; $(\!|alg|\!)$ is known as the fold for algebra (A, alg) (Hutton, 1999).

Any compositional semantics of $CL\ s$ programs can be formalised as a fold with an appropriate algebra. For example, one straightforward semantics is as an algebra on the carrier $s \rightarrow s$, i.e., interpreting programs as state-transformation functions.

$sem :: CL\ s \rightarrow (s \rightarrow s)$
$sem = (\!|alg|\!)\ \textbf{where}$
$\quad alg :: CL_F\ s\ (s \rightarrow s) \rightarrow (s \rightarrow s)$
$\quad alg\ Skip_F \qquad\qquad = id$
$\quad alg\ (Update_F\ f\ p) \;= f \ggg p$
$\quad alg\ (If_F\ c\ p\ q\ r) \quad\; = conditional\ c\ p\ q \ggg r$
$\quad alg\ (While_F\ c\ p\ q) = \textbf{let}\ while = conditional\ c\ (p \ggg while)\ q$
$\qquad\qquad\qquad\qquad\qquad\quad\; \textbf{in}\ \ while$
$\quad conditional :: (s \rightarrow Bool) \rightarrow (s \rightarrow s) \rightarrow (s \rightarrow s) \rightarrow (s \rightarrow s)$
$\quad conditional\ c\ t\ e = (\lambda s \rightarrow (c\ s, s)) \ggg$
$\qquad\qquad\qquad\qquad\qquad (\lambda(b, s) \rightarrow \textbf{if}\ b\ \textbf{then}\ t\ s\ \textbf{else}\ e\ s)$

Here, $(\ggg)$ is forward function composition: $f \ggg g = g \circ f$.

Note that sem is not only a fold over the abstract syntax, but also a monoid morphism from the $CL\ S$ monoid to $\langle S \rightarrow S, id, (\ggg) \rangle$.

$sem\ skip \quad = id$
$sem\ (p \mathbin{\raise0.3ex{\tiny\circ}\atop\raise-0.3ex{\tiny\circ}} q) = sem\ p \ggg sem\ q$

The above has set out our general approach to defining a language and its semantics, illustrating it on the simplest (useful) language possible. We now add probability.

12.4.2 Adding probability: CL → pGCL

The probabilistic version of CL is called PCL, following Haskell's (upper-case) convention for type constructors. It is effectively the *pGCL* of (McIver and Morgan, 2005), in turn derived from the seminal work of (Kozen, 1983). Its difference from CL is that state updates in PCL are probabilistic, i.e., an update does not assign a single new state, but rather a probability distribution over (new) states. For instance, we will be able to express that the variable x in our running example is decremented probabilistically by either 1 (probability $2/3$) or 2 (probability $1/3$), as here:

```
y := 0;
while (x > 0) {
   y := y + x;
   x := x - (1 2/3⊕ 2);
}
```
(12.8)

Similarly, we will make the conditionals in our program probabilistic. For instance, the following program's while loop chooses with probability $1/2$ on each iteration whether to apply the test $x > 0$ or $x > 1$ for termination:

```
y := 0;
while (x > 0 1/2⊕ x > 1) {
   y := y + x;
   x := x - 1;
}
```

We can also model the probabilistic choice between entire statements rather than merely expressions. For instance,

```
(y := y + 1) 5/6⊕ (x := x + 1)
```

is short-hand for

```
if (true 5/6⊕ false) {
   y := y + 1
} else {
   x := x + 1
}
```

The probabilistic nature of state updates is reflected as follows in the abstract syntax:

data PCL s
    = Skip
    | Update (s →ᴅ s) (PCL s)
    | If (s →ᴅ Bool) (PCL s) (PCL s) (PCL s)
    | While (s →ᴅ Bool) (PCL s) (PCL s)

where → in (12.6) has been replaced by the Kleisli arrow →ᴅ for the probability monad $\mathbb{D}$, so that $A →_D B$ is the type of probabilistic programs from A to B:

type $a →_D b = a → Dist\ b$

The abstract syntax of our first probabilistic example (12.8) becomes:

$example_2$ :: PCL S
$example_2$ =
    update ($\lambda s → return\ (s.y := 0)$) ⨟
    while ($\lambda s → return\ (s.x > 0)$)
        (update ($\lambda s → return\ (s.y := (s.y + s.x))$) ⨟
            update ($\lambda s → (s.x := (s.x − 1))\ _{2/3}⊕\ (s.x := (s.x − 2))$))))

Observe that what was written earlier in the example as an assignment of a probabilistically chosen value is represented here as abstract syntax in the form of a probabilistic choice between assignments of pure values.

We obtain an interpreter for PCL by reusing the constructions of §12.4.1, simply adapting the target of the monoid morphism *sem* from the monoid $\langle s → s, id, (\ggg) \rangle$ of endofunctions with function composition to the monoid $\langle s →_D s, return, (>=>) \rangle$ of Kleisli arrows with forward Kleisli composition.

sem_D :: Ord s ⇒ PCL s → (s →ᴅ s)
sem_D = ⦇alg⦈ *where*
    alg :: Ord s ⇒ PCL_F s (s →ᴅ s) → (s →ᴅ s)
    alg $Skip_F$ = return
    alg ($Update_F$ f p) = f >=> p
    alg (If_F c p q r) = conditional c p q >=> r
    alg ($While_F$ c p q) = *let* while = conditional c (p >=> while) q
                            in while
    conditional :: (Ord s) ⇒ s →ᴅ Bool → (s →ᴅ s) → (s →ᴅ s) → (s →ᴅ s)
    conditional c p q = ($\lambda s → fmap\ (\lambda b → (b,s))\ (c\ s)$) >=>
                        ($\lambda(b,s) →$ *if* b *then* p s *else* q s)

*12.4.3 Adding observations: pGCL → **Kuifje***

Finally, we extend PCL with 'observations' to yield our *QIF* language "Kuifje". Observations are probabilistically chosen values that the computation outputs, or 'leaks', as a side-effect. For instance, in our running example we express that we can observe x at the end of each iteration by adding *observe x* there:

```
y := 0;
while (x > 0) {
    y := y + x;
    x := x - (1 2/3⊕ 2);
    observe x
}
```
$$(12.9)$$

To express that we will observe either *x* or *y*, with equal probability, we would write

```
y := 0;
while (x > 0) {
    y := y + x;
    x := x - (1 2/3⊕ 2);
    observe x 1/2⊕ observe y
}
```
$$(12.10)$$

And finally, we can express that we either observe *x* or observe *y but we don't know which* with

```
y := 0;
while (x > 0) {
    y := y + x;
    x := x - (1 2/3⊕ 2);
    observe (x 1/2⊕ y)
}
```
$$(12.11)$$

As an example of that important distinction, suppose there were a secret number x uniformly distributed with $0 \leq x < 3$, and that with probability $1/2$ either x mod 2 or x ÷ 2 were revealed in an observation, i.e. either its low- or high-order bit. If the observer knew whether mod or ÷ had been used, then afterwards

knowing that mod *was used:*
with probability $1/3$ she would be able to conclude that x was either 0 or 2, assigning equal probability to each;
with probability $1/6$ she would be able to conclude that x was certainly 1.
knowing that ÷ *was used:*
with probability $1/3$ she would be able to conclude that x was either 0 or 1, assigning equal probability to each; and

with probability $^1/_6$ she would be able to conclude that x was certainly 2.

On the other hand, if she did *not* know which of mod or ÷ had been used, then afterwards

not knowing which of mod *or* ÷ *was used:*
with probability $^2/_3$ she would be able to conclude that x was either 0,1 or 2, with probabilities $^1/_2$, $^1/_4$ and $^1/_4$ respectively; and
with probability $^1/_3$ she would be able to conclude that x was equally likely to be 1 or 2.

There's no denying that this is a subtle distinction – but it is a real one, and our programming language expresses it easily. [18]

To support observations – and to obtain our third and final language *Kuifje* – we add a new constructor *Observe* to the type *PCL*, based on a datatype *Bits* that allows the observation to be effectively of any type; in fact "*Bits*" is a temporary expedient that, below, will allow us to construct in Haskell the lists of heterogeneous element-type that accumulate the observations made. In our final presentation, these lists will disappear – taking "*Bits*" with them.

```
data Kuifje s
  = Skip
  | Update (s →ᴅ s) (Kuifje s)
  | If (s →ᴅ Bool) (Kuifje s) (Kuifje s) (Kuifje s)
  | While (s →ᴅ Bool) (Kuifje s) (Kuifje s)
  | Observe (s →ᴅ Bits) (Kuifje s)              — added
```

The new form *Observe f p* uses *f* to probabilistically determine a sequence of bits from the current state, observe them and then proceed with program *p*. Here a sequence of bits is simply a list of booleans.

```
type Bit  = Bool
type Bits = [Bit]
```

The new basic combinator

```
observe :: ToBits a ⇒ (s →ᴅ a) → Kuifje s
observe f = Observe (fmap toBits ∘ f) skip
```

allows us to observe values of any type *a* whose conversion to *Bits* has been defined via the *ToBits* type class

```
class ToBits a where
  toBits :: a → Bits
```

---

[18] An explanation of the precise probabilities above is given in App. 12A.

For instance, *Int* values can be observed as bits through a binary encoding (here, *quot* is division rounding towards zero, so the encoding consists of a sign bit followed by a list of binary digits, least significant first; thus, −6 is encoded as [*True, False, True, True*]):

> **instance** *ToBits Int* **where**
>   *toBits n* = (*n* < 0) : *unfoldr* (λ*m* → **if** *m* ≡ 0
>   **then** *Nothing*
>   **else** *Just* (*odd m, quot m* 2)) *n*

For syntax, the new constructor requires only a straightforward extension of the composition function (⨾):

> (⨾) :: *Kuifje s* → *Kuifje s* → *Kuifje s*
> *Skip*   ⨾ *k* = *k*
> *Update f p* ⨾ *k* = *Update f* (*p* ⨾ *k*)
> *While c p q* ⨾ *k* = *While c p* (*q* ⨾ *k*)
> *If c p q r*   ⨾ *k* = *If c p q* (*r* ⨾ *k*)
> *Observe f p* ⨾ *k* = *Observe f* (*p* ⨾ *k*)   — added

The abstract syntax tree of the first example (12.9) with observations is:

> *example₃ₐ* :: *Kuifje S*
> *example₃ₐ* =
>   *update* (λ*s* → *return* (*s.y* := 0)) ⨾
>   *while* (λ*s* → *return* (*s.x* > 0))
>   (*update* (λ*s* → *return* (*s.y* := (*s.y* + *s.x*))) ⨾
>   *update* (λ*s* → (*s.x* := (*s.x* − 1)) ₂/₃⊕ (*s.x* := (*s.x* − 2))) ⨾
>   *observe* (λ*s* → *return* (*s.x*)))

For the second (12.10), it is

> *example₃ᵦ* :: *Kuifje S*
> *example₃ᵦ* =
>   *update* (λ*s* → *return* (*s.y* := 0)) ⨾
>   *while* (λ*s* → *return* (*s.x* > 0))
>   (*update* (λ*s* → *return* (*s.y* := (*s.y* + *s.x*))) ⨾
>   *update* (λ*s* → (*s.x* := (*s.x* − 1)) ₂/₃⊕ (*s.x* := (*s.x* − 2))) ⨾
>   *cond* (λ*s* → *True* ₁/₂⊕ *False*)
>   (*observe* (λ*s* → *return* (*s.x*)))
>   (*observe* (λ*s* → *return* (*s.y*))))

And for the third (12.11) it is

$example_{3c} :: Kuifje\ S$
$example_{3c} =$
  $update\ (\lambda s \rightarrow return\ (s.y := 0))\ \mathbf{\overset{\circ}{,}}$
  $while\ (\lambda s \rightarrow return\ (s.x > 0))$
    $(update\ \ (\lambda s \rightarrow return\ (s.y := (s.y + s.x))))\ \mathbf{\overset{\circ}{,}}$
      $update\ \ (\lambda s \rightarrow (s.x := (s.x - 1))\ _{2/3}\oplus\ (s.x := (s.x - 2))))\ \mathbf{\overset{\circ}{,}}$
      $observe\ (\lambda s \rightarrow (s.x)\ _{1/2}\oplus\ (s.y)))$

For semantics, however, the domain of interpretation requires a more significant change. Indeed, we augment the distribution monad *Dist* with the capabilities of a *Bits*-writer monad to accommodate the list of accumulated observations: [19] Thus we interpret programs as Kleisli arrows $s \rightarrow_{DB} s$ of this augmented monad.

type $a \rightarrow_{DB} b = a \rightarrow Dist\ (Bits, b)$

Again because of our general approach, the structure of the interpreter remains largely the same, because most cases are parametric in the underlying monad: first we had $s \rightarrow s$; then we had $s \rightarrow_D s$ and now we have $s \rightarrow_{DB} s$. The two cases that require attention are *Update* and *Observe*.

$sem_{DB} :: Kuifje\ s \rightarrow (s \rightarrow_{DB} s)$
$sem_{DB} = (|alg\,p|)\ \mathbf{where}$
  $alg_P :: (Ord\ s) \Rightarrow Kuifje_F\ s\ (s \rightarrow_{DB} s) \rightarrow (s \rightarrow_{DB} s)$
  $alg_P\ Skip_F \qquad\qquad = \lambda x \rightarrow return\ ([\,],x)$
  $alg_P\ (Update_F\ f\ p) \ = uplift\ f >\!\!=\!\!> p$
  $alg_P\ (If_F\ c\ p\ q\ r) \quad = conditional\ c\ p\ q >\!\!=\!\!> r$
  $alg_P\ (While_F\ c\ p\ q) = \mathbf{let}\ while = conditional\ c\ (p >\!\!=\!\!> while)\ q$
  $\qquad\qquad\qquad\qquad\qquad \mathbf{in}\ \ while$
  $alg_P\ (Observe_F\ f\ p) = obsem\ f >\!\!=\!\!> p$

In the case of *Update* we lift the update function f from the distribution monad to the augmented distribution monad, by adding an empty sequence of observations.

$uplift :: (a \rightarrow_D b) \rightarrow (a \rightarrow_{DB} b)$
$uplift\ f = fmap\ (\lambda b \rightarrow ([\,],b)) \circ f$

In the case of *Observe* we extract the observation and return it alongside the current state.

$obsem :: (s \rightarrow_D Bits) \rightarrow (s \rightarrow_{DB} s)$
$obsem\ f = \lambda s \rightarrow fmap\ (\lambda w \rightarrow (w,s))\ (f\ s)$

---

[19] This list of observations becomes ever longer as the program executes; but in §12.5.3 the whole list, and *Bits*, will be 'quotiented away'.

Finally, while we preserve the definition of *If* and *While* in terms of the more primitive *conditional*, we do modify the conditional to leak its argument.

$$conditional :: (Ord\ s) \Rightarrow (s \rightarrow_D Bool) \rightarrow (s \rightarrow_{DB} s) \rightarrow (s \rightarrow_{DB} s) \rightarrow (s \rightarrow_{DB} s)$$
$$conditional\ c\ p\ q = obsem\ (fmap\ toBits \circ c) >=>$$
$$(\lambda([b], s) \rightarrow return\ ([b], (b, s))) >=>$$
$$(\lambda(b, s) \rightarrow if\ b\ then\ p\ s\ else\ q\ s)$$

The consequence is that the programs *skip* and *cond* $(\lambda s \rightarrow True\ _{1/2}\oplus False)$ *skip skip* now have different semantics:

$$> sem_{DB}\ skip\ ()$$
$$1 \div 1 \quad ([\,], ())$$
$$> sem_{DB}\ (cond\ (\lambda s \rightarrow True\ _{1/2}\oplus False)\ skip\ skip)\ ()$$
$$1 \div 2 \quad ([False], ())$$
$$1 \div 2 \quad ([True], ())$$

There are two good reasons for having leaking conditionals. It is a common (though not universal) assumption in *QIF*, a pragmatic principle that one should not 'branch on high'. Much more important, however, is that it enables a compositional hyper-semantics, as we explain in Section 12.5.3.

12.5 Hyper-distributions: from leaked values
to leaked information

In §12.4 we defined the syntax and semantics of our language in three stages, of which Kuifje – with probabilistic choice and observations – was the final outcome. We now undertake a major abstraction, removing the sequence of observed values but leaving behind the information-flow effect they induce.

12.5.1 Abstracting from observed values

If an observer is interested only in information flow about the value of a program's final state, then – we will argue – the values of the observations themselves are irrelevant. An example of this is spies who speak different languages. If they are to report the value of a secret Booolean, it makes no difference whether they say "True/False" or "Waar/Onwaar" or "Vrai/Faux" as long as their controller knows the correspondence between the observed utterance and the hidden value that caused it. Thus in our *Bit*-sequence semantics it should not matter whether the observations are say

```
        ["true","true","false"]
  or    ["waar","waar","onwaar"]
  or    ["vrai","vrai","faux"].
```

They all three result in exactly the same information flow.

The abstraction we are about to implement, motivated by that, allows a drastic simplification of the sem_{DB} semantics: we throw away the sequences of *Bits*, but we retain the distinctions they made. Further, if we propagate the abstraction to the leaves of the abstract syntax tree, we never have to construct the sequences in the first place – and then we can throw away the *Bits* type itself. Here is how it is done.

In the above interpretation, the type $S \to Dist\ (Bits, S)$ denotes a map from initial states of type S to probability distributions of sequences of observed *Bits* together with a final state of type S.

The resulting distributions *dp* of type $Dist\ (Bits, S)$ are isomorphic to pairs (d, f) of type $(Dist\ Bits, Bits \to Dist\ S)$, where the domain of f is restricted to bit sequences that occur with non-zero probability in d. This isomorphism is witnessed by the functions *toPair* and *fromPair*.

> *toPair* :: $(Ord\ s) \Rightarrow Dist\ (Bits, s) \to (Dist\ Bits, Bits \to Dist\ s)$
> *toPair dp* = (d, f)
>   **where**
> d = *fmap fst dp*
> $f\ ws$ = **let** $dpws = D\ [(s, p) \mid ((ws', s), p) \leftarrow runD\ dp, ws' \equiv ws]$
>   **in** $D\ [(s, p\ /\ weight\ dpws) \mid (s, p) \leftarrow runD\ dpws]$
> *fromPair* :: $(Dist\ Bits, Bits \to Dist\ s) \to Dist\ (Bits, s)$
> *fromPair* (d, f) = *join* $(fmap\ (\lambda ws \to fmap\ (\lambda s \to (ws, s))\ (f\ ws))\ d)$

The function *toPair* allows us to determine the likelihood of each possible trace of observations, together with the conditional distribution of possible states that the trace induces.

For instance, for the program over two Booleans

> $example_4$ :: $Kuifje\ (Bool, Bool)$
> $example_4$ = *observe* $(\lambda(b_1, b_2) \to b_1\ _{1/2}\oplus b_2)$

and the uniform distribution of Boolean pairs as input distribution

> *boolPairs* :: $Dist\ (Bool, Bool)$
> *boolPairs* = *uniform* $[(b_1, b_2) \mid b_1 \leftarrow bools, b_2 \leftarrow bools]$
>   **where** $bools = [True, False]$

we can see the distribution of observations

> *fst* (*toPair* (*boolPairs* $\ggg$ *sem*$_{DB}$ *example*$_4$))
$1 \div 2$ [*False*]
$1 \div 2$ [*True*]

that is the sequence [*False*] with probability $^1\!/_2$ and the sequence [*True*] the same; and their respective conditional distributions of final states

> *snd* (*toPair* (*boolPairs* $\ggg$ *sem*$_{DB}$ *example*$_4$)) [*False*]
$1 \div 2$ (*False, False*)
$1 \div 4$ (*False, True*)
$1 \div 4$ (*True, False*)   (12.12)

that is that if *False* is observed, the posterior distribution of states is as above, and similarly

> *snd* (*toPair* (*boolPairs* $\ggg$ *sem*$_{DB}$ *example*$_4$)) [*True*]
$1 \div 4$ (*False, True*)
$1 \div 4$ (*True, False*)
$1 \div 2$ (*True, True*)   (12.13)

If *True* is observed, the posterior distribution of states is as here instead.

If we do not care about the particular trace of observations – our postulate – but are only interested in the variation of distributions of final states, we can eliminate the sequences of observations altogether while retaining however the conditional distributions they determine. This yields so-called hyper-distributions, i.e., distributions of distributions, of type *Dist* (*Dist s*). Each of the 'inner' distributions of the hyper has as its own 'outer' probability the probability that was assigned to the no-longer-present *Bits*-sequence that gave rise to it. We do that with this function:

multiply :: (*Dist Bits, Bits* $\rightarrow$ *Dist s*) $\rightarrow$ *Dist* (*Dist s*)
multiply (*d,f*) = *fmap f d*

Thus, putting everything together, we can compute the hyper-distribution of final states as follows from a given distribution of initial states.

hyper :: (*Ord s*) $\Rightarrow$ *Kuifje s* $\rightarrow$ (*Dist s* $\rightarrow$ *Dist* (*Dist s*))
hyper p d$_0$ = *multiply* (*toPair* (*d*$_0$ $\ggg$ *sem*$_{DB}$ *p*))   (12.14)

That yields the following result on our example program, where the outers are on the left and the inners are on the right:

> *hyper example*$_4$ *boolPairs*
$1 \div 2$ $1 \div 4$ (*False, True*)

$$
1 \div 2 \quad
\begin{array}{ll}
1 \div 4 & (\textit{True}, \textit{False}) \\
1 \div 2 & (\textit{True}, \textit{True}) \\
1 \div 2 & (\textit{False}, \textit{False}) \\
1 \div 4 & (\textit{False}, \textit{True}) \\
1 \div 4 & (\textit{True}, \textit{False})
\end{array}
$$

12.5.2 Hyper-distributions in theory: why?

Although the definition of *hyper* calculates the sequences of observations, which we can then remove, we will see in §12.5.3 below that these two steps can be fused into one so that only the abstractions are used, and the *Bits*-sequences are never constructed.

First however we look at the theoretical reasons for doing this.

Our model of a *QIF*-aware program is as an initial-state to final-state mechanism that chooses its final state probabilistically, depending on the initial state, and might release information about the state at the same time. The fundamental insight *in theory* is that the actual value of the leak is unimportant: the leak's only role is in allowing an adversary to make deductions about what the state must have been at that point in order for that leak-value to have been observed. That is, we have decided as a design principle that the two programs

$$\textit{observe } b \quad \text{and} \quad \textit{observe } (\textit{not } b)$$

are the same: each one, if executed, will allow the adversary to deduce the (current) value of *b* because, knowing the source-code, she also knows (in this example) whether she must negate the leak or not; and – beyond leaking *b* – they are operationally the same, since neither changes the state. This being so, we use hyper-distributions in the (denotational) theory to abstract from those output values; and the result is that two programs are behaviourally equal just when their denotations are equal – i.e. this way we achieve full abstraction.

Further, this 'tidiness' in the semantic structures allows us in a more extensive presentation to discuss the domain structure of the semantic space: its refinement order; whether it is complete; how fixed-points are found etc. This is extensively discussed in other work (McIver et al., 2014b).

12.5.3 Hyper-distributions in practice: why?

If we accept the arguments in §12.5.2 just above, that we are interested only in the hyper-distribution of final states for a given distribution of initial states then, as we have suggested, *hyper* is not the most efficient way to compute it: *hyper* first computes the full distribution *Dist* (*Bits*, *s*) before condensing it to the usually much more compact hyper-distribution *Dist* (*Dist s*). In this section we explain how that can be implemented. We work directly with the more compact hyper-distributions throughout: programs are interpreted as hyper-arrows, and the writer-monad is no longer used; and this increased efficiency is the 'why' of hyper-distributions in practice. Thus we define

$$\textbf{\textit{type }} a \rightarrow_{\text{DD}} b = Dist\ a \rightarrow Dist\ (Dist\ b)$$

which happens to form a monoid as well: $\langle s \rightarrow_{\text{DD}} s, return, \texttt{>=>}\rangle$. Indeed, we can derive the *hyper* semantics directly as a fold *sem*$_{\text{DD}}$,

$$
\begin{aligned}
&sem_{\text{DD}} :: (Ord\ s) \Rightarrow Kuifje\ s \rightarrow (s \rightarrow_{\text{DD}} s) \\
&sem_{\text{DD}} = (\!|alg_H|\!)
\end{aligned}
\tag{12.15}
$$

by solving the "fold fusion" equation for the algebra *alg*$_H$

$$post \circ alg_P\ =\ alg_H \circ fmap\ hyper \tag{12.16}$$

where

$$
\begin{aligned}
&post :: Ord\ s \Rightarrow (s \rightarrow_{\text{DB}} s) \rightarrow (s \rightarrow_{\text{DD}} s) \\
&post\ t = \lambda d \rightarrow multiply\ (toPair\ (d \texttt{>>=} t))
\end{aligned}
$$

Using the following three properties of *post*

$$post\ return = return \tag{12.17}$$

$$post\ (f \texttt{>=>} g) = post\ f \texttt{>=>} post\ g \tag{12.18}$$

$$post\ (\lambda s \rightarrow (f\ s)\ {}_w\!\oplus (g\ s)) = \lambda d \rightarrow (post\ f\ d)\ {}_w\!\oplus (post\ g\ d) \tag{12.19}$$

it is possible to verify[20] that the definition of *alg*$_H$ below satisfies (12.16).

$$
\begin{aligned}
&alg_H :: (Ord\ s) \Rightarrow Kuifje_{\text{F}}\ s\ (s \rightarrow_{\text{DD}} s) \rightarrow (s \rightarrow_{\text{DD}} s) \\
&alg_H\ Skip_{\text{F}} \qquad\qquad = return \\
&alg_H\ (Update_{\text{F}}\ f\ p) \ = huplift\ f \texttt{>=>} p \\
&alg_H\ (If_{\text{F}}\ c\ p\ q\ r) \quad\ = conditional\ c\ p\ q \texttt{>=>} r \\
&alg_H\ (While_{\text{F}}\ c\ p\ q) = \textbf{\textit{let}}\ while = conditional\ c\ (p \texttt{>=>} while)\ q \\
&\qquad\qquad\qquad\qquad\quad\ \textbf{\textit{in}}\ while \\
&alg_H\ (Observe_{\text{F}}\ f\ p) = hobsem\ f \texttt{>=>} p
\end{aligned}
$$

$$
\begin{aligned}
&conditional :: Ord\ s \Rightarrow (s \rightarrow_{\text{D}} Bool) \rightarrow (s \rightarrow_{\text{DD}} s) \rightarrow (s \rightarrow_{\text{DD}} s) \rightarrow (s \rightarrow_{\text{DD}} s) \\
&conditional\ c\ t\ e = \lambda d \rightarrow \\
&\quad \textbf{\textit{let}}\ d' = d \texttt{>>=} \lambda s \rightarrow c\ s \texttt{>>=} \lambda b \rightarrow return\ (b, s)
\end{aligned}
$$

---

[20] Note that Equation 12.19 only holds when there are no two inputs x and y such that $f\ x$ and $g\ y$ yield the same observations. This is the case for two branches of a conditional, which, because they leak their condition, always yield disjoint observations.

$$w_1 = sum\ [\,p \mid ((b,s),p) \leftarrow runD\ d',b\,]$$

$$w_2 = 1 - w_1$$

$$d_1 = D\ [\,(s,p\ /\ w_1) \mid ((b,s),p) \leftarrow runD\ d',b\,]$$

$$d_2 = D\ [\,(s,p\ /\ w_2) \mid ((b,s),p) \leftarrow runD\ d',not\ b\,]$$

$$h_1 = t\ d_1$$

$$h_2 = e\ d_2$$

$$\mathbf{in\ if}\quad null\ (runD\ d_2)\ \mathbf{then}\ h_1$$

$$\mathbf{else\ if}\ null\ (runD\ d_1)\ \mathbf{then}\ h_2$$

$$\mathbf{else}\ \ join\ (h_1\ {}_{w_1}\!\oplus h_2)$$

$$huplift :: Ord\ s \Rightarrow (s \rightarrow_{\mathrm{D}} s) \rightarrow (s \rightarrow_{\mathrm{DD}} s)$$

$$huplift\ f = return \circ (\!\ggg\! f)$$

Because sem_{DD} immediately abstracts over the observations and never collects them in a (homogeneously-typed) list, we do not first have to convert them to *Bits*. This means that we can generalize our syntax of programs to observations of arbitrary type o:

```
data Kuifje s
   = Skip
   | Update (s →ᴅ s) (Kuifje s)
   | If (s →ᴅ Bool) (Kuifje s) (Kuifje s) (Kuifje s)
   | While (s →ᴅ Bool) (Kuifje s) (Kuifje s)
   | ∀o . (Ord o, ToBits o) ⇒ Observe (s →ᴅ o) (Kuifje s)
```

and interpret them without requiring a *ToBits* instance.

$$hobsem :: (Ord\ s, Ord\ o) \Rightarrow (s \rightarrow_{\mathrm{D}} o) \rightarrow (s \rightarrow_{\mathrm{DD}} s)$$

$$hobsem\ f = multiply \circ toPair \circ (\!\ggg\! obsem\ f)$$

$$\mathbf{where}$$

$$\quad obsem :: Ord\ o \Rightarrow (a \rightarrow_{\mathrm{D}} o) \rightarrow (a \rightarrow_{\mathrm{D}} (o,a))$$

$$\quad obsem\ f = \lambda x \rightarrow fmap\ (\lambda w \rightarrow (w,x))\ (f\ x)$$

$$\quad toPair :: (Ord\ s, Ord\ o) \Rightarrow Dist\ (o,s) \rightarrow (Dist\ o, o \rightarrow Dist\ s)$$

$$\quad toPair\ dp = (d,f)$$

$$\quad\quad \mathbf{where}$$

$$\quad\quad\quad d\ \ = fmap\ fst\ dp$$

$$\quad\quad\quad f\ ws = \mathbf{let}\ dpws = D\ [\,(s,p) \mid ((ws',s),p) \leftarrow runD\ dp, ws' \equiv ws\,]$$

$$\quad\quad\quad\quad\quad\quad \mathbf{in}\ \ D\ [\,(s,p\ /\ weight\ dpws) \mid (s,p) \leftarrow runD\ dpws\,]$$

$$\quad multiply :: (Dist\ o, o \rightarrow Dist\ s) \rightarrow Dist\ (Dist\ s)$$

$$\quad multiply\ (d,f) = fmap\ f\ d$$

In summary, with sem_{DD} from (12.15) we obtain the same results as with sem_{DB} (12.12,12.13) – but without the need for post-processing:

> sem_{DD} $example_4$ $boolPairs$

$1 \div 2$	$1 \div 4$	(*False, True*)
	$1 \div 4$	(*True, False*)
	$1 \div 2$	(*True, True*)
$1 \div 2$	$1 \div 2$	(*False, False*)
	$1 \div 4$	(*False, True*)
	$1 \div 4$	(*True, False*)

12.6 Case Studies

12.6.1 The Monty Hall problem

The (in)famous Monty Hall problem (Rosenhouse, 2009) concerns a quiz-show where a car is hidden behind one of three curtains. The other two curtains conceal goats. The show's host is Monty Hall, and a contestant (Monty's adversary) is trying to guess which curtain conceals the car.

Initially, the contestant believes the car is equally likely to be behind each curtain. She chooses one of the three, reasoning (correctly) that her chance of having chosen the car is $1/3$; but the host does not open the curtain. Instead Monty opens one of the two other curtains, making sure that a goat is there. (Thus if the contestant has chosen the car – though she does not know that – he will open either of the other two curtains; but if she has not chosen the car he opens the (unique) other curtain that hides a goat. Either way, from her point of view, he has opened a curtain where there is a goat.)

Monty Hall then says "Originally you had a one-in-three chance of getting the car. But now there are only two possible positions for the car: the curtain you chose, and the other closed curtain. Would you like to change your mind?" The notorious puzzle is then "Should she change?"

A qualitative (i.e. non-quantitative) approach to this, relying on intuition, suggests that

(i) Since Monty Hall could have opened a goat-curtain no matter where the car is, his doing so conveys nothing; and

(ii) Since the contestant still does not know where the car is, nothing has been leaked.

But a quantitative approach enables more sophisticated reasoning.[21] Even though the

---

[21] ...but also sometimes unsophisticated too: "Since there are now only two doors, the chance of the car's being behind the door already chosen has risen to $1/2$."

contestant does not know for sure where the car is, after Monty's action, is it really true that she knows *no* more than before? Or has she perhaps learned something, but not everything? Has *some* information flowed? There are many compelling informal arguments for that.[22] But here we give one based on the information-flow semantics of Kuifje.

We declare the three-element type *Door*

data *Door* = *DoorA* | *DoorB* | *DoorC* **deriving** (*Eq, Show, Ord*)

and describe Monty's action with a single Kuifje statement: choose a door that is neither the door already chosen by the contestant nor the one with the car. This is the *hall* program just below, with argument *ch* for the contestant's choice; its initial state *d* is where the car is:

hall :: *Door* → *Kuifje Door*
hall ch = *observe* (*λd* → *uniform* ([*DoorA, DoorB, DoorC*] \\ [*d, ch*]))

The list [*DoorA, DoorB, DoorC*] \\ [*d, ch*] is those doors that were not chosen by the contestant *and* don't conceal the car: there can be one or two of them, depending on whether the contestant (so far, unknowingly) chose the car.[23]

If the contestant initially chooses *DoorA*, then we obtain the following hyper-distribution of the car's door after observing the goat revealed by Monty:

doors = *uniform* [*DoorA, DoorB, DoorC*]
monty = *sem*$_{\text{DD}}$ (*hall DoorA*) *doors*

> *monty*

$1 \div 2$	$1 \div 3$	*DoorA*
	$2 \div 3$	*DoorB*
$1 \div 2$	$1 \div 3$	*DoorA*
	$2 \div 3$	*DoorC*

(12.20)

It expresses that the contestant will know (or *should* realise) that the car is with probability $^2/_3$ behind the still-closed curtain. The two $^1/_2$ 'outer' probabilities reflects (given she chose *DoorA*) that the remaining closed door is equally likely to be *DoorB* or *DoorC*.[24] Since the program treats all doors in the same way, the same argument holds even if another initial door was chosen: in every case, it is better to change.

---

[22] For those who still doubt: Suppose there were 100 doors, 99 goats and one car. The contestant chooses one door, and Monty opens 98 others with goats behind every one. . .

[23] The operator (\\) removes all elements of the right list from the left list.

[24] That can happen in two ways. If she chose the car (unknowingly) at *DoorA*, then Monty is equallty likely to open *DoorB* or *DoorC*; if she did not choose the car, it is equally likely to be behind *DoorB* or *DoorC*, and thus equally likely that Monty will open *DoorC* or *DoorB* respectively.

Since we have captured the result hyper in the variable *monty*, we can carry this analysis a bit further. (Note that we do not have to re-run the program: the output hyper *monty* contains all we need for the analysis.) Recall that the *Bayes Vulnerability bv* of a distribution (for which we wrote $V()$ in Fig. 12.4) is precisely the maximum probability of any element:

bv :: *Ord a* $\Rightarrow$ *Dist a* $\rightarrow$ *Prob*
bv = *maximum* $\circ$ *map snd* $\circ$ *runD* $\circ$ *reduction*

and that this represents a rational adversary's strategy in guessing a secret whose distribution is known: guess the secret of (possibly equal) greatest probability. To use *bv* in the situation above, where there are *two* possible distributions the contestant might face, we simply average her best-chance over each of the two distributions' likelihood of occurring. For the first, with probability $^1/_2$, she will be able to guess correctly with probability $^2/_3$, giving $^1/_2 \times {}^2/_3 = {}^1/_3$ for the overall probability that Monty will reveal *DoorC* and the car will be behind *DoorB*. We get $^1/_3$ for the other alternative (it is effectively the same, with the doors changed), and so her overall probability of finding the car is $^1/_3 + {}^1/_3 = {}^2/_3$.

That process can be automated by defining

condEntropy :: (*Dist a* $\rightarrow$ *Rational*) $\rightarrow$ *Dist* (*Dist a*) $\rightarrow$ *Rational*
condEntropy e h = *average* (*fmap e h*) **where**
    average :: *Dist Rational* $\rightarrow$ *Rational*   — Average a distr. of *Rational*'s.
    average d = *sum* [$r \times p$ | $(r,p) \leftarrow$ *runD d*]

which for any entropy, that is *bv* in the case just below, gives its average when applied to all the inners of a hyper – yielding the conditional entropy. Thus we get

  > *condEntropy bv monty*
  $2 \div 3$

for the (smart) contestant's chance of getting her new car.

12.6.2 A defence against side-channels

Our second example here concerns a side-channel attack on the well known fast-exponentiation algorithm used for public-key encryptions.

The algorithm is given in pseudo-code at Fig. 12.7. As usual we assume that the program code is public, so that any side channels caused e.g. by 'branching on high' might allow an adversary to make deductions about the inputs: in this case, a careful analysis might be used to distinguish between the two branches of the **IF**, [25] as

---

[25] For example it could be a timing leak.

```
VAR B ← Base.                                    Global variables.
    E ← Exponent.
    p ← To be set to Bᴱ.

BEGIN VAR b,e:= B,E                              Local variables.
  p:= 1
  WHILE e≠0 DO
    VAR r:= e MOD 2
    IF r≠0 THEN p:= p*b FI                        ← Side channel.
    b,e:= b²,e÷2
  END
END
{ p = Bᴱ }
```

Here we are assuming that the 'branch on high' is the undesired side-channel: by detecting whether or not the branch is taken, the adversary can learn the bits of exponent E – which is the secret key – one by one. When the loop ends, she will have learned them all.

Figure 12.7 Insecure implementation of public/private key encryption.

```
Global variables.
VAR B ← Base.                                    Global variables.
    D ← Set of possible divisors.

    p ← To be set to Bᴱ.
    E:= uniform(0..N-1)    Choose exponent uniformly at random.

BEGIN VAR b,e:= B,E                              Local variables.
  p:= 1
  WHILE e≠0 DO
    VAR d:= uniform(D)    ← Choose divisor uniformly from set D.
    VAR r:= e MOD d
    IF r≠0 THEN p:= p*bʳ FI                       ← Side channel.
    b,e:= bᵈ,e÷d
  END
END
{ p = Bᴱ }          What does the adversary know about E at this point?
```

Here the side channel is much less effective: although the adversary learns whether r=0, she knows nothing about d except that it was chosen uniformly from D, and thus learns little about e, and hence E at that point. A typical choice for D would be [2, 3, 5]. When the loop ends, she will have learned something about E, but not all of it. (In order to be able to analyse the program's treatment of E as a secret, we have initialised it uniformly from N possible values.)

Figure 12.8 Obfuscated implementation of public/private key encryption.

indicated in Fig. 12.7, which is equivalent to determining whether the current value of e is divisible by 2. That occurs each time the loop iterates, and an adversary who has access to this (e.g. by analysing timing) would therefore be able to figure out exactly the initial value of E one bit at a time – and E is in fact the encryption key.

A defence against this side channel attack was proposed by (Walter, 2002) and is implemented at Fig. 12.8. His idea is that rather than attempting to close the side channel, instead one can reduce its effectiveness. The problem with the implementation at Fig. 12.7 is that 2 is always used as a divisor, which is why the ith branching at the IF-statement is correlated exactly with the i'th bit of the original secret E. In Fig. 12.8, that correlation is attenuated by adding an extra variable d, used as divisor in place of 2 – and it is selected independently at random on each iteration. That obfuscates the relationship between e and the branching at the IF-statement, because the adversary does not know which value of d is being used. The information transmitted by the channel is therefore no longer exactly correlated with the i'th bit of the secret.

To compare the two programs we used the semantics of Kuifje to compute the final hyper-distribution resulting from Fig. 12.8 for an example range of E, determined by N. We assume that all the variables are hidden, as we are only interested in the information flowing through the side channel and what it tells us about e's divisibility by d. [26]

Below is a translation of our obfuscated algorithm Fig. 12.8 into Kuifje. All variables are global, so the state space is:

data *SE* = *SE* {$_b$*ase,* $_e$*xp, e, d, p* :: *Integer*}

And we initialise the state as follows:

initSE :: *Integer* → *Integer* → *SE*
initSE base exp = *SE* {$_b$*ase* = *base,* $_e$*xp* = *exp, e* = 0, *d* = 0, *p* = 0}

And here is the body of the algorithm, based on Fig. 12.8, taking a list *ds* of divisors:

exponentiation :: [*Integer*] → *Kuifje SE*
exponentiation ds =
   update (λ*s* → *return* (*s.e* := (*s.exp*))) ⨟
   update (λ*s* → *return* (*s.p* := 1)) ⨟
   while (λ*s* → *return* (*s.e* ≠ 0))
     (*update* (λ*s* → *uniform* [*s.d* := *d'* | *d'* ← *ds*]) ⨟
     cond (λ*s* → *return* (*s.e* 'mod' *s.d* ≠ 0))
      (*update* (λ*s* → *return* (*s.p* := ((*s.p*) × ((*s.base*) ↑ (*s.e* 'mod' *s.d*))))) ⨟
       update (λ*s* → *return* (*s.e* := (*s.e* − (*s.e* 'mod' *s.d*)))))))   — Then

---

[26] We are not, in this analysis, considering a brute force attack that could invert the exponentiation.

$$skip \, \text{\textbf{;}} \hspace{5cm} — \text{Else}$$
$$update \, (\lambda s \to return \, (s.base := ((s.base) \uparrow (s.d)))) \, \text{\textbf{;}}$$
$$update \, (\lambda s \to return \, (s.e := (s.e \text{ `}div\text{` } s.d)))$$
$$) \hspace{9cm} (12.21)$$

Finally, we project the program's output onto a hyper retaining only the variable E (that is $_exp$), using the following function:

$$project :: Dist \, (Dist \, SE) \to Dist \, (Dist \, Integer)$$
$$project = fmap \, (fmap \, (\lambda s \to s.exp))$$

In the two runs below we choose E uniformly from $[0 .. 15]$, that is a 4-bit exponent (secret key). The first case *hyper2* is effectively the conventional algorithm of Fig. 12.7, because we restrict the divisor d to being 2 every time:

$$hyper2 = project \, (sem_{\text{DD}} \, (exponentiation \, [2])$$
$$(uniform \, [initSE \, 6 \, exp \mid exp \leftarrow [0 .. 15]]))$$

The value of *hyper2*, that is what is known about E after calculating the power p, is shown in Fig. 12.9. The first column (all $1 \div 16$, that is $^1/_{16}$) shows that there are sixteen possible outcomes distributed just as the hidden input E was, that is uniformly. The second- and third columns show that in each of those outcomes, the adversary will know for certain ($1 \div 1$) what the secret ket E was. That is, with probability $^1/_{16}$ she will know for certain (i.e. with probability $^1/_1$) that it was 0, with probability $^1/_{16}$ that it was 1, with $^1/_{16}$ it was 2 etc. If the prior distribution were different, then the outer of the hyper would be correspondingly different: but in each case the second column, the inners, would be "probability 1" throughout. Compare that with the "perfect channel" of Fig. 12.5 – it has the same effect, making a hyper all of whose inners are point distributions.

The second case *hyper235*, again with uniform choice of E over 4 bits, is what we are more interested in: it is not a perfect channel for E. In that case we can see what happens with divisor d's being chosen uniformly from $[2, 3, 5]$:

$$hyper235 = project \, (sem_{\text{DD}} \, (exponentiation \, [2, 3, 5])$$
$$(uniform \, [initSE \, 6 \, exp \mid exp \leftarrow [0 .. 15]]))$$

The value of *hyper235* is shown in Fig. 12.10. Surprisingly, there are still cases where E is learned exactly by the adversary: for example, with probability $^1/_{432}$ she will learn that E=12 is certain (and similarly 13, 14, 15). But her probability $^1/_{432}$ of learning that is very low. On the other hand, with a higher probability $^{41}/_{144}$, i.e. about $^1/_3$, the adversary will learn only that E is in the set $\{3..14\}$ with certain probabilities. Thus in the second case the hyper shows that with low probability the adversary learns a lot, but with high probability the adversary learns only a little.

We now discuss further the significance of *hyper235* resulting from running the

> *hyper2*

$1 \div 16$	$1 \div 1$	0
$1 \div 16$	$1 \div 1$	1
$1 \div 16$	$1 \div 1$	2
$1 \div 16$	$1 \div 1$	3
$1 \div 16$	$1 \div 1$	4
$1 \div 16$	$1 \div 1$	5
$1 \div 16$	$1 \div 1$	6
$1 \div 16$	$1 \div 1$	7
$1 \div 16$	$1 \div 1$	8
$1 \div 16$	$1 \div 1$	9
$1 \div 16$	$1 \div 1$	10
$1 \div 16$	$1 \div 1$	11
$1 \div 16$	$1 \div 1$	12
$1 \div 16$	$1 \div 1$	13
$1 \div 16$	$1 \div 1$	14
$1 \div 16$	$1 \div 1$	15

Figure 12.9 Hyper *hyper2* produced by running the program of Fig. 12.8 when d=[2].

exponentiation program when d can be 2,3 or 5. A rational adversary will guess that the value of *exp* is the one of highest probability: thus in the case $^{41}/_{144}$ mentioned above, she will guess that *exp* is 7. To find out her overall probability of guessing correctly, we take the average of those maxima.

As in the previous example (§12.6.1) we use the Bayes Vulnerability *bv* of a distribution, the maximum probability of any element:

bv :: *Ord a* $\Rightarrow$ *Dist a* $\rightarrow$ *Prob*
bv = *maximum* ∘ *map snd* ∘ *runD* ∘ *reduction*

and we average that value over *hyper235* using *condEntropy*:

condEntropy :: (*Dist a* $\rightarrow$ *Rational*) $\rightarrow$ *Dist* (*Dist a*) $\rightarrow$ *Rational*
condEntropy e h = *average* (*fmap e h*) **where**
    average :: *Dist Rational* $\rightarrow$ *Rational*   — Average a distr. of *Rational*'s.
    average d = *sum* [$r \times p$ | $(r,p) \leftarrow$ *runD d*]

yielding the conditional entropy:

> *condEntropy bv hyper235*
$7 \div 24$ (12.22)

We see that her chance of guessing *exp* is now less than $^1/_3$, significantly less than the 'can guess with certainty' of *hyper2*:

> *condEntropy bv hyper2*
$1 \div 1$

> *hyper235*

1 ÷ 16	1 ÷ 1	0
7 ÷ 48	3 ÷ 7	1
	2 ÷ 7	2
	1 ÷ 7	3
	1 ÷ 7	4
5 ÷ 36	3 ÷ 20	2
	3 ÷ 20	3
	1 ÷ 10	4
	3 ÷ 20	5
	3 ÷ 20	6
	1 ÷ 20	8
	1 ÷ 20	9
	1 ÷ 10	10
	1 ÷ 20	12
	1 ÷ 20	15
41 ÷ 144	3 ÷ 41	3
	3 ÷ 41	4
	5 ÷ 41	5
	3 ÷ 41	6
	6 ÷ 41	7
	5 ÷ 41	8
	4 ÷ 41	9
	1 ÷ 41	10
	3 ÷ 41	11
	2 ÷ 41	12
	3 ÷ 41	13
	3 ÷ 41	14
31 ÷ 432	3 ÷ 31	4
	6 ÷ 31	6
	2 ÷ 31	8
	3 ÷ 31	9
	6 ÷ 31	10
	5 ÷ 31	12
	6 ÷ 31	15

7 ÷ 72	1 ÷ 14	5
	1 ÷ 7	7
	1 ÷ 14	8
	1 ÷ 21	9
	1 ÷ 14	10
	3 ÷ 14	11
	1 ÷ 14	12
	4 ÷ 21	13
	5 ÷ 42	14
17 ÷ 216	3 ÷ 34	6
	3 ÷ 34	8
	3 ÷ 34	9
	5 ÷ 34	10
	3 ÷ 17	12
	3 ÷ 17	14
	4 ÷ 17	15
2 ÷ 27	3 ÷ 32	7
	3 ÷ 32	9
	3 ÷ 32	10
	1 ÷ 4	11
	3 ÷ 16	13
	3 ÷ 32	14
	3 ÷ 16	15
1 ÷ 108	1 ÷ 4	8
	3 ÷ 4	12
5 ÷ 432	1 ÷ 5	9
	3 ÷ 5	13
	1 ÷ 5	14
1 ÷ 108	1 ÷ 4	10
	1 ÷ 2	14
	1 ÷ 4	15
1 ÷ 144	1 ÷ 3	11
	2 ÷ 3	15
1 ÷ 432	1 ÷ 1	12
1 ÷ 432	1 ÷ 1	13
1 ÷ 432	1 ÷ 1	14
1 ÷ 432	1 ÷ 1	15

Figure 12.10 Hyper *hyper234* produced by running the program of Fig. 12.8 when d=[2, 3, 5].

A more interesting situation however is one where we look at the adversary in more abstract terms: it is not the secret key E that she wants, but rather the money she can get by using it. If that were say \$1, then her expected profit from an attack on *hyper235* is from (12.22) of course \$$^{161}/_{1296}$, i.e. about 12 cents. But now – even more abstractly – we imagine that if she guesses incorrectly, she is caught in the act and is punished: the extra abstraction is then that we assign a notional cost to her of say \$5 for being punished. In this setting then, one might imagine that she would never bother to guess the key: as we saw, her probability of guessing correctly is only about $^1/_8$, and thus of guessing incorrectly is $^7/_8$, giving an expected profit of $^1/_8\times1 - ^7/_8\times5$, i.e. a *loss* of about \$4.25.

If that *were* so then, since she is rational, she would not guess at all: it is too risky because she will lose on average \$4.25 every time she does. But it is *not* so: that is the wrong conclusion. Recall for example that with probability $^1/_{432}$ she will learn that *exp* was 12 (and similarly for 13, 14, 15) [27] – and in those cases, she *will* guess. With a bit of arithmetic, we capture the true scenario of gaining \$1 if the guess is correct and losing \$5 if guess is incorrect as follows:

> *jail* :: *Ord a* $\Rightarrow$ *Dist a* $\rightarrow$ *Rational*
> *jail d* = **let** *m* = *maximum* (*map snd* (*runD* (*reduction d*))) **in**
> $\quad\quad$ $(1 \times m - 5 \times (1 - m))$ '*max*' 0

where the term $1\times m - 5\times(1-m)$ represents her expected (abstract) profit, and bounding below by 0 encodes her strategy that if that profit is negative, she won't risk a guess at all. Now we find

> $>$ *condEntropy jail hyper235*
> $31 \div 432$
> $>$ *condEntropy jail hyper2*
> $1 \div 1$

– that is, that by choosing rationally to guess the password only when her expected gain is non-negative, the adversary gains 7 cents on average. We see also just above that in the 2-only case she gets the full \$1 on average, because she has no risk of guessing incorrectly: the value of E is completely revealed.

Note that the calculations and experiments we just carried out were on the hyper-distributions *hyper2* and *hyper235* and did *not* require the program *exponentiation* at (12.21) to be re-run on each experiment. Just one run captures in the resulting *hyper* all the information we need to evaluate various attacker strategies (like *bv* and *jail*).

Finally, we note that Kuifje is not able currently to deal with the large inputs required for realistic cryptographic computations. As our examples show however, it is a useful experimental tool to increase the understanding of the underlying risks associated with those computations, for example side channels in implementations of cryptography, and what can be done about them.

---

[27] There is also the case where *exp* is 0, in which case she learns that for sure – and guesses 0. In practical circumstances that choice of *exp* would be forbidden; but to keep things simple in the presentation, we have left it in.

12.7 Conclusion

12.7.1 Related work

This chapter brings together two ideas for the first time: quantitative information flow for modelling security in programs, and functional programming's generic use of monads to incorporate computational effects in programming languages. The result is a clean implementation of a security-based semantics for programs written in Haskell.

What makes this synthesis possible is that information flows can be modelled in program semantics using the Giry Monad for probabilistic semantics (Giry, 1981) which, as explained above, is applied to the type $\mathbb{D}X$ rather than the more familiar X for some state space.

Quantitative information flow for modelling confidentiality was described by (Gray, 1990) and in even earlier work by (Millen, 1987), establishing a relationship between information channels and non-interference of (Goguen and Meseguer, 1984) and the strong dependence of (Cohen, 1977). This last treatment of non-interference turned out however to be unable to impose the weaker security guarantees which are required for practical implementations – it does not allow for partial information flows, for example, which are very difficult and perhaps even impossible to eradicate.

The *channel model* for information flow was mentioned by (Chatzikokolakis et al., 2008) for studying anonymity protocols and was further developed by (Alvim et al., 2012) to include the ideas of gain functions to generalise entropies and secure refinement to enable robust comparisons of information flows between channels. Both of these ideas were already present in earlier work (McIver et al., 2010) which described a model for quantitative information flow in a sequential programming context. A special case of that model are programs which only leak information without updating variables. Such programs correspond exactly to channels.

(McIver et al., 2015) demonstrated that information flow in programs (and therefore channels too) can be expressed in terms of the Giry monad, unifying the sequential program operator for programs and 'parallel composition' for channels. The idea of refinement's merging posterior behaviour is a generalisation of the way ignorance is handled in qualitative model for information flow (Morgan, 2006, 2009) which is similarly based on monads (for sets rather than distributions).

The abstraction for information flow and state updates that is required for this monadic program semantics is inspired by Hidden Markov Models (Baum and Petrie, 1966), but does not assume that all Markov updates and channel leaks are the same – this generalisation was not present in the original concrete model. Others have also used a concrete version of Hidden Markov Models for analysing information flow in programs (Clark et al., 2005a,b) and do not consider refinement.

Probability in sequential program semantics to express randomisation (but not information flow) was originally due to (Kozen, 1981) although it was not presented in the monadic form used here; that seems to be due to (Lawvere, 1962) and then later brought to a wider audience by (Giry, 1981), as mentioned above.

Haskell's use of monads goes back to (Moggi, 1991), who famously showed that monads provide a semantic model for computational effects, and (Jones and Plotkin, 1989) used this to present a monadic model of a probabilistic lambda calculus. (Wadler, 1992) promoted Moggi's insight within functional programming, with the consequence that monads now form a mainstream programming abstraction, especially in the Haskell programming language. In particular, several people (Ramsey and Pfeffer, 2002; Erwig and Kollmansberger, 2006; Gibbons and Hinze, 2011) have explored the representation of probabilistic programs as Kleisli arrows for the probability monad.

12.7.2 Discussion

The approach we have taken to providing an executable model of *QIF* is as an *embedded domain-specific language* (Hudak, 1996; Gibbons, 2013) called Kuifje, hosted within an existing general-purpose language. That is, we have not taken the traditional approach of designing a standalone language for *QIF*, and building a compiler that translates from *QIF* concrete syntax to some more established language. Instead, we have defined a datatype *Kuifje* to represent *QIF* abstract syntax trees as values, a semantic domain $\rightarrow_{\text{DD}}$ to represent the behaviour of *QIF* programs, and a translation function *hyper* :: *Ord s* $\Rightarrow$ *Kuifje s* $\rightarrow$ (*s* $\rightarrow_{\text{DD}}$ *s*) from abstract syntax to semantic domain – all within an existing host language. In our case, that host language is Haskell, although that fact is not too important – we could have chosen OCaml, or Scala, or F#, or any one of a large number of alternatives instead.

Embedded DSLs offer a number of benefits over standalone languages, especially when it comes to early exploratory studies. For example, one can reuse existing tools such as type-checkers, compilers, and editing modes, rather than having to build one's own; moreover, programs in the DSL may exploit features of the host language such as definition mechanisms, modules, and basic datatypes, so these do not have to be added explicitly to the language. These benefits make it quick and easy to build a prototype for the purposes of studying a new language concept. On the other hand, programs in the embedded DSL have to be encoded as abstract syntax trees, and written using the syntactic conventions of the host language, rather than enjoying a free choice of notation best suited to the task; this can be a bit awkward. Once DSL design decisions have been explored and the language design is stable, and the number of users and uses starts to grow, it is easier to justify the additional effort of developing a standalone implementation, perhaps taking the embedded DSL implementation as a starting point.

Our Haskell implementation is inspired by work on *algebraic effects and han-*

dlers (Pretnar, 2015), a language concept that assigns meaning to a syntax tree built out of effectful operations by folding over it with an appropriate algebra known as a handler. While the conventional approach of algebraic effects and handlers applies to trees that have a free-monad structure, our approach is an instance of the generalized framework of (Pieters et al., 2017) that admits handlers for trees with a generalized monoid structure (Rivas and Jaskelioff, 2017) like our plain monoids.

The monoidal representation of programs as state transformers, while relatively simple, has one big limitation: it requires that the type of the initial state is the same as that of intermediate states and of the final state. This means that the program cannot introduce local and result variables, or drop the initial variables and local variables. This leads to awkward models where the initial state contains dummy values for local variables that are initialized in the program. We can overcome this limitation and model heterogenous state by moving – within the framework of generalized monoids – from plain monoids over set to Hughes' *arrows* (Hughes, 2000), which are monoids in a category of so-called *profunctors*.

Acknowledgements

We are grateful for the helpful comments of Nicolas Wu and other members of IFIP Working Group 2.1 on *Algorithmic Languages and Calculi*. Annabelle McIver and Carroll Morgan thank the Australian Research Council for its support via grants DP120101413 and DP141001119; Morgan thanks the Australian Government for its support via CSIRO and Data61. Tom Schrijvers thanks the Research Foundation – Flanders (FWO). Gibbons and Schrijvers thank the Leibniz Center for Informatics: part of this work was carried out during Dagstuhl Seminar 18172 on *Algebraic Effect Handlers go Mainstream*.

Appendix 12A *A-priori-* and *a-posteriori* distributions

In §12.4.3 an example compared two programs that released information about a variable x, initially distributed uniformly so that $0 \leq x < 3$. Here we show how those numbers are calculated. Note that this is not an innovation of this chapter: we are merely filling in the background of the conventional treatment of priors (*a priori* distributions) and posteriors (*a posteriori* distributions), for those who might not be familiar with them.

In our example x is initially either 0, 1 or 2 with probability $1/3$ for each, i.e. the uniform distribution: this is called *a priori* because it is what the observer believes *before* any leaks have occurred. *Prior* is short for *a-priori* distribution.

If x mod 2 is leaked, then the observer will see either 0 – when x is 0 or 2; or 1 when x is 1. The 0 observation occurs with probability $2/3$, because that is the probability that **x** is 0 or 2; observation 1 occurs with remaining probability $^1/_3$. In the 0 case, the observer reasons that **x** cannot be 1; and that its probability of being 0 or 2 is $^1/_2$ each, because their initial probabilities were equal. This is the *a posteriori* distribution, conditioned on the observation's being 0, so that **x** is equally likely to be 0 or 2, and cannot be 1. In the 1 case, she reasons that **x** must be 1 (and can't be 0 or 2).

The corresponding calculations if **x** ÷ 2 is leaked are that when 0 is observed, she reasons that **x** is equally likely to be 0 or 1; and if she sees 1, she knows for sure that **x** is 2.

Now if the choice is made between $x \bmod 2$ and $x \div 2$ with probability $^1/_2$, and the observer knows whether mod or ÷ is used then, whichever it turns out to have been used, she will be able to carry out the corresponding reasoning above. And so overall her conclusions are the weighted sum of the separate outcomes, i.e. their average in this case. Thus:

- with probability $^1/_2 \times ^2/_3 = ^1/_3$ she will know that **x** is either 0 or 2 (with equal probability for each, as explained above);
- with probability $^1/_2 \times ^1/_3 = ^1/_6$ she will know that **x** is 1;
- with probability $^1/_2 \times ^2/_3 = ^1/_3$ she will know that **x** is either 0 or 1; and
- with probability $^1/_2 \times ^1/_3 = ^1/_6$ she will know that **x** is 2.

The other situation is when the observer does *not* know whether mod or (÷) was used. In that case she will see 0 with probability $^1/_2 \times ^2/_3 + ^1/_2 \times ^2/_3 = ^2/_3$, either because mod was used and **x** was 0 or 2, or because (÷) was used and **x** was 0 or 1. And in that case 0 is twice as likely as each of the other two, so that the posterior is that **x** is 0 with probability $^1/_2$ and is 1 or 2 with probability $^1/_4$ each. When she sees 1, with probability $^1/_2 \times ^1/_3 + ^1/_2 \times ^1/_3 = ^1/_3$, she will reason *a posteriori* that **x** is equally likely to be 1 or 2.

These two cases are handled automatically by the semantics we have defined. The first is modelled by a conditional, leaking which branch is taken:

> *modOrDiv*₁ :: *Kuifje Int*
> *modOrDiv*₁ =
>   *cond* (λs → *uniform* [*True, False*])
>   (*observe* (λx → *return* (x ʻmodʻ 2)))
>   (*observe* (λx → *return* (x ʻdivʻ 2)))

Its effect is as follows:

> > *sem*_DD *modOrDiv*₁ (*uniform* [0 . . 2])
> 1 ÷ 3   1 ÷ 2 0
>   1 ÷ 2 1

$$1 \div 3 \quad 1 \div 2 \quad 0$$
$$1 \div 2 \quad 2$$
$$1 \div 6 \quad 1 \div 1 \quad 1$$
$$1 \div 6 \quad 1 \div 1 \quad 2$$

The second case is modelled by a probabilistic observation

$$modOrDiv_2 :: Kuifje\ Int$$
$$modOrDiv_2 = observe\ (\lambda x \rightarrow (x\ `mod`\ 2)\ _{1/2}\oplus (x\ `div`\ 2))$$

whose effect is

$$> sem_{\mathrm{DD}}\ modOrDiv_2\ (uniform\ [0..2])$$
$$2 \div 3 \quad 1 \div 2 \quad 0$$
$$1 \div 4 \quad 1$$
$$1 \div 4 \quad 2$$
$$1 \div 3 \quad 1 \div 2 \quad 1$$
$$1 \div 2 \quad 2$$

Appendix 12B A password checker

The state is a record of five fields: a password $_pw$ and a guess $_gs$, each a list of characters; a loop counter $_i$; a list $_l$ of indices still to check; and a Boolean result $_ans$. Each of the programs uses either $_i$ or $_left$ to control the loop, but not both; for simplicity, we use a common state record for them all the programs.

data $SP = SP\ \{_pw :: [Char], _gs :: [Char], _l :: [Int], _i :: Int, _ans :: Bool\}$
  deriving $(Show, Eq, Ord)$

Here is some boilerplate that invokes Template Haskell to generate a lens (a particular higher-order function) for each of the state variables: each acts as a getter and setter for its associated variable.

$makeLenses\ ''\ SP$

Function *makeState* takes a value for the password *pw* and for the guess *gs* and produces a state containing those values (setting the other variables to appropriate defaults):

$$makeState :: [Char] \rightarrow [Char] \rightarrow SP$$
$$makeState\ pw\ gs = SP\ \{_pw = pw, _gs = gs, _l = [\ ], _i = 0, _ans = True\}$$

At the end of the run, we will project the five-variable hyper onto a hyper for *pw* alone, since that is the secret the adversary is trying to discover:

```
basicI :: Int → Kuifje SP
basicI n =
    update (λs → return (s.i := 0)) ⨾                — i := 0;
    update (λs → return (s.ans := True)) ⨾           — ans := true
    while (λs → return (s.ans ∧ s.i < n))            — while (ans ∧ i < N) do
    (                                                — begin
        cond (λs → return ((s.pw !! s.i) ≠ (s.gs !! s.i)))   —   if (pw [i] ≠ gs [i])
            (update (λs → return (s.ans := False)))          —     then ans := false
            skip ⨾                                           —     else skip
        (update (λs → return (s.i := (s.i + 1))))            —   i++
    )                                                — end
```

Figure 12.11 Basic password checker, with early exit

$projectPw :: Dist\ (Dist\ SP) → Dist\ (Dist\ [Char])$
$projectPw = fmap\ (fmap\ (λs → s.pw))$

A number of versions of the program now follow. Each starts not from an initial
state, but rather from an initial distribution over states. We will make that a uniform
distribution over all permutations of a password, and a single fixed guess.

$initialDist\ pw\ gs = uniform\ [makeState\ pw'\ gs\ |\ pw' ← permutations\ pw]$

The first program, shown in Figure 12.11, checks the guess against the password
character-by-character, and exits the loop immediately if a mismatch is found.

   Now we prepare to run the program and use *projectPw* to discover the hyper over
pw that results.

$hyperI\ pw\ gs = projectPw\ (sem_{DD}\ (basicI\ (length\ pw))\ (initialDist\ pw\ gs))$

Here we choose as possible passwords all permutations of "abc" and actual guess
"abc". It yields the following output, showing that the early exit does indeed leak
information about the password: how long a prefix of it agrees with the guess:

```
> hyperI "abc" "abc"
1 ÷ 6      1 ÷ 1       "abc"
1 ÷ 6      1 ÷ 1       "acb"
2 ÷ 3      1 ÷ 4       "bac"
           1 ÷ 4       "bca"
           1 ÷ 4       "cab"
           1 ÷ 4       "cba"
```

The first inner, with probability $^1/_6$, is the case where the password is correctly
guessed: only then will the loop run to completion, because of our choice of
passwords and guess – if the guess is correct for the first two characters, it must be
correct for the third also.

```
basicL :: Int → Kuifje SP
basicL n =
    update (λs → return (s.i := 0)) ;              — i := 0;
    update (λs → return (s.ans := True)) ;         — ans := true
    while (λs → return (s.i < n))                  — while i < N do
    (                                              — begin
        cond (λs → return ((s.pw !! s.i) ≠ (s.gs !! s.i)))   —   if (pw [i] ≠ gs [i])
            (update (λs → return (s.ans := False)))          —     then ans := false
        skip ;                                              —     else skip
        (update (λs → return (s.i := (s.i + 1)))))          —   i++
    )                                              — end
```

Figure 12.12 Basic password checker, without early exit

The second inner corresponds to the loop's exiting after the second iteration: here, again because of the particular values we have chosen, the only possibility is that the first letter of the guess is correct but the second and third are swapped.

The third inner is the case where the loop is exited after one iteration: then the first letter must be incorrect (2 possibilities), and the second and third can be in either order (2 more possibilities), giving $^1/_{2\times2}$ for the inner probabilities.

For our second example of this program, we use a guess `"axc"` that is not one of the possible passwords: here, as just above, the $^2/_3$ inner corresponds to an exit after the first iteration. Unlike the above, there is a $^1/_3$ inner representing exit after the second iteration – guaranteed because the second character `"x"` of the guess is certainly wrong. In this case however, the adversary learns nothing about whether the password ends with `"bc"` or with `"cb"`.

```
> hyperI "abc" "axc"
1 ÷ 3       1 ÷ 2      "abc"
            1 ÷ 2      "acb"
2 ÷ 3       1 ÷ 4      "bac"
            1 ÷ 4      "bca"
            1 ÷ 4      "cab"
            1 ÷ 4      "cba"
```

In our second program *basicL* we try to plug the leak that *basicI* contains simply by removing the loop's early exit. It is shown in Fig. 12.12.

We run it with

hyperL pw gs = projectPw (sem$_{DD}$ *(basicL (length pw)) (initialDist pw gs))*

and obtain this surprising result:

```
> hyperL "abc" "abc"
```

```
basicM :: Int → Kuifje SP
basicM n =
    update (λs → return (s.i := 0)) ⨟           — i := 0;
    update (λs → return (s.ans := True)) ⨟       — ans := true
    while (λs → return (s.i < n))                — while i < N do
    (                                            — begin
        (update (λs → return (s.ans :=            —    ans:=
            (s.ans ∧ (s.pw !! s.i) ≡ (s.gs !! s.i))))) ⨟  —        ans ∧ (pw [i] = gs [i]);
        (update (λs → return (s.i := (s.i + 1))))  —    i++
    )                                            — end
```

Figure 12.13 Basic password checker, without early exit and without leaking conditional

$1 \div 6$	$1 \div 1$	"abc"
$1 \div 6$	$1 \div 1$	"acb"
$1 \div 6$	$1 \div 1$	"bac"
$1 \div 3$	$1 \div 2$	"bca"
	$1 \div 2$	"cab"
$1 \div 6$	$1 \div 1$	"cba"

Still the program is leaking information about the password, even though the loop runs to completion every time – and this, we now realise, is because the condition statement within the loop is leaking its condition. We knew that, but had perhaps forgotten it: remember "Don't branch on high."

Our next attempt therefore is to replace the leaking conditional with an assignment of a conditional expression, which is how we make the Boolean $pw [i] \neq gs [i]$ unobservable. That is shown in Fig. 12.13, and we find

hyperM pw gs – projectPw (sem$_{DD}$ (basicM (length pw)) (initialDist pw gs))

> hyperM "abc" "abc"		
$1 \div 1$	$1 \div 6$	"abc"
	$1 \div 6$	"acb"
	$1 \div 6$	"bac"
	$1 \div 6$	"bca"
	$1 \div 6$	"cab"
	$1 \div 6$	"cba"

indicating that in this case the adversary discovers nothing about the password at all: the resulting hyper, projected onto *pw*, is a singleton over an inner whose probabilities are simply those we knew before running the program in the first place.

But at this point we should wonder why the adversary does not discover the

```
basicN :: Int → Kuifje SP
basicN n =
    update (λs → return (s.i := 0)) ⨟              — i := 0;
    update (λs → return (s.ans := True)) ⨟         — ans := true
    while (λs → return (s.i < n))                  — while i < N do
    (                                              — begin
        (update (λs → return (s.ans :=            —    ans:=
            (s.ans ∧ (s.pw !! s.i) ≡ (s.gs !! s.i))))) ⨟   —    ans ∧ (pw [i] = gs [i]);
        (update (λs → return (s.i := (s.i + 1))))  —    i++
    ) ⨟                                            — end;
    observe (λs → return (s.ans))                  — observe ans
```

Figure 12.14 Basic password checker, success observed

password when she guesses correctly; and we should wonder as well why we haven't noticed that issue before. . .

The reason is that in our earlier examples the adversary was learning whether she had guessed correctly merely by observing the side channel! That is, the leak was so severe she did not even have to look to see whether the password checker had accepted her guess or not. Only now, with the side channel closed, do we discover that we have accidentally left off the final **observe** *ans* that models the adversary's learning the result of her guess. We remedy that in Fig. 12.14, and find

$$hyperN\ pw\ gs = projectPw\ (sem_{\mathrm{DD}}\ (basicN\ (length\ pw))\ (initialDist\ pw\ gs))$$

> *hyperN* "abc" "abc"

$1 \div 6$	$1 \div 1$	"abc"
$5 \div 6$	$1 \div 5$	"acb"
	$1 \div 5$	"bac"
	$1 \div 5$	"bca"
	$1 \div 5$	"cab"
	$1 \div 5$	"cba"

that is that with probability $1/6$ the adversary learns the password exactly, because she guessed it correctly; but when she guesses incorrectly, she finds none of the passwords she didn't guess to be any more likely than any other.

And now – finally – we come to our obfuscating password checker that compares the characters of the password and the guess in a randomly chosen order. It is in Fig. 12.15.

Running *basicR* we discover that in the $1/6$ case the adversary guesses the password correctly, she is of course still certain what it is. But now, when she does *not* guess correctly, she knows much less than she did in the case *hyperI*, where we began, where early exit leaked the length of the longest matching prefix.

```
basicR :: Int → Kuifje SP
basicR n =
    update (λs → return (s.l := [0 .. n − 1]))⨾        — l := [0, ... , n − 1];
    update (λs → return (s.ans := True))⨾              — ans := true;
    while (λs → return (s.ans ∧ not (null (s.l))))     — while (ans ∧ l ≠ [ ]) do
    (                                                  — begin
        update (λs → uniform [s.i := j | j ← s.l])⨾    —     i := uniform (l);
        (update (λs → return (s.ans :=                 —     ans:=
            (s.ans ∧ (s.pw !! s.i) ≡ (s.gs !! s.i)))))⨾ —         ans ∧ (pw [i] = gs [i]);
        (update (λs → return (s.l := (s.l \\ [s.i])))) —         l := l − {i}
    )⨾                                                 — end;
    observe (λs → return (s.ans))                      — observe ans
```

Figure 12.15 Randomized password checker

$$hyperR \; pw \; gs = projectPw \; (sem_{DD} \; (basicR \; (length \; pw))) \; (initialDist \; pw \; gs))$$

```
> hyperR "abc" "abc"
1 ÷ 6      1 ÷ 1      "abc"
2 ÷ 3      1 ÷ 6      "acb"
           1 ÷ 6      "bac"
           1 ÷ 4      "bca"
           1 ÷ 4      "cab"
           1 ÷ 6      "cba"
1 ÷ 6      1 ÷ 3      "acb"
           1 ÷ 3      "bac"
           1 ÷ 3      "cba"
```

The difference in security between *basicI* and *basicR* is clearly revealed by taking the conditional Bayes entropy of each, i.e. (as we saw in the *exponential* example) the probability that an adversary will be able to guess the password after running the checker. We find

```
> condEntropy bv (hyperR "abc" "abc")
7 ÷ 18
> condEntropy bv (hyperI "abc" "abc")
1 ÷ 2
```

that is that the chance is $^1/_2$ for the "check in ascending order" version *basicI*, but it is indeed slightly less, at $^7/_{18}$, in the case that the order is random.

For longer passwords, printing the hyper is not so informative; but still we can give the conditional Bayes vulnerability (and other entropies too). We find for example that the obfuscated algorithm, even with its early exit, reduces the probability of guessing the password by half:

> *condEntropy bv* (*hyperI* "abcde" "abcde")

$1 \div 24$

> *condEntropy bv* (*hyperR* "abcde" "abcde")

$13 \div 600$

There are other entropies, of course: one of them is "guessing entropy" which is the average number of tries required to guess the secret: the adversary's strategy is to guess possible secret values one-by-one in decreasing order of their probability. [28]
We define

$ge :: Ord\ a \Rightarrow Dist\ a \rightarrow Prob$

$ge = sum \circ zipWith\ (*)\ [1 ..] \circ sortBy\ (flip\ compare) \circ map\ snd \circ$
    $\quad runD \circ reduction$

and find

> *condEntropy ge* (*hyperR* "abc" "abc")

$7 \div 3$

> *condEntropy ge* (*hyperI* "abc" "abc")

$2 \div 1$

that is that the average number of guesses for a three-character password is just more than in the sequential case, where the average number of guesses is exactly 2.
For five-character passwords (of which there are 5! = 120) we find

> *condEntropy ge* (*hyperR* "abcde" "abcde")

$5729 \div 120$

> *condEntropy ge* (*hyperI* "abcde" "abcde")

$1613 \div 40$

that is about 47 guesses for the obfuscated version, on average, versus about 40 guesses for the sequential version. For six-character passwords we find

> *condEntropy bv* (*hyperI* "abcdef" "abcdef")

$1 \div 120$

> *condEntropy bv* (*hyperR* "abcdef" "abcdef")

$3 \div 800$

> *condEntropy ge* (*hyperI* "abcdef" "abcdef")

$20571 \div 80$

> *condEntropy ge* (*hyperR* "abcdef" "abcdef")

$214171 \div 720$

[28] This does not mean that the adversary runs the password checker many times: rather it means that she runs it once (only) and, on the basis of what she learns, makes successive guesses "on paper" as to what the password actually is.

```
basicS :: Int → Kuifje SP
basicS n =
    update (λs → return (s.l := [0 .. n − 1])) ⸵        — l := [0, . . . , n − 1];
    update (λs → return (s.ans := True)) ⸵              — ans := true;
    while (λs → return (s.ans ∧ not (null (s.l))))      — while (ans ∧ l ≠ [ ]) do
    (                                                   — begin
        update (λs → uniform [s.i := j | j ← s.l]) ⸵    —     i := uniform (l);
        cond (λs → return ((s.pw !! s.i) ≠ (s.gs !! s.i)))  —     if (pw [i] ≠ gs [i])
            (update (λs → return (s.ans := False)))     —         then ans := false
            skip ⸵                                      —         else skip
        (update (λs → return (s.l := (s.l \\ [s.i]))))  —         l := l − {i}
    ) ⸵                                                 — end;
    observe (λs → return (s.ans))                       — observe ans
```

Figure 12.16 Randomized password checker, but with conditional reinstated.

which is about probability 0.008 vs. 0.004 for Bayes vulnerability, and expected guesses 257 vs. 297 for guessing entropy of the sequential vs. randomised versions respectively. Those results suggest that the extra security might not be worth the effort of the obfuscation, at least in these examples.

Finally, we might wonder that – since now we are again allowing an early (though obfuscated) exit – whether there is any longer a reason to replace our original conditional in *basicI* and *basicL* with the "atomic" assignment to *ans* in *basicM* and its successors. After all, now that the loop's exit is (once again) observable, the adversary knows what the "answers" *ans* must have been: a succession of *true*'s and then perhaps a *false*. The randomisation of *i* ensures however that, so to speak, she does not know the questions. Thus (one last time) we re-define our program:

hyperS pw gs = projectPw (sem$_{DD}$ (basicS (length pw)) (initialDist pw gs))

```
> hyperS "abc" "abc"
1 ÷ 6     1 ÷ 1     "abc"
2 ÷ 3     1 ÷ 6     "acb"
          1 ÷ 6     "bac"
          1 ÷ 4     "bca"
          1 ÷ 4     "cab"
          1 ÷ 6     "cba"
1 ÷ 6     1 ÷ 3     "acb"
          1 ÷ 3     "bac"
          1 ÷ 3     "cba"
```

And indeed we find replacing the conditional seems to offer no extra security.

References

Alvim, Mário S., Chatzikokolakis, Kostas, Palamidessi, Catuscia, and Smith, Geoffrey. 2012 (June). Measuring Information Leakage using Generalized Gain Functions. Pages 265–279 of: *Proc. 25th IEEE Computer Security Foundations Symposium (CSF 2012)*.

Baum, L. E., and Petrie, T. 1966. Statistical Inference for Probabilistic Functions of Finite State Markov Chains. *The Annals of Mathematical Statistics*, **37**(6), 1554–1563.

Chatzikokolakis, Konstantinos, Palamidessi, Catuscia, and Panangaden, Prakash. 2008. Anonymity protocols as noisy channels. *Information and Computation*, **206**(2), 378–401. Joint Workshop on Foundations of Computer Security and Automated Reasoning for Security Protocol Analysis (FCS-ARSPA 06).

Clark, D., Hunt, S., and Malacaria, P. 2005a. Quantitative Information Flow, Relations and Polymorphic Types. *J. Logic and Computation*, **15**(2), 181–199.

Clark, David, Hunt, Sebastian, and Malacaria, Pasquale. 2005b. Quantified Interference for a While Language. *Electr. Notes Theor. Comput. Sci.*, **112**, 149–166.

Cohen, E.S. 1977. Information Transmission in Sequential Programs. *ACM SIGOPS Operatings Systems Review*, **11**(5), 133–9.

Denning, Dorothy. 1982. *Cryptography and Data Security*. Reading: Addison-Wesley.

Erwig, Martin, and Kollmansberger, Steve. 2006. Probabilistic Functional Programming in Haskell. *Journal of Functional Programming*, **16**(1), 21–34.

Feller, W. 1971. *An Introduction to Probability Theory and its Applications*. second edn. Vol. 2. Wiley.

Gibbons, Jeremy. 2013. Functional Programming for Domain-Specific Languages. Pages 1–28 of: Zsók, Viktória, Horváth, Zoltán, and Csató, Lehel (eds), *Central European Functional Programming School*. Lecture Notes in Computer Science, vol. 8606. Springer.

Gibbons, Jeremy, and Hinze, Ralf. 2011 (Sept.). Just do It: Simple Monadic Equational Reasoning. Pages 2–14 of: *International Conference on Functional Programming*.

Giry, Michèle. 1981. A Categorical Approach to Probability Theory. In: Banachewski, B. (ed), *Categorical Aspects of Topology and Analysis*. Lecture Notes in Mathematics, vol. 915. Springer.

Goguen, J.A., and Meseguer, J. 1984. Unwinding and Inference Control. Pages 75–86 of: *Proc. IEEE Symp on Security and Privacy*. IEEE Computer Society.

Gray, J.W. 1990. Probabilistic interference. Pages 170–179 of: *IEEE Symposium on Security and Privacy*.

Hudak, Paul. 1996. Building Domain-Specific Embedded Languages. *ACM Computing Surveys*, **28**(4es), 196.

Hughes, John. 2000. Generalising Monads to Arrows. *Science of Computer Programming*, **37**(1-3), 67–111.

Hutton, Graham. 1999. A Tutorial on the Universality and Expressiveness of Fold. *Journal of Functional Programming*, **9**(4), 355–372.

Jones, Claire, and Plotkin, Gordon D. 1989. A Probabilistic Powerdomain of Evaluations. Pages 186–195 of: *Logic in Computer Science*. IEEE Computer Society.

Kiselyov, Oleg, and Shan, Chung-chieh. 2009. Embedded Probabilistic Programming. Pages 360–384 of: Taha, Walid Mohamed (ed), *IFIP TC2 Working Conference on Domain-Specific Languages*. Lecture Notes in Computer Science, vol. 5658. Springer.

Kozen, D. 1983. A Probabilistic PDL. Pages 291–7 of: *Proceedings of the 15th ACM Symposium on Theory of Computing*. New York: ACM.

Kozen, Dexter. 1981. Semantics of Probabilistic Programs. *Journal of Computer and System Sciences*, **22**(3), 328–350.

Lawvere, F. William. 1962. *The Category of Probabilistic Mappings*. Manuscript.

Malcolm, Grant. 1990. Data Structures and Program Transformation. *Science of Computer Programming*, **14**(2-3), 255–279.

McIver, A.K., and Morgan, C.C. 2005. *Abstraction, Refinement and Proof for Probabilistic Systems*. Monographs in Computer Science. New York: Springer Verlag.

McIver, Annabelle, Meinicke, Larissa, and Morgan, Carroll. 2010. Compositional Closure for Bayes Risk in Probabilistic Noninterference. Pages 223–235 of: *Automata, Languages and Programming, 37th International Colloquium, ICALP 2010, Bordeaux, France, July 6-10, 2010, Proceedings, Part II*.

McIver, Annabelle, Morgan, Carroll, Smith, Geoffrey, Espinoza, Barbara, and Meinicke, Larissa. 2014a. Abstract Channels and Their Robust Information-Leakage Ordering. Pages 83–102 of: Abadi, Martín, and Kremer, Steve (eds), *Principles of Security and Trust - Third International Conference, POST 2014, Held as Part of the European Joint Conferences on Theory and Practice of Software, ETAPS 2014, Grenoble, France, April 5-13, 2014, Proceedings*. Lecture Notes in Computer Science, vol. 8414. Springer.

McIver, Annabelle, Meinicke, Larissa, and Morgan, Carroll. 2014b. Hidden-Markov Program Algebra with Iteration. *Mathematical Structures in Computer Science*.

McIver, Annabelle, Morgan, Carroll, and Rabehaja, Tahiry. 2015. Abstract Hidden Markov Models: a monadic account of quantitative information flow. In: *Proc. LiCS 2015*.

Millen, J. K. 1987 (April). Covert Channel Capacity. Pages 60–60 of: *1987 IEEE Symposium on Security and Privacy*.

Moggi, Eugenio. 1991. Notions of Computation and Monads. *Information and Computation*, **93**(1).

Morgan, C.C. 2006. *The Shadow Knows:* Refinement of Ignorance in Sequential Programs. Pages 359–78 of: *Math Prog Construction*.

Morgan, C.C. 2009. *The Shadow Knows:* Refinement of Ignorance in Sequential Programs. *Science of Computer Programming*, **74**(8), 629–653.

Peyton Jones, Simon L. 2003. The Haskell 98 Language. *Journal of Functional Programming*, **13**.

Pieters, Ruben, Schrijvers, Tom, and Rivas, Exequiel. 2017. Handlers for Non-Monadic Computations. In: *Implementation and Application of Functional Programming Languages*.

Pretnar, Matija. 2015. An Introduction to Algebraic Effects and Handlers. *Electronic Notes in Theoretical Computer Science*, **319**, 19–35.

Ramsey, Norman, and Pfeffer, Avi. 2002. Stochastic Lambda Calculus and Monads of Probability Distributions. Pages 154–165 of: Launchbury, John, and Mitchell, John C. (eds), *Principles of Programming Languages*. ACM.

Rivas, Exequiel, and Jaskelioff, Mauro. 2017. Notions of Computation as Monoids. *Journal of Functional Programming*, **27**, e21.

Rosenhouse, Jason. 2009. *The Monty Hall Problem: The Remarkable Story of Math's Most Contentious Brain Teaser.* Oxford University Press.

Shannon, C.E. 1948. A mathematical theory of communication. *Bell System Technical Journal*, **27**, 379–423, 623–656.

Smith, Geoffrey. 2009. On the Foundations of Quantitative Information Flow. Pages 288–302 of: de Alfaro, Luca (ed), *Proc. 12th International Conference on Foundations of Software Science and Computational Structures (FoSSaCS '09)*. Lecture Notes in Computer Science, vol. 5504.

Wadler, Philip. 1992. Monads for Functional Programming. In: Broy, Manfred (ed), *Program Design Calculi: Proceedings of the Marktoberdorf Summer School*.

Walter, Colin D. 2002. MIST: An Efficient, Randomized Exponentiation Algorithm for Resisting Power Analysis. Pages 53–66 of: *Topics in Cryptology - CT-RSA 2002, The Cryptographer's Track at the RSA Conference, 2002, San Jose, CA, USA, February 18-22, 2002, Proceedings.*

13

Luck: A Probabilistic Language for Testing

Lampropoulos Leonidas, Benjamin C. Pierce and Li-yao Xia
University of Pennsylvania
Diane Gallois-Wong and Cătălin Hriţcu
INRIA Paris
John Hughes
Chalmers University

Abstract: Property-based random testing *à la* QuickCheck requires building efficient generators for well-distributed random data satisfying complex logical predicates, but writing these generators can be difficult and error prone. This chapter introduces a probabilistic domain-specific language in which generators are conveniently expressed by decorating predicates with lightweight annotations to control both the distribution of generated values and the amount of constraint solving that happens before each variable is instantiated. This language, called *Luck*, makes generators easier to write, read, and maintain.

We give Luck a probabilistic formal semantics and prove several fundamental properties, including the soundness and completeness of random generation with respect to a standard predicate semantics. We evaluate Luck on common examples from the property-based testing literature and on two significant case studies, showing that it can be used in complex domains with comparable bug-finding effectiveness and a significant reduction in testing code size compared to handwritten generators.

13.1 Introduction

Since being popularized by QuickCheck (Claessen and Hughes, 2000), property-based random testing has become a standard technique for improving software quality in a wide variety of programming languages (Arts *et al.*, 2008; Lindblad, 2007; Hughes, 2007; Pacheco and Ernst, 2007) and for streamlining interaction with proof assistants (Chamarthi *et al.*, 2011; Bulwahn, 2012a; Owre, 2006; Dybjer *et al.*, 2003; Paraskevopoulou *et al.*, 2015).

When using a property-based random testing tool, one writes *properties* in the form of executable predicates. For example, a natural property to test for a list

[a] From *Foundations of Probabilistic Programming*, edited by Gilles Barthe, Joost-Pieter Katoen and Alexandra Silva published 2020 by Cambridge University Press.

reverse function is that, for any list xs, reversing xs twice yields xs again. In QuickCheck notation:

```
prop_reverse xs  =   (reverse (reverse xs) == xs)
```

To test this property, QuickCheck generates random lists until either it finds a counterexample or a predetermined number of tests succeed.

An appealing feature of QuickCheck is that it offers a library of property combinators resembling standard logical operators. For example, a property of the form p ==> q, built using the implication combinator ==>, will be tested automatically by generating *valuations* (assignments of random values, of appropriate type, to the free variables of p and q), discarding those valuations that fail to satisfy p, and checking whether any of the ones that remain are counterexamples to q.

QuickCheck users soon learn that this default generate-and-test approach sometimes does not give satisfactory results. In particular, if the precondition p is satisfied by relatively few values of the appropriate type, then most of the random inputs that QuickCheck generates will be discarded, so that q will seldom be exercised. Consider, for example, testing a simple property of a school database system: that every student in a list of registeredStudents should be taking at least one course,

```
prop_registered studentId =
  member studentId registeredStudents ==>
  countCourses studentId > 0
```

where, as usual:

```
member x [] = False
member x (h:t) = (x == h) || member x t
```

If the space of possible student ids is large (e.g., because they are represented as machine integers), then a randomly generated id is very unlikely to be a member of registeredStudents, so almost all test cases will be discarded.

To enable effective testing in such cases, the QuickCheck user can provide a *generator*, a probabilistic program that produces inputs satisfying p – here, a generator that always returns student ids drawn from the members of registeredStudents. Indeed, QuickCheck provides a library of combinators for defining such generators. These combinators also allow fine control over the *distribution* of generated values – a crucial feature in practice (Claessen and Hughes, 2000; Hriţcu *et al.*, 2013; Groce *et al.*, 2012).

Custom generators work well for small to medium-sized examples, but writing them can become challenging as p gets more complex – sometimes turning into a research contribution in its own right! For example, papers have been written about random generation techniques for well-typed lambda-terms (Pałka *et al.*, 2011; Fetscher *et al.*, 2015; Tarau, 2015) and for "indistinguishable" machine states that can be used for finding bugs in information-flow monitors (Hriţcu *et al.*, 2013, 2016). Moreover, if we aim to test an *invariant* property (e.g., type preservation), then the same condition will appear in both the precondition and the conclusion of the property, requiring that we express this condition both as a boolean predicate p and as a generator whose outputs all satisfy p. These two artifacts must then be kept in sync, which can become both a maintenance issue and a rich source of confusion in the testing process. These difficulties are not hypothetical: Hriţcu *et al.*'s machine-state generator (Hriţcu *et al.*, 2013) is over 1500 lines of tricky Haskell, while Pałka *et al.*'s generator for well-typed lambda-terms (Pałka *et al.*, 2011) is over 1600 even trickier ones. To enable effective property-based random testing of complex software artifacts, we need a better way of writing predicates and corresponding generators.

A natural idea is to derive an efficient generator for a given predicate p directly from p itself. Indeed, two variants of this idea, with complementary strengths and weaknesses, have been explored by others – one based on local choices and backtracking, one on general constraint solving. Our language, Luck, synergistically combines these two approaches.

The first approach can be thought of as a kind of incremental generate-and-test: rather than generating completely random valuations and then testing them against p, we instead walk over the structure of p, instantiating each unknown variable x at the first point where we meet a constraint involving x. In the member example above, on each recursive call, we make a random choice between the branches of the | |. If we choose the left, we instantiate x to the head of the list; otherwise we leave x unknown and continue with the recursive call to member on the tail. This has the effect of traversing the list of registered students and picking one of its elements. It is important to carefully control the probabilities guiding this choice to avoid getting a distribution which is very skewed towards early elements.

This process resembles *narrowing* from functional logic programming (Antoy, 2000; Hanus, 1997; Lindblad, 2007; Tolmach and Antoy, 2003). It is attractively lightweight, admits natural control over distributions (as we will see in the next section), and has been used successfully (Fischer and Kuchen, 2007; Christiansen and Fischer, 2008; Reich *et al.*, 2011; Gligoric *et al.*, 2010), even in challenging domains such as generating well-typed programs to test compilers (Claessen *et al.*, 2014; Fetscher *et al.*, 2015).

However, choosing a value for an unknown when we encounter the *first* constraint on it risks making choices that do not satisfy *later* constraints, forcing us to backtrack and make a different choice when the problem is discovered. For example, consider the notMember predicate:

```
notMember x []      =   True
notMember x (h:t)   =   (x /= h) && notMember x t
```

Suppose we wish to generate values for x such that notMember x ys for some given list ys. When we first encounter the constraint x /= h, we generate a value for x that is not equal to the known value h. We then proceed to the recursive call of notMember, where we *check* that the chosen x does not appear in the list's tail. Since the values in the tail are not taken into account when choosing x, this may force us to backtrack if our choice of x was unlucky. If the space of possible values for x is not much bigger than the length of ys – say, just twice as big – then we will backtrack 50% of the time. Worse yet, if notMember is used to define another predicate – e.g., distinct, which tests whether each element of an input list is different from all the others – and we want to generate a list satisfying distinct, then notMember's 50% chance of backtracking will be compounded on each recursive call, leading to unacceptably low rates of successful generation.

The second existing approach uses a *constraint solver* to generate a diverse set of valuations satisfying a predicate.[1] This approach has been widely investigated, both for generating inputs directly from predicates (Carlier *et al.*, 2010; Seidel *et al.*, 2015; Gotlieb, 2009; Köksal *et al.*, 2011) and for symbolic-execution-based testing (Godefroid *et al.*, 2005; Sen *et al.*, 2005; Cadar *et al.*, 2008; Avgerinos *et al.*, 2014; Torlak and Bodík, 2014), which additionally uses the system under test to guide generation of inputs that exercise different control-flow paths. For notMember, gathering a set of disequality constraints on x before choosing its value avoids any backtracking.

However, *pure* constraint-solving approaches do not give us everything we need. They do not provide effective control over the distribution of generated valuations. At best, they might guarantee a *uniform* (or near uniform) distribution (Chakraborty *et al.*, 2014), but this is typically not the distribution we want in practice (see Section 13.2). Moreover, the overhead of maintaining and solving constraints can make these approaches significantly less efficient than the more lightweight, local approach of needed narrowing when the latter does not lead to backtracking, as for instance in member.

The complementary strengths and weaknesses of local instantiation and global constraint solving suggest a hybrid approach, where limited constraint propagation, under explicit user control, is used to refine the domains (sets of possible values) of unknowns before instantiation. This chapter explores such an approach by introducing

---

[1] Constraint solvers can, of course, be used to *directly* search for counterexamples to a property of interest by software model checking (Blanchette and Nipkow, 2010; Jackson, 2011; Ball *et al.*, 2011; Jhala and Majumdar, 2009, etc.). We are interested here in the rather different task of quickly generating a large number of diverse inputs, so that we can thoroughly test systems like compilers whose state spaces are too large to be exhaustively explored.

a probabilistic domain-specific language, *Luck*, for writing generators via lightweight annotations on predicates. In Section 13.2 we illustrate Luck's novel features using binary search trees as an example. We also place Luck's design on a firm formal foundation, by defining a probabilistic core calculus and establishing key properties: the soundness and completeness of its probabilistic generator semantics with respect to a straightforward interpretation of expressions as predicates (Section 13.3).

Finally, we provide a prototype interpreter (Section 13.4) using a custom constraint solver that supports per-variable sampling. We evaluate Luck's expressiveness on a collection of common examples from the random testing literature (Section 13.5) and on two significant case studies, demonstrating that Luck can be used (1) to find bugs in a widely used compiler (GHC) by randomly generating well-typed lambda terms and (2) to help design information-flow abstract machines by generating "low-indistinguishable" machine states.

This chapter is accompanied by several auxiliary materials: (1) a Coq formalization of the narrowing semantics of Luck and machine-checked proofs of its properties (available at `https://github.com/QuickChick/Luck`) (Section 13.3.3); (2) the prototype Luck interpreter and a battery of example programs, including all the ones we used for evaluation (also at `https://github.com/QuickChick/Luck`) (Section 13.5); (3) an extended version of the paper this chapter is based on (Lampropoulos *et al.*, 2017) with full definitions and paper proofs for the whole semantics (`https://arxiv.org/abs/1607.05443`).

13.2 Luck by Example

Figure 13.1 shows a recursive Haskell predicate `bst` that checks whether a given tree with labels strictly between `low` and `high` satisfies the standard binary-search tree (BST) invariant (Okasaki, 1999). It is followed by a QuickCheck generator `genTree`, which generates BSTs with a given maximum depth, controlled by the `size` parameter. This generator first checks whether `low + 1 >= high`, in which case it returns the only valid BST satisfying this constraint – the `Empty` one. Otherwise, it uses QuickCheck's `frequency` combinator, which takes a list of pairs of positive integer weights and associated generators and randomly selects one of the generators using the probabilities specified by the weights. In this example, $\frac{1}{size+1}$ of the time it creates an `Empty` tree, while $\frac{size}{size+1}$ of the time it returns a `Node`. The `Node` generator is specified using monadic syntax: first it generates an integer `x` that is strictly between `low` and `high`, and then the left and right subtrees `l` and `r` by calling `genTree` recursively; finally it returns `Node x l r`.

The generator for BSTs allows us to efficiently test conditional properties of the form "if `bst` t then ⟨*some other property of* t⟩," but it raises some new issues of its own. First, even for this simple example, getting the generator right is a bit tricky

Binary tree datatype (in both Haskell and Luck):

```
data Tree a = Empty | Node a (Tree a) (Tree a)
```

Test predicate for BSTs (in Haskell):

```
bst :: Int -> Int -> Tree Int -> Bool
bst low high tree =
  case tree of
    Empty -> True
    Node x l r ->
      low < x && x < high
      && bst low x l && bst x high r
```

QuickCheck generator for BSTs (in Haskell):

```
genTree :: Int -> Int -> Int -> Gen (Tree Int)
genTree size low high
  | low + 1 >= high = return Empty
  | otherwise =
      frequency [(1, return Empty),
                 (size, do
                   x <- choose (low + 1, high - 1)
                   l <- genTree (size `div` 2) low x
                   r <- genTree (size `div` 2) x high
                   return (Node x l r))]
```

Luck generator (and predicate) for BSTs:

```
sig bst :: Int -> Int -> Int -> Tree Int -> Bool
fun bst size low high tree =
  if size == 0 then tree == Empty
  else case tree of
        | 1     % Empty -> True
        | size % Node x l r ->
          ((low < x && x < high) !x)
          && bst (size / 2) low x l
          && bst (size / 2) x high r
```

Figure 13.1 Binary Search Tree tester and two generators

(for instance because of potential off-by-one errors in generating x), and it is not immediately obvious that the set of trees generated by the generator is exactly the set accepted by the predicate. Worse, we now need to maintain two similar but distinct artifacts and keep them in sync. We can't just throw away the predicate and keep the generator because we often need them both, for example to test properties like "the `insert` function applied to a BST and a value returns a BST." As predicates and generators become more complex, these issues can become quite problematic (e.g., Hriţcu *et al.*, 2013). Enter Luck.

The bottom of Figure 13.1 shows a Luck program that represents *both* a BST predicate *and* a generator for random BSTs. Modulo variations in concrete syntax, the Luck closely code follows the Haskell `bst` predicate. The significant differences are: (1) the *sample-after expression* `!x`, which controls when node labels are generated, and (2) the `size` parameter, which is used, as in the generator, to annotate the branches of the `case` with relative weights. Together, these enable us to give the program both a natural interpretation as a predicate (by simply ignoring weights and sampling expressions) and an efficient interpretation as a generator of random trees with the same distribution as the QuickCheck version. For example, evaluating the top-level query `bst 10 0 42 u = True` – i.e., "generate values `t` for the unknown `u` such that `bst 10 0 42 t` evaluates to `True`" – will yield random binary search trees of size up to 10 with node labels strictly between 0 and 42, with the same distribution as the QuickCheck generator `genTree 10 0 42`.

An *unknown* in Luck is a special kind of value, similar to logic variables found in logic programming languages and unification variables used by type-inference algorithms. Unknowns are typed, and each is associated with a domain of possible values from its type. Given an expression *e* mentioning some set *U* of unknowns, our goal is to generate *valuations* over these unknowns (maps from *U* to concrete values) by iteratively refining the unknowns' domains, so that, when any of these valuations is substituted into *e*, the resulting concrete term evaluates to a desired value (e.g., `True`).

Unknowns can be introduced both explicitly, as in the top-level query above (see also Section 13.4), and implicitly, as in the generator semantics of `case` expressions. In the `bst` example, when the `Node` branch is chosen, the pattern variables `x`, `l`, and `r` are replaced by fresh unknowns, which are then instantiated by evaluating the body of the branch.

Varying the placement of unknowns in the top-level `bst` query yields different behaviors. For instance, if we change the query to `bst 10 ul uh u = True`, replacing the `low` and `high` parameters with unknowns `ul` and `uh`, the domains of these unknowns will be refined during tree generation and the result will be a generator for random valuations (`ul ↦ i`, `uh ↦ j`, `u ↦ t`) where `i` and `j` are lower and upper bounds on the node labels in `t`.

Alternatively, we can evaluate the top-level query `bst 10 0 42 t = True`, replacing `u` with a concrete tree `t`. In this case, Luck will return a trivial valuation only if `t` is a binary search tree; otherwise it will report that the query is unsatisfiable. A less useful possibility is that we provide explicit values for `low` and `high` but choose them with `low > high`, e.g., `bst 10 6 4 u = True`. Since there are no satisfying valuations for `u` other than `Empty`, Luck will now generate only `Empty` trees.

A *sample-after expression* of the form `e !x` controls instantiation of unknowns. Typically, `x` will be an unknown `u`, and evaluating `e !u` will cause `u` to be instantiated to a concrete value (after evaluating e to refine the domains of all of the unknowns in e). If x reduces to a value v rather than an unknown, we similarly instantiate any unknowns appearing within v.

As a concrete example, consider the compound inequality constraint 0 < x && x < 4. A generator based on pure narrowing (as in Gligoric *et al.*, 2010), would instantiate x when the evaluator meets the first constraint where it appears, namely 0 < x (assuming left-to-right evaluation order). We can mimic this behavior in Luck by writing ((0 < x) !x) && (x < 4). However, picking a value for x at this point ignores the constraint x < 4, which can lead to backtracking. If, for instance, the domain from which we are choosing values for x is 32-bit integers, then the probability that a random choice satisfying 0 < x will also satisfy x < 4 is minuscule. It is better in this case to write (0 < x && x < 4) !x, instantiating x after the entire conjunction has been evaluated and all the constraints on the domain of x recorded and thus avoiding backtracking completely. Finally, if we do not include a sample-after expression for x here at all, we can further refine its domain with constraints later on, at the cost of dealing with a more abstract representation of it internally in the meantime. Thus, sample-after expressions give Luck users explicit control over the tradeoff between the expense of possible backtracking – when unknowns are instantiated early – and the expense of maintaining constraints on unknowns – so that they can be instantiated late (e.g., so that x can be instantiated after the recursive calls to bst).

Sample-after expressions choose random values with *uniform* probability from the domain associated with each unknown. While this behavior is sometimes useful, effective property-based random testing often requires fine control over the distribution of generated test cases. Drawing inspiration from the QuickCheck combinator library for building complex generators, and particularly frequency (which we saw in genTree (Figure 13.1)), Luck also allows weight annotations on the branches of a case expression which have a frequency-like effect. In the Luck version of bst, for example, the unknown tree is either instantiated to an Empty tree $\frac{1}{1+size}$ of the time or partially instantiated to a Node (with fresh unknowns for x and the left and right subtrees) $\frac{size}{1+size}$ of the time.

Weight annotations give the user control over the probabilities of local choices. These do not necessarily correspond to a specific posterior probability, but the QuickCheck community has established techniques for guiding the user in tuning local weights to obtain good testing. For example, the user can wrap properties inside a collect x combinator; during testing, QuickCheck will gather information on x, grouping equal values to provide an estimate of the posterior distribution that is being sampled. The collect combinator is an effective tool for adjusting frequency weights and dramatically increasing bug-finding rates (e.g., Hriţcu *et al.*, 2013). The Luck implementation provides a similar primitive.

One further remark on uniform sampling: while *locally* instantiating unknowns uniformly from their domain is a useful default, generating *globally* uniform distributions of test cases is usually not what we want, as this often leads to inefficient testing in practice. A simple example comes from the information flow control experiments of Hriţcu *et al.* (2013). There are two "security levels," called *labels*, Low and High, and pairs of integers and labels are considered "indistinguishable" to a Low observer if the labels are equal and, if the labels are Low, so are the integers. In Haskell:

```
indist (v1,High) (v2,High)  =  True
indist (v1,Low ) (v2,Low)   =  v1 == v2
indist _           _        =  False
```

If we use 32-bit integers, then for every Low indistinguishable pair there are 2^{32} High ones! Thus, a uniform distribution over indistinguishable pairs means that we will essentially never generate pairs with Low labels. Clearly, such a distribution cannot provide effective testing; indeed, Hriţcu *et al.* found that the best distribution was somewhat skewed in favor of Low labels.

We can easily validate this intuition using a probabilistic programming framework with emphasis on efficient sampling: R2 (Nori *et al.*, 2014). We can model indistinguishability using the following probabilistic program, where labels are modeled by booleans:

```
double v1 = Uniform.Sample(0, 10);
double v2 = Uniform.Sample(0, 10);
bool l1 = Bernoulli.Sample(0.5);
bool l2 = Bernoulli.Sample(0.5);

Observer.Observe(l1==l2 && (v1==v2 || l1));
```

Two pairs of doubles and booleans will be indistinguishable if the booleans are equal and, if the booleans are false, so are the doubles. As predicted, all generated samples have their booleans set to true. Of course, one could probably come up with a better prior or use a tool that allows arbitrary conditioning to skew the distribution appropriately. If, however, for such a trivial example the choices are non-obvious, imagine replacing pairs of doubles and booleans with arbitrary lambda terms and indistinguishability by a well-typedness relation. Coming up with suitable priors that lead to efficient testing would become an ambitious research problem on its own!

13.3 Semantics of Core Luck

We next present a core calculus for Luck – a minimal subset into which the examples in the previous section can in principle be desugared. The core omits primitive booleans and integers and replaces datatypes with binary sums, products, and iso-recursive types.

We begin in Section 13.3.1 with the syntax and standard *predicate semantics* of the core. (We call it the "predicate" semantics because, in our examples, the result of evaluating a top-level expression will typically be a boolean, though this expectation is not baked into the formalism.) We then build up to the full generator semantics in three steps. First, we give an interface to a *constraint solver* (Section 13.3.2), abstracting over the primitives required to implement our semantics. Then we define a probabilistic *narrowing semantics*, which enhances the local-instantiation approach to random generation with QuickCheck-style distribution control (Section 13.3.3). Finally, we introduce a *matching semantics*, building on the narrowing semantics, that unifies constraint solving and narrowing into a single evaluator (Section 13.3.4). The key properties of the generator semantics (both narrowing and matching versions) are soundness and completeness with respect to the predicate semantics (Section 13.3.6); informally, whenever we use a Luck program to generate a valuation that satisfies some predicate, the valuation will satisfy the boolean predicate semantics (soundness), and it will generate every possible satisfying valuation with non-zero probability (completeness).

13.3.1 Syntax, Typing, and Predicate Semantics

The syntax of Core Luck is given in Figure 13.2. Except for the last line in the definitions of values and expressions, it is a standard simply typed call-by-value lambda calculus with sums, products, and iso-recursive types. We include recursive lambdas for convenience in examples, although in principle they could be encoded using recursive types.

Values include unit, pairs of values, sum constructors (L and R) applied to values (and annotated with types, to eliminate ambiguity), first class recursive functions (*rec*), *fold*-annotated values indicating where an iso-recursive type should be "folded," and *unknowns* drawn from an infinite set. The standard expression forms include variables, unit, functions, function applications, pairs with a single-branch pattern-matching construct for deconstructing them, value tagging (L and R), pattern matching on tagged values, and *fold/unfold*. The nonstandard additions are unknowns (u), *instantiation* ($e \leftarrow (e_1, e_2)$), *sample* ($!e$) and *after* ($e_1 \; ; \; e_2$) expressions.

The "after" operator, written with a backwards semicolon, evaluates both e_1 and e_2 in sequence. However, unlike the standard sequencing operator $e_1; e_2$, the result of $e_1 \; ; \; e_2$ is the result of e_1; the expression e_2 is evaluated just for its side-effects. For example, the sample-after expression e !x of the previous section is desugared

$$v ::= () \mid (v,v) \mid L_T \ v \mid R_T \ v$$
$$\mid \ rec \ (f : T_1 \rightarrow T_2) \ x = e \mid fold_T \ v$$
$$\mid \ u$$
$$e ::= x \mid () \mid rec \ (f : T_1 \rightarrow T_2) \ x = e \mid (e \ e)$$
$$\mid \ (e,e) \mid case \ e \ of \ (x,y) \rightarrow e$$
$$\mid \ L_T \ e \mid R_T \ e \mid case \ e \ of \ (L \ x \rightarrow e) \ (R \ x \rightarrow e)$$
$$\mid \ fold_T \ e \mid unfold_T \ e$$
$$\mid \ u \mid e \leftarrow (e,e) \mid \ !e \mid e \ ; e$$
$$\overline{T} ::= X \mid 1 \mid \overline{T} + \overline{T} \mid \overline{T} \times \overline{T} \mid \mu X. \overline{T}$$
$$T ::= X \mid 1 \mid T + T \mid T \times T \mid \mu X. T \mid T \rightarrow T$$
$$\Gamma ::= \emptyset \mid \Gamma, x : T$$

Figure 13.2 Core Luck Syntax

to a combination of sample and after: $e \ ; \ !x$. If we evaluate this snippet in a context where x is bound to some unknown u, then the expression e is evaluated first, refining the domain of u (amongst other unknowns); then the sample expression $!u$ is evaluated for its side effect, instantiating u to a uniformly generated value from its domain; and finally the result of e is returned as the result of the whole expression. A reasonable way to implement $e_1 \ ; \ e_2$ using standard lambda abstractions would be as $(\lambda x. (\lambda\_. \ x) \ e_2) \ e_1$. However, there is a slight difference in the semantics of this encoding compared to our intended semantics – we will return to this point in Section 13.3.4.

Weight annotations like the ones in the `bst` example can be desugared using *instantiation expressions*. For example, assuming a standard encoding of binary search trees (*Tree* = $\mu X. \ 1 + int \times X \times X$) and naturals, plus syntactic sugar for constant naturals:

$$case \ (unfold_{Tree} \ tree \ < -(1, size)) \ of \ (L \ x \rightarrow \dots)(R \ y \rightarrow \dots)$$

Most of the typing rules are standard (these can be found in the extended version of the paper). The four non-standard rules are given in Figure 13.3. Unknowns are typed: each will be associated with a domain (set of values) drawn from a type $\overline{T}$ that does not contain arrows. Luck does not support constraint solving over functional domains (which would require something like higher-order unification), and the restriction of unknowns to non-functional types reflects this. To remember the types of unknowns, we extend the typing context to include a component U, a map from unknowns to non-functional types. When the variable typing environment $\Gamma = \emptyset$, we write $U \vdash e : T$ as a shorthand for $\emptyset; U \vdash e : T$. An unknown u has type $\overline{T}$ if $U(u) = \overline{T}$. If e_1 and e_2 are well typed, then $e_1 \ ; \ e_2$ shares the type of e_1. An

$$\text{T-U} \quad \frac{U(u) = \overline{T}}{\Gamma; U \vdash u : \overline{T}} \qquad \text{T-After} \quad \frac{\Gamma; U \vdash e_1 : T_1 \quad \Gamma; U \vdash e_2 : T_2}{\Gamma; U \vdash e_1 \mathbin{;} e_2 : T_1}$$

$$\text{T-Bang} \quad \frac{\Gamma; U \vdash e : \overline{T}}{\Gamma; U \vdash {!}e : \overline{T}} \qquad \text{T-Narrow} \quad \frac{\Gamma; U \vdash e : \overline{T}_1 + \overline{T}_2 \quad \Gamma; U \vdash e_l : nat \quad \Gamma \vdash e_r : nat}{\Gamma; U \vdash e \leftarrow (e_l, e_r) : \overline{T}_1 + \overline{T}_2}$$

$$nat := \mu X.\, 1 + X$$

Figure 13.3 Typing Rules for Nonstandard Constructs

$$\text{P-Narrow} \quad \frac{\begin{array}{ccc} e \Downarrow v & e_1 \Downarrow v_1 & e_2 \Downarrow v_2 \\ & [\![v_1]\!] > 0 & [\![v_2]\!] > 0 \end{array}}{e \leftarrow (e_1, e_2) \Downarrow v} \qquad \text{P-Bang} \quad \frac{e \Downarrow v}{!e \Downarrow v}$$

$$\text{P-After} \quad \frac{e_1 \Downarrow v_1 \quad e_2 \Downarrow v_2}{e_1 \mathbin{;} e_2 \Downarrow v_1}$$

$$\begin{aligned} [\![fold_{nat}\, (L_{1+nat}\, ())]\!] &= 0 \\ [\![fold_{nat}\, (R_{1+nat}\, v)]\!] &= 1 + [\![v]\!] \end{aligned}$$

Figure 13.4 Predicate Semantics for Nonstandard Constructs

instantiation expression $e \leftarrow (e_l, e_r)$ is well typed if e has sum type $\overline{T}_1 + \overline{T}_2$ and e_l and e_r are natural numbers. A sample expression $!e$ has the (non-functional) type $\overline{T}$ when e has type $\overline{T}$.

The predicate semantics for Core Luck, written $e \Downarrow v$, are defined as a big-step operational semantics. We assume that e is closed with respect to ordinary variables and free of unknowns. The rules for the standard constructs are unsurprising (see the extended version). The only non-standard rules are the ones for narrow, sample and after expressions, which are essentially ignored (Figure 13.4). With the predicate semantics we can implement a naive generate-and-test method for generating valuations satisfying some predicate by generating arbitrary well-typed valuations and filtering out those for which the predicate does not evaluate to `True`.

13.3.2 Constraint Sets

The rest of this section develops an alternative probabilistic generator semantics for Core Luck. This semantics will use *constraint sets* $\kappa \in C$ to describe the possible values that unknowns can take. For the moment, we leave the implementation of constraint sets open (the one used by our prototype interpreter is described in the extended version of the chapter), simply requiring that they support the following operations:

$$
\begin{array}{llll}
[\![\cdot]\!] & :: & C-> Set\ Valuation \\
U & :: & C-> Map\ \mathcal{U}\ \overline{T} \\
\textit{fresh} & :: & C \to \overline{T}^* \to (C \times \mathcal{U}^*) \\
\textit{unify} & :: & C \to Val \to Val \to C \\
SAT & :: & C \to Bool \\
[\cdot] & :: & C \to \mathcal{U} \to Maybe\ Val \\
\textit{sample} & :: & C \to \mathcal{U} \to C^*
\end{array}
$$

Here we describe these operations informally, deferring technicalities until after we have presented the generator semantics (Section 13.3.6).

A constraint set κ denotes a set of valuations ($[\![\kappa]\!]$), representing the solutions to the constraints. Constraint sets also carry type information about existing unknowns: $U(\kappa)$ is a mapping from κ's unknowns to types. A constraint set κ is *well typed* ($\vdash \kappa$) if, for every valuation σ in the denotation of κ and every unknown u bound in σ, the type map $U(\kappa)$ contains u and $\emptyset; U(\kappa) \vdash \sigma(u) : U(\kappa)(u)$.

Many of the semantic rules will need to introduce fresh unknowns. The *fresh* function takes a constraint set κ and a sequence of (non-functional) types of length k; it draws the next k unknowns (in some deterministic order) from the infinite set $\mathcal{U}$ and extends $U(\kappa)$ with the respective bindings.

The main way constraints are introduced during evaluation is unification. Given a constraint set κ and two values, each potentially containing unknowns, *unify* updates κ to preserve only those valuations in which the values match.

SAT is a total predicate that holds on constraint sets whose denotation contains at least one valuation. The totality requirement implies that our constraints must be decidable.

The value-extraction function $\kappa[u]$ returns an optional (non-unknown) value: if in the denotation of κ, all valuations map u to the same value v, then that value is returned (written $\{v\}$); otherwise nothing (written $\emptyset$).

The *sample* operation is used to implement sample expressions ($!e$): given a constraint set κ and an unknown $u \in U(\kappa)$, it returns a list of constraint sets representing all possible concrete choices for u, in all of which u is completely determined – that is $\forall \kappa \in (sample\ \kappa\ u). \exists v.\ \kappa[u] = \{v\}$. To allow for reasonable implementations of this interface, we maintain an invariant that the input unknown to *sample* will always have a finite denotation; thus, the resulting list is also finite.

13.3.3 Narrowing Semantics

As a first step toward a probabilistic semantics for Core Luck that incorporates both constraint solving and local instantiation, we define a simpler *narrowing* semantics.

This semantics is of some interest in its own right, in that it extends traditional "needed narrowing" with explicit probabilistic instantiation points, but its role here is as a subroutine of the matching semantics in Section 13.3.4.

The narrowing evaluation judgment takes as inputs an expression e and a constraint set κ. As in the predicate semantics, evaluating e returns a value v, but now it also depends on a constraint set κ and returns a new constraint set κ'. The latter is intuitively a refinement of κ – i.e., evaluation will only remove valuations.

$$e \dashv \kappa \Downarrow_q^t \kappa' \vDash v$$

The semantics is annotated with a representation of the sequence of random choices made during evaluation, in the form of a *trace* t. A trace is a sequence of *choices*: integer pairs (m, n) with $0 \leq m < n$, where n denotes the number of possibilities chosen among and m is the index of the one actually taken. We write ϵ for the empty trace and $t \cdot t'$ for the concatenation of two traces. We also annotate the judgment with the probability q of making the choices represented in the trace. Recording traces is useful after the fact in calculating the total probability of some given outcome of evaluation (which may be reached by many different derivations), but they play no role in determining how evaluation proceeds.

We maintain the invariant that both the input constraint set κ and the input expression e are well typed, the latter with respect to an empty variable context and unknown context $U(\kappa)$. Another invariant is that every constraint set κ that appears as input to a judgment is satisfiable and the restriction of its denotation to the unknowns in e is finite. These invariants are established at the top-level (see Section 13.4). The finiteness invariant ensures the output of *sample* will always be a finite collection and therefore the probabilities involved will be positive rational numbers. They also guarantee termination of constraint solving, as we will see in Section 13.3.4. Finally, we assume that the type of every expression has been determined by an initial type-checking phase. We write e^T to show that e has type T. This information is used in the semantic rules to type fresh unknowns.

The narrowing semantics is given in Figure 13.5 for the standard constructs (omitting *fold/unfold* and **N-R** and **N-Case-R** rules analogous to the **N-L** and **N-Case-L** rules shown) and in Figure 13.6 for instantiation expressions; Figure 13.8 and Figure 13.7 give some auxiliary definitions. Most of the rules are intuitive. A common pattern is sequencing two narrowing judgments $e_1 \dashv \kappa \Downarrow_{q_1}^{t_1} \kappa_1 \vDash v$ and $e_2 \dashv \kappa_1 \Downarrow_{q_2}^{t_2} \kappa_2 \vDash v$. The constraint-set result of the first narrowing judgment (κ_1) is given as input to the second, while traces and probabilities are accumulated by concatenation ($t_1 \cdot t_2$) and multiplication ($q_1 * q_2$). We now explain the rules in detail.

Rule **N-Base** is the base case of the evaluation relation, handling values that are not handled by other rules by returning them as-is. No choices are made, so the probability of the result is 1 and the trace is empty.

$$\textbf{N-Base} \quad \frac{v = ()\ \vee\ v = (rec\ (f : T_1 \to T_2)\ x = e')\ \vee\ v \in \mathcal{U}}{v \dashv \kappa \Downarrow_1^\epsilon \kappa \vDash v}$$

$$\textbf{N-Pair} \quad \frac{e_1 \dashv \kappa \Downarrow_{q_1}^{t_1} \kappa_1 \vDash v_1 \qquad e_2 \dashv \kappa_1 \Downarrow_{q_2}^{t_2} \kappa_2 \vDash v_2}{(e_1, e_2) \dashv \kappa \Downarrow_{q_1 * q_2}^{t_1 \cdot t_2} \kappa_2 \vDash (v_1, v_2)}$$

$$\textbf{N-CasePair-P} \quad \frac{e \dashv \kappa \Downarrow_q^t \kappa_a \vDash (v_1, v_2) \qquad e'[v_1/x, v_2/y] \dashv \kappa_a \Downarrow_{q'}^{t'} \kappa' \vDash v}{case\ e\ of\ (x, y) \to e' \dashv \kappa \Downarrow_{q*q'}^{t \cdot t'} \kappa' \vDash v}$$

$$\textbf{N-CasePair-U} \quad \frac{\begin{array}{c} e \dashv \kappa \Downarrow_q^t \kappa_a \vDash u \\ (\kappa_b, [u_1, u_2]) = fresh\ \kappa_a\ [\overline{T}_1, \overline{T}_2] \\ \kappa_c = unify\ \kappa_b\ (u_1, u_2)\ u \\ e'[u_1/x, u_2/y] \dashv \kappa_c \Downarrow_{q'}^{t'} \kappa' \vDash v \end{array}}{case\ e^{\overline{T}_1 \times \overline{T}_2}\ of\ (x, y) \to e' \dashv \kappa \Downarrow_{q*q'}^{t \cdot t'} \kappa' \vDash v}$$

$$\textbf{N-L} \quad \frac{e \dashv \kappa \Downarrow_q^t \kappa' \vDash v}{L_{T_1 + T_2}\ e \dashv \kappa \Downarrow_q^t \kappa' \vDash L_{T_1 + T_2}\ v}$$

$$\textbf{N-Case-L} \quad \frac{e \dashv \kappa \Downarrow_q^t \kappa_a \vDash L_T\ v_l \qquad e_l[v_l/x_l] \dashv \kappa_a \Downarrow_{q'}^{t'} \kappa' \vDash v}{case\ e\ of\ (L\ x_l \to e_l)(R\ x_r \to e_r) \dashv \kappa \Downarrow_{q*q'}^{t \cdot t'} \kappa' \vDash v}$$

$$\textbf{N-Case-U} \quad \frac{\begin{array}{c} e \dashv \kappa \Downarrow_{q_1}^{t_1} \kappa_a \vDash u \\ (\kappa_0, [u_l, u_r]) = fresh\ \kappa_a\ [\overline{T}_l, \overline{T}_r] \\ \kappa_l = unify\ \kappa_0\ u\ (L_{\overline{T}_l | \overline{T}_r}\ u_l) \qquad \kappa_r = unify\ \kappa_0\ u\ (R_{\overline{T}_l + \overline{T}_r}\ u_r) \\ choose\ 1\ \kappa_l\ 1\ \kappa_r \to_{q_2}^{t_2} i \\ e_i[u_i/x_i] \dashv \kappa_i \Downarrow_{q_3}^{t_3} \kappa' \vDash v \end{array}}{case\ e^{\overline{T}_l + \overline{T}_r}\ of\ (L\ x_l \to e_l)(R\ x_r \to e_r) \dashv \kappa \Downarrow_{q_1 * q_2 * q_3}^{t_1 \cdot t_2 \cdot t_3} \kappa' \vDash v}$$

$$\textbf{N-App} \quad \frac{\begin{array}{c} e_0 \dashv \kappa \Downarrow_{q_0}^{t_0} \kappa_a \vDash (rec\ (f : T_1 \to T_2)\ x = e_2) \\ e_1 \dashv \kappa_a \Downarrow_{q_1}^{t_1} \kappa_b \vDash v_1 \\ e_2[(rec\ (f : T_1 \to T_2)\ x = e_2)/f, v_1/x] \dashv \kappa_b \Downarrow_{q_2}^{t_2} \kappa' \vDash v \end{array}}{(e_0\ e_1) \dashv \kappa \Downarrow_{q_0 * q_1 * q_2}^{t_0 \cdot t_1 \cdot t_2} \kappa' \vDash v}$$

Figure 13.5 Narrowing Semantics of Standard Core Luck Constructs

$$\textbf{N-After} \quad \frac{e_1 \dashv \kappa \Downarrow^{t_1}_{q_1} \kappa_1 \vDash v_1 \quad e_2 \dashv \kappa_1 \Downarrow^{t_2}_{q_2} \kappa_2 \vDash v_2}{e_1 \,;\, e_2 \dashv \kappa \Downarrow^{t_1 \cdot t_2}_{q_1 * q_2} \kappa_2 \vDash v_1}$$

$$\textbf{N-Bang} \quad \frac{e \dashv \kappa \Downarrow^{t}_{q} \kappa_a \vDash v \quad sampleV \; \kappa_a \; v \Rightarrow^{t'}_{q'} \kappa'}{!e \dashv \kappa \Downarrow^{t \cdot t'}_{q * q'} \kappa' \vDash v}$$

$$\textbf{N-Narrow} \quad \frac{\begin{array}{c} e \dashv \kappa \Downarrow^{t}_{q} \kappa_a \vDash v \\ e_1 \dashv \kappa_a \Downarrow^{t_1}_{q_1} \kappa_b \vDash v_1 \qquad\qquad e_2 \dashv \kappa_b \Downarrow^{t_2}_{q_2} \kappa_c \vDash v_2 \\ sampleV \; \kappa_c \; v_1 \Rightarrow^{t'_1}_{q'_1} \kappa_d \qquad\qquad sampleV \; \kappa_d \; v_2 \Rightarrow^{t'_2}_{q'_2} \kappa_e \\ nat_{\kappa_e}(v_1) = n_1 \qquad n_1 > 0 \qquad nat_{\kappa_e}(v_2) = n_2 \qquad n_2 > 0 \\ (\kappa_0, [u_1, u_2]) = fresh \; \kappa_e \; [\overline{T}_1, \overline{T}_2] \\ \kappa_l = unify \; \kappa_0 \; v \; (L_{\overline{T}_1 + \overline{T}_2} \; u_1) \qquad \kappa_r = unify \; \kappa_0 \; v \; (R_{\overline{T}_1 + \overline{T}_2} \; u_2) \\ choose \; n_1 \; \kappa_l \; n_2 \; \kappa_r \rightarrow^{t'}_{q'} i \end{array}}{e^{\overline{T}_1 + \overline{T}_2} < -(e^{nat}_1, e^{nat}_2) \dashv \kappa \Downarrow^{t \cdot t_1 \cdot t_2 \cdot t'_1 \cdot t'_2 \cdot t'}_{q * q_1 * q_2 * q'_1 * q'_2 * q'} \kappa_i \vDash v}$$

Figure 13.6 Narrowing Semantics for Non-Standard Expressions

$$\frac{SAT(\kappa_1) \qquad SAT(\kappa_2)}{choose \; n \; \kappa_1 \; m \; \kappa_2 \rightarrow^{[(0,2)]}_{n/(n+m)} l} \qquad\qquad \frac{\neg SAT(\kappa_1) \qquad SAT(\kappa_2)}{choose \; n \; \kappa_1 \; m \; \kappa_2 \rightarrow^{\epsilon}_{1} r}$$

$$\frac{SAT(\kappa_1) \qquad SAT(\kappa_2)}{choose \; n \; \kappa_1 \; m \; \kappa_2 \rightarrow^{[(1,2)]}_{m/(n+m)} r} \qquad\qquad \frac{SAT(\kappa_1) \qquad \neg SAT(\kappa_2)}{choose \; n \; \kappa_1 \; m \; \kappa_2 \rightarrow^{\epsilon}_{1} l}$$

Figure 13.7 Auxiliary relation *choose*

Rule **N-Pair**: To evaluate (e_1, e_2) given a constraint set κ, we sequence the derivations for e_1 and e_2.

Rules **N-CasePair-P**, **N-CasePair-U**: To evaluate the pair elimination expression *case e of* $(x, y) \rightarrow e'$ in a constraint set κ, we first evaluate e in κ. Typing ensures that the resulting value is either a pair or an unknown. If it is a pair (**N-CasePair-P**), we substitute its components for x and y in e' and continue evaluating. If it is an unknown u of type $\overline{T}_1 \times \overline{T}_2$ (**N-CasePair-U**), we first use $\overline{T}_1$ and $\overline{T}_2$ as types for fresh unknowns u_1, u_2 and remember the constraint that the pair (u_1, u_2) must unify with u. We then proceed as above, this time substituting u_1 and u_2 for x and y.

The first pair rule might appear unnecessary since, even in the case where the scrutinee evaluates to a pair, we could generate unknowns, unify, and substitute, as in **N-CasePair-U**. However, unknowns in Luck only range over non-functional

$$\frac{sample\ \kappa\ u = S \qquad S[m] = \kappa'}{sampleV\ \kappa\ u \Rightarrow^{[(m,|S|)]}_{1/|S|} \kappa'}$$

$$\frac{}{sampleV\ \kappa\ () \Rightarrow^{\epsilon}_{1} \kappa} \qquad \frac{sampleV\ \kappa\ v \Rightarrow^{t}_{q} \kappa'}{sampleV\ \kappa\ (fold_T\ v) \Rightarrow^{t}_{q} \kappa'}$$

$$\frac{sampleV\ \kappa\ v \Rightarrow^{t}_{q} \kappa'}{sampleV\ \kappa\ (L_T\ v) \Rightarrow^{t}_{q} \kappa'} \qquad \frac{sampleV\ \kappa\ v \Rightarrow^{t}_{q} \kappa'}{sampleV\ \kappa\ (R_T\ v) \Rightarrow^{t}_{q} \kappa'}$$

$$\frac{sampleV\ \kappa\ v_1 \Rightarrow^{t_1}_{q_1} \kappa_1 \qquad sampleV\ \kappa_1\ v_2 \Rightarrow^{t_2}_{q_2} \kappa'}{sampleV\ \kappa\ (v_1, v_2) \Rightarrow^{t_1 \cdot t_2}_{q_1 * q_2} \kappa'}$$

Figure 13.8 Auxiliary relation *sampleV*

types $\overline{T}$, so this trick does not work when the type of the e contains arrows. The **N-CasePair-U** rule also shows how the finiteness invariant is preserved: when we generate the unknowns u_1 and u_2, their domains are unconstrained, but before we substitute them into an expression used as "input" to a subderivation, we unify them with the result of a narrowing derivation, which already has a finite representation in κ_a.

Rule **N-L**: To evaluate $L_{T_1+T_2}\ e$, we evaluate e and tag the resulting value with $L_{T_1+T_2}$, with the resulting constraint set, trace, and probability unchanged. $R_{T_1+T_2}\ e$ is handled similarly (the rule is elided) .

Rules **N-Case-L,N-Case-U**: As in the pair elimination rule, we first evaluate the discriminee e to a value, which must have one of the shapes $L_T\ v_l$, $R_T\ v_r$, or $u \in \mathcal{U}$, thanks to typing. The cases for $L_T\ v_l$ (rule **N-Case-L**) and $R_T\ v_r$ (elided) are similar to **N-CasePair-P**: v_l or v_r can be directly substituted for x_l or x_r in e_l or e_r. The unknown case (**N-Case-U**) is similar to **N-CasePair-U** but a bit more complex. Once again e shares with the unknown u a type $\overline{T}_l + \overline{T}_r$ that does not contain any arrows, so we can generate fresh unknowns u_l, u_r with types $\overline{T}_l$, $\overline{T}_r$. We unify $L_{\overline{T}_l+\overline{T}_r}\ v_l$ with u to get the constraint set κ_l and $R_{\overline{T}_l+\overline{T}_r}\ v_r$ with u to get κ_r. We then use the auxiliary relation *choose* (Figure 13.7), which takes two integers n and m (here equal to 1) as well as two constraint sets (here κ_l and κ_r), to select either l or r. If exactly one of κ_l and κ_r is satisfiable, then *choose* will return the corresponding index with probability 1 and an empty trace (because no random choice were made). If both are satisfiable, then the resulting index is randomly chosen. Both outcomes are equiprobable (because of the 1 arguments to *choose*), so the probability is one half in each case. This uniform binary choice is recorded in the trace t_2 as either $(0, 2)$ or $(1, 2)$. Finally, we evaluate the expression corresponding to the chosen index, with the corresponding unknown substituted for the variable. The satisfiability checks enforce the invariant that constraint sets are satisfiable, which in turn ensures that κ_l and κ_r cannot both be unsatisfiable at the same time, since there must exist at least one valuation in κ_0 that maps u to a value (either L or R) which ensures that the corresponding unification will succeed.

Rule **N-App**: To evaluate an application $(e_0 \ e_1)$, we first evaluate e_0 to $rec \ (f :$ $T_1 \to T_2) \ x = e_2$ (since unknowns only range over arrow-free types $\overline{T}$, the result cannot be an unknown) and its argument e_1 to a value v_1. We then evaluate the appropriately substituted body, $e_2[(rec \ (f : T_1 \to T_2) \ x = e_2)/f, v_1/x]$, and combine the various probabilities and traces appropriately.

Rule **N-After** is similar to **N-Pair**; however, the value result of the derivation is that of the first narrowing evaluation, implementing the reverse form of sequencing described in the introduction of this section.

Rule **N-Bang**: To evaluate $!e$ we evaluate e to a value v, then use the auxiliary relation *sampleV* (Figure 13.8) to completely instantiate v, walking down the structure of v. When unknowns are encountered, *sample* is used to produce a list of constraint sets S; with probability $\frac{1}{|S|}$ (where $|S|$ is the size of the list) we can select the mth constraint set in S, for each $0 \le m < |S|$.

Rule **N-Narrow** is similar to **N-Case-U**, modulo the "weight" arguments e_1 and e_2. These are evaluated to values v_1 and v_2, and *sampleV* is called to ensure that they are fully instantiated in all subsequent constraint sets, especially κ_e. The relation $nat_{\kappa_e}(v_1) = n_1$ walks down the structure of the value v_1 (like *sampleV*) and calculates the unique natural number n_1 corresponding to v_1: when the input value is an unknown, $nat_\kappa(u) = n$ holds if $\kappa[u] = v'$ and $[\![v]\!] = n$, where the notation $[\![v]\!]$ is defined in Figure 13.4. The rest of the rule is the same as **N-Case-U**, but with the computed weights n_1 and n_2 given as arguments to *choose* to shape the distribution.

Using the narrowing semantics, we can implement a more efficient method for generating valuations than the naive generate-and-test described in Section 13.3.1: instead of generating arbitrary valuations we only lazily instantiate a subset of unknowns as we encounter them. This method has the additional advantage that, if a generated valuation yields an unwanted result, the implementation can backtrack to the point of the latest choice, which can drastically improve performance (Claessen *et al.*, 2014).

Unfortunately, using the narrowing semantics in this way can lead to a lot of backtracking. To see why, consider three unknowns, $u_1, u_2,$ and u_3, and a constraint set κ where each unknown has type Bool (i.e., $1 + 1$) and the domain associated with each contains both True and False ($L_{1+1} \ ()$ and $R_{1+1} \ ()$). Suppose we want to generate valuations for these three unknowns such that the conjunction $u_1 \ \&\& \ u_2 \ \&\& \ u_3$ holds, where $e_1 \ \&\& \ e_2$ is shorthand for *case* e_1 *of* $(L \ x \to e_2)(R \ y \to$ False$)$. If we attempt to evaluate the expression $u_1 \ \&\& \ u_2 \ \&\& \ u_3$ using the narrowing semantics, we first apply the **N-Case-U** rule with $e = u_1$. That means that u_1 will be unified with either L or R (applied to a fresh unknown) with equal probability, leading to a False result for the entire expression 50% of the time. If we choose to unify u_1 with an L, then we apply the **N-Case-U** rule again, returning either False or u_3 (since unknowns are values – rule **N-Base**) with equal probability. Therefore, we will have generated a desired valuation only 25% of the time; we will need to backtrack 75% of the time.

The problem here is that the narrowing semantics is agnostic to the desired result of the whole computation – we only find out at the very end that we need to backtrack. But we can do better. . .

13.3.4 Matching Semantics

In this section we present a *matching* semantics that takes as an additional input a *pattern* (a value not containing lambdas but possibly containing unknowns) and propagates this pattern backwards to guide the generation process. By allowing our semantics to look ahead in this way, we can often avoid case branches that lead to non-matching results. The matching judgment is again a variant of big-step evaluation; it has the form

$$p \Leftarrow e \dashv \kappa \Uparrow_q^t \kappa^?$$

where p can mention the unknowns in $U(\kappa)$ and where the metavariable $\kappa^?$ stands for an *optional* constraint set ($\emptyset$ or $\{\kappa\}$) returned by matching. Returning an option allows us to calculate the probability of backtracking by summing the q's of all failing derivations. (The combined probability of failures and successes may be less than 1, because some reduction paths may diverge.)

We keep the invariants from Section 13.3.3: the input constraint set κ is well typed and so is the input expression e (with respect to an empty variable context and $U(\kappa)$); moreover κ is satisfiable, and the restriction of its denotation to the unknowns in e is finite. To these invariants we add that the input pattern p is well typed in $U(\kappa)$ and that the common type of e and p does not contain any arrows (e can still contain functions and applications internally; these are handled by calling the narrowing semantics).

The rules except for *case* are similar to the narrowing semantics. Figure 13.9 shows several; the rest appear in the extended version.

Rule **M-Base**: To generate valuations for a unit value or an unknown, we unify v and the target pattern p under the input constraint set κ. Unlike **N-Base**, there is no case for functions, since the expression being evaluated must have a non-function type.

Rules **M-Pair**, **M-Pair-Fail**: To evaluate (e_1, e_2), where e_1 and e_2 have types $\overline{T}_1$

$$\textbf{M-Base} \; \frac{v = () \;\vee\; v \in \mathcal{U} \quad \kappa' = \textit{unify } \kappa \; v \; p}{p \Leftarrow v \dashv \kappa \Uparrow_1^\epsilon \textit{ if } SAT(\kappa') \textit{ then } \{\kappa'\} \textit{ else } \emptyset}$$

$$\textbf{M-Pair} \; \frac{\begin{array}{c}(\kappa',[u_1,u_2]) = \textit{fresh } \kappa \; [\overline{T}_1,\overline{T}_2] \\ \kappa_0 = \textit{unify } \kappa' \; (u_1,u_2) \; p \\ u_1 \Leftarrow e_1 \dashv \kappa_0 \Uparrow_{q_1}^{t_1} \{\kappa_1\} \quad u_2 \Leftarrow e_2 \dashv \kappa_1 \Uparrow_{q_2}^{t_2} \kappa_2^?\end{array}}{p \Leftarrow (e_1^{\overline{T}_1}, e_2^{\overline{T}_2}) \dashv \kappa \Uparrow_{q_1 * q_2}^{t_1 \cdot t_2} \kappa_2^?}$$

$$\textbf{M-Pair-Fail} \; \frac{\begin{array}{c}(\kappa',[u_1,u_2]) = \textit{fresh } \kappa \; [\overline{T}_1,\overline{T}_2] \\ \kappa_0 = \textit{unify } \kappa' \; (u_1,u_2) \; p \\ u_1 \Leftarrow e_1 \dashv \kappa_0 \Uparrow_{q_1}^{t_1} \emptyset\end{array}}{p \Leftarrow (e_1^{\overline{T}_1}, e_2^{\overline{T}_2}) \dashv \kappa \Uparrow_{q_1}^{t_1} \emptyset}$$

$$\textbf{M-App} \; \frac{\begin{array}{c}e_0 \dashv \kappa \Downarrow_{q_0}^{t_0} \kappa_0 \vDash (\textit{rec } f \; x = e_2) \\ e_1 \dashv \kappa_0 \Downarrow_{q_1}^{t_1} \kappa' \vDash v_1 \\ p \Leftarrow e_2[(\textit{rec } f \; x = e_2)/f, v_1/x] \dashv \kappa' \Uparrow_{q_2}^{t_2} \kappa^?\end{array}}{p \Leftarrow (e_0 \; e_1) \dashv \kappa \Uparrow_{q_0 * q_1 * q_2}^{t_0 \cdot t_1 \cdot t_2} \kappa^?}$$

$$\textbf{M-After} \; \frac{p \Leftarrow e_1 \dashv \kappa \Uparrow_{q_1}^{t_1} \{\kappa_1\} \quad e_2 \dashv \kappa_1 \Downarrow_{q_2}^{t_2} \kappa_2 \vDash v}{p \Leftarrow e_1 \; ; \; e_2 \dashv \kappa \Uparrow_{q_1 * q_2}^{t_1 \cdot t_2} \{\kappa_2\}}$$

Figure 13.9 Matching Semantics of Selected Core Luck Constructs

and $\overline{T}_2$, we first generate fresh unknowns u_1 and u_2. We unify the pair (u_1, u_2) with the target pattern p, obtaining a new constraint set κ'. We then proceed as in **N-Pair**, evaluating e_1 against pattern u_1 and e_2 against u_2, threading constraint sets and accumulating traces and probabilities. **M-Pair** handles the case where the evaluation of e_1 succeeds, while **M-Pair-Fail** handles failure: if evaluating e_1 yields $\emptyset$, the whole computation immediately yields $\emptyset$ as well; e_2 is not evaluated, and the final trace and probability are t_1 and q_1.

Rules **M-App**, **M-After**: To evaluate an application $e_0 \; e_1$, we use the narrowing semantics to reduce e_0 to $\textit{rec } f \; x = e_2$ and e_1 to a value v_1, then evaluate $e_2[(\textit{rec } f \; x = e_2)/f, v_2/x]$ against the original p. In this rule we cannot use a pattern during the evaluation of e_1: we do not have any candidates! This is the main reason for introducing the sequencing operator as a primitive $e_1 \; ; \; e_2$ instead of encoding it using lambda abstractions. In **M-After**, we evaluate e_1 against p and then evaluate e_2 using narrowing, just for its side effects. If we used lambdas to encode sequencing, e_1 would be narrowed instead, which is not what we want.

$$(\kappa_0, [u_1, u_2]) = fresh\ \kappa\ [\overline{T}_1, \overline{T}_2]$$
$$(L_{\overline{T}_1 + \overline{T}_2}\ u_1) \Leftarrow e \dashv \kappa_0 \Uparrow_{q_1}^{t_1} \{\kappa_1\}$$
$$(R_{\overline{T}_1 + \overline{T}_2}\ u_2) \Leftarrow e \dashv \kappa_0 \Uparrow_{q_2}^{t_2} \{\kappa_2\}$$

$$p \Leftarrow e_1[u_1/x_l] \dashv \kappa_1 \Uparrow_{q'_1}^{t'_1} \kappa_a^? \qquad p \Leftarrow e_2[u_2/y_r] \dashv \kappa_2 \Uparrow_{q'_2}^{t'_2} \kappa_b^?$$

M-Case-1 $\qquad \kappa^? = combine\ \kappa_0\ \kappa_a^?\ \kappa_b^?$

$$\frac{}{p \Leftarrow case\ e^{\overline{T}_1 + \overline{T}_2}\ of\ (L\ x_l \rightarrow e_1)(R\ y_r \rightarrow e_2) \dashv \kappa}$$
$$\Uparrow_{q_1 * q_2 * q'_1 * q'_2}^{t_1 \cdot t_2 \cdot t'_1 \cdot t'_2}\ \kappa^?$$

where *combine* $\kappa\ \emptyset\ \emptyset = \emptyset$
   combine $\kappa\ \{\kappa_1\}\ \emptyset = \{\kappa_1\}$
   combine $\kappa\ \emptyset\ \{\kappa_2\} = \{\kappa_2\}$
   combine $\kappa\ \{\kappa_1\}\ \{\kappa_2\} = union\ \kappa_1\ (rename\ (U(\kappa_1) - U(\kappa))\ \kappa_2)$

$$(\kappa_0, [u_1, u_2]) = fresh\ \kappa\ [\overline{T}_1, \overline{T}_2]$$
$$(L_{\overline{T}_1 + \overline{T}_2}\ u_1) \Leftarrow e \dashv \kappa_0 \Uparrow_{q_1}^{t_1} \emptyset$$
$$(R_{\overline{T}_1 + \overline{T}_2}\ u_2) \Leftarrow e \dashv \kappa_0 \Uparrow_{q_2}^{t_2} \{\kappa_2\}$$

M-Case-2 $\qquad p \Leftarrow e_2[u_2/y] \dashv \kappa_2 \Uparrow_{q'_2}^{t'_2} \kappa_b^?$

$$\frac{}{p \Leftarrow case\ e^{\overline{T}_1 + \overline{T}_2}\ of\ (L\ x \rightarrow e_1)(R\ y \rightarrow e_2) \dashv \kappa \Uparrow_{q_1 * q_2 * q'_2}^{t_1 \cdot t_2 \cdot t'_2}\ \kappa_b^?}$$

Figure 13.10 Matching Semantics for Constraint-Solving *case*

The interesting rules are the ones for *case* when the type of the scrutinee does not contain functions. For these rules, we can actually use the patterns to guide the generation that occurs during the evaluation of the scrutinee as well. Instead of choosing which branch to follow with some probability (50% in **N-Case-U**), we evaluate both branches, just like a constraint solver would exhaustively search the entire domain.

Before looking at the rules in detail, we need to extend the constraint set interface with two new functions:

$$rename \quad :: \quad \mathcal{U}^* \rightarrow C \rightarrow C$$
$$union \quad :: \quad C \rightarrow C \rightarrow C$$

The *rename* operation freshens a constraint set by replacing all the unknowns in a given sequence with freshly generated ones. The *union* of two constraint sets intuitively denotes the union of their corresponding denotations.

Two of the rules appear in Figure 13.10. (A third is symmetric to **M-Case-2**; a fourth handles failures.) We independently evaluate *e* against both an *L* pattern and an R pattern. If both of them yield failure, then the whole evaluation yields failure (elided). If exactly one succeeds, we evaluate just the corresponding branch (**M-Case-2** or the other elided rule). If both succeed (**M-Case-1**), we evaluate both branch bodies and combine the results with *union*. We use *rename* to avoid conflicts, since we may generate the same fresh unknowns while independently computing $\kappa_a^?$ and $\kappa_b^?$. If desired, the user can ensure that only one branch will be executed by using an instantiation expression before the *case* is reached. Since e will then begin with a concrete constructor, only one of the evaluations of e against the patterns L and R will succeed, and only the corresponding branch will be executed.

The **M-Case-1** rule is the second place where the need for finiteness of the restriction of κ to the input expression e arises. In order for the semantics to terminate in the presence of (terminating) recursive calls, it is necessary that the domain be finite. To see this, consider a simple recursive predicate that holds for every number:

$$rec \; (f : nat \rightarrow bool) \; u = case \; unfold_{nat} \; u \; of \; (L \; x \rightarrow \texttt{True})(R \; y \rightarrow (f \; y))$$

Even though f terminates in the predicate semantics for every input u, if we allow a constraint set to map u to the infinite domain of all natural numbers, the matching semantics will not terminate. While this finiteness restriction feels a bit unnatural, we have not found it to be a problem in practice – see Section 13.4.

13.3.5 Example

To show how all this works, let's trace the main steps of the matching derivations of two given expressions against the pattern `True` in a given constraint set. We will also extract probability distributions about optional constraint sets from these derivations.

We are going to evaluate $A := (0 < u \;\&\&\; u < 4) \; ; \; !u$ and $B := (0 < u \; ; \; !u) \;\&\&\; u < 4$ against the pattern `True` in a constraint set κ, in which u is independent from other unknowns and its possible values are $0, \ldots, 9$. Similar expressions were introduced as examples in Section 13.2; the results we obtain here confirm the intuitive explanation given there.

Recall that we are using a standard Peano encoding of naturals: $nat = \mu X. \; 1 + X$, and that the conjunction expression $e_1 \;\&\&\; e_2$ is shorthand for $case \; e_1 \; of \; (L \; a \rightarrow e_2)(R \; b \rightarrow \texttt{False})$. We elide folds for brevity. The inequality $a < b$ can be encoded as $lt \; a \; b$, where:

$$lt = rec \; (f : nat \rightarrow nat{-} > bool) \; x = rec \; (g : nat \rightarrow bool) \; y =$$
$$case \; y \; of \quad (L \; \_ \rightarrow \texttt{False})$$
$$(R \; y_R \rightarrow case \; x \; of \quad (L \; \_ \rightarrow \texttt{True})$$
$$(R \; x_R \rightarrow f \; x_R \; y_R))$$

Many rules introduce fresh unknowns, many of which are irrelevant: they might be directly equivalent to some other unknown, or there might not exist any reference to them. We use the same variable for two constraint sets which differ only in the addition of a few irrelevant variables in one.

Evaluation of *A* We first derive $\mathtt{True} \Leftarrow (0 < u) \dashv \kappa \Uparrow_1^\epsilon \{\kappa_0\}$. Since in the desugaring of $0 < u$ as an application *lt* is already in *rec* form and both 0 and u are values, the constraint set after the narrowing calls of **M-App** will stay unchanged. We then evaluate *case u of* $(L\_ \to \mathtt{False})(R\ y_R \to \ldots)$. Since the domain of u contains both zero and non-zero elements, unifying u with $L_{1+nat}\ u_1$ and $R_{1+nat}\ u_2$ (**M-Base**) will produce some non-empty constraint sets. Therefore, rule **M-Case-1** applies. Since the body of the left hand side of the match is $\mathtt{False}$, the result of the left derivation in **M-Case-1** is $\emptyset$ and in the resulting constraint set κ_0 the domain of u is $\{1,\ldots,9\}$.

Next, we turn to $\mathtt{True} \Leftarrow (0 < u\ \&\&\ u < 4) \dashv \kappa \Uparrow_1^\epsilon \{\kappa_1\}$, where, by a similar argument following the recursion, the domain of u in κ_1 is $\{1,2,3\}$. There are 3 possible narrowing-semantics derivations for $!u$: (1) $!u \dashv \kappa_1 \Downarrow_{1/3}^{[(0,3)]} \kappa_1^A \vDash u$, (2) $!u \dashv \kappa_1 \Downarrow_{1/3}^{[(1,3)]} \kappa_2^A \vDash u$, and (3) $!u \dashv \kappa_1 \Downarrow_{1/3}^{[(2,3)]} \kappa_3^A \vDash u$, where the domain of u in κ_i^A is $\{i\}$. (We have switched to narrowing-semantics judgments because of the rule **M-After**.) Therefore all the possible derivations for $A = (0 < u\ \&\&\ u < 4)\ ;\ !u$ matching $\mathtt{True}$ in κ are:

$$\mathtt{True} \Leftarrow A \dashv \kappa \Uparrow_{1/3}^{[(i-1,3)]} \{\kappa_i^A\} \qquad \text{for } i \in \{1,2,3\}$$

From the set of possible derivations, we can extract a probability distribution: for each resulting optional constraint set, we sum the probabilities of each of the traces that lead to this result. Thus the probability distribution associated with $\mathtt{True} \Leftarrow A \dashv \kappa$ is

$$[\{\kappa_1^A\} \mapsto \frac{1}{3};\quad \{\kappa_2^A\} \mapsto \frac{1}{3};\quad \{\kappa_3^A\} \mapsto \frac{1}{3}].$$

Evaluation of *B* The evaluation of $0 < u$ is the same as before, after which we narrow $!u$ directly in κ_0 and there are 9 possibilities: $!u \dashv \kappa_0 \Downarrow_{1/9}^{[(i-1,9)]} \kappa_i^B \vDash u$ for each $i \in \{1,\ldots,9\}$, where the domain of u in κ_i^B is $\{i\}$. Then we evaluate $\mathtt{True} \Leftarrow u < 4 \dashv \kappa_i^B$: if i is 1, 2 or 3 this yields $\{\kappa_i^B\}$; if $i > 3$ this yields a failure $\emptyset$. Therefore the possible derivations for $B = (0 < u\ ;\ !u)\ \&\&\ u < 4$ are:

$$\mathtt{True} \Leftarrow B \dashv \kappa \Uparrow_{1/9}^{[(i-1,9)]} \{\kappa_i^B\} \qquad \text{for } i \in \{1,2,3\}$$

$$\mathtt{True} \Leftarrow B \dashv \kappa \Uparrow_{1/9}^{[(i-1,9)]} \emptyset \qquad \text{for } i \in \{4,\ldots,9\}$$

We can again compute the corresponding probability distribution:

$$[\{\kappa_1^B\} \mapsto \frac{1}{9}; \quad \{\kappa_2^B\} \mapsto \frac{1}{9}; \quad \{\kappa_3^B\} \mapsto \frac{1}{9}; \quad \emptyset \mapsto \frac{2}{3}]$$

Note that if we were just recording the probability of an execution and not its trace, we would not know that there are six distinct executions leading to $\emptyset$ with probability $\frac{1}{9}$, so we would not be able to compute its total probability.

The probability associated with $\emptyset$ (0 for A, 2/3 for B) is the probability of backtracking. As stressed in Section 13.2, A is much better than B in terms of backtracking – i.e., it is more efficient in this case to instantiate u only after all the constraints on its domain have been recorded. For a more formal treatment of backtracking strategies in Luck using Markov Chains, see Gallois-Wong (2016).

13.3.6 Properties

We close our discussion of Core Luck by summarizing some key properties; more details and proofs can be found in the extended version. Intuitively, we show that, when we evaluate an expression e against a pattern p in the presence of a constraint set κ, we can only remove valuations from the denotation of κ (*decreasingness*), any derivation in the generator semantics corresponds to an execution in the predicate semantics (*soundness*), and every valuation that matches p will be found in the denotation of the resulting constraint set of some derivation (*completeness*).

Since we have two flavors of generator semantics, narrowing and matching, we also present these properties in two steps. First, we present the properties for the narrowing semantics; their proofs have been verified using Coq. Then we present the properties for the matching semantics; for these, we have only paper proofs, but these proofs are quite similar to the narrowing ones (details are in the extended version; the only real difference is the case rule).

We begin by giving the formal specification of constraint sets. We introduce one extra abstraction, the *domain* of a constraint set κ, written $dom(\kappa)$. This domain corresponds to the unknowns in a constraint set that actually have bindings in $[\![\kappa]\!]$. For example, when we generate a fresh unknown u from κ, u does not appear in the domain of κ; it only appears in the denotation after we use it in a unification. The domain of κ is a subset of the set of keys of $U(\kappa)$. When we write that for a valuation and constraint set $\sigma \in [\![\kappa]\!]$, it also implies that the unknowns that have bindings in σ are exactly the unknowns that have bindings in $[\![\kappa]\!]$, i.e., in $dom(\kappa)$. We use the overloaded notation $\sigma|_x$ to denote the restriction of σ to x, where x is either a set of unknowns or another valuation.

Specification of fresh

$$(\kappa', u) = fresh\ \kappa\ T \implies \begin{cases} u \notin U(\kappa) \\ U(\kappa') = U(\kappa) \oplus (u \mapsto T) \\ [\![\kappa']\!] = [\![\kappa]\!] \end{cases}$$

Intuitively, when we generate a fresh unknown u of type T from κ, u is really fresh for κ, meaning $U(\kappa)$ does not have a type binding for it. The resulting constraint set κ' has an extended unknown typing map, where u maps to T and its denotation remains unchanged. That means that $dom(\kappa') = dom(\kappa)$.

Specification of sample

$$\kappa' \in sample\ \kappa\ u \implies \begin{cases} U(\kappa') = U(\kappa) \\ SAT(\kappa') \\ \exists v.\ [\![\kappa']\!] = \{\ \sigma \mid \sigma \in [\![\kappa]\!],\ \sigma(u) = v\ \} \end{cases}$$

When we sample u in a constraint set κ and obtain a list, for every member constraint set κ', the typing map of κ remains unchanged and all of the valuations that remain in the denotation of κ' are the ones that mapped to some specific value v in κ. We also require a completeness property from *sample*, namely that if we have a valuation $\sigma \in [\![\kappa]\!]$ where $\sigma(u) = v$ for some u, v, then is in some member κ' of the result:

$$\left. \begin{array}{c} \sigma(u) = v \\ \sigma \in [\![\kappa]\!] \end{array} \right\} \implies \exists \kappa'. \begin{cases} \sigma \in [\![\kappa']\!] \\ \kappa' \in sample\ \kappa\ u \end{cases}$$

Specification of unify

$$U(unify\ \kappa\ v_1\ v_2) = U(\kappa)$$
$$[\![unify\ \kappa\ v_1\ v_2]\!] = \{\ \sigma \in [\![\kappa]\!] \mid \sigma(v_1) = \sigma(v_2)\ \}$$

When we unify in a constraint set κ two well-typed values v_1 and v_2, the typing map remains unchanged while the denotation of the result contains the valuations from κ that when substituted into v_1 and v_2 make them equal.

Specification of union

$$\left. \begin{array}{c} U(\kappa_1)|_{U(\kappa_1) \cap U(\kappa_2)} = U(\kappa_2)|_{U(\kappa_1) \cap U(\kappa_2)} \\ union\ \kappa_1\ \kappa_2 = \kappa \end{array} \right\} \implies \begin{cases} U(\kappa) = U(\kappa_1) \cup U(\kappa_2) \\ [\![\kappa]\!] = [\![\kappa_1]\!] \cup [\![\kappa_2]\!] \end{cases}$$

To take the *union* of two constraint sets, their typing maps must obviously agree on any unknowns present in both. The denotation of the *union* of two constraint sets is then just the union of their corresponding denotations.

Properties of the Narrowing Semantics The first theorem, *decreasingness* states that we never add new valuations to our constraint sets; our semantics can only refine the denotation of the input κ.

Theorem 13.1 (Decreasingness).

$$e \dashv \kappa \Downarrow_q^t \kappa' \vDash v \implies \kappa' \leq \kappa$$

Soundness and completeness can be visualized as follows:

$$
\begin{array}{ccc}
e_p & \xrightarrow{\quad\Downarrow\quad} & v_p \\
{\scriptstyle \sigma \in \llbracket \kappa \rrbracket}\Big\uparrow & & \Big\uparrow{\scriptstyle \sigma' \in \llbracket \kappa' \rrbracket} \\
e \dashv \kappa & \xrightarrow[\quad\Downarrow_q^t\quad]{} & v \vDash \kappa'
\end{array}
$$

Given the bottom and right sides of the diagram, soundness guarantees that we can fill in the top and left. That is, any narrowing derivation $e \dashv \kappa \Downarrow_t^q \kappa' \vDash v$ corresponds to some derivation in the predicate semantics, with the additional assumption that all the unknowns in e are included in the domain of the input constraint set κ (or that e is well typed in κ).

Theorem 13.2 (Soundness).

$$
\left.
\begin{array}{l}
e \dashv \kappa \Downarrow_t^q \kappa' \vDash v \\
\sigma'(v) = v_p \ \wedge\ \sigma' \in \llbracket \kappa' \rrbracket \\
\forall u.\, u \in e \implies u \in dom(\kappa)
\end{array}
\right\}
\implies \exists \sigma\ e_p.
\left\{
\begin{array}{l}
\sigma'|_\sigma \equiv \sigma \\
\sigma \in \llbracket \kappa \rrbracket \\
\sigma(e) = e_p \\
e_p \Downarrow v_p
\end{array}
\right.
$$

Completeness guarantees the opposite direction: given a predicate derivation $e_p \Downarrow v_p$ and a "factoring" of e_p into an expression e and a constraint set κ such that for some valuation $\sigma \in \llbracket \kappa \rrbracket$ substituting σ in e yields e_p, if is well typed, there is always a nonzero probability of obtaining some factoring of v_p as the result of a narrowing judgment.

Theorem 13.3 (Completeness).

$$
\left.
\begin{array}{l}
e_p \Downarrow v_p \\
\sigma(e) = e_p \\
\sigma \in \llbracket \kappa \rrbracket \ \wedge \vdash \kappa \\
\emptyset; U(\kappa) \vdash e : T
\end{array}
\right\}
\implies
\begin{array}{l}
\exists v\ \kappa'\ \sigma'\ q\ t. \\
\left\{
\begin{array}{l}
\sigma'|_\sigma \equiv \sigma \ \wedge\ \sigma' \in \llbracket \kappa' \rrbracket \\
\sigma'(v) = v_p \\
e \dashv \kappa \Downarrow_q^t \kappa' \vDash v
\end{array}
\right.
\end{array}
$$

Properties of the Matching Semantics The decreasingness property for the matching semantics is very similar to the narrowing semantics: if the matching semantics yields $\{\kappa'\}$, then κ' is smaller than the input κ.

Theorem 13.4 (Decreasingness).

$$p \Leftarrow e \dashv \kappa \Uparrow^t_q \{\kappa'\} \implies \kappa' \leq \kappa$$

Soundness is again similar to the matching semantics.

Theorem 13.5 (Soundness).

$$\left. \begin{array}{l} p \Leftarrow e \dashv \kappa \Uparrow^t_q \{\kappa'\} \\ \sigma'(p) = v_p \wedge \sigma' \in [\![\kappa']\!] \\ \forall u. \, (u \in e \vee u \in p) \Rightarrow u \in dom(\kappa) \end{array} \right\} \implies \exists \sigma \, e_p. \left\{ \begin{array}{l} \sigma'|_\sigma \equiv \sigma \\ \sigma \in [\![\kappa]\!] \\ \sigma(e) = e_p \\ e_p \Downarrow v_p \end{array} \right.$$

For the completeness theorem, we need to slightly strengthen its premise; since the matching semantics may explore both branches of a *case*, it can fall into a loop when the predicate semantics would not (by exploring a non-terminating branch that the predicate semantics does not take). Thus, we require that all input valuations result in a terminating execution.

Theorem 13.6 (Completeness).

$$\left. \begin{array}{l} e_p \Downarrow v_p \wedge \sigma \in [\![\kappa]\!] \\ \emptyset; U(\kappa) \vdash e : \overline{T} \wedge \vdash \kappa \\ \sigma(e) = e_p \wedge \sigma(p) = v_p \\ \forall \sigma' \in [\![\kappa]\!]. \, \exists v'. \, \sigma'(e) \Downarrow v' \end{array} \right\} \implies \begin{array}{l} \exists \kappa' \, \sigma' \, q \, t. \\ \left\{ \begin{array}{l} \sigma'|_\sigma \equiv \sigma \\ \sigma' \in [\![\kappa']\!] \\ p \Leftarrow e \dashv \kappa \Uparrow^t_q \{\kappa'\} \end{array} \right. \end{array}$$

13.4 Implementation

We next describe the Luck prototype: its top level, its treatment of backtracking and its probability-preserving pattern match compiler. We refer the reader to the extended version for the constraint set implementation.

At the Top Level The inputs provided to the Luck interpreter consist of an expression e of type *bool* containing zero or more free unknowns $\vec{u}$ (but no free variables), and an initial constraint set κ providing types and finite domains[2] for each unknown in $\vec{u}$, such that their occurrences in e are well typed ($\emptyset; U(\kappa) \vdash e : 1 + 1$).

---

[2] This restriction to finite domains appears to be crucial for our technical development to work, as discussed in the previous section. In practice, we have not yet encountered a situation where it was important to be able to generate examples of *unbounded* size (as opposed to examples up to some large maximum size). We do

The interpreter matches e against True (that is, L_{1+1} ()), to derive a refined constraint set κ':

$$L_{1+1} \ () \ \Leftarrow \ e \ \dashv \ \kappa \ \Uparrow_q^t \ \{\kappa'\}$$

This involves random choices, and there is also the possibility that matching fails (and the semantics generates $\emptyset$ instead of $\{\kappa'\}$). In this case, a simple *global* backtracking approach could simply try the whole thing again (up to an ad hoc limit). While not strictly necessary for a correct implementation of the matching semantics, some *local* backtracking allows wrong choices to be reversed quickly and leads to an enormous improvement in performance (Claessen *et al.*, 2015). Our prototype backtracks locally in calls to *choose*: if *choose* has two choices available and the first one fails when matching the instantiated expression against a pattern, then we immediately try the second choice instead. Effectively, this means that if e is already known to be of the form $L\_\_$, then narrow will not choose to instantiate it using $R\_\_$, and vice versa. This may require matching against e twice, and our implementation shares work between these two matches as far as possible. (It also seems useful to give the user explicit control over where backtracking occurs, but we leave this for future work.)

After the interpreter matches e against True, all the resulting valuations $\sigma \in [\![\kappa']\!]$ should map the unknowns in $\vec{u}$ to some values. However, there is no guarantee that the generator semantics will yield a κ' mapping every $\vec{u}$ to a unique values. The Luck top-level then applies the *sample* constraint set function to each unknown in $\vec{u}$, ensuring that $\sigma|_{\vec{u}}$ is the same for each σ in the final constraint set. The interpreter returns this common $\sigma|_{\vec{u}}$ if it exists, and backtracks otherwise.

Pattern Match Compiler In Section 13.2, we saw an example using a standard Tree datatype and instantiation expressions assigning different weights to each branch. While the desugaring of simple pattern matching to core Luck syntax is straightforward (Section 13.3.1), nested patterns – as in Figure 13.11 – complicate things in the presence of probabilities. We expand such expressions to a tree of simple case expressions that match only the outermost constructors of their scrutinees. However, there is generally no unique choice of weights in the expanded predicate: a branch from the source predicate may be duplicated in the result. We guarantee the intuitive property that the *sum* of the probabilities of the clones of a branch is proportional to the weights given by the user, but that still does not determine the individual probabilities that should be assigned to these clones.

sometimes want to generate structures containing large numbers, since they can be represented efficiently, but here, too, choosing an enormous finite bound appears to be adequate for the applications we've tried. The implementation allows for representing all possible ranges of a corresponding type up to a given size bound. Such bounds are initialized at the top level, and they are propagated (and reduced a bit) to fresh unknowns created by pattern matching before these unknowns are used as inputs to the interpreter.

```
data T = Var Int | Lam Int T | App T T

sig isRedex :: T -> Bool                        -- Original
fun isRedex t =
  case t of
  | 2 % App (Lam _ _) _ -> True                 -- 2/3
  | 1 % _ -> False                              -- 1/3

sig isRedex :: T -> Bool                        -- Expansion
fun isRedex t =
  case t of
  | 1 % Var _ -> False                          -- 1/9
  | 1 % Lam _ _ -> False                        -- 1/9
  | 7 % App t1 _ -> case t1 of
                    | 1 % Var _ -> False        -- 1/18
                    | 12 % Lam _ _ -> True      -- 2/3
                    | 1 % App _ _ -> False      -- 1/18
```

Figure 13.11 Expanding case expression with a nested pattern and a wildcard. Comments show the probability of each alternative.

The most obvious way to distribute weights is to simply share the weight equally with all duplicated branches. But the probability of a single branch then depends on the total number of expanded branches that come from the same source, which can be hard for users to determine and can vary widely even between sets of patterns that appear similar. Instead, Luck's default weighing strategy works as follows. For any branch B from the source, at any intermediate case expression of the expansion, the subprobability distribution over the immediate subtrees that contain at least one branch derived from B is uniform. This makes modifications of the source patterns in nested positions affect the distribution more locally.

In Figure 13.11, the `False` branch should have probability $\frac{1}{3}$. It is expanded into four branches, corresponding to subpatterns `Var _`, `Lam _ _`, `App (Var _) _`, `App (App _ _) _`. The latter two are grouped under the pattern `App _ _`, while the former two are in their own groups. These three groups receive equal shares of the total probability of the original branch, that is $\frac{1}{9}$ each. The two nested branches further split that into $\frac{1}{18}$. On the other hand, `True` remains a single branch with probability $\frac{2}{3}$. The weights on the left of every pattern are calculated to reflect this distribution.

13.5 Evaluation

To evaluate the expressiveness and efficiency of Luck's hybrid approach to test case generation, we tested it with a number of small examples and two significant case

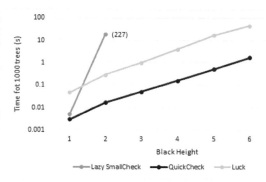

Figure 13.12 Red-Black Tree Experiment

studies: generating well-typed lambda terms and information-flow-control machine states. The Luck code is generally much smaller and cleaner than that of existing handwritten generators, though the Luck interpreter takes longer to generate each example – around 20× to 24× for the more complex generators.

Small Examples The literature on random generation includes many small examples – list predicates such as `sorted`, `member`, and `distinct`, tree predicates like BSTs (Section 13.2) and red-black trees, and so on. In the extended version we show the implementation of many such examples in Luck, illustrating how to write predicates and generators together with minimal effort.

We use red-black trees to compare the efficiency of our Luck interpreter to generators provided by commonly used tools like QuickCheck (random testing), SmallCheck (exhaustive testing) and Lazy SmallCheck (Runciman *et al.*, 2008). Lazy SmallCheck leverages Haskell's laziness to greatly improve upon out-of-the-box QuickCheck and SmallCheck generators in the presence of sparse preconditions, by using partially defined inputs to explore large parts of the search space at once. Using both Luck and Lazy SmallCheck, we attempted to generate 1000 red black trees with a specific black height bh – meaning that the depth of the tree can be as large as $2 \cdot bh + 1$. Results are shown in Figure 13.12. Lazy SmallCheck was able to generate all 227 trees of black height 2 in 17 seconds, fully exploring all trees up to depth 5. When generating trees of black height 3, which required exploring trees up to depth 7, Lazy SmallCheck was unable to generate 1000 red black trees within 5 minutes. At the same time, Luck lies consistently within an order of magnitude of a very efficient handwritten QuickCheck generator that generates valid Red-Black trees directly. Using rejection-sampling approaches by generating trees and discarding those that don't satisfy the red-black tree invariant (e.g., QuickCheck or SmallCheck's ==>) is prohibitively costly: these approaches perform much worse than Lazy SmallCheck.

Well-Typed Lambda Terms Using our prototype implementation we reproduced the experiments of Pałka *et al.* (2011), who generated well-typed lambda terms in order to discover bugs in GHC's strictness analyzer. We also use this case study to indirectly compare to two narrowing-based tools that are arguably closer to Luck and that use the same case study to evaluate their work: Claessen *et al.* (2014, 2015) and Fetscher *et al.* (2015).

We encoded a model of simply typed lambda calculus with polymorphism in Luck, providing a large typing environment with standard functions from the Haskell Prelude to generate interesting well-typed terms. The generated ASTs were then pretty-printed into Haskell syntax and each one was applied to a partial list of the form: `[1,2,undefined]`. Using the same version of GHC (6.12.1), we compiled each application twice: once with optimizations (`-O2`) and once without and compared the outputs.

A straightforward Luck implementation of a type system for the polymorphic lambda calculus was not adequate for finding bugs efficiently. To improve its performance we borrowed tricks from the similar case study of Fetscher *et al.*, seeding the environment with monomorphic versions of possible constants and increasing the frequency of `seq`, a basic Haskell function that introduces strictness, to increase the chances of exercising the strictness analyzer. Using this, we discovered bugs similar to those found by Pałka *et al.* and Fetscher *et al.*. For example, the `[Int] -> [Int]` function

```
seq (id (\a -> seq a id) undefined),
```

when fed the singleton list `[undefined]`, yields an exception immediately with `-O0` (following the semantics of `seq`), but prints the toplevel constructor of the result `[` before raising the exception if compiled with `-O1`.

Luck's generation speed was slower than that of Pałka's handwritten generator. We generated terms of average size 50 (internal nodes), and, grouping terms together in batches of 100, we got a total time of generation, unparsing, compilation and execution of around 35 seconds per batch. This is a slowdown of 20x compared to that of Pałka's. However, our implementation is a total of 82 lines of fairly simple code, while the handwritten development is 1684 lines, with the warning "... the code is difficult to understand, so reading it is not recommended" in its distribution page (Pałka, n.d.).

The derived generators of Claessen *et al.* (2014) achieved a 7x slowdown compared to the handwritten generator, while the Redex generators (Fetscher *et al.*, 2015) also report a 7× slowdown in generation time for their best generator. However, by seeding the environment with monomorphised versions of the most common constants present in the counterexamples, they were able to achieve a time per counterexample on par with the handwritten generator.

Information-Flow Control For a second large case study, we reimplemented a method for generating information-flow control machine states (Hriţcu *et al.*, 2013). Given an abstract stack machine with data and instruction memories, a stack, and a program counter, one attaches *labels* – security levels – to runtime values, propagating them during execution and restricting potential flows of information from *high* (secret) to *low* (public) data. The desired security property, *termination-insensitive noninterference*, states that if we start with two indistinguishable abstract machines s1 and s2 (i.e., all their low-tagged parts are identical) and run each of them to completion, then the resulting states s1' and s2' are also indistinguishable.

Hriţcu *et al.* found that efficient testing of this property could be achieved in two ways: either by generating instruction memories that allow for long executions and checking for indistinguishability at each low step (called *LLNI*, low-lockstep noninterference), or by looking for counter-examples to a stronger invariant (strong enough to *prove* noninterference), generating two arbitrary indistinguishable states and then running for a single step (*SSNI*, single step noninterference). In both cases one must first generate one abstract machine s and then *vary* s, to generate an indistinguishable one s'. In writing a generator for variations, one must reverse the indistinguishability predicate between states and then keep the two artifacts in sync.

We first investigated the stronger property (SSNI), by encoding the indistinguishability predicate in Luck and using our prototype to generate small, indistinguishable pairs of states. In 216 lines of code we were able to describe both the predicate and the generator for indistinguishable machines. The same functionality required >1000 lines of complex Haskell code in the handwritten version. The handwritten generator is reported to generate an average of 18400 tests per second, while the Luck prototype generates 1450 tests per second, around 12.5 times slower.

The real promise of Luck, however, became apparent when we turned to LLNI. Hriţcu *et al.* (2013) generate long sequences of instructions using *generation by execution*: starting from a machine state where data memories and stacks are instantiated, they generate the current instruction ensuring it does not cause the machine to crash, then allow the machine to take a step and repeat. While intuitively simple, this extra piece of generator functionality took significant effort to code, debug, and optimize for effectiveness, resulting in more than 100 additional lines of code. The same effect was achieved in Luck by the following 6 intuitive lines, where we just put the previous explanation in code:

```
sig runsLong :: Int -> AS -> Bool
fun runsLong len st =
    if len <= 0 then True
    else case step st of
        | 99 % Just st' -> runsLong (len - 1) st'
```

```
| 1 % Nothing   -> True
```

We evaluated our generator on the same set of buggy information-flow analyses as in (Hrițcu *et al.*, 2013). We were able to find all of the same bugs, with similar effectiveness (number of bugs found per 100 tests). However, the Luck generator was 24 times slower (Luck: 150 tests/s, Haskell: 3600 tests/s). We expect to be able to improve this result (and the rest of the results in this section) with a more efficient implementation that compiles Luck programs to QuickCheck generators directly, instead of interpreting them in a minimally tuned prototype.

This prototype gives the user enough flexibility to achieve effectiveness similar to state-of-the-art generators, while significantly reducing the amount of code and effort required, suggesting that the Luck approach is promising and pointing towards the need for a real, optimizing implementation.

13.6 Related Work

Luck lies in the intersection of many different topics in programming languages, and the potentially related literature is huge. Here, we present just the closest related work; a more comprehensive treatment of related work can be found in the extended version of the paper.

Property-Based Testing The works that are most closely related to our own are the narrowing based approaches of (Gligoric *et al.*, 2010), (Claessen *et al.*, 2014, 2015) and (Fetscher *et al.*, 2015). Gligoric *et al.* use a "delayed choice" approach, which amounts to needed-narrowing, to generate test cases in Java. Claessen *et al.* exploit the laziness of Haskell, combining a narrowing-like technique with FEAT (Duregård *et al.*, 2012), a tool for functional enumeration of algebraic types, to efficiently generate near-uniform random inputs satisfying some precondition. Fetscher *et al.* (2015) also use an algorithm that makes local choices with the potential to backtrack in case of failure. Moreover, they add a simple version of constraint solving, handling equality and disequality constraints. This allows them to achieve excellent performance in testing GHC for bugs (as in Pałka *et al.*, 2011) by monomorphizing the polymorphic constants of the context as discussed in the previous section. However, both tools provide limited (locally, or globally, uniform) distribution guarantees, with no user control over the resulting distribution.

Another interesting related approach appears in the inspiring work of Bulwahn (2012b). In the context of Isabelle's (Nipkow *et al.*, 2002) QuickCheck (Bulwahn, 2012a), Bulwahn automatically constructs enumerators for a given precondition via a compilation to logic programs using mode inference. Lindblad (2007) and (Runciman *et al.*, 2008) also provide support for exhaustive testing using narrowing-based techniques. Instead of implementing mechanisms that resemble narrowing in standard functional languages, Fischer and Kuchen (Fischer and Kuchen, 2007) leverage the built-in engine of the functional logic programming language Curry (Hanus *et al.*, 1995) to enumerate tests satisfying a coverage criterion. While exhaustive testing is useful and has its own merits and advantages over random testing in a lot of domains, we turn to random testing because the complexity of our applications – testing noninterference or optimizing compilers – makes enumeration impractical.

Probabilistic programming Semantics for probabilistic programs share many similarities with the semantics of Luck (Milch *et al.*, 2005; Goodman *et al.*, 2008; Gordon *et al.*, 2014), while the problem of generating satisfying valuations shares similarities with probabilistic sampling (Mansinghka *et al.*, 2009; Łatuszyński *et al.*, 2013; Chaganty *et al.*, 2013; Nori *et al.*, 2014). For example, the semantics of PROB in the recent probabilistic programming survey of Gordon *et al.* (Gordon *et al.*, 2014) takes the form of probability distributions over valuations, while Luck semantics can be viewed as (sub)probability distributions over constraint sets, which induces a distribution over valuations. Moreover, in probabilistic programs, observations serve a similar role to preconditions in random testing, creating problems for simplistic probabilistic samplers that use *rejection sampling* – i.e., generate and test. Recent advances in this domain, like the work on Microsoft's R2 Markov Chain Monte Carlo sampler (Nori *et al.*, 2014), have shown promise in providing more efficient sampling, using pre-imaging transformations in analyzing programs. An important difference is in the type of programs usually targeted by such tools. The difficulty in probabilistic programming arises mostly from dealing with a large number of complex observations, modeled by relatively small programs. For example, Microsoft's TrueSkill (Herbrich *et al.*, 2006) ranking program is a very small program, powered by millions of observations. In contrast, random testing deals with very complex programs (e.g., a type checker) and a single observation (`observe true`).

13.7 Conclusions and Future Work

In this chapter we introduced Luck, a language for writing generators in the form of lightly annotated predicates. We presented the semantics of Luck, combining local instantiation and constraint solving in a unified framework and exploring their interactions. We described a prototype implementation of this semantics and used it to repeat state-of-the-art experiments in random generation. The results showed the potential of Luck's approach, allowing us to replicate the distribution yielded by the handwritten generators with reduced code and effort. The prototype was slower by an order of magnitude, but there is still significant room for improvement.

In the future it will be interesting to explore ways to improve the performance of our interpreted prototype, by compiling Luck into generators in a mainstream language and by experimenting with other domain representations. We also want to investigate Luck's equational theory, showing that the encoded logical predicates satisfy the usual logical laws. Moreover, the backtracking strategies in our implementation can be abstractly modeled on top of our notion of choice-recording trace; Gallois-Wong (Gallois-Wong, 2016) shows promising preliminary results using Markov chains for this.

Another potential direction for future work is automatically deriving smart shrinkers. Shrinking, or delta-debugging, is crucial in property-based testing, and it can also require significant user effort and domain specific knowledge to be efficient (Regehr *et al.*, 2012). It would be interesting to see if there is a counterpart to narrowing or constraint solving that allows shrinking to preserve desired properties.

References

Antoy, Sergio. 2000. A Needed Narrowing Strategy. Pages 776–822 of: *Journal of the ACM*, vol. 47. ACM Press.

Arts, Thomas, Castro, Laura M., and Hughes, John. 2008. Testing Erlang Data Types with QuviQ QuickCheck. Pages 1–8 of: *7th ACM SIGPLAN Workshop on Erlang*. ACM.

Avgerinos, Thanassis, Rebert, Alexandre, Cha, Sang Kil, and Brumley, David. 2014. Enhancing symbolic execution with Veritesting. Pages 1083–1094 of: *36th International Conference on Software Engineering, ICSE '14, Hyderabad, India: May 31–June 07, 2014*.

Ball, Thomas, Levin, Vladimir, and Rajamani, Sriram K. 2011. A decade of software model checking with SLAM. *Commun. ACM*, **54**(7), 68–76.

Blanchette, Jasmin Christian, and Nipkow, Tobias. 2010. Nitpick: A Counterexample Generator for Higher-Order Logic Based on a Relational Model Finder. Pages 131–146 of: *First International Conference on Interactive Theorem Proving (ITP)*. LNCS, vol. 6172. Springer.

Bulwahn, Lukas. 2012a. The New Quickcheck for Isabelle – Random, Exhaustive and Symbolic Testing under One Roof. Pages 92–108 of: *2nd International Conference on Certified Programs and Proofs (CPP)*. LNCS, vol. 7679. Springer.

Bulwahn, Lukas. 2012b. Smart Testing of Functional Programs in Isabelle. Pages 153–167 of: *18th International Conference on Logic for Programming, Artificial Intelligence, and Reasoning (LPAR)*. LNCS, vol. 7180. Springer.

Cadar, Cristian, Dunbar, Daniel, and Engler, Dawson. 2008. KLEE: unassisted and automatic generation of high-coverage tests for complex systems programs. Pages 209–224 of: *8th USENIX conference on Operating systems design and implementation*. OSDI. USENIX Association.

Carlier, Matthieu, Dubois, Catherine, and Gotlieb, Arnaud. 2010. Constraint Reasoning in FocalTest. Pages 82–91 of: *5th International Conference on Software and Data Technologies*. SciTePress.

Chaganty, Arun T., Nori, Aditya V., and Rajamani, Sriram K. 2013 (April). Efficiently Sampling Probabilistic Programs via Program Analysis. In: *Artificial Intelligence and Statistics (AISTATS)*.

Chakraborty, Supratik, Meel, Kuldeep S., and Vardi, Moshe Y. 2014. Balancing Scalability and Uniformity in SAT Witness Generator. Pages 60:1–60:6 of: *Proceedings of the 51st Annual Design Automation Conference*. DAC '14. New York, NY, USA: ACM.

Chamarthi, Harsh Raju, Dillinger, Peter C., Kaufmann, Matt, and Manolios, Panagiotis. 2011. Integrating Testing and Interactive Theorem Proving. Pages 4–19 of: *10th International Workshop on the ACL2 Theorem Prover and its Applications*. EPTCS, vol. 70.

Christiansen, Jan, and Fischer, Sebastian. 2008. EasyCheck – Test Data for Free. Pages 322–336 of: *9th International Symposium on Functional and Logic Programming (FLOPS)*. LNCS, vol. 4989. Springer.

Claessen, Koen, and Hughes, John. 2000. QuickCheck: a lightweight tool for random testing of Haskell programs. Pages 268–279 of: *5th ACM SIGPLAN International Conference on Functional Programming (ICFP)*. ACM.

Claessen, Koen, Duregård, Jonas, and Pałka, Michał H. 2014. Generating Constrained Random Data with Uniform Distribution. Pages 18–34 of: *Functional and Logic Programming*. LNCS, vol. 8475. Springer.

Claessen, Koen, Duregård, Jonas, and Palka, Michal H. 2015. Generating constrained random data with uniform distribution. *J. Funct. Program.*, **25**.

Duregård, Jonas, Jansson, Patrik, and Wang, Meng. 2012. Feat: Functional Enumeration of Algebraic Types. Pages 61–72 of: *Proceedings of the 2012 Haskell Symposium*. Haskell '12. New York, NY, USA: ACM.

Dybjer, Peter, Haiyan, Qiao, and Takeyama, Makoto. 2003. Combining Testing and Proving in Dependent Type Theory. Pages 188–203 of: *16th International Conference on Theorem Proving in Higher Order Logics (TPHOLs)*. LNCS, vol. 2758. Springer.

Fetscher, Burke, Claessen, Koen, Palka, Michal H., Hughes, John, and Findler, Robert Bruce. 2015. Making Random Judgments: Automatically Generating Well-Typed Terms from the Definition of a Type-System. Pages 383–405 of: *24th European Symposium on Programming*. LNCS, vol. 9032. Springer.

Fischer, Sebastian, and Kuchen, Herbert. 2007. Systematic generation of glass-box test cases for functional logic programs. Pages 63–74 of: *9th International ACM SIGPLAN Conference on Principles and Practice of Declarative Programming (PPDP)*. ACM.

Gallois-Wong, Diane. 2016 (Aug.). *Formalising Luck: Improved Probabilistic Semantics for Property-Based Generators*. Inria Internship Report.

Gligoric, Milos, Gvero, Tihomir, Jagannath, Vilas, Khurshid, Sarfraz, Kuncak, Viktor, and Marinov, Darko. 2010. Test generation through programming in UDITA. Pages 225–234 of: *32nd ACM/IEEE International Conference on Software Engineering*. ACM.

Godefroid, Patrice, Klarlund, Nils, and Sen, Koushik. 2005. DART: directed automated random testing. Pages 213–223 of: *ACM SIGPLAN Conference on Programming Language Design and Implementation*. PLDI. ACM.

Goodman, Noah D., Mansinghka, Vikash K., Roy, Daniel M., Bonawitz, Keith, and Tenenbaum, Joshua B. 2008. Church: a language for generative models. Pages 220–229 of: *UAI 2008, Proceedings of the 24th Conference in Uncertainty in Artificial Intelligence, Helsinki, Finland, July 9-12, 2008*.

Gordon, Andrew D., Henzinger, Thomas A., Nori, Aditya V., and Rajamani, Sriram K. 2014. Probabilistic programming. Pages 167–181 of: Herbsleb, James D., and Dwyer, Matthew B. (eds), *Proceedings of the on Future of Software Engineering, FOSE 2014, Hyderabad, India, May 31–June 7, 2014*. ACM.

Gotlieb, Arnaud. 2009. Euclide: A Constraint-Based Testing Framework for Critical C Programs. Pages 151–160 of: *ICST 2009, Second International Conference on Software Testing Verification and Validation, 1-4 April 2009, Denver, Colorado, USA*.

Groce, Alex, Zhang, Chaoqiang, Eide, Eric, Chen, Yang, and Regehr, John. 2012. Swarm Testing. Pages 78–88 of: *Proceedings of the 2012 International Symposium on Software Testing and Analysis*. ISSTA 2012. New York, NY, USA: ACM.

Hanus, M., Kuchen, H., and Moreno-Navarro, J.J. 1995. Curry: A Truly Functional Logic Language. Pages 95–107 of: *Proc. ILPS'95 Workshop on Visions for the Future of Logic Programming*.

Hanus, Michael. 1997. A Unified Computation Model for Functional and Logic Programming. Pages 80–93 of: *24th ACM SIGPLAN-SIGACT Symposium on Principles of Programming Languages (POPL)*. ACM Press.

Herbrich, Ralf, Minka, Tom, and Graepel, Thore. 2006. TrueSkill[TM]: A Bayesian Skill Rating System. Pages 569–576 of: *Advances in Neural Information Processing Systems 19, Proceedings of the Twentieth Annual Conference on Neural Information Processing Systems, Vancouver, British Columbia, Canada, December 4-7, 2006*.

Hriţcu, Cătălin, Hughes, John, Pierce, Benjamin C., Spector-Zabusky, Antal, Vytiniotis, Dimitrios, Azevedo de Amorim, Arthur, and Lampropoulos, Leonidas. 2013. Testing Noninterference, Quickly. Pages 455–468 of: *18th ACM SIGPLAN International Conference on Functional Programming (ICFP)*. ACM.

Hriţcu, Cătălin, Lampropoulos, Leonidas, Spector-Zabusky, Antal, Azevedo de Amorim, Arthur, Dénès, Maxime, Hughes, John, Pierce, Benjamin C., and Vytiniotis, Dimitrios. 2016. Testing Noninterference, Quickly. *Journal of*

Functional Programming (JFP); Special issue for ICFP 2013, **26**(Apr.), e4 (62 pages). Technical Report available as arXiv:1409.0393.

Hughes, John. 2007. QuickCheck Testing for Fun and Profit. Pages 1–32 of: *9th International Symposium on Practical Aspects of Declarative Languages (PADL)*. LNCS, vol. 4354. Springer.

Jackson, Daniel. 2011. *Software Abstractions: Logic, Language, and Anlysis*. The MIT Press.

Jhala, Ranjit, and Majumdar, Rupak. 2009. Software model checking. *ACM Comput. Surv.*, **41**(4).

Köksal, Ali Sinan, Kuncak, Viktor, and Suter, Philippe. 2011. Scala to the Power of Z3: Integrating SMT and Programming. Pages 400–406 of: *23rd International Conference on Automated Deduction*. LNCS, vol. 6803. Springer.

Lampropoulos, Leonidas, Gallois-Wong, Diane, Hritcu, Catalin, Hughes, John, Pierce, Benjamin C., and Xia, Li-yao. 2017. Beginner's Luck: a language for property-based generators. Pages 114–129 of: *Proceedings of the 44th ACM SIGPLAN Symposium on Principles of Programming Languages, POPL 2017, Paris, France, January 18-20, 2017*.

Łatuszyński, Krzysztof, Roberts, Gareth O., and Rosenthal, Jeffrey S. 2013. Adaptive Gibbs samplers and related MCMC methods. *The Annals of Applied Probability*, **23**(1), 66–98.

Lindblad, Fredrik. 2007. Property Directed Generation of First-Order Test Data. Pages 105–123 of: *8th Symposium on Trends in Functional Programming*. Trends in Functional Programming, vol. 8. Intellect.

Mansinghka, Vikash K., Roy, Daniel M., Jonas, Eric, and Tenenbaum, Joshua B. 2009. Exact and Approximate Sampling by Systematic Stochastic Search. Pages 400–407 of: *Proceedings of the Twelfth International Conference on Artificial Intelligence and Statistics, AISTATS 2009, Clearwater Beach, Florida, USA, April 16-18, 2009*.

Milch, Brian, Marthi, Bhaskara, Russell, Stuart J., Sontag, David, Ong, Daniel L., and Kolobov, Andrey. 2005. BLOG: Probabilistic Models with Unknown Objects. Pages 1352–1359 of: *IJCAI-05, Proceedings of the Nineteenth International Joint Conference on Artificial Intelligence, Edinburgh, Scotland, UK, July 30-August 5, 2005*.

Nipkow, Tobias, Wenzel, Markus, and Paulson, Lawrence C. 2002. *Isabelle/HOL: A Proof Assistant for Higher-order Logic*. Berlin, Heidelberg: Springer-Verlag.

Nori, Aditya V., Hur, Chung-Kil, Rajamani, Sriram K., and Samuel, Selva. 2014. R2: An Efficient MCMC Sampler for Probabilistic Programs. In: *AAAI Conference on Artificial Intelligence (AAAI)*. AAAI.

Okasaki, Chris. 1999. Red-Black Trees in a Functional Setting. *Journal of Functional Programming*, **9**(4), 471–477.

Owre, Sam. 2006. Random Testing in PVS. In: *Workshop on Automated Formal Methods*.

Pacheco, Carlos, and Ernst, Michael D. 2007. Randoop: feedback-directed random testing for Java. Pages 815–816 of: *22nd ACM SIGPLAN Conference on Object-Oriented Programming Systems And Applications*. OOPSLA. ACM.

Pałka, Michał H. *Testing an optimising compiler by generating random lambda terms*. http://www.cse.chalmers.se/~palka/testingcompiler/.

Pałka, Michał H., Claessen, Koen, Russo, Alejandro, and Hughes, John. 2011. Testing an Optimising Compiler by Generating Random Lambda Terms. Pages 91–97 of: *Proceedings of the 6th International Workshop on Automation of Software Test*. AST '11. New York, NY, USA: ACM.

Paraskevopoulou, Zoe, Hriţcu, Cătălin, Dénès, Maxime, Lampropoulos, Leonidas, and Pierce, Benjamin C. 2015. Foundational Property-Based Testing. Pages 325–343 of: Urban, Christian, and Zhang, Xingyuan (eds), *6th International Conference on Interactive Theorem Proving (ITP)*. LNCS, vol. 9236. Springer.

Regehr, John, Chen, Yang, Cuoq, Pascal, Eide, Eric, Ellison, Chucky, and Yang, Xuejun. 2012. Test-case reduction for C compiler bugs. Pages 335–346 of: *ACM SIGPLAN Conference on Programming Language Design and Implementation, PLDI '12, Beijing, China, June 11–16, 2012*.

Reich, Jason S., Naylor, Matthew, and Runciman, Colin. 2011. Lazy Generation of Canonical Test Programs. Pages 69–84 of: *23rd International Symposium on Implementation and Application of Functional Languages*. LNCS, vol. 7257. Springer.

Runciman, Colin, Naylor, Matthew, and Lindblad, Fredrik. 2008. SmallCheck and Lazy SmallCheck: automatic exhaustive testing for small values. Pages 37–48 of: *1st ACM SIGPLAN Symposium on Haskell*. ACM.

Seidel, Eric L., Vazou, Niki, and Jhala, Ranjit. 2015. Type Targeted Testing. Pages 812–836 of: *Programming Languages and Systems: 24th European Symposium on Programming, ESOP 2015, Held as Part of the European Joint Conferences on Theory and Practice of Software, ETAPS 2015, London, UK, April 11-18, 2015. Proceedings*.

Sen, Koushik, Marinov, Darko, and Agha, Gul. 2005. CUTE: a concolic unit testing engine for C. Pages 263–272 of: *10th European software engineering conference held jointly with 13th ACM SIGSOFT international symposium on Foundations of software engineering*. ESEC/FSE-13. ACM.

Tarau, Paul. 2015. On Type-directed Generation of Lambda Terms. In: *Proceedings of the Technical Communications of the 31st International Conference on Logic Programming (ICLP 2015), Cork, Ireland, August 31–September 4, 2015*.

Tolmach, Andrew P., and Antoy, Sergio. 2003. A monadic semantics for core Curry. *Electr. Notes Theor. Comput. Sci.*, **86**(3), 16–34.

Torlak, Emina, and Bodík, Rastislav. 2014. A lightweight symbolic virtual machine for solver-aided host languages. Page 54 of: *ACM SIGPLAN Conference on Programming Language Design and Implementation*. ACM.

Tabular: Probabilistic Inference from the Spreadsheet

Andrew D. Gordon
Microsoft Research and University of Edinburgh
Claudio Russo[a]
DFINITY, Zürich
Marcin Szymczak[b]
RWTH Aachen University
Johannes Borgström
Uppsala University
Nicolas Rolland[a] and Thore Graepel[a]
University College London
Daniel Tarlow[a]
Google Research, Brain Team, Montreal

Abstract: Tabular is a domain-specific language for expressing probabilistic models of relational data. Tabular has several features that set it apart from other probabilistic programming languages including: (1) programs and data are stored as spreadsheet tables; (2) programs consist of probabilistic annotations on the relational schema of the data; and (3) inference returns estimations of missing values and latent columns, as well as parameters. Our primary implementation is for Microsoft Excel and relies on Infer.NET for inference. Still, the language can be called independently of Excel and can target alternative inference engines.

14.1 Overview

Probabilistic programming languages promise to make machine learning more accessible by allowing users to write their generative models as computer programs and providing generic inference engines capable of performing inference on all valid programs expressible in the given language. However, as most of the currently existing languages are essentially probabilistic extensions of conventional programming languages, they are arguably not ideally suited for the job.

For one thing, they are still difficult to use for people who are not professional programmers. Meanwhile, many people who may want to use probabilistic mod-

[a]   The work was conducted while the authors were at Microsoft Research
[b]   The work was conducted while the author was at University of Edinburgh and Oxford University
[c]   From *Foundations of Probabilistic Programming*, edited by Gilles Barthe, Joost-Pieter Katoen and Alexandra Silva published 2020 by Cambridge University Press.

elling are domain experts, for instance business analysts, who often have limited programming experience and could find, for instance, systems based on functional (Goodman et al., 2008; Wood et al., 2014) or logic (Van den Broeck et al., 2010) programming baffling. Secondly, most existing languages require all the necessary data to be loaded and placed in the right data structures. This can often be problematic and require a large amount of data pre-processing, which could be a nuisance even for experienced programmers and statisticians.

The Tabular language, first presented by Gordon et al. (2014b), takes a different approach. Instead of extending an ordinary programming language with primitives for sampling and conditioning, Tabular extends schemas of relational databases with probabilistic model expressions and annotations. This idea is based on the observation that in model-based Bayesian machine learning, the starting point is not the model itself, but the dataset to which one wants to fit a model, which has to be stored in some sort of database – for example a spreadsheet. In Tabular, the probabilistic model is built on top of the data, and the input database does not need to be manipulated before being fed to the program.

A key strength of Tabular is that it is easier to use than standard programming languages, because it does not require the user to write an actual program from scratch – all that the user has to do to define a model is to annotate a database schema with probabilistic expressions explaining how they believe the data was generated and add latent columns for the unknown quantities of interest. Moreover, Tabular's design allows it to be integrated with environments such as spreadsheet applications, that are familiar to users who are not professional programmers. Indeed, Tabular has been implemented as an Excel plugin and both the model and the input database are specified as Excel spreadsheets. Inference results are also saved to a spreadsheet, which allows for easier post-processing and visualisation. The command-line version of Tabular is open source and the source code is available at `https://github.com/TabularLang/CoreTabular`.

In this chapter, we present a new, substantially enhanced version of Tabular, which features user-defined functions and queries on inference results. We endow Tabular with a structural, dependent type system, which helps understand the sample space of a program and catch common modelling mistakes. We define a reduction relation reducing Tabular programs with function applications to Core models containing only simple expressions and corresponding directly to factor graphs. We also demonstrate by example how these features make Tabular a useful language for Bayesian modelling.

This chapter is based on Chapter 4 of Szymczak (2018), which is itself an extended version of Gordon et al. (2015).

14.2 Introduction and Examples

In this section, we introduce Tabular informally, explaining its features by example.

14.2.1 Probabilistic Programming in Tabular

A Tabular program is constructed by extending a database schema with:

- *Latent columns* representing unknown parameters, not present in the database, which we want to infer from the data,
- *Annotations* defining roles of respective columns in the probabilistic model (input variables, modelled output variables, local variables),
- *Model expressions*, which express our belief about how the values in the given column of the database were generated.

In the simplest case, model expressions are ordinary expressions written in a first-order functional language with random draws. We refer to schemas and tables containing only such simple expressions as Core schemas and tables. Other kinds of models include function applications and indexed models, which will be discussed later.

Let us begin the presentation of Tabular with an example based on one from Gordon et al. (2014b), which implements the TrueSkill model (Herbrich et al., 2007) for ranking players in online video games. Suppose we have a database containing the outcomes of past matches between some players. This database can have the following schema (where we assume that each table has an implicit, integer-valued ID column, serving as the primary key of the table):

table Players	
Name	**string**
table Matches	
Player1	**link**(Players)
Player2	**link**(Players)
Win1	**bool**

where Win1 is true if the match was won by Player 1 and false if Player 2 won the match (we assume there are no draws). Based on these past results, we want to infer the relative skills of the players.

According to the TrueSkill model, we quantify the *performance* of a given player in a certain match by a numeric value, which is a noisy copy of the player's skill. We assume that each match was won by the player with higher performance value. We can implement this model in Tabular by extending the above schema as follows[1]:

---

[1] As explained in Section 14.3, in the formal syntax of Tabular, each column has a global and local name, because of issues with α-conversion. In the introductory examples in this section, we only give each column one name, serving both as a global and local identifier, to simplify presentation.

table Players			
Name	**string!det**	**input**	
Skill	**real!rnd**	**output**	Gaussian(100.0, 100.0)
table Matches			
Player1	**link(Players)!det**	**input**	
Player2	**link(Players)!det**	**input**	
Perf1	**real!rnd**	**output**	Gaussian(Player1.Skill, 100.0)
Perf2	**real!rnd**	**output**	Gaussian(Player2.Skill, 100.0)
Win1	**bool!rnd**	**output**	Perf1 > Perf2

We have added one new column, not present in the database, to the Players table and two columns to the Matches table. The Players table now has a Skill attribute. This column is not expected to be present in the input database – its distribution is to be inferred from the observed data. By assigning the expression Gaussian(100.0, 100.0) to this column, we have defined the prior distribution on players' skills to be a Gaussian with mean 100 and variance 100. Similarly, the values of the Perf1 and Perf2 columns are, in the generative interpretation of the model, drawn from Gaussians centred at the skills of the corresponding players (the expression Player1.Skill is a reference to the value of Skill in the row of Players linked to by Player1, and similarly for Player2.Skill). Finally, the observed Win1 column is assigned the expression Perf1 > Perf2, which expresses the condition that in every row of the Matches table, Perf1 must be greater than Perf2 if Win1 in this row is **true** in the database, and not greater than Perf2 if Win1 is **false** – otherwise, the values of the parameters would be inconsistent with the observations.

The types in the second schema include **det** and **rnd** annotations which specify whether the data in the given column is deterministic (known in advance) or random (to be inferred by the inference algorithm). These annotations, which we call *spaces*, are used by the type system to catch information flow errors, such as supposedly deterministic data depending on random variables. Tabular columns can also be in space **qry**, which will be discussed later.

To perform inference in the above model, we need to parametrise it on a particular dataset. In Tabular, like in BUGS (Gilks et al., 1994) and Stan (Carpenter et al., 2017), input data is decoupled from the program and is loaded by the compiler from a separate data source. This approach makes it possible to run inference in the same model with multiple datasets without modifying the model. The TrueSkill model, as implemented above, was designed to be applied to databases containing thousands of matches and players, but the following is a valid tiny input database for this schema:

Players

ID	Name
0	"Alice"
1	"Bob"
2	"Cynthia"

Matches

ID	Player1	Player2	Win1
0	0	1	**false**
1	1	2	**false**

In this example, we have only three players, Alice, Bob and Cynthia, and we assume that Bob beat Alice in the first match and was beaten by Cynthia in the second one.

The default inference algorithm of Tabular, Expectation Propagation (Minka, 2001), adds the approximate distributions of unobserved random columns to the input database. The output database for the above tiny example is as follows:

Players

ID	Name	Skill
0	"Alice"	Gaussian(95.25, 82.28)
1	"Bob"	Gaussian(100.0, 70.66)
2	"Cynthia"	Gaussian(104.8, 82.28)

Matches

ID	P1	P2	Perf1	Perf2	Win1
0	0	1	Gaussian(90.49, 129.1)	Gaussian(104.8, 123.6)	**false**
1	1	2	Gaussian(95.25, 123.6)	Gaussian(109.5, 129.1)	**false**

This matches our intuition that Cynthia, having beaten the winner of the first match, is most likely to be the best of the three players, and Alice is probably the weakest.

In addition to the style of inference described above, called *query-by-latent-column*, Tabular also supports *query-by-missing-value*, where the database has some missing entries for one or many **output** columns and the goal is to compute the distributions on the missing values. For example, if we want to predict the outcome of an upcoming match between Alice and Cynthia, we can extend the matches table as follows:

Matches

ID	Player1	Player2	Win1
0	0	1	**false**
1	1	2	**false**
2	0	2	?

The Tabular inference engine will then compute the distribution of Win1 in the third column.

Matches

ID	P1	P2	Perf1	Perf2	Win1
0	0	1	Gaussian(90.49, 129.1)	Gaussian(104.8, 123.6)	**false**
1	1	2	Gaussian(95.25, 123.6)	Gaussian(109.5, 129.1)	**false**
2	0	2	Gaussian(95.25, 182.3)	Gaussian(104.8, 182.3)	Bernoulli(0.3092)

14.2.2 User-Defined, Dependently-Typed Functions

Tabular supports *functions*, which are defined in the same way as ordinary tables and can be used to abstract away arbitrary repeated blocks of code which only differ by some values used in the model expressions. Functions can help users make their schemas shorter and more concise. Tabular already comes with a library of predefined functions, representing, for instance, commonly used conjugate models, and new functions can be defined by the user.

To illustrate how functions can be used in Tabular, let us consider the well-known problem of inferring the bias of a coin from the outcomes of coin tosses. Assuming that each bias (between 0 and 1) is equally likely, this model can be represented in Tabular as follows:

table Coins			
V	real!rnd[2]	static output	Dirichlet[2]([1.0, 1.0])
Flip	mod(2)!rnd	output	Discrete[2](V)

where Dirichlet[2]([1.0, 1.0]) is just the uniform distribution on pairs of two probabilities adding up to 1, and Discrete[2](V) draws 0 or 1 (representing tails and heads, respectively) with probability proportional to the corresponding component of V.

This model, in which the parameter to the discrete distribution has a uniform Dirichlet prior, is an instance of the *Conjugate Discrete* model. Conjugate Discrete, which is a building block of many more complex models, is defined in the standard function library as follows:

fun CDiscrete			
N	int!det	static input	
R	real!det	static input	
V	real!rnd[N]	static output	Dirichlet[N]([for i < N → R])
ret	mod(N)!rnd	output	Discrete[N](V)

The arguments of this function, N and R, denote, respectively, the length of the parameter vector and the value of each component of the hyperparameter vector passed to the prior (the higher the value of R, the closer together the components of the parameter vector are expected to be). This function also demonstrates the use of dependent types: **real!rnd**[N] indicates that the given random column is an array of reals of size determined by the variable N, and **mod**(N)!**rnd** denotes a non-negative random integer smaller than N. It is worth noting that in the definition of CDiscrete we could alternatively make the entire pseudocount vector passed to Dirichlet[N] an argument of type **real!det**[N].

With this function in place, we can rewrite the coin toss model as follows:

table Coins			
Flip	mod(2)!rnd	output	CDiscrete(N=2, R=1.0)

where setting R to 1.0 guarantees that the prior distribution on probabilities V of heads and tails is uniform.

The reduction algorithm presented later in this chapter reduces this table to the form shown earlier, modulo renaming of column names.

Tabular also supports *indexing* function applications, which results in turning static parameters of the model into arrays, indexed by a categorical variable (that is, a discrete random variable with a finite domain). For example, suppose that in the above problem we have two coins with different biases, and we always toss one of them, chosen at random with equal probability. To infer the biases of the coins, we can adapt the above Tabular program as follows:

table Coins			
CoinUsed	mod(2)!rnd	output	Discrete[2]([0.5, 0.5])
Flip	int!rnd	output	CDiscrete(N=2, R=1.0)[CoinUsed < 2]

Now, we have two copies of the bias vector V, one for each coin, and at each row, the vector indicated by the random variable CoinUsed is used.

14.2.3 Query Variables

Another novel feature of Tabular is the **infer** operator, which can be used to extract properties of an inferred distribution, such as its mean (in case of, say, a Gaussian) or bias (in case of a Bernoulli distribution). These properties can then be used to compute some pseudo-deterministic data dependent on the inference results.

For instance, in the above biased coin example, we might be interested in extracting the actual bias of the coin, as a numeric value rather than a distribution. Since the posterior distribution of the bias is a Dirichlet distribution, parametrized by the "pseudocounts" of the numbers of heads and tails, the bias itself is the count of heads divided by the sum of the counts. Using the **infer** operator, we can compute it as follows:

table Coins			
V	real!rnd[2]	static output	Dirichlet[2]([1.0, 1.0])
Flip	mod(2)!rnd	output	Discrete[2](V)
counts	real!qry[2]	static local	infer.Dirichlet[2].pseudocount(V)
Bias	real!qry	static output	counts[1]/(counts[1]+counts[0])

For instance, if we apply this model to a tiny database consisting of three coin flip outcomes, two of them being heads and one being tails, the inference algorithm returns the following static quantities:

Coins		
V	counts	Bias
Dirichlet(2, 3)	[2,3]	0.6

In the expression **infer**.Dirichlet[2].pseudocount(V), Dirichlet[2] denotes the type of distribution from which we want to extract a property, pseudocount is the name of the parameter we want to extract (in Tabular, all distributions have named parameters) and V is the column in which the distribution is defined.

All columns containing calculations dependent on the result of a query are in the **qry** space. Columns in this space can only reference random variables via the **infer** operator.

After adding the **infer** operator, we now have three different kinds of columns in Tabular: deterministic columns, whose values are known before inference; random columns, whose distributions are to be inferred and may depend on deterministic columns, and query columns, depending on inferred distributions. The values or distributions of these columns (in all rows) must be computed in the right order, for instance, a random column cannot depend on the result of a query. To make sure that there are no erroneous dependencies in the program, the columns are split into three spaces: **det**, **rnd** and **qry**; space annotations ensure that the constraints on dependencies between columns are preserved.

14.2.4 Related Work

Probabilistic programming is becoming an increasingly popular approach to Bayesian inference and many new languages following different paradigms were created recently. These include functional languages like Fun (Borgström et al., 2013), Church (Goodman et al., 2008), Anglican (Wood et al., 2014), Venture (Mansinghka et al., 2014), WebPPL (Goodman and Stuhlmüller, 2014) and monad-bayes (Ścibior et al., 2015), procedural languages like R2 (Nori et al., 2014), Infer.NET (Minka et al., 2012) and Stan (Carpenter et al., 2017), logical languages such as ProbLog (Van den Broeck et al., 2010) and even an implementation of the probabilistic process algebra ProPPA (Georgoulas et al., 2014). Recently, a new class of probabilistic languages marrying Bayesian modelling with deep neural networks saw the light of day. These include Pyro (Bingham et al., 2018) and ProbTorch (Siddharth et al., 2017).

Designing a language involves a trade-off between expressiveness and performance. In this respect, probabilistic languages can be roughly divided into two groups: universal, Turing-complete languages such as R2 and Church and its descendants, which allow creation of arbitrary probabilistic models (including nonparametric models with unbounded numbers of random variables) but can only use a limited range of sampling-based inference algorithms, and more restricted languages like Infer.NET and BUGS (Gilks et al., 1994), in which models correspond to factor graphs and which can therefore use a wider class of inference algorithms, including algorithms for factor graphs. Tabular belongs to the second class and uses Expectation Propagation (Minka, 2001) as its default inference algorithm.

In terms of the paradigm and user interface, the two probabilistic programming

packages most related to Tabular are BayesDB (Mansinghka et al., 2015) and Scenarios (Wu et al., 2016). BayesDB is a probabilistic package based on relational
database schemas. Its modelling language is a probabilistic extension of SQL,
which is significantly different from the approach taken by Tabular, where models
are written by directly annotating database schemas. Scenarios is a commercial
Excel plugin which allows defining probabilistic models in a spreadsheet environment. The difference between Scenarios and Tabular is that the former is shallowly
embedded in Excel and defines probabilistic models via special Excel functions,
while Tabular is a standalone probabilistic language which simply uses Excel as a
convenient development environment. Because of its shallow embedding within a
dynamically typed formula language, Scenarios does not have a static type system.

14.2.5 Retrospective and Related Projects

Tabular was first presented by Gordon et al. (2014b) as a language based on database
schemas, with a standalone implementation in the form of a GUI program interfac-
ing directly with a relational database. This initial version of the language did not
support functions – models were either simple expressions or predefined conjugate
models from a small, fixed library. Tabular had a non-dependent type system without spaces, in which the type of a schema was a quintuple of nested record types,
whose components specified the types of hyperparameters, parameters, inputs and
latent and observed variables of the model defined by the table. The semantics of
Tabular was defined by means of translation to Fun (Borgström et al., 2013), a first-
order, functional probabilistic programming language. Post-processing of inference
results had to be done outside Tabular.

A revised version of the language, described by Gordon et al. (2015), added
support for user-defined functions and queries, as described earlier in this section.
The original type system was replaced by a simpler one, in which types themselves
have a similar form to Core Tabular tables. The new type system supports basic dependent types and provides space annotations dividing columns into deterministic,
random and query columns. The semantics of the new version of Tabular consists
of a reduction system reducing schemas with functions and indexing to the Core
form and a semantics of Core Tabular models (omitted in this chapter, see the long
version of the aforementioned paper (Gordon et al., 2014a)), defined directly in
terms of measure theory. Reduction to Core form is proven type-sound.

Further improvements to Tabular were presented in the doctoral dissertation of
Szymczak (2018), which introduced double column names to fix a problem with
α-conversion and presented a more rigorous proof of type soundness of schema reduction. The dissertation also described a new, arguably more rigorous and elegant,
semantics of Core Tabular models.

Fabular, presented by Borgström et al. (2016), extends Tabular with hierarchical linear regression formulas, extending the formula notation used by R packages such as `lmer`. Such formulas allow for a concise representation of a wide class of models and can be used in Tabular like any other model expressions.

Additionally in his Master's dissertation, Hutchison (2016) presented a generative grammar allowing dynamic creation of Tabular programs, which could serve as a basis for an automated model suggestion tool for Tabular. Hence, Tabular was used as part of a study of the internet-based trade in specimens of endangered species of plants (Vaglica et al., 2017).

14.3 Syntax of Tabular

Having introduced Tabular informally, we now present the formal syntax of the language. Since programs and data are decoupled in Tabular, we need to define the syntax for both Tabular databases and schemas.

14.3.1 Syntax of Databases

A Tabular database is a tuple $DB = (\delta_{in}, \rho_{sz})$, consisting of two maps whose domain is the set of names of tables in the database. The first map, $\delta_{in} = [t_i \mapsto \tau_i{}^{i \in 1..n}]$, assigns to each table another map $\tau_i = [c_j \mapsto a_j{}^{j \in 1..m_i}]$ mapping each column c_i to an attribute a_i. An *attribute* $a_j = \ell_j(V_j)$ consists of a *level* ℓ_j and a *value* V_j, which can be a scalar s (that is, an integer, a real or a Boolean) or an array of values. The level of an attribute can be either **static**, in which case the given column has only one value accross all rows, or **inst**, which means that the column has one value per row. In the latter case, V_j is actually an array of values, with one value per row. Column names c_j have the same form as external column names in schemas (described below), except that they are not allowed to be empty.

The second map, $\rho_{sz} = [t_i \mapsto sz_i{}^{i \in 1..n}]$, simply stores the sizes of tables. The value of each **inst**-level attribute of table t_i must be an array of size sz_i.

Any value V_j in the database can be *nullable*, that is, any **static** attribute can have an empty value (denoted ?) and in any **inst** attribute, any number of component values can be empty. An empty value in a row of an **output** column means that the distribution on the given row and column is to be inferred from other data by the inference algorithm.

Databases, Tables, Attributes, and Values:

$\delta_{in} ::= [t_i \mapsto \tau_i{}^{i \in 1..n}]$	table map
$c, o ::= b_1.(\ldots).b_n$	column name
$\rho_{sz} ::= [t_i \mapsto sz_i{}^{i \in 1..n}]$	table size map

$a ::= \ell(V)$	attribute value: V with level ℓ
$V ::= ? \mid s \mid [V_0, \dots, V_{n-1}]$	nullable value
$\ell, pc ::= \textbf{static} \mid \textbf{inst}$	level (**static** < **inst**)
$\tau ::= [c_j \mapsto a_j{}^{j \in 1..m}]$	table in database

For example, the input database for the TrueSkill example from Section 14.2.1 can be written as follows using the formal syntax of databases:

$$[\text{Players} \mapsto [\text{ID} \mapsto \textbf{inst}([0,1,2])],$$
$$\text{Matches} \mapsto [\text{ID} \mapsto \textbf{inst}([0,1,2]), \text{Player1} \mapsto \textbf{inst}([0,1,0]),$$
$$\text{Player2} \mapsto \textbf{inst}([1,2,2]), \text{Win1} \mapsto \textbf{inst}([0,0,?])]]$$

where player names are omitted (they are insignificant for the model, and the formal syntax of Tabular does not allow strings[2]) and **true** and **false** are represented by 1 and 0, respectively.

14.3.2 Syntax of Core Schemas

We begin by giving the syntax of Core schemas, which have a straightforward interpretation as factor graphs. We first define the basic building blocks of a Tabular column.

Index Expressions, Spaces and Dependent Types of Tabular:

$e ::=$	index expression
$\quad x$	variable
$\quad s$	scalar constant
$\quad \textbf{sizeof}(t)$	size of a table
$S ::= \textbf{bool} \mid \textbf{int} \mid \textbf{real}$	scalar type
$spc ::= \textbf{det} \mid \textbf{rnd} \mid \textbf{qry}$	space
$T, U ::= (S \,!\, spc) \mid (\textbf{mod}(e) \,!\, spc) \mid T[e]$	(attribute) type
$c, o ::= \_ \mid b_1.(\dots).b_n$	external column name
$\text{space}(S \,!\, spc) \triangleq spc \quad \text{space}(\textbf{mod}(e) \,!\, spc) \triangleq spc \quad \text{space}(T[e]) \triangleq \text{space}(T)$	

An *index expression* is a constant, a variable (referencing a previous column or an array index) or a **sizeof** expression, returning the size of the given table (that is, **sizeof**(t) returns $\rho_{sz}(t)$ if ρ_{sz} is the map of table sizes). A *scalar type* is one of **bool**, **int** or **real**. These correspond to scalar types in conventional languages. A *space* of a column, being part of its type, can be either **det**, **rnd** or **qry**, depending on

---

[2] The implementation of Tabular does support strings and implicitly converts them to integers

whether the column is deterministic, random or at query-level. An attribute *type* can be either a scalar type S with a space, a dependent bounded integer type **mod**(e), whose bound is defined by the indexed expression e, with a space, or a recursively defined array type $T[e]$, where T is an arbitrary type and e an index expression defining the size of the array. We use **link**(t) as a shorthand for **mod**(**sizeof**(t)). An *external column name*, used to reference a column from another table or to access a field of a reduced function body, is either empty (denoted by _) or consists of a sequence of one or more *atomic names* b_i, separated by dots.

The space operator, used in the remainder of this chapter, returns the unique space annotation nested within the given type.

As an example, consider the type of the Flip column in the Coins table in Section 14.2.2, **mod**(2)!**rnd**. This is a type of random non-negative integer-valued expressions bounded by 2 (that is, admitting only values 0 and 1). It is clear by definition of space that space(**mod**(2)!**rnd**) = **rnd**. Moreover, the type of the V column in CDiscrete in Section 14.2.2, **real**!**rnd**[N], is a type of arrays of size N (where the variable N represents a deterministic non-negative integer), whose elements all have type **real**!**rnd** (that is, are random real-valued expressions). The space of this type is given by space(**real**!**rnd**[N]) = space(**real**!**rnd**) = **rnd**.

Expressions of Tabular:

$E, F ::=$	expression
e	index expression
$g(E_1,\ldots,E_n)$	deterministic primitive g
$D[e_1,\ldots,e_m](F_1,\ldots,F_n)$	random draw from distribution D
if E **then** F_1 **else** F_2	if-then-else
$[E_1,\ldots,E_n] \mid E[F]$	array literal, lookup
$[\textbf{for } x < e \rightarrow F]$	for loop (scope of index x is F)
infer.$D[e_1,\ldots,e_m].c(E)$	parameter c of inferred marginal of E
$E : t.c$	dereference link E to instance of c
$t.c$	dereference static attribute c of t

This grammar of expressions, defining models of the particular columns of the table, is mostly standard for a first-order probabilistic functional language. The expression $D[e_1,\ldots,e_m](F_1,\ldots,F_n)$ represents a draw from a primitive distribution D with hyperparameters determined by the index expressions $e_1,\ldots,e_m$ and parameters defined by the expressions $F_1,\ldots,F_n$. The operator **infer**.$D[e_1,\ldots,e_m].c(E)$ returns an approximate value of the parameter c of the posterior distribution of expression E, expected to be of the form $D[e_1,\ldots,e_m]$. Access to columns defined in previous tables is provided via the operators $t.c$ and $E : t.c$, referencing, respectively, the static attribute with global name c of table t and the E-th row of **inst**-level attribute with global name c of table t. We assume a fixed (but extensible) collection of distributions and deterministic primitives, such as addition, multiplication and comparison.

Distribution signatures are parametrized by *spc*, to distinguish the use of corresponding distributions in random models and inside queries. The signatures of distributions include the following:

Distributions: $D_{spc} : [x_1 : T_1, \ldots, x_m : T_m](c_1 : U_1, \ldots, c_n : U_n) \to T$

Bernoulli$_{spc}$: (bias : **real!**spc) $\to$ **bool!rnd**

Beta$_{spc}$ :: (a : **real!**spc, b : **real!**spc) $\to$ **real!rnd**

Discrete$_{spc}$: [N : **int!det**](probs : **real!**spc[N]) $\to$ **mod**(N)**!rnd**

Dirichlet$_{spc}$: [N : **int!det**](pseudocount : (**real!**spc)[N]) $\to$ (**real!rnd**)[N]

Gamma$_{spc}$: (shape : **real!**spc, scale : **real!**spc) $\to$ **real!rnd**

Gaussian$_{spc}$: (mean : **real!**spc, variance : **real!**spc) $\to$ **real!rnd**

VectorGaussian$_{spc}$:

  [N : **int!det**](mean : (**real!**spc)[N], covariance : **real!**spc[N][N]) $\to$

    (**real!rnd**[N])

The names of parameters of distributions are fixed and not α-convertible, as they can be referenced by name by the **infer** operator.

Random draws and the **infer** operator were already used in examples in Sections 14.2.2 and 14.2.3. For instance, the expression Dirichlet[2]([1.0, 1.0]) in the column V in table Coins is a random draw from the Dirichlet distribution with the single hyperparameter N (denoting the length of the parameter array and the output array) set to 2 and the single parameter pseudocount (of type (**real!**spc)[2]) set to the array [1.0, 1.0]. Meanwhile, Gaussian([100.0, 100.0]) in the Skill column in table Players is the Gaussian distribution with parameters mean and variance both set to 100. The list of hyperparameters is empty, because (as is clear from the signature) the Gaussian distribution admits no hyperparameters.

The **infer** operator is used in column counts in table Coins in Section 14.2.3. In the expression **infer**.Dirichlet[2].pseudocount(V), V is the name of the column whose posterior distribution we are interested in, Dirichlet[2] is the expected type and hyperparameter vector of that distribution (which we know because of conjugacy) and pseudocount is the name of the parameter of the Dirichlet posterior distribution in column V whose expected value we want to obtain. In other words, if the posterior distribution of the column V returned by the inference algorithm is Dirichlet[2][c_1, c_2], the expression **infer**.Dirichlet[2].pseudocount(V) returns [c_1, c_2], which is the value of the pseudocount parameter of Dirichlet[2][c_1, c_2].

The list of random primitives can be extended by adding multiple signatures for different parametrisations of the same distribution – for instance, the Gaussian distribution, parametrised above by its mean and variance, can also be parametrised by mean and precision (inverse of variance). This parametrisation is convenient when defining the conjugate Gaussian model.

Distributions: $D_{spc} : [x_1 : T_1, \ldots, x_m : T_m](c_1 : U_1, \ldots, c_n : U_n) \to T$

GaussianFromMeanAndPrecision$_{spc}$:
  (mean : **real!**spc, prec : **real!**spc) $\to$ **real!rnd**

In the rest of this chapter, we will abbreviate GaussianFromMeanAndPrecision as GaussianMP.

The syntax of Core Tabular schemas is as follows:

Core Tabular Schemas:

$\mathbb{S} ::= [] \mid (t_1 = \mathbb{T}_1) :: \mathbb{S}$	(database) schema
$\mathbb{T} ::= [] \mid (c \triangleright x : T \; \ell \; viz \; M) :: \mathbb{T}$	table (or function) (scope of x is $\mathbb{T}$)
$viz ::= $ **input** $\mid$ **local** $\mid$ **output**	visibility
$M, N ::= \epsilon \mid E$	model expression

A Tabular *schema* $\mathbb{S}$ consists of any number of named *tables* $\mathbb{T}$, each of which is a sequence of *columns*. Every column in Core Tabular has a *field name c* (also called a *global* or *external name*), an *internal name x* (also called a *local name*), a *type T* (as defined earlier), a *level* (**static** or **inst**), a *visibility* (**input**, **output** or **local**) and a *model expression*, which is empty for **input** columns and is a simple expression E for other types of columns. The **local** visibility is just like **output**, except that **local** columns are not exported to the type of the schema (as defined by the type system, described in Section 14.5), and so can be considered local variables. The default level of a column is **inst**, and we usually omit the level if it is not **static**.

Tables and schemas can also be represented in the formal syntax using list notation. We define $[(c_1 \triangleright x_1 : T_1 \; \ell_1 \; viz_1 \; M_1), \ldots, (c_n \triangleright x_n : T_n \; \ell_n \; viz_n \; M_n)]$ and $[t_1 = \mathbb{T}_1, \ldots, t_n = \mathbb{T}_n]$ to be syntactic sugar for $(c_1 \triangleright x_1 : T_1 \; \ell_1 \; viz_1 \; M_1) :: \ldots :: (c_n \triangleright x_n : T_n \; \ell_n \; viz_n \; M_n) :: []$ and $(t_1 = \mathbb{T}_1) :: \ldots :: (t_n = \mathbb{T}_n) :: []$, respectively.

To illustrate the formal syntax of Tabular, let us consider again the simple Coins table, which was presented in the grid-based form at the beginning of Section 14.2.2. If we specify the global and local names explicitly, this table has the following form:

table Coins			
V ▷ V	**real!rnd[2]**	**static output**	Dirichlet[2]([1.0, 1.0])
Flip ▷ Flip	**mod(2)!rnd**	**output**	Discrete[2](V)

In the formal Tabular syntax, this table would be written as follows:

$$[(V \triangleright V : \textbf{real!rnd}[2] \textbf{ static output } \text{Dirichlet}[2]([1.0, 1.0]),$$

$$(\text{Flip} \triangleright \text{Flip} : \textbf{mod}(2)\textbf{!rnd inst output } \text{Discrete}[2](V))]$$

The schema consisting of just this single table is:

$$[\text{Coins} = [(V \triangleright V : \textbf{real!rnd}[2] \textbf{ static output } \text{Dirichlet}[2]([1.0, 1.0]),$$

$$(\text{Flip} \triangleright \text{Flip} : \textbf{mod}(2)\textbf{!rnd inst output } \text{Discrete}[2](V))]]$$

In the rest of this chapter, col denotes a single column $(c \triangleright x : T \ \ell \ viz \ M)$ of a table, where its components are unimportant.

Motivation for double column names In the syntax of the new version of Tabular presented in the paper which was the starting point for this work (Gordon et al., 2015), each column only has one name. This causes a problem with alpha-conversion: if a column is visible outside the given table, then its name cannot be alpha-convertible, since renaming the column would break references to it from outside the table. On the other hand, alpha-conversion is necessary for the substitution and function reduction to work properly. To mitigate this issue, we now follow the standard approach used in module systems, first presented by Harper and Lillibridge (1994): we give each column two names, a local, alpha-convertible name, which is only in scope of a given table, and a global, fixed field name, which can only be used outside the table (or function). In practice, we can assume that the internal and external name are initially the same.

14.3.3 Syntax of Schemas with Functions and Indexing

Tabular supports two additional kinds of model expressions: *function applications* and *indexed models*.

A function is represented as a Core table whose last column is identified by the name ret and has visibility **output**. A function $\mathbb{T}$ can be applied to a list of named *arguments R*, whose types and number must match the types and number of **input** columns in the function table. Note that function arguments are identified by the field name of the corresponding column. The reduction algorithm (presented in Section 14.4) reduces a column containing a function application to the body of the function with all **input** columns removed and the input variables in subsequent model expressions replaced by the corresponding arguments.

The output column of a function can be referenced in the "caller" table simply by the (local) name of the "caller" column. Other columns can be referenced by means of a new operator $e.c$, where e is expected to be the local name x of the "caller" column and c is the field name of the referenced column of the function table (we need to use the field name, because the local name is only in scope inside the function).

An *indexed model* $M[e_{index} < e_{size}]$ represents the model M with all **rnd static** attributes turned into arrays of size e_{size} and references to them replaced by array lookups extracting the element at index e_{index}.

Full Tabular Schemas:

$E ::= \cdots \mid e.c$	expression
$M, N ::= \cdots \mid M[e_{index} < e_{size}] \mid \mathbb{T}\, R$	model expression
$R ::= [\,] \mid (c = e) :: R$	function arguments

Function arguments can also be represented using the standard list notation as $R = (c_1 = e_1, \ldots, c_n = e_n)$. The function field reference is only defined to be $e.c$ rather than $x.c$ in order for substitution to be well-defined. The indexing operator is only meaningful if it is applied (possibly multiple times) to a function application, since it has no effect on basic expressions.

In the Coins example in Section 14.2.2, a predefined function (from the standard library) was referenced in the main table by its name. Indeed, in the implementation, functions are always defined outside of the main schema and are called by identifiers. In the formal syntax, however, functions are inlined. For instance, to represent the function call CDiscrete(N = 2, R = 1.0) formally, we need to substitute CDiscrete with its body. The resulting function application looks as follows:

$$[(\mathsf{N} \triangleright \mathsf{N} : \textbf{int!det static input } \epsilon),$$
$$(\mathsf{R} \triangleright \mathsf{R} : \textbf{real!det static input } \epsilon),$$
$$(\mathsf{V} \triangleright \mathsf{V} : \textbf{real!rnd}[\mathsf{N}] \textbf{ static input } \mathsf{Dirichlet}[\mathsf{N}]([\textbf{for } i < \mathsf{N} \rightarrow R)),$$
$$(\mathsf{ret} \triangleright \mathsf{ret} : \textbf{mod}(\mathsf{N})\textbf{!rnd}[\mathsf{N}] \textbf{ static input } \mathsf{Dirichlet}[\mathsf{N}]([\textbf{for } i < \mathsf{N} \rightarrow R))]$$
$$(\mathsf{N} = 2, \mathsf{R} = 1)$$

Free Variables and Core *Columns*

The free variables $\mathrm{fv}(\mathbb{T})$ of a table $\mathbb{T}$ are all local variables used in column types and model expressions which are not bound by column declarations or for-loops. Formally, the operator $\mathrm{fv}(\mathbb{T})$ can be defined inductively in the usual way. Unbound occurrences of field names are not considered free variables, as they are a separate syntactic category.

The predicate Core states that the given schema, table or column is in Core form, as defined earlier.

14.4 Reduction to Core Tabular

We now define the reduction relation which reduces arbitrary well-typed Tabular schemas (with function applications and indexing) to a Core form. Before discussing the technical details of reduction, we present an example which will guide our development. This time we make the distinction between local and field names explicit, to illustrate how substitution and renaming work.

Consider the following function implementing the widely used Conjugate Gaussian model, whose output is drawn from a Gaussian with mean modelled by another Gaussian and precision (inverse of variance) drawn from a Gamma distribution:

fun CG			
M ▷ M	real!det	static input	
P ▷ P	real!det	static input	
Mean ▷ Mean	real!rnd	static output	GaussianMP(M,P)
Prec ▷ Prec	real!rnd	static output	Gamma(1.0, 1.0)
ret ▷ ret	real!rnd	output	GaussianMP(Mean, Prec)

Suppose we want to use this function to model eruptions of the Old Faithful geyser in the Yellowstone National Park. The eruptions of this geyser, known for its regularity, can be split into two clusters based on their duration and time elapsed since the previous eruption: some eruptions are shorter and occur more frequently, others are longer but one has to wait longer to see them. Given a database consisting of eruption durations and waiting times (not split into clusters), we want to infer the means and precisions of the distributions of durations and waiting times in each of the two clusters. If we simply modelled the duration and waiting time with a call to CG, we would obtain a single distribution for the mean and precision of each quantity, but we can turn each Mean and Prec column into an array of size 2 by combining the function calls with indexing.

table Faithful			
cluster ▷ cluster	mod(2)!rnd	output	(CDiscrete(N=2)
duration ▷ duration	real!rnd	output	CG(M=0.0, P=1.0)[cluster<2]
time ▷ time	real!rnd	output	CG(M=60.0, P=1.0)[cluster<2]

14.4.1 Reducing Function Applications

Before we introduce the reduction of indexed models, let us consider a simplified version of the above model, with just function applications:

table Faithful			
duration ▷ duration	real!rnd	output	CG(M=0.0, P=1.0)
time ▷ time	real!rnd	output	CG(M=60.0, P=1.0)

To reduce the duration and time columns to Core form, we must expand the applications. This is done by just replacing the given column with the body of the function with the arguments substituted for the input variables. The field name of the last column, always expected to be the keyword ret, is replaced by the name of the "caller" column, and the field names of previous columns are prefixed with the field name of the "caller" column. This is done to ensure that field names in the reduced table are unique, even if the same function is used several times.

Meanwhile, local names can be refreshed (by alpha-conversion), to make sure they do not clash with variables which are free in the remainder of the "caller" table or the remaining arguments. References to the columns of the function in the "caller" table (of the form $x.c$) are then replaced with the refreshed local column names.

In the end, the above table reduces to the following form:

table Faithful			
duration.Mean ▷ Mean	**real!rnd**	**static output**	GaussianMP(0.0,1.0)
duration.Prec ▷ Prec	**real!rnd**	**static output**	Gamma(1.0,1.0)
duration ▷ duration	**real!rnd**	**output**	GaussianMP(Mean,Prec)
time.Mean ▷ Mean	**real!rnd**	**static output**	GaussianMP(60.0,1.0)
time.Prec ▷ Prec	**real!rnd**	**static output**	Gamma(1.0,1.0)
time ▷ time	**real!rnd**	**output**	GaussianMP(Mean,Prec)

Just like in ordinary languages, variable definitions can be overshadowed by more closely scoped binders. The variable Mean in the duration column refers to the definition in the column with external name duration.mean, and Mean in column time refers to the definition in the column with field name time.Mean, and similarly with Prec.

Binders and Capture-avoiding Substitutions: $\mathbb{T}\{e/x\}$, $\mathbb{T}\langle y/x.c\rangle$

In order to define the reduction rules, we first need two capture-avoiding substitution operators on tables: $\mathbb{T}\{e/x\}$, which replaces free occurrences of the variable x with the index expression e, and $\mathbb{T}\langle y/x.c\rangle$, which replaces function field references $x.c$ with a single local variable y. These substitutions can be formally defined inductively, as usual. Here we omit these formal definitions (which can be found in Szymczak, 2018) and show by example how the second, slightly less standard, operator works.

Let us consider again the simplified version of the Old Faithful model from the beginning of this section, but this time using different local variable and field names, to emphasise the fact that they are not the same thing:

table Faithful			
duration ▷ x	**real!rnd**	**output**	CG(M=0.0, P=1.0)
time ▷ x'	**real!rnd**	**output**	CG(M=60.0, P=1.0)

Suppose we want to calculate the mean of the posterior distribution of the mean of duration (using the **infer** operator, described in 14.2.3). To this end, we need to add an additional column to the above table, which references the column with field name Mean in the reduced application of CG in the column duration. As field names are not binders, we need to use the local name x of the column duration. On the other hand, as the local names of the columns of CG are not visible outside the function CG itself, we need to access the column Mean of CG by using its field name. Hence, the reference has the form x.Mean, and the full table is the following:

table Faithful			
duration ▷ x	real!rnd	output	CG(M=0.0, P=1.0)
time ▷ x'	real!rnd	output	CG(M=60.0, P=1.0)
duration_mean ▷ z	real!qry	output	infer.Gaussian.mean(x.Mean)

When the function application in column duration is reduced (as described later), and the column Mean of the application of CG in duration is turned into a column with local name y in the main table, we need to substitute references to the (no longer existing) parameter Mean of the model in column x with the variable y in the rest of the table by using the operator $\langle y/_{x.c} \rangle$. Applying this substitution to the last two columns of the above table yields:

time ▷ x'	real!rnd	output	CG(M=60.0, P=1.0)
duration_mean ▷ z	real!qry	output	infer.Gaussian.mean(y)

One might be concerned that the substitution $\langle y/_{x.c} \rangle$ would not work correctly if the function application pointed to by x was assigned to another variable z, for example in a part of a table of the form:

field1 ▷ z	real!rnd	output	x
field2 ▷ z'	real!rnd	output	z.c

However, it is impossible to assign a function application to another variable in Tabular, as it is impossible to reference a function application as a whole. If a variable x referencing a function application is used on its own (not in a field reference $x.c$), it always denotes the *last column* of the reduced application, not the application itself. The expression $z.c$ in the above table is not well-typed, as z does not refer to a function.

Reduction Relation

The reduction is defined by means of the small-step reduction relation, reducing one column of the function table at a time, being the least relation closed under the set of rules presented below.

Reduction to Core Tabular:

$\mathbb{T} \to \mathbb{T}'$	table reduction

The judgment $\mathbb{T} \to \mathbb{T}'$ states that table $\mathbb{T}$ reduces to $\mathbb{T}'$ in one step. In the reduction rules, we normally use o for the (field) name of the "caller" column and c for the name of a column in the function table, to disambiguate between the two. The reduction system is deterministic and the assumptions guarantee that at most one rule applies to each table (the same applies to the reduction rules for indexed models and schemas presented in the following sections).

Reduction Rules for Tables: $\mathbb{T} \to \mathbb{T}'$

(RED APPL OUTPUT) (for Core($\mathbb{T}$))

$$\frac{y \notin \mathrm{fv}(\mathbb{T}', R) \cup \{x\} \quad c \neq \mathsf{ret}}{\begin{aligned}&(o \triangleright x : T\ \ell\ viz\ ((c \triangleright y : T'\ \ell'\ \mathbf{output}\ E) :: \mathbb{T})\ R) :: \mathbb{T}' \to \\ &\quad (o.c \triangleright y : T'\ (\ell \wedge \ell')\ viz\ E) :: (o \triangleright x : T\ \ell\ viz\ \mathbb{T}\ R) :: \mathbb{T}'\langle y/_{x.c}\rangle\end{aligned}}$$

(RED APPL LOCAL) (for Core($\mathbb{T}$))

$$\frac{y \notin \mathrm{fv}(\mathbb{T}', R) \cup \{x\}}{\begin{aligned}&(o \triangleright x : T\ \ell\ viz\ ((c \triangleright y : T'\ \ell'\ \mathbf{local}\ E) :: \mathbb{T})\ R) :: \mathbb{T}' \to \\ &\quad (\_ \triangleright y : T'\ (\ell \wedge \ell')\ \mathbf{local}\ E) :: (o \triangleright x : T\ \ell\ viz\ \mathbb{T}\ R) :: \mathbb{T}'\end{aligned}}$$

(RED APPL INPUT) (for Core($\mathbb{T}$))

$$\frac{}{\begin{aligned}&(o \triangleright x : T\ \ell\ viz\ (c \triangleright y : T'\ \ell'\ \mathbf{input}\ \epsilon) :: \mathbb{T}\ (c = e) :: R) :: \mathbb{T}' \to \\ &\quad (o \triangleright x : T\ \ell\ viz\ \mathbb{T}\ \{e/_y\}\ R) :: \mathbb{T}'\end{aligned}}$$

(RED APPL RET)

$$\frac{}{\begin{aligned}&(o \triangleright x : T\ \ell\ viz\ [(\mathsf{ret} \triangleright y : T'\ \ell'\ \mathbf{output}\ E)]\ []) :: \mathbb{T}' \to \\ &\quad (o \triangleright x : T'\ (\ell \wedge \ell')\ viz\ E) :: \mathbb{T}'\end{aligned}}$$

(RED TABLE RIGHT)

$$\frac{\mathbb{T} \to \mathbb{T}' \quad \mathrm{Core}(col)}{col :: \mathbb{T} \to col :: \mathbb{T}'}$$

The (RED APPL OUTPUT) rule (in which *viz* is expected to be **local** or **output**) reduces a single **output** column of a function by appending it to the main table, preceded by the "caller" column with the unevaluated part of the application $\mathbb{T}\ R$ (which will be reduced in the following steps). If the function was called from a **static** column, the level of the reduced function column is changed to **static**. Similarly, if the function was called from a **local** column, the visibility of the reduced column is dropped to **local**. Because the reduced column is appended to the main table, it has to be referenced using its internal name (recall that field names are not binders). Hence, all references to it, of the form $x.c$, are replaced with its internal name y. Meanwhile, the global name of the reduced column is prefixed by the field name of the "caller" column.

To avoid capturing free variables which are not bound by the reduced column in the original top-level table, y is required not to be free in $\mathbb{T}'$ and R. This is always possible, because tables are identified up to alpha-conversion of internal column names, so *y* can be refreshed if needed (formally, the reduction relation is a relation on alpha-equivalence classes of syntactic terms).

(RED APPL LOCAL) is similar, except that we do not need to substitute *y* for *x.c* in $\mathbb{T}$, because the given column is not visible outside the function. The external name of a reduced column can be empty, because local columns are not exported.

The (RED APPL INPUT) rule removes an input column and replaces all references to it in the rest of the function with the corresponding argument.

The last column of a function is reduced by (RED APPL RET), which simply replaces the application of the single ret column to the empty argument list with the expression from the said column. The level is also changed to **static** if the ret column was **static**. The internal and field names of the top-level column are left unchanged, and the names of the last column of the function are discarded, because the last column of a function is always referenced by the name of the "caller" table.

(RED TABLE RIGHT) is a congruence rule, allowing us to move to the next column of the main table if the current first column is already in Core form.

Example of Function Reduction To see how the reduction rules work, let us consider again the simplified version of the Old Faithful example with the additional duration_mean column:

table Faithful			
duration ▷ x	real!rnd	output	CG(M=0.0, P=1.0)
time ▷ x'	real!rnd	output	CG(M=60.0, P=1.0)
duration_mean ▷ z	real!qry	output	infer.Gaussian.mean(x.Mean)

The reduction rules reduce the duration column first. In the beginning, the rule (RED APPL INPUT) is applied twice, and reduces the columns M and P of the function CG in duration, replacing references to M and P in the body of CG with corresponding arguments. The reduced table has the following form:

table Faithful			
duration ▷ x	real!rnd	output	CG'()
time ▷ x'	real!rnd	output	CG(M=60.0, P=1.0)
duration_mean ▷ z	real!qry	output	infer.Gaussian.mean(x.Mean)

where CG' is the following partially evaluated function:

fun CG'			
Mean ▷ Mean	real!rnd	static output	GaussianMP(0.0, 1.0)
Prec ▷ Prec	real!rnd	static output	Gamma(1.0, 1.0)
ret ▷ ret	real!rnd	output	GaussianMP(Mean, Prec)

The next rule to be applied is (RED APPL OUTPUT), which reduces the first column Mean of CG' and replaces references to it, of the form *x*.Mean, with the local name of the reduced column (which we can assume is still Mean, as the name does not conflict with any other variable), in the rest of the top-level table by using the field substitution operator. The reduced table has the following form:

table Faithful			
duration.Mean ▹ Mean	real!rnd	**static output**	GaussianMP(0.0,1.0)
duration ▹ x	real!rnd	**output**	CG''()
time ▹ x'	real!rnd	**output**	CG(M=60.0, P=1.0)
duration_mean ▹ z	real!qry	**output**	infer.Gaussian.mean(Mean)

where CG'' is:

fun CG''			
Prec ▹ Prec	real!rnd	**static output**	Gamma(1.0, 1.0)
ret ▹ ret	real!rnd	**output**	GaussianMP(Mean, Prec)

Note that Mean in CG'' refers to the column defined outside the function (which is in scope of CG'', as functions are assumed to be defined inline, even though the implementation uses named functions).

The remaining columns of function applications are reduced similarly, except that the local name Mean in the second application of CG has to be changed by α-conversion, as Name is free in the last column of the top-level table.

14.4.2 Reducing Indexed Models

In order to reduce a column with an indexed function application, we need to transform the function into an indexed form before applying it to the arguments. In the case of the duration column of the original table of the running example, this transformation needs to turn the expressions in all **static rnd** columns into arrays of size 2, with each element modelled by the original expression, and replace all references to these columns in the rest of the table with array accesses, returning the component at index cluster.

For instance, applying indexing [cluster < 2] to the function CG yields the following indexed function

M ▹ M	real!det	static input	
P ▹ P	real!det	static input	
Mean ▹ Mean	real!rnd	static output	[for _ < 2 → GaussianMP(M,P)]
Prec ▹ Prec	real!rnd	static output	[for _ < 2 → Gamma(1.0, 1.0)]
ret ▹ ret	real!rnd	output	GaussianMP(Mean[cluster], Prec[cluster])

parametrised on the free variable cluster defined outside the function.

Reducing the application of this function to (M = 0.0, P = 1.0) in the duration column gives the following table:

duration.Mean ▹ Mean	real!rnd[2]	static output	[for _ < 2 → GaussianMP(0.0,1.0)]
duration.Prec ▹ Prec	real!rnd[2]	static output	[for _ < 2 → Gamma(1.0,1.0)]
duration ▹ duration	real!rnd	output	GaussianMP (Mean[cluster], Prec[cluster])

More generally, table indexing is formalised via the operator $\text{index}_A(\mathbb{T}, e_1, e_2)$, where $\mathbb{T}$ is the table (reduced application) to index, e_1 and e_2 are, respectively, the index variable and the number of clusters and A is the (initially empty) set of **static**

rnd columns, which needs to be available to convert variables into array accesses correctly.

We disallow indexing tables with **qry** columns, since substituting a reference to a query column with an array access with a random index would break the information flow constraints, so indexed query columns would not have a well-defined semantics. Below, the predicate NoQry states that a given Core table or model has no **qry**-level columns. The requirement that tables with **qry** columns cannot be indexed is enforced by the type system, presented in Section 14.5.

The indexing operator makes use of a new capture-avoiding substitution operator: $E[A, e]$ denotes E with every variable x in the set of variables A (supposed to contain only **static rnd** variables) replaced with the array access $x[e]$, as long as the syntax allows it. For instance, $\text{Gaussian}(x, y)[\{x, y\}, i]$ is $\text{Gaussian}(x[i], y[i])$, but $(\text{Discrete}[z](y))[\{z, y\}, i]$ is $\text{Discrete}[z](y[i])$, and not $\text{Discrete}[z[i]](y[i])$, because hyperparameters of distributions are index expressions, so they cannot be array accesses. However, we do not need to worry about variables which cannot be replaced with array accesses, such as z above, as (in non-**qry** columns of functions) they are always expected to be deterministic or occur in function field references of the form $x.c$, while indexing is only supposed to modify random variables referencing Core columns. We elide the formal definition of the operator, which can be found in Szymczak (2018).

The indexing operator is defined inductively below.

Table Indexing: $\text{index}_A(\mathbb{T}, e_1, e_2)$, **where** $\text{NoQry}(\mathbb{T})$

$\text{index}_A([], e_1, e_2) \triangleq []$

$\text{index}_A((c \triangleright x : T \text{ static } viz E) :: \mathbb{T}, e_1, e_2) \triangleq$
$\quad (c \triangleright x : T[e_2] \text{ static } viz [\textbf{for } i < e_2 \rightarrow E[A, i]]) :: \text{index}_{A \cup \{x\}}(\mathbb{T}, e_1, e_2)$
$\quad \quad \text{if } viz \neq \textbf{input} \text{ and } \textbf{rnd}(T) \text{ and } x \notin \text{fv}(e_1) \cup \text{fv}(e_2) \cup A \text{ and } i \notin \text{fv}(E)$

$\text{index}_A((c \triangleright x : T \ell \textbf{ input } \epsilon) :: \mathbb{T}, e_1, e_2) \triangleq$
$\quad (c \triangleright x : T \ell \textbf{ input } \epsilon) :: \text{index}_A(\mathbb{T}, e_1, e_2) \text{ if } x \notin \text{fv}(e_1) \cup \text{fv}(e_2) \cup A$

$\text{index}_A((c \triangleright x : T \ell viz E) :: \mathbb{T}, e_1, e_2) \triangleq$
$\quad (c \triangleright x : T \ell viz E[A, e_1]) :: \text{index}_A(\mathbb{T}, e_1, e_2)$
$\quad \quad \text{otherwise if } x \notin \text{fv}(e_1) \cup \text{fv}(e_2) \cup A.$

Unsurprisingly, indexing an empty table returns an empty table. In any **static rnd** column, the model expression E is turned into an array of e_2 elements, each modelled by E. Since E may contain references to previous **static rnd** columns of the original table, which have been turned into arrays, we must replace these references (by means of the $E[A, i]$ operator) with array accesses, returning values at indices corresponding to the positions of the expressions. Before index is applied recursively to the rest of the table, the variable x is added to the set A of **rnd static** variables, so that each reference to x in subsequent **rnd static** and **rnd inst** columns would be replaced with an appropriate array access.

Input columns are left unchanged by index, and in **inst**-level random columns, references to previous **static rnd** columns are replaced by array accesses returning the e_1-th component. Note that $E[A, i]$ leaves expressions in deterministic columns unchanged, because all variables in the set A are expected to be random.

With the index operator in place, we can define the reduction relation reducing indexed models.

Reduction to Core Tabular:

$M \to M'$	model reduction

The above judgment, which states that indexed model M reduces to M' in one step (that is, that M' is M with one level of indexing eliminated), is derived by the following rules:

Reduction Rules for Models: $M \to M'$

(RED INDEX)

$$\frac{\text{Core}(\mathbb{T}) \quad \text{NoQry}(\mathbb{T})}{(\mathbb{T} \ R)[e_{index} < e_{size}] \to (\text{index}_\varnothing(\mathbb{T}, e_{index}, e_{size})) \ R}$$

(RED INDEX INNER)

$$\frac{M \to M'}{M[e_{index} < e_{size}] \to M'[e_{index} < e_{size}]}$$

(RED INDEX EXPR)

$$\frac{}{E[e_{index} < e_{size}] \to E}$$

Reduction Rules for Tables: $\mathbb{T} \to \mathbb{T}'$

(RED MODEL)

$$\frac{M \to M'}{(c \triangleright x : T \ \ell \ viz \ M) :: \mathbb{T} \to (c \triangleright x : T \ \ell \ viz \ M') :: \mathbb{T}}$$

The (RED INDEX) rule applies the index operator to the function table in an application, returning a pure function application which will be reduced at table level. The (RED INDEX INNER) rule simply allows reducing a model nested in an indexed expression, in case this model is an indexed model itself. Since simple expressions have no static parameters of their own, indexing a simple expression has no effect, so the (RED INDEX EXPR) rule just discards the indexing. The (RED MODEL) rule allows reducing a model (other than a function application) in a column of a table.

14.4.3 Reducing Schemas

Finally, we can define the reduction relation for schemas:

Reduction to Core Tabular:

$\mathbb{S} \to \mathbb{S}'$	schema reduction

The judgment $\mathbb{S} \to \mathbb{S}'$ states that the schema $\mathbb{S}$ reduces to $\mathbb{S}'$ in one step – that is, $\mathbb{S}'$ is $\mathbb{S}$ with one table reduced to Core form. This judgment is derived by the following two rules:

Reduction Rules for Schemas: $\mathbb{S} \to \mathbb{S}'$

(RED SCHEMA LEFT)
$$\frac{\mathbb{T} \to \mathbb{T}'}{(t = \mathbb{T}) :: \mathbb{S} \to (t = \mathbb{T}') :: \mathbb{S}}$$

(RED SCHEMA RIGHT)
$$\frac{\mathbb{S} \to \mathbb{S}' \quad \mathsf{Core}(\mathbb{T})}{(t = \mathbb{T}) :: \mathbb{S} \to (t = \mathbb{T}) :: \mathbb{S}'}$$

The (RED SCHEMA LEFT) rule reduces the first table, while (RED SCHEMA RIGHT) proceeds to the following table if the first one has already been fully reduced.

Putting all these rules together, we can finally reduce the Old Faithful model to Core form:

table faithful			
cluster.V ▹ V	real!rnd[2]	**static output**	Dirichlet[2]([**for** i < 2 → 1.0])
cluster ▹ cluster	mod(2)!rnd	**output**	Discrete[2](V)
duration.Mean ▹ Mean	real!rnd[2]	**static output**	[**for** i < 2 → GaussianMP(0.0, 1.0)]
duration.Prec ▹ Prec	real!rnd[2]	**static output**	[**for** i < 2 → Gamma(1.0, 1.0)]
duration ▹ duration	real!rnd	**output**	GaussianMP(Mean[cluster], Prec[cluster])
time.Mean ▹ Mean	real!rnd[2]	**static output**	[**for** i < 2 → GaussianMP(60.0, 1.0)]
time.Prec ▹ Prec	real!rnd[2]	**static output**	[**for** i < 2 → Gamma(1.0, 1.0)]
time ▹ time	real!rnd	**output**	GaussianMP(Mean[cluster], Prec[cluster])

As noted before, a Tabular model in Core form has a straightforward interpretation as a factor graph. Assuming that the table faithful has n rows, the reduced Old Faithful model corresponds to the (directed) factor graph shown in Figure 14.1, in which we use abbreviated variable names (for example dM for duration.Mean) to make the presentation cleaner:

The boxes with solid edges are *plates*, which create multiple copies of given variables and factors – for instance, we have n values of dM_i, one for each i, each drawn from the same distribution GaussianMP(0.0, 1.0). The boxes with dotted lines are *gates* (Minka and Winn, 2009), which select a factor based on the value of a categorical variable (c_j in this case). While the graph above is directed to make the dependency structure explicit, the arrow heads can be removed to obtain a standard, undirected factor graph.

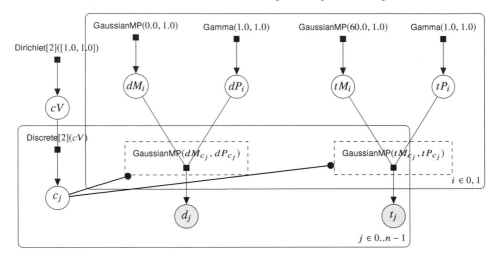

Figure 14.1 Reduced Old Faithful model as a factor graph

Once a schema is reduced to Core form, the Tabular backend can perform inference on it using Expectation Propagation or another algorithm provided by Infer.NET. Figure 14.2 presents the results of inference shown as in the Excel interface and visualised by Excel plots. A new column assignment has been added to the model – this column uses the **infer** operator to assign each eruption to the more likely cluster.

14.5 Type System

Type systems are useful in probabilistic languages because they specify the domain of each random variable and ensure that each random draw is used where a value in the given domain is expected. Thus, types guide the modelling process and help prevent incorrect dependencies between variables.

As seen in examples in the previous sections, Tabular makes use of basic dependent types and determinacy and binding time annotations. All the type constraints in Tabular are checked statically, which allows some modelling errors to be caught before the inference procedure is started, thus saving the user time on debugging.

Tabular's type system ensures that the role of each variable in the program is immediately clear and checks that each random variable is defined on the right domain. Dependent types additionally allow checking array sizes and bounds on categorical variables in functions, even though these may depend on function arguments. This helps to check that functions are indeed correctly defined and make the right use of their arguments. Moreover, because of space annotations, the compiler

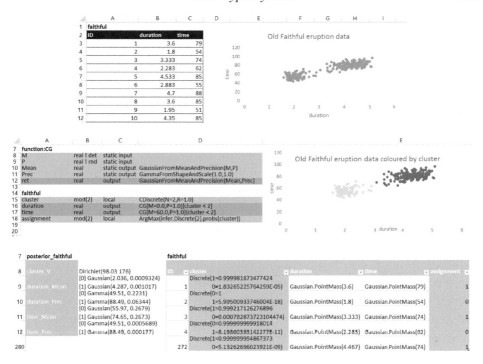

Figure 14.2 Old Faithful inference results in Excel

can split a Tabular program into the probabilistic model and the post-processing code, and process them at the right time in the pipeline – the user is not required to define **rnd** and **qry** variables in separate blocks. These annotations also disallow models which the default inference engine cannot handle, such as mixture models with an random number of components.

In this section, we define the Tabular type system formally and present the type soundness property of the reduction system shown in Section 14.4 (whose proof can be found in Szymczak (2018)).

In addition to the column types introduced in Section 14.3, we also give types to model expressions, tables and schemas. These types define the spaces of input and output variables of the probabilistic models defined by programs or their parts.

Limitations of the Type System The type system does not enforce conjugacy, which is required by the default inference engine of Tabular, because we wanted to keep the developments in this chapter independent of a particular inference algorithm. Moreover, well-typedness of a Tabular program does not guarantee that Expectation Propagation inference will always succeed. Lack of conjugacy and other algorithm-specific issues may result in the inference algorithm failing at runtime, in which case an error message from the inference backend is shown to the user in the implementation.

14.5.1 Syntax of Tabular Types

To each model and table, we assign a type Q (hereafter called Q-type), which consists of a list of column names (local and field names), column types, levels and visibilities (which cannot be **local**, because local attributes of tables and functions are not exported to types). A single component of type Q is just a table column without a model expression. The Q-types used here are akin to right-associating dependent record types (Pollack, 2002), except that in their inhabitants, the values of fields may depend on previous fields, like in translucent sums (Harper and Lillibridge, 1994).

The type Sty of a schema is just a list of table identifiers paired with corresponding table types. These types are notably simpler than the nested record types used in the original formulation of Tabular (Gordon et al., 2014b).

We define three predicates on Q-types: **fun**(Q), which means that the given type Q is a valid function type, whose last column is marked as the return column, **table**(Q), which states that Q has no deterministic **static** columns and can type a top-level (i.e. non-function) table, and red(Q), which states that Q is the type of a reduced function application, having no **input** columns.

Table and Schema Types:

$Q ::= [] \mid (c \triangleright x : T\ \ell\ viz) :: Q$	table type (scope of x is Q, $viz \neq$ **local**)
$Sty ::= (t : Q) :: Sty$	schema type
fun(Q) iff $viz_n =$ **output** and $c_n =$ ret	
table(Q) iff for each $i \in 1..n$, $\ell_i =$ **static** $\Rightarrow$ **rnd**$(T_i) \vee$ **qry**(T_i)	
red(Q) iff **table**(Q) and for each $i \in 1..n$, $viz_i =$ **output**	

The predicate **table**(Q) ensures that no top-level columns can be referenced in subsequent column types (because only **static det** columns can appear in types), which guarantees that all column types in Core tables (including reduced tables) are closed, except possibly for table size references. This property is necessary because columns can be referenced from other tables, and any variables in a type would be free outside the table in which the corresponding column was defined.

We define fv(Q) to be the set of local variables in column types in Q which are not bound by column definitions.

Schemas, tables, models and expressions are all typechecked in a given typing environment Γ, which is an ordinary typing environment except that it has three kinds of entries (for variables denoting previous Core columns, for previous tables and for reduced function applications) and the entries for Core columns include level annotations as well as column types (recall that column types themselves contain binding type annotations).

Tabular Typing Environments:

$$\Gamma ::= \varnothing \mid (\Gamma, x :^{\ell} T) \mid (\Gamma, t : Q) \mid (\Gamma, x : Q) \qquad \text{environment}$$

The *domain* dom(Γ) of an environment Γ is the set of all variables and table names in the environment:

Below is the list of all judgments of the Tabular type system, which will be described in the remainder of this section.

Judgments of the Tabular Type System:

$\Gamma \vdash \diamond$	environment Γ is well-formed
$\Gamma \vdash T$	in Γ, type T is well-formed
$\Gamma \vdash^{pc} e : T$	in Γ at level pc, index expression e has type T
$\Gamma \vdash Q$	in Γ, table type Q is well-formed
$\Gamma \vdash Sty$	in Γ, schema type Sty is well-formed
$\Gamma \vdash T <: U$	in Γ, T is a subtype of U
$\Gamma \vdash^{pc} E : T$	in Γ at level pc, expression E has type T
$\Gamma \vdash^{pc} R : Q \to Q'$	R sends function type Q to model type Q'
$\Gamma \vdash^{pc} M : Q$	model expression M has model type Q
$\Gamma \vdash^{pc} \mathbb{T} : Q$	table $\mathbb{T}$ has type Q
$\Gamma \vdash \mathbb{S} : Sty$	schema $\mathbb{S}$ has type Sty

Tabular programs and types are identified up to α-conversion of internal column names and variables bound by **for**-loops.

14.5.2 Type Well-formedness and Expression Types

We begin by discussing the well-formedness rules for environments and column and table types and typing rules for index expressions (which are mutually dependent). We do not present all the rules in detail to save space.

The judgment $\Gamma \vdash \diamond$ holds if the variable names in Γ are unique and all (column and table) types in Γ are well-formed. The column type well-formedness judgment $\Gamma \vdash T$ requires all index expressions in T to be deterministic integers well-formed in Γ. For instance, the well-formedness rule for $T = U[e]$ has the following form:

(TYPE ARRAY)

$$\frac{\Gamma \vdash U \quad \Gamma \vdash^{\text{static}} e : \text{int} \,!\, \text{det}}{\Gamma \vdash U[e]}$$

The judgment $\Gamma \vdash^{pc} e : T$ states that the index expression e has type T in Γ and only depends on data at level up to pc. Recall that **static** < **inst**. Typing rules for constants and table sizes are trivial, but if e is a variable, then it can correspond to either a variable in Γ or the last column of a Q-type in Γ:

Selected Rules for Index Expressions:

<table>
<tr>
<td>

(INDEX VAR) (for $\ell \leq pc$)

$$\dfrac{\Gamma \vdash \diamond \quad \Gamma = \Gamma_1, x :^\ell T, \Gamma_2}{\Gamma \vdash^{pc} x : T}$$

</td>
<td>

(FUNREFRET)

$$\dfrac{\Gamma \vdash \diamond \quad \Gamma = \Gamma', x : Q, \Gamma'' \quad Q = Q' @ [(\text{ret} \triangleright y : T \, \ell \, \textbf{output})] \quad \ell \leq pc}{\Gamma \vdash^{pc} x : T}$$

</td>
</tr>
</table>

Next, we define well-formedness rules for Q-types and schema types:

Formation Rules for Table and Schema Types: $\Gamma \vdash Q \quad \Gamma \vdash Sty$

<table>
<tr>
<td>

(TABLE TYPE [])

$$\dfrac{\Gamma \vdash \diamond}{\Gamma \vdash []}$$

</td>
<td>

(TABLE TYPE INPUT)

$$\dfrac{\Gamma \vdash T \quad \Gamma, x :^\ell T \vdash Q \quad c \notin \text{names}(Q)}{\Gamma \vdash (c \triangleright x : T \, \ell \, \textbf{input}) :: Q}$$

</td>
<td>

(TABLE TYPE OUTPUT)

$$\dfrac{\Gamma \vdash T \quad \Gamma, x :^\ell T \vdash Q \quad c \notin \text{names}(Q)}{\Gamma \vdash (c \triangleright x : T \, \ell \, \textbf{output}) :: Q}$$

</td>
</tr>
<tr>
<td>

(SCHEMA TYPE [])

$$\dfrac{\Gamma \vdash \diamond}{\Gamma \vdash []}$$

</td>
<td colspan="2">

(SCHEMA TYPE TABLE)

$$\dfrac{\Gamma \vdash Q \quad \textbf{table}(Q) \quad \Gamma, t : Q \vdash Sty}{\Gamma \vdash (t : Q) :: Sty}$$

</td>
</tr>
</table>

These rules simply require all column types in a Q-type and all table types in a schema type to be well-formed (in the environments formed by preceding columns and tables), all local identifiers to be unique and all field names to be unique within the Q-types in which they are defined. Tables in a schema must also satisfy the **table** predicate.

Every expression in Tabular belongs to one of the three spaces **det**, **rnd** and **qry**, determined by the expression's type. We want to allow information flow from **det** to **rnd** space, because it is harmless to use a deterministic value where a value potentially "tainted" by randomness is expected. Similarly, we want to allow flow from **det** to **qry**. However, since we assume **qry** columns to be deterministic given the inferred posterior distributions of **rnd** columns, we do not allow **qry** columns to reference **rnd** columns directly – information flow from **rnd** to **qry** is only possible via the **infer** operator, which references posterior distributions of random variables, rather than random variables themselves.

We also disallow flows from **qry** to **det** and **rnd**, because we want to ensure that a run of a Tabular program consists of a single round of inference, determining the posterior distributions of **rnd** columns, followed by a single post-processing phase, which computes the values of **qry** columns given the (already known) approximate distributions of **rnd** columns. Tabular does not support nested inference, where, for instance, a **rnd** column used in the second round of inference could depend on a **qry** column computed after the first round of inference.

We embed these restrictions in the type system by means of a subtyping relation on column types. We first define a preorder $\leq$ on spaces as the least reflexive relation satisfying **det** $\leq$ **rnd** and **det** $\leq$ **qry**. We also define a (partial) least upper bound $spc \vee spc'$.

Least upper bound: $spc \vee spc'$ (**if** $spc \leq spc'$ **or** $spc' \leq spc$)

$spc \vee spc = spc$ **det** $\vee$ **rnd** = **rnd**   **det** $\vee$ **qry** = **qry**

(The combination **rnd** $\vee$ **qry** is intentionally not defined.)

We can lift the $\vee$ operation to types in the straightforward way.

We define the subtyping judgment $\Gamma \vdash T <: U$ to hold if and only if both T and U are well-formed in Γ, they are of the same form and space$(T) \leq$ space(U).

Selected Typing Rules for Expressions: $\Gamma \vdash^{pc} E : T$

(DEREF STATIC)

$\Gamma \vdash \diamond \qquad \Gamma = \Gamma', t : Q, \Gamma''$

$Q = Q'@\lfloor(c \triangleright x : T \text{ **static** } viz)\rfloor@Q''$

$\overline{\Gamma \vdash^{pc} t.c : T}$

(DEREF INST)

$\Gamma \vdash^{pc} E : \text{link}(t) \,!\, spc$

$\Gamma = \Gamma', t : Q, \Gamma''$

$Q = Q'@\lfloor(c \triangleright x : T \text{ **inst** } viz)\rfloor@Q''$

$\overline{\Gamma \vdash^{pc} E : t.c : T \vee spc}$

(RANDOM) (where $\sigma(U) \triangleq U\{e_1/x_1\} \ldots \{e_m/x_m\}$)

$D_\text{rnd} : [x_1 : T_1, \ldots, x_m : T_m](c_1 : U_1, \ldots, c_n : U_n) \to T$

$\Gamma \vdash^\text{static} e_i : T_i \quad \forall i \in 1..m \quad \Gamma \vdash^{pc} F_j : \sigma(U_j) \quad \forall j \in 1..n \quad \Gamma \vdash \diamond$

$\{x_1, \ldots, x_m\} \cap (\bigcup_i \text{fv}(e_i)) = \varnothing \quad x_i \neq x_j \text{ for } i \neq j$

$\overline{\Gamma \vdash^{pc} D[e_1, \ldots, e_m](F_1, \ldots, F_n) : \sigma(T)}$

(INFER) (where $\sigma(U) \triangleq U\{e_1/x_1\} \ldots \{e_m/x_m\}$)

$D_\text{qry} : [x_1 : T_1, \ldots, x_m : T_m](c_1 : U_1, \ldots, c_n : U_n) \to T$

$\Gamma \vdash^\text{static} e_i : T_i \quad \forall i \in 1..m \quad \Gamma \vdash^{pc} E : \sigma(T) \quad j \in 1..n$

$\{x_1, \ldots, x_m\} \cap (\bigcup_i \text{fv}(e_i)) = \varnothing \quad x_i \neq x_j \text{ for } i \neq j$

$\overline{\Gamma \vdash^{pc} \text{**infer**}.D[e_1, \ldots, e_m].c_j(E) : \sigma(U_j)}$

(FUNREF)

$\Gamma \vdash \diamond \qquad \Gamma = \Gamma', x : Q, \Gamma''$

$Q = Q'@[(c \triangleright y : T \, \ell \, viz)]@Q''$

$\ell \leq pc \quad c \neq \text{ret}$

$\overline{\Gamma \vdash^{pc} x.c : T}$

Above, we present some of the non-standard typing rules for basic model expressions. Most of them are similar to the typing rules of Fun (Borgström et al., 2013), the language on which the grammar of expressions is based, except that they also handle spaces. We also need to add rules for dereference operators, function column accesses and the **infer** primitive.

The rule (DEREF STATIC) checks that there is an entry for table t in the environment and that its Q-type has column c with type T. (DEREF INST) is similar, except that it typechecks a reference to an **inst**-level column. The index E must be an integer bounded by the size of table t. An instance dereference is only deterministic if both the index and the reference column are deterministic, and a reference to the value of a deterministic column at a random index (or vice versa) is random (and similarly for queries), so we need to join the type of the referenced column with the space of the index.

The (RANDOM) rule requires all hyperparameters $e_1, \ldots, e_m$ of a distribution to be static and have the right types, as specified by the distribution signature. Since the types $U_1, \ldots, U_n$ of parameters and the output type T may depend on these hyperparameters, we need to substitute their values in these types. This is done by the σ operator. The expressions $F_1, \ldots, F_n$ defining parameter values must check against the corresponding types $U_1, \ldots, U_n$ in the signature of the distribution with hyperparameter values substituted by σ. The requirements that the (α-convertible) formal hyperparameter names $x_1, \ldots, x_m$ and free variables in $e_1, \ldots, e_m$ are disjoint and that no hyperparameter name appears twice guarantee that the substitution σ is well-defined.

To see how the (RANDOM) rule works, consider the expression Discrete[2](V) in table Coins in Section 14.2.2. While typechecking the (original, functionless) Coins table, Discrete[2](V) is typeckecked at level **inst** in the environment $\Gamma = $ V :**static** **real!rnd**[2]. The signature of the Discrete distribution in space **rnd** is Discrete$_{rnd}$: [N : **int!det**](probs : **real!rnd**[N]) $\rightarrow$ **mod**(N)!**rnd**. In Discrete[2](V), the value of the only hyperparameter N is $e_1 = 2$, which obviously checks against the type **int!det** in the signature. After substituting this value for N in the type of the only parameter probs, we get **real!rnd**[2]. We need to check that $\Gamma \vdash^{\textbf{inst}}$ V : **real!rnd**[2]. This follows instantly from (INDEX VAR), because V has exactly the type **real!rnd**[2] in Γ. Thus, the expression typechecks correctly and the output type, obtained by substituting 2 for N in **mod**(N)!**rnd**, is **mod**(2)!**rnd**.

The (INFER) rule has a similar form to (RANDOM), but instead of typing the distribution arguments, it checks whether the type of the expression E defining the distribution of interest (and normally expected to reference a previous column), matches the output type T in the signature of the distribution D (with hyperparameters $x_1, \ldots, x_m$ again substituted by their values $e_m, \ldots, e_m$). As **infer**.$D[e_1, \ldots, e_m].c_j(E)$ is supposed to return the expected value of the parameter c_j of the posterior distribution of expression E, the type of **infer**.$D[e_1,\ldots,e_m].c_j(E)$ is the type of the argument c_j in the signature of D, again with the hyperparameter values substituted.

Note that the rule uses the **qry** version of the signature of D, in which the types of arguments are in **qry**-space. This ensures that the type of a post-inference query is in **qry**-space, and thus the query is not part of the probabilistic model.

Let us demonstrate how the rule works by going back to the example in Section 14.2.3. As the table Coins with the additional **qry**-level columns counts and Bias is typechecked, the expression **infer**.Dirichlet[2].pseudocount(V) is typeckeched at level **static** in environment Γ = V :^{static} **real!rnd**[2], Flip :^{inst} **mod**(2)!**rnd**. The signature of Dirichlet in **qry**-space is Dirichlet$_{\text{qry}}$: [N : **int!det**](pseudocount : (**real!qry**)[N]) $\rightarrow$ (**real!rnd**)[N]. As in the above example for (RANDOM), the value of the only hyperparameter N, which is 2, must be checked at level **static** against the type of N in the signature of Dirichlet$_{\text{qry}}$ – that is, **int!det**.

As the posterior distribution of V is expected to be Dirichlet with N = 2, we need to check that the type of the column referenced by V actually matches the output type of Dirichlet with the given hyperparameter, which we obtain by substituting 2 for N in (**real!rnd**)[N]. Looking at the environment Γ, we immediately see that $\Gamma \vdash^{\text{static}}$ V : **real!rnd**[2] indeed holds.

The parameter of the Dirichlet posterior of V whose expected value the **infer** operator is supposed to return is pseudocount, which has type (**real!qry**)[N] in the signature. After substituting N by its value, this type becomes (**real!qry**)[2]. Hence, this is the type of the entire expression **infer**.Dirichlet[2].pseudocount(V).

The (FUNREF) rule defines the type of a column access to be the type of the given column in the type of the reduced table, as long as this column is visible at level pc.

All the other typing rules (including the subsumption rule) are standard.

14.5.3 Model Types

Before we extend the type system to compound models, we define typing rules for function argument lists. The judgment $\Gamma \vdash^{pc} R : Q \rightarrow Q'$ means that applying a function of type Q to R at level pc yields a table of type Q'. The typing rules for arguments are presented below. Recall that in functions called at **static** level, the level of every column is reduced to **static**, hence the need to join ℓ with pc in output types.

Typing Rules for Arguments: $\Gamma \vdash^{pc} R : Q \rightarrow Q'$

(ARG INPUT)

$$\frac{\Gamma \vdash^{\ell \wedge pc} e : T \quad \Gamma \vdash^{pc} R : Q\{e/x\} \rightarrow Q'}{\Gamma \vdash^{pc} ((c = e) :: R) : ((c \triangleright x : T \; \ell \; \textbf{input}) :: Q) \rightarrow Q'}$$

(ARG OUTPUT)

$$\frac{\Gamma, x :^{\ell \wedge pc} T \vdash^{pc} R : Q \to Q' \qquad c \neq \text{ret} \qquad x \notin \text{fv}(R)}{\Gamma \vdash^{pc} R : ((c \triangleright x : T \ \ell \ \textbf{output}) :: Q) \to ((c \triangleright x : T \ (\ell \wedge pc) \ \textbf{output}) :: Q')}$$

(ARG RET)

$$\frac{\Gamma \vdash T}{\Gamma \vdash^{pc} R : (\text{ret} \triangleright x : T \ \ell \ \textbf{output}) \to (\text{ret} \triangleright x : T \ (\ell \wedge pc) \ \textbf{output})}$$

The (ARG INPUT) rule typechecks the argument e, substitutes it for the input variable x and proceeds with checking the rest of R, without copying the input column x to the output type. If the column level ℓ is **static**, e must be a static expression to be a valid argument, and if pc is **static**, then e may be referenced in the subsequent **static** columns of the reduced table, hence we need to typecheck e at level $\ell \wedge pc$. The following rule, (ARG OUTPUT), just adds x to the environment (as it may appear in the types of subsequent columns) and proceeds with processing the rest of Q, copying the current column into the output with updated level.

Finally, (ARG RET) just checks the well-formedness of the type of the output column and updates its level.

In order to simplify typechecking indexed models, we also define an indexing operator for Q-types, which changes the types of all non-input **static rnd** columns in Q into array types.

Indexing a Table Type: $Q[e]$

$$\varnothing[e] \triangleq \varnothing$$

$$((c \triangleright x : T \ \textbf{inst} \ viz) :: Q)[e] \triangleq (c \triangleright x : T \ \textbf{inst} \ viz) :: (Q[e]) \quad \text{if } x \notin \text{fv}(e)$$

$$((c \triangleright x : T \ \textbf{static} \ viz) :: Q)[e] \triangleq (c \triangleright x : T \ \textbf{static} \ viz) :: (Q[e])$$
$$\quad \text{if } viz = \textbf{input} \text{ or } \textbf{det}(T) \text{ and } x \notin \text{fv}(e)$$

$$((c \triangleright x : T \ \textbf{static} \ viz) :: Q)[e] \triangleq (c \triangleright x : T[e] \ \textbf{static} \ viz) :: (Q[e])$$
$$\quad \text{if } viz \neq \textbf{input} \text{ and } \textbf{rnd}(T) \text{ and } x \notin \text{fv}(e)$$

We also need to make sure function tables are Core and have no trailing **local** and **input** columns:

Table and Schema Types:

$$\textbf{fun}(\mathbb{T}) \text{ iff Core}(\mathbb{T}) \text{ and } \mathbb{T} = \mathbb{T}_1 @ [(\text{ret} \triangleright x : T \ \ell \ \textbf{output} \ E)]$$

where @ denotes table concatenation.

The typing rules for (non-simple) models can now be defined as follows:

Typing Rules for Model Expressions: $\Gamma \vdash^{pc} M : Q$

(MODEL APPL)

$$\frac{\Gamma \vdash^{pc} \mathbb{T} : Q \quad \mathsf{fun}(\mathbb{T}) \quad \Gamma \vdash^{pc} R : Q \to Q'}{\Gamma \vdash^{pc} \mathbb{T}\,R : Q'}$$

(MODEL INDEXED)

$$\frac{\Gamma \vdash^{pc} M : Q \quad \Gamma \vdash^{pc} e_{index} : \mathsf{mod}(e_{size})\,!\,\mathsf{rnd} \quad \mathsf{NoQry}(M)}{\Gamma \vdash^{pc} M[e_{index} < e_{size}] : Q[e_{size}]}$$

The (MODEL APPL) rule typechecks the function table and the argument lists, returning the output type of the argument typing judgment. Meanwhile, (MODEL INDEXED) uses the Q-type indexing to construct the type of an indexed model from the type of its base model. As stated in Section 14.4, only tables with no **qry** columns can be indexed, so we need to ensure that the table nested in M satisfies NoQry.

14.5.4 Table Types

The rules below are used for typechecking both top-level tables and function tables, which can be called from **static** columns, so we need to add the pc level to the typing judgment. To preserve information flow restrictions, a model expression in a column at level ℓ can only reference variables at level at most ℓ. Similarly, expressions in a function at level pc cannot use variables at level greater than pc. Hence, all model expressions are typechecked at level $\ell \wedge pc$.

Tables with Core *columns*

We start with rules for typechecking Core columns. The operator names(Q), used below and in the rest of this section, returns the set of global names of all columns in Q.

Typing Rules for Tables - Core columns: $\Gamma \vdash^{pc} \mathbb{T} : Q$

(TABLE [])   (TABLE INPUT)

$$\frac{}{\Gamma \vdash \diamond}{\Gamma \vdash^{pc} [] : []} \qquad \frac{\Gamma, x :^{\ell \wedge pc} T \vdash^{pc} \mathbb{T} : Q \quad c \notin \mathsf{names}(Q)}{\Gamma \vdash^{pc} (c \triangleright x : T\ \ell\ \mathbf{input}\ \epsilon) :: \mathbb{T} : (c \triangleright x : T\ (\ell \wedge pc)\ \mathbf{input}) :: Q}$$

(TABLE CORE OUTPUT)

$$\frac{\Gamma \vdash^{\ell \wedge pc} E : T \quad \Gamma, x :^{\ell \wedge pc} T \vdash^{pc} \mathbb{T} : Q \quad c \notin \mathsf{names}(Q)}{\Gamma \vdash^{pc} (c \triangleright x : T\ \ell\ \mathbf{output}\ E) :: \mathbb{T} : (c \triangleright x : T\ (\ell \wedge pc)\ \mathbf{output}) :: Q}$$

(TABLE CORE LOCAL) (where $x \notin \mathsf{fv}(Q)$)

$$\frac{\Gamma \vdash^{\ell \wedge pc} E : T \quad \Gamma, x :^{\ell \wedge pc} T \vdash^{pc} \mathbb{T} : Q}{\Gamma \vdash^{pc} (c \triangleright x : T\ \ell\ \mathbf{local}\ E) :: \mathbb{T} : Q}$$

The (TABLE []) rule is obvious. The (TABLE INPUT) rule just adds the variable x to the environment (at level $\ell \wedge viz$) and checks the rest of the table. The (TABLE CORE OUTPUT) rule checks the model expression E and then typechecks the rest of the table in the environment extended with x. The type of the current column (with level joined with pc) is concatenated with the (recursively derived) type of the rest of the table. (TABLE CORE LOCAL) is similar to (TABLE CORE OUTPUT), except that the type of the current column does not appear in the table type and x cannot be free in Q (otherwise Q could contain a variable not defined in the environment Γ in the conclusion of the rule).

Example: checking Core Tabular functions To illustrate how the typing rules for Core tables work, recall the functions CDiscrete from Section 14.2.2 and CGaussian from Section 14.4. In this and the following examples, we will use the same column-based notation for Q-types as for Tabular tables.

The function CDiscrete has the following form, with local and field names:

fun CDiscrete			
N ▷ N	int!det	static input	
R ▷ R	real!det	static input	
V ▷ V	real!rnd[N]	static output	Dirichlet[N]([for i < N → R])
ret ▷ ret	mod(N)!rnd	output	Discrete[N](V)

To typecheck CDiscrete in an empty environment at level **inst**, we first add the arguments N and R to the environment, by applying (TABLE INPUT).

Now, let $\Gamma = $ N :^{static} **int!det**, R :^{static} **real!det**. Then, by inspecting the signature of Dirichlet and applying (RANDOM), we can show that

$$\Gamma \vdash^{\text{inst}} \text{Dirichlet}[N]([\textbf{for } i < N \to R]) : \textbf{real} \ ! \ \textbf{rnd}[N]$$

By applying (RANDOM) again, we get

$$\Gamma, V :^{\text{static}} \textbf{real} \ ! \ \textbf{rnd}[N] \vdash^{\text{inst}} \text{Discrete}[N](V) : \textbf{mod}(N) \ ! \ \textbf{rnd}$$

By (TABLE CORE OUTPUT), the last column has type

ret ▷ ret	mod(N)!rnd	output

in the environment $\Gamma, V :^{\text{static}} \textbf{real} \ ! \ \textbf{rnd}[N]$. Applying (TABLE CORE OUTPUT) again adds the column

V ▷ V	real!rnd[N]	static output

to this type. Finally, by applying (TABLE INPUT) twice, we get the type of CDiscrete:

N ▷ N	int!det	static input
R ▷ R	real!det	static input
V ▷ V	real!rnd[N]	static output
ret ▷ ret	mod(N)!rnd	output

Similarly, CG can be shown to have the following type in the empty environment:

M ▹ M	real!det	static input
P ▹ P	real!det	static input
Mean ▹ Mean	real!rnd	static output
Prec ▹ Prec	real!rnd	static output
ret ▹ ret	real!rnd	output

Example: typing function applications Recall the coin flip example from Section 14.2.2, shown here with double column names:

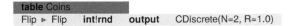

table Coins			
Flip ▹ Flip	int!rnd	output	CDiscrete(N=2, R=1.0)

This example contains a single call to CDiscrete. By the argument typing rules, we have

$$\varnothing \vdash^{\textbf{inst}} (N = 2, R = 1.0) : Q_{CD} \rightarrow Q'_{CD}$$

where Q_{CD} is the type of CDiscrete, shown above, and Q_{CD}' is the type of the reduced function application, having the following form:

V ▹ V	real!rnd[2]	static output
ret ▹ ret	mod(2)!rnd	output

By (MODEL APPL), the type of the function application is Q'_{CD}:

$$\varnothing \vdash^{\textbf{inst}} \text{CDiscrete}(N = 2, R = 1.0) : Q'_{CD}$$

Example: indexing model types In the Old Faithful example, we applied indexing [cluster < 2] to the application CG(M = 0.0, P = 1.0). It can be easily shown (like in the example above) that in any environment Γ, this application has the following type Q'_{CG}:

Mean ▹ Mean	real!rnd	static output
Prec ▹ Prec	real!rnd	static output
ret ▹ ret	real!rnd	output

According to the (MODEL INDEXED) rule, in an environment Γ such that $\Gamma \vdash^{\textbf{inst}}$ cluster : **mod ! rnd**, the indexed application CG(M = 0.0, P = 1.0)[cluster < 2] has the following type:

Mean ▹ Mean	real!rnd[2]	static output
Prec ▹ Prec	real!rnd[2]	static output
ret ▹ ret	real!rnd	output

Full Tabular Tables

To typecheck columns with non-basic models, we need a prefixing operator for Q-types and two additional rules.

Prefixing function type column names: $c.Q$

$$c.((d \triangleright x : T \; \ell \; viz) :: Q) = (c.d \triangleright x : T \; \ell \; viz) :: c.Q \qquad\qquad \text{if } d \neq \mathsf{ret}$$
$$c.([(\mathsf{ret} \triangleright x : T \; \ell \; viz)]) = [(c \triangleright x : T \; \ell \; viz)]$$
$$c.([(d \triangleright x : T \; \ell \; viz)]) = [(c.d \triangleright x : T \; \ell \; viz)] \qquad\qquad \text{if } d \neq \mathsf{ret}$$

Typing Rules for Tables: $\Gamma \vdash^{pc} \mathbb{T} : Q$

(TABLE OUTPUT)
$$\dfrac{\Gamma \vdash^{\ell \wedge pc} M : Q_c \quad \Gamma, x : Q_c \vdash^{pc} \mathbb{T} : Q \quad Q_c = Q'_c @ [(\mathsf{ret} \triangleright y : T \; \ell' \; \mathbf{output})] \quad \mathsf{names}(c.Q_c) \cap \mathsf{names}(Q) = \varnothing}{\Gamma \vdash^{pc} (c \triangleright x : T \; \ell \; \mathbf{output} \; M) :: \mathbb{T} : (c.Q_c) @ Q}$$

(TABLE LOCAL)
$$\dfrac{\Gamma \vdash^{\ell \wedge pc} M : Q_c \quad \Gamma, x : Q_c \vdash^{pc} \mathbb{T} : Q \quad Q_c = Q'_c @ [(\mathsf{ret} \triangleright y : T \; \ell' \; \mathbf{output})]}{\Gamma \vdash^{pc} (\epsilon \triangleright x : T \; \ell \; \mathbf{local} \; M) :: \mathbb{T} : Q}$$

The (TABLE OUTPUT) rule typechecks the model M and then recurses into the rest of the table with the environment extended with the type Q_c of M, assigned to x. Note that local attributes of M cannot be referenced in $\mathbb{T}$. This is a design choice – local columns in functions are only meant to be used locally. (TABLE LOCAL) is similar, except it does not export the type of the model.

Example: typing tables with compound models Recall the coin flip model:

table Coins			
Flip ▷ Flip	mod(2)!rnd	output	CDiscrete(N=2, R=1.0)

We have already shown that the application CDiscrete(N = 2, R = 1.0) has the following type:

V ▷ V	real!rnd[2]	static output
ret ▷ ret	mod(2)!rnd	output

By (TABLE OUTPUT), the type of the Coins table is:

Flip.V ▷ V	real!rnd[2]	static output
Flip ▷ Flip	mod(2)!rnd	output

Similarly, we can show that the Old Faithful model from the beginning of Section 14.4.1 has the following type:

cluster.V ▷ V	real!rnd[2]	static output
cluster ▷ cluster	mod(2)!rnd	output
duration.Mean ▷ Mean	real!rnd[2]	static output
duration.Prec ▷ Prec	real!rnd[2]	static output
duration ▷ duration	real!rnd	output
time.Mean ▷ Mean	real!rnd[2]	static output
time.Prec ▷ Prec	real!rnd[2]	static output
time ▷ time	real!rnd	output

Example: accessing function fields Let us consider once again the simplified version of the Old Faithful model with an additional column containing a function field access:

table Faithful			
duration ▹ x	real!rnd	output	CG(M=0.0, P=1.0)
time ▹ x'	real!rnd	output	CG(M=60.0, P=1.0)
duration_mean ▹ z	real!qry	output	infer.Gaussian.mean(x.Mean)

As shown before, each application of CG has the following type Q'_{CG}:

Mean ▹ Mean	real!rnd	static output
Prec ▹ Prec	real!rnd	static output
ret ▹ ret	real!rnd	output

According to the typing rules, if the initial typing environment is empty, the final column is checked in the environment $\Gamma = x : Q'_{CG}, x' : Q'_{CG}$. This final column must be typechecked by the (TABLE CORE OUTPUT) rule, which requires that

$$\Gamma \vdash^{inst} \text{infer.Gaussian.mean(x.Mean)} : \textbf{real} ! \textbf{rnd}$$

By (INFER), this only holds if

$$\Gamma \vdash^{inst} \text{x.Mean} : \textbf{real} ! \textbf{rnd}$$

The environment Γ can be easily shown to be well-formed. Since x has type Q'_{CG} in the environment, and this Q-type has a column with field name Mean and type **real** ! **rnd**, the above judgment can be derived with (FUNREF).

14.5.5 Schema Types

We round off the description of the type system with the following two self-explanatory rules for schemas:

Typing Rules for Schemas: $\Gamma \vdash \mathbb{S} : Sty$

(SCHEMA [])	(SCHEMA TABLE)
$\Gamma \vdash \diamond$	$\Gamma \vdash^{inst} \mathbb{T} : Q \quad \textbf{table}(Q) \quad \Gamma, t : Q \vdash \mathbb{S} : Sty$
$\overline{\Gamma \vdash [] : []}$	$\overline{\Gamma \vdash (t = \mathbb{T}) :: \mathbb{S} : (t : Q) :: Sty}$

Top-level tables in a schema are typechecked at level **inst**, because they can define both **static** and **inst**-level columns. The table typing judgment only includes the level parameter because it is also used for typing functions, which can be called from **static** columns.

14.5.6 Type Soundness and Termination of Reduction

In this section, we present the key property of the reduction system: every well-typed schema reduces to a Core schema with the same type. To prove the type soundness property, we need to state and prove three separate propositions: type preservation, progress and termination of reduction. The proofs of these properties are mostly standard inductive proofs and are omitted in this chapter. They can be found in Szymczak (2018).

The type preservation proposition states that if a schema can be reduced, this reduced schema is well-typed and has the same type as the original schema:

Proposition 14.1 (Type preservation)
(1) *If $\Gamma \vdash^{pc} M : Q$ and $M \to M'$, then $\Gamma \vdash^{pc} M' : Q$*
(2) *If $\Gamma \vdash^{inst} \mathbb{T} : Q$ and $\mathbb{T} \to \mathbb{T}'$, then $\Gamma \vdash^{inst} \mathbb{T}' : Q$*
(3) *If $\Gamma \vdash \mathbb{S} : Sty$ and $\mathbb{S} \to \mathbb{S}'$, then $\Gamma \vdash \mathbb{S}' : Sty$.*

The progress property states that every well-typed schema which is not in Core form can be reduced.

Proposition 14.2 (Progress)
(1) *If $\Gamma \vdash^{pc} \mathbb{T} : Q$ then either Core($\mathbb{T}$) or there is $\mathbb{T}'$ such that $\mathbb{T} \to \mathbb{T}'$.*
(2) *If $\Gamma \vdash^{pc} \mathbb{S} : Sty$ then either Core($\mathbb{S}$) or there is $\mathbb{S}'$ such that $\mathbb{S} \to \mathbb{S}'$.*

The final property needed for the type soundness theorem is termination of reduction:

Proposition 14.3 (Termination)   *There does not exist an infinite chain of reductions $\mathbb{S}_1 \to \mathbb{S}_2 \to \cdots$.*

By putting these propositions together, we obtain the key theoretical result of this chapter, the type soundness theorem (where we write $\to^*$ for the reflexive and transitive closure of the reduction relation):

Theorem 14.4   *If $\varnothing \vdash \mathbb{S} : Sty$, then $\mathbb{S} \to^* \mathbb{S}'$ for some unique $\mathbb{S}'$ such that Core($\mathbb{S}'$) and $\varnothing \vdash \mathbb{S}' : Sty$.*

Proof   By Propositions 14.1 and 14.2, we can construct a maximal chain of reductions $\mathbb{S} \to \mathbb{S}_1 \to \mathbb{S}_2 \cdots$ such that $\varnothing \vdash \mathbb{S}_i : Sty$ for all i and either Core($\mathbb{S}_i$) or $\mathbb{S}_i \to \mathbb{S}_{i+1}$. By Proposition 14.3, we know that this chain must be finite, so we must have Core($\mathbb{S}_i$) for some $\mathbb{S}_i$. The uniqueness of this $\mathbb{S}_i$ follows from the determinacy of the reduction rules.   □

14.6 Conclusions

We have presented a new, significantly extended version of the Tabular schema-based probabilistic programming language, with user-defined functions serving as reusable, modular model components, a primitive for computing quantities depending on inference results, useful in decision theory, and dependent types for catching common modelling errors.

We endowed the language with a rigorous metatheory, strengthening its design. We have defined a system of structural types, in which each table or model type shows the variables used in the model, their domains, determinacies, numbers of instances (one or many) and roles they play in the model. We have shown how to reduce compound models to the Core form, directly corresponding to a factor graph, by providing a set of reduction rules akin to operational semantics in conventional languages, and have proven that this operation is type-sound.

One possible direction of future work is adding support for inference in time-series models. Another possible extension is to allow nested inference Rainforth (2018); Mantadelis and Janssens (2011) by extending the lattice of spaces, so that the distributions computed in one run of inference could be queried by the probabilistic model "active" in the following run. The new lattice would include indexed spaces of the form $\mathbf{rnd}_i$ and $\mathbf{qry}_i$, where the result of **infer** applied to a random variable in $\mathbf{rnd}_i$ would be in $\mathbf{qry}_i$ and data in $\mathbf{rnd}_{i+1}$ could reference columns in space $\mathbf{qry}_i$.

References

Bingham, Eli, Chen, Jonathan P., Jankowiak, Martin, Obermeyer, Fritz, Pradhan, Neeraj, Karaletsos, Theofanis, Singh, Rohit, Szerlip, Paul, Horsfall, Paul, and Goodman, Noah D. 2018. Pyro: Deep Universal Probabilistic Programming. *arXiv preprint arXiv:1810.09538*.

Borgström, Johannes, Gordon, Andrew D., Greenberg, Michael, Margetson, James, and Gael, Jurgen Van. 2013. Measure Transformer Semantics for Bayesian Machine Learning. *Logical Methods in Computer Science*, **9**(3). Preliminary version at ESOP'11.

Borgström, Johannes, Gordon, Andrew D., Ouyang, Long, Russo, Claudio, Ścibior, Adam, and Szymczak, Marcin. 2016. Fabular: Regression Formulas As Probabilistic Programming. Pages 271–283 of: *Proceedings of the 43rd Annual ACM SIGPLAN-SIGACT Symposium on Principles of Programming Languages*. POPL '16. New York, NY, USA: ACM.

Carpenter, Bob, Gelman, Andrew, Hoffman, Matthew D., Lee, Daniel, Goodrich, Ben, Betancourt, Michael, Brubaker, Marcus, Guo, Jiqiang, Li, Peter, and Riddell, Allen. 2017. Stan: A probabilistic programming language. *Journal of Statistical Software*, **76**(1).

Georgoulas, Anastasis, Hillston, Jane, Milios, Dimitrios, and Sanguinetti, Guido.

2014. Probabilistic Programming Process Algebra. Pages 249–264 of: *Quantitative Evaluation of Systems - 11th International Conference, QEST 2014, Florence, Italy, September 8-10, 2014. Proceedings*.

Gilks, W R, Thomas, A, and Spiegelhalter, D. J. 1994. A language and program for complex Bayesian modelling. *The Statistician*, **43**, 169–178.

Goodman, Noah, Mansinghka, Vikash K., Roy, Daniel M., Bonawitz, Keith, and Tenenbaum, Joshua B. 2008. Church: a language for generative models. Pages 220–229 of: *Uncertainty in Artificial Intelligence (UAI'08)*. AUAI Press.

Goodman, Noah D., and Stuhlmüller, Andreas. 2014. *The Design and Implementation of Probabilistic Programming Languages*. http://dippl.org.

Gordon, Andrew D., Russo, Claudio, Szymczak, Marcin, Borgström, Johannes, Rolland, Nicolas, Graepel, Thore, and Tarlow, Daniel. 2014a. *Probabilistic Programs as Spreadsheet Queries*. Tech. rept. MSR–TR–2014–135. Microsoft Research.

Gordon, Andrew D., Graepel, Thore, Rolland, Nicolas, Russo, Claudio, Borgstrom, Johannes, and Guiver, John. 2014b. Tabular: A Schema-driven Probabilistic Programming Language. Pages 321–334 of: *Proceedings of the 41st ACM SIGPLAN-SIGACT Symposium on Principles of Programming Languages*. POPL '14. New York, NY, USA: ACM.

Gordon, Andrew D., Russo, Claudio V., Szymczak, Marcin, Borgström, Johannes, Rolland, Nicolas, Graepel, Thore, and Tarlow, Daniel. 2015. Probabilistic Programs as Spreadsheet Queries. Pages 1–25 of: Vitek, Jan (ed), *Programming Languages and Systems (ESOP 2015)*. Lecture Notes in Computer Science, vol. 9032. Springer.

Harper, Robert, and Lillibridge, Mark. 1994. A Type-theoretic Approach to Higher-order Modules with Sharing. Pages 123–137 of: *Proceedings of the 21st ACM SIGPLAN-SIGACT Symposium on Principles of Programming Languages*. POPL '94. New York, NY, USA: ACM.

Herbrich, Ralf, Minka, Tom, and Graepel, Thore. 2007. TrueSkill™: A Bayesian Skill Rating System. Pages 569–576 of: Schölkopf, B., Platt, J. C., and Hoffman, T. (eds), *Advances in Neural Information Processing Systems 19*. MIT Press.

Hutchison, Dylan. 2016. ModelWizard: Toward Interactive Model Construction. *CoRR*, **abs/1604.04639**.

Mansinghka, Vikash K., Selsam, Daniel, and Perov, Yura N. 2014. Venture: a higher-order probabilistic programming platform with programmable inference. *CoRR*, **abs/1404.0099**.

Mansinghka, Vikash K., Tibbetts, Richard, Baxter, Jay, Shafto, Patrick, and Eaves, Baxter. 2015. BayesDB: A probabilistic programming system for querying the probable implications of data. *CoRR*, **abs/1512.05006**.

Mantadelis, Theofrastos, and Janssens, Gerda. 2011. Nesting Probabilistic Inference. *CoRR*, **abs/1112.3785**.

Minka, T., Winn, J.M., Guiver, J.P., and Knowles, D.A. 2012. *Infer.NET 2.5*. Microsoft Research Cambridge. http://research.microsoft.com/infernet.

Minka, Thomas P. 2001. Expectation Propagation for approximate Bayesian inference. Pages 362–369 of: *Uncertainty in Artificial Intelligence (UAI'01)*. Morgan Kaufmann.

Minka, Tom, and Winn, John. 2009. Gates. Pages 1073–1080 of: Koller, D., Schuurmans, D., Bengio, Y., and Bottou, L. (eds), *Advances in Neural Information Processing Systems 21*. Curran Associates, Inc.

Nori, Aditya V., Hur, Chung-Kil, Rajamani, Sriram K., and Samuel, Selva. 2014. R2: An Efficient MCMC Sampler for Probabilistic Programs. Pages 2476–2482 of: *Proceedings of the Twenty-Eighth AAAI Conference on Artificial Intelligence*. AAAI'14. AAAI Press.

Pollack, Robert. 2002. Dependently Typed Records in Type Theory. *Formal Aspects of Computing*, **13**, 386–402.

Rainforth, Tom. 2018. Nesting Probabilistic Programs. Pages 249–258 of: Globerson, Amir, and Silva, Ricardo (eds), *Proceedings of the Thirty-Fourth Conference on Uncertainty in Artificial Intelligence, UAI 2018, Monterey, California, USA, August 6-10, 2018*. AUAI Press.

Ścibior, Adam, Ghahramani, Zoubin, and Gordon, Andrew D. 2015. Practical probabilistic programming with monads. Pages 165–176 of: Lippmeier, Ben (ed), *Proceedings of Haskell 2015*. ACM.

Siddharth, N., Paige, Brooks, van de Meent, Jan-Willem, Desmaison, Alban, Goodman, Noah D., Kohli, Pushmeet, Wood, Frank, and Torr, Philip. 2017. Learning Disentangled Representations with Semi-Supervised Deep Generative Models. Pages 5927–5937 of: Guyon, I., Luxburg, U. V., Bengio, S., Wallach, H., Fergus, R., Vishwanathan, S., and Garnett, R. (eds), *Advances in Neural Information Processing Systems 30*. Curran Associates, Inc.

Szymczak, Marcin. 2018. *Programming Language Semantics as a Foundation for Bayesian Inference*. Ph.D. thesis, University of Edinburgh.

Vaglica, V., Sajeva, M., McGough, H. N., Hutchison, D., Russo, C., Gordon, A. D., Ramarosandratana, A. V., Stuppy, W., and Smith, M. J. 2017. Monitoring internet trade to inform species conservation actions. *Endangered Species Research*, **32**, 223–235.

Van den Broeck, Guy, Thon, Ingo, van Otterlo, Martijn, and De Raedt, Luc. 2010. DTProbLog: A Decision-theoretic Probabilistic Prolog. Pages 1217–1222 of: *Proceedings of the Twenty-Fourth AAAI Conference on Artificial Intelligence*. AAAI'10. AAAI Press.

Wood, Frank, Meent, Jan Willem, and Mansinghka, Vikash. 2014. A New Approach to Probabilistic Programming Inference. Pages 1024–1032 of: Kaski, Samuel, and Corander, Jukka (eds), *Proceedings of the Seventeenth International Conference on Artificial Intelligence and Statistics*. Proceedings of Machine Learning Research, vol. 33. Reykjavik, Iceland: PMLR.

Wu, Mike, Perov, Yura N., Wood, Frank D., and Yang, Hongseok. 2016. Spreadsheet Probabilistic Programming. *CoRR*, **abs/1606.04216**. (see also the Scenarios tool at `invrea.com`).

15

Programming Unreliable Hardware

Michael Carbin
Massachusetts Institute of Technology
Sasa Misailovic
University of Illinois

Abstract: Emerging high-performance architectures are anticipated to contain unreliable components that may exhibit *soft errors*, which silently corrupt the results of computations. Full detection and masking of soft errors is challenging, expensive, and, for some applications, unnecessary. For example, approximate computing applications (such as multimedia processing, machine learning, and big data analytics) can often naturally tolerate soft errors.

We present Rely, a programming language that enables developers to reason about the quantitative reliability of an application – namely, the probability that it produces the correct result when executed on unreliable hardware. Rely allows developers to specify the reliability requirements for each value that a function produces.

We present a static quantitative reliability analysis that verifies quantitative requirements on the reliability of an application, enabling a developer to perform sound and verified reliability engineering. The analysis takes a Rely program with a reliability specification and a hardware specification that characterizes the reliability of the underlying hardware components and verifies that the program satisfies its reliability specification when executed on the underlying unreliable hardware platform. We demonstrate the application of quantitative reliability analysis on six computations implemented in Rely.

15.1 Introduction

Reliability is a major concern in the design of computer systems. The current goal of delivering systems with negligible error rates restricts the available design space and imposes significant engineering costs. And as other goals such as energy efficiency, circuit scaling, and new features and functionality continue to grow in importance, maintaining even current error rates will become increasingly difficult.

[a] From *Foundations of Probabilistic Programming*, edited by Gilles Barthe, Joost-Pieter Katoen and Alexandra Silva published 2020 by Cambridge University Press.

In response to this situation, researchers have developed numerous techniques for detecting and masking errors in both hardware (Ernst et al., 2003) and software (Reis et al., 2005; Perry et al., 2007; de Kruijf et al., 2010). Because these techniques typically come at the price of increased execution time, increased energy consumption, or both, they can substantially hinder or even cripple overall system performance.

Many computations, however, can easily tolerate occasional errors. An *approximate computation* (including many multimedia, financial, machine learning, and big data analytics applications) can tolerate occasional errors in its execution and/or the data that it manipulates (Rinard, 2006; Misailovic et al., 2010; Carbin and Rinard, 2010). A *checkable computation* can be augmented with an efficient checker that verifies either the exact correctness (Blum and Kanna, 1989; Leveson et al., 1990) or the approximate acceptability of the results that the computation produces. If the checker does detect an error, it can reexecute the computation to obtain an acceptable result.

For both approximate and checkable computations, operating without (or with at most selectively applied) mechanisms that detect and mask errors can produce (1) faster and more energy efficient execution that (2) delivers acceptably accurate results often enough to satisfy the needs of their users.

15.1.1 Background

Approximate computations have emerged as a major component of many computing environments. Motivated in part by the observation that approximate computations can often acceptably tolerate occasional computation and/or data errors (Rinard, 2006; Misailovic et al., 2010; Carbin and Rinard, 2010), researchers have developed a range of new mechanisms that forgo exact correctness to optimize other objectives. Typical goals include maximizing program performance subject to an accuracy constraint and altering program execution to recover from otherwise fatal errors (Rinard et al., 2004).

Software Techniques Most software techniques deploy *unsound transformations –* transformations that change the semantics of an original exact program. Proposed mechanisms include skipping tasks (Rinard, 2006), loop perforation (skipping iterations of time-consuming loops) (Misailovic et al., 2010; Sidiroglou et al., 2011), sampling reduction inputs (Zhu et al., 2012), multiple selectable implementations of a given component or components (Baek and Chilimbi, 2010; Ansel et al., 2011; Hoffman et al., 2011; Zhu et al., 2012), dynamic knobs (configuration parameters that can be changed as the program executes) (Hoffman et al., 2011) and synchronization elimination (forgoing synchronization not required to produce an acceptably accurate result) (Misailovic et al., 2013). The results show that aggressive techniques such as loop perforation can deliver up to a four-fold performance improvement with acceptable changes in the quality of the results that the application delivers.

Hardware Techniques The computer architecture community has begun to investigate new designs that improve performance by breaking the traditional fully reliable digital abstraction that computer hardware has traditionally sought to provide. The goal is to reduce the cost of implementing a reliable abstraction on top of physical materials and manufacturing methods that are inherently unreliable. For example, researchers are investigating designs that incorporate aggressive device and voltage scaling techniques to provide low-power ALUs and memories. A key aspect of these components is that they forgo traditional correctness checks and instead expose timing errors and bitflips with some non-negligible probability (de Kruijf et al., 2010; Esmaeilzadeh et al., 2012; Leem et al., 2010; Liu et al., 2011; Narayanan et al., 2010; Palem, 2005; Sampson et al., 2011).

In this work, we focus on hardware techniques that manifest as *soft errors* – errors that occur in the system nondeterministically. They may affect the values computed by individual instruction executions or data stored in individual memory locations. We can associate the probability of soft-error occurrence with each (unprotected) instruction. However, soft errors do not last over multiple instruction executions or permanently damage the hardware.

15.1.2 Reasoning About Approximate Programs

Approximate computing violates the traditional contract that the programming system must preserve the standard semantics of the program. It therefore invalidates standard paradigms and motivates new, more general, approaches to reasoning about program correctness, and acceptability.

One key aspect of approximate applications is that they typically contain *critical* regions (which must execute without error) and *approximate* regions (which can execute acceptably even in the presence of occasional errors) (Rinard, 2006; Carbin and Rinard, 2010). Existing systems, tools, and type systems have focused on helping developers identify, separate, and reason about the binary distinction between critical and approximate regions (Rinard, 2006; Carbin and Rinard, 2010; Liu et al., 2011; Sampson et al., 2011; Esmaeilzadeh et al., 2012). However, in practice, no computation can tolerate an unbounded accumulation of errors – to execute acceptably, executions of even approximate regions must satisfy some minimal requirements.

Approximate computing therefore raises a number of fundamental new research questions. For example, what is the probability that an approximate program will produce the same result as a corresponding original exact program? How much do the results differ from those produced by the original program? And is the resulting program safe and secure?

Because traditional correctness properties do not provide an appropriate conceptual framework for addressing these kinds of questions, we instead work with *acceptability properties* – the minimal requirements that a program must satisfy for acceptable use in its designated context. We identify three kinds of acceptability properties and use the following program (which computes the minimum element `min` in an `N`-element array) to illustrate these properties:

```
int min = INT_MAX;
for (int i = 0; i < N; ++i)
    if (a[i] < min) min = a[i];
```

Integrity Properties: Integrity properties are properties that the computation must satisfy to produce a successful result. Examples include both computation-independent properties (no out of bounds accesses, null dereferences, divide by zero errors, or other actions that would crash the computation) and computation-dependent properties (for example, the computation must return a result within a given range). One integrity property for our example is that accesses to the array `a` must always be within bounds.

Reliability Properties: Reliability properties characterize the probability that the produced result is correct. Reliability properties are often appropriate for approximate computations executing on unreliable hardware platforms that exhibit occasional nondeterministic errors. A potential reliability property for our example program is that `min` must be the minimum element in `a[0]-a[N-1]` with probability at least 95%.

Accuracy Properties: Accuracy properties characterize how accurate the produced result must be. For example, an accuracy property might state that the transformed program must produce a result that differs by at most a specified percentage from the result that a corresponding original program produces (Misailovic et al., 2011; Zhu et al., 2012). Alternatively, a potential accuracy property for our example program might require the `min` to be within the smallest `N/2` elements `a[0]-a[N-1]`. Such an accuracy property might be satisfied by, for example, a loop perforation transformation that skips `N/2-1` of the loop iterations.

In other research, we have developed techniques for reasoning about integrity properties (Carbin et al., 2012, 2013a) and both worst-case and probabilistic accuracy properties (Misailovic et al., 2011; Zhu et al., 2012; Carbin et al., 2012). We have extended the research presented in this chapter to include combinations of reliability and accuracy properties (Misailovic et al., 2014), and more recently to reason about message-passing parallel programs with approximate communication (Fernando et al., 2019).

15.1.3 Verifying Reliability (Contributions)

To meet the challenge of reasoning about reliability, we present a programming language, Rely, and an associated program analysis that computes the *quantitative reliability* of the computation – i.e., the probability with which the computation produces a correct result when parts of the computation execute on unreliable hardware. Specifically, given a hardware specification and a Rely program, the analysis computes, for each value that the computation produces, a conservative probability that the value is computed correctly despite the possibility of soft errors.

Rely supports and is specifically designed to enable partitioning a program into *critical* regions (which must execute without error) and *approximate* regions (which can execute acceptably even in the presence of occasional errors) (Rinard, 2006; Carbin and Rinard, 2010). In contrast to previous approaches, which support only a binary distinction between critical and approximate regions, quantitative reliability can provide precise static probabilistic acceptability guarantees for computations that execute on unreliable hardware platforms. This chapter describes the following contributions we initially presented in Carbin et al. (2013b).

Quantitative Reliability Specifications We present quantitative reliability specifications, which characterize the probability that a program executed on unreliable hardware produces the correct result, as a constructive method for developing applications. Quantitative reliability specifications enable developers who build applications for unreliable hardware architectures to perform sound and verified reliability engineering.

Language We present Rely, a language that enables developers to specify reliability requirements for programs that allocate data in unreliable memory regions and use unreliable arithmetic/logical operations.

Quantitative Reliability Analysis We present a program analysis that verifies that the dynamic semantics of a Rely program satisfies its quantitative reliability specifications. For each function, the analysis computes a symbolic reliability precondition that characterizes the set of valid specifications for the function. The analysis then verifies that the developer-provided specifications are valid according to the reliability precondition.

15.2 Example

Figure 15.1 presents the syntax of the Rely language. Rely is an imperative language for computations over integers, floats (not presented), and multidimensional arrays.

$$
\begin{array}{rcl}
n & \in & \text{Int}_\text{M} \\
r & \in & \mathbb{Q} \\
x, \ell & \in & \text{Var} \\
a & \in & \text{ArrVar}
\end{array}
\qquad
\begin{array}{rcl}
e \in Exp & \to & n \mid x \mid (Exp) \mid Exp \ iop \ Exp \\
b \in BExp & \to & \texttt{true} \mid \texttt{false} \mid Exp \ cmp \ Exp \mid (BExp) \mid \\
& & BExp \ lop \ BExp \mid \texttt{!} BExp \mid \texttt{!} . BExp \\
CExp & \to & e \mid a
\end{array}
$$

$$
\begin{array}{rcl}
m & \in & \text{MVar} \\
V & \to & x \mid a \mid V, x \mid V, a \\
RSpec & \to & r \mid \texttt{R}(V) \mid r * \texttt{R}(V) \\
T & \to & \texttt{int} \mid \texttt{int} <RSpec>
\end{array}
\qquad
\begin{array}{rcl}
F & \to & (T \mid \texttt{void}) \ ID \ (P^*) \ \{ \ S \ \} \\
P & \to & P_0 \ [\texttt{in} \ m] \\
P_0 & \to & \texttt{int} \ x \mid T \ a \ (n) \\
S & \to & D^* \ S_s \ S_r^?
\end{array}
$$

$$
\begin{array}{rcl}
D & \to & D_0 \ [\texttt{in} \ m] \\
D_0 & \to & \texttt{int} \ x \ [= Exp] \mid \texttt{int} \ a \ [n^+] \\
S_s & \to & \texttt{skip} \mid x = Exp \mid x = a \ [Exp^+] \mid a \ [Exp^+] = Exp \mid \\
& & ID \ (CExp^*) \mid x = ID \ (CExp^*) \mid \texttt{if}_\ell \ BExp \ S \ S \mid S \ \texttt{;} \ S \\
& & \texttt{while}_\ell \ BExp \ [: n] \ S \mid \texttt{repeat}_\ell \ n \ S \\
S_r & \to & \texttt{return} \ Exp
\end{array}
$$

Figure 15.1 Rely's Language Syntax

To illustrate how a developer can use Rely, Figure 15.2 presents a Rely-based implementation of a pixel block search algorithm derived from that in the x264 video encoder (x264, 2013).

The function `search_ref` searches a region (`pblocks`) of a previously encoded video frame to find the block of pixels that is most similar to a given block of pixels (`cblock`) in the current frame. The motion estimation algorithm uses the results of `search_ref` to encode `cblock` as a function of the identified block. This is an approximate computation that can trade correctness for more efficient execution by approximating the search to find a block. If `search_ref` returns a block that is not the most similar, then the encoder may require more bits to encode `cblock`, potentially decreasing the video's peak signal-to-noise ratio or increasing its size. However, previous studies on soft error injection (de Kruijf et al., 2010) and more aggressive transformations like loop perforation (Misailovic et al., 2010; Sidiroglou et al., 2011) have demonstrated that the quality of x264's final result is only slightly affected by perturbations of this computation.

15.2.1 Reliability Specifications

The function declaration on Line 6 specifies the types and reliabilities of `search_ref`'s parameters and return value. The parameters of the function are `pblocks(3)`, a three-dimensional array of pixels, and `cblock(2)`, a two-dimensional array of pixels. In addition to the standard signature, the function declaration contains *reliability specifications* for each result that the function produces.

Rely's reliability specifications express the reliability of a function's results – when executed on an unreliable hardware platform – as a function of the reliabil-

```
1   #define nblocks 20
2   #define height  16
3   #define width   16
4
5   int<0.99*R(pblocks, cblock)>
6   search_ref (
7    int<R(pblocks)> pblocks(3) in urel,
8    int<R(cblock)> cblock(2) in urel)
9   {
10    int minssd = INT_MAX,
11        minblock = -1 in urel;
12    int ssd, t, t1, t2 in urel;
13    int i = 0, j, k;
14
15    repeat nblocks  {
16      ssd = 0;
17      j = 0;
18      repeat height {
19        k = 0;
20        repeat width {
21          t1 = pblocks[i,j,k];
22          t2 = cblock[j,k];
23          t = t1 -. t2;
24          ssd = ssd +. t *. t;
25          k = k + 1;
26        }
27        j = j + 1;
28      }
29
30      if (ssd <. minssd) {
31        minssd = ssd;
32        minblock = i;
33      }
34
35      i = i + 1;
36    }
37    return minblock;
38  }
```

Figure 15.2 Rely Code for Motion Estimation

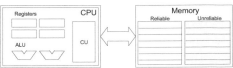

Figure 15.3 Machine Model.

```
reliability spec {
   operator (+.) = 1 - 10^-7;
   operator (-.) = 1 - 10^-7;
   operator (*.) = 1 - 10^-7;
   operator (<.) = 1 - 10^-7;
   memory rel {rd = 1, wr = 1};
   memory urel {rd = 1 - 10^-7, wr = 1};
}
```

Figure 15.4 Hardware Reliability Specification

$$(3) \quad \{Q_0 \wedge A_{ret} \leq r_0^4 \cdot \mathcal{R}(i, ssd, minssd)$$
$$\wedge\ A_{ret} \leq r_0^4 \cdot \mathcal{R}(\ minblock, ssd, minssd)\}$$
```
if (ssd <. minssd) {
```
$$(2) \quad \{Q_0 \wedge A_{ret} \leq r_0 \cdot \mathcal{R}(i, \ell_{30})\}$$
```
  minssd = ssd;
```
$$\{Q_0 \wedge A_{ret} \leq r_0 \cdot \mathcal{R}(i, \ell_{30})\}$$
```
  minblock = i;
```
$$\{Q_0 \wedge A_{ret} \leq r_0 \cdot \mathcal{R}(minblock, \ell_{30})\}$$
```
} else {
```
$$(2) \quad \{Q_0 \wedge A_{ret} \leq r_0 \cdot \mathcal{R}(minblock, \ell_{30})\}$$
```
  skip;
```
$$\{Q_0 \wedge A_{ret} \leq r_0 \cdot \mathcal{R}(minblock, \ell_{30})\}$$
```
}
```
$$(1) \quad \{Q_0 \wedge A_{ret} \leq r_0 \cdot \mathcal{R}(minblock, \ell_{30})\}$$

Figure 15.5 `if` Statement Analysis in Last Iteration

ities of its inputs. The specification for the reliability of `search_ref`'s result is `int<0.99*R(pblocks,cblock)>`. This states that the return value is an integer with a reliability that is at least 99% of the **joint reliability** of the parameters `pblocks` and `cblock` (denoted by `R(pblocks, cblock)`). The joint reliability of a set of parameters is the probability that they all have the correct value when passed in from the caller. The joint reliability is a key abstraction for our verification; we will formalize it in Section 15.4.2.

The reliability specification holds for all possible values of the joint reliability of `pblocks` and `cblock`. For instance, if the contents of the arrays `pblocks` and `cblock` are fully reliable (correct with probability one), then the return value is correct with probability 0.99.

In Rely, arrays are passed by reference and the execution of a function can, as a side effect, modify an array's contents. The reliability specification of an array therefore allows a developer to constrain the *reliability degradation* of its contents. Here `pblocks` has an output reliability specification of R(pblocks) (and similarly for `cblock`), meaning that all of `pblock`'s elements are at least as reliable when the function exits as they were on entry to the function.

15.2.2 Unreliable Computation

Rely targets hardware architectures that expose both reliable operations (which always execute correctly) and more energy-efficient unreliable operations (which execute correctly with only some probability). Specifically, Rely supports reasoning about reads and writes of unreliable memory regions and unreliable arithmetic/logical operations.

Memory Region Specification Each parameter declaration also specifies the memory region in which the data of the parameter is allocated. Memory regions correspond to the physical partitioning of memory at the hardware level into regions of varying reliability. Here `pblocks` and `cblock` are allocated in an unreliable memory region named `urel`.

Lines 10-13 declare the local variables of the function. By default, variables in Rely are allocated in a default, fully reliable memory region. However, a developer can also optionally specify a memory region for each local variable. For example, the variables declared on Lines 10-12 reside in `urel`.

Unreliable Operations The operations on Lines 23, 24, and 30 are unreliable arithmetic/logical operations. In Rely, every arithmetic/logical operation has an unreliable counterpart that is denoted by suffixing a period after the operation symbol. For example, "-." denotes unreliable subtraction and "<." denotes unreliable comparison.

Using these operations, `search_ref`'s implementation *approximately* computes the index (`minblock`) of the most similar block, i.e. the block with the minimum distance from `cblock`. The `repeat` statement on line 15, iterates a constant `nblock` number of times, enumerating over all previously encoded blocks. For each encoded block, the `repeat` statements on lines 18 and 20 iterate over the `height*width` pixels of the block and compute the sum of the squared differences (`ssd`) between each pixel value and the corresponding pixel value in the current block `cblock`. Finally, the computation on lines 30 through 33 selects the block that is – approximately – the most similar to `cblock`.

15.2.3 Hardware Semantics

Figure 15.3 illustrates the conceptual machine model behind Rely's reliable and unreliable operations; the model consists of a CPU and a memory.

CPU The CPU consists of (1) a register file, (2) arithmetic logical units that perform operations on data in registers, and (3) a control unit that manages the program's execution.

The arithmetic-logical unit can execute reliably or unreliably. We have represented this in Figure 15.3 by physically separate reliable and unreliable functional units, but this distinction can be achieved through other mechanisms, such as dual-voltage architectures (Esmaeilzadeh et al., 2012). Unreliable functional units may omit additional checking logic, enabling the unit to execute more efficiently but also allowing for soft errors that may occur due to, for example, power variations within the ALU's combinatorial circuits or particle strikes. As is provided by existing computer architecture proposals (Sampson et al., 2011; Esmaeilzadeh et al., 2012), the control unit of the CPU reliably fetches, decodes, and schedules instructions; given a virtual address in the application, the control unit correctly computes a physical address and operates only on that address.

Memory Rely supports machines with memories that consist of an arbitrary number of memory partitions (each potentially of different reliability), but for simplicity Figure 15.3 partitions memory into two regions: reliable and unreliable. Unreliable memories can, for example, use decreased DRAM refresh rates to reduce power consumption at the expense of increased soft error rates (Liu et al., 2011; Sampson et al., 2011).

Hardware Reliability Specification

We abstract the behavior of the unreliable hardware platforms through a reliability specification. It specifics the reliability of arithmetic/logical and memory operations. Figure 15.4 presents a hardware reliability specification that is inspired by the results from existing computer architecture literature (Ernst et al., 2003; Liu et al., 2011). Each entry specifies the reliability – the probability of a correct execution – of arithmetic operations (e.g., +.) and memory read/write operations.

For ALU operations, the presented reliability specification uses the reliability of an unreliable multiplication operation that we selected from Ernst et al. (2003, Figure 9). For memory operations, the specification uses the probability of a bit flip in a memory cell that we selected from Liu et al. (2011, Figure 4) with extrapolation to the probability of a bit flip within a 32-bit word. Note that a memory region specification includes two reliabilities: the reliability of a read (`rd`) and the reliability of a write (`wr`).

15.2.4 Reliability Analysis

Given a Rely program, Rely's reliability analysis verifies that each function in the program satisfies its reliability specification when executed on unreliable hardware. The analysis takes as input a Rely program and a *hardware reliability specification*.

The analysis consists of two components: the **precondition generator** and the **precondition checker**. For each function, the precondition generator produces a precondition that characterizes the reliability of the function's results given a hardware reliability specification that characterizes the reliability of each unreliable operation. The precondition checker then determines if the function's specifications satisfy the constraint. If so, then the function satisfies its reliability specification when executed on the underlying unreliable hardware in that the reliability of its results exceed their specifications.

Design As a key design point, the analysis generates preconditions according to a conservative approximation of the semantics of the function. Specifically, it characterizes the reliability of a function's result according to the probability that the function computes that result fully reliably.

To illustrate the intuition behind this design point, consider the evaluation of an integer expression e. The reliability of e is the probability that it evaluates to the same value n in an unreliable evaluation as in the fully reliable evaluation. There are two ways that an unreliable evaluation can return n: (1) the unreliable evaluation of e encounters no faults and (2) the unreliable evaluation possibly encounters faults, but still returns n by chance.

Rely's analysis conservatively approximates the reliability of a computation by only considering the first scenario. This design point simplifies the reasoning to the task of computing the probability that a result is reliably computed as opposed to reasoning about a computation's input distribution and the probabilities of all executions that produce the correct result. As a consequence, the analysis requires as input only a hardware reliability specification that gives the probability with which each arithmetic/logical operation and memory operation executes correctly. The analysis is therefore oblivious to a computation's input distribution and does not require a full model of how soft errors affect its result.

Precondition Generator

For each function, Rely's analysis generates a *reliability precondition* that conservatively bounds the set of valid specifications for the function. A reliability precondition is a conjunction of predicates of the form $A_{out} \leq r \cdot \mathcal{R}(X)$, where A_{out} is a placeholder for a developer-provided reliability specification for an output with name *out*, r is a numerical value between 0 and 1, and the term $\mathcal{R}(X)$ is the joint reliability of the set X of variables (including the function parameters) on entry to the function.

The analysis starts at the end of the function from a postcondition that must be true when the function returns and then works backward to produce a precondition such that if the precondition holds before execution of the function, then the postcondition holds at the end of the function.

Postcondition The postcondition for a function is the constraint that the reliability of each array argument exceeds that given in its specification. For `search_ref`, the postcondition Q_0 is

$$Q_0 = A_{\texttt{pblocks}} \leq \mathcal{R}(\texttt{pblocks}) \wedge A_{\texttt{cblock}} \leq \mathcal{R}(\texttt{cblock}),$$

which specifies that the reliability of the arrays `pblocks` and `cblock` $- \mathcal{R}(\texttt{pblocks})$ and $\mathcal{R}(\texttt{cblock})$ – should be at least that specified by the developer – $A_{\texttt{pblocks}}$ and $A_{\texttt{cblock}}$.

Precondition Generation The analysis of the body of the `search_ref` function starts at the `return` statement. Given the postcondition Q_0, the analysis creates a new precondition Q_1 by conjoining to Q_0 a predicate that states that the reliability of the return value ($r_0 \cdot \mathcal{R}(\texttt{minblock})$) is at least that of its specification (A_{ret}):

$$Q_1 = Q_0 \wedge A_{ret} \leq r_0 \cdot \mathcal{R}(\texttt{minblock}).$$

The reliability of the return value is the probability of correctly reading `minblock` from unreliable memory – which is $r_0 = 1 - 10^{-7}$ according to the hardware reliability specification – multiplied by $\mathcal{R}(\texttt{minblock})$, the probability that the preceding computation correctly computed and stored `minblock`.

Loops The statement that precedes the `return` statement is the `repeat` statement on Line 15. A key difficulty with reasoning about the reliability of variables modified within a loop is that if a variable is updated unreliably and has a loop-carried dependence then its reliability monotonically decreases as a function of the number of loop iterations. Because the reliability of such variables can, in principle, decrease arbitrarily in an unbounded loop, Rely provides both an unbounded loop statement (with an associated analysis) and an alternative *bounded loop* statement that lets a developer specify a compile-time bound on the maximum number of its iterations that therefore bounds the reliability degradation of modified variables. The loop on Line 15 iterates `nblocks` times and therefore decreases the reliability of any modified variables `nblocks` times. Because the reliability degradation is bounded, Rely's analysis uses unrolling to reason about the effects of a bounded loop.

Conditionals The analysis of the body of the loop on Line 15 encounters the `if` statement on Line 30.[1] This `if` statement uses an unreliable comparison operation on `ssd` and `minssd`, both of which reside in unreliable memory. The reliability of `minblock` when modified on Line 32 therefore also depends on the reliability of this expression because faults may force the execution down a different path.

Figure 15.5 presents a Hoare logic style presentation of the analysis of the conditional statement. The analysis works in three steps; the preconditions generated by each step are numbered with the corresponding step.

Step 1 To capture the implicit dependence of a variable on an unreliable condition, Rely's analysis first uses latent *control flow variables* to make these dependencies explicit. A control flow variable is a unique program variable (one for each statement) that records whether the conditional evaluated to *true* or *false*. We denote the control flow variable for the `if` statement on Line 30 by ℓ_{30}.

To make the control flow dependence explicit, the analysis adds the control flow variable to all joint reliability terms in Q_1 that contain variables modified within the body of the `if` conditional (`minssd` and `minblock`).

Step 2 The analysis next recursively analyses both the "then" and "else" branches of the conditional, producing one precondition for each branch. As in a standard precondition generator (e.g., weakest-preconditions) the assignment of `i` to `minblock` in the "then" branch replaces `minblock` with `i` in the precondition. Because reads from `i` and writes to `minblock` are reliable (according to the specification) the analysis does not introduce any new r_0 factors.

Step 3 In the final step, the analysis leaves the scope of the conditional and conjoins the two preconditions for its branches after transforming them to include the direct dependence of the control flow variable on the reliability of the `if` statement's condition expression.

The reliability of the `if` statement's expression is greater than or equal to the product of (1) the reliability of the `<.` operator (r_0), (2) the reliability of reading both `ssd` and `minssd` from unreliable memory (r_0^2), and (3) the reliability of the computation that produced `ssd` and `minssd` ($\mathcal{R}(\texttt{ssd},\texttt{minssd})$). The analysis therefore transforms each predicate that contains the variable ℓ_{30}, by multiplying the right-hand side of the inequality with r_0^3 and replacing the variable ℓ_{30} with `ssd` and `minssd`.

This produces the precondition Q_2:

$$Q_2 = Q_0 \wedge A_{ret} \leq r_0^4 \cdot \mathcal{R}(\texttt{i},\texttt{ssd},\texttt{minssd}) \wedge A_{ret} \leq r_0^4 \cdot \mathcal{R}(\texttt{minblock},\texttt{ssd},\texttt{minssd}).$$

---

[1] This happens after encountering the increment of `i` on Line 35, which does not modify the current precondition because it does not reference `i`.

Simplification After unrolling a single iteration of the loop that begins at Line 15, the analysis produces

$$Q_0 \wedge A_{ret} \leq r_0^{2564} \cdot \mathcal{R}(\texttt{pblocks}, \texttt{cblock}, \texttt{i}, \texttt{ssd}, \texttt{minssd})$$

as the precondition for a single iteration of the loop's body. The constant 2564 represents the number of unreliable operations within a single loop iteration.

Note that there is one less predicate in this precondition than in Q_2. As the analysis works backwards through the program, it uses a simplification technique that identifies that a predicate $A_{ret} \leq r_1 \cdot \mathcal{R}(X_1)$ *subsumes* another predicate $A_{ret} \leq r_2 \cdot \mathcal{R}(X_2)$. Specifically, the analysis identifies that $r_1 \leq r_2$ and $X_2 \subseteq X_1$, which together mean that the second predicate is a weaker constraint on A_{ret} than the first and can therefore be removed. This follows from the fact that the joint reliability of a set of variables is less than or equal to the joint reliability of any subset of the variables – regardless of the distribution of their values.

This simplification is how Rely's analysis achieves scalability when there are multiple paths in the program. Specifically, the simplified precondition is a lower bound of the reliability specification of all its program paths.

Final Precondition When the analysis reaches the beginning of the function after fully unrolling the loop on Line 15, it has a precondition that bounds the set of valid specifications as a function of the reliability of the parameters of the function. For `search_ref`, the analysis generates the precondition $A_{ret} \leq 0.994885 \cdot \mathcal{R}(\texttt{pblocks}, \texttt{cblock}) \wedge A_{\texttt{pblocks}} \leq \mathcal{R}(\texttt{pblocks}) \wedge A_{\texttt{cblock}} \leq \mathcal{R}(\texttt{cblock})$.

Precondition Checker

The final precondition is a conjunction of predicates of the form $A_{out} \leq r \cdot \mathcal{R}(X)$, where A_{out} is a placeholder for the reliability specification of an output. Because reliability specifications are all of the form $r \cdot \mathcal{R}(X)$ (Figure 15.1), each predicate in the final precondition (where each A_{out} is replaced with its specification) is of the form form $r_1 \cdot \mathcal{R}(X_1) \leq r_2 \cdot \mathcal{R}(X_2)$, where $r_1 \cdot \mathcal{R}(X_1)$ is a reliability specification and $r_2 \cdot \mathcal{R}(X_2)$ is computed by the analysis. Similar to the analysis's simplifier (Section 15.2.4), the precondition checker verifies the validity of each predicate by checking that (1) r_1 is less than r_2 and (2) $X_2 \subseteq X_1$.

For `search_ref`, the analysis computes the predicates

$$0.99 \cdot \mathcal{R}(\texttt{pblocks}, \texttt{cblock}) \leq 0.994885 \cdot \mathcal{R}(\texttt{pblocks}, \texttt{cblock}),$$
$$\mathcal{R}(\texttt{pblocks}) \leq \mathcal{R}(\texttt{ pblocks}), \text{ and also } \mathcal{R}(\texttt{cblock}) \leq \mathcal{R}(\texttt{cblock}).$$

Because these predicates are valid according to the checking procedure, `search_ref` satisfies its reliability specification when executed.

15.3 Language Semantics

Because soft errors may probabilistically change the execution path of a program, we model the semantics of a Rely program with a probabilistic transition system. Specifically, the dynamic semantics defines probabilistic transition rules for each arithmetic/logical operation and each read/write on an unreliable memory region.

Over the next several sections, we develop a small-step semantics that specifies the probability of each individual transition of an execution. In Section 15.3.4, we provide big-step definitions that specify the probability of an entire execution.

15.3.1 Preliminaries

Rely's semantics is given in the terms of an abstract machine that consists of a heap and a stack. The heap is an abstraction over the physical memory of the concrete machine, including its various reliable and unreliable memory regions. Each variable (both scalar and array) is allocated in the heap. The stack consists of frames – one for each function invocation – which contain references to the locations of each allocated variable. This conceptual model of local variables does not need to be concretized in the compilation model. For example, placing local variables in a reliable stack can achieve competitive performance (Misailovic et al., 2014).

Hardware Reliability Specification A hardware reliability specification $\psi \in \Psi = (iop + cmp + lop + M_{op}) \to \mathbb{Q}_{\geq 0}$ is a finite map from arithmetic/logical operations (iop, cmp, lop) and *memory region operations* (M_{op}) to reliabilities (i.e., the probability that the operation executes correctly).

Arithmetic/logical operations iop, cmp, and lop include both reliable and unreliable versions of each integer, comparison, and logical operation. The reliability of each reliable operation is 1 and the reliability of an unreliable operation is as provided by a specification (Section 15.2.3).

The finite maps $rd \in M \to M_{op}$ and $wr \in M \to M_{op}$ define memory region operations as reads and writes (respectively) on memory regions $m \in M$, where M is the set of all memory regions in the reliability specification.

The hardware reliability specification 1_ψ denotes the specification for fully reliable hardware in which all arithmetic/logical and memory operations have reliability 1.

References Given a finite, contiguous address space Loc, a *reference* is a tuple $\langle n_b, \langle n_1, \ldots, n_k \rangle, m \rangle \in \text{Ref}$ consisting of a base address $n_b \in \text{Loc}$, a dimension descriptor $\langle n_1, \ldots, n_k \rangle$, and a memory region m. Base addresses and the components of dimension descriptors range over the finite set of bounded-width machine integers $n \in \text{Int}_M$.

References describe the location, dimensions, and memory region of variables in the heap. For scalars, the dimension descriptor is the single-dimension, single-element descriptor $\langle 1 \rangle$. The projections π_{base} and π_{dim} select the base address and the dimension descriptor of a reference, respectively.

Frames, Stacks, Heaps, and Environments A *frame* $\sigma \in \Sigma = \text{Var} \rightarrow \text{Ref}$ is a finite map from variables to references. A *stack* $\delta \in \Delta ::= \sigma \mid \sigma :: \Delta$ is a non-empty list of frames. A *heap* $h \in H = \text{Loc} \rightarrow \text{Int}_M$ is a finite map from addresses to machine integers. An *environment* $\varepsilon \in \text{E} = \Delta \times H$ is a stack and heap pair, $\langle \delta, h \rangle$.

Memory Allocator The abstract memory allocator *new* is a partial function that executes reliably. It takes a heap h, a memory region m, and a dimension descriptor and returns a fresh address n_b that resides in memory region m and a new heap h' that reflects updates to the internal memory allocation data structures.

Auxiliary Probability Distributions Each nondeterministic choice in Rely's semantics must have an underlying probability distribution so that the set of possible transitions at any given small step of an execution constitutes a probability distribution – i.e., the probabilities of all possibilities sum up to one. In Rely, there are two points at which an execution can make a nondeterministic choice: (1) the result of an incorrect execution of an unreliable operation and (2) the result of allocating a new variable in the heap.

The discrete probability distribution $P_f(n_f \mid op, n_1, ..., n_k)$ models the manifestation of a soft error during an incorrect execution of an operation. Specifically, it gives the probability that an incorrect execution of an operation op on operands $n_1, \ldots, n_k$ produces a value n_f that is different from the correct result of the operation. This distribution is inherently tied to the properties of the underlying hardware.

The discrete probability distribution $P_m(n_b, h' \mid h, m, d)$ models the semantics of a nondeterministic memory allocator. It gives the probability that a memory allocator returns a fresh address n_b and an updated heap h' given an initial heap h, a memory region m, and a dimension descriptor d.

We define these distributions only to support a precise formalization of the dynamic semantics of a program; they do not need to be specified for a given hardware platform or a given memory allocator to use Rely's analysis.

15.3.2 Semantics of Expressions

Figure 15.6 presents a selection of the rules for the dynamic semantics of integer expressions. The labeled probabilistic small-step evaluation relation $\langle e, \sigma, h \rangle \xrightarrow{\theta, p}_\psi e'$ states that from a frame σ and a heap h, an expression e evaluates in one step with

$$\dfrac{\text{E-VAR-C}}{\langle x, \sigma, h \rangle \xrightarrow{C,\, \psi(rd(m))}_{\psi} h(n_b)}$$

$$\dfrac{\text{E-VAR-F}}{\langle x, \sigma, h \rangle \xrightarrow{\langle F, n_f \rangle,\, p}_{\psi} n_f}$$

$$\dfrac{\text{E-IOP-R1}}{\langle e_1, \sigma, h \rangle \xrightarrow{\theta,\, p}_{\psi} e_1'}{\langle e_1 \; iop \; e_2, \sigma, h \rangle \xrightarrow{\theta,\, p}_{\psi} e_1' \; iop \; e_2}$$

$$\dfrac{\text{E-IOP-R2}}{\langle e_2, \sigma, h \rangle \xrightarrow{\theta,\, p}_{\psi} e_2'}{\langle n \; iop \; e_2, \sigma, h \rangle \xrightarrow{\theta,\, p}_{\psi} n \; iop \; e_2'}$$

$$\dfrac{\text{E-IOP-C}}{\langle n_1 \; iop \; n_2, \sigma, h \rangle \xrightarrow{C,\, \psi(iop)}_{\psi} iop(n_1, n_2)}$$

$$\dfrac{\text{E-IOP-F}}{p = (1 - \psi(iop)) \cdot P_f(n_f \mid iop, n_1, n_2)}{\langle n_1 \; iop \; n_2, \sigma, h \rangle \xrightarrow{\langle F, n_f \rangle,\, p}_{\psi} n_f}$$

Figure 15.6 Dynamic Semantics of Integer Expressions

probability p to an expression e' given a hardware reliability specification ψ. The label $\theta \in \{C, \langle C, n \rangle, \langle F, n_f \rangle\}$ denotes whether the transition corresponds to a correct (C or $\langle C, n \rangle$) or a faulty ($\langle F, n_f \rangle$) evaluation of that step. For a correct transition $\langle C, n \rangle$, $n \in Int_M$ records a nondeterministic choice made for that step. For a faulty transition $\langle F, n_f \rangle$, $n_f \in Int_M$ represents the value that the fault introduced in the semantics of the operation.

To illustrate the meaning of the rules, consider the rules for variable reference expressions. A variable reference x reads the value stored in the memory address for x. A variable reference can be evaluated in two ways:

- Correct [E-VAR-C]. The variable reference evaluates correctly and successfully returns the integer stored in x. This happens with probability $\psi(rd(m))$, where m is the memory region in which x allocated. This probability is the reliability of reading from x's memory region.

- Faulty [E-VAR-F]. The variable reference experiences a fault and returns another integer n_f. The probability that the faulty execution returns a specific integer n_f is $(1 - \psi(rd(m))) \cdot P_f(n_f \mid rd(m), h(n_b))$. P_f is the distribution that gives the probability that a failed memory read operation returns a value n_f instead of the true stored value $h(n_b)$ (Section 15.3.1).

15.3.3 Semantics of Statements

Figure 15.7 presents the semantics of the scalar and control flow fragment of Rely. The labeled probabilistic small-step execution relation $\langle s, \varepsilon \rangle \xrightarrow{\theta,\, p}_{\psi} \langle s', \varepsilon' \rangle$ states that execution of the statement s in the environment ε takes one step yielding a statement s' and an environment ε' with probability p under the hardware reliability specification ψ. As in the dynamic semantics for expressions, a label θ denotes

E-DECL-R

$$\frac{\langle e, \sigma, h \rangle \xrightarrow{\theta, p}_\psi e'}{\langle \text{int } x = e \text{ in } m, \langle \sigma :: \delta, h \rangle \rangle \xrightarrow{\theta, p}_\psi \langle \text{int } x = e' \text{ in } m, \langle \sigma :: \delta, h \rangle \rangle}$$

E-DECL

$$\frac{\langle n_b, h' \rangle = new(h, m, \langle 1 \rangle) \qquad p_m = P_m(n_b, h' \mid h, m, \langle 1 \rangle)}{\langle \text{int } x = n \text{ in } m, \langle \sigma :: \delta, h \rangle \rangle \xrightarrow{\langle C, n_b \rangle, p_m}_\psi \langle x = n, \langle \sigma[x \mapsto \langle n_b, \langle 1 \rangle, m \rangle] :: \delta, h' \rangle \rangle}$$

E-ASSIGN-R

$$\frac{\langle e, \sigma, h \rangle \xrightarrow{\theta, p}_\psi e'}{\langle x = e, \langle \sigma :: \delta, h \rangle \rangle \xrightarrow{\theta, p}_\psi \langle x = e', \langle \sigma :: \delta, h \rangle \rangle}$$

E-ASSIGN-C

$$\frac{\langle n_b, \langle 1 \rangle, m \rangle = \sigma(x) \qquad p = \psi(wr(m))}{\langle x = n, \langle \sigma :: \delta, h \rangle \rangle \xrightarrow{C, p}_\psi \langle \text{skip}, \langle \sigma :: \delta, h[n_b \mapsto n] \rangle \rangle}$$

E-ASSIGN-F

$$\frac{\langle n_b, \langle 1 \rangle, m \rangle = \sigma(x) \qquad p = (1 - \psi(wr(m))) \cdot P_f(n_f \mid wr(m), h(n_b), n)}{\langle x = n, \langle \sigma :: \delta, h \rangle \rangle \xrightarrow{\langle F, n_f \rangle, p}_\psi \langle \text{skip}, \langle \sigma :: \delta, h[n_b \mapsto n_f] \rangle \rangle}$$

E-IF

$$\frac{\langle b, \sigma, h \rangle \xrightarrow{\theta, p}_\psi b'}{\langle \text{if}_\ell \ b \ s_1 \ s_2, \langle \sigma :: \delta, h \rangle \rangle \xrightarrow{\theta, p}_\psi \langle \text{if}_\ell \ b' \ s_1 \ s_2, \langle \sigma :: \delta, h \rangle \rangle}$$

E-IF-TRUE

$$\frac{}{\langle \text{if}_\ell \ true \ s_1 \ s_2, \varepsilon \rangle \xrightarrow{C, 1}_\psi \langle s_1, \varepsilon \rangle}$$

E-IF-FALSE

$$\frac{}{\langle \text{if}_\ell \ false \ s_1 \ s_2, \varepsilon \rangle \xrightarrow{C, 1}_\psi \langle s_2, \varepsilon \rangle}$$

E-SEQ-R1

$$\frac{\langle s_1, \varepsilon \rangle \xrightarrow{\theta, p}_\psi \langle s_1', \varepsilon' \rangle}{\langle s_1 \ ; \ s_2, \varepsilon \rangle \xrightarrow{\theta, p}_\psi \langle s_1' \ ; \ s_2, \varepsilon' \rangle}$$

E-SEQ-R2

$$\frac{}{\langle \text{skip} \ ; \ s_2, \varepsilon \rangle \xrightarrow{C, 1}_\psi \langle s_2, \varepsilon \rangle}$$

E-WHILE

$$\frac{}{\langle \text{while}_\ell \ b \ s, \varepsilon \rangle \xrightarrow{C, 1}_\psi \langle \text{if}_\ell \ b \ \{s \ ; \ \text{while}_\ell \ b \ s\} \ \{\text{skip}\}, \varepsilon \rangle}$$

E-WHILE-BOUNDED

$$\frac{}{\langle \text{while}_\ell \ b : n \ s, \varepsilon \rangle \xrightarrow{C, 1}_\psi \langle \text{if}_\ell \ b \ \{s \ ; \ \text{while}_\ell \ b : (n-1) \ s\} \ \{\text{skip}\}, \varepsilon \rangle}$$

Figure 15.7 Dynamic Semantics of Statements

whether the transition evaluated correctly (C or $\langle C, n \rangle$) or experienced a fault ($\langle F, n_f \rangle$). The semantics of the statements in the language is largely similar to that of traditional presentations except that the statements have the ability to encounter faults during execution.

The semantics we present here is designed to allow unreliable computation at all points in the application – subject to the constraint that the application is still memory safe and exhibits control flow integrity.

Memory Safety To protect references that point to memory locations from corruption, the stack is allocated in a reliable memory region and stack operations – i.e., pushing and popping frames – execute reliably. To prevent out-of-bounds memory accesses that may occur due to an unreliable array index computation, Rely requires that each array read and write include a bounds check. These bounds check computations execute reliably. We presented the semantics of memory accesses in Carbin et al. (n.d.).

Control Flow Integrity To prevent execution from taking control flow edges that do not exist in the program's static control flow graph, Rely assumes that (1) instructions are stored, fetched, and decoded reliably (as supported by existing unreliable processor architectures (Sampson et al., 2011; Esmaeilzadeh et al., 2012)) and (2) targets of control flow branches are reliably computed. These two properties allow for the control flow transfers in the rules [E-IF-TRUE], [E-IF-FALSE], and [E-SEQ-R2] to execute reliably with probability 1.

Note that the semantics does not require a specific underlying mechanism to achieve reliable execution and, therefore, an implementation can use any applicable software or hardware technique (Reis et al., 2005; Perry et al., 2007; de Kruijf et al., 2010; Feng et al., 2010; Pattabiraman et al., 2008; Schlesinger et al., 2011; Hiller et al., 2002; Thomas and Pattabiraman, 2013).

15.3.4 Big-step Notations

We use the following big-step execution relations in this paper.

Definition 15.1 (Big-step Trace Semantics).

$$\langle s, \varepsilon \rangle \xrightarrow{\tau, p}_{\psi} \varepsilon' \equiv \langle s, \varepsilon \rangle \xrightarrow{\theta_1, p_1}_{\psi} \ldots \xrightarrow{\theta_n, p_n}_{\psi} \langle \texttt{skip}, \varepsilon' \rangle$$
$$\text{where } \tau = \theta_1, \ldots, \theta_n \text{ and } p = \prod_i p_i$$

The big-step trace semantics is, conceptually, a reflexive transitive closure of the small-step execution relation that records a trace of the execution. We define a *trace*, $\tau \in T ::= \cdot \mid \theta :: T$, as the sequence of small-step transition labels, $\tau = \theta_1 :: \ldots :: \theta_n :: \cdot$. The *probability of a trace*, p, is the product of the probabilities of each transition, $p = \prod_{i=1}^{n} p_i$.

Definition 15.2 (Big-step Aggregate Semantics).

$$\langle s, \varepsilon \rangle \xrightarrow{p}_{\psi} \varepsilon' \text{ where } p = \sum \{ p_\tau \mid \exists \tau \in T. \langle s, \varepsilon \rangle \xrightarrow{\tau, p_\tau}_{\psi} \varepsilon' \}$$

The big-step aggregate semantics computes the aggregate probability (over all finite length traces) that a statement s evaluates to an environment ε' from an environment ε given a hardware reliability specification ψ. The big-step aggregate semantics therefore gives the total probability that a statement s starts from an environment ε and terminates in an environment ε'.[2]

Termination and Errors An unreliable execution of a statement may experience a run-time error (due to an out-of-bounds array access) or not terminate at all. The big-step aggregate semantics does not collect such executions. Therefore, the sum of the probabilities of the big-step transitions from an environment ε may not equal to 1. Specifically, let $p \in E \to \mathbb{R}_{\geq 0}$ be a measure for the set of environments reachable from ε, i.e., $\forall \varepsilon'.\langle s, \varepsilon \rangle \overset{p(\varepsilon')}{\Longrightarrow}_{\psi} \varepsilon'$. Then p is *subprobability* measure, i.e., $0 \leq \sum_{\varepsilon' \in E} p(\varepsilon') \leq 1$ (Kozen, 1981).

15.4 Semantics of Quantitative Reliability

We next present definitions that give a semantic meaning to the reliability of a Rely program.

15.4.1 Paired Execution

The *paired execution* semantics is the primary execution relation that enables one to reason about the reliability of a program. Specifically, the relation pairs the semantics of the program when executed reliably with its semantics when executed unreliably.

Definition 15.3 (Paired Execution). $\qquad \varphi \in \Phi = E \to \mathbb{R}_{\geq 0}$

$$\langle s, \langle \varepsilon, \varphi \rangle \rangle \Downarrow_{\psi} \langle \varepsilon', \varphi' \rangle \text{ such that } \langle s, \varepsilon \rangle \overset{1}{\Longrightarrow}_{1_{\psi}} \varepsilon' \text{ and}$$
$$\varphi'(\varepsilon'_u) = \sum \{\!\!\{ \varphi(\varepsilon_u) \cdot p_u \mid \varepsilon_u \in E, \langle s, \varepsilon_u \rangle \overset{p_u}{\Longrightarrow}_{\psi} \varepsilon'_u \}\!\!\}$$

The relation states that from a *configuration* $\langle \varepsilon, \varphi \rangle$ consisting of an environment ε and an *unreliable environment distribution* φ, the paired execution of a statement s yields a new configuration $\langle \varepsilon', \varphi' \rangle$.

The environments ε and ε' are related by the fully reliable execution of s. Namely, an execution of s from an environment ε yields ε' under the fully reliable hardware model 1_{ψ}.

The unreliable environment distributions φ and φ' are probability mass functions that map an environment to the probability that the unreliable execution of the program is in that environment. In particular, φ is a distribution on environments before the unreliable execution of s whereas φ' is the distribution on environments

---

[2] The inductive (versus co-inductive) interpretation of T yields a countable set of finite-length traces and therefore the sum over T is well-defined.

$$[\![P]\!] \in \mathcal{P}(\mathrm{E} \times \Phi) \qquad [\![\texttt{true}]\!] = \mathrm{E} \times \Phi \qquad [\![\texttt{false}]\!] = \varnothing \qquad [\![P_1 \wedge P_2]\!] = [\![P_1]\!] \cap [\![P_2]\!]$$

$$[\![R_1 \le R_2]\!] = \{\langle \varepsilon, \varphi \rangle \mid [\![R_1]\!](\varepsilon, \varphi) \le [\![R_2]\!](\varepsilon, \varphi)\}$$

$$[\![R]\!] \in \mathrm{E} \times \Phi \to \mathbb{R}_{\ge 0} \qquad [\![r]\!](\varepsilon, \varphi) = r \qquad [\![R_1 \cdot R_2]\!](\varepsilon, \varphi) = [\![R_1]\!](\varepsilon, \varphi) \cdot [\![R_2]\!](\varepsilon, \varphi)$$

$$[\![\mathcal{R}(X)]\!](\varepsilon, \varphi) = \sum_{\varepsilon_u \in \mathcal{E}(X, \varepsilon)} \varphi(\varepsilon_u) \qquad \mathcal{E} \in \mathcal{P}(\mathrm{Var} + \mathrm{ArrVar}) \times \mathrm{E} \to \mathcal{P}(\mathrm{E})$$

$$\mathcal{E}(X, \varepsilon) = \{\varepsilon' \mid \varepsilon' \in \mathrm{E} \wedge \forall v.\, v \in X \Rightarrow \mathrm{equiv}(\varepsilon', \varepsilon, v)\})$$

$$\mathrm{equiv}(\langle \sigma' :: \delta', h' \rangle, \langle \sigma :: \delta, h \rangle, v) = \forall i.\, 0 \le i < \mathrm{len}(v, \sigma) \Rightarrow h'(\pi_{\mathrm{base}}(\sigma'(v)) + i) = h(\pi_{\mathrm{base}}(\sigma(v)) + i)$$

$$\mathrm{len}(v, \sigma) = \mathrm{let}\ \langle n_0, \ldots, n_k \rangle = \pi_{\mathrm{dim}}(\sigma(v))\ \mathrm{in} \prod_{0 \le i \le k} n_i$$

Figure 15.8 Predicate Semantics

after executing s. These distributions specify the probability of reaching a specific environment as a result of faults during the execution.

The unreliable environment distributions are discrete because E is a countable set (Lemma 15.4). Therefore, φ' can be defined pointwise: for any environment $\varepsilon_u' \in \mathrm{E}$, the value of $\varphi'(\varepsilon_u')$ is the probability that the unreliable execution of the statement s results in the environment ε_u' given the distribution on possible starting environments, φ, and the aggregate probability p_u of reaching ε_u' from any starting environment $\varepsilon_u \in \mathrm{E}$ according to the big-step aggregate semantics. In general, φ' is a subprobability measure because it is defined using the big-step aggregate semantics, which is also a subprobability measure (Section 15.3.4).

Lemma 15.4 (Discrete Distribution). *The probability space of unreliable environments* (E, φ) *is discrete.*

Sketch   A probability distribution is discrete if it is defined on a countable sample space. Therefore, we need to prove that the set E is countable. We can accomplish it by proving that both the stack and the heap are countable. We demonstrate the former by observing that the number of variables in each stack frame is finite, and the number of frames is countable. We demonstrate the latter by noting that the number of locations is finite, and each is of the finite size. Full proof is available in Carbin et al. (n.d.).   □

15.4.2 Reliability Predicates and Transformers

The paired execution semantics enables a definition of the semantics of statements as transformers on *reliability predicates* that bound the reliability of program variables. A reliability predicate P is a predicate of the form:

$$P \rightarrow \texttt{true} \mid \texttt{false} \mid R \le R \mid P \wedge P$$
$$R \rightarrow r \mid \mathcal{R}(X) \mid R \cdot R$$

A predicate can either be the constant `true`, the constant `false`, a comparison between *reliability factors* (R), or a conjunction of predicates. A reliability factor is real-valued quantity that is either a rational constant r in the range $[0, 1]$; a joint reliability factor $\mathcal{R}(X)$ that gives the probability that all program variables in the set X have the same value in the unreliable execution as they have in the reliable execution; or a product of reliability factors, $R \cdot R$.

This combination of predicates and reliability factors enables a developer to specify bounds on the reliability of variables in the program, such as $0.99999 \le \mathcal{R}(\{x\})$, which states that the probability that x has the correct value in an unreliable execution is at least 0.99999.

Semantics of Reliability Predicates.

Figure 15.8 presents the denotational semantics of reliability predicates via the semantic function $[\![P]\!]$. The denotation of a reliability predicate is the set of configurations that satisfy the predicate. A key new element in the semantics of this predicate language is the semantics of joint reliability factors.

Joint Reliability Factor A joint reliability factor $\mathcal{R}(X)$ represents the probability that an unreliable environment ε_u sampled from the unreliable environment distribution φ has the same values for all variables in the set X as that in the reliable environment ε. To define this probability, we use the function $\mathcal{E}(X, \varepsilon)$, which gives the set of environments that have the same values for all variables in X as in the environment ε. The denotation of a joint reliability factor is then the sum of the probabilities of each of these environments according to φ.

Auxiliary Definitions We define predicate satisfaction and validity as:

$$\langle \varepsilon, \varphi \rangle \models P \quad \equiv \quad \langle \varepsilon, \varphi \rangle \in [\![P]\!]$$
$$\models P \quad \equiv \quad \forall \varepsilon. \forall \varphi. \langle \varepsilon, \varphi \rangle \models P$$

Reliability Transformer

Given a semantics for predicates, it is now possible to view the paired execution of a program as a *reliability transformer* – namely, a transformer on reliability predicates that is reminiscent of Dijkstra's Predicate Transformer Semantics (Dijkstra, 1975).

Definition 15.5 (Reliability Transformer).
$$\psi \models \{P\}\, s\, \{Q\} \equiv$$
$$\forall \varepsilon. \forall \varphi. \forall \varepsilon'. \forall \varphi'. (\langle \varepsilon, \varphi \rangle \models P \wedge \langle s, \langle \varepsilon, \varphi \rangle \rangle \Downarrow_\psi \langle \varepsilon', \varphi' \rangle) \Rightarrow \langle \varepsilon', \varphi' \rangle \models Q$$

The paired execution of a statement s is a transformer on reliability predicates, denoted $\psi \models \{P\}\ s\ \{Q\}$. Specifically, the paired execution of s *transforms* P to Q if for all $\langle \varepsilon, \varphi \rangle$ that satisfy P and for all $\langle \varepsilon', \varphi' \rangle$ yielded by the paired execution of s from $\langle \varepsilon, \varphi \rangle$, $\langle \varepsilon', \varphi' \rangle$ satisfies Q. The paired execution of s transforms P to Q for any P and Q where this relationship holds.

Reliability predicates and reliability transformers enable Rely to use symbolic predicates to characterize and constrain the shape of the unreliable environment distributions before and after execution of a statement. This approach provides a well-defined domain in which to express Rely's reliability analysis as a generator of constraints on the shape of the unreliable environment distributions for which a function still satisfies its specification.

15.5 Reliability Analysis

For each function in a program, Rely's reliability analysis generates a symbolic *reliability precondition* with a precondition generator style analysis. The reliability precondition is a reliability predicate that constrains the set of specifications that are valid for the function. Specifically, the reliability precondition is the conjuction of the terms of the form $R_i \leq R_j$ where R_i is the reliability factor for a developer-provided specification of a function output and R_j is a reliability factor that gives a conservative lower bound on the reliability of that output. If the reliability precondition is valid, then the developer-provided specifications are valid for the function.

15.5.1 Preliminaries

Transformed Semantics We formalize Rely's analysis over a transformed semantics of the program that is produced via a source-to-source transformation function $\mathcal{T}$ that performs two transformations:

- **Conditional Flattening:** Each conditional has a unique *control flow variable* ℓ associated with it that $\mathcal{T}$ uses to flatten a conditional of the form $\text{if}_\ell\ (b)\ \{s_1\}\ \{s_2\}$ to the sequence $\ell = b\ ;\ \text{if}_\ell\ (\ell)\ \{s_1\}\ \{s_2\}$. This transformation reifies the control flow variable as an explicit program variable that records the value of the conditional.
- **SSA:** The transformation function also transforms a Rely program to a SSA renamed version of the program. The ϕ-nodes for a conditional include a reference to the control flow variable for the conditional. For example, $\mathcal{T}$ transforms a sequence of statements of the form

$$\ell = b\ ;\ \text{if}_\ell\ (\ell)\ \{x = 1\}\ \{x = 2\}$$

to the sequence of statements

$$\ell = b \; ; \; \texttt{if}_\ell \; (\ell) \; \{x_1 = 1\} \; \{x_2 = 2\} \; ; \; x = \phi(\ell, x_1, x_2).$$

We rely on standard treatments for the semantics of ϕ-nodes (Barthe et al., 2012) and arrays (Knobe and Sarkar, 1998). We also note that $\mathcal{T}$ applies the SSA transformation such that a reference of a parameter at any point in the body of the function refers to its initial value on entry to the function. This property naturally gives a function's reliability specifications a semantics that refers to the reliability of variables on entry to the function.

These two transformations together make explicit the dependence between the reliability of a conditional's control flow variable and the reliability of variables modified within.

Auxiliary Maps The map $\Lambda \in \text{Var} \to M$ is a map from program variables to their declared memory regions. We compute this map by inspecting the parameter and variable declarations in the function. The map $\Gamma \in \text{Var} \to R$ is the unique map from the outputs of a function – namely, the return value and arrays passed as parameters – to the reliability factors (Section 15.4.2) for the developer-provided specification of each output. We allocate a fresh variable named ret that represents the return value of the program.

Substitution A substitution $e_0[e_2/e_1]$ replaces all occurrences of the expression e_1 with the expression e_2 within the expression e_0. Multiple substitution operations are applied from left to right. The substitution matches set patterns. For instance, the pattern $\mathcal{R}(\{x\} \cup X)$ represents a joint reliability factor that contains the variable x, alongside with the remaining variables in the set X. Then, the result of the substitution $r_1 \cdot \mathcal{R}(\{x, z\})[r_2 \cdot \mathcal{R}(\{y\} \cup X)/\mathcal{R}(\{x\} \cup X)]$ is the expression $r_1 \cdot r_2 \cdot \mathcal{R}(\{y, z\})$.

15.5.2 Precondition Generation

The analysis generates preconditions according to a conservative approximation of the paired execution semantics. Specifically, it characterizes the reliability of a value in a function according to the probability that the function computes that value – including its dependencies – fully reliably given a hardware specification.

Figure 15.9 presents a selection of Rely's reliability precondition generation rules. The generator takes as input a statement s, a postcondition Q, and (implicitly) the maps Λ and Γ. The generator produces as output a precondition P, such that if P holds before the paired execution of s, then Q holds after.

We have designed the analysis so that Q is the constraint over the developer-provided specifications that must hold at the end of execution of a function. Because arrays are passed by reference in Rely and can therefore be modified, one property

$$\rho \in (Exp + BExp) \rightarrow \mathbb{Q}_{\geq 0} \times \mathcal{P}(Var) \qquad \rho(n) = (1, \varnothing) \qquad \rho(x) = (\psi(rd(\Lambda(x))), \{x\})$$

$$\rho(e_1 \ iop \ e_2) = (\rho_1(e_1) \cdot \rho_1(e_2) \cdot \psi(iop), \ \rho_2(e_1) \cup \rho_2(e_2)) \qquad \rho_1(e) = \pi_1(\rho(e)) \qquad \rho_2(e) = \pi_2(\rho(e))$$

$$
\begin{aligned}
RP_\psi \ &\in \ S \times P \rightarrow P \\
RP_\psi(\texttt{return } e, Q) \ &= \ Q \wedge \Gamma(\text{ret}) \leq \rho_1(e) \cdot \mathcal{R}(\rho_2(e)) \\
RP_\psi(x = e, Q) \ &= \ Q \, [(\rho_1(e) \cdot \psi(wr(\Lambda(x))) \cdot \\
&\qquad \mathcal{R}(\rho_2(e) \cup X))/\mathcal{R}(\{x\} \cup X)] \\
RP_\psi(x = a[e_1, \dots, e_n], Q) \ &= \ Q \, [((\textstyle\prod_i \rho_1(e_i)) \cdot \psi(rd(\Lambda(a))) \cdot \psi(wr(\Lambda(x))) \cdot \\
&\qquad \mathcal{R}(\{a\} \cup (\textstyle\bigcup_i \rho_2(e_i)) \cup X))/\mathcal{R}(\{x\} \cup X)] \\
RP_\psi(a[e_1, \dots, e_n] = e, Q) \ &= \ Q \, [(\rho_1(e) \cdot (\textstyle\prod_i \rho_1(e_i)) \cdot \psi(wr(\Lambda(a))) \cdot \\
&\qquad \mathcal{R}(\rho_2(e) \cup (\textstyle\bigcup_i \rho_2(e_i)) \cup \{a\} \cup X))/\mathcal{R}(\{a\} \cup X)] \\
RP_\psi(\texttt{skip}, Q) \ &= \ Q \\
RP_\psi(s_1 \ ; \ s_2, Q) \ &= \ RP_\psi(s_1, RP_\psi(s_2, Q)) \\
RP_\psi(\texttt{if}_\ell \ \ell \ s_1 \ s_2, Q) \ &= \ RP_\psi(s_1, Q) \wedge RP_\psi(s_2, Q) \\
RP_\psi(x = \phi(\ell, x_1, x_2), Q) \ &= \ Q \, [\mathcal{R}(\{\ell, x_1\} \cup X)/\mathcal{R}(\{x\} \cup X)] \wedge \\
&\qquad Q[\mathcal{R}(\{\ell, x_2\} \cup X)/\mathcal{R}(\{x\} \cup X)] \\
RP_\psi(\texttt{while}_\ell \ b : 0 \ s, Q) \ &= \ Q \\
RP_\psi(\texttt{while}_\ell \ b : n \ s, Q) \ &= \ RP_\psi(\mathcal{T}(\texttt{if}_{\ell_n} \ b \ \{s \ ; \ \texttt{while}_\ell \ b : (n-1) \ s\} \ \texttt{skip}), Q) \\
RP_\psi(\texttt{int } x = e \ \texttt{in } m, Q) \ &= \ RP_\psi(x = e, Q) \\
RP_\psi(\texttt{int } a[n_0, \dots, n_k] \ \texttt{in } m, Q) \ &= \ Q \, [\mathcal{R}(X)/\mathcal{R}(\{a\} \cup X)]
\end{aligned}
$$

Figure 15.9 Reliability Precondition Generation

that must hold at the end of execution of a function is that each array must be at least as reliable as implied by its specification. The analysis captures this property by setting the initial Q for the body of a function to

$$\bigwedge_{a_i} \Gamma(a_i) \leq \mathcal{R}(a_i')$$

where a_i is the i-th array parameter of the function and a_i' is an SSA renamed version of the array that contains the appropriate value of a_i at the end of the function. This constraint therefore states that the reliability implied by the specifications must be less than or equal to the actual reliability of each input array at the end of the function. As the precondition generator works backwards through the function, it generates a new precondition that – if valid at the beginning of the function – ensures that Q holds at the end.

Reasoning about Expressions

The topmost part of Figure 15.9 first presents the rules for reasoning about the reliability of evaluating an expression. The reliability of evaluating an expression depends on two factors: (1) the reliability of the operations in the expression and (2) the reliability of the variables referenced in the expression. The function $\rho \in (Exp + BExp) \rightarrow \mathbb{Q}_{\geq 0} \times \mathcal{P}(Var)$ computes the core components of these two factors. It returns a pair consisting of (1) the probability of correctly executing all operations in the expression and (2) the set of variables referenced by the expression. The projections ρ_1 and ρ_2 return each component, respectively. Using these projections, the reliability of an expression e – given any reliable environment and unreliable environment distribution – is therefore *at least* $\rho_1(e) \cdot \mathcal{R}(\rho_2(e))$, where $\mathcal{R}(\rho_2(e))$ is the joint reliability of all the variables referenced in e. The rules for boolean and relational operations are defined analogously.

Generation Rules for Statements

As in a precondition generator, the analysis works backwards from the end of the program to the beginning. We have therefore structured the discussion of the statements starting with function returns.

Function Returns When execution reaches a function return, `return e`, the analysis must verify that the reliability of the return value is greater than the reliability that the developer specified. To verify this, the analysis rule generates the additional constraint $\Gamma(\text{ret}) \leq \rho_1(e) \cdot \mathcal{R}(\rho_2(e))$. This constrains the reliability of the return value, where $\Gamma(\text{ret})$ is the reliability specification for the return value.

Assignment For the program to satisfy a predicate Q after the execution of an assignment statement $x = e$, then Q must hold given a substitution of the reliability of the expression e for the reliability of x. The substitution $Q[(\rho_1(e) \cdot \psi(wr(\Lambda(x)))) \cdot \mathcal{R}(\rho_2(e) \cup X))/\mathcal{R}(\{x\} \cup X)]$ binds each reliability factor in which x occurs – $\mathcal{R}(\{x\} \cup X)$ – and replaces the factor with a new reliability factor $\mathcal{R}(\rho_2(e) \cup X)$ where $\rho_2(e)$ is the set of variables referenced by e.

The substitution also multiplies the reliability factor by $\rho_1(e) \cdot \psi(wr(\Lambda(x)))$, which is the probability that e evaluates fully reliably and its value is reliably written to the memory location for x.

Array loads and stores The reliability of a load, $x = a[e_1, \ldots, e_n]$, depends on the reliability of the indices $e_1, \ldots, e_n$, the reliability of the values stored in a, and the reliability of reading from a's memory region. The rule's implementation is similar to that for assignment.

The reliability of an array store $a[e_1, \ldots, e_n] = e$ depends on the reliability of the source expression e, the reliability of the indices $e_1, \ldots, e_n$, and the reliability of writing to a. Note that the rule preserves the presence of a within the reliability term. By doing so, the rule ensures that it tracks the full reliability of all the elements within a.

Conditional For the program to satisfy a predicate Q after a conditional statement of the form `if`$_\ell$ b s_1 s_2, each branch must satisfy Q. The rule therefore generates a precondition that is a conjunction of the results of the analysis of each branch.

Phi-nodes The rule for a ϕ-node $x = \phi(\ell, x_1, x_2)$ captures the implicit dependence of the effects of control flow on the value of a variable x. For the merged value x, the rule establishes Q by generating a precondition that ensures that Q holds independently for both x_1 and x_2, given an appropriate substitution. Note that the rule also includes ℓ in the substitution; this explicitly captures x's dependence on ℓ. The flattening statement inserted before a conditional (Section 15.5.1), later replaces the reliability of ℓ with that of its dependencies.

Bounded `while` **and** `repeat` Bounded `while` loops, `while`$_\ell$ $b : n$ s, and `repeat` loops, `repeat` n s, execute their bodies at most n times. Execution of such a loop therefore satisfies Q if P holds beforehand, where P is the result of invoking the analysis on n sequential copies of the body. The rule implements this approach via a sequence of bounded recursive calls to transformed versions of itself.

Unbounded `while` We present the analysis for unbounded `while` loops in the section that follows.

Function Calls The analysis for functions is modular and takes the reliability specification from the function declaration and substitutes the reliabilities of the function's formal arguments with the reliabilities of the expressions that represent the function's actual arguments. We presented the rule for function calls in Carbin et al. (n.d.).

Unbounded `while` *Loops*

An unbounded loop, `while`$_\ell$ b s, may execute for a number of iterations that is not bounded statically. The reliability of a variable that is modified unreliably within a loop and has a loop-carried dependence is a monotonically decreasing function of the number of loop iterations. The only sound approximation of the reliability of such a variable is therefore zero. However, unbounded loops may also update a variable reliably. In this case, the reliability of the variable is the joint reliability of its dependencies. We have designed an analysis for unbounded `while` loops to distinguish these two cases as follows:

Dependence Graph The analysis first constructs a dependence graph for the loop. Each node in the dependence graph corresponds to a variable that is read or written within the condition or body of the loop. There is a directed edge from the node for a variable x to the node for a variable y if the value of y depends on the value of x. The analysis additionally classifies each edge as reliable or unreliable meaning that a reliable or unreliable operation creates the dependence.

There is an edge from the node for a variable x to the node for the variable y if one of the following holds:

- **Assignment:** there is an assignment to y where x occurs in the expression on the right hand side of the assignment; this condition captures direct data dependencies. The analysis classifies such an edge as reliable if every operation in the assignment (i.e., the operations in the expression and the write to memory) are reliable. Otherwise, the analysis marks the edge as unreliable. The rules for array load and store statements are similar, and include dependencies induced by the computation of array indices.
- **Control Flow Side Effects:** y is assigned within an `if` statement and the `if` statement's control flow variable is named x; this condition captures control dependencies. The analysis classifies each such edge as reliable.

The analysis uses the dependence graph to identify the set of variables in the loop that are *reliably updated*. A variable x is reliably updated if all simple paths (and simple cycles) to x in the dependence graph contain only reliable edges.

Fixpoint Analysis Given a set of reliably updated variables X_r, the analysis next splits the postcondition Q into two parts. For each predicate $R_i \leq r \cdot \mathcal{R}(X)$ in Q (where R_i is a developer-provided specification), the analysis checks if the property $\forall x \in X . x \in \text{modset}(s) \Rightarrow x \in X_r$ holds, where $\text{modset}(s)$ computes the set of variables that may be modified by s. If this holds, then all the variables in X are either modified reliably or not modified at all within the body of the loop. The analysis conjoins the set of predicates that satisfy this property to create the postcondition Q_r and conjoins the remaining predicates to create Q_u.

The analysis next iterates the function $F(A)$ starting from `true`, where $F(A) = Q_r \wedge RP_\psi(\mathcal{T}(\text{if}_\ell \ b \ s \ \text{skip}), A)$, until it reaches a fixpoint. The resulting predicate Q_r' is a translation of Q_r such the joint reliability of a set of variables is replaced by the joint reliability of its dependencies.

Lemma 15.6 (Termination). *Iteration of $F(A)$ terminates.*

This follows from the monotonicity of RP and the fact that the range of $F(A)$ is finite (given a simplifier that removes redundant predicates and produces a canonical, symbolic predicate representation – which we present a subsumption-based variant in Section 15.5.3) – together, forming finite descending chains. The key intuition is that the set of rational constants in the precondition before and after an iteration does not change (because all variables are reliably updated) and the set of variables that can occur in a joint reliability factor is finite. Therefore, there are a finite number of unique preconditions in the range of $F(A)$.

Final Precondition In the last step, the analysis produces a final precondition that preserves the reliability of variables that are reliably updated by conjoining Q_r'

with the predicate $Q_u[(R_i \leq 0)/(R_i \leq R_j)]$, where R_i and R_j are joint reliability factors. The substitution on Q_u sets the joint reliability factors that contain unreliably updated variables to zero.

Properties

Rely's analysis is sound with respect to the transformer semantics presented in Section 15.4.

Theorem 15.7 (Soundness). $\psi \models \{RP_\psi(s, Q)\}\ s\ \{Q\}$

This theorem states that if a configuration $\langle \varepsilon, \varphi \rangle$ satisfies a generated precondition and the paired execution of s yields a configuration $\langle \varepsilon', \varphi' \rangle$, then $\langle \varepsilon', \varphi' \rangle$ satisfies Q. Alternatively, s transforms the precondition generated by the analysis to Q.

We demonstrate the basic constructions for reasoning about soundness of the analysis via a detailed presentation of the soundness of the rule for assignment.

Lemma 15.8 (Soundness of Assignment).

$$\psi \models \{A \leq \rho_p(e) \cdot \psi(wr(x)) \cdot R(X/\{x\} \cup \rho_{var}(e))\}$$
$$x = e$$
$$\{A \leq R(X)\}$$

Outline By the definition of the reliability transformer, this judgment is equivalent to proving that $A \leq [\![R(X)]\!](\varepsilon', \varphi')$ given the two premises:
(1) $A \leq [\![\rho_p(e) \cdot \psi(wr(x)) \cdot R(Y)]\!](\varepsilon, \varphi)$ and
(2) $\langle s, \varepsilon, \varphi \rangle \Downarrow_\psi \langle \varepsilon', \varphi' \rangle$ where $Y = (X - \{x\}) \cup \rho_{var}(e)$.
   We establish this theorem by proving that

$$[\![\rho_p(e) \cdot \psi(wr(x)) \cdot R(Y)]\!](\varepsilon, \varphi) \leq [\![R(X)]\!](\varepsilon', \varphi')$$

and then using the transitivity of $\leq$, namely, that $A \leq [\![\rho_p(e) \cdot \psi(wr(x)) \cdot R(Y)]\!](\varepsilon, \varphi) \leq [\![R(X)]\!](\varepsilon', \varphi')$ This follows from the following definitions and lemmas.

Lemma 15.9 (Initial Reliability).
If $ins = \{\varepsilon_u \mid equiv(\varepsilon, \varepsilon_u, Y)\}$ *then* $[\![R(Y)]\!](\varepsilon, \varphi) = \sum_{\varepsilon_u \in ins} \varphi(\varepsilon_u)$.

This lemma is a restatement of the semantics of joint reliability factors as laid out in Section 15.4.

Lemma 15.10 (Final Reliability).
If $outs \subseteq \{\varepsilon'_u \mid equiv(\varepsilon', \varepsilon'_u, X)\}$ *then* $\sum_{\varepsilon_u \in outs} \varphi'(\varepsilon_u) \leq [\![R(X)]\!](\varepsilon', \varphi')$.

This lemma is also a restatement of the semantics of joint reliability factors.

Definition 15.11 (Unreliable Execution Summary). An *unreliable execution summary* is a tuple $(\varepsilon_u, \tau, p, \varepsilon_u') \in U = \{(\varepsilon_u, \tau, p, \varepsilon_u') \mid \langle x = e, \varepsilon_u \rangle \overset{\tau, p}{\Longrightarrow}_\psi \varepsilon_u'\}$ such that from an environment ε_u, execution of the statement $x = e$ under the reliability model ψ proceeds following a trace τ with probability p and yields an environment ε_u'.

Unreliable execution summaries enable us to construct a conservative approximation of the paired execution semantics:

Lemma 15.12 (Paired Execution Approximation).
If execs $\subseteq U$ and $\langle s, \varepsilon, \varphi \rangle \Downarrow_\psi \langle \varepsilon', \varphi' \rangle$ then

$$\left(\sum_{ex \in execs} \varphi(\pi_{\varepsilon_u}(ex)) \cdot \pi_p(ex) \right) \leq \sum_{ex \in (execs)} \varphi'(\pi_{\varepsilon_u'}(ex)).$$

This lemma states that for any set of execution summaries *execs* the sum – over all summaries – of the product of the probability of each summary's initial state (according to φ) and the probability of the execution's trace p is less than or equal to the sum of the probability of each summary's final state according to φ'.

This lemma follows from the definition of the paired execution semantics provided in Section 15.4. According to the paired execution semantics, the probability of any final state ε_u' – i.e., $\varphi'(\varepsilon_u')$ – is the sum over all states ε_u of the aggregate probability (as defined by the aggregate big-step semantics) that the unreliable program reaches ε_u'. Additionally, the aggregatate probability is the sum over all unreliable traces that reach ε_u' from ε_u. This sum is therefore bounded from below by the sum over any subset of all states and traces.

Definition 15.13 (Fully Reliable Execution Summaries). Let the set of fully reliable execution summaries be

$$execs_c = \{(\varepsilon_u, \tau, p, \varepsilon_u') \mid (\varepsilon_u, \tau, p, \varepsilon_u') \in U \wedge \varepsilon_u \in$$
$$\{\varepsilon_u \mid \text{equiv}(\varepsilon, \varepsilon_u, Y)\} \wedge \text{correct}(\tau)\},$$

where correct(τ) is a predicate that is true only if the trace τ is a list of the form C^+ (C transition label indicates that a transition executed reliably).

The set of fully reliable execution summaries characterizes the set of pairs of environments ε_u and ε_u' where ε_u has the correct values for the set of variables Y and execution from ε_u proceeds fully reliably to ε_u'.

Proof Using the set of fully reliable executions, we can build our proof of the main theorem. Via Lemma 15.9, we know that

$$[\![\rho_p(e) \cdot \psi(wr(x)) \cdot \mathcal{R}(Y)]\!](\varepsilon, \varphi) = \rho_p(e) \cdot \psi(wr(x)) \cdot \sum_{\varepsilon_u \in ins} \varphi(\varepsilon_u)$$

$$= \sum_{\varepsilon_u \in ins} \varphi(\varepsilon_u) \cdot \rho_p(e) \cdot \psi(wr(x))$$

$$= \sum_{ex \in execs_c} \varphi(\pi_{\varepsilon_u}(ex)) \cdot \pi_p(ex)$$

This fact is true because all initial environments ε_u have the same values for all variables in Y and $\rho_p(e) \cdot \psi(wr(x))$ is the probability that the statement executes correctly.

Continuing on from this right-hand side, we use the paired execution approximation and Lemma 15.10 to complete our proof:

$$\sum_{ex \in execs_c} \varphi(\pi_{\varepsilon_u}(ex)) \cdot \pi_p(ex) \le \sum_{ex \in execs_c} \varphi'(\pi_{\varepsilon'_u}(ex)).$$

$$\le [\![\mathcal{R}(X)]\!](\varepsilon', \varphi')$$

The first step follows from the fact that $execs_c \subseteq U$. The second step fact follows from the fact that $\pi_{\varepsilon'_u}(execs_c) \subseteq \{\varepsilon'_u \mid \text{equiv}(\varepsilon', \varepsilon'_u, X)\}$. We know that $\pi_{\varepsilon'_u}(execs_c) \subseteq \{\varepsilon'_u \mid \text{equiv}(\varepsilon', \varepsilon'_u, X)\}$. because if (1) all values referenced in e have the correct value and (2) both e and the assignment to x execute reliably, then x has the correct value (and the remaining variables in X have the same correct values as they have not been modified). We can therefore conclude that $A \le [\![\rho_p(e) \cdot \psi(wr(x)) \cdot \mathcal{R}(Y)]\!](\varepsilon, \varphi) \le [\![\mathcal{R}(X)]\!](\varepsilon', \varphi')$ □

15.5.3 Specification Checking

As the last step of the analysis for a function, the analysis checks the developer-provided reliability specifications for the function's outputs as captured by the precondition generator's final precondition. Because each specification has the form $r \cdot \mathcal{R}(X)$ (Figure 15.1) the precondition is a conjunction of predicates of the form $r_1 \cdot \mathcal{R}(X_1) \le r_2 \cdot \mathcal{R}(X_2)$. While these joint reliability factors represent arbitrary and potentially complex distributions of the values of X_1 and X_2, there is a simple and sound (though not complete) procedure to check the validity of each predicate in a precondition that follows from the *ordering* of joint reliability factors.

Proposition 15.14 (Ordering). *For two sets of variables X and Y, if $X \subseteq Y$ then $\mathcal{R}(Y) \le \mathcal{R}(X)$.*

The proposition states that the joint reliability of a set of variables Y is less than or equal to the joint reliability of any subset of the variables – regardless of the distribution of their values.

Proof (Sketch) First, we consider the case when all variables in X and Y are scalars. Let U_Y be the set passed as the argument at the base case of the recursion started by the call $\text{rel}(Y, \varepsilon, \varphi, E)$ and U_X be the set passed as the argument at the base case of the recursion started by the call $\text{rel}(X, \varepsilon, \varphi, E)$. Then, if $X \subseteq Y$, the set $U_Y \subseteq U_X$, since the variables in $Y \backslash X$ provide additional restrictions on the states that are contained in U_Y. The theorem statement follows from the inequality $\sum_{v \in U_X} \varphi(v) \geq \sum_{v \in U_Y} \varphi(v)$.

If a is an array variable, then the function rel adds a constraint for each element of a. Then, we can apply the same argument for each such obtained sets U_X and U_Y. This property holds for each array element, and is not affected by the minimum operator in the function rel. □

As a consequence of the ordering of joint reliability factors, there is a simple and sound method to check the validity of a predicate.

Corollary 15.15 (Predicate Validity). *If $r_1 \leq r_2$ and $X_2 \subseteq X_1$ then* $\models r_1 \cdot \mathcal{R}(X_1) \leq r_2 \cdot \mathcal{R}(X_2)$.

The constraint $r_1 \leq r_2$ is a comparison of two rational numbers and the constraint $X_2 \subseteq X_1$ is an inclusion of finite sets. Note that both types of constraints are decidable and efficiently checkable.

Checking Because the predicates in the precondition generator's output are mutually independent, it is possible to use Corollary 15.15 to check the validity of the full precondition by checking the validity of each predicate.

Our implementation performs simplification transformations after each precondition generator step to simplify numerical expressions and remove predicates that are trivially valid or *subsumed* by another predicate.

Proposition 15.16 (Predicate Subsumption)*A predicate $r_1 \cdot \mathcal{R}(X_1) \leq r_2 \cdot \mathcal{R}(X_2)$ subsumes (i.e., soundly replaces) another predicate $r_1' \cdot \mathcal{R}(X_1') \leq r_2' \cdot \mathcal{R}(X_2')$ if $r_1' \cdot \mathcal{R}(X_1') \leq r_1 \cdot \mathcal{R}(X_1)$ and $r_2 \cdot \mathcal{R}(X_2) \leq r_2' \cdot \mathcal{R}(X_2')$.*

This property follows directly from the ordering of joint reliability factors. We provide the proof in Carbin et al. (n.d., Section C.3).

15.6 Related Work

Integrity Almost all approximate computations have critical regions that must execute without error for the computation as a whole to execute acceptably. *Dynamic criticality analyses* automatically change different regions of the computation or internal data structures, and observe how the change affects the program's output, e.g. Rinard (2006); Carbin and Rinard (2010); Misailovic et al. (2010). In addition, specification-based *static criticality analyses* let the developer identify and separate critical and approximate program regions, e.g., Liu et al. (2011); Sampson et al. (2011). Carbin et al. (2012) present a verification system for relaxed approximate programs based on a relational Hoare logic. The system enables rigorous reasoning about the integrity and worst-case accuracy properties of a program's approximate regions.

In contrast to the prior static analyses that focus on the binary distinction between reliable and approximate computations, Rely allows a developer to specify and verify that even approximate computations produce the correct result *most of the time*. Overall, this additional information can help developers better understand the effects of deploying their computations on unreliable hardware and exploit the benefits that unreliable hardware offers.

Accuracy In addition to reasoning about how often a computation may produce a correct result, it may also be desirable to reason about the accuracy of the result that the computation produces. Dynamic techniques observe the accuracy impact of program transformations, e.g., Rinard (2006), Misailovic et al. (2010), Ansel et al. (2011), Baek and Chilimbi (2010), Sidiroglou et al. (2011), or injected soft errors, e.g., de Kruijf et al. (2010), Liu et al. (2011), Sampson et al. (2011). Empirical techniques like Approxilyzer (Venkatagiri et al., 2015, 2019) present systematic exploration of the impact of soft errors on individual program instructions, including the accuracy of the result. Researchers have developed static techniques that use probabilistic reasoning to characterize the accuracy impact of various sources of uncertainty (Misailovic et al., 2011; Chaudhuri et al., 2011; Zhu et al., 2012). And of course, the accuracy impact of the floating point approximation to real arithmetic has been extensively studied in numerical analysis.

Fault Tolerance and Resilience Researchers have developed various software, hardware, or mixed approaches for detection and recovery from specific types of soft errors that guarantee a reliable program execution, e.g., Reis et al. (2005), Perry et al. (2007), de Kruijf et al. (2010). For example, Reis et al. (2005) present a compiler that replicates a computation to detect and recover from single event upsets. These techniques are complementary to Rely – each can provide implementations of operations that need to be reliable (as specified by the developer or required by Rely) to preserve memory safety and control flow integrity.

Follow up works Since publishing the original paper (Carbin et al., 2013b), we and other researchers have extended this research in various directions. We developed the Chisel optimization system to automate the placement of approximate operations and data (Misailovic et al., 2014). Chisel extends the Rely reliability specifications (that capture acceptable frequency of errors) with absolute error specifications (that also capture acceptable magnitude of errors). It formulates an integer optimization problem to automatically navigate the tradeoff space and generate an approximate computation that provides maximum energy savings while satisfying both the reliability and absolute error specifications.

Several static analyses studied the interactions between safety and reliability. Decaf (Boston et al., 2015) presents a type system that incorporates reliability specifications with EnerJ type annotations. FlexJava (Park et al., 2015) presents a static analysis for inferring annotations on approximate variables. Leto (Boston et al., 2018) provides a flexible interface for expressing custom hardware error models and a verification framework that can prove various properties about programs that execute on such hardware. Aloe (Joshi et al., 2020) adds support for analyzing recovery blocks to Rely.

More recently, researchers also extended the reliability analysis to other kinds of computations. Hung et al. (2019) extend the reliability analysis to quantum programs. Fernando et al. (2019) presented an approach for analyzing message-passing parallel programs with unreliable computation and/or communication.

15.7 Conclusion

The software and hardware communities have grown accustomed to the digital abstraction of computing: the computing substrate is designed to either faithfully execute an operation or detect and report that an error has occurred. This abstraction has enabled a process whereby increased performance capability in the substrate enables the development of increasingly larger and more complicated computing systems that are composed of less complicated, modularly-specified components.

Emerging trends in the scalability of existing hardware design techniques, however, jeopardize the hope that future gains in computing performance will still be accompanied by a digital abstraction. Instead, future high-performance computing platforms may produce uncertain results and, therefore, it may no longer be possible to use traditional techniques to modularly compose components to execute on these platforms.

While there is an immediate opportunity for our work to enable the reasoning needed to reliably achieve better performance in the face of uncertainty, the true motivation for this work is that the nature of computing itself has changed. Emerging applications, such as machine learning, multimedia, and data analytics are inherently uncertain computations that operate over uncertain inputs. Moreover, emerging uncertain computational substrates, such as intermittently powered devices, biological devices, and quantum computing, create new possibilities for where computation can take place and even what can be computed itself.

Going forward, this work will enable the software and hardware communities to discard the notion that they must rely on the digital abstraction to build computing systems. Instead, emerging computing systems will use abstractions of acceptability that will enable these systems to exploit not only the performance benefits of uncertain substrates, but also the new possibilities that these platforms offer for computation.

Acknowledgments

We thank Martin Rinard, our advisor and the co-authors of the conference version of this chapter (Carbin et al., 2013b). We also thank Vimuth Fernando for proofreading the draft. This research was supported in part by the National Science Foundation (Grants CCF-0905244, CCF-1036241, CCF-1138967, CCF-1138967, and IIS-0835652), the United States Department of Energy (Grant DE-SC0008923), and DARPA (Grants FA8650-11-C-7192, FA8750-12-2-0110).

References

Ansel, J., Wong, Y., Chan, C., Olszewski, M., Edelman, A., and Amarasinghe, S. 2011. Language and compiler support for auto-tuning variable-accuracy algorithms. CGO.

Baek, W., and Chilimbi, T. M. 2010. Green: a framework for supporting energy-conscious programming using controlled approximation. PLDI.

Barthe, G., Demange, D., and Pichardie, D. 2012. A formally verified SSA-Based middle-end: Static single assignment meets compcert. ESOP.

Blum, M., and Kanna, S. 1989. Designing programs that check their work. STOC.

Boston, Brett, Sampson, Adrian, Grossman, Dan, and Ceze, Luis. 2015. Probability type inference for flexible approximate programming. In: *OOPSLA*.

Boston, Brett, Gong, Zoe, and Carbin, Michael. 2018. Leto: verifying application-specific hardware fault tolerance with programmable execution models. In: *OOPSLA*.

Carbin, M., and Rinard, M. 2010. Automatically Identifying Critical Input Regions and Code in Applications. ISSTA.

Carbin, M., Misailovic, S., and Rinard, M. *Verifying Quantitative Reliability of Programs that Execute on Unreliable Hardware (Appendix)*. http://groups.csail.mit.edu/pac/rely.

Carbin, M., Kim, D., Misailovic, S., and Rinard, M. 2012. Proving Acceptability Properties of Relaxed Nondeterministic Approximate Programs. PLDI.

Carbin, M., Kim, D., Misailovic, S., and Rinard, M. 2013a. Verified integrity properties for safe approximate program transformations. PEPM.

Carbin, M., Misailovic, S., and Rinard, M. 2013b. Verifying Quantitative Reliability for Programs That Execute on Unreliable Hardware. OOPSLA.

Chaudhuri, S., Gulwani, S., Lublinerman, R., and Navidpour, S. 2011. Proving Programs Robust. FSE.

de Kruijf, M., Nomura, S., and Sankaralingam, K. 2010. Relax: an architectural framework for software recovery of hardware faults. ISCA.

Dijkstra, Edsger W. 1975. Guarded commands, nondeterminacy and formal derivation of programs. *Communications of the ACM*, **18**(August), 453–457.

Ernst, D., Kim, N. S., Das, S., Pant, S., Rao, R., Pham, T., Ziesler, C., Blaauw, D., Austin, T., Flautner, K., and Mudge, T. 2003. Razor: A low-power pipeline based on circuit-level timing speculation. MICRO.

Esmaeilzadeh, H., Sampson, A., Ceze, L., and Burger, D. 2012. Architecture support for disciplined approximate programming. ASPLOS.

Feng, S., Gupta, S., Ansari, A., and Mahlke, S. 2010. Shoestring: probabilistic soft error reliability on the cheap. ASPLOS.

Fernando, V., Joshi, K., and Misailovic, S. 2019. Verifying Safety and Accuracy of Approximate Parallel Programs via Canonical Sequentialization. OOPSLA.

Hiller, M., Jhumka, A., and Suri, N. 2002. On the placement of software mechanisms for detection of data errors. DSN.

Hoffman, H., S. Sidiroglou, M. Carbin, S. Misailovic, A. Agarwal, and Rinard, M. 2011. Dynamic Knobs for Responsive Power-Aware Computing. ASPLOS.

Hung, Shih-Han, Hietala, Kesha, Zhu, Shaopeng, Ying, Mingsheng, Hicks, Michael, and Wu, Xiaodi. 2019. Quantitative robustness analysis of quantum programs. *Proceedings of the ACM on Programming Languages*, **3**(POPL), 31.

Joshi, Keyur, Fernando, Vimuth, and Misailovic, Sasa. 2020. Aloe: Verifying Reliability of Approximate Programs in the Presence of Recovery Mechanisms. CGO. ACM.

Knobe, K., and Sarkar, V. 1998. Array SSA form and its use in parallelization. POPL.

Kozen, D. 1981. Semantics of probabilistic programs. *Journal of Computer and System Sciences*.

Leem, L., Cho, H., Bau, J., Jacobson, Q., and Mitra, S. 2010. ERSA: error resilient system architecture for probabilistic applications. DATE.

Leveson, N., Cha, S., Knight, J. C., and Shimeall, T. 1990. The use of self checks and voting in software error detection: An empirical study. *IEEE TSE*.

Liu, S., Pattabiraman, K., Moscibroda, T., and Zorn, B. 2011. Flikker: Saving DRAM refresh-power through critical data partitioning. ASPLOS.

Misailovic, S., Sidiroglou, S., Hoffmann, H., and Rinard, M. 2010. Quality of service profiling. ICSE.

Misailovic, S., Roy, D., and Rinard, M. 2011. Probabilistically Accurate Program Transformations. SAS.

Misailovic, S., Kim, D., and Rinard, M. 2013. Parallelizing Sequential Programs With Statistical Accuracy Tests. *ACM TECS Special Issue on Probabilistic Embedded Computing*.

Misailovic, S., Carbin, M., Achour, S., Qi, Z., and Rinard, M. 2014. Chisel: Reliability- and Accuracy-aware Optimization of Approximate Computational Kernels. OOPSLA.

Narayanan, S., Sartori, J., Kumar, R., and Jones, D. 2010. Scalable stochastic processors. DATE.

Palem, K. 2005. Energy aware computing through probabilistic switching: A study of limits. *IEEE Transactions on Computers*.

Park, Jongse, Esmaeilzadeh, Hadi, Zhang, Xin, Naik, Mayur, and Harris, William. 2015. Flexjava: Language support for safe and modular approximate programming. In: *FSE*.

Pattabiraman, K., Grover, V., and Zorn, B. 2008. Samurai: protecting critical data in unsafe languages. EuroSys.

Perry, F., Mackey, L., Reis, G.A., Ligatti, J., August, D.I., and Walker, D. 2007. Fault-tolerant typed assembly language. PLDI.

Reis, G., Chang, J., Vachharajani, N., Rangan, R., and August, D. 2005. SWIFT: Software Implemented Fault Tolerance. CGO.

Rinard, M. 2006. Probabilistic accuracy bounds for fault-tolerant computations that discard tasks. ICS.

Rinard, M., Cadar, C., Dumitran, D., Roy, D.M., Leu, T., and Beebee Jr, W.S. 2004. Enhancing server availability and security through failure-oblivious computing. OSDI.

Sampson, A., Dietl, W., Fortuna, E., Gnanapragasam, D., Ceze, L., and Grossman, D. 2011. EnerJ: approximate data types for safe and general low-power computation. PLDI.

Schlesinger, C., Pattabiraman, K., Swamy, N., Walker, D., and Zorn, B. 2011. YARRA: An Extension to C for Data Integrity and Partial Safety. CSF.

Sidiroglou, S., Misailovic, S., Hoffmann, H., and Rinard, M. 2011. Managing Performance vs. Accuracy Trade-offs With Loop Perforation. FSE.

Thomas, A., and Pattabiraman, K. 2013. Error Detector Placement for Soft Computation. DSN.

Venkatagiri, Radha, Mahmoud, Abdulrahman, Hari, Siva Kumar Sastry, and Adve, Sarita V. 2015. Approxilyzer: Towards a systematic framework for instruction-level approximate computing and its application to hardware resiliency. In: *MICRO*.

Venkatagiri, Radha, Ahmed, Khalique, Mahmoud, Abdulrahman, Misailovic, Sasa, Marinov, Darko, Fletcher, Christopher W, and Adve, Sarita V. 2019. gem5-Approxilyzer: An Open-Source Tool for Application-Level Soft Error Analysis. In: *DSN*.

x264. 2013. http://www.videolan.org/x264.html.

Zhu, Z., Misailovic, S., Kelner, J., and Rinard, M. 2012. Randomized Accuracy-Aware Program Transformations for Efficient Approximate Computations. POPL.